Introduction to **POLITICS**

Introduction to
POLITICS

fourth edition

Robert GARNER
Peter FERDINAND
Stephanie LAWSON

OXFORD
UNIVERSITY PRESS

OXFORD
UNIVERSITY PRESS

Great Clarendon Street, Oxford, OX2 6DP,
United Kingdom

Oxford University Press is a department of the University of Oxford.
It furthers the University's objective of excellence in research, scholarship,
and education by publishing worldwide. Oxford is a registered trade mark of
Oxford University Press in the UK and in certain other countries

© Robert Garner, Peter Ferdinand, Stephanie Lawson 2020

The moral rights of the authors have been asserted

First edition 2009
Second edition 2012
Third edition 2016

Impression: **5**

Public sector information reproduced under Open Government Licence v3.0
(http://www.nationalarchives.gov.uk/doc/open-government-licence/open-government-licence.htm)

Published in the United States of America by Oxford University Press
198 Madison Avenue, New York, NY 10016, United States of America

British Library Cataloguing in Publication Data
Data available

Library of Congress Control Number: 2019949833

ISBN 978–0–19–882061–1

Printed in Great Britain by
Ashford Colour Press Ltd, Gosport, Hampshire

BRIEF CONTENTS

DETAILED CONTENTS

ABOUT THE AUTHORS

ROBERT GARNER is a Professor of Politics at the University of Leicester. He has published widely in the area of environmental politics in general and the politics and philosophy of animal rights in particular. His books include *Animals, Politics and Morality* (Manchester University Press, 2004), *The Political Theory of Animal Rights* (Manchester University Press, 2005), *Animal Ethics* (Polity Press, 2005), *A Theory of Justice for Animals* (Oxford University Press, 2013), and *Environmental Political Thought* (Palgrave, 2019).

PETER FERDINAND is an Emeritus Reader in Politics and International Studies and former Director of the Centre for Studies in Democratization at the University of Warwick. He is a former Head of the Asia-Pacific Programme at the Royal Institute of International Affairs (Chatham House). He is the author of *Communist Regimes in Comparative Perspective: The Evolution of the Soviet, Chinese and Yugoslav Models* (1992) and *Governance in Pacific Asia* (2012). He has edited books on politics and political economy in Taiwan, Central Asia, Hong Kong, and on the Internet and democracy. His interests are in the politics of Pacific Asia, the former Soviet Union, democratization, political economy, and new rising world powers.

STEPHANIE LAWSON holds honorary professorships in Politics and International Relations at Macquarie University and in the Department of Pacific Affairs, Australian National University. She is also a Senior Research Associate, Faculty of Humanities, University of Johannesburg.

GUIDED TOUR OF THE TEXTBOOK FEATURES

This textbook is enriched with a range of learning features to help you navigate the text and reinforce your understanding of politics. This guided tour shows you how to get the most out of your textbook.

Reader's Guides at the beginning of each chapter set the scene for the themes and issues to be discussed, and indicate the scope of the chapter's coverage.

READER'S GUIDE

This chapter will begin by seeking to define the nature of politics asking whether politics is an inevitable feature of all human socie examining the boundary problems inherent in an analysis of the Two are particularly notable. Should politics be defined narrowl state, or should it be broadly defined to encompass other social politics equivalent to consensus and cooperation, so that politi event of conflict and war? The chapter then goes on to disti

Key Concept Boxes throughout the text draw out and clearly explain important ideas.

KEY CONCEPT BOX 1.2
Civil Society

A term that is usually taken to refer to a range of private institut vidual and the state. This would include what are now referred t ing things that people have in common, such as business, trade so on. Hegel, the eighteenth- and early nineteenth-century Gert between the family, civil society, and the state, each offering ing aration. Others would want to include the family as an institut

Key Debate Boxes in each chapter highlight key areas of contention and challenge you to think critically about important issues in the text.

KEY DEBATE BOX 10.3
Are Human Rights a 'Western' Construct?

In the aftermath of the Second World War, the newly created establish a better world that would never revert to the injustic adopted the Universal Declaration of Human Rights in 1948, whic human beings are born free and equal in dignity and rights'. Articl one without exception is entitled to these freedoms and rights (f However, Article 29(2) clarifies that limitations on the exercise

Key Quote Boxes throughout the text draw out important and influential statements.

KEY QUOTE BOX 9.8
Fanon on Violence in Decolonization . . .

[D]ecolonization is always a violent phenomenon . . . The naked for us the searing bullets and bloodstained knives which emanat first, this will only come to pass after a murderous and decisive tagonists. . . . [Because, he argued, colonization had been force could only succeed by force—] . . . the agents of government spea '[C]olonialism . . . is violence in its natural state, and it will only

Case Study Boxes demonstrate how political ideas, concepts, and issues manifest in the real world.

CASE STUDY BOX 11.3
The Indian General Election 2014

The Indian general election in 2014 marked a turning point in In tion, widespread expert expectations were that national politics paralysis caused by an 'inevitable' coalition government, with thir in the lower house of parliament, the Lok Sabha. However, with of caste or regional identity rather than policies, the nationalist B tunning victory. For the first time since 1984, a party in India

Short Biography Boxes provide you with more information on key political thinkers and their ideas.

> **SHORT BIOGRAPHY** BOX 5.5
> John Rawls (1921–2002)
>
> John Rawls was an American academic who spent most of his Philosophy at Harvard University. Despite his retiring dispositic involved in political debate, Rawls's major work, *A Theory of Justic* one of the most influential works of political philosophy in the t than 300,000 copies in the USA alone. His rights-based theory o discipline in apparent decline but also provided a major challe

Key Points at the end of each section draw out the most important points and arguments from the text.

> **KEY POINTS**
>
> • Politics is usually predicated on the existence of competing societies of any complexity.
> • For most commentators politics is inevitable precisely be differences that have to be tackled in some way.
> • Different versions of 'endism' proclaim the dominance of libera cannot be sustained in the face of ongoing ideological conflic

Cross-references throughout the book help you to make connections between the chapters and deepen your understanding of particular topics.

> 960) and Francis Fukuyama (1992) respectively. 1945 period, liberal democratic values gradually d. This appeared to be confirmed by the collapse al system in 1989. However, whilst it is true that munism in Russia and Eastern Europe has been Vest has made it more difficult for left-of-centre not follow that we have reached the end of ide-
>
> ➡ See Chapter 2 for a discussion of human nature.

Glossary terms appear in colour throughout the text and are defined in a glossary at the end of the book, helping you expand your vocabulary and aiding your exam revision.

> We are living through a time of worldwide disruption and populism, identity politics, nationalism, isolationism, prot ments of people are putting considerable pressure on states of government. At the same time, the global balance of pow ing in a way not experienced since the Second World War, ur international order. We have sought not only to look at need stand from our many witnesses the roots of this upheaval UK's 'bedrock' relationship with its key ally of past deca

Key questions at the end of every chapter help you to check your understanding of core themes and critically reflect on the chapter material.

> **KEY QUESTIONS**
>
> 1. How do norms and methods inform the development of the
> 2. What were the major factors behind the rise of liberal inter eth century and what did early theorists hope to achieve?
> 3. In what way does the right to national self-determination st nation-state idea?
> 4. Why did E. H. Carr describe early liberals as utopians, and

Further reading lists are provided at the end of each chapter to help you take your learning further and to locate they key academic literature relevant to the chapter topic.

> **FURTHER READING**
>
> Bryson, V. (2003), *Feminist Political Theory: An Introduction* (Basing This is an excellent introduction.
> Garner, R. (2019), *Environmental Political Thought: Interests, Values* Globe Press). A comprehensive, and up to date, account of the major debates in
> Gray, J. (2003), *Al Qaeda and What it Means to be Modern* (Londor

GUIDED TOUR OF THE ONLINE RESOURCES

The Online Resources that accompany this book provide students and instructors with a range of ready-to-use teaching and learning resources.

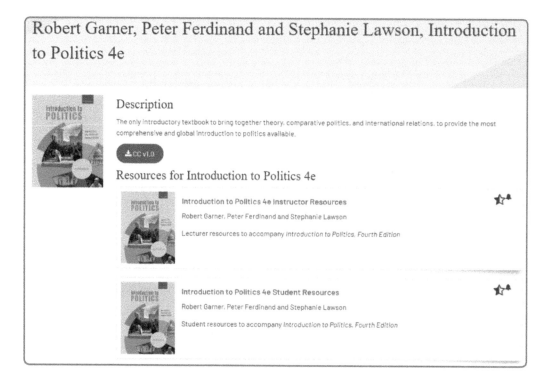

FOR STUDENTS
- Learn more about the people behind the theory with the 'Key Thinkers' resource
- Test your understanding of the chapter content and receive instant feedback with self-marking multiple-choice questions
- Revise key terms and concepts with an online flashcard glossary

FOR REGISTERED LECTURERS
- Encourage students to think critically with political scenario exercises
- Reinforce key themes from each chapter with suggested discussion questions for use in seminars
- Use the adaptable PowerPoint slides as the basis for a lecture presentation, or as hand-outs in class
- Save time preparing assessments and seminars with a fully updated test bank of questions

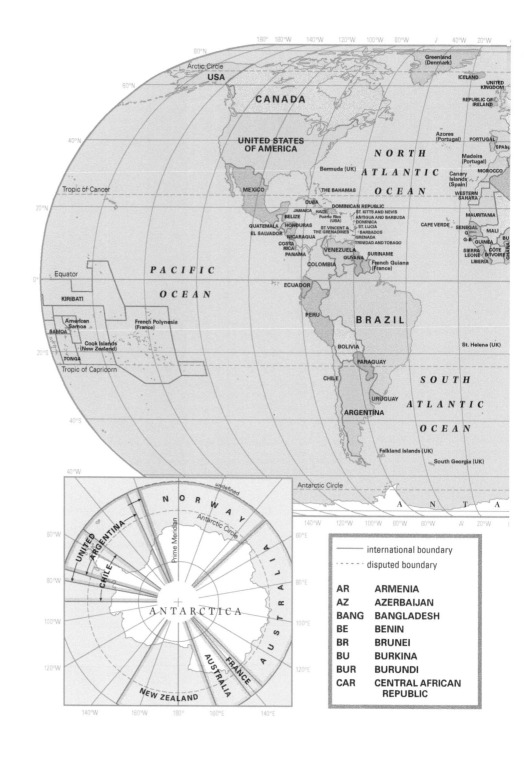

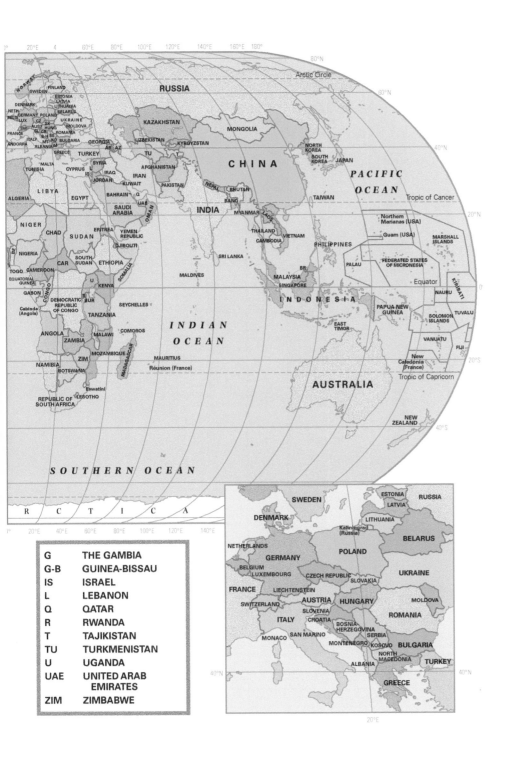

G	THE GAMBIA
G-B	GUINEA-BISSAU
IS	ISRAEL
L	LEBANON
Q	QATAR
R	RWANDA
T	TAJIKISTAN
TU	TURKMENISTAN
U	UGANDA
UAE	UNITED ARAB EMIRATES
ZIM	ZIMBABWE

INTRODUCTION: THE NATURE OF POLITICS AND POLITICAL ANALYSIS

BY ROBERT GARNER

READER'S GUIDE

This chapter will begin by seeking to define the nature of politics and the political before asking whether politics is an inevitable feature of all human societies. Some time is spent examining the boundary problems inherent in an analysis of the nature of the political. Two are particularly notable. Should politics be defined narrowly, in the context of the state, or should it be broadly defined to encompass other social institutions? Second, is politics equivalent to consensus and cooperation, so that politics does not exist in the event of conflict and war? The chapter then goes on to distinguish between different forms of political analysis—the empirical, the normative, and the semantic—and outlines different approaches to the study of politics. Finally, it is asked whether politics can ever be a science to rival subjects in the natural sciences.

1

WHAT IS POLITICS?

Politics is a many-sided activity which is impervious to one simple definition. A crucial question is to ask what are the boundaries of the political? Should we draw them narrowly, at the risk of rejecting much of what might fairly be described as politics, or should we draw them widely, at the risk of diluting the term to the point of meaninglessness?

Definitional rigour is not helped by the fact that politics is often popularly regarded in a pejorative sense, associated with corruption, intrigue, and conflict. The close association of politics with power, or more especially the abuse of power, compounds the negative associations, as does the perception that many politicians in the contemporary period are only 'in it for themselves'. US President Trump's promise, made during his 2016 election campaign, to 'drain the swamp' of Washington DC initially referred to conflicts of interest created by the political lobbying industry, but the phrase also stands as a more general metaphor, at least for Trump supporters, for almost everything that appears to be wrong at the centre of American politics.

One commentator has noted that the popular association of politics with the apparent pursuit of the material self-interest of politicians in the contemporary period is 'oddly antithetical to its very *raison d'etre*'—that is the realization of the 'collective good' (Hay, 2002: 3). Most contemporary politicians would say that this is actually what motivated them to seek public office in the first place, and there is no doubt that many do genuinely believe that it lies at the heart of their calling. The view of politics as essential to the realization of a common or collective good has appeared in the work of political thinkers from the ancient Greeks onwards.

In the ancient and pre-modern periods, in addition to Aristotle, political philosophers such as Plato (427–327 BC), Cicero (106–43 BC), St Augustine of Hippo (354–430), and St Thomas Aquinas (1225–74) all articulated conceptions of the common good, and highlighted the task of politics in achieving this. In the Arab/Muslim world, too, philosophers such as Ibn Rushd (1126–98) saw the purpose of government and politics as creating the conditions for the pursuit of the good life while much of classical Hindu political philosophy in South Asia and the Confucian tradition of thought in East Asia centred on similar themes. In the modern period, political philosophers such as Jean-Jacques Rousseau (1712–78) and John Stuart Mill (1806–73) regarded participation in political life as an honourable activity that ought to be encouraged. The essentially noble purpose of politics is therefore evident in a broad range of philosophical traditions. Here, it is interesting to note that in the ancient Greek world, the term *idiotes* (idiot) referred specifically to a citizen who took no interest in the affairs of the polis.

The pejorative critique of politics actually provides, though, a clue to what politics is about. For it might be argued that politics is associated with adversarial behaviour precisely because it reflects the conflictual nature of society, or, to use a less value-laden term, the fact that all societies of any complexity contain a range of different interests and values. Indeed, one popular definition of politics is that it is the process by which groups representing divergent interests and values make collective decisions. There are two assumptions here. The first is that all societies of any complexity must contain diversity, that humans will always have different interests and values, and therefore there will always be a need for a mechanism whereby these different interests and values are reconciled. The second assumption is that scarcity is also an inevitable characteristic of all societies. Since there is not enough to go around of the goods that people want, there needs to be some mechanism whereby these goods can be distributed.

Politics would seem, then, in the words of the American political scientist Harold Lasswell (1936), to be about 'Who Gets What, When, How?' Clearly, of great importance here is the way in which economic goods are distributed, as these are crucially important in determining the nature of society and the well-being of those who live within it. As we shall see in Chapter 5, competing theories of distributive justice focus on a particular ordering of economic goods. However, there are other goods that humans value. Status, for instance, is seen to be particularly important. For most people, for example, the granting of an honour, whether by the state or an organization within civil society, is regarded as valuable, even though no monetary reward is attached to it.

The study of politics prior to the nineteenth century was almost exclusively concerned with a study of values; that is, politics was equated with philosophy. Political philosophers asked, what is the good life? What, in other words, is the best kind of society for us to live in? Many different answers to this question have been provided but, as Stoker (2006: 6) points out, a 'central divide for much of the last two centuries has been between those who prefer liberty over equality and those who prefer equality over liberty'. This of course raises the question of the balance between the two. In the present period, there is evidence of a widening gap between rich and poor in many countries. Of equal importance in the twenty-first century is the conflict between liberty and the value of security—a theme which has become increasingly prominent in the wake of '9/11' and the heightened sense of threat from terror attacks.

IS POLITICS INEVITABLE?

If we define politics in terms of differences, conflicts, and scarcity, then it might be, and has by many been suggested, that politics is an inevitable feature of all societies. Not all agree with this. For some, such a claim seriously underestimates the possibility of greater social cohesion based around agreement on core values. Marxists, in particular, suggest that, since differences of interests in society centre on the existence of competing social classes, the creation of a classless society offers the prospect of a society based on consensus and cooperation, one in which politics and the state are not necessary.

Politics, for Marx then, is seen in negative terms. It is about class conflict. Political power, as Marx and Engels famously insisted in the *Communist Manifesto* (1976: 105), is 'merely the organised power of one class for oppressing another'. It logically follows from this that, once that conflict is ended through the overthrow of capitalism, there are no competing classes and therefore, by definition, no politics. For others, this Marxist vision is unrealistic—'ideal fancy' in Berlin's words (1969: 118) since it fails to take into account human nature's tendency towards difference, striving, and competition.

Other, more recent versions of the 'end of politics' are associated with the 'end of ideology' and 'end of history' theses proposed by Daniel Bell (1960) and Francis Fukuyama (1992) respectively. An argument common to both is that in the post-1945 period, liberal democratic values gradually assumed a position of dominance across the world. This appeared to be confirmed by the collapse of communism as a viable economic and political system in 1989. However, whilst it is true that the Cold War is now a thing of the past, that communism in Russia and Eastern Europe has been dismantled, and that growing affluence in the West has made it more difficult for left-of-centre parties to garner political support, it simply does not follow that we have reached the end of ideology, let alone history.

➡ See Chapter 2 for a discussion of human nature.

A cursory glance at world affairs seems to put this end of ideology thesis to the sword. As this book will reveal, in the world there are a number of alternatives to the liberal democratic model. Some of these alternatives have similarities with Western liberal democracy but also significant differences. The post-communist regimes of Eastern Europe, for instance, operate very differently because of their limited experience of democratic norms. Many East Asian regimes (such as China, Malaysia, Singapore, and so on) have put a greater focus on economic development, sometimes at the expense of civil liberty and democratic procedures. The difficulty of establishing liberal democratic principles in Iraq is also indicative of the limited application of the end of history approach. Finally, other alternatives are obviously completely different from the Western liberal democratic model. This applies to military regimes, often found in Africa, and Islamic regimes, particularly of the fundamentalist variety as in Iran, that put religious norms before liberty and democracy. The fact that some authoritarian regimes, such as China, have experienced rapid economic growth belies the claim that there is a causal relationship between prosperity and the existence of liberal democratic values and institutions (Dryzek and Dunleavy, 2009: 335).

Many fundamental conflicts remain in the world that require political resolution. Some are based on territory, others are based on political values, the most insoluble containing elements of both. Here, the uncompromising ideology of nationalism is all too apparent. The Israel/Palestine conflict, in which competing nationalisms make apparently irreconcilable claims, is one such case. And there have been cases in Western Europe where resort to violence has only recently been eliminated, as in Northern Ireland and the Basque country of Spain. Widely divergent views over such issues as immigration and multiculturalism have also generated much conflict as has the emergence of identity politics. As Gamble (2000: 108) points out, 'The notion that there are no longer any great ideological issues in the world . . . becomes bizarre in relation to the vast populations . . . in Africa, in Asia, in Latin America and in the former territories of the Soviet Union' who live under regimes that do not subscribe to all, or some, liberal democratic principles.

There is another sense in which politics is said to be superfluous, identified and challenged by Gamble (2000). Gamble seeks to challenge what he sees as the pessimistic acceptance in the modern world that humans can no longer influence their destiny. According to this position, the forces of 'bureaucracy, technology and the global market' have led to the 'disenchantment of the world, in which the ability to change that world . . . has been lost and lost irrevocably' (14). So-called globalization, in particular, signals the end of national autonomy. It no longer matters what allegedly sovereign governments do because we are controlled by global economic forces that no one can alter. As a result, the 'space for politics is shrinking, and with it the possibility to imagine or to realise any serious alternative to our present condition. This it seems is our fate' (Gamble, 2000: 2–3).

Such pessimism is, in part at least, a cause of the alleged 'crisis of politics' seen in declining political participation and the emergence of an 'anti-politics' discourse in Western democracies. (Flinders, 2012: 10–15; Heywood, 2013: 443–5). The term 'anti-politics' is now used variously to describe a distrust of career politicians, a rejection of partisan politics as embodied in dominant party systems, a disengagement with mainstream politics or 'politics as usual', and a turn to populism. Anti-politics has recently been identified with the 2016 'Brexit' vote in the UK, the campaign for which was spearheaded by the previously marginal UK Independence Party (UKIP), and in the 2016 US presidential election in which Donald Trump gained support from many who saw him as not a politician.

➡ See Chapter 6 for a discussion of nationalism.

➡ See Chapter 7 for a discussion of multiculturalism.

➡ See Chapter 2 for a discussion of identity politics.

➡ See Chapters 2, 21, and 22 for a discussion of globalization.

➡ See Chapters 7 and 15 for a discussion of populism.

➡ See Chapter 4 for a discussion of contemporary challenges to democracy.

Should we really be so pessimistic about contemporary politics and the prospect of positive change? It would be wrong to suggest that there are no constraints, some of them severe, acting upon human will. We may have to deal with the realities of the global market and dehumanizing technologies, but it would be equally wrong to conclude that human agency has no impact. Rather, there is a tension between impersonal forces and human will, a tension 'between politics and fate', that must be recognized and tackled.

KEY POINTS

- Politics is usually predicated on the existence of competing interests and values in all societies of any complexity.
- For most commentators politics is inevitable precisely because all societies contain differences that have to be tackled in some way.
- Different versions of 'endism' proclaim the dominance of liberal democratic values, but this cannot be sustained in the face of ongoing ideological conflicts around the world.
- Contemporary politics in Western democracies appears to have generated much pessimism about the capacity of politics to actually deliver the good life, as reflected in the phenomenon of 'anti-politics'.

POLITICAL QUESTIONS

Politics, then, is essentially a mechanism for deciding, in Lasswell's words, 'Who Gets What, When, How?' If we all had the same interests and values, and there was enough of everything to go around, there would be no need to make such decisions. We could have everything we wanted. Politics is predicated on the assumption that this is not the case. As a result, students of politics ask a number of questions about the decisions that are taken.

In the first place, they will ask what values do and what should the decisions made serve? Do they serve, for instance, the values of justice or liberty, and if so, what do we mean by justice and liberty? Is a just decision one that is made in the interests of the few, the many, or all? Second, students of politics will ask who makes and should make the decisions? Is it one person who makes the decisions, or a few, many, or all? Is there anything special, it will be asked further, about democratic forms of government? Are we more obliged to obey decisions taken in a democratic way than in other ways? These types of question formed the basis of Aristotle's famous six-fold classification of political systems (**see Box 1.1 and Table 1.1**).

The third main question that students of politics will ask is why are those taking decisions able to enforce them? Here, it is important to make a distinction between power and authority, concepts which are central to politics. We could say that rulers are able to enforce their decisions either because they have the power to do so or because they have the authority to do so. The former implies some form of coercion or sanction; that those with power are able to cause those without power to behave in a way they would not otherwise have done. Clearly, a regime that relies exclusively on the exercise of power, in the sense described above, is likely to be inefficient and unstable. Such a regime will only survive if it is able to impose coercion continually, a time-consuming and difficult exercise.

1

Aristotle (384–322 BC) argued that a symbol of good government was the degree to which the rulers ruled in the interests of all and not a sectional interest. As a result, he developed a six-fold classification containing three 'proper' forms of government and three 'deviant' forms of government. His preferred form of government was a monarchy. Democracy is regarded as a deviant form of government because it is regarded by Aristotle as the rule of the poor in their own interests, thereby equivalent to mob rule. However, he also thought (as was echoed by Winston Churchill's comment many centuries later) that democracy is the least bad form of government (Cunningham, 2002: 7).

Photo 1.1 Aristotle, a Greek philosopher during the classical period in Ancient Greece. *Wellcome Collection*

Table 1.1 Political systems according to Aristotle

Number ruling	Rulers rule in interest of . . .	
	. . . All	. . . Themselves
One	Monarchy	Tyranny
Few	Aristocracy	Oligarchy
Many	Polity	Democracy

Source: Dahl (1991: 59).

If a set of rulers has authority, on the other hand, force will not be necessary since authority is defined in terms of legitimacy. Authority, then, is defined here as legitimate power in the sense that rulers can produce acceptance by the ruled, not because they can exercise coercion but because the ruled recognize the right of the rulers to exercise power. Converting power into authority, then, should be the goal of any set of rulers.

➜ See Chapter 3 for an exploration of the concepts of power and authority.

KEY POINTS

- Assuming differences of values and interests, politics becomes a study of which values and interests come to dominate, who is responsible for these decisions, and with what justification.
- Politics involves the exercise of power, but issues of authority and legitimacy moderate the manner in which it is exercised.

THE BOUNDARIES OF THE POLITICAL: (1) STATE, SOCIETY, AND THE INTERNATIONAL COMMUNITY

We have seen that politics is presaged on differences that human beings have, and how these differences, in interests and values, can be managed in a world where scarcity is inevitable. However, this only takes us so far in a definitional sense, because it does not touch upon boundary problems. Much of the definitional controversy surrounding politics relates to these boundary problems. Where does politics begin and end? For Leftwich (1984: 10), this is the 'single most important factor involved in influencing the way people implicitly or explicitly conceive of politics'.

For some, politics ought to be defined narrowly. According to this view, politics is associated with the activities of the state and the public realm, or with a particular type of decision-making based on building compromise and consensus. As a result, institutions other than the state, and dispute-resolving through violence or suppression, although important in their own right, are beyond the scope of politics. For others, as we shall see later, this narrow drawing of the boundary is to miss much of importance that might fairly be described as political.

Politics has traditionally been associated with the activities of the state. This narrow definition certainly helps to distinguish politics, however artificially, from other social sciences such as sociology and economics. As a result, subfields of politics such as political sociology and political economy focus on the relationship between the state and society and the economy respectively. The state has traditionally been the centre of much political analysis because it has been regarded as the highest form of authority in a society. Put another way, in the words of the great German sociologist Max Weber (1864–1920), the state has a 'monopoly of the legitimate use of physical force in enforcing its order within a given territorial area' (Gerth and Mills, 1946: 77–8).

Such authority is tantamount to sovereignty. The state is sovereign in the sense that it is the supreme law-making body within a particular territory. Ultimately, it has the power of life and death over individuals. It can decide to put people to death for crimes they have committed, and it can demand that individuals fight for their country in wars with other sovereign states. Defined

1

→ See Chapter 14 for a discussion of civil society.

in such a way, the state can be distinguished from the government in the sense that it is a much larger entity, containing not just political offices but also bureaucratic institutions, the judiciary, military, and police and security services. The state can also be distinguished from civil society which consists of those non-governmental institutions—such as pressure groups, business organizations, and trade unions—to which individuals belong. It is these institutions that provide linkages between the individual and the state. **See Box 1.2.**

Without doubt, to include the activities of the state in a study of politics is necessary, albeit not necessarily sufficient. As we will see in Part 2 of this book, the study of government—its legislative, executive, and judicial functions—occupies a great deal of the political analyst's time. Moreover, Chapters 2 and 3 reveal that the question of state power is central to the study of politics. Since the sixteenth century, political theory has been associated with—and has helped shape the character of—the nation-state, the varying types of which are described in Chapter 2. Political theory is intrinsically linked to a study of political obligation. Why should we, it is asked, obey the state? Is there any particular form of the state that we can obey rather than others? Can we obey any state?

→ See Chapter 4 for a discussion of political obligation.

Similarly, concepts such as freedom and justice, examined in Chapter 5, were largely concerned with, in the former case, what limits ought to be placed on the state and, in the latter, what distribution of goods ought the state to pursue. Most of the ideologies covered in Chapters 6 and 7 are equally concerned with principles by which the state ought to be organized.

Although questions of political power tend to focus on the state, some seek to draw the boundaries of the political much wider. For these scholars, we can talk sensibly about politics existing in various types of group from the family to the international community. One fundamental question for students of politics, for instance, is the degree to which politics now exists beyond the state at a higher supranational level. There have always been those who have argued that the state is an oppressive institution and therefore ought not to exist (Hoffman, 1995). Arguably too, now, the focus of politics has begun to shift because in a practical sense we are living in a world which is becoming increasingly interdependent, where the forces of so-called globalization are placing increasing constraints on what individual so-called 'sovereign' states can do on their own.

→ See Chapter 17 for a discussion of realism.

It is certainly the case that the academic study of international relations has grown enormously in the past few years. The fact that a third of this book is devoted to the relationship between states—rather than politics within the state, or with comparisons between states—is a reflection of the growing importance of this field. That said, it should also be recognized that the traditional so-called 'realist' approach to international relations still has the state as the key actor. In this model, the difficulty of securing agreement between states can act as a significant handicap on the successful resolution of supranational problems.

KEY CONCEPT BOX 1.2
Civil Society

A term that is usually taken to refer to a range of private institutions existing between the individual and the state. This would include what are now referred to as interest groups representing things that people have in common, such as business, trade unions, religion, ethnicity, and so on. Hegel, the eighteenth- and early nineteenth-century German philosopher, distinguished between the family, civil society, and the state, each offering increasing degrees of social integration. Others would want to include the family as an institution within civil society.

The forces of globalization, discussed in various places in this book, question not only the sovereign state, but also political theory itself which grew up to theorize it. At the extremes, we could defend to the hilt the state-specific nature of much political thought by denying the claims made by advocates of globalization. Conversely, we could accept these claims and render the dominant state-specific school of political theory as redundant. What is certain is that political theorists will increasingly have to grapple with the impact of globalization. Indeed, this is already beginning to happen. The case for cosmopolitan theories of democracy and justice, for instance, is considered in Chapters 4 and 5 respectively. Moreover, those ideologies—such as environmentalism and multiculturalism—which are predicated on the reality of increasing interconnectedness of the peoples and nations of the world, form part of the subject matter of Chapter 7.

Another dent in the argument of those who draw the boundaries of the political in a narrow sense comes from those who argue that politics exists in the institutions of society below the state. Hay (2002: 3), for instance, makes this abundantly clear when he insists that 'the political should be defined in such a way as to encompass the entire sphere of the social'. Leftwich (1984) substantially agrees, arguing that 'politics is at the heart of *all* collective social activity, formal and informal, public and private, in *all* human groups, institutions and societies'. The term governance, often preferred now to government, reflects this by drawing the boundaries of the governmental process much wider to include not just the traditional institutions of government but also the other inputs into decisions affecting society such as the workings of the market and the role of interest groups. Indeed, this concurs with everyday discourse where it is common to hear about politics taking place in business organizations, universities, churches, sport, and the family.

As Part 3 of this book will show, the student of international relations is faced with a very complex world of relations not just between states but with an enormous range of non-state actors and forces. This is reflected in fields as varied as international political economy, international organizations, and security studies. The challenge to international relations in the present period is to integrate insights from domestic and comparative studies, including studies in political theory, into a broader conception of the 'international'. As we shall see, this has prompted some scholars to abandon the very term 'international'—and 'relations'—favouring instead terms such as 'global politics' or 'world politics'.

Some ideological traditions concur with this wider view of politics. Radical feminists, for instance, see power deriving from patriarchy meaning literally the rule of the father—in personal relationships and the family, and therefore the personal realm is acutely political. This is what is meant by the radical feminism slogan 'the personal is the political'. Classical Marxists, likewise, insist that political power derives from dominance in the economic realm. Similarly, whatever its internal divisions, and there are many, Islamic thought, deriving from religious scriptures, delves into all aspects of the social sphere down to the family and normative prescriptions that individuals are meant to follow. To deny the political nature of this thought further alienates politics from much of importance in the contemporary world.

➡ See Chapters 7 and 18 for a discussion of feminism.

Despite Leftwich's limitation above, it can also be questioned whether the boundaries of the political should stop at the human species. There would seem to be a strong case for incorporating at least some species of non-human animals as beings who are morally considerable and ought to have their interests considered in the political process (Garner, 2005; Donaldson and Kymlicka, 2011). An even more radical position seeks to extend the boundaries of the political to encompass the whole of the natural world, a position designated as dark green ecology (Dobson, 2007).

➡ See Chapter 7 for a discussion on environmentalism.

There is an apparent danger in expanding the boundaries of the political in the ways suggested in the preceding discussion. If we do so, does not politics cease to be a distinctive discipline? How would we distinguish, say, between the work of the sociologist and that of the political analyst? Does not politics, in a very real sense, lose its separate identity?

Hay's response here is that this critique is confusing politics as an arena with politics as a process (2002: 72). For Hay, the distinctiveness of politics lies not in the arena within which it takes place but in 'the emphasis it places on the political aspect of social relations'. This 'political aspect' is then defined in terms of the 'distribution, exercise and consequences of power'. Politics, then, is about power, and occurs wherever the exercise of power takes place. Hay is not suggesting, then, that politics explains everything there is to be known, or even the most important things to be known, about social relationships. Other disciplines—sociology, economics, psychology, cultural studies—have important explanatory roles too. 'Though politics may be everywhere', Hay (2002: 75) continues, 'nothing is exhaustively political'. As Dahl (1991: 4) explains, people 'experience many relationships other than power and authority: love, respect, dedication, shared beliefs and so on'.

THE BOUNDARIES OF THE POLITICAL: (2) POLITICS AS CONSENSUS OR CONFLICT?

There are those who suggest that politics is the art of finding peaceful resolutions to conflict, through compromise and the building of consensus. In so far as this fails to happen and military conflict or any kind of violence results as a consequence, then politics can be said to have been rejected or failed. Bernard Crick is perhaps the best-known advocate of this position. For him, politics is 'only one possible solution to the problem of order' (1962: 18). It is, for Crick, the preferable way to resolve conflicts. Politics is, for him then, a 'great and civilizing human activity' associated with admirable values of toleration and respect and fortitude (15).

In contrast to tyranny and oligarchy, both of which are concerned with coercing those who disagree with the ruling elite, political rule, for Crick, is concerned with incorporating competing groups in society. He argues that conciliation is most likely to occur when power is widely spread in society so that no one small group can impose its will on others. Unfortunately, as he recognizes, politics is a rare activity that is too often rejected in favour of violence and suppression. He therefore calls for its values to be promoted and persevered with.

Similar arguments are put forward by Gerry Stoker (2006) and Matthew Flinders (2012). The former argues that politics not only expresses the reality of disagreement and conflict in society but is also 'one of the ways we know of how to address and potentially patch up the disagreements that characterize our societies without resource to illegitimate coercion or violence' (7). For Flinders (2012: 5) likewise, the 'simple essence' of politics is a 'commitment to stability and compromise through social dialogue'.

Both Flinders and Stoker further argue that much of the present discontent about politics is misplaced. Our expectations are too high and have increased at a time when politicians are increasingly able to achieve less (Flinders, 2012: 18–35). Rather than judging it by too exacting standards it should be recognized that politics, by its very nature, is messy, muddled, and, in a very real sense, 'designed to disappoint' (Stoker, 2006: 10). Although 'democratic politics may not be perfect . . . it remains vastly superior to any other form of regime' (Flinders, 2012: 2).

It might be best to describe the arguments put forward by Crick, Stoker, and Flinders as representing a particular kind of politics. Crick has been criticized for linking politics closely with the practices of liberal democracies where power is commonly assumed to be widely dispersed. It would seem strange if our definition forces us into a position which holds that those countries governed undemocratically by economic, religious, or military elites are not practising politics but should, as Crick implies, aspire to it. Flinders and Stoker, as their arguments described in the last paragraph attest, avoid this lack of clarity by explicitly engaging in a defence of *democratic* politics rather than politics per se.

It is true that conflicts and differences are at the heart of politics, but if we can only talk about politics when agreements are reached, and compromises made then it would seem to be a very limited activity. In this sense, it is probably sensible to talk of the resort to force and violence and military conflict as politics by another means, as in the famous dictum by the nineteenth-century Prussian military strategist, Carl von Clausewitz. **See Box 1.3**.

KEY QUOTE BOX 1.3
The Nature of Politics

[A political system is] any persistent pattern of human relationships that involves, to a significant extent, control, influence, power or authority. (Dahl, 1991: 4)

[Politics is the] art of governing mankind by deceiving them. (Issac D'Israeli, quoted in Crick, 1962: 16)

[Politics] can be simply defined as the activity by which differing interests within a given unit of rule are conciliated by giving them a share in power in proportion to their importance to the welfare and the survival of the whole community. (Crick, 1962: 21)

Politics is a phenomenon found in and between all groups, institutions (formal and informal) and societies, cutting across public and private life. It is involved in all the relations, institutions and structures which are implicated in the activities of production and reproduction in the life of societies ... Thus, politics is about power; about the forces which influence and reflect its distribution and use; and about the effect of this on resource use and distribution ... it is not about Government or government alone. (Held and Leftwich, 1984: 144)

Politics is designed to disappoint—that is the way that the process of compromise and reconciliation works. Its outcomes are often messy, ambiguous and never final. (Stoker, 2006: 10)

KEY POINTS

- Defining politics is beset by boundary problems.
- Some argue that the boundaries of the political ought to be drawn narrowly, recognizing the state as the key political institution. Others argue that politics ought to be drawn far more broadly to encompass power relations in social institutions such as the family or political institutions at the supranational level.
- The second boundary problem concerns the subject matter of politics, rather than its location. Here, there are those, such as Crick, who seek to define politics in terms of consensus-building and cooperation. For many, however, this definition is unduly limiting. Politics is not absent in undemocratic regimes or in periods of civil or international strife.

THE STUDY OF POLITICS

The study of politics dates back to at least the Greeks in the fifth century BC, the Greek philosophers Plato and Aristotle credited with being the founding fathers. Despite this, politics only became an independent discipline in higher education at the beginning of the twentieth century, previously being subsumed under other disciplines such as law, philosophy, and history. The American Political Science Association, the body of academics specializing in political studies, was formed in 1903 and its British equivalent, the Political Studies Association, in 1950 (Lowndes, Marsh, and Stoker, 2018: 2). Canada, Finland, India, China, and Japan all had political studies associations before the UK did. There are now over 50 national and regional studies associations affiliated to the International Political Science Association which was established in 1949 (see http://www.ipsa.org/about-ipsa/history).

The teaching of politics has traditionally distinguished between the study of political ideas (sometimes also referred to as theory or philosophy), the study of political institutions and processes within states, and the relations between states. This book is structured around these distinctions, yet, as we shall have cause to emphasize later in this introduction, they are far from being mutually exclusive. As Part 1 of this book shows, the study of political ideas contains a mix of conceptual analysis, coverage of the key figures in the history of political thought, and discussion of ideologies. The study of institutions and processes, too, covered in Part 2, can take a number of forms such as the examination of the institutions of a single state, comparisons of the institutions and processes of a number of states, political history, electoral politics, and public administration. Finally, students of international politics, examined in Part 3, focus, among other things, on the role of states or of a range of supranational actors and institutions, either historically or contemporaneously.

THE RISE AND FALL OF NORMATIVE ANALYSIS

In all three branches of the study of politics at least three major kinds of political analysis are utilized. First, students of politics engage in normative analysis. This type of political analysis asks questions of a valuational kind and seeks to identify what is good or better with a view to recommending what we ought to want. It asks, for instance, whether, when, and why we ought to value freedom, or democracy or equality and why we should obey the state. Many of the so-called 'greats' in the history of political thought, ranging from Plato's *Republic* through Thomas Hobbes's *Leviathan* to a more recent major work of political philosophy, John Rawls's *A Theory of Justice*, have all sought to set out what constitutes the 'good life', the kind of society and polity within which it would be desirable for us to live.

For much of the twentieth century, among the three forms of analysis identified above, normative analysis was the poor relation. In academia, a great deal of emphasis was placed on empirical political science and also on 'analytical' political philosophy, in which the meaning of concepts and the relation between them was considered. This was the so-called 'behavioural' revolution in which number crunching, particularly in relation to the study of electoral behaviour, was the gold standard. In this climate, pontificating on what kind of society and polity we ought to have—the basis of normative analysis—was regarded as, at best, unnecessary and, at worst, meaningless.

A variety of intellectual and practical political reasons have been put forward to explain what Peter Lasslett (1956: vii) described as the 'death of political philosophy'. Some see the nineteenth century as the last great age of political philosophy and put its decline down to the growth of secularism. As Dahl (1991: 120) points out, 'values could no longer be successfully justified by basing them on divinely revealed religious truths'. In addition, the status of philosophy in general had taken a hammering by virtue of the fact that the senseless destruction of human life in the Holocaust had occurred in what was regarded as the most philosophically sophisticated country in Europe (Horton, 1984: 115).

Another factor was the emergence, in the 1950s and 1960s—in the West at least—of consensus politics whereby widespread agreement on fundamental political principles was accompanied by economic prosperity. There was little purchase in justifying alternative political arrangements when the present ones—based on the mixed economy, the welfare state, and the nuclear deterrent—were working so well.

In the academic world, the decline of normative analysis was partly a product of the rise in status of positivism, an approach that seeks to apply the scientific methodology of the natural sciences to social phenomena (**see Box 1.4**). This approach was associated in particular with the French social scientist Auguste Comte (1798–1856), who argued that the scientific stage of history now upon us would dominate.

An extreme version of positivism was a school of thought known as logical positivism, centring around a group of philosophers known as the 'Vienna Circle' (see Ayer, 1971). For logical positivists, only statements which are empirically verifiable *and* those which sought to say something about the meaning of concepts and the relations between them are legitimate. Normative statements, seeking to make claims of a valuational kind, are regarded as meaningless.

Normative political philosophy began to make a comeback in the 1960s and 1970s, partly as a result of the decline in consensus politics, itself a product of mounting economic problems, and partly because of the emergence of new and innovative works of political philosophy, most notably Rawls's *A Theory of Justice*. Despite this, however, it should be recognized that a great deal of contemporary political philosophy is much more cautious and tentative than the grand narratives of the past. A number of contemporary political philosophers have noted the discrepancy between the abstract normative work of some political philosophy, in which ideal political and moral principles are advocated, and the difficulty of applying such principles in the non-ideal real world. John Rawls's theory of justice, discussed in Chapter 5, is often taken to be the classical example of an ideal theory. As he writes (1971: 9), 'the nature and aims of a perfectly just society is the fundamental part of the theory of justice'.

Advocates of so-called 'non-ideal' theory are not claiming simply that political pragmatism should prevail over normative political philosophy, but rather that any political philosophy which

---

! KEY CONCEPT BOX 1.4
Positivism

An approach which holds that science must limit itself to those things that are observable, thereby insisting upon a clear separation between fact and value. At the extreme, positivism—in the form of the doctrine known as logical positivism—holds that only those statements that can be investigated by observation, and those that can be examined semantically, are worthwhile. Normative questions are regarded as more or less meaningless.

does not take account of the non-ideal world in which it is attempting to influence, and address is *normatively* deficient (Farrelly, 2007). That is, it is being claimed here that normative political principles, such as those present in many theories of justice, are not logically independent from questions relating to non-ideal constraints, whether they concern unsympathetic social, economic, or historical circumstances, moral disagreement, or human nature. This boils down to the well-known moral principle that 'ought implies can'. As Farrelly (2007: 845) points out, 'there is some conceptual incoherence involved in saying "This is what justice involves, but there is no way it could be implemented" '. In other words, a valid *theory* of justice must be relevant to the eradication of at least some current injustices.

What is clear is that normative questions present problems of a peculiar nature for the student of politics. As we shall see later, empirical facts can play a part in the resolution of normative questions. However, for most scholars it still remains impossible to derive normative statements merely from empirical facts. This is the famous dictum that it is impossible to derive an ought from an is. Consider the premise that 'she is old and lonely, and her health is frail' followed by the conclusion that 'you ought to help her' (Thomas, 1993: 14). Clearly, the conclusion does not follow from the premise unless we add another clause along the lines that 'we ought to help those who are old, lonely, and frail'. This, of course, is another normative statement not capable of empirical confirmation.

Given that we cannot resolve normative questions merely by invoking empirical facts, how then can we judge the validity of a normative statement? In other words, does this not mean that the logical positivists were right after all that normative statements are meaningless and attempts to adjudicate between competing values is a worthless exercise? As Dahl (1991: 118) asks, does this mean that asking the question whether democracy is better than dictatorship is equivalent to asking whether 'you like coffee better than tea'?

There is 'no easy answer' (Wolff, 1996: 3) to this normative conundrum. One possible solution is offered by Dworkin (1987: 7–8), who cleverly argues that it is mistaken to regard modern political theories as offering different foundational values. Rather, he suggests, they all have a commitment to egalitarianism in the sense that they all hold that humans are worth the same and have an equal value. Even if Dworkin is right, and it might be argued that he overestimates the compatibility between mainstream ideologies such as liberalism and socialism, it still remains the case that other political ideologies clearly do not hold that humans have an equal value; and yet, without any apparent means of assessing their worth, we are committed to saying that, say, slavery is as good as freedom, or racism is as good as racial tolerance. Intuitively, most of us would want to deny this relativism. How are we to judge between competing political and moral values?

In the first place, a relativist position does exaggerate the degree to which judgements on the validity of competing belief systems are not possible. Nagel (1987: 232), for instance, argues convincingly that it is possible to dismiss a particular belief 'in terms of errors in their evidence, or identifiable errors in drawing conclusions from it, or in argument, judgement and so forth'. Moreover, there are surely some conceptions of the good—health, bodily integrity, wealth, even liberty—to which everyone might aspire (Waldron, 1989: 74–5) as well as 'conceptions of the good which are manifestly unreasonable' (Arneson, 2000: 71). Of course, we may never be certain about the competing value of many conceptions of the good but, as Arneson (2000: 77) points out, 'if one sets the threshold of supporting reasons for public policy at the level of certainty, it is doubtful that any proposed policy can pass'.

EMPIRICAL AND SEMANTIC ANALYSIS

The second type of analysis common to politics, as well as most other academic disciplines, is empirical. Empirical analysis seeks to identify observable phenomena in the real world with a view to establishing what is, rather than what ought to be. Empirical analysis, of course, is the basis of the natural sciences, and many so-called *positivist* political analysts seek to bring to bear what they see as the impartial and value-free methods of the natural sciences to the study of political phenomena.

The third type of analysis commonly used in politics is analysis of a semantic kind. As its name suggests, this form of analysis is concerned with clarifying the meaning of the concepts we use. This is an important function in political studies. Many of the concepts used in politics have no commonly accepted definition, and, indeed, have been described as 'essentially contested concepts' (Gallie, 1955–6). Defining what we mean by key terms such as democracy and freedom, then, is a crucial starting point.

In reality, the three forms of political analysis described above are not used independently of each other. As Wolff (1996: 3) succinctly points out, 'studying how things are helps to explain how things can be and studying how they can be is indispensable for assessing how they ought to be'. Thus, in the first place, normative claims are, at least partly, based on empirical knowledge. In the case of Hobbes, to give one example, the normative claim that we ought to rely on an all-powerful sovereign to protect us derives from the largely empirical assumption that human nature is so brutally competitive that there is a great risk to our security without the protection of the so-called 'Leviathan'. Conversely, a great deal of empirical analysis presupposes some normative assumptions. This can be seen, in particular, in our choice of investigation. Thus, students of politics choose, say, to investigate the causes of war because it is assumed that war is undesirable and therefore, we should try to eliminate it.

➜ See Chapter 2 for a discussion on human nature.

It is instructive at this point to appreciate the differences between what might be called empirical and normative political theory. From a positivist perspective, the former refers to the generation of testable hypotheses of political phenomena. An example would be a hypothesis which postulated that democracy can only flourish in societies with a market economy and private ownership. The latter, on the other hand, is usually taken to mean the normative goal of judging to which political goals we ought to aspire. In other words, it would ask whether a democratic political framework or a capitalist economic framework is desirable in the first place.

Two main responses should be made to the claim that we can separate political 'theory' from the study of political institutions and processes. First, those who study government without recognition of the key normative questions raised by political philosophers will only receive a partial picture of their discipline. Systems of government created by human beings are a reflection of normative beliefs. The American Constitution, to give one prime example, is a product of the vision of the 'Founding Fathers' of what a modern polity ought to be like, and developments in the constitution since its creation, allowing, for example, for universal suffrage for the election of the President, reflect modern normative thinking.

In addition to the importance of normative theorizing, it should also be noted that theorizing of an empirical kind is also, as we will see in the chapters in Part 2, a central part of the study of political institutions and processes (Savigny and Marsden, 2011: 5–8). Theories are used in empirical work to try to order and make sense of the mass of information political researchers unearth, and to try and identify and explain relationships between observable phenomena. Knowing about particular political institutions or sets of them is only part of the objective and doing so properly is obviously essential. But locating them within a broader pattern of regularities is equally important and ultimately more satisfying. These sorts of issues provoke questions such as: why do parties exist? Is it possible to identify general patterns of their interactions? What general principles underlie electoral systems? How can we explain the behaviour of interest groups? In a similar vein, much of the theoretical literature surrounding the study of relationships between states, considered in Chapters 17 and 18, has an empirical dimension, although it should also be noted that most of these theories—whether it is explicit or not—also have a distinctive normative basis.

A key element of the empirical approach to the study of political institutions and processes is the comparative method. Here, political analysts seek to develop testable generalizations by examining political phenomena across different political systems or historically within the same political system. To attempt an answer to the hypothesis posed above—that democracy requires the free market and private ownership—it is necessary to engage in a comparative examination of different regimes so that the relationship between political and economic variables can be better understood. It also, it might be added, requires semantic analysis of the concept of democracy, a term subject to many different definitions, as discussed in Chapter 4. To take another example, the proposition that electoral systems using a form of proportional representation tend to produce political and economic instability can be tested by comparing their use with regimes using alternatives such as the first-past-the-post system.

This book deliberately sets out to introduce you to politics from all regions of the world. A great many politics students concentrate on Europe and the USA. Many students become passionately interested in them. So later chapters, for example, outline the reasons why political parties emerged in the USA, and contrast the different approaches to policy-making in the UK and France. Other students are more attracted by politics in the developing world or in other regions. This is an equally legitimate object of study. So we discuss Islamic understandings of justice, the problems of the African state, and the debate over the merits of presidentialism in Latin America and the Philippines. What is vital is that we use consistent and compatible approaches to the analysis of institutions, whether in the developed or the developing world, so that we can identify similarities and differences in the ways in which apparently similar institutions operate in different parts of the world. There is no doubt that institutions such as the state, political parties, or civil society look different when they are studied in Europe or the USA, as compared with other regions of the world. We want to encourage you to develop a sophisticated understanding of the similarities and the differences, their strengths and weaknesses.

DEDUCTIVE AND INDUCTIVE METHODS

The most important approaches to the empirical study of politics can be divided into those using deductive reasoning, on the one hand, and those using inductive reasoning, on the other. The deductive method, sometimes known as the top-down approach, starts from a general theoretical proposition and works down to the specific, aiming to test the theory in question by examining the relevant data. The inductive method, which works in the opposite, bottom-up, direction, moves from the observation of specific data to general propositions, aiming to generate rather than test theories. The deductive method is associated with so-called rational choice theories of politics, and the inductive approach is most often associated with an approach known as **behaviouralism**. (**See Box 1.5**.) Both approaches had the effect of moving politics away from the formalistic and legalistic study of institutions and, particularly, constitutions.

Rational choice approaches to politics have become an increasingly important branch of the discipline. They focus on politics being a response to the problem of collective action, which, as this book will show, has applications in both the study of political institutions and processes, and the study of international relations. In general, rational choice approaches start by making certain fundamental assumptions about human behaviour from which hypotheses or theories are deduced before being tested against the facts in the real world. The assumptions made are that human beings are essentially rational, utility maximizers, who will follow the path of action most likely to benefit them. This approach has been used in so-called 'game theory' where individual behaviour is applied to particular situations. These 'games' reveal how difficult it can be for rational individuals to reach optimal outcomes, not least because of the existence of free-riders—actors who calculate that they can reap the benefits of collective action without paying any of the costs. In political science, the best-known applications can be found in the fields of voting and party competition and in interest group politics.

➡ See Chapter 4 for a discussion of Downs's model of party competition.

One problem with the deductive method is precisely that its fundamental assumptions remain just that: assumptions which many regard as, at best, simplifications and, at worst, entirely inaccurate descriptions of human behaviour. Moreover, rational choice theory is awash with hypotheses about various aspects of the political process but is short on empirical tests of these hypotheses (Hay, 2002: 39–40). It is evident that rational choice theory is better able to predict outcomes deriving from certain stated premises than developing accurate empirical theories of the real world.

Inductive approaches to politics, in contrast to deductive approaches, start with empirical observation from which explanatory generalizations are generated. For deductive approaches, then, theory is deduced from first principles before being tested, whereas for inductive approaches, theory follows observation and generalization. A classic version of inductivism is an approach known as behaviouralism which dominated Western, and particularly American, political studies, in the 1950s and 1960s (**see Box 1.5**). The behaviouralists focused on political topics which, like voting behaviour, are quantifiable. Thus, to give one commonly cited example, empirical data on British voting behaviour during this period generated the generalization that voting is class-based, with the working class tending to vote Labour and the middle and upper classes tending to vote Conservative.

➡ See Chapter 14 for a discussion of interest groups.

KEY CONCEPT BOX 1.5
Behaviouralism

An approach that developed, particularly in the USA, in the post-1945 period. It stresses the importation of the scientific method in the study of social phenomena. Objective measurement of the social world is the goal, values to be completely jettisoned from social enquiry. There is an assumption that human behaviour is capable of being measured in a precise way and generalizations derived from it. It reached its height of influence in political studies in the 1960s. Since then, it has been increasingly challenged by those who doubt the value-free nature of political studies and social enquiry in general.

The weaknesses of the inductive method mirror those of the deductive method. While, as we saw, the latter approach is strong on theory but not so much on empirical testing, the reverse is true of the former. The inductive approach, in other words, tends to focus more on gathering empirical data than it does on the generation of theory. This traditional positivism was famously revised by the philosopher of science Karl Popper (1902–94), who argued that rather than generating empirical data from which a hypothesis can be derived, the scientific method should be concerned with seeking to falsify a hypothesis. This had the effect, among other things, of making truth claims temporary; only as good as the next successful attempt to refute them. Verification can never be conclusive, but falsification can be. More to the point, for our purposes here, it meant that positivists have tended, since Popper, to move away from using the inductive method and have shown more interest in the generation of hypotheses to be refuted.

Another weakness of the inductive method is that the type of hypotheses generated by inductivism tends not to be explanatory—in the sense of offering a causal link between generalizations. Rather, they tend to be merely patterns of statistical correlation (Hay, 2002: 79). Finding correlations between phenomena is not the same as the one explaining the other. To give an example, the identification of a statistical correlation between, say, social class and voting behaviour does not, by itself, explain why this correlation exists.

KEY POINTS

- Political analysis involves three main approaches: empirical, normative, and semantic.
- Theorizing normatively about politics remains difficult and often contentious. While recognizing this, it should be noted that one can exaggerate these difficulties, and a moral relativism is not the inevitable consequence of political philosophy.
- In practice, these three forms of political analysis are not mutually exclusive. We need to know what is, before we can talk sensibly about what ought to be. Similarly, empirical analysis presupposes some normative assumptions.
- Empirical political analysis tends to use either inductive or deductive reasoning. The former can be illustrated by behaviouralism, the latter by rational choice theory.

CAN POLITICS BE A SCIENCE?

It is often asked whether social sciences, such as politics, can be, or ought to aim to be, scientific. This debate is a 'complex, voluminous and multi-faceted' one (Hay, 2002: 75), and we can only touch upon its major themes here. To a certain extent, the answer to the question depends on whether we adopt a loose or rigid definition of science. Politics is quite clearly a science in the sense that it 'offers ordered knowledge based on systematic enquiry' (Lowndes, Marsh, and Stoker, 2018: 9). Indeed, according to this definition, even normative analysis, when undertaken in a systematic way, can be described as scientific. A more rigid definition would involve applying the methodology of the natural sciences to the political realm, as is attempted in the behavioural approach discussed above. Here, an appropriate definition of science might be 'the ability to generate neutral, dispassionate and objective knowledge claims' (Hay, 2002: 87).

The attractions of developing a value-free and objective account of politics where we can iden-tify the 'truth' about political phenomena are obvious. However, the claims about a science of politics at this more rigid level can be challenged on two main grounds. In the first place, one can question whether the methods of natural science can be transferred to a social science such as politics. At a second, more fundamental, level, one can question whether the whole scientific enterprise, in both natural and social settings, is a valid and useful exercise.

At the first level, it is the social element of politics which is the key. Human beings, it is suggest-ed, are unpredictable and are not amenable to unbending scientific laws in the way that, say, the workings of molecules are in the natural sciences. In other words, as Hay (2002: 50) points out, what makes the social sciences qualitatively different from the natural sciences is that the 'former must deal with conscious and reflective subjects, capable of acting differently under the same stimuli, whereas the units which comprise the latter can be assumed inanimate, unreflexive and hence entirely predictable in response to external stimuli'.

The unpredictability of human beings not only leads us to question the application of the 'sci-entific' method to the field of social studies, it also reminds us that social researchers often face ethical dilemmas in their work. We cannot treat human, or indeed animal, subjects with the same impunity that natural sciences treat inanimate objects. Humans and animals, can feel emotional and physical distress that researchers have to take into account. Moreover, the prescriptions that might emanate from social research, or that might be derived from it by others, can have impor-tant ethical dimensions. An example here would be the implications of social research that led to claims being made about the importance of race, or gender, in determining intelligence and, therefore, moral and political worth.

The only way of avoiding the conclusion that a science of society is difficult, if not impossible, because of the unpredictable nature of human beings, is to adopt an approach which claims that human behaviour can be determined. As we saw in the case of rational choice theory, however, it is doubtful if assumptions about human behaviour made in such accounts would stand the test of empirical observation. In addition, the study of politics is not value-free. As we saw earlier, we impose our own assumptions and norms on our work from the very start of a research project, the choice of which is imbued with our own sense of its importance. We might want to argue, too, that politics *should* be about values and norms. To attempt to exclude them is to miss much of what is valuable in a study of the political.

At a more fundamental level, the core of the scientific project has been challenged. Here, it might be argued that it is unfair to criticize politics for not being a science because there is no true value-free science in the first place. We should therefore question the claim that there can be a value-free exercise to which we can attach the label 'science', rather than solely questioning the scientific merits of politics. As Hay (2002: 87) remarks, the natural scientist, just like the social sci-entist, is 'socially and politically embedded within a complex and densely structured institutional and cultural landscape which they cannot simply escape by climbing the ivory tower of academe to look down with scientific dispassion and disinterest on all they survey'.

This idea that 'scientific' knowledge is, in part at least, socially constructed is the basis of the contemporary, so-called, 'interpretivist' approach which has emerged to challenge positivism (see Bevir and Rhodes, 2002). To understand this critique a little better, it is important to under-stand the difference between the terms ontology and epistemology. Following Hay (2002: 61), we can say that ontology 'relates to *being*, to what *is*, to what *exists*'. In other words, an ontology asks what is there to know? For our purposes here, the key ontological question relates to whether there is a political world out there capable of being observed or whether this 'reality' is, at least to some degree, created by the meanings or ideas we impose upon it. Epistemology refers to the task of 'acquiring knowledge of that which exists' (63). In other words, it concerns itself with what can be known about what exists.

The definitional diversion is important because it enables us to make sense of the fundamental claims being made by those who insist that the study of politics can be a science. Thus, those adopting behavioural or rational choice approaches adopt a foundationalist ontology and a positivist epistemology, meaning, in short, an acceptance that a real world exists out there which can be discovered by empirical observations. Increasingly, though, this approach has been challenged by those writing from a so-called interpretivist standpoint. These scholars have ontologically challenged the very idea that there is an objective reality out there that is waiting for us to discover. As a result, rather than seeking to discover an objective reality that does not really exist, we should seek to examine the meanings that human beings themselves impose. From this perspective, then, a science of politics is impossible.

KEY POINTS

- Behaviouralists, in particular, suggest that politics can have the scientific rigour of the natural sciences.
- Two challenges to this view were noted. In the first place, one can question whether the methods of natural science can be transferred to a social science such as politics.
- At a second, more fundamental, level, one can question whether the whole scientific enterprise, in both natural and social settings, is a valid and useful exercise.

CONCLUSION

This chapter has sought to introduce you to certain basic definitional features of politics, and some central themes within political analysis. The difficulty of studying politics, because of the lack of consensus on its meaning, has not been disguised. We suggest that having an open mind to what is 'political' prevents undue conservatism which would miss much that is important in the real world. The rest of this book operates in this vein.

Part 1, Chapters 2–7, continues the exploration of political ideas and ideologies, focusing on the state, power and democracy, freedom and justice, and traditional and new political ideologies. Part 2, Chapters 8–15, focuses on the study of political institutions and processes, with chapters on the main elements of the political system: institutions and states; law, constitutions, and federalism; voters, elections, legislatures, and legislators; executives, bureaucracies, policy studies, and governance; political parties; civil society, interests groups, and the media; and democratization and authoritarianism. It will become apparent that the vast majority of political thinkers whose ideas are discussed in this book are white European males. This is an understandable reflection of the dominance of white men in Western political thought. As something of a corrective to this, though we have also added in this edition a separate chapter on non-Western approaches to politics. Part 3, Chapters 16–22, deals with relationships between states. This section starts with a definition of key terms, and a historical account of the development of the states' system, before going on to examine international relations theory, international security, diplomacy and foreign policy, international organizations, and, finally, international political economy.

KEY QUESTIONS

1. What is politics?
2. Is politics synonymous with the state?
3. Is politics an inevitable feature of all societies?
4. What is the difference between normative and empirical analysis in the study of politics?
5. Can politics be a science?
6. Should politics be seen in a positive light?
7. What is the case for defining politics narrowly?
8. How can we evaluate between competing normative claims?
9. What is meant by inductive and deductive approaches to political studies?
10. 'Politics is generally disparaged as an activity which is shrinking in importance and relevance' (Andrew Gamble). Discuss.

FURTHER READING

Crick, B. (1962), *In Defence of Politics* (London: Weidenfeld & Nicolson).
This is a classic case for a particular interpretation of politics.

Dahl, R. (1991), *Modern Political Analysis* (Englewood Cliffs, NJ: Prentice-Hall).
This is a classic account of the study of politics by a legendary American academic.

Gamble, A. (2000), *Politics and Fate* (Cambridge: Polity Press).
Like Crick, this seeks to defend politics, but from the perspective of those who would decry the ability of humans to control their destiny.

Hay, C. (2002), *Political Analysis* (Basingstoke: Palgrave).
This cannot be bettered as a comprehensive and accessible account of different approaches to political science. Hard going at times but worthwhile.

Lowndes, V., Marsh, D., and Stoker, G. (eds) (2018), *Theory and Methods in Political Science* (London: Palgrave, 4th edn).
This is an extremely useful collection of articles setting out the field.

Savigny, H., and Marsden, L. (2011), *Doing Political Science and International Relations: Theories in Action* (Basingstoke: Palgrave).
A very accessible account of the nature of political analysis which adopts an issue-based approach in order to make sense of some very complex ideas.

Stoker, G. (2006), *Why Politics Matter* (Basingstoke: Palgrave).
This is a modern version of Crick's work, which defines politics in terms of consensus and democracy.

 For additional material and resources, please visit the Online Resources at:
www.oup.com/he/garner4e

concepts and
IDEOLOGIES

by Robert Garner

POLITICS AND THE STATE

READER'S GUIDE

This chapter begins by stressing the importance of the state and sovereignty to the study of politics. An attempt is made to provide an empirical typology of the state, before going on to outline various theories about the distribution of power in the state—namely pluralism, elitism, Marxism, and New Right theories. The chapter then proceeds to examine different views about what the role of the state ought to be, from the minimalist state recommended by classical liberal theory, to the pursuit of distinctive social objectives as recommended, in particular, by communitarian thinkers. Finally, empirical and normative challenges to the state are reviewed.

THE POLITICAL IMPORTANCE OF THE STATE

For many centuries, the state has been the dominant form of political organization such that 'no concept is more central to political discourse and political analysis' (Hay and Lister, 2006: 1). It is only a slight exaggeration to say that the state determines how we live and how we die. Virtually all of the land in the world is claimed by a state, of which there are now nearly 200. Indeed, the state's role in the economy and society has increased progressively, particularly since the advent of the 'welfare' state in the post 1945 period.

Despite its political importance, the state is a notoriously difficult concept to define. Some argue that 'the state is not a suitable concept for political theory, since it is impossible to define it'

(Hoffman and Graham, 2006: 22). The fact that the state is difficult to define, however, does not seem to be reason enough to refuse to try and define it, unless it is thought that the state does not actually exist, which virtually no one is claiming.

A classic definition of the state is provided by Weber who regards it as an institution claiming a 'monopoly of the legitimate use of physical force in enforcing its order within a given territorial area'. The state is therefore inextricably linked with sovereignty. Above all, this concept was developed by the French political philosopher Jean Bodin (1529–96) and the English jurist William Blackstone (1723–80). The idea of the sovereign state denotes its superiority as the highest form of authority in a particular territory. There is, therefore, no higher authority within that territory, and, equally importantly, no external challenge to this authority. As Chapters 8 and 17 will describe in detail, sovereign states emerged in the fifteenth and sixteenth centuries in Europe, replacing feudal societies which shared authority between the aristocracy and the Catholic Church (Tilly, 1975). Subsequent to this, most countries in the world have adopted, often through colonial rule, the sovereign state model, although stateless societies still exist in small communities of people, such as nomadic tribes.

➡ See Chapter 8 for a discussion of the rise of the European state system.

The usefulness of the concept of sovereignty as a description of political reality, however, is debatable. In constitutional theory, states are sovereign but, in reality, states have always faced challenges from within and outside their borders, thereby, in practice, limiting their autonomy. In this sense, sovereignty has always been something of a myth. Here, there is a crucial distinction between *de jure* sovereignty, which refers to a legal right to rule supremely, and *de facto* sovereignty, which refers to the actual distribution of political power. As Held (1989: 216) points out: 'Sovereignty has been an important and useful concept for legal analysis, but it can be a misleading notion if applied uncritically as a political idea.' For example, the concept of sovereignty is of little use when discussing the phenomena of so-called 'failed states', where—as in Somalia—the state is unable to perform the functions of sovereignty.

A TYPOLOGY OF THE STATE

A classification of the state is usually organized around the degree to which it intervenes in society and the economy. At one end of this continuum is the so-called night-watchman state in which the state concentrates on ensuring external and internal security, playing little role in civil society and the economy where the economic market is allowed to operate relatively unhindered. The idea of a night-watchman state was a central characteristic of classical liberal thought and played a large part in shaping nineteenth-century British politics. It sees the state as having a protective role, seeking to uphold the rights—to life, liberty, and property—of individuals against external and internal threats.

➡ See Chapter 8 for a discussion of weak states.

➡ See Chapter 22 for an exploration of the relationship between the state and economic institutions.

The notion of a minimal state is an ideal type which has probably existed nowhere in reality. The degree, and character, of state intervention in the world today, however, differs enormously. In the so-called developmental state, for instance, there is a strong relationship between state and private economic institutions with the goal of securing rapid economic development. This model has been particularly prevalent in East Asia, where states have developed rapidly since 1945. Japan is the prime example of a developmental state (Johnson, 1995), but the model is also relevant to South Korea and even Malaysia, a so-called illiberal democracy, a concept which will be discussed later.

Developmental states should not be confused with social democratic states which have a broader social and political objective. They are associated with attempts to secure greater social and economic equality, rather than just economic development. One of the criticisms of post-1945 British political and economic development is that Britain adopted a social democrat approach but neglected the developmental aspect (Marquand, 1988). This failure, it is argued, has hindered the social democratic project because greater social and economic equality is greatly assisted by general economic prosperity which provides a great deal more resources to redistribute.

States can also be defined in terms of their relationship to democracy or popular control of political leaders. Here, a useful distinction is to be made between liberal democracies, illiberal democracies, and authoritarian regimes (Hague and Harrop, 2007: 7–9). Liberal democracies—such as the USA, the UK, and Germany—are characterized by free and fair elections involving universal suffrage, together with a liberal political framework consisting of a relatively high degree of personal liberty and the protection of individual rights. Liberal democracy is now the dominant state form existing in much of the world, in Europe, North and South America, Australasia, Japan, India, and South Africa, although in recent years democracy would seem to be in retreat (see Chapter 4).

Illiberal democracies—such as Russia and Malaysia—are characterized by elections but relatively little protection of rights and liberties, and state control over the means of communication. This creates a situation where opposition leaders and parties are disadvantaged and, as a result, there are relatively few transfers of power through elections.

➡ See Chapter 4 for an account of democratic recession.

Authoritarian regimes can be characterized in terms of the absence of fair elections and therefore the accountability of political rulers. About a third of people in the world live under regimes that can be described as authoritarian, most notably China—which contains just under 20 per cent of the world's population—and many states in the Middle East. The political elites in such regimes can derive from the military, royalty, ruling parties, or merely be individual dictators.

The degree of intervention in the economy and society can vary enormously in authoritarian regimes. At the extreme end is the totalitarian state, so-called because the state intervenes—often through a brutal and oppressive state police—in all aspects of social and economic life,

Photo 2.1 Vladimir Putin, President of Russia (2012–present), which can be categorized as an illiberal democracy. *The Russian Presidential Press and Information Office*

2

under the guise of a transformative ideology. While liberal state theory postulates the existence of a civil society in which the state intervenes relatively rarely, in totalitarian states civil society is eclipsed. Totalitarianism is very much a twentieth-century phenomenon—associated, in particular, with Nazi Germany, Stalin's Soviet Union, and East Germany—although Iran, since the Islamic revolution in the late 1970s, has a number of totalitarian features.

KEY POINTS

- However difficult it is to define, the state is undoubtedly a crucial institution for the political analyst.
- Sovereignty is a key, defining feature of the state, although it is a concept that, arguably, has greater legal than political importance.
- It is possible to develop an empirical typology of the state from the minimalist night-watchman state, approximated to by nineteenth-century capitalist regimes at one end of the spectrum, to the totalitarian state of the twentieth century at the other.

THE STATE AND POWER

Another dimension of the state relates to the relationship with power. Theories of the state more often than not provide different accounts of power distribution. These theories are primarily empirical accounts, seeking to describe the reality of power distribution rather than a normative aspiration. Clearly, it is essential to have an understanding of the concept of power itself, a task which is undertaken in Chapter 3. For now, it is necessary to note that an evaluation of the validity of the empirical theories of the state discussed in this chapter depends, to a large extent, on the way in which the concept of power is defined and operationalized.

The need for an overarching theory of the state emerges from the need to be selective, to have some guide to the choosing of relevant information from the mass of factual evidence that can be unearthed. Choosing a theory of the state constitutes the analyst's criteria for selection and enables him or her to avoid drowning in a sea of information. In this chapter, we will look at three major theories of the state: pluralism, elitism, and Marxism, as well as considering the New Right approach to the state. The feminist approach to the state is outlined in Chapter 3.

➡ See Chapter 3 for a discussion of the feminist approach to the state.

Pluralism

By the end of the 1960s, the pluralist approach, associated above all with the work of the American political scientist Robert Dahl (1963, 1971), dominated Western political science. It is possible to distinguish between different varieties of pluralism. In the classical pluralist position, society is seen as being composed of thousands of activities that have the effect of creating many different groups of all shapes and sizes. For pluralists, the existence of, often competing, groups is a natural feature of all societies of any complexity. The only way in which these groups can be prevented is through suppression, as they had been, for instance, in the old Soviet system.

For pluralists, the role of the state can also be defined in terms of the activities of groups. In this *political* pluralism, the state's role is to regulate and mediate between these groups. Some pluralists see the state as a neutral arbiter in this system, whereas some see it as a group in itself competing against others in society. The outputs of government are the result of group pressure. What governments do will be a mirror image of the balance of power of groups within society (**see Figure 2.1**). It is important to note that pluralists are not saying here that all groups or interests are equal. Rather, pluralists are claiming that there are no predominant classes or interests within society, that all groups are able to make their voices heard in the political process, and that all groups get at least something of what they want.

Power in society for pluralists is diffuse or fragmented. In other words, in a pluralist state, most interest groups will be able to influence public policy outcomes to at least some extent. Dahl defines modern liberal democratic politics in terms of 'minorities rule' rather than majority rule, or polyarchy rather than democracy, to illustrate that politics is based upon the permanent interplay of numerous groups each constituting a minority. Successful political parties, then, are those that are able to forge a majority coalition of minority groups.

➡ See Chapter 14 for a detailed discussion of interest groups.

The pluralist conclusion that power is fragmented is based upon a number of related arguments. The first is that the bases upon which power rests are variable; that is, political influence is not dependent upon one particular resource. Rather, there are a variety of important resources—wealth, organization, public support, a group's position in the economy, the ability to exercise, or threaten to exercise, sanctions—which are not the preserve of a small number of groups. For example, a group of key workers such as miners or doctors may not be particularly wealthy or even have public support but can garner influence through the crucial functions they perform. Second, even though it may seem that in a particular issue area one group or small set of groups is influential, the same groups are not influential in other issue areas. Farmer's organizations, for instance, do not have a role in, say, health or education policy. Third, more often than not, it is the case that an influential group in a policy arena is challenged by a 'countervailing influence'. In the economic sphere, for instance, the influence of business groups is checked by the role of trade unions.

Pluralism to Elitism Continuum

The position we have just described can be classified as classical pluralism. It is possible to envisage a number of other approaches or theories of the state on a continuum between classical pluralism and classical elitism. The first of these is elite pluralism, sometimes described as democratic elitism. This revision of classical pluralism came about in the late 1950s and early 1960s following a sustained criticism of it. One of the major challengers was the American sociologist C. Wright Mills (1956), who argued that power in American society is concentrated in the hands of a powerful elite, dominating the economic, military, and governmental spheres.

➡ See Chapter 4 for a discussion of the elitist theory of democracy.

The pluralist response to this led by Dahl (1958) was to accept that the classical pluralist assumption, that there is widespread participation in decision-making and that groups are themselves internally egalitarian, was misplaced. The existence of political elites, a small group of people playing a disproportionate role in groups, was accepted. Far from undermining the pluralist position, however, scholars such as Dahl suggested that it still existed because these political elites have divided interests and compete with each other to achieve their aims. Politics may be

2

hierarchical, then, but rather than one homogeneous elite group, there are a multiplicity of competing elites. Pluralists, for instance, would see business as divided between, say, a financial and a manufacturing sector. Political power for pluralists can be represented diagrammatically, then, by a succession of pyramids and not just one (**see Figure 2.2**).

Yet further down the continuum between pluralism and elitism is corporatism (**see Box 2.1**). Traditionally, corporatism referred to the top-down model where the state, as in the fascist model, incorporates economic interests in order to control them and civil society in general. This is also the corporatist model that can be applied to authoritarian states, particularly in Asia. Modern societal or neo-corporatism, on the other hand, reflects a genuine attempt by governments to incorporate economic interests into the decision-making process (Held, 1989: 65). This modern version of societal corporatism shares, with pluralism, the belief that groups are a crucial part of the political system. Corporatism denies, however, that the competition between groups was as widespread, equitable, and fragmented as pluralists had suggested. Instead, corporatism points to the critical role played by economic elites. Government outputs are a product of a tripartite relationship between elites in government, business, and the trade unions. The insider role of economic elites was sanctioned by the state in return for the cooperation of these key interests in securing the support of their members for government policy.

CASE STUDY BOX 2.1
Corporatism in Europe

Corporatism, or neo-corporatism to be precise, has been traditionally prevalent in certain European states—such as Austria, Norway, Sweden, and the Netherlands—whereas New Zealand, Canada, the UK, and the USA have traditionally been regarded as the least corporatist, and thereby closer to the pluralist model (Lijphart and Crepaz, 1991). Until the 1970s, corporatism was largely applauded for its economic success. Since then, corporatism has decayed to some extent. A survey of Scandinavian corporatism, for instance, reveals that since the mid-1970s there has been a decline in the number of corporatist actors in public bodies, and the degree to which governments base decisions on corporatist-style agreements (Blom-Hansen, 2000).

The form of corporatism we have been describing is shorn of much of the negative connotations associated with the top-down variety, associated with fascist regimes and authoritarian regimes such as China, which involve the state incorporating key interests in order to control them. Neo-corporatism, by contrast, is seen as a way of incorporating, and modifying, the key interests within civil society. It is argued that it has served a vital aggregation function.

Neo-corporatism has not, however, escaped criticism. In the first place, it is argued that governments tend, in practice, to be unduly influenced by business interests in corporatist arrangements. Even if trade unions are successfully integrated, neo-corporatism is still regarded as less open and democratic than a pluralist system because it is hierarchically organized, with power residing in the hands of economic elites. From the perspective of the New Right corporatism is condemned for failing to allow the market free rein, and thereby acceding to the, it is argued, unrealistic demands of sectional interests.

Elitism

At the other end of the spectrum from classical pluralism is the ruling elite theory of the state. While classical pluralists hold that Western liberal democracies have diffuse power structures, with a plurality of groups competing to influence the government, ruling elite theory holds that all society, whatever democratic rhetoric proclaims, is ruled by a single, unified, and self-conscious elite. Whereas the diagrammatical representation of elite pluralism is a series of pyramids, elitism can be represented by one pyramid containing an elite and the masses (**see Figure 2.3**).

Elitism is particularly associated with a group of Italian scholars writing at the turn of the twentieth century (in particular, Robert Michels, Gaetano Mosca, and Vilfredo Pareto), although their work was built upon by later, mainly American, writers. The original elitists were concerned primarily with refuting Marx's vision of a future egalitarian society. For them, a ruling elite was an inevitable feature of all complex societies. The elitists claim to have discovered, in the words of Robert Michels, an 'iron law of oligarchy'; that is, in organizations of any complexity, whether they be political parties or interests groups, there will always be a dominant group controlling them. Elites come to dominate because of the resources they can muster, their psychological character-istics, or their position within society. Unlike Marxism, or ruling-class theory, no one resource is necessarily crucial, so that it is possible to conceive of elites based upon military, administrative, and religious factors, as much as economic ones.

Later scholarship on elitism came from the USA. Unlike the earlier Italian version, modern elitism has ceased to be anti-Marxist and has, instead, become a critique of pluralism. In other words, elitist thinkers such as James Burnham (1941) and C. Wright Mills (1956) have identified empirically the rule of elites but, rather than regarding this as inevitable or desirable, have argued that it is illegitimate and ought to be challenged.

Marxism and the State

An alternative to elitism is Marxism or ruling-class theory. Marxism has been a remarkably influ-ential political ideology with, at one time, a large proportion of the world's population living under regimes proclaiming to be inspired by Marx's ideas. Marxism, of course, derives its inspiration from the work of the nineteenth-century German thinker Karl Marx (1818–83). Marxism shares with elitism an acceptance of the fact that modern capitalist societies are dominated by a united, self-interested ruling group. Democracy in such societies, therefore, is a sham. Despite elections, the influence of the masses is minimal.

There are, however, two crucial differences between elitism and Marxism. In the first place, unlike elitists, Marxists are very specific about the character of the ruling group in capitalist soci-eties. As we saw, elitists envisage ruling groups with a variety of resources. For Marx, the ruling group in pre-communist societies is always that social group or class that controls the means of production, and therefore has economic power. In capitalist society, then, the dominant class is the bourgeoisie and the dominated class is the proletariat (or working class), the latter defined in terms of its non-ownership of the means of production (**see Figure 2.4**).

Marx produced a voluminous and disorganized body of literature, and it has been interpret-ed in a number of ways. The dominant interpretation of Marx attaches to him the view that it is pointless for the working class to seek emancipation through gaining the vote and winning

→ See
Chapter 3 for a
discussion of
Marxist ideas on
state power.

power through elections. This is not where real power lies. Rather, power lies within the economic sphere of society. In other words, those who have economic power also have political power. The working class, therefore, needs to win power by attacking its source in the economic sphere. Having said that, there is some evidence that Marx was prepared to accept a greater autonomy for the state and that it was not perceived as simply the vehicle of the dominant class. This idea of the 'relative autonomy' of the state was taken up by later Marxists.

The second key difference between elitism and Marxism is that for the latter a communist revolution will bring about a truly egalitarian society, one in which a hierarchical society is abolished. By contrast, the earlier elitists argued, in response to Marx, that a hierarchical system of power relations is an inevitable feature of all societies of any complexity, and it is a utopian dream to think otherwise. Marx spent very little time describing in detail what this egalitarian society would look like, mainly because of his insistence that the downfall of capitalism would produce such a society, whatever he thought ought to happen, **see Box 2.2**.

The New Right Theory of the State

A slightly different theory of the state was provided by a number of commentators, writing from the 1970s onwards, who can be classified as the New Right, a position whose antecedents were liberal free market advocates such as Hobbes, Locke, and Adam Smith. According to this position,

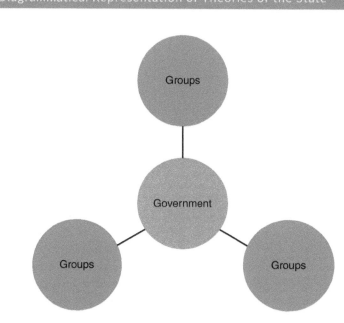

KEY CONCEPT BOX 2.2
A Diagrammatical Representation of Theories of the State

Figure 2.1 Pluralist theory of the state

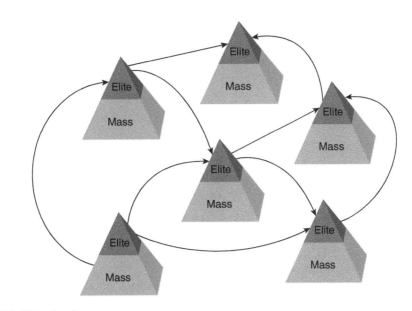

Figure 2.2 Elite pluralism

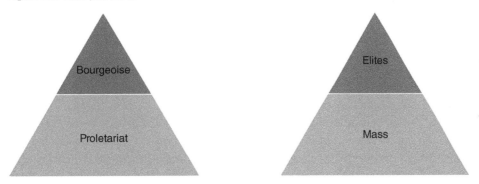

Figure 2.3 Marxist theory of the state   Figure 2.4 Elitist theory of the state

the state has a tendency to expand its activities far beyond what is healthy for society. There are two main forces at work here. The first is external. Here, in a process that is coined as the 'economic consequences of democracy' (Britten, 1977), competitive electoral politics encourages politicians to offer ever-increasing benefits in order to attract votes, and once elected, governments then find it very difficult to meet the promises made to individuals and groups, sometimes sailing perilously close to bankruptcy.

The second force at work here for New Right thinkers is internal. Here, it is argued, in what has been called the 'over-supply thesis' (Dunleavy and O'Leary, 1987: 117–19), the state bureaucracy has a tendency to expand because it is in its self-interest to do so (Niskanen, 1971). To increase intervention and 'big' government, bureaucrats will forge relationships with interest groups. Both the bureaucrats and the groups have a vested interest in governments offering more, mainly financial, benefits.

2

For the New Right, then, the pluralist theory of the state is wrong on two main counts. First, the state is not neutral but serves its own interests. Second, the liberal democratic polity does not encourage stability and equilibrium as pluralists suggest. Rather, it has a tendency to lead to governing failure. The end result is 'a hyperpluralism of powerful groups confronting weak governments' (Dearlove and Saunders, 2000: 220).

The Empirical Dimension of the State

We have focused so far in this chapter on the empirical reality of the state—what the state does. When the role of the state is discussed, it is necessary to distinguish between the functions that the state does play, as a matter of fact, and the functions that it ought to play, as a matter of value. The theories of the state discussed previously have both empirical and normative dimensions to them. An empirical analysis of a theory of the state would examine the degree to which it reflects the reality of any particular political system. As we shall see in Chapter 3, assessing the empirical adequacy of a theory of the state has a great deal to do with how political power is measured.

➡ See Chapter 3 for a more developed critique of pluralism.

Here, we should just briefly note that an empirical critique of pluralism would be to say that it exaggerates the extent to which power is fragmented in liberal democratic societies. Indeed, pluralism has been criticized on the grounds that it too readily assumes that groups have a reasonable chance of influencing policy-making, whereas there is strong evidence to suggest that certain interests are much more powerful than others. We could engage, too, in an empirical critique of the elitist and Marxist theories of the state. Is it really credible to argue, for instance, that a ruling elite or a ruling class remains entirely untroubled by representative machinery in liberal democracies? Certainly, in addition, one can challenge many, if not all, of the claims made by Marx about the future direction of capitalism. Indeed, as we shall see in Chapter 6, post-Marxian Marxists did adapt classical Marxism to very different circumstances.

➡ See Chapter 6 for a discussion of the development of socialist ideas.

The New Right approach was most influential in the 1970s and 1980s, particularly following the election of Thatcher in Britain and Regan in the US. As Keynesian ideas were perceived to have failed, neo-liberal ideas came to predominate. Ironically, though, the success of political parties and politicians advocating neo-liberal solutions to perceived economic problems does tend to question the demand-side analysis the New Right put forward. That is, the claim that voters would not vote for parties that sought to control public spending and reduce the role of the state has proven wide of the mark.

According to Dryzek and Dunleavy (2009: 331–3), however, the New Right—or market liberal approach as they call it—has declined in influence. Issues such as the threat of terrorism—particularly in France and the US—climate change, and the perceived negative impact of globalization on the indigenous working class, have emphasized again the need for a strong interventionist state. Moreover, the financial crisis which erupted in 2008 was, for many, a product of the limited regulation of financial institutions. Trump's election in the US in 2016 reflected this new constituency for a state willing to use its power to correct market failures, control its borders, and to take a tougher stance on external threats.

In defence of the New Right approach, it seeks to explain the financial crisis in terms of the self-interested vote maximization of politicians who encouraged voters to borrow and spend money with little regard to their ability to pay it back (Minford, 2010). However, the fact that a strong state response—in terms of using tax revenues to bail out failed financial institutions—was an essential rejoinder has further dented confidence in a market liberal approach. Finally, Dryzek and Dunleavy (2009) note the massively increased technological capacity which makes an efficient state-planned economy more realistic than it was before.

KEY POINTS

- There are a number of empirical theories of the state arranged on a continuum from classical pluralism at one end to ruling elite and Marxist theory at the other.
- Whereas pluralism sees the power structure as diffuse and fragmented, ruling elite and Marxist theories sees it as concentrated.
- The two key differences between ruling elite and Marxism are, first, that for the latter the dominant group is always that class that owns the means of production, distribution, and exchange, whereas for the former the source of power can be varied. Second, Marxism postulates the existence of a future egalitarian society whereas ruling-elite theory sees elites as an inevitable feature of all societies.
- The New Right theory of the state offers a different take on the role of the state, focusing on a critique of the collectivist state rather than a description of the distribution of power.
- It is possible to distinguish between an empirical and a normative examination of the state. In empirical terms, we can criticize pluralism, elitism, Marxism and New Right theory for their failure adequately to describe the reality of the world as it is.

THE ROLE OF THE STATE: WHAT OUGHT THE STATE TO DO?

Theories of the state can also be assessed on normative grounds; in other words, we can explore the degree to which they constitute adequate representations of how the state *ought* to be organized. The work produced in this area represents the core of political philosophy, which has as its fundamental aim the identification of the ideal polity and the good society. This question will occupy us also in Chapters 4 and 5, particularly in the context of the crucial question of political obligation. Here, however, we will merely sketch out some of the major answers to this normative question.

Pluralism and the Politics of Identity

There are two main normative critiques that can be made of pluralism. Firstly, the revised elite version of pluralism might be criticized from a normative perspective on the grounds that it dismisses the importance of political participation. Thus, instead of accepting the competition between political elites as the best that can be achieved, political philosophers have argued that this is unacceptable from a democratic perspective and we ought to look at ways in which opportunities to participate can be enhanced.

Second, it can be argued that the pluralist theory of the state devalues the idea of the general or public interest. Indeed, pluralism almost glories in the differences between people. It therefore accepts as given the, rather pessimistic, view that society consists of a diverse range of competing,

➡ See Chapter 4 for a discussion of the elitist theory of democracy.

and sometimes hostile, interests. There is no-doubt, in practice, that the divisive character of Western liberal democracies has been enhanced by the emergence of identity politics (**see Box 2.3**). It is true, of course, that campaigns against oppression by different identity groups have had many positive consequences such as the establishment of civil rights, the much greater awareness of abuse against women, and legislative equality for members of the gay community. Most would agree that we live in a much more tolerant age. However, there is also a negative side to identity politics. Of particular relevance in the context of a normative critique of pluralism is its propensity to encourage divisions and extreme polarization within society whilst the ties that bind us have been lost sight of (Fukuyama, 2018).

The divisiveness of identity politics occurs because separate (and to some extent inaccessible) identities, which have become increasingly narrow and specialized, are vigorously protected against outsiders. This has led, arguably, to a diminution of free speech when it is deemed justifiable to render illegitimate arguments deemed to be offensive to a group's sense of self-worth. It has also led to conflicts between identity groups, such as that between some feminists and the trans community. It is to some extent true, too, that identity politics has fragmented the left as left-wing parties have increasingly focused on promoting the interests of a range of identity groups—for instance, in the context of American politics, African Americans, the LGBT community, Hispanics, Native Americans, Asian Americans, women, and so on—and less on their traditional concern for economic equality. As a result, the left has increasingly ignored the plight of its traditional constituency, the white working class and has lost 'a sense of what we share as citizens and what binds us' (Lilla, 2017: 9). At the same time, the right has responded by promoting an identity politics of its own emphasizing a white national identity with divisive racial, ethnic, and sometimes religious, connotations (Kaufmann, 2018).

 See Chapter 6 for a discussion of nationalism.

As Fukuyama (2018: 117, 122) comments, then, diversity 'is not an unalloyed good'. Although societies 'need to protect the marginalised and excluded' they also 'need to achieve common goals via deliberation and consensus'. For him, the remedy is the development of larger and more integrative national identities, a civic, and not ethnic, version of nationalism.

KEY CONCEPT BOX 2.3
Identity Politics

In recent years identity politics, sometimes referred to as the politics of difference, has become a pronounced feature of modern liberal democratic societies. It is a cultural movement based on a demand for recognition and respect by particular groups of people centred on their race, ethnicity, gender, sexual orientation, or nationality. For identity groups on the progressive left, liberal societies promote the interests and values of dominant groups (whites, men and the economically well-off) and undermine and marginalize other groups who are regarded as inferior and less valuable. As a result, identity politics is about redressing negative perceptions by reasserting the value and dignity of the particular oppressed group. Well-known examples of identity politics in action are the #MeToo and the Black Lives Matter movements. Identity politics has been, partly at least, the product of globalization and increased migration which has created much more culturally diverse societies in the West. This has led to the promotion of multiculturalism as a response, which in turn has led to the emergence of an identity politics on the right centring on white nationalism.

See Chapter 7 for a discussion of multiculturalism.

A Normative Account of Elitism, Marxism, and New Right Theory

As a description of the state, elitism makes no value judgement about the validity of elite rule. From this perspective, classical elitists at least are saying that, whether we like it or not, modern societies are dominated by a ruling elite. Students often confuse this empirical claim for a normative one. A normative justification for elite rule would argue that the best ought to rule, uncluttered by the less able masses. The Greek philosopher Plato offers just such a scenario, justifying the rule of the so-called 'philosopher kings'. The modern theory of democratic elitism, examined in Chapter 4, is also based partly on a normative claim that elites ought to be left alone to govern because the masses tend to have authoritarian values. According to this position, mass participation in politics tends to result in instability and a climate of crisis (Dye, 2000). In these circumstances, apathy is to be encouraged.

The normative character of **Marxism**, and socialism in general, is very apparent. Marx himself sought to distinguish his 'scientific' version of socialism from what he called the 'utopian' socialism that preceded him. Therefore, Marx claims that the laws of historical development will, whether we like it or not, result in the downfall of capitalism and the creation of a communist state. By contrast, ethical socialists seek to promote socialism and persuade people that it is a desirable form of social organization. Quite clearly, though, Marx does think that communism is a more desirable form of society than capitalism. Indeed, some Marxist scholars think that Marx was much less of a historical determinist than is often claimed, that there is still a role for human agency in effecting change.

Finally, the New Right theory also has strong normative underpinnings. Thus, state intervention, it is argued, encourages individuals to overly rely on the state to provide welfare support, thereby stifling individual initiative and self-help. Finally, it is also unjust, failing to reward individual effort appropriately. Such claims, of course, are open to challenge. For instance, competing theories of justice argue that need or equality, and not merit, should be the underlying justification for determining the distribution of resources.

The Liberal Social Contract Tradition

A classic means of determining what the role of the state ought to be is provided by the liberal **social contract** tradition. This is particularly associated with the work of the seventeenth-century liberal political thinkers Thomas Hobbes (1588–1679) and John Locke (1632–1704). Rousseau also employed the social contract, although, for reasons that will be explored in Chapter 5, it is questionable whether he can be described as a liberal. The social contract tradition is based around the idea of an imaginary **state of nature**, where individuals exist without government. In other words, it is argued that in order to find out what form of government is justified and why, we should try to consider what life would be like without the state. Social contract theorists envisage individuals coming together to decide the nature of the political system under which they will live. This approach was also adopted by a twentieth-century liberal political philosopher, John Rawls, whose ideas we will consider in Chapter 4.

➡ See Chapter 5 for an exploration of Rawls's Theory of Justice.

Despite using the same social contract **methodology**, Hobbes and Locke provide very different versions of an ideal state. Much of the difference revolves around the issue of **human nature**, a key variable in political thought (see Plant, 1991: ch. 1). Hobbes famously paints a picture of

2

Photo 2.2 English philosopher John Locke (1632–1702). *Wellcome Collection*

human nature as egotistical and competitive. Without government, life is very insecure. Indeed, in a well-known phrase, life in the state of nature, for Hobbes, is described as 'solitary, poor, nasty, brutish and short' (1651/1992: 186). As a result, a political system is necessary in order to impose order and ensure security, both from the risk of external threat and from the threat of internal conflict. The ideal political system for Hobbes, then, is an all-powerful sovereign which Hobbes describes as the *Leviathan*.

 For Hobbes's influence on international theory, see Chapter 17.

John Locke, writing a little later, appears to be much less pessimistic about human nature and the ability of human beings to rub along without undue conflict. Because there are no immediate security considerations for Locke, individuals should choose to live under political rule only when it protects what individuals have in the state of nature (1690/1998). For Locke, individuals have natural rights, given by God, and these natural rights ought to be protected by the state, **see Box 2.4**. Locke promotes what became known as negative rights. These rights—to life, liberty, and property—are rights against societal and state interference.

> **! KEY CONCEPT** BOX 2.4
> Natural Rights

It is common to make a distinction between natural rights and legal rights. Legal rights are those which exist within a particular society at a particular time. They are simply statements, then, of what the existing law is. Natural rights, on the other hand, are rights which humans are said to possess irrespective of the particular legal and political system under which they live. These are said to derive from natural law, a higher law, handed down from nature or God. In a more

→ secular age, what were previously described as natural rights have been renamed as human rights (Woods, 2014).

Modern liberal thinkers, writing particularly after 1945, have argued for the existence of positive rights. These are rights to things, such as free education and healthcare, that are enshrined in the United Nations Universal Declaration of Human Rights established in 1948. These positive rights have the potential to conflict with the negative rights promoted by Locke. In particular, the right to own property can conflict with other, more positive rights, and some political thinkers writing particularly from a Marxist perspective have criticized Locke for seeking to defend a possessive individualism which justifies selfishness, greed, and vast inequalities (Macpherson, 1962).

The Night-Watchman State

Both Locke and Hobbes were apologists for a free market economy and limited state interference, a tradition current in liberal thought up to the end of the nineteenth century. Classical liberals advocate a minimal state in order to maximize freedom. A modern version of this justification is provided by a group of thinkers and political actors known as the New Right, whose theory of the state we encountered previously. The political-popularizers of the New Right were leaders such as Thatcher and Reagan, but the academic ballast was provided by political economists such as Friedrich von Hayek and Milton Friedman, as well as political philosophers such as Robert Nozick.

→ See Chapter 6 for a discussion of liberalism.

The New Right challenged the state interventionism that had become standard in post-1945 liberal democracies, centring on the welfare state, the mixed economy, and the use of demand management economic theory developed by John Maynard Keynes (1883–1946). Here, the state would seek to increase demand in the economy through public spending on various schemes, and these would be reined in when the increased demand threatened to create inflationary pressures. For the New Right school of thought, state intervention is counterproductive. It encourages individuals to overly rely on the state to provide welfare support, thereby stifling individual initiative and self-help. It is also inefficient, propping up unprofitable economic concerns and stifling the emergence of new lean and relevant ones. Finally, it is also unjust, failing to reward individual effort appropriately.

→ See Chapter 5 for a discussion of Nozick and the minimal state.

Utilitarianism

Another strand of liberal thought is the philosophy known as utilitarianism. The utilitarian theory of the state is associated with the work of the British political thinker Jeremy Bentham (1748–1832). Bentham argues that the key to judging the effectiveness of a government is the degree to which it promotes the greatest happiness, or, as he sometimes put it, the greatest happiness of the greatest number (1948). Happiness, for Bentham, is associated with pleasure. In so far as governments do

Photo 2.3 Jeremy Bentham, the founder of modern Utilitarianism. *Wellcome Collection*

➡ See Chapter 4 for a description of the utilitarian theory of democracy.

maximize happiness then they are valid, if they fall short of this goal then they are not. Bentham came to think that only if they are accountable to the electorate will rulers seek to maximize the happiness of all, rather than their own happiness. This forms the basis of the utilitarian theory of democracy.

The chief advantage of utilitarianism as a general ethical theory as well as a guide to political action is that it is flexible enough to justify the attainment of what most would regard as important social goals. By focusing on the happiness of the community, rather than the protection of individual rights, it is able to sanction the kind of collective goals associated with the welfare state. On the downside, utilitarianism, or at least the classical version associated with Bentham, has been criticized for its aggregative character, **see Box 2.5**.

Liberalism and Communitarianism

➡ See Chapter 5 for a further discussion of the harm principle.

The classical liberal theory of the state, which is closely associated with pluralism, holds that the state should remain neutral as between different conceptions of the good. A liberal society's function, Arblaster (1984: 45) suggests, 'is to serve individuals, and one of the ways in which it should do this is by respecting their autonomy, and not trespassing on their rights to do as they please as long as they can do so without harm to others'. This harm principle, associated with J. S. Mill, is central to the liberal emphasis on freedom and toleration. It is also the central theme of John Rawls's later work as laid out in his *Political Liberalism* (1993).

For much of its history, the major ideological opponent of liberalism came from the left, from Marxism in particular. In more recent years, however, the liberal theory of the neutral state has been challenged by a body of thought known as communitarianism. The label communitarian embraces a wide variety of views. In general, communitarian thinkers seek to re-establish the state as an institution with a role to play in uniting society around a shared set of values. This contrasts greatly with the liberal insistence that the state should allow a plurality of belief systems to

> ### KEY DEBATE BOX 2.5
> #### Rights versus Utilitarianism
>
> Traditionally, the two dominant approaches to ethics have been rights and utilitarianism. Until relatively recently, it was utilitarianism that held sway, but since the Second World War, rights theory has made a significant comeback. The following points should be borne in mind when considering the merits of the two approaches:
>
> - Utilitarianism is a secular theory. It therefore 'does not depend on the existence of God, or a soul, or any other dubious metaphysical entity' (Kymlicka, 2002: 11). Earlier versions of rights tended to have such a religious overtone.
> - By focusing on the consequences of an action, and not the motives of those responsible, utilitarians ask us to consider those who are affected by it, a laudable goal. On the other hand, utilitarianism is intuitively mistaken in assuming that there is nothing amiss in an action taken for malicious motives that inadvertently produces a desirable outcome. Conversely, it seems odd to condemn an action taken for the best of motives that produces undesirable consequences.
> - Utilitarianism 'provides a clear and definite procedure for determining which acts are right or wrong' (Brandt, 1992: 113). By contrast, rights theory struggles with what to do in situations where rights conflict. For example, should the right to free healthcare or education be more important than the right to the fruits of one's own property?
> - Utilitarianism is flexible enough to justify the attainment of what most would regard as important social goals. It is therefore more flexible and less individualistic than rights. On the other hand, as a deontological theory, rights theory, unlike utilitarianism, seeks to protect individuals whose fundamental interests cannot, under normal circumstances, be sacrificed in order to promote the general welfare (Dworkin, 1978). It therefore avoids the aggregative consequences of utilitarianism, thereby ensuring that individual interests cannot be sacrificed for some greater good. As a result, 'it avoids the very counter-intuitive solutions to questions of distributive justice' that utilitarianism offers (Carruthers, 1992: 27). In Jones's words (1994: 62): 'There is no end to the horror stories that can be concocted to illustrate the awful possibilities that utilitarianism might endorse.' The persecution of a racial minority in the interests of a racist majority is one such example among many other possibilities.
>
> #### Questions
> 1. What are the implications of adopting a utilitarian approach to public policy?
> 2. What criticisms can you make of a political discourse based on rights?

exist, **see Box 2.6**. The form of state represented by communitarianism is *perfectionist* as opposed to the neutral state advocated by liberal thinkers.

The State and the General Will

In many ways, the antecedents of communitarianism are those political philosophers, such as Jean-Jacques Rousseau (1712–78) and Georg Friedrich Hegel (1770–1831), who suggested that the state and morality are inextricably linked. Thus, for Rousseau, the state should be judged by the degree to which it upholds the general will. This is the will that binds people together and can be contrasted with the selfish or partial will existing within everyone.

2

→ See
Chapters 4 and 5
for more on the
general will.

→ See
Chapter 6 for an
exploration of
anarchism.

> ### KEY DEBATE BOX 2.6
> #### Communitarianism versus Liberalism
>
> Since the 1970s, communitarianism has provided a more potent ideological challenge to liberalism than conservatism and socialism. Defining the basic thrust of communitarianism is difficult because of the disparate nature of its adherents, coming from the right and left of the political spectrum. The essence of the communitarian approach is an attack on what is perceived to be the asocial individualism of liberalism. This attack is both methodological and normative (Avineri and de-Shalt, 1992: 2).
>
> - Methodologically, communitarians argue that human behaviour is best understood in the context of the social, historical, and cultural environments of individuals. Thus, 'it is the kind of society in which people live that affects their understanding both of themselves and of how they should lead their lives' (Mulhall and Swift, 1996: 13).
> - Some communitarian writing suggests that the basis of the communitarian critique of liberalism is the normative assertion that liberal theory accurately reflects the individualistic nature of modern society and that therefore this society ought to be transformed. Others suggest, methodologically, that liberal theory misrepresents the reality of modern societies where social ties are more important in determining the belief-systems of individuals than liberal theory has realized (Walzer, 1990).
>
> Normatively, communitarians emphasize the value of communal existence, and the importance of being bound together by a shared vision of the good promoted by a perfectionist state—part of a tradition that can be traced back to Aristotle—on which particular emphasis is placed by MacIntyre (1985).
>
> #### Questions
> 1. What is the communitarian critique of liberal political thought?
> 2. Evaluate the communitarian case against liberalism.

Rousseau thinks that the general will can only emerge in small-scale communities. The German philosopher Hegel, on the other hand, seeks to apply a very similar objective for the state to modern nineteenth-century Prussia. Hegel distinguished between the state, civil society, and the family, seeing the state as the embodiment of the general interest, in which the partiality and self-interest of civil society and the family would be superseded. This elevated view of the state is in sharp contrast to Marx's wholly negative view of the state as an instrument of exploitation. In fact, Marx was originally a follower of Hegel but came to see that the reality of the state in Prussia was very different from the glorified version of it provided by Hegel. As a result, Marx came to see that the point of political philosophy was not, as Hegel had thought, to interpret the world, but to change it, **see Box 2.7**.

The Anarchist Theory of the State

The normative theories we have identified do not challenge the need for some form of state to organize political affairs. Anarchists, however, question the very need for a state. Although anarchist thought dates back to the nineteenth century, and has preoccupied the minds of some great political theorists, its impact on modern politics is limited.

SHORT BIOGRAPHY BOX 2.7
Georg Wilhelm Friedrich Hegel (1770–1831)

The German philosopher Hegel was born in Stuttgart in 1770. After a varied career as a personal tutor and a headteacher in a school, Hegel took the post of Professor of Philosophy at the University of Heidelberg in 1816. Two years later he was invited to take the prestigious chair of philosophy at the University of Berlin, where he stayed until his death in 1831.

His main work of political theory was the *Philosophy of Right*, published in 1821 (1942). His starting point is to deal with the political and social dissatisfaction existing in the Prussia of his day, social fragmentation being the major difficulty. He moves from an attempt to suggest reforms to create a more homogeneous society to, in the *Philosophy of Right*, a philosophical understanding of the modern world. Very basically, he argues that if we appreciate the unifying role played by the state, transcending the partial unity provided by the family and civil society, then we can be happy with our world.

Hegel has often been seen as an apologist for what was, in reality, a repressive and far from inclusive regime existing in Prussia during his day. His most eminent critic was Karl Marx who had been an advocate of Hegel's philosophy in his younger days. He turns Hegel's philosophy on its head by arguing, first, that human history can be explained by the developing of material forces rather than, as Hegel had argued, by the development of the mind or the realm of ideas. Second, Marx argued that the point of philosophy was to change the world rather than merely explaining it. In other words, Marx argued that in order to achieve the goal Hegel had set—a unified and inclusive polity—it was necessary to change it so that, in particular, the existing divisive class system was abolished.

Photo 2.4 German philosopher Georg Wilhelm Friedrich Hegel distinguished between the state, civil society, and the family. *Library of Congress*

Anarchists' abhorrence of the state is based on its corrupting influence, which undermines a human being's tendency to be morally upstanding. This basic principle, however, raises more questions than it answers; for instance, who is to perform the functions of the state? How are the egalitarian aspirations of the dominant socialist strand of anarchism to be achieved without authority structures to enforce it? If there is a need for some authority structure—as some anarchists recognize—can this be consistent with the claim that this will inevitably lead to a loss of freedom?

KEY POINTS

- A normative critique of pluralism focuses on its downgrading of the public or general interest, a phenomenon that is enhanced by the growing importance of identity politics in the West, while a normative account of elitism focuses on the degree to which elites ought to rule.

- The liberal social contract tradition, represented most notably by Hobbes and Locke, provides different reasons to justify the state, the former focusing on security, the latter on the protection of natural rights.

- Other normative theories of the state seek to justify a limited role (the New Right), the state's pursuit of happiness or preference satisfaction (utilitarianism), the upholding of moral pluralism (liberalism), and a critique of the state in general (anarchism).

- One of the key debates in modern political theory is that between the liberal and the communitarian theory of the state. The former upholds a version of moral pluralism, whereas the latter seeks moral uniformity. The antecedents of the communitarian position reside in the attempts, by political philosophers such as Rousseau and Hegel, to justify obedience to a state promoting the general will.

WHITHER THE STATE?

The state is now under sustained attack as a variety of scholars seek to challenge its utility and very existence. There are empirical and normative dimensions to this debate. From the former perspective, it is suggested that certain modern developments have made the state increasingly redundant. From the latter perspective is the long-standing view that the state is an exploitative institution that ought to be done away with. This derives its major impetus from the ideas of Marx. **see Box 2.8**.

Is The State 'Hollowing Out'?

The 'hollowing out' thesis (Jessop, 1990) suggests that, in a variety of ways, the state no longer plays the significant role that it used to. The major slant here is the globalization thesis. This is the view that the world has become so economically and politically interdependent that there is little room for manoeuvre for nation-states. To the extent that this is true, there is clearly a gap between the political theory of the sovereign state, articulated at the beginning of this chapter, and the reality of politics in the modern world. Globalization undoubtedly, then, has a significant impact on political studies as an academic discipline. The focus of politics, and particularly

KEY DEBATE BOX 2.8
The Marxist Theory of the State

The state has always been criticized by anarchist thinkers and is regarded by Marxists as an exploitative institution that ought to be transcended. The dominant interpretation of classical Marxism (the Marxism associated with the writings of Karl Marx himself) operates with a very simplistic definition of politics and the state. For classical Marxists, the state is merely a vehicle for the exercise of power by the dominant class, so that once classes are abolished, the state itself is abolished, or, in the words of Marx's collaborator Fredrich Engels, 'withers away'. A communist society requires no enforcing state because the end of capitalism transforms human nature fundamentally. In other words, once classes are abolished, then conflict between individuals that is significant is a thing of the past.

Many scholars have argued that this is all too simplistic (see Plamenatz, 1963: 351–408).

- In the first place, it is argued that complex societies contain many different sources of division or conflict. Getting rid of classes therefore only ends one source of conflict. Others, based on aspects of life, such as religion, culture, or types of work, will still exist and have to be dealt with presumably by an institution such as the state. The experience of the communist states of Eastern Europe backs up this critique of Marxism, for once the constraints of communist control were released, numerous interests, previously suppressed, emerged. As a result, it might be argued too that politics resumed, after it had been artificially suppressed.

- Moreover, the transformation of human nature envisaged by Marx, it is argued, is also overly simplistic. There is something in the claim that to reduce the level of economic inequality will have an impact on the behaviour of individuals, reducing crime based on acquisitiveness. Marx is justly famous for having pointed this out. However, it is a large step from this to the claim that society can exist effectively without the need for differential rewards as incentives for contributing to it. One of the problems here is Marx's assumption that communism would end material scarcity, which, from the perspective of the twenty-first century, seems remarkably misplaced. As a result of all of these factors, it seems likely that a state would be necessary in a communist regime in order to achieve the desired egalitarian goals. Some would argue that this involves the illegitimate suppressing of the natural urge that individuals have to be different and better than others. Others would argue that this is a necessary price to pay in order to create a fairer and more equal society.

Questions
1. Describe Marx's theory of the state and politics.
2. Critically examine the case for and against Marx's theory of the state.

political theory, has been on the nation-state. In addition, the dominant tradition in international relations has been the realist tradition, which postulates a state system consisting of individual autonomous and competing sovereign states. Globalization challenges both assumptions.

The issue of globalization will be considered in more detail later in this book. For now, it should be noted that we can adopt empirical and normative approaches to it (Dryzek and Dunleavy, 2009: ch. 14). From an empirical perspective, the major impetus behind globalization is the

➜ See
Chapter 22 for a
discussion of the
relationship
between the
state and
international
economic
institutions.

internationalization of the economy. With the growth of multinational corporations—which have emerged to rival the power of states—and the liberalization of world trade, it is argued, the economic policies of individual states are now determined elsewhere (Ohmae, 1995). Partly as a result of greater economic interdependence—together with improved communication technology and the emergence of global environmental problems—supranational institutions (whether they be intergovernmental organizations, such as the World Trade Organization, or non-governmental organizations, such as Greenpeace) have emerged to challenge further the power of states.

As a result, critics argue, the realist school postulating the key role of sovereign states is time-bound, dating from the Peace of Westphalia in 1648. We are now, it is suggested, in a period of 'new medievalism' where 'as in medieval Europe, sovereignty is shared among societies that interact in an ongoing way' (Cunningham, 2002: 203; see also Slaughter, 2003: 190). Others argue that the globalization thesis exaggerates the reality, that sovereign states still have a great deal of autonomy and were never, anyway, as self-contained as is often made out (Robertson, 1992). In recent years, the case for the reassertion of the state's central role in politics has been precipitated by a number of factors. These include the need for states to deal with terrorism (which has led to extra spending on security and tighter border controls), and the state's role in facilitating economic recovery after the 2008 financial crash.

From a normative perspective, it can be argued that the liberation of world markets is a positive development, facilitating greater prosperity. In addition, global problems—such as those concerned with the environment—require global solutions that are beyond the reach of sovereign states. Finally, it is argued that globalization also facilitates cosmopolitanism, the goal of achieving peace, toleration, and justice in a world where we owe our allegiances to humanity—a form of global citizenship—rather than to partial entities such as the state (Heater, 1999). Others do not see the nation-state as an obstacle to cosmopolitanism, and suggest that a system of markets unencumbered by the state is a negative phenomenon, exacerbating inequality in the world and increasing exploitation, particularly in developing countries.

One final point here is that it is not just globalization that represents a threat to the autonomy of the nation-state. In addition, as we saw in the introduction to this book, the reality of decision-making is that the state is in partnership with a range of social and economic institutions. Government has now been replaced by governance. Included in those now sharing power with the state are sub-state institutions such as, in Britain, the Scottish and Welsh authorities established by devolution proposals in recent years, as well as the supranational institutions that are the subject of the globalization debate. This overlapping system of governance has been described as neo-medievalism as a result of its similarity to the system of authority in the Europe of the Middle Ages before the emergence of the state.

CONCLUSION

In this chapter, we attempted to define the state, before going on to provide empirical typologies of it, and a consideration of various interpretations of how the state ought to be organized. We saw that one of the most important typologies of the state centres on the distribution of power. Here, we identified empirical theories of the state on a continuum from the open and diffuse picture painted by classical pluralism to the closed and hierarchical picture painted by elitists and

Marxists. These theories can be criticized on empirical grounds—they do not provide an accurate description of how the state is organized—and on normative grounds—they do not provide polities to which we ought to aspire.

Certainly, theories of the state, with the possible exception of Marxism, do not emphasize enough the external constraints operating on the state in the modern world, and these globalizing tendencies will be a constant theme of this book. Chapters 4 and 5 will continue an exploration of how the state ought to be organized, and what it ought to do. In the next chapter, however, we will look closely at the concept of power, not least because this will help us to understand how difficult it is to investigate which of the theories of the state is the most accurate description of a particular political system.

KEY QUESTIONS

1. What is the state?
2. Can we do without the state?
3. Compare and contrast the pluralist, elitist, and Marxist theories of the state.
4. How far does the American political system exhibit the characteristics of the pluralist theory of the state?
5. Critically examine the Marxist theory of the state.
6. Which normative theory of the state do you find most convincing?
7. Evaluate the strengths and weaknesses of identity politics.
8. How effective is the communitarian critique of liberalism?
9. In the light of 9/11, the financial crisis, and the growing threat of climate change, the New Right theory of the state is seriously flawed. Discuss.
10. Are the state's days numbered?

FURTHER READING

Dryzek, J. and Dunleavy, P. (2009), *Theories of the Democratic State* (Basingstoke: Palgrave).
  Written by two leading political scientists, this is an excellent introduction to competing theories of the state and, indeed, political science in general. It has an excellent chapter on globalization.

Fukuyama, F. (2018), *Identity: Contemporary Identity Politics and the Struggle for Recognition* (London: Profile).
  This is an articulate critique of identity politics and what to do about it.

Hay, C. et al. (eds) (2006), *The State: Theories and Issues* (Basingstoke: Palgrave).
  This is a very useful book with chapters on various aspects of the debate about the state.

Held, D. et al. (2005), *Debating Globalization* (Cambridge: Polity).
  This provides a very useful collection of articles on globalization taking all sides of the debate.

2

Hoffman, J. (1995), *Beyond the State* (Cambridge: Polity).

This provides a normative critique of the state, while also outlining the different approaches considered in this chapter.

James, A. (1986), *Sovereign Statehood* (London: Allen & Unwin).

This is a detailed conceptual account of sovereignty. James argues that the concept remains useful in understanding modern politics.

Jessop, B. (2015) *The State: Past, Present, Future* (Cambridge: Polity Press).

This is a short but extremely useful book on debates about the role of the state.

Parry, G. (1969), *Political Elites* (London: Allen & Unwin).

This is a relatively old book but still cannot be bettered for the way in which it expertly surveys the literature on both classical elitism and pluralist versions of elitism.

Savigny, H. and Marsden, L. (2011), *Doing Political Science and International Relations: Theories in Action* (Basingstoke: Palgrave Macmillan).

Chapter 3 of this book contains a useful overview of theories of the state. Case studies applying theories of the state to the credit crunch issue are instructive.

Woods, K. (2014), *Human Rights* (Basingstoke: Palgrave Macmillan).

A comprehensive, empirical and normative, account of the concept of rights.

 For additional material and resources, please visit the Online Resources at:
www.oup.com/he/garner4e

POLITICAL POWER, AUTHORITY, AND THE STATE

READER'S GUIDE

This chapter explores the concept of power. It starts by defining power in the context of authority, before going on to discuss the classic threefold typology of authority put forward by the German sociologist Max Weber. Some conceptual questions about power are then asked—'is it the same as force?', 'must it be exercised deliberately?', 'is it a good thing?', and 'can we ever eliminate it?' The rest of the chapter is concerned with examining the methodological problems inherent in the measurement of power, particularly in relation to the theories of the state discussed in Chapter 2.

POWER AND AUTHORITY

Power and authority are central concepts in politics. As Hay (2002: 168) states, in only slightly exaggerated terms, 'power is to political analysis what the economy is to economics'. Politics is about competing interests and values, and a key question is what interests and values come out on top in practice. To discover this, we need to know something about power, since those who have power over others can determine which interests and values will be adopted by political decision-makers.

3

CASE STUDY BOX 3.1
The United States Supreme Court: Authority, Power, and Legitimacy

One useful example of the distinction between power and authority is the role of the Supreme Court in the USA. The Supreme Court is often said to be the most powerful arm of the American political system because of its established right (of judicial review) to declare actions of the executive and legislative branches as unconstitutional. This means that the decisions of elected bodies can be overridden by an unelected body. Members of the Supreme Court are chosen by the president and confirmed by the senate but once appointed remain as justices for life unless removed for wrongdoing.

It is often asked whether the Supreme Court's apparent power is worrying in a democratic polity. The court has made many important political decisions relating to such controversial issues as race, abortion, and capital punishment, and yet its members are not elected and made accountable to the people. Presidents appoint justices, when the opportunity arises, in order to alter or maintain the ideological balance of the court, and the ideological bias they create can exist long after a particular president has left office.

One retort to the claim that the Supreme Court is exercising illegitimate power is to invoke the distinction between power and authority. Thus, it is important to note that the Supreme Court has no army or police force with which to enforce its decisions. In other words, it is unable to exercise power or, at the very least, it has to share power with the executive and legislative branches of the federal government. As a result, in order for its decisions to be accepted without the threat of coercion, the court relies on its authority. In other words, it has authority but not power. The Supreme Court would almost certainly lose its authority, and therefore its legitimacy, if it made decisions that are too divorced from public opinion. Supreme Court justices are, therefore, constrained by the need to remain an authoritative institution in the American polity.

To give an example, in a well-known judgment (Brown versus Board of Education of Topeka) the Court ruled that racial segregation of children in public schools was unconstitutional. For many in the southern states, this decision was unacceptable and many schools and local officials sought to defy it. In one celebrated case, in Little Rock Arkansas in 1957, President Eisenhower deployed federal troops to enable black students to attend high school and thus implement the Supreme Court ruling. School segregation was commonplace in the South until Congress passed civil rights legislation in 1968.

A common way of distinguishing between power and authority is to equate the former with coercion and the latter with consent. Authority, then, is defined here as legitimate power in the sense that rulers can produce acceptance by the ruled, not because they can exercise coercion but because the ruled recognize the right of the rulers to exercise power. Converting power into authority, then, is highly desirable. **See Box 3.2**. As Goodwin (2014: 346) points out: 'Where coercion creates obedience at a high cost in manpower and equipment, authority can control both the minds and the behaviour of individuals at a very low cost.'

In terms of the exercise of power, there would seem to be two possible answers to the difficulty of applying coercion. One is to rule through so-called ideological control. In this scenario, rulers are able to maintain control through manipulating the preferences of the ruled so that these preferences reflect the interests of the rulers. Such control—associated with elitist thinkers and Marxist critiques of capitalist society—is much more effective in that it obviates the need for permanent scrutiny and coercion of the ruled. Nevertheless, as we shall see, its validity does depend upon the debatable assumption that individual preferences can be manipulated in such a way.

Some political theorists seek to link authority with philosophy and power with sociological analysis (Barry, 2000: 83). Here, authority is linked with moral and political philosophy with what ought to be, while power is conceived of as an empirical concept, with what is. This distinction, though, is problematic. As we noted previously, authority can be a product of manipulation. Or, if one is suspicious of claims that people can be easily brainwashed, it might be argued that people are simply wrong, that they recognize as legitimate the wrong set of leaders.

There is no doubt, for instance, that Hitler had a great deal of authority within German society and yet few would want to claim that we therefore ought to regard the Nazi regime as legitimate. At the very least, we can agree with Goodwin's (2014: 350) assertion that 'a state's authority in the eyes of the people is not necessarily an indicator of its justice'. A linked argument is the case for saying that power is preferable to authority precisely on the grounds that, whereas the latter can be based upon manipulation, the former is based on coercion. And, in the case of coercion, it is possible to recognize and act upon it (Goodwin, 2014: 351).

The second answer to the problem of coercion makes no such assumptions about the 'real' interests of the ruled. Rather, it simply asks how can any set of rulers make themselves legitimate in the eyes of the ruled? In other words, how can rulers convert power into authority? No set of rulers can survive very long without at least some authority. This, then, raises another question: on what is authority based? The question of when and why political systems are legitimate is a crucial one for political theorists. It is a topic we touched on in Chapter 2 when looking at what role, if any, the state ought to have, and it is a question to which we shall return in Chapter 4 when we examine the claims of democracy.

The best-known attempt to come up with an analysis of the basis of authority was provided by Max Weber (Gerth and Mills, 1946). Weber regarded so-called 'legal–rational' authority as the predominant basis for authority in the modern world. To give an example of this, the American president is obeyed, not because he is charismatic or because he claims to have a divine right to rule, but because he holds the office of the president. We can go further than this. In the modern Western world, and indeed in many other parts of the world now, political institutions are accepted because they are subject to democratic principles. In other words, nowadays, the holder of the office of the American president has authority because he is elected. Indeed, the president remains the only part of the American polity whose constituency is the entire American electorate, **see Box 3.2**.

As Hoffman and Graham (2006: 5–11) rightly point out, although we can define power and authority separately, in practice all governments use both. Even in a democracy some exercise of power is necessary. This is not least because decisions taken by a majority (the classic way decisions are taken in a democracy) leave a minority who may be resentful that their view did not prevail. Thus, even though democratic states exercise much more authority than authoritarian states who exercise more power, the former have to exercise power at least some of the time and the latter always have some authority.

3

KEY CONCEPT BOX 3.2
Weber and Authority

Max Weber (1864–1920), the German sociologist and social theorist, developed a threefold classification of authority. He recognized that these were ideal types, and all societies were likely to contain elements of the three types. Weber argued that the modern world exhibits a greater tendency towards legal–rational authority.

- **Traditional authority:** authority derived from traditional customs and values. A major example would be the principle of the divine right of kings, prevalent in European monarchies, whereby monarchies were said to be ordained by God to rule.
- **Charismatic authority:** authority derived from the personality traits of an individual. This is often associated with the leaders of authoritarian or totalitarian regimes, not least because such charismatic leaders tend to emerge at a time of crisis. This form of authority may be less important in modern, liberal democracies where authority tends to be based upon status and not personal qualities. However, charisma still plays some part, being part of a political leader's armoury, particularly now that the media image of leaders is important, even in parliamentary systems such as Britain. Weber regarded charismatic authority as inherently unstable. This is because, since authority rests with an individual and not a set of rules, the death of this individual, or her loss of authority, will immediately lead to instability.
- **Legal–rational authority:** authority derived from the status of an office as part of a system of constitutional rules, in a democratic country, or a religious document such as the Qur'an in Islamic regimes.

Photo 3.1 German sociologist Max Weber classified authority into three categories: traditional, charismatic, and legal-rational. *Alamy (library image): Keystone Press/Alamy Stock Photo*

To put another spanner in the works, the distinction between authority and power is further clouded by the (likely) possibility that authority is granted to an institution, or an individual, precisely because it has power. It is true that, not only do democratic regimes have to exercise power, but also totalitarian regimes usually have some degree of authority, even if it is the charismatic authority associated with political leaders such as Stalin and Hitler.

As Heywood (2015: 127–30) points out, the concept of authority is now particularly contentious. Many bemoan the decline of authority, reflecting what they see as the decline of social deference. Conservative thinkers, therefore, seek to justify its importance, emphasizing the need for people to be led and protected (Scruton, 2001). Those from a liberal perspective, by contrast, while recognizing the importance of authority for social stability, also promote liberty which can challenge authority.

➡ See Chapter 4 for a discussion of the problem of majority rule.

CONCEPTUAL QUESTIONS ABOUT POWER

The meaning of power can be teased out a little further if we consider a number of questions about it.

Is Power the Same As Force?

It is often argued that there is a conceptual difference between power and force or coercion (Barry, 2000: 89–90). Power can be, and usually is, exercised by the threat of force. However, it might be argued that the actual use of force means that power has failed. For example, the USA clearly used a great deal of force in Vietnam, as well as, more recently, in Iraq. However, it palpably failed to gain obedience in the former and it is headed the same way in the latter. As Lukes (2005: 70) points out, 'having the means of power is not the same as being powerful'.

Must Power Be Exercised Deliberately?

There are some who argue that power must be exercised deliberately. As Bertrand Russell (1872–1970), the great twentieth-century British philosopher, insisted, power is 'the production of *intended* results: the unforeseen effects of our influence on others cannot be called power' (1938: 25). The argument here is that it sounds intuitively odd to accord power to someone who has benefited from a situation which that person has not created. Nelson Polsby (1980: 208), the American political scientist, sums this up nicely by using the example of taxi drivers and the weather. Thus, taxi drivers surely benefit when it rains but they do not cause it to rain. It is merely an unplanned effect of the rain. As he points out, it is mistaken to regard this as an exercise of power by taxi drivers since showing that taxi drivers benefit from the rain 'falls short of showing that these beneficiaries created the status quo, act in a meaningful way to maintain it, or could, in the future, act effectively to deter changes in it'. As a result, 'Who benefits? . . . is a different question from who governs?' (209).

This debate is important because it relates to the argument (outlined later) put forward by some Marxists and elitists that the ruling class or elite exercises power, not because of its own agency, but because economic structures automatically benefit it and disadvantage others. It is to outcomes that we ought to look then if we want to see the true location of power. Of course, this sits uneasily with the claim that power is about intended effects; about, in other words, agency over structure. Maybe this is merely a matter of semantics. We can dispute that certain structures—the capitalist system, for instance—do inevitably benefit some and disadvantage others. What we cannot do is to dispute the effect of structures that do actually benefit some and disadvantage others. This may not be an exercise of power, if we define power in terms of intended effects, but it is clearly politically significant. Maybe domination, rather than power, is a better word to use in this situation.

Is Power A Good Thing?

Some political thinkers would argue that whether or not power is good depends upon the uses to which it is put. From this perspective, using power to achieve certain desired outcomes is positive. As Lukes (2005: 109) points out, there are 'manifold ways in which power over others can be productive, transformative, authoritative and compatible with dignity'. By contrast, using power to harm others is negative. From a liberal perspective, however, power is always undesirable because 'every exercise of power involves the imposition of someone's values upon another' (Barry, 2000: 99). This is why liberals recommend limitations on power in the form, for instance, of a separation of powers to prevent one branch of government from exercising too much power.

It is not clear, however, that the exercise of power is necessarily undesirable, whatever the consequences. It is logically possible, for instance, to think of a situation where A might know B's real interests better than B does herself, so that A exercising power over B would be to act in B's interests. An example here would be the relationship between a parent and a child. Liberals could still contend, however, that such a power relationship is illegitimate because, whatever the motive, the exercise of power still infringes the individual's freedom. There are two responses to this. The first is to say that we are faced with a choice between two incommensurable concepts (freedom and intervention for good) and there is no sure-fire way of arbitrating between them. The second is to say that it is logically possible, however unlikely, for A to use her power to insist that B is free. Using the law to abolish human slavery would be a good example of this. It is possible to conceive of someone who wishes to remain in slavery and, in this case, power would be used to make them free.

Can We Eliminate Power?

A related question is, whether it is ever possible for power to be dispensed with. Can a society in which no one exercises power over anyone else exist? Here, the work of the French philosopher Michel Foucault (1926–84) is instructive. Foucault is usually taken as offering a challenge to the work of those, such as Habermas (1929–), Marcuse (1898–1979), and Lukes, who, as we shall see later, imply that power is illegitimately exercised and ought therefore to be curtailed. For Foucault, power is ubiquitous, it is everywhere, and power relations between individuals are inevitable.

In his work *Discipline and Punish* (1977), for instance, Foucault argues that the history of legal punishment in France is superficially progressive because extremely violent punishment gave way to regimented incarceration. In reality, however, these are only two ways of achieving the same objective. Both involve power relations and both involve domination. History, for Foucault, then, is 'an endlessly repeated play of domination' (quoted in Hay, 2002: 191). Because power is ubiquitous, there is no possibility of liberation from it, although we can, as Foucault shows, change its focus and implementation. Lukes (2005: 107), who disputes this conclusion (and also denies that Foucault should be interpreted in this way) asks the question raised by Foucault, should we give up thinking 'of the very possibility of people being more or less free from others' power to live as their own nature and judgment dictate?' Foucault answers this in the affirmative. Lukes is less pessimistic.

KEY POINTS

- The concepts of power and authority are usually taken to differ over the issue of legitimacy, the former implying the use or threat of sanctions, the latter reflecting a set of rulers' right to rule.
- A key question for students of politics is the degree to which power is converted into authority. Weber's threefold classification remains the best-known attempt. He argues that modern political authority is legal-rational in nature rather than being based on tradition or charisma.
- Typical questions asked about power, upon which different answers are provided, include whether power is the same as force, whether power can be said to be exercised without the intention of doing so, whether the exercise of power can ever be good, and, a related question, whether we can ever eliminate power relationships.

POWER AND THEORIES OF THE STATE

We saw in the last chapter that theories of the state centre on the distribution of power. These theories might be used to describe the power structures in different societies. We might be justified, for instance, in claiming that various clearly undemocratic regimes in the world exhibit characteristics equivalent to ruling-elite theory, or even Marxist theory, whereas the liberal democratic regimes in the West are more clearly pluralist oriented.

The debate about power has applied overwhelmingly to liberal democracies. This is partly because participants in the debate have been Western political scientists, particularly from the USA, concerned with analysing liberal democratic political systems. More significantly, it reflects the fact that the power debate has been used to both defend and challenge the claim that political power in liberal democracies is widely spread rather than concentrated. That is, in non-democratic states it is assumed that the pluralist model does not apply.

There are, of course, authoritarian states in the world that have survived and, in some cases, prospered despite the influence of the democratic ideal. However we define them, and whatever their strengths, one thing is for sure: they are not democracies. They therefore do not exhibit the characteristics of the pluralist theory of the state. The point of the Marxist and elitist challenge to the pluralist model, then, is to demonstrate that, despite the democratic rhetoric, the pluralist model is not an accurate description of so-called liberal democracies either.

The first observation to make in an analysis of competing theories of power is that we cannot claim that all of these theories of the state correctly analyse the power structure existing in any one polity. In other words, we cannot claim that a country such as the UK is at one and the same time capable of being explained in Marxist and pluralist terms. A pluralist account of UK politics would look very different from a Marxist account (see the discussion in Dearlove and Saunders, 2000: ch. 9). Having said this, it is possible to argue that, at a micro level, different policy networks within a particular polity area exhibit different power structures some being more open than others (see Smith, 1993, and the discussion in Chapter 13).

Second, we need to ask how we go about determining which of these theories of the state provides a more accurate description of reality in, say, Britain or the USA? Such a task is enormously difficult, partly because of the problems involved in measuring the exercise of power. These stem largely from the fact that, as we shall see, power has been conceptualized in a number of different ways. These different conceptualizations of power were articulated in a classic account of the concept provided by Stephen Lukes (2005) in a book originally published in 1974.

This became known as the 'faces of power' debate, because Lukes distinguishes between three dimensions or faces of power, himself preferring the third dimension as the most comprehensive. He starts, however, by offering us a definition of power which, he holds, is universally acceptable. This definition is as follows: 'A exercises power over B when A affects B in a manner contrary to B's interests' (Lukes, 2005: 30). This only takes us so far because there is disagreement over the way in which A can act contrary to B's interests.

PLURALISM AND LUKES' THREE DIMENSIONS OF POWER

The way in which power is conceptualized has a significant bearing on the empirical validity of theories of the state. To see how this is so, let us return to the pluralist theory of the state. Pluralists adopt a decision-making approach to measuring power, which is equivalent to the first dimension of power. The first face of power is where, in Robert Dahl's words, 'A has power over B to the extent that he can get B to do something that B would not otherwise do' (quoted in Lukes, 2005: 16).

This first face of power is otherwise known as the decision-making approach, in that the method used by pluralist researchers is to look at the decisions made and the preferences of those groups involved in decision-making in a particular set of policy domains. It is then suggested that if a group's aims are met, or partly met, then they have power (see Hewitt, 1974). If no one group gets its way on all occasions, then the pluralist model is affirmed. The advantage of the decision-making approach utilizing the first face of power is that it is eminently researchable. Indeed, numerous so-called 'community power' studies in the late 1950s and 1960s were undertaken in the USA, most of which confirmed the pluralist theory of the state (Dahl, 1963; Polsby, 1980).

Clearly, the decision-making approach could lead to non-pluralist conclusions; that is, it is possible that one group or a small number of groups get their way in the decisions made and the decision-making approach will pick this up. However, critics of pluralism suggest that the pluralist methodology is more than likely to generate pluralist conclusions (Morriss, 1975). In the first place, the pluralist methodology makes no attempt to rank issues in order of importance.

Clearly, some issues are more important than others, and it may be the case that an elite group allows other groups to prevail in the lesser issues while ensuring that it gets its way in the more important ones, **see Box 3.3**.

Second, it is assumed that the barriers to entry for groups in the political system are low. That is, pluralists assume that if a group of people have a case to put or a grievance to express, then it is easy for them to enter the decision-making arena to express it. Clearly, however, this is a dubious assumption. Some groups—such as the unemployed or the homeless—may not have the resources or the expertise to organize effectively even if they wanted to. Other groups may not bother to organize because they anticipate little success. By focusing on the active groups in the decision-making arena, therefore, pluralists may well miss a range of interests which, for whatever reason, never appear within it.

Moreover, third, there is the related assumption that those issues discussed in the decision-making arena are the most important ones. In other words, it ignores the possibility that an elite group,

KEY DEBATE BOX 3.3
The First Face of Power and Its Critics

Pluralists typically adopt a decision-making methodology, what Lukes (2005) describes as the first face of power. The decision-making approach is illustrated in **Table 3.1**. This table shows the outcome of four issues on which three groups took positions.

Table 3.1 shows that all the groups to a range of decisions got their way at least some of the time. For example, the decisions taken on 1 and 2 met with the approval of Groups A and B while Group C achieved its goal on Issue 4. Pluralists would conclude from this that no one group was able to get its way on all issues, and that power is therefore widely dispersed.

It is possible that the decision-making approach can generate non-pluralist conclusions. In the example in **Table 3.1**, for instance, it might have been found that Group A got its way on all four issues and groups B and C lost out. However, the critics of pluralism suggest that the decision-making approach as set out in **Table 3.1** is likely to generate pluralist conclusions.

One of the reasons for this, the critics argue, is that pluralists tend to assume that all issues are of the same political importance as all others. As **Table 3.1** illustrates, this can distort the political reality. What it misses is the possibility that an elite group gets its way on the most important issue or issues, leaving other groups to get their way on the less important ones. Therefore, in the example, **Table 3.2**, Group C gets its way on fewer issues but yet gets its way on the issue weighted most highly (Issue 4).

Table 3.1 The pluralist decision-making approach

	Issue 1	Issue 2	Issue 3	Issue 4	Total
Group A	WON	WON	LOST	LOST	2
Group B	WON	WON	WON	LOST	3
Group C	LOST	LOST	LOST	WON	1

Source: Adapted from Hay (2002: 174).

Table 3.2 Pluralism and issue preferences

	Issue 1	Issue 2	Issue 3	Issue 4	Total
Weighting	1	1	1	5	
Group A	WON	WON	LOST	LOST	2
Group B	WON	WON	WON	LOST	3
Group C	LOST	LOST	LOST	WON	5

Source: Adapted from Hay (2002: 177).

Imagine, for instance, that groups A and B are trade unions and Group C is a business organization. Further, imagine that Issues 1–3 establish for workers an extra fifteen minutes' break at various parts of the working day, and Issue 4 grants to employers a right to prohibit strike action. Clearly, Issue 4 is much more important for business interests and is a serious restriction on trade unions; yet, a pluralist methodology would fail to take this into account as an exercise of power by one group.

Questions

1. What criticisms have been made of the decision-making approach to measuring power?
2. What impact do these criticisms have on the validity of the pluralist theory of the state?

or indeed a ruling class, can determine what will and will not be discussed. It is here that the second and third faces of power identified by Lukes can be invoked. The second face of power involves what Bachrach and Baratz (1963)—two American political scientists working in the 1960s—described as 'non-decision-making'. Here, an elite group operating behind the scenes can prevent certain issues from ever entering the decision-making arena.

For Bachrach and Baratz, then, power has two faces: the readily observable type as defined by the first dimension and a not so readily observable realm of non-decision—making. Power, for them, 'is also exercised when A devotes his energies to creating or reinforcing social and political values and institutional practices that limit the scope of the political process to public consideration of only those issues which are comparatively innocuous to A' (Bachrach and Baratz, 1970: 7). Non-decision-making, it is being suggested, usually operates in the interests of the most powerful who stand to gain most from inaction. Bachrach and Baratz advocate using both faces of power to gain a more rounded picture of the power structure. The first focuses on decisions actually made. The second is when 'power has the effect of preventing an issue from reaching the point where a decision is required' (Shorten, 2016: 151).

Although undoubtedly difficult, it is possible to identify cases of non-decision-making, where issues of importance to some groups have not appeared on the political agenda. A number of empirical studies (for example, Crenson, 1971; Blowers, 1984) have attempted to show how this has occurred. A starting point is to identify covert grievances, grievances that clearly exist but which are never openly discussed. The next step is to identify reasons for non-decision-making. A number of possibilities present themselves. Issues may be excluded because of the use of force. Equally, they may be excluded because there is consensus among politicians on an issue, therefore denying the electorate a choice. Similarly, issues can be excluded by the use of rules or procedures. In the latter category can be included filibustering, a common tactic in the US Congress, as well as the common tactic of taking the heat out of an issue by referring it to a legislative committee or, in the British context, a Royal Commission, thereby postponing the need to make a decision.

Another cause of non-decision-making is the so-called 'law of anticipated reactions'. We have already seen how this can impact on a group's decision not to enter the decision-making arena. It can also, however, influence the attitude of decision-makers themselves. A study by the American political scientist Charles Lindblom (1977), for instance, argued that business interests hold a privileged position in the decision-making arena because of their position in the economy; that is, governments recognize that businesses can help to deliver desirable economic scenarios—low unemployment and inflation—and as a result will always be likely to concede to business demands. This power of business is enhanced even further when governments have to deal with multinational companies who have the option to take their businesses to another country.

The crucial point here is that business interests do not have to lobby decision-makers or demonstrate on the street to be heard. Pluralist researchers adopting the decision-making approach will not, therefore, identify business interests as one of a number of interests with a stated position. Rather, governments will automatically consider business peoples' interests because they anticipate their influence.

The first and second faces of power assume that political actors are aware of their own interests. The second, and much more insidious, way in which an elite group or ruling class can set the political agenda, it is suggested, is their ability to shape the demands which groups articulate in the decision-making arena. This is the third dimension of power, or power as 'preference manipultion' (Shorten, 2016: 152), **see Box 3.4**. For Lukes (2005: 27), 'A may exercise power over B by getting him to do what he does not want to do, but he also exercises power over him by influencing, shaping, or determining his very wants', **see Box 3.5**.

For Lukes, then, the exercise of power may not involve conflict (because individuals who are being dominated are not aware of it). The exercise of power does, though, require 'latent conflict' in the sense that there is a gap 'between the interests of those exercising power and the *real interests*' of those being dominated (Lukes, 2005: 28). Consider this example. Wealthy oil companies regularly fund studies which seek to deny the existence or scale of man-made climate change. These studies, of dubious scientific validity, cloud the judgement of people, thus allowing the oil companies to continue making huge profits from the burning of fossil fuels.

The critique of pluralists here is that they take it for granted that the preferences expressed by individuals and groups are in their interests. No attempt is made by pluralists to ascertain how individuals and groups come to hold the preferences they do. For elitists and Marxists this is a serious omission, since the ability of dominant groups to exercise ideological control is a key aspect of the exercise of power. By shaping individual preferences—through control over the means of communication and socialization—a ruling elite or class can prevent demands which challenge its interests from ever reaching the political agenda (for example, see the discussion of the power of the media in Chapter 14). In this way, an apparently pluralistic polity—with freedom of association, free elections, and so on—is, in reality, nothing of the sort.

➡ See Chapter 14 for a discussion of the power of the media.

3

CASE STUDY BOX 3.4
Crenson, Lukes, and Air Pollution

Stephen Lukes, in his now classic study of power, argues that it is possible to determine empir-ically cases where individuals can be manipulated so that the wants they express are different from their actual interests. He cites the well-known study by the American political scientist Matthew Crenson that looked at air pollution policy in two American cities as an example of how this can be done (Lukes, 2005: 44–8).

Crenson (1971) asks why the issue of air pollution was raised in some American cities but not in others. He looks in detail at two cities in the state of Indiana. One, East Chicago, introduced air pollution controls in 1949 and the other, Gary, waited until 1962. Crenson's explanation for this is that the latter city was dominated by one powerful steel company whose reputation for power prevented the issue from being raised, and when it was impossible to ignore, influenced the content of the legislation that emerged. It was not just that the industry prevented support-ers of pollution control from getting a hearing (an example of non-decision-making), although that was part of the story. In addition, support for pollution controls was weak because, Crenson (1971: 27) claims, there was an element of ideological control too in which 'local political insti-tutions and political leaders' exercised 'considerable control over what people choose to care about and how forcefully they articulate their cares'.

Lukes argues that Crenson's study reveals a genuine case where the real interests of people are different from the wants they express. As he remarks, 'there is good reason to expect that, other things being equal, people would rather not be poisoned', and yet it appears they were prepared to be (Lukes, 2005: 48).

Using this study in support of the third face of power is, as a number of commentators have noted, enormously problematic. The assumption both Crenson and Lukes make is that it was in the interests of people in East Chicago and Gary to have pollution control legislation. Therefore, in Gary, the people articulated their 'real' interests and achieved pollution control legislation whereas in East Chicago they did not. However, this assumption is dubious, to say the least. It could equally be argued that residents of Gary were well aware of the benefits that air pollution legislation might bring but were equally aware of the economic drawbacks. They were well aware, in other words, that paying the costs of such legislation would make the company less profitable and might lead to redundancies and reduced pay.

It may or may not be the case that pollution control legislation has economic consequences. Arguably, at the level of the individual industrial unit, unemployment and reduced pay would be the result of pollution control, although the benefits to society as a whole (including economic ones) may outweigh these costs. That, however, is little consolation to those whose livelihoods depend upon continued employment at the unit being threatened. This would be the case par-ticularly where, as in Gary, one company dominates the economy.

Questions
1. What is Lukes' third face of power?
2. How far do you agree with Lukes' claim that Crenson's study provides an example of the third face of power in action?

> **KEY QUOTE** BOX 3.5
> The Third Face of Power
>
> Is it not the most insidious exercise of power to prevent people, to whatever degree, from having grievances by shaping their perceptions, cognitions, and preferences in such a way that they accept their role in the existing order of things, either because they can see or imagine no alternative to it, or because they see it as natural or unchangeable, or because they value it as divinely ordained and beneficial?   (Lukes, 2005: 28)

KEY POINTS

- Determining the empirical validity of the theories of the state discussed in Chapter 2 depends on an analysis of power.
- Pluralists use what Lukes calls the first face of power, focusing on the decision-making arena.
- This approach, while capable of producing non-pluralist conclusions, does not, it is argued, provide the complete picture. It misses, first, the possibility that a political elite or ruling class can avoid making decisions on certain key issues (the second face of power) and can, second, ensure that the wants expressed by political actors are not those that will damage the interests of the ruling group.

INTERESTS AND POWER

Despite the force of their arguments, the critics of pluralism are faced with well-rehearsed methodological difficulties of their own—for if power is exercised in more subtle ways, how do we go about measuring it? We saw that it is possible, albeit difficult, to identify non-decision-making but how do we go about determining if individual preferences have been shaped by dominant forces in society?

The assumption of the third face of power is that one can distinguish between what individuals or groups perceive to be in their interests, and what is, in fact, actually in their interests. This requires the researcher to 'discover' the existence of 'objective' interests, which can then be contrasted with the interests that individuals perceive themselves as having. Now, it is not impossible to conclude accurately that someone is acting against their best interests. Imagine, for instance, that the dominant ideology of a university, accepted by all of the students, is that it is necessary go out drinking the night before an exam on the spurious grounds that this will enhance their performance the following day. Imagine further that the university has shares in a local brewery and that it is likely to further benefit when students fail their exams and have to pay additional fees to resit them. Here, it is possible to conclude that an ideology (accepted by the students) benefits those in power and is not in the interests of the students.

Unfortunately, however, the identification of cases where individuals are clearly acting against their best interests are rarely as simple as that. Take the issue of climate change mentioned previously. To qualify as an example of the third face of power, it would have to be shown that action to tackle climate change is in everybody's real interests. An argument could be made, however, that this is not always the case, or not obviously so. It may be, for instance, that action on climate change will significantly damage the economic interests of some people. It may also be the case that, although we can admit that climate change will ultimately lead to serious problems, that these will mainly affect future generations, so current people can safely ignore the problem. Take, as another example, the issue of smoking (Dearlove and Saunders, 2000: 368). Are we to say that those who continue to smoke, despite being aware of the health problems caused by it, are acting against their best interests? In some cases, undoubtedly, people would have given up smoking if they had been aware of the damage it was going to cause to their health; but others, well aware of the potential health costs, may insist that they want to continue smoking because of other perceived benefits—that it relaxes them, prevents them putting on weight, provides an ice breaker in social situations—or because they value other things over a long life. In these situations, are we still to say that these people are acting against their best interests?

There is an ever-present danger here of being extremely and unjustifiably patronizing towards individuals, a 'we know best' mentality. In reality, the researcher has to be careful to avoid his or her own subjective preferences from intervening, **see Box 3.6**. For example, imagine that one finds that there is widespread support for the existence of nuclear weapons and the argument that this acts as a deterrent against hostile powers also holding nuclear weapons. For the political analyst to argue that this belief is not in the interests of those holding it requires the imposition of an extremely contentious—and therefore political—judgement that, for instance, nuclear weapons are expensive and only encourage other countries to have them too. Others, of course, argue that the nuclear deterrent is in the interests of the people because it helps to maintain peace. Many political questions are similarly subjective and it is difficult to sustain the view that support for one value over another constitutes a failure to act in one's own interests. If a poor person, for instance, prefers freedom over equality are we to say that person is being manipulated? Such a position risks illegitimately denying the importance of one particular view of how society is organized over another.

One innovative critique of the third face of power is provided by Scott (1990). He argues that researchers tend to confuse willing compliance, suggesting ideological manipulation, with a political strategy exercised by dominated groups. Such groups may superficially absorb and articulate the dominant world view of the rulers, but underneath a counter-culture exists which challenges these dominant norms. This kind of strategy, Scott argues, is apparent in cases of

> ## KEY QUOTE BOX 3.6
> ### A Critique of the Third Face of Power
>
> The problem (with the third face of power) . . . is the deeply condescending conception of the social subject as an ideological dupe that it conjures up. Not only is this wretched individual incapable of perceiving her/his true interests . . . But rising above the ideological mists is the enlightened academic who from his/her perch in the ivory tower may look down to discern the genuine interests of those not similarly blessed. (Hay, 1997: 47–8)

slavery, serfdom, caste domination, and, at a micro level, in relations between prisoners and warders and teachers and students. Lukes (2005: 127–8) does not challenge the ingenuity of Scott's research, but raises doubts about the correctness of its interpretation. Scott ignores the public evidence suggesting the willing compliance of dominant groups, in favour of focusing on private transcripts which, he claims, reveal a deliberate strategy of quiescence. But why should we regard this evidence as more important than other information suggesting ideological conformity? At the very least, it 'does not show there is also not widespread consent and resignation' (Lukes, 2005: 131).

POLITICAL ELITES

Given the difficulty of establishing that real interests are being thwarted, many critics of pluralism fall back on the existence of political elites. Here, it is argued, if it can be shown that those occupying the top positions in a variety of institutions have similar social and educational backgrounds, then this provides evidence of the possibility that a ruling elite or class does exist. This approach is, superficially at least, a fruitful one. In almost every elite group in a society such as Britain, those occupying the top positions are drawn disproportionately from the middle and upper classes and from those with public school and Oxbridge educations. Similarly, C. Wright Mills (1956), in his study of American centres of power, found overlapping social and educational backgrounds.

The problem with the political elite approach, however, is that it arguably does not tell us very much at all about the exercise of power. Common sense tells us that political elites exist, but their existence is not necessarily incompatible with the pluralist position. As we saw in Chapter 2, pluralists accept the existence of elites but argue that, provided these elites compete with each other, the basis of the pluralist position is maintained. To demonstrate the existence of a ruling elite or class, we have to establish that there is a coherent, conscious, and conspiratorial group which dominates decision-making.

➡ See Chapter 2, for an exploration of pluralists' attitudes towards elites.

In other words, establishing the existence of a ruling elite or class requires us to ask two additional questions. First, how far do elite groups share a common set of values and beliefs which is distinct from the rest of society? Second, how far do the aims of elite groups prevail? It is by no means clear that either of these conditions exist in a liberal democracy such as Britain, although the extent to which they do should, in principle, be capable of being researched. The problem is that it requires the type of empirical research of observable phenomena that critics of pluralism have already rejected.

KEY POINTS

- It is extremely difficult to show conclusively that a political preference is not in the real interests of those who express it.
- Elite background studies do tend to reveal similar patterns of recruitment. However, the existence of a shared social and educational background does not prove the existence of a ruling elite or class.

MARXISM AND POWER

The methodological problems we have identified above are as applicable to Marxist accounts as they are to elitist ones. Marxists, for instance, have emphasized the ability of the ruling class to exercise ideological control over the proletariat. They are therefore subject to the same critique that it is difficult to distinguish 'real' interests from perceived interests.

➡ See Chapter 6 for an exploration of post-Marxian Marxism.

Marx famously pointed out that, 'the ideas of the ruling class are in every epoch the ruling ideas' (McLellan, 1980: 184). As a result of ideological control, the proletariat, for Marxists, are subject to 'false consciousness', and this explains their lack of revolutionary fervour. Marx tended to assume that a revolutionary class consciousness would arise spontaneously as a result of objective economic developments. As we shall see in Chapter 6, subsequent Marxists such as Lenin have argued for the need for a revolutionary party to articulate and promote the proletariat's 'real' interests.

The concept of false consciousness is a theme developed by many post-Marxian Marxists. The Italian Marxist Antonio Gramsci (1891–1937), for instance (from whom Lukes borrows extensively), emphasized the ability of the ruling class ideologically to manipulate the proletariat through their 'hegemony', and regarded the role of intellectuals as crucial in challenging this domination (1971). Similarly, the neo-Marxist thinker Herbert Marcuse (1898–1979) stressed that the capitalist state creates a situation where a large part of the population are led to believe that the state is benign, if not beneficial, whereas the reality is that the state is exerting power. The evidence for this is provided by those occasions when the state is forced to react violently to public protest (1964).

Marxists, like elitists, have struggled to explain how it is that the ruling class rules despite the existence of universal suffrage and competitive elections. Marx himself, of course, had not faced this problem as he was writing at a time when the suffrage was limited to a small number of wealthy men. Later Marxists, such as Ralph Miliband (1924–94), have tended to fall back on three arguments here (1978). In the first place, they note the similar social and educational backgrounds of state and economic elites. Again, however, this falls prey to the critique previously outlined, that such backgrounds do not show conclusively the existence of a cohesive, conspiratorial ruling class.

Second, Marxists, such as Miliband, argue that business interests represent a particularly powerful interest group. Again, the power of business can be challenged on pluralist grounds, by noting the countervailing power of non-business interests and also by the state which Marxists have arguably failed to show always acts in the interests of business. Third, Marxists (as well as elitists) argue that we ought to focus, not on the way decisions are made and who is involved in the decision-making arena, but on the outcomes of decision-making. Who wins and who loses from the decisions taken? According to the who wins and who loses position, we only have to look, it is argued, at the inequalities in most societies, including liberal democracies, to see that a particular group benefits. As Westergaard and Resler (1975: 141) state in their classic, Marxist, account of the class structure:

> Power is visible only through its consequences: they are the first and the final proof of the existence of power. The continuing inequalities of wealth, income and welfare that divide the population are . . . the most visible manifestations of the division of power in a society such as Britain.

From this, it is assumed that the group that benefits exercises power, and therefore that an elitist or Marxist approach is a more accurate description of modern political systems.

We saw earlier in this chapter that it is questionable whether outcomes such as these can be equated with power without the intended actions of a human agent. More specifically, although it is true that a great deal of inequality does still exist in most capitalist societies, it would be wrong to claim that universal suffrage and the coming to power of left-of-centre governments has had no impact on the distribution of resources. The creation of the welfare state and the introduction of free education in modern liberal democracies has undoubtedly improved the lives of many people. Indeed, arguably, the consequences of affluence, not least relating to the environment, have become as big a problem in the developed world as poverty.

Marxists counter the argument that the welfare state and other social reforms 'disprove' their central thesis. In the first place, they would argue that the creation of the welfare state was instrumental for the owners of capital because good healthcare and educational provision is essential for a productive workforce. Second, there is the argument that reforms benefiting the working class are made only when social unrest would have been the result had concessions not been made.

Both of these arguments have their problems. In the first place, not all social benefits can be shown to be in the direct interests of the dominant economic class. Some, such as, say, measures to improve productivity might be, but it is difficult to see free higher education in subjects in the humanities and social sciences in the same way. Second, the argument that reforms have averted social unrest and even revolution is weak, partly because it is impossible to disprove. We cannot possibly know for sure what the consequences of not granting concessions would have been. Moreover, if the ruling classes are continually making concessions, then the question must be asked: how far do they remain a ruling class?

A more sophisticated Marxist account, which takes account of some of the weaknesses outlined, is the structural Marxism associated mainly with the Greek Marxist Nicos Poulantzas (1936–79), who in the late 1960s and 1970s engaged in a sustained debate with Miliband, the exponent of a more traditional Marxism (Poulantzas, 1973, 1976). Poulantzas, a disciple of the French structuralist Marxist Louis Althusser (1918–90), moves us from an account based on agency to one based on structure; that is, he argues that benefits in society may be distributed in a particular way not because of the intentional actions of individuals but because of the structure of the situation. In the economic sphere, capitalists, however kind and philanthropic they may be, are forced to act in particular ways—increasing profit primarily by bringing down wages—if they want to remain in business.

State personnel, too, are forced to act in ways that support the logic of the capitalist system. For Poulantzas, the state is able to act autonomously from the bourgeoisie, but this enables it to act in the long-term interests of the dominant class, even if, in some instances, the short-term interests of this class are set aside. Offering concessions to prevent social unrest is one such strategy. Offering free healthcare and education is not in the short-term interests of the bourgeoisie because paying for it eats into their profits. In the long term, however, the ruling class benefits because of the creation of a healthier, more productive workforce, and a climate less likely to result in social unrest.

By emphasizing structure over agency, Poulantzas, it might be argued, still falls foul of the claim that power can only be exercised deliberately. More specifically, he has been criticized for

➡ See Chapter 7 for a discussion of the relationship between economic growth and environmental protection.

failing to explain why it is that the state behaves in the way he says it does (Hay, 1999). In other words, if the state is not directly controlled by the ruling class, why is it that it still acts in its long-term interests? Even more peculiar, why is it that it has autonomy which is only relative? There is an air of mysticism here which, perhaps, is the result of not paying enough attention to the attitudes and actions of individuals.

KEY POINTS

- Marxists also emphasize the role of both ideological control and elite background studies, and therefore face similar problems to those seeking to justify a ruling-elite position.
- Marxists also face difficulty in trying to explain how a ruling class can still be said to rule in a liberal democracy where universal suffrage has long been the norm and in which a welfare state now exists.
- Marxists tend to argue that universal suffrage does not dent the power of business interests, and that, in any case, much social welfare reform is in the interests of the dominant class.
- The structural Marxism associated with Poulantzas attempts, not always successfully, to deal with these problems. Political actors are forced to act in ways that promote the capitalist system because of the structure of the situation. Moreover, the state acts in the long-term interests of capitalism, even though in the short term it may seem to damage the interests of the class that is said to rule.

FEMINISM AND POWER

So far, we have focused on power relations between groups and classes and between individuals and elites. Feminists would argue that this is to miss the crucial reality of gendered power relations. For feminists, the issue of state power by itself is not of great significance. Liberal feminists, as we will see in a later chapter, critically observe that men tend to dominate the key powerful positions within the public sphere, whether it be in political or business institutions. With adequate pressure applied, however, liberal feminists suggest that the representation of women by women is possible, and the state can be persuaded to adopt reforms that are in their interests. As such, they would seem to be accepting of the pluralist theory of the state. Radical feminists, on the other hand, argue that it is not power in the state that ought to be the chief focus, but the patriarchal—or male-dominated—character of the private sphere. It is this insight—that the family can be the site of power, oppression, and violence—that is feminism's major contribution to the debate about power. In this sense, the radical feminist approach is similar to the Marxist theory of the state in that the state is not seen as an autonomous entity.

➡ See Chapter 7 for a discussion of feminism as an ideology

Of particular importance in feminist state theory is Carol Pateman's notion of a 'sexual contract' (Pateman, 1988). The traditional liberal social contract theory, associated with English political philosophers such as Thomas Hobbes and John Locke, holds that states can only be legitimate if individuals agree to the terms of the state before it is created. Pateman argues that this liberal social contract relies upon an unstated, but essential, sexual contract in which women accept the dominant position of men in return for being protected and cared for. It is men, therefore, who have the power in the public sphere to act on behalf of women. Only when this inequality in the private sphere is tackled, Pateman argues, can the equality, as envisaged by liberal political theorists such as Hobbes and Locke, be realized. The solution cannot come from liberalism, however, because it is an ideology that frowns upon state intervention in the private sphere.

3

➜ See Chapters 2 and 4 for a discussion of liberal social contract theory and Chapter 7 for a discussion of feminism.

KEY POINTS

- A feminist theory of power emphasizes gender, rather than classes, or individuals.
- For liberal feminists, gendered inequality in the distribution of powerful positions in the public sphere is the chief focus. Radical feminists, on the other hand, emphasize male dominance within the private sphere which liberal political thought is ill-equipped to tackle.

CONCLUSION

It is to be hoped that this chapter has been able to demonstrate how crucial the concept of power is to a study of politics. We have seen that semantic, **normative**, and empirical questions about power abound: what is it? Is it a good thing? How is it distributed? The answers to all of these questions are contested. Answers to the empirical question remain, perhaps, most disputed. Indeed, here, we reached something of an impasse.

On the one hand, we suspect that the conceptualization of power adopted by pluralists, although eminently quantifiable and researchable, is, at the very least, incomplete. On the other hand, the conceptualization of power most favoured by elitists and Marxists, although persuasive, is problematic because it appears unresearchable. This explains why the debate between exponents of competing theories of the state continues. This debate is, perhaps, less intensive than it was thirty years ago and this is partly, at least, to do with the question marks being raised against the efficacy of the state in an increasingly globalized world.

KEY QUESTIONS

1. What is the difference between power and authority?
2. Is power a good thing?
3. Design a research project to determine whether the pluralist theory of the state accurately describes the distribution of political power in any one country with which you are familiar.
4. Find examples of issues which have been referred to legislative committees or Royal Commissions. How far do these examples provide evidence of non-decision-making?
5. Is power as thought control a viable concept?
6. How important is the fact that most political elites in a country such as Britain have similar educational backgrounds?
7. Is economic inequality a product of the exercise of power?

3

FURTHER READING

Bachrach, P. and Baratz, M. (1963), 'Decisions and Non-Decisions', *American Political Science Review*, 57: 632–42.

This is a much-cited critique of the pluralist theory of the state which emphasizes the importance of non-decision-making.

Blowers, A. (1984), *Something in the Air: Corporate Power and the Environment* (London: Harper & Row).

This is an interesting British case study relevant to theories of power.

Crenson, M. (1971), *The Un-Politics of Air Pollution* (Baltimore: Johns Hopkins University Press).

This is a study which attempts to put into operation Lukes' critique of the pluralist decision-making methodology.

Dahl, R. (1963), *Who Governs?* (New Haven, CT: Yale University Press).

This is the classic example of the decision-making methodology associated with pluralism.

Lukes, S. (2005), *Power: A Radical View* (Basingstoke: Palgrave Macmillan, 2nd edn).

This is a celebrated account of power. This repeats the original account published in 1974 but also includes an essay defending it against critics.

Miliband, R. (1978), *The State in Capitalist Society* (New York: Basic Books).

This is the best-known modern defence of the Marxist theory of the state.

 For additional material and resources, please visit the Online Resources at:
www.oup.com/he/garner4e

DEMOCRACY AND POLITICAL OBLIGATION

READER'S GUIDE

This chapter has two major aims: first, to explore key aspects of democratic theory, and second, to examine the case for democracy being the major grounding for political obligation. The first objective will be fulfilled by examining the historical evolution of the term, the debate between advocates of the protective theory and the participatory theory of democracy, and the new directions democratic theory has taken in recent years. The second will be fulfilled by outlining why it is that democracy is seen as the major grounding for political obligation, examining alternatives to democracy, and considering the majoritarian implications of democracy.

WHAT IS DEMOCRACY?

Like many other political concepts, democracy is a term with no precise and agreed meaning. Finding a definitional consensus for democracy is not helped by its emotive connotations. Democracy is a 'good' word. It is almost universally regarded in a favourable light. There are few countries in the world that would want to be labelled as undemocratic. Indeed, partly because of the collapse of the old Soviet Union and its satellites: 'Around two-thirds of all the countries in the world have a basic set of democratic institutions built around competitive elections that enable all adult citizens to choose and remove their government leaders' (Stoker, 2006: 7).

This expansion of competitive elections has led to the growing importance of so-called illiberal democracies or, as they are sometimes called, competitive authoritarian regimes or semi-democracies (Levitsky and Way, 2002; Zakaria, 2003). As we saw in Chapter 2, these are regimes in which, while elections are not blatantly rigged, elected rulers pay little heed to the protection of individual rights (such as free speech) once in power, and therefore opposition to rulers, who are able to manipulate electoral outcomes through control of the media and the use of the state apparatus, is difficult. As a result, the turnover of political leaders through competitive elections is small.

➡ See Chapter 2 for a description of illiberal democracy.

The existence of illiberal democracies, however, raises a conundrum for students of democracy. For, while it is surely stretching the concept to breaking point if we insist that the label 'democratic' can be applied to, say, one-party states—for example, in China (which describes itself as a 'democratic dictatorship') or in the old Soviet bloc countries—it is not so clear-cut that we should deny the democracy label to competitive authoritarian states.

It is probably the case that democracy does, justifiably, mean different things to different people; the question is, whether there is a core of meaning on which we can all agree. Very basically, democracy refers to a regime whereby political power is widely spread, where power in some way rests with the people. Democracy, then, has something to do with political equality. As Arblaster (2002: 7) points out, this definition is sufficiently vague to allow for a number of interpretations. Lively (1975: 30) suggests seven possibilities:

1. That all should govern, in the sense that all should be involved in legislating, in deciding on general policy, in applying laws, and in governmental administration.
2. That all should be personally involved in crucial decision-making, that is to say in deciding general laws and matters of general policy.
3. That rulers should be accountable to the ruled; they should, in other words, be obliged to justify their actions to the ruled and be removable by the ruled.
4. That rulers should be accountable to the representatives of the ruled.
5. That rulers should be chosen by the ruled.
6. That rulers should be chosen by the representatives of the ruled.
7. That rulers should act in the interests of the ruled.

Lively argues that numbers 1 to 4 are justified in being described as democratic whereas 5 to 7 are not (ibid.: 33–42). The crucial defining characteristic is accountability. The latter three definitions provide no means whereby the rulers can be removed by the ruled and therefore cannot be defined as versions of democracy. Number 7 allows for the inclusion of regimes, such as those subscribing to communism, who claim, despite the lack of competitive elections, to be democratic because the real interests of the many are promoted by rulers who are aiming for social and economic equality (Macpherson, 1966: 12–22).

This claim—that the democratic label can be attached to a regime whose rulers, however they are chosen, govern in the interests of all—is a logical mistake. The outcomes of a political system are separate from the means by which its rulers are chosen. It may be the case, as we will see later, that democracy (in the sense of a political system requiring regular competitive elections) is the most effective way of ensuring that rulers do act in the interests of the ruled. It may also be the case that the achievement of political equality requires a degree of economic equality. Ultimately, though, a benign dictatorship with the interests of her people at heart is not impossible. Many one-party communist states, of course, were far from being benign, arguably precisely because their leaders were not accountable. It is also questionable whether illiberal democracies, where rulers are able to manipulate elections and transfers of power are rare, uphold the accountability rule and can therefore be described as truly democratic. To add an extra layer of complexity, we will see later in the chapter that liberal democracies do not escape criticism from a democratic perspective because of the potential conflict between majoritarian decision-making and the protection of individual rights.

Focusing on the first four of Lively's typology, we are still left with considerable variation. The first two are forms of direct democracy, whereas the latter two are forms of representative democracy. Direct democracy refers to a system whereby the people rule directly. The first definition on Lively's list seems impossible to be realized in anything but a very small-scale society. Even the second raises huge difficulties. Representative democracy is a more realistic proposition. This is where the people choose others to represent their interests. There can also be stronger and weaker versions of representative democracy. British MPs, invoking the great eighteenth-century parliamentarian Edmund Burke (1729–97), for instance, have for long insisted upon their independence from their constituents, so that on at least some issues (mainly moral ones such as capital punishment and abortion) they vote according to their conscience. Of course, it is debatable how far MPs can remain aloof from their constituents' views without negative consequences befalling them at a future election, as the debate over Brexit has illustrated (**see Box 4.1**).

CASE STUDY BOX 4.1
MPs, Brexit, and the EU Referendum

An interesting illustration of competing theories of representation has occurred in the context of the UK Referendum on the European Union. Held in June 2016, the result was a narrow victory for the leave side of the debate. There has been much subsequent debate about the role of Parliament and MPs in the post-referendum climate, and much delay in making a final decision. Theresa May's failure to get Parliamentary approval for a deal negotiated with the EU ultimately led to her resignation. The current position is that the UK has left the EU, under the terms negotiated by Boris Johnson's Government. Many (on the leave side) argued that MPs should simply follow the will of the people irrespective of whether or not a deal could be agreed. Some even suggested that Parliament should have no role in the implementation of the referendum verdict. Others argued that Parliament should have had the final say, at least on the terms of the exit from the EU, if not the actual decision whether or not to leave. A prominent leave supporter took a case to the Supreme Court to establish that Parliament should be involved. Significantly,

4

Photo 4.1 Britain's exit from the EU ('Brexit;) raised many questions about representation.
Shutterstock RF: Ink Drop/Shutterstock.com

the vast majority of MPs in both major parties voted to accept the decision to invoke Article 50 allowing the UK to leave the EU despite the fact that a majority of them supported remaining. The fear of an electoral backlash, particularly against Labour MPs (stunningly realized at the 2019 election) was the chief reason for the decision not to go against the popular will by seeking to revoke Article 50. This reveals the limited utility of the Burkean model of representation in a democracy with regular elections. Nevertheless, MPs have remained committed to the view that they should have the final say on what the UK's approach should be.

> **KEY POINTS**
>
> - The concept of democracy has a core meaning. It is about popular rule or the rule of the people. This can be interpreted in a wide variety of ways, although some regimes clearly do not exhibit any characteristics of the people having power, and others limit it extensively.
> - Lively suggests that democracy requires the people to make decisions directly, or to choose, and be able to remove, those who make decisions on the people's behalf.

HISTORY

Democracy is a Greek term containing two words: *demos*, meaning the citizens within a city-state, and *kratos*, meaning power or rule (Arblaster, 2002: 15). The term was used to describe the practice of the Greek city-states. Many contemporary democratic theorists and activists look back to the Greek city-states with great affection, regarding them as providing a participatory model of democracy of which modern liberal democracies fall far short. In actual fact, direct democracy was possible precisely because a considerable number of people—most notably women, slaves, and foreigners—were excluded and did a great deal of the work that enabled citizens to engage in politics.

For much of its history, democracy has been regarded in a negative light. The Greek philosophers—Plato and Aristotle, for instance—argued that democracy was synonymous with mob rule and was a perverted form of government, although the latter regarded democracy as the least bad of the three 'deviant' forms of rule: democracy, tyranny, and oligarchy. (**See Box 4.2**.) Much the same picture applied to successive political thinkers. For instance, neither of the key English political theorists of the seventeenth century, John Locke and Thomas Hobbes, were democrats.

The French and American Revolutions

The tide began to turn with the French and American revolutions of the eighteenth century. Both revolutions proclaimed democracy as one of their goals, and both were influenced by the writings of the French political philosopher, Jean-Jacques Rousseau. The Americans endorsed democracy but were still wary of it. The Founding Fathers of the US Constitution, and most notably James Madison (1751–1836), were very keen to rid themselves of the absolute monarchy

Photo 4.2 Plato was an ancient Greek philosopher did not support democracy.
Shutterstock RF: Vangelis aragiannis/Shutterstock.com

The utilitarian theory of democracy is associated with the nineteenth-century British political thinker Jeremy Bentham, who developed the theory in association with his chief disciple, James Mill. Bentham had initially not been concerned about democracy, feeling that an enlightened despot was just as likely to pursue the utilitarian aim of the greatest happiness. He came to change his mind after the failure of the British government to implement any of his schemes of reform.

The utilitarian theory of democracy is based on the premise that democracy is necessary to ensure that those in government will remain accountable to those they govern. Bentham and Mill argued that, left to their own devices, members of government will maximize their own pleasure. They will only pursue the greatest happiness for all if their positions in power are dependent upon it. The function of elections is, therefore, a protective device to ensure that the preferences of the people are taken into account by decision-makers.

of George III. However, they were equally concerned about the effects of introducing majoritarianism. Majority tyranny was, they thought, the ever-present danger of democracy. As a result, the Founding Fathers created a constitution that set up a directly elected legislature, the House of Representatives, but at the same time checked it by separating power between it and the senate (the other part of the legislature), the executive branch headed by the president, and the judiciary, headed by the supreme court.

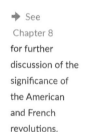

➜ See Chapter 8 for further discussion of the significance of the American and French revolutions.

The Nineteenth-Century Move Towards Democracy

By the nineteenth century, democracy was beginning to take on more popular connotations in theory and practice. Many countries began the long and slow road towards universal suffrage. In theoretical terms, the so-called utilitarian theory of democracy associated with Jeremy Bentham and James Mill was extremely influential. (**See Box 4.2.**)

As the Marxist political theorist C. B. Macpherson (1911–87) pointed out (1977: 23–43), the utilitarian theory was the first attempt to seek to apply democracy to a class-divided capitalist industrial society. This gave rise to liberal democracy, which denotes the linking of democracy with the kind of liberal principles originally associated with the industrial middle class. The linking together of democracy and capitalism raised the crucial question of how to reconcile political equality—to which democracy in its purest sense amounts—with economic inequality. The fear of many property owners at the time was that the arrival of universal suffrage would result in a political programme designed to create greater economic equality, thereby putting their privileged position at considerable risk. Despite the rise of the Labour Party in Britain and similar socialist parties elsewhere, there was no great move towards a socialist political programme. Macpherson (1977: 62), and other left-wing academics such as Miliband (1972), argued that this was the product of trade union and Labour Party leaders betraying the revolutionary potential of the working-class.

KEY POINTS

• For much of its history, democracy has been regarded in a negative light.

• The turning point was the French and American revolutions in the eighteenth century, after which democracy became a more desirable concept.

• The nineteenth century saw a sustained attempt to achieve universal suffrage in practice and to justify it in theory. The utilitarian theory of democracy, associated with James Mill and Bentham, was really the first attempt to try to justify incorporating democracy into a class-divided society. This raises the question, why did the advent of democracy not bring about a more economically equal society?

Democracy Under Challenge

In the last thirty years or so, the democratic landscape has been transformed again with a doubling of the number of states having competitive elections. So, in 1970 only about thirty-five countries had electoral democracies whereas this had increased to about 120 by the early years of the twenty-first century. This was largely a product of the collapse of the Soviet bloc and the emergence of independent states in Eastern Europe, but democracy has also emerged in Southern Europe (Greece, Portugal, and Spain), Latin America (for example, Venezuela), and parts of Africa (for example, Botswana) and Asia (for example, Malaysia). From a democratic perspective, this has undoubtedly been an advance, even though, as we saw, the democratic credentials of the many illiberal states that have accompanied this wave of **democratization** can be questioned.

➡ See Chapter 15 for an explanatory account of democratization.

Since the early part of the present century, however—in what Diamond (2015) has called a period of 'democratic recession'—the progress of democracy has stalled. Some of the democracies created in recent years—such as Hungary, Turkey, Thailand, and Russia—have slipped back into authoritarianism. Moreover, authoritarian regimes, most notably China, have become more confident and self-assured. In addition, previously strong and stable liberal democracies in the West are experiencing a crisis of confidence, as witnessed by declining levels of political participation, disenchantment with political elites, and the rise of populist movements directly pitting the 'people' against the political establishment, which is painted as corrupt, inefficient, and self-serving.

➡ See Chapter 15 for a further discussion of the Arab Spring.

The democratic promise of the Arab Spring (a series of protests against authoritarian regimes in North Africa and the Middle East) which began in Tunisia in 2010 was also largely thwarted. For instance, the Syrian dictator Assad (supported by Iran and Russia) fought back against opposition to his regime before the country sunk into civil war, a fate that also befell Libya, Yemen, and Iraq. In Egypt, democratic elections resulted in victory for the Muslim Brotherhood as the dictator Hosni Mubarak was disposed in 2011, but the democratic promise was short-lived as two years later the military staged a successful coup. In the Arab world, only Tunisia can lay claim to be a fully democratic state. After twenty-three years in power, the country's ruler—Zine El Abidine Ben Ali—was deposed in 2011, after a sustained period of popular unrest, leading to the establishment of a pluralistic representative democracy.

➡ See Chapters 7 and 15 for a discussion of populism.

It is worth speculating why the forward march of democracy has seemingly stalled. One issue that is clearly important is the perception that Western democracies have underperformed, not least economically. It may be that legitimacy is based, in practice, not on the intrinsic value of democracy but on its capacity to produce desirable consequences. It has been thought for a long time that performance constitutes the primary base of the legitimacy of authoritarian regimes, most notably in China (Yang and Zhao, 2015), and there is a startling contrast between China's successful economic performance and the travails of the West, particularly since the financial crash of 2008.

The relationship between democracy and performance serves to remind us that democracy is a procedure, a method of making decisions, but there is no guarantee that this procedure will produce outcomes that we might desire. This is partly an issue of the role of experts. In a democracy, where political equality is the major objective, the views of experts carry no greater weight that those of ordinary voters. And yet, as Plato argued many centuries ago, there is strong case for the rule of the most able.

The potential discrepancy between procedure and outcome is also partly an issue of values. That is, we might value a particular goal—for example, liberty, equality, a clean environment— but there is no guarantee that a democratic procedure will guarantee the outcome we may desire. We can make two points about this. The first is that most values are contested. That is, for every person who values a freer society, there will be one who values a more equal one. Given this, there needs to be some device to decide which goal, for now at least, predominates. A democratic system would then, of course, give those who lost out the chance to refight, and possibly win, the argument at some time in the future. The second point is that some goals and values might be so important that we want to insulate them against majority decisions taken in a democracy (the issue of majoritarianism is considered later in this chapter).

> **KEY POINTS**
>
> - In the final quarter of the twentieth century there was an enormous expansion of regimes introducing competitive elections and proclaiming themselves democratic.
> - More recently, the credentials of democracy have been challenged as the confidence of authoritarian regimes has grown. This has been, at least partly, caused by the underperformance of Western democracies which, in turn, reflects the contingent relationship between democratic procedures and outcomes.

THE CLASSICAL VERSUS THE ELITIST THEORY OF DEMOCRACY

By the twentieth century, democracy was largely shorn of its negative connotations. In academic political theory, the major dispute in the post-1945 period was over two competing theories of democracy. On the one hand was the elitist theory of democracy (also sometimes called the 'revisionist' or 'protective' theory). This theory is particularly associated with the Austrian economist and sociologist Joseph Schumpeter (1883–1950), who articulated his theory in the much-cited book *Capitalism, Socialism and Democracy*, originally published in 1942. Against this is the classical theory of democracy, sometimes also referred to as the 'participatory' or 'developmental' theory (**see Box 4.3**).

→ See Chapter 2 for an exploration of elitism.

Schumpeter was reacting to what he saw as the inevitable role played by elites in modern polities. He therefore recognized the importance of the Italian elitists whom we encountered in Chapter 2. However, far from agreeing with their conclusion that democracy is a sham, Schumpeter argues that democracy can be reconciled with elitism. Schumpeter identifies what he describes as the prevailing classical theory of democracy, which he takes to be a model emphasizing the active participation of citizens in the making of political decisions. This model is associated with the practice of the Greek city-states, and the theories of Rousseau and the nineteenth-century British political theorist, John Stuart Mill. For Schumpeter, however, this model is both unrealistic and undesirable.

The classical model is unrealistic, Schumpeter argues, because mass participation is not a characteristic of modern democratic societies. Empirically, most people appear happy to leave politics to a class of political elites. The classical model is also undesirable, Schumpeter argues, because the masses tend to be irrational and are liable to have authoritarian values and be seduced by charismatic and dictatorial leaders, a view echoed by Kornhauser (1960). It is no accident that Schumpeter was writing at a time when the rise of fascism in Germany and Italy had brought to power such leaders with the apparent consent, some of it enthusiastic, of a large proportion of the masses. Far from being a threat to democracy, then, elites become the protectors of democracy against the authoritarian values of the masses.

Schumpeter seeks to replace this classical theory of democracy with what he perceives to be a more desirable alternative. In a well-known passage, Schumpeter (1961: 269) redefines democracy as 'that institutional arrangement for arriving at political decisions in which individuals acquire the power to decide by means of a competitive struggle for the people's vote'. What is notable about this definition is that there is no emphasis on participation. Decisions are to be

---

KEY DEBATE BOX 4.3
Advocates of the Protective and Participatory Theories of Democracy

Protective theory	Developmental theory
Bentham	Greek city-states
James Mill	Rousseau
Schumpeter	J. S. Mill
Downs	Cole
	Bachrach
	Pateman

Questions
1. Is it possible to reconcile elitism with democracy?
2. Is participatory democracy politically realistic?

left to a political elite. What makes the system democratic, for Schumpeter, is the competition between elites. The voters in this model do not even choose between different sets of policies but, rather, simply choose between different teams of leaders who then decide what policies to carry out.

Schumpeter's account has been built upon by other political scientists. In particular, account has been taken of intermediary groups such as trade unions and business organizations with elites of their own who compete with each other in trying to persuade the political leadership to adopt their policies. Kornhauser (1960) argued that this system of elites safeguards liberal democracies from totalitarian regimes and from 'mass society' in general. Without the various intermediary groups, atomized individuals provide an opportunity for an elite to mobilize them and this may lead to the overthrow of the existing regime and its replacement by a new elite who may have totalitarian intentions.

This elitist theory of democracy held sway in political science circles for twenty or so years after the end of the Second World War. It was reinforced by the so-called 'economic theory of democracy' which built on the earlier utilitarian model. **See Box 4.4**. These types of theory

KEY DEBATE BOX 4.4
The Economic Theory of Democracy and Its Critics

One version of the protective theory of democracy is the so-called economic theory of democracy. This is associated with the American political scientist Anthony Downs (1930–), who wrote a hugely influential book on this issue in the late 1950s (1957). It is a good example of the use of the rational choice approach to political science (see Chapter 1, Introduction).

Downs develops a sophisticated explanatory 'economic theory' of democracy, in which he tries to account for the nature of voter choice and party competition. Downs's theory is labelled economic because it shares certain fundamental principles with economics. In particular, advocates of the economic theory of democracy assume certain characteristics of human behaviour from which the theory is deduced. Humans are regarded as individualistic utility maximizers whose aim is to achieve benefits for themselves at the least possible cost.

For Downs, the behaviour of politicians and voters is analogous to the behaviour of producers and consumers in the economy.

* Political parties and politicians are equivalent to producers. Just as producers seek to maximize profit, politicians seek to maximize votes. Their only goal is to win power.
* Likewise, just as consumers seek the best buy for their money, voters seek to 'buy' at the cheapest possible price the set of policies that will serve their interests the most. As a result, parties must offer the voters what they want, or they will not win enough votes to gain power.

Based on these simple principles, Downs constructs a whole model of competitive party politics. He suggests that voters can be located on an ideological continuum from left to right, and that political parties will seek to place themselves at the point where the majority of voters are situated, the vote maximization position.

There have been a number of pertinent criticisms of this model.

- It is overly simplistic. For example, it is inadequate to focus on just one ideological continuum, since that does not take into account the complexities of voter preferences. Moreover, voter choice is not simply about competing ideologies. A crucial dimension of voter choice is voter perceptions of the competence of politicians. This is not easily located on the kind of spectrum Downs uses.
- It is by no means certain that voters and politicians behave in the way that Downs tells us they do.
  - Evidence suggests that at least some voters use their vote in an altruistic way on the grounds of principle rather than merely in their own self-interest.
  - Similarly, to describe politicians as merely vote maximizers is surely too simplistic. Parties may recognize that they have to win votes in order to gain power, but this is different from saying that they have no principles they want to promote.
  - Even more devastating for the economic theory of democracy is the evidence which suggests that many voters do not have the level of sophistication that the economic theory demands (Robertson, 1976: 177–81). According to the alternative party identification model, voters choose between parties, not on the basis of their perceptions of a party's particular policies, but because they have a long-standing psychological identification with a party. As a result, their support for a party does not change when the party's policies change.
  - The economic theory of democracy also finds it difficult to explain why most people bother to vote at all (Barry, 1970: 13–22). For the economic theory, voting is a cost which is only worth paying if the benefits of voting outweigh these costs. Given this, it is only worthwhile voting if the vote makes a difference to the result. The chances of one vote making this amount of difference are minimal.
  - The economic theory of democracy takes voter preferences as given. It therefore neglects to consider the possibility that these preferences are shaped by powerful forces in society, and not least by the political parties themselves, particularly when they have governmental power (Dunleavy and Ward, 1981).

Questions

1. What is 'economic' about the economic theory of democracy?
2. Do voters and politicians behave in the ways suggested by the economic theory of democracy?
3. Is there any point in voting?

can be classified as 'protective' models of democracy, in the sense that they are concerned with ensuring that political leaders are accountable to the wishes of the voters. They are concerned, therefore, with democracy as a means to an end of voter utility maximization.

An alternative model can be described as a 'participatory' or 'developmental' model of democracy. This is enshrined in the classical theory of democracy, although this label contains as many differences as similarities. The developmental model is more concerned with democracy as an end in itself; that is, participation is itself enriching. It is not, as for the protective theory, a burden to be undertaken in order to ensure that politicians are accountable. Rather, participation is to be valued for the positive effect it has on individual characteristics. Individuals who participate, it is argued, become more virtuous and intelligent, they understand the need for cooperation, and their own self-worth increases as does their status in the eyes of others.

The antecedents of the developmental model are in the practice of the Greek city-states and the political philosophy of Rousseau, J. S. Mill, and the unjustly neglected British socialist thinker G. D. H. Cole (1889–1959) (Wright, 1979). Support for it began to re-emerge in the 1960s. A new breed of radical democratic theorists began to challenge the elite theory (Duncan and Lukes, 1964; Bachrach, 1967; Pateman, 1970). They argued that, by abandoning the participatory element, the elitist theory of democracy had lost sight of the true meaning of democracy. Any notion of rule by the people had been abandoned. What was needed, then, was the rediscovery of participation in the political process.

Assessing the validity of these competing theories of democracy is a difficult task, not least because the meaning of the concept is disputed. Two observations about these competing models of democracy are pertinent here. One is that if democracy can be defined first and foremost as political equality, then the elite theory of democracy stretches the label to its absolute limits. Schumpeter was, arguably, trying to say that the rule of political elites, albeit in a competitive environment, is for a variety of reasons preferable to mass participation in politics. As a result, democracy ought to be limited in the interests of other goals such as stability and efficiency. In other words, Schumpeter is really espousing a mixed form of government combining democracy with other values. The problem is that, by the time Schumpeter was writing, democracy had such positive connotations that it was difficult for him to admit to wanting to limit it.

On the other hand, we can say that advocates of the developmental model must be able to show that their version of democracy is not undesirable and unrealistic, and this, indeed, is what much of the developmental literature seeks to do. For example, advocates of this model would say that political apathy is not inevitable, that people can be encouraged to participate more and, once they start, they will improve at it. Some may, perhaps, be less likely as a result to exhibit authoritarian values. Political apathy, they would continue, is partly a product of the lack of participation in decision-making in the working environment. Of great importance to the developmentalists, therefore, is industrial democracy (Pateman, 1970). As Lively (1975: 38) astutely remarks, 'it does not follow from the fact that "classical" democracy does not exist that it cannot ever exist; nor does it force us to redefine democracy, for it might just as well lead us to the conclusion that Western systems are not democracies or are only imperfect democracies'.

Finally, advocates of the developmental model have to show that participation is possible (Arblaster, 2002: 84–5). Here, technological developments would seem to be on their side, offering the possibility of greater involvement in politics through, for instance, the use of the Internet and interactive-TV technology. In a large complex society, the use of referendums, whereby all electors vote on a particular issue, is a direct democratic way of increasing involvement. They are used in many countries, particularly Switzerland and the USA, and were used, very successfully, to decide on Scottish independence in 2014.

KEY POINTS

- The modern debate has been between exponents of the elite theory of democracy, on the one hand, and the participatory theory of democracy, on the other.

- In the post-1945 period, the elitist theory, associated above all with Schumpeter, held sway. The classical theory, associated with participation and citizen involvement in decision-making, was regarded as undesirable and unrealistic.

- The elitist theory began to be challenged from the 1960s by a new breed of participationists, eager to show the developmental possibilities of greater citizen involvement. The success of their enterprise depends on showing that greater participation is both desirable and realistic.

WHY IS DEMOCRACY REGARDED AS SPECIAL?

Politics in the West, and, indeed, much of the world, has become synonymous with democracy. Democracy is regarded as indispensable. But why is this? What is it about democracy that is so special? The usual answer to this question is that democracy is regarded as special because it is put forward as the main reason why we should obey the rules and laws of a political system. In other words, if one were to ask why it is that we are obliged to accept and obey the laws of our society, then the answer would be because they are democratically made.

This question of political obligation—on what grounds should we obey the laws of the state?—has been one of the central preoccupations of political philosophy. At a more general level, political philosophers ask how can the state be justified, or, to put it another way, what makes the state legitimate? What, that is, is the ideal state which we would recommend for humans to live under? The issue of political obligation is important because of its compulsory nature. If we join a voluntary organization, such as a pressure group or a church, we have to accept the rules of that organization but if we do not like them, we have the option of leaving. For most of us, we do not have the same option when it comes to the state. Some people may be able to go and live somewhere more to their liking, but for most people, that is not an option, and it is certainly not an option to live in a stateless society. Most of us do not have a choice when it comes to accepting the laws of the state, or at least if we choose not to obey the state, then we can expect sanctions to be applied against us.

➡ See Chapter 2 for a discussion of the liberal social contract tradition.

Democracy seems to offer us the ideal grounding for political obligation because if we make the laws under which we live, then they are likely to be in our interests and therefore we get what we want. In other words, we do not lose anything as a result of being in a political community. Democracy, then, has a strong claim to be the political system that would be chosen by people in the state of nature scenario that we saw in Chapter 2 has been a device used by social contract theorists. In other words, if a group of people came together to form a political system, the advantages of choosing democratic principles would be that they would all get a say in the laws under which they have to live. Government by consent, then, is an important principle for liberal social contract theorists because it can be argued that, if we consent to the laws under which we live, the freedom existing in the state of nature would be maintained in a democratic political system.

4

The concept of consent derives principally from John Locke, the seventeenth-century English political philosopher, who argued that since we have a natural right to freedom, only our consent can justify political power being exercised over us. Of course, we then have to ask, what precisely is it that counts as consent? Political philosophers have got themselves into a bit of a muddle trying to answer this question. Most notoriously, Locke argued that consent need not be expressly given, in the sense that someone has to actually formally register their consent. Instead, Locke argued, consent can also be given tacitly, in the sense that it does not require a formal act. Locke (1690/1988: 177) argues, then, that providing that an individual lives under a particular political jurisdiction, gaining the benefits—whatever they may be—of doing so, then that person can be said to have consented to political rule.

Clearly, this is problematic, not least because for most people there is little choice but to live where they are. Political philosophers tend to argue, therefore, that consent must be expressed. Moreover, it must be continuous, since no subsequent generation can be bound by the consent of their predecessors. But how is this to be achieved? One suggestion is that voting serves this function. That is, when we vote, irrespective of the outcome, we accept—or consent to—the political order under which we live. This clearly provides an option not to consent—by not voting or spoiling a ballot paper. It follows logically that those who do not choose to vote are withholding consent and are not then obliged to obey the state.

There are a number of problems with regarding the democratic procedure of voting as a way in which we can be obligated to the state. The obvious problem here is those who vote are not primarily, if at all, knowingly consenting to the political system. Likewise, many who fail to vote clearly do so for reasons other than registering their lack of consent. Moreover, even if we choose not to vote, we will be forced by the state to obey laws in any case, so non-voting has no purchase in this regard. Voting, by itself then, is not an express act of consent, and incurs the same problem as residence (Hyams, 2015: 12–13). Moreover, it may be that when we vote we find ourselves in a minority. The question then is are we still morally obliged to obey in this circumstance even when we have not got what we want from a decision? (see the discussion later in this chapter). A related question is: are we obliged to obey any decisions provided they are democratically made? Here, it is possible to conceive of a situation where we are so morally opposed to a decision, even if it is made democratically, that we feel unable to obey it. Decisions made on issues such as abortion and the use of animals in scientific experiments fall, for some people, into this category.

ALTERNATIVE SOURCES OF POLITICAL OBLIGATION

It should be recognized that democracy and consent are not the only possible reasons for political obligation. We could also focus on substantive outcomes, on what the state actually does, rather than on the procedures involved in making decisions, in order to determine the state's legitimacy. If we adopt this different approach, there are a variety of possible candidates. Here we can reprise some of the normative accounts of the state provided in Chapter 2:

➡ See Chapter 2 for an account of competing normative theories of the state.

We Ought to Obey the State Because it Provides us With Security

This idea, as we saw, is associated with the seventeenth-century British political theorist Thomas Hobbes. To reiterate, Hobbes argues that a sovereign who is strong enough to enforce stability is worth obeying. As soon as the sovereign's power weakens, however, and security can no longer be guaranteed, we have no obligation to obey.

We Ought to Obey the State Because it Protects Our Natural Rights

This idea is associated with another British political thinker, John Locke. He argues that humans possess natural rights, given by God, before they enter into a political community. As a result, for such a political community to be legitimate, it must uphold and protect these rights. If it fails to do so, then we are entitled to revolt against it. Two brief observations at this point can be made about this approach to political obligation. The first is that, although Locke was not a democrat, his theory is not necessarily incompatible with democracy. Most democrats would argue that rights should be protected and would say that this is more likely to happen if the people have an influence on what the state does. There are some problems with this, though, which we will come back to later.

The second observation to note is that the key problem with rights as a grounding for political obligation is that it leaves open the question of *what* rights exist. Locke himself argued that the crucial rights to protect are the rights to liberty, life, and property. The problem with these rights is that they might be used to defend the status quo, to defend inequality and privilege. As we pointed out in Chapter 2, however, it is equally plausible to claim that we have other rights too—the right not to starve, for instance, or the right to a home, or education, or healthcare. Of course, these latter—social and economic—rights may conflict with the negative ones. It may be necessary, for example, to constrain, or even eliminate, property rights in order to generate enough resources to provide free healthcare or education.

More pertinently, from the perspective of the subject matter of this chapter, a democratic decision taken with the will of the majority may lead to the sacrifice of negative rights in favour of the achievement of more positive ones. Alternatively, the achievement of positive rights may be used as a reason, or as an excuse, for a failure to introduce democracy. For example, in China, the political leadership published a White Paper on democracy in 2005 in which the postponement of democratic reforms was justified partly on the grounds that economic development, and the achievement of better standards of living, were a priority (see web links). The upholding of (at least some) rights, then, is not necessarily compatible with democracy. Again, the consequences of this will be explored a little later in the chapter.

We Ought to Obey the State When it Maximises Happiness

From a utilitarian perspective, our obligation to obey the state depend upon the degree to which it maximises happiness. The state should therefore stop individuals causing pain to others through a rigorous system of punishment. Moreover, the state also has a paternalistic role to ensure that individuals do pursue what is in their best interests and therefore maximize their own happiness. Bentham came to think that only if they are accountable to the electorate will rulers seek to maximize the happiness of all, rather than their own happiness. As we saw earlier in this chapter, this forms the basis of the utilitarian theory of democracy.

We Ought to Obey the State When it Pursues the General Will

The idea of the general will has been a popular theme in political theory but it is particularly associated with the eighteenth-century French philosopher, Jean-Jacques Rousseau. For Rousseau, the general will can be contrasted with the selfish, particular, wills of individuals. It is tantamount, then, to the common good, something that is in the general interest of the

Photo 4.3 Jean Jacques Rousseau.
Shutterstock RF via DAM: Georgios Kollidas/
Shutterstock.com

community, that is, in the collective interests of society. This general will, then, amounts to more than the sum of particular wills. Rather, it is a genuine collective will, irrespective of the particular wills of members of the community. This approach to political obligation holds that if the state pursues this common or general interest—and not particular interests—then we have an obligation to obey it. Hegel adopts a very similar theory, whereby the state pursues the common interest, thereby transcending the particular interests pursued by families and by civil society.

Rousseau's arguments are more complex than has been suggested so far. We can coax them out by looking at what might be regarded as a key problem with his theory. We might respond to Rousseau and other advocates of the general will by asking what is so good about it? Why are we obliged to accept it? Why should I not be selfish and encourage the state to pursue a programme that is in my own selfish interests? We might answer by saying that we ought to obey the general will because it is the right and moral thing to do. The problem with this is that some people may deny the importance of this moral edict and still say 'I'm still not going to obey the general will because, on this occasion at least, it is not in my interests to do it'.

It is at this point that Rousseau's argument becomes a little more complex and contentious, for he wants to claim that not only should we promote the general will, but that this is what we *really* want to do. He even goes as far as to say that if we are forced to accept the general will, then we are being *forced to be free* (Rousseau, 1913). We are being forced to be free because we are being forced to accept what we really want to do.

This is not the place to engage in a sustained critical analysis of Rousseau's political theory. We can say that it is heavily dependent on the very existence of a community's collective will. Some political theorists suggest that that idea is a fiction. Of course, if this is the case, it becomes a potentially dangerous doctrine, open to abuse by a dictator who justifies tyrannical measures on the spurious grounds that they are in the 'public' or 'collective' interest (Talmon, 1952). Here, critics have been particularly scathing about the implications of Rousseau's claim that it is legitimate to force someone to be free. This aspect of Rousseau's theory relies on a particular conception of freedom and we will return to it in more detail in Chapter 5.

For now, if we accept that Rousseau is right and that we all do really want to pursue the general will, it is important to recognize that he has arguably solved the problem of political obligation. Remember that the study of political obligation is concerned with finding a political system which we can all obey because we want to. If we can do this, then we do not lose any freedom by joining together with others to create a political community. Rousseau (1913: 191) sets out his task as follows.

> The problem is to find a form of association which will defend and protect with the whole common force the person and goods of each associate, and in which each, while uniting himself with all, may still obey himself alone, and remain as free as before. This is the fundamental problem of which the social contract provides the solution.

Rousseau's answer is that we can all obey a political system that pursues the general will and remain as free as we were before, because the general will is what we all want. In other words, what the state wants to do, if it pursues the general will, can be unanimously accepted as representing the will of all. As we will see later, democracy finds it difficult, if not impossible, to achieve unanimity, and this raises question marks against its claim to provide an ideal form of political obligation.

➜ See Chapter 5 for a discussion of Rousseau's idea of the general will and its implications for freedom.

KEY POINTS

- Democracy is often regarded as the most important source of political obligation. This is because it is a political system that allows people to make decisions under which they can live. The freedom that individuals have in an imaginary state of nature is therefore maintained.

- There are, of course, others reasons we might invoke to explain our political obligation. We might, for instance, want to obey the state because it provides us with security (Hobbes) or because it protects our rights (Locke) or because it promotes the general will (Rousseau) or maximises happiness (Bentham).

- If Rousseau is right that we always really want the state to promote the general will, he has made a case for a solution to the problem of political obligation. This is because even if we oppose the general will, we can be forced to follow it which is tantamount to being forced to be free. Our allegiance to the state, therefore, makes us as free as we were before a political community was created.

IS DEMOCRACY SPECIAL? THE PROBLEM OF MAJORITY RULE

After that detour, we will go back now and, armed with knowledge of alternative approaches to political obligation, further consider democracy's claim to be the ideal form of political obligation. Democracy, as we saw, is regarded as the primary modern ground for political obligation because if we participate in the making of the laws under which we live, these laws are likely to be in our interests and therefore we get what we want. The principal problem with democracy, however, is that we are very rarely going to arrive at unanimous decisions. As a result, democratic government means, in practice, following the view of the majority.

There are a number of problems with the majoritarian principle. In the first place, it is well documented that where there are more than two alternatives on which voters can have preferences, then it is difficult to reach a majority decision (Lively, 1975: 14–15). Of course, in practice too, many governments in the UK and presidents in the USA are not elected with the majority of votes. This is explained by the use of the first-past-the-post, or plurality rule, electoral system, where the winning candidate merely has to gain more votes than any other candidate. This system is used in the UK, the USA, Canada, Jamaica, and India, although most countries now use electoral systems where there is a more proportional relationship between the seats won and the votes cast. This avoids the discrepancies that can occur in countries using plurality rule voting where there are more than two significant parties.

Even if majority rule can be established, it is far from clear that it is the most appropriate political mechanism. For one thing, pure majority rule leaves open the possibility that a government can be elected with majority support, but which then intends to deny the principle of majoritarianism in the future. The best example of this was in Algeria in 1991 when the Islamic Salvation Front won a majority of the seats (although not the votes) in the country's first multiparty elections. With a doubtful commitment to multiparty democracy, the military intervened, cancelling the second round, and banning all political parties based on religion. This was then followed by a violent civil war. This raises the question whether it is ever justified on democratic grounds to prevent a government with a majority of votes and/or seats from taking power.

Even if the principle of majoritarianism is maintained, however, there is the problem that arises from the fact that some people in every decision made are going to find themselves in a minority. Rousseau's solution to this problem is to say: 'provided that the laws carried are in accord with the general will, everyone unanimously will want to accept them because it is the right or moral thing to do'. For Rousseau, then, there is no problem with the minority. However, Rousseau's assertion that everyone would and should willingly accept the general will is contentious, to say the least. Therefore, if we assume that Rousseau's solution to the minority problem is flawed, then we are still left with the problem of the lack of unanimity; that is, if we accept that democratic decisions are those taken by majority votes, then what happens to those who find themselves in a minority? Do we still expect them to obey the law even though they did not support it and does this not risk the minority being exploited by the majority to the extent that their rights are infringed? (**See Box 4.5.**)

There are some political philosophers who want to suggest that we cannot expect such people to obey a law which they did not support. One such political theorist, Robert Paul Wolff, in his book *In Defense of Anarchism* (1970), argues that those who find themselves in a minority are not obliged to accept the law; and because there is no solution to the majority rule problem, no government can ever be legitimate, requiring everyone to be obligated to it. For Wolff, the only legitimate kind of society is one that preserves individual autonomy. This, for Wolff, is an anarchist society, a society without government.

In practice, of course, we may just have to accept that democracy is not perfect, and console ourselves with the thought that at least a majority rule decision ensures that more people than not are on the winning side. What we can say is that the position of minorities is made much worse if the same people find themselves permanently in a minority. Usually, this does not happen because there are shifting or fluid minorities; that is, everyone can expect to be in a minority from time to time. As a result, the majority in any particular instance is less likely to harm the

4 Democracy and Political Obligation 87

CASE STUDY BOX 4.5
Democracy, Rights, and Hunting

One interesting example of the potential conflict between the application of majoritarianism and the protection of rights is the debate about hunting in the UK. The hunting community has used a variety of arguments to support the continuation of hunting, but one recent strategy has been to employ the ideals of liberalism and the protection of individual rights. Here it has been argued that, despite the fact that hunting has been regularly opposed by a majority of British people in opinion polls and a majority of MPs in the House of Commons, it still does not justify a ban because it is illegitimate for a majority to impose its own moral views on the minority. To take such an action is a serious infringement of rights. This rights defence of hunting, however, fell on deaf ears despite the hunting community's attempt to undermine the legislative ban by appealing to the Human Rights Act.

minority's interests fundamentally, because those in the majority know that at some future point, they may find themselves in the minority.

The persecution of a minority is much more likely to take place where there is a permanent majority and a permanent minority. The classic case of this is in Northern Ireland, where traditionally most issues have been decided on ethno-nationalist lines with Protestants in the majority and Catholics in the minority on key issues. Clearly, such a situation is likely to cause problems and it was the persistent discrimination faced by the minority Catholic community that led to the resurgence of the troubles in the late 1960s. A form of rule known as consociational democracy, involving the sharing of power in divided societies, is one possible solution to this problem of entrenched minorities.

See Chapter 10 for a further discussion of consociationalism.

KEY POINTS

- The problem with democracy as a source of a political obligation is that few, if any, decisions are going to be made unanimously. As a result, the minority are going to have to accept decisions with which they disagree, thereby reducing their freedom.
- Some political philosophers, most notably Wolff, argue that because of the minority rule problem, no state can ever be legitimate.
- Fluid minorities are less of a problem than permanent minorities. The latter are more likely to lead to the oppression of a minority.

NEW DIRECTIONS IN DEMOCRATIC THOUGHT

Traditionally, thinking about democracy has been based on a number of assumptions (Saward, 2001). Three are particularly important. The first is that democracy only applies to the political unit of the nation state. That is, democracy refers to the character of the political institutions in any particular sovereign state. The second is that democracy is principally about the aggregation of preferences. That is, it is assumed that a democratic outcome is one that measures accurately the preferences of the electorate in devices such as elections and referendums. Providing that all adults are allowed to register a preference, the outcome is regarded as a democratic one. Little interest or concern has traditionally been expressed about how these preferences are created in the first place. The third assumption is that the membership of the political community is settled. Debates about the extent of the democratic community have, it is said, been resolved now that universal suffrage has been achieved.

Recent developments in democratic theory challenge all three of these assumptions. In this chapter, we look at four theories which illustrate this change of direction in democratic theory.

Associative Democracy

This approach, associated most notably with Paul Hirst (1996), provides an alternative to the state-centric focus of much democratic thought. Associative democracy seeks to reduce the role of the state by advocating the democratic role of voluntary, self-governing associations within civil society. It therefore seeks to provide a 'Third Way' between free-market capitalism and state socialism. The state's role is to be reduced, but decisions are not to be left to the vagaries of the market. Rather, it envisages considerable political participation and decision-making beyond the reaches of the formal state.

Cosmopolitan Democracy

The associative theory of democracy challenges the assumption that democracy must be focused on the state. Another, better known, theory that also challenges that assumption is the cosmopolitan theory of democracy. Here it is suggested (e.g. by Held, 2006: 304–9) that given that citizens of nation-states are increasingly affected, if not dominated, by forces happening beyond the boundaries of the particular nation-state within which they live, then what matters now is ensuring that global forces are controlled by democratic means. This requires that the international level of inclusion be at the level of the individual and not, or not exclusively, the state. As Weale (2007: 239) points out: 'Just as democracy had to make the transition from the city-state to the nation-state, so it must now make the transition to the international global order.'

An alternative approach to the undemocratic implications of globalization is to 'urge *strengthening* the sovereignty of (democratic) states by defending their internal political structures against external constraint and interference' (Cunningham, 2002: 201). Of course, the cosmopolitan model is based on the assumption that globalization is a reality; a position challenged by those holding a realist view of international relations that still puts the nation-state at the centre of political analysis. It is also based on the principle that state representation is insufficiently democratic. This is because states are unequal in power and influence, and therefore, the political influence of individuals varies depending on which nation-state they live in.

Democratic theorists, cosmopolitan democrats argue, should therefore be focusing on ensuring that international institutions are both effective controllers of global developments and that they themselves are under democratic control. A number of institutional arrangements have been suggested. Held (2006: 306), for one, suggests the creation of regional parliaments with the power to make decisions binding in international law, and the introduction of referendums across national boundaries. The EU would be a good model of this. Archibugi (1995), similarly, proposes the creation of a Second Assembly within the UN, to coexist alongside the General Assembly. Representation would be based on population size, so that the most populated states would get more seats than less populated states. Such a system would therefore allow people from autocratic states to have some democratic representation.

Where the existing sovereign state fits into this model is not clear and, as Hoffman and Graham (2006: 119) point out, this rather undermines the radical force of Held's argument. For them (123), the 'concept of a "cosmopolitan democracy" can only be coherently sustained if the international community ceases to be composed of states'. This, of course, raises the prospect of how realistic cosmopolitan democracy is, an issue we raised in the context of 'ideal' theory in the introduction to this volume. Even if it is realistic for the representation of states to coexist with the representation of individuals at the international level, problems remain. Chief among these are the issues of whether a viable international institution of individuals is possible given the scale of representation required, and the lack of a common cultural heritage. Added to this is the relevance of such an institution given that institutions representing states are still likely to be necessary if viable international agreements are to be arrived at (Weale, 2007: 239–41).

Deliberative Democracy

The third new direction in democratic theory challenges the assumption that democracy is merely about the aggregation of preferences. Deliberative democracy, heavily influenced by the ideas of the German philosopher Jurgen Habermas, has become the most written and talked about new theory of democracy (**see Box 4.6**) and there is now an extensive and varied literature on the subject—Elstub and McLaverty (2014) provide a comprehensive review. Because of the extent and variety of the literature, it is probably misleading to talk about one account of deliberative democracy. Nevertheless, it is possible to elicit a number of key features shared among a vast majority of the exponents of deliberative democracy.

The first feature is that democracy ought not to be defined either in terms of the aggregation of pre-existing preferences in a vote at elections or in a referendum, nor in terms of a reflection of the balance of competing interests within civil society, as the pluralist model has it. Rather, for advocates of deliberative democracy, collective decisions are only legitimate if they are made after reasoned and detailed discussion. Second, it is held that genuinely deliberative arenas ought to be as inclusive as possible with all points of view and social characteristics represented, and an equal chance to participate offered to all of those who are present. Third, during deliberation, self-interest should be put aside, as should strategic behaviour designed to achieve as much as possible of a pre-existing agenda. Instead, mutual respect of, and empathy for, the arguments of others is encouraged. Deliberative democracy, then, encourages participants to be open to the views of others, to listen to what they have to say and empathize with their point of view. There is a supposed 'moralizing effect' of deliberation (Niemeyer, 2004). That is, genuine deliberation involves the advancement of arguments by citizens about what is right, and in the general or public interest, and not about what is in the self-interest of participants. One can contrast genuine deliberation here with the dominance of powerful vested interests which, it is said, is prevalent in traditional interest group politics.

4

A number of criticisms have been made of deliberative democracy, as follows.

1. It is unrealistic to expect anything other than a small minority will be able to engage in genuine deliberation. To create a universal deliberative system involving everyone is impossible because of time, logistical, and resource constraints. This would seem to mean that we have a choice. We can opt for a genuinely deliberative system which is politically unequal because only a few will be able to take part. It may, for instance, be only political elites such as professional politicians who are able to engage in genuine deliberation. The alternative is to maximize participation to enhance political equality through, for instance, increasing the number of referendums held. This would be done, though, at the expense of deliberation. We would therefore seem to be faced with a choice between deliberation and political equality (Parkinson, 2006).

2. Some empirical research has found that human beings do not always behave in the way that deliberative democracy theory says that they will (Mutz, 2008). There is, for instance, an inability and/or unwillingness to understand complex social, political, and economic issues, and a tendency to follow the dominant majority in group settings, to fit in with the crowd.

3. In addition, although there is some evidence from the research of actual deliberative events undertaken that people's views are sometimes transformed, it is - not surprisingly perhaps - less likely that those with a strong opinion on a topic will change their view on a topic or empathize with the views of others. The implication of this is that deliberation only really works on issues which matter less to people.

4. There is evidence that participant's views can be transformed by the provision of information they were not aware of before. It should be pointed out, however, that this can be separated from the deliberation process itself. That is, one could endeavour to provide comprehensive and balanced information on an issue without requiring those making a decision to then deliberate about it.

5. Some political theorists have argued that without some fundamental reforms to the balance of power among competing interests in contemporary liberal democracies, deliberatively democracy merely reproduces existing inequalities, advantaging the already powerful. These inequalities are based, in part, on finance, but also go wider, and include the type of communication (rational and formal debate) valued by advocates of deliberative democracy and the possibility of discourse hegemony (Young, 2000).

6. The emphasis placed on minimizing difference and conflict in deliberative theory has been criticized by some for unrealistically denying the real purpose of politics, which is predicated on the existence of widely diverse interests and values (Mouffe, 2005).

Questions

1. How does deliberative democracy differ from conventional theories of democracy?
2. Critically examine the claims made for deliberative democracy.

Fourth, the inclusive communication and social learning inherent in the deliberative process, it is suggested, leads to better decisions in the sense that they are more informed, more effective, more just, and therefore more legitimate. Finally, and probably most important, deliberation, it is argued, increases the possibility of a consensus being arrived at and the transformation of the views of participants. What is important, then, is not what the preferences are at the start of deliberation but what they are *after* deliberation.

Advocates of deliberative democracy differ about the best site for deliberation. Some focus on the benefits of small-scale so-called 'minipublics', such as citizen juries and deliberative polls—the latter involving a small section of the population engaging in debates about an issue and being polled before and after the deliberation in order to see if their views have altered (Fishkin, Jowell, and Luskin, 2002). Other deliberative theorists, by contrast, talk in terms of deliberative political institutions such as legislatures (Steiner et al., 2004) or of a 'deliberative system' within civil society (Dryzek, 2010). Advocates of deliberative democracy differ too over who should do the deliberating. Deliberative participants can be ordinary members of the public or elite policy-makers. They can also be partisans, with a definite view about a topic or non-specialists with no particular position or vested interest. Deliberative theorists differ in addition over the collective goal of deliberation. Some think that the goal is consensus where no disagreement between the participants remains, whereas other advocates think that an acceptance of the legitimacy of the procedure is all that matters, and the best we can achieve. In the latter camp, Gutmann and Thompson (1996) are particularly notable: they argue that the goal of deliberation is what they call an 'economy of moral disagreement' in the sense that there is a greater acceptance of the terms of difference and disagreement. In other words, differences of opinion are acceptable providing there is a greater recognition and empathy with the views you disagree with.

Ecological Democracy

The fourth and final new democratic theory can be described as ecological democracy because the impetus for it has come mainly from green political theorists who have sought to explore the relationship between the objectives of the environmental movement, on the one hand, and the political process, on the other. They start with the question: should environmentalists be democrats? The conventional answer is that the relationship between environmentalism and democracy is a contingent one. That is, sometimes the democratic process might produce outcomes that environmentalists are happy with. Sometimes, it will not. The relationship between democracy and environmentalism is a contingent one because democracy is a process (a theory of agency) and environmentalism is substantive (a theory of value). There is no guarantee that any particular theory of agency will support a particular theory of value (Goodin, 1992: 168). In the case of the environment, in other words, there is absolutely no guarantee that any particular democratically elected legislature or executive is going to be concerned enough about it to consider prioritizing it above other political issues.

It might be thought that that is all there is to it. Two responses to the contingency conclusion, however, have followed. The first is the suggestion that deliberative democracy is more likely to produce political outcomes favourable to environmental protection (Smith, 2003). The second is the suggestion by some green political thinkers that the membership of the democratic

4

community ought to be expanded. As we saw, with the attainment of universal suffrage this question of who is to be a member of the democratic political community (who counts that is) was regarded as settled. Some green political theorists, however, question this assumption. They argue that restricting the political community to currently living humans is too restrictive because it has the effect of excluding other entities that have important interests who are entitled to have these interests represented.

One such important group is future generations. Future generations have important interests which may conflict with ours. For example, we may want to maximize our economic prosperity, but this may cause irreversible environmental problems for generations to come. We might use up all of a particular resource so there is none left for those not yet born or we might pollute the planet so that the quality of life for future generations will be much reduced or even non-existent. Even more radical is the claim that democracy is illegitimately anthropocentric. That is, it is too focused on humans. After all, non-humans—animals and nature as a whole—have interests which may conflict with ours. And these interests will be ignored if only humans are members of the democratic political community (Garner, 2017).

Academic literature has emerged that tries to work out how we might incorporate the interests of the currently excluded. Ingenious schemes have been proposed in which humans act as proxies for future generations and nature whose representatives are allocated some seats in legislative assemblies (Dobson, 1996). An alternative suggestion is for the creation of counter-majoritarian devices designed to impede the will of the majority (Ekeli, 2009). So, for instance, it could be written into a constitution that any Act of Parliament has to show that its provisions would not seriously damage the interests of future generations or nature (Hayward, 2005). Other means that have been suggested for helping the political system to incorporate the interests of future generations include giving more political power to the young, on the grounds that the young have a greater interest in the future than older citizens do.

Merely stating that future generations and nature have interests, of course, does not, by itself, justify extending the boundary of the *demos* to include them (**see Box 4.7**). The ecological view of democracy relies upon a particular principle of inclusion. This is the so-called 'all affected' principle (Goodin, 2007). This is one answer to the so-called 'boundary problem' or problem of inclusion in democratic theory which asks: how do we decide who is to be included in the *demos*? Who is to count as 'the people'? The all-affected principle responds by saying that 'everyone affected by decisions made has a categorical right to participate in the process of making those decisions'.

> ### KEY DEBATE BOX 4.7
> #### A Critique of Ecological Democracy
>
> The ecological theory of democracy is dependent on the validity of the all-affected principle as an answer to the boundary problem in democratic theory. But this is only one answer to the boundary problem. We might, for instance, want to say that inclusion in the *demos* requires significant cognitive capacities. After all, we restrict the franchise to prevent children from voting on the grounds that we do not regard them as sufficiently competent to participate in politics. If we adopt this approach, then it also provides a justification for excluding non-humans from
>
>

democratic inclusion. That does not mean that we have no moral obligations to non-human animals, only that they do not have a democratic right that their interests be represented.

There are also objections to including future generations within a democratic polity. Can we really know what their interests are? Can we really know all the effects of our actions to make a solid assessment of the impact our actions will have on future generations? In the so-called non-identity problem, can we owe obligations to those who probably would not have existed had we not damaged the environment in the first place (Parfit, 1984)? How far down the line must we go—one generation, two, three, four? And do all of these generations have the same weight of interest as ours? Should not the interests of currently living humans take precedence over those of future generations? For these reasons and others, some scholars have argued that even if we must take the interests of future generations into account, their interests cannot carry the same weight as ours and should be discounted gradually in line with how far away from us in time they are (Page, 2006).

Questions

1. How should we decide who is to be included in a democratic polity?
2. What are the problems associated with the all-affected principle as an answer to the boundary problem in democratic theory?

KEY POINTS

- Traditional democratic thinking has been based on a number of assumptions concerning the site of democratic institutions, the measuring of democratic decisions, and the boundary of the democratic community.
- New theories of democracy challenge all of these assumptions.
- The state-centric character of traditional democratic theory and practice is challenged by the associative and cosmopolitan theories of democracy; the aggregative measuring of preferences is challenged by deliberative democracy and the widely accepted limits to the democratic community is challenged by ecological theories of democracy.

CONCLUSION

We have seen, in this chapter that, however democracy is defined, it is almost universally feted, despite its contemporary difficulties. When we come to examine its claims to be the most important grounding for political obligation, however, we come up against the problem of what to do with the minority consequences of majoritarianism. We could reject democracy in favour of some version of the general will, whereby it is claimed that unanimity can be achieved, or we can recognize and deal with the minorities question.

The obvious solution to the problem of minorities is to introduce some device protecting their interests. Many political systems, including the USA, do just this by including a bill of rights protecting individuals against the majority. In the USA, this was included precisely because the Founding Fathers were concerned about the potential dangers of majority rule or majority tyranny as they called it. The problem here is that it must be questioned how democratic such a bill of rights is. Again, using the Supreme Court in the USA as an example, its members are not elected and not removable except under the most extraordinary circumstances.

The protection of some rights—such as the right to free speech, the right to form political associations, and, of course, the right to life—is essential for democracy to function. As we pointed out earlier, however, it is not clear that all rights, such as the right to property, are consistent with democracy. Maybe our conclusion should be that democracy is not as special as we previously thought. Perhaps it does not provide us with an adequate theory of political obligation, because of the problem of minorities, and maybe we should regard other principles, such as the protection of individual rights, as more important, **see Box 4.5**.

In many ways, the debate about the implications of majoritarianism might be regarded as rather old-fashioned now. A widespread feeling that modern democratic politics, dominated by money, powerful interests, and the media, is deeply flawed—coupled with the rise of globalization and the ominous threat of climate change—has led to challenges to the central assumptions of traditional democratic theory. Equally, perhaps it should be asked whether democracy, particularly of the participationist and deliberative variety, is the most appropriate way to deal with some of the world's most intractable problems. In this context, should not, it might be asked, the role of experts be allowed full rein in order that the interests of the whole planet are put before the self-interested utility maximizing that passes for electoral choice in much of the democratic world?

KEY QUESTIONS

1. What is democracy?
2. Distinguish between direct democracy, democratic elitism, representative democracy, and deliberative democracy. Which is to be preferred?
3. Is democracy special?
4. How far is it true to say that we are witnessing a 'democratic recession'?
5. Are we obliged to obey decisions taken democratically?
6. Why should we obey the state?
7. Is democracy consistent with a class-divided society?
8. Discuss the relationship between democracy and majority rule.
9. Is cosmopolitan democracy possible and desirable?

FURTHER READING

Elstub, S. and McLaverty, P. (2014), *Deliberative Democracy: Issues and Cases* (Edinburgh: Edinburgh University Press).
A current review of the most important contemporary development in democratic theory.

Held, D. (2006), *Models of Democracy* (Cambridge: Polity, 3rd edn).
This is probably the best general text on democracy, coupling comprehensive descriptions with astute evaluation.

Macpherson, C. B. (1977), *The Life and Times of Liberal Democracy* (Oxford: Oxford University Press).
This is a contentious account of the development of democratic thought and practice. Compelling reading.

Shapiro, I. (2003), *The Moral Foundations of Politics* (New Haven, CT: Yale University Press).
This is an admirably concise account of the answers given by political theorists to the question of political obligation.

Weale, A. (2007), *Democracy* (Basingstoke: Palgrave).
A sound introduction to the major themes in democratic theory, now in its 2nd edition.

Wolff, R. P. (1970), *In Defense of Anarchism* (New York: Harper & Row).
This is short and controversial but essential reading on the problem of political obligation.

 For additional material and resources, please visit the Online Resources at:
www.oup.com/he/garner4e

FREEDOM AND JUSTICE

READER'S GUIDE

This chapter explores two related, but distinct, political concepts—justice and freedom. The difficulty of defining freedom is revealed by virtue of an examination of various competing constraints on our freedom. Berlin's argument that there are only two types of freedom is challenged by those who perceive there to be numerous conceptions of the concept. The chapter then explores the degree to which freedom is desirable. Various alternative values—equality, paternalism, happiness—that might conflict with freedom are considered, mainly in the context of the political thought of John Stuart Mill. In the second part of the chapter, the concept of justice is explored. Various criteria for determining the meaning of justice are identified and discussed mainly in the context of the major competing theories of justice provided by Rawls and Nozick. Finally, the chapter considers alternative theories of justice which challenge the conventional liberal view that theories of justice should focus only on the nation-state and are applicable only to human beings.

CONSTRAINTS ON OUR FREEDOM

Like most other political concepts, freedom—or liberty (the terms are used interchangeably here)—is a difficult concept to define. Like democracy, part of the problem is that freedom is regarded as a 'good' concept, one which all governments should pursue. The reality, however, is that there may be good grounds for limiting freedom to pursue other goods that are valued. A starting point is to say that freedom is the opposite of constraint. Therefore, a common-sense definition of freedom is the absence of constraints or the absence of impediments. The problem is this only takes us so far, because most of the definitional controversy over freedom concerns the content of these constraints. In other words, political philosophers disagree about what counts as a constraint. We might profitably begin, then, with an attempt to outline various possible constraints on our freedom.

Freedom and Democracy

The first possible constraint is *non-democratic forms of government*. In other words, how far is our freedom restricted by living in a non-democratic society? The answer would seem to be that there is no necessary relationship between freedom and the absence of democracy. It is possible to conceive of a benign dictatorship which grants a considerable degree of freedom to its people. Conversely, a democracy polity could conceivable limit freedom in a variety of ways, as, for instance, in the limits on abortion existing in states such as Ireland. As Berlin (1969: 130) correctly points out: 'The answer to the question "Who governs me?" is logically distinct from the question "How far does government interfere with me?".'

Freedom and Physical Coercion

Perhaps the most obvious constraint on our freedom is when we are *physically coerced* by others. Here, we are unfree when others physically constrain us from doing what we want to do. The most obvious, and extreme, examples are imprisonment and slavery. It has been argued too that, in this category, an obvious restriction on freedom is the existence of law backed by sanctions. However, this is not as clear-cut as it first appears since we are, of course, free to break the law and either try to avoid detection or accept the punishment that comes with it. It seems odd, however, to exclude the law as a constraint on our freedom. A response to this suggested by Barry (2000: 196) is to say that in many cases the costs of breaking the law—such as a long prison sentence or even the death penalty—are so high that, to all intents and purposes, they are equivalent to physical constraints.

Freedom and Physical Incapacity

We might want to add *physical incapacity* to this list, in the sense that we are unfree because we cannot do something that physical impairment prevents us from doing. This might refer to a situation where an individual does not have an ability that other humans do, such as the ability to walk, or conditions which affect all humans, such as our inability to fly. These constraints, although clearly impediments, might not be worthwhile pursuing in so far as the situation is unalterable or beyond the control of human action. It is a different matter, however, if someone's disability is alterable and lack of resources prevents that person from living a normal life. In this case, the case for utilizing the language of freedom is compelling. In other words, human **agency** is necessary for an impediment to count as a constraint on our freedom.

Freedom, Rationality, and Morality

Some political theorists would also want to say that our freedom can be limited by a lack of *rationality* or *morality*. Only rational or moral behaviour, then, can be truly free. There is clearly something in the rationality argument. For example, we would not regard the supervision and direction of a person with senile dementia as a constraint on their freedom in the same way we would in the case of a normal healthy adult. In the same way, we do not regard the supervision and direction of children in the same way as we would with adults.

There are also weaknesses with the attempt to link freedom and rationality. We might want to say that supervising and directing the behaviour of children or adults with senile dementia is a genuine restriction on their freedom (after all, we are preventing them from doing what they want to do) but that this restriction is justified in the pursuit of other goals, in this case protecting their safety. In addition, there are dangers in claiming that only rational behaviour is free, because it is by no means clear what the content of rational behaviour is. At the very least, this can encourage political leaders to impose their own version of rationality on to others and justify paternalistic action on the grounds that it makes those subject to it freer.

Some of the arguments about equating freedom with rationality can also be applied to morality. Morality in this context is usually taken to mean behaviour that is selfless rather than selfish. In other words, we are free in so far as we behave morally or altruistically, acting in accordance with the common interest, or what Rousseau (1913) describes as the **general will**. Conversely, we are unfree in so far as we behave immorally or selfishly. This view, that freedom is linked to morality, is a central feature of one version of the so-called 'positive' theory of liberty. The main advocate is Jean-Jacques Rousseau. The credibility of this approach to freedom depends on the validity of the assertion that what we really want to do is to behave morally, and in so far as we do not behave morally, we are not doing what we really want to do. We become unfree, therefore, if we behave selfishly because ultimately, we do not want to be selfish. It is in this sense that Rousseau, as we saw in Chapter 4, can argue that we can be 'forced to be free'.

➡ See Chapter 4 for more on the idea of the general will and its implications for freedom and democracy.

In response to the attempt to link freedom with morality, we might want to say that it seems to confuse two very different values. There may be a case when it makes sense to say that we can be freed from our desires—as in the case of, say, a paedophile who genuinely wants to behave in a different way. However, this requires a recognition from the individual himself that his behaviour is unacceptable, coupled with a desire to change it. The notion of forcing someone to be free goes further than this by arguing that someone can be coerced into behaving differently. There may be a case for saying that this is justifiable, and the state does intervene (as in the case of paedophiles) to try to change behaviour. However, it seems more appropriate to say in such cases that the state is imposing society's moral standards on individuals, not in order to make people freer but on the grounds that the moral principle is important enough to justify sacrificing freedom for.

Freedom and Psychology

The penultimate constraint to be identified refers to *psychological* influences on our behaviour. We have previously seen that we can be constrained by physical coercion. It might also be argued that we can be equally constrained psychologically; that is, we can be forced to behave in ways we really do not want to because of outside influences that affect the way we think. A very powerful example of this is advertising. It is often claimed that advertising creates wants that would otherwise not be there. This can apply to general commercial advertising as well as political advertising by parties and the state. A classic example here is the banning, in the UK and elsewhere, of tobacco advertising, on the ground that it encourages the dangerous habit of smoking that then creates an addiction difficult to shake off. The ability of a ruling group to influence, if not determine, the way that the masses think is an example of the 'third dimension' of power that we encountered in Chapter 3.

➤ See Chapter 3 for an exploration of the three dimensions of power.

5

Freedom and Economic Impediments

The final constraint that we can identify relates to *economic impediments*. If we regard freedom as merely the absence of externally imposed physical coercion, we would seem to be saying that freedom is best achieved if the state and society leave people largely to their own devices. Some political thinkers argue, however, that the state can, by intervening in the lives of individuals, do a great deal to increase freedom. In other words, an individual is not really free to develop as a human being and enjoy freedom if she does not have enough to eat, or a roof over her head. This links freedom with power. As Gray (1991: 42) points out, 'for liberty to exist in any real sense, the agent must have the power to exercise it'. By intervening to provide, at least, a basic standard of living below which individuals cannot fall, then the state can play a positive role in increasing the freedom of individuals to make something of their lives.

As with grounding freedom on notions of rationality and morality, however, it might be argued that advocates of this version of positive liberty are confusing liberty with other values; that is, preventing poverty, homelessness, and unemployment might be justified for a whole host of reasons, but these reasons are not the same as freedom. Clarity demands, it might be argued, that we should say that state intervention limits freedom in order to secure greater economic equality.

KEY POINTS

- Since freedom is defined as the absence of constraints, the identification of constraints on our freedom is a useful starting point.
- Possible constraints can be divided into those that are external to us, and those that are internal to us, the latter including such characteristics as rationality and morality.

DETERMINING THE NATURE OF FREEDOM

The previous discussion might lead us to suggest that we cannot resolve the question about the meaning of freedom. One way out of this impasse is to take on board a formulation suggested by MacCallum (1967). He argues that all genuine statements about freedom must contain three elements involving X (the agent), Y (the constraint), and Z (the objective). In this triadic relationship, X is free from Y to do or be Z. Political philosophers, he argued, have disagreed over what ought to be included as X, Y, and Z but all have operated with the same conception. Thus, those who emphasize the importance of physical constraints (the Y factor) interpret the agent (the X factor) as an actual self and the objective (the Z factor) as an action. Those, on the other hand, who emphasize the importance of lack of rationality and morality as constraints, interpret the agent as a real (rational or moral) self and the objective as a state of mind.

The problem with MacCallum's formulation is that it only takes us so far. This is because, as we saw in the first section, political philosophers disagree on the content of the X, Y, and Z elements. As Gray (1991: 14) points out, MacCallum's formulation does not 'eliminate conceptual issues in relation to liberty, but simply displaces or conceals them as conceptual issues about what constitutes an X or Y or Z factor'. Better then to adopt the position that while 'there is only one *concept* of freedom . . . there are many *conceptions* of that concept' (6).

Negative and Positive Freedom

The view that there are many conceptions of freedom has been disputed by those who argue that essentially freedom can be divided into negative and positive varieties. The distinction between negative and positive freedom dates back to the Ancient Greeks (Gray, 1991: 7) but it is particularly associated with the Oxford political philosopher, Isaiah Berlin (1909–97). Berlin famously argued, in an article first published in 1958, that these represent the two main, and distinct, conceptions of freedom. The negative conception is concerned with the question: 'What is the area within which the subject . . . is or should be left to do or be what he is able to do or be, without interference by other persons?' The positive conception, on the other hand, is concerned with the question: 'What, or who, is the source of control or interference that can determine someone to do, or be, this rather than that?' (Berlin, 1969: 121–2.) Therefore, Berlin seeks to distinguish between the *area* of control, emphasized by negative liberty, and the *source* of control, emphasized by positive freedom. The ability of individuals to be self-governing, then, is crucial for advocates of the latter.

Berlin's purpose in making this distinction was primarily to defend negative liberty against advocates of the positive version. Indeed, he was vociferously opposed to the latter version, seeing it as an enemy of real freedom. This was because he argued that self-government usually involved the argument that genuine freedom requires that the 'real' (rational or moral) self be established over the 'actual' self. Berlin emphasized the illiberal implications of this move, discussed earlier in this chapter.

Berlin's approach has been heavily criticized (Gray, 1991: 8–11). In terms of the debate about the meaning of freedom, it is argued that Berlin has not demonstrated the existence of only two diametrically opposed conceptions of freedom. Positive freedom can be interpreted in a way that makes it close to the negative variety. As Barry (2000: 204) points out, the emphasis on self-mastery in the former may be interpreted as merely another means whereby constraints on individuals can be removed, with the difference being that these constraints are internal as opposed to the external variety emphasized by the latter. What we are then left with is still a number of different conceptions of freedom—based on the nature of the constraints—and not two different conceptions, as Berlin maintains.

> **KEY POINTS**
>
> - MacCallum argues that a single conception of freedom can be identified, including statements about the agent, the constraint, and the objective.
> - Berlin argues, by contrast, that there are only two types of freedom—negative and positive varieties.
> - Other political philosophers dispute both interpretations, arguing that there are many conceptions of freedom, each having a different interpretation of the nature of the agent, the constraint, and the nature of the objective to which freedom is directed.

IS FREEDOM SPECIAL?

Justifying freedom is a very different exercise from defining its character. The two, of course, are linked in the sense that our assessment of the value of freedom will be dependent on what we think it is. It might be argued, for instance, that we can justifiably limit freedom in favour of greater equality. If, however, we have defined freedom in such a way that it requires state intervention in order to equalize resources so that freedom can be realized effectively by many people, then the two concepts are not as diametrically opposed as first thought.

Bearing this in mind, we can outline a number of justifications for freedom. Some political philosophers argue that there ought to be a presumption in favour of freedom (Benn, 1971); that is, the burden of proof ought to rest with those who would limit freedom. However, this begs the question of *why* freedom ought to have such an exalted status. In other words, it presupposes some pre-existing argument in favour of freedom.

One such argument is that freedom is a basic human right (Hart, 1967). However, this argument also depends upon a prior argument in favour of rights, in general, and a right to freedom in particular. Dworkin (1978) seeks to provide such a justification by arguing that those freedoms that are necessary to ensure that individuals are treated with equal concern and respect (so-called 'strong' liberties) should be inviolable. Again, however, Dworkin tends to take as given the importance of his equality principle. Moreover, Dworkin's argument for upholding strong liberties has been criticized for its subjectivity. Is it not a matter of opinion which liberties are to count as strong ones that uphold the right to equal concern and respect? (Gray, 1991: 106). This is particularly problematic if we accept that cultural pluralism—where competing norms of behaviour are regarded as acceptable—is deemed to be desirable, **see Box 5.1**.

Mill, Utilitarianism, and Freedom

One of the best-known defences of freedom was put forward by the British political philosopher, John Stuart Mill. Mill does not seek to justify a right to liberty. Rather, his arguments are coloured by his utilitarianism. In other words, Mill is arguing that freedom is conducive to the greatest happiness. There is another aspect to his thought that is important to note here too. Mill's mentor, Jeremy Bentham, had not sought to provide any content to happiness or pleasure. For him, it is

Photo 5.1 John Stuart Mill argued that freedom is essential to create the greatest happiness.
Shutterstock RF: Everett Historical/Shutterstock.com

KEY DEBATE BOX 5.1
Freedom and Cultural Pluralism

Consider the following two cases:

1. In 2004, religious symbols in schools were banned by the French National Assembly. This included a ban on Muslim girls wearing a veil, and the wearing of Jewish skullcaps, Sikh turbans, and conspicuous Christian crosses (Mookherjee, 2015: 161–6).

2. It is estimated that well over 100 million women have been subject to circumcision. This practice (involving either the removal of some of or the entire clitoris) can lead to serious physical and psychological problems, yet it is justified on cultural and religious grounds and is still widely practised in Western and Southern Asia, the Middle East, and large parts of Africa. It has also been estimated that several thousand girls are circumcised every year in Britain.

These examples raise the important complication added by cultural pluralism to issues of freedom. Cultural pluralism describes a situation where different cultures adopt different norms of behaviour. On the one hand, should we seek, as in the first example, to limit cultural pluralism in the interest of national unity, thereby reducing freedom? On the other, as in the second example, should we allow cultural diversity even when this practice itself harms and denies freedom to others? The problem for those who would impose a universal standard of right and wrong, whereby it is not justified in restricting freedom for some things but is for others, is that they risk being accused of cultural imperialism.

Questions
1. What is the relationship between cultural pluralism and freedom?
2. Is a ban on the wearing of religious symbols inimical to freedom?

the quantity of pleasure gained in any particular act that is crucial. Mill, on the other hand, famously revises the Benthamite principle by arguing that certain types of pleasure—what he calls the higher pleasures—are more valuable and ought to be pursued by individuals and the state. These are the pleasures associated with cerebral activities—literature, music, art, and so forth—as opposed to the bodily and more base pleasures (Mill, 1972).

Having established the basics of Mill's position, we can examine his theory of liberty. His essay *On Liberty*, originally published in 1859, is divided into two parts. In the first, he seeks to argue the case for the maximum possible freedom of thought and discussion. Even if an opinion being expressed is palpably false or hurtful to the sensibilities of others, Mill argues that it still should not be censored. True beliefs, he argues, will gain in vigour when they have to be upheld against objections, and false beliefs are more likely to be seen as such if they are open to public challenge. Mill strongly believes, too, that freedom of thought and expression is a means to social progress. Society, in other words, will be stronger if a wider variety of opinions and lifestyles are tried and tested.

In the second part of the essay, Mill seeks to argue the case for freedom of action. Here, Mill makes the well-known distinction between self and other regarding actions. This is the so-called harm principle. Only those actions that harm others (affecting them adversely) should be prevented by public opinion or the state. Self-regarding actions are not to be interfered with. We are entitled to warn of the dangers of pursuing a particular self-regarding path, but we cannot, according to Mill, physically restrain someone in order to prevent them from acting in a way that they choose, even if by so doing we strongly suspect they will harm themselves in the process. Mill is very clear, here, that actions which others find offensive, but which do not cause them physical or financial harm, are not to be seen as 'other' regarding.

Freedom, Happiness, and Paternalism

Mill's thoughts on liberty have been very influential in determining the nature of state intervention in modern liberal societies. Laws legalizing homosexuality between consenting adults in many liberal democratic states, for instance, owe much to Mill's distinction between self and other regarding actions, **see Box 5.2**.

In formulating a critique of Mill, it is crucial, first, to note how his arguments for freedom are strongly influenced by the utilitarian framework of his thought. Thus, he argues for maximizing

CASE STUDY BOX 5.2
The Wolfenden Report

In the 1950s, at a time when homosexual acts were illegal in the UK, the government set up a Departmental Committee, under Sir John Wolfenden, to consider both homosexual offences and prostitution. Wolfenden's influential report, published in 1957, put forward the argument that 'homosexual behaviour between consenting adults in private be no longer a criminal offence'. The grounds for this recommendation, derived from Mill, was that such acts were self-regarding. Despite the recommendations of the report, however, it was not until July 1967 that homosexuality finally became legal in England and Wales.

freedom of thought and discussion on the grounds that it will lead to social progress, through the development of greater knowledge. Knowledge was important for Mill because it facilitated the development of the higher pleasures. Likewise, Mill advocates freedom of action partly on the grounds that he thought humans were the best judges of what they want to do, and partly because he thought that making people free to choose what to do with their lives would be character-forming. In both cases, Mill is making the claim, then, that freedom makes humans happier.

It is by no means clear, however, that social progress will result from maximizing freedom of thought and discussion. Mill was arguably much too optimistic that in the marketplace of ideas, rationality and truth will prevail. It seems equally possible that the truth will need to be protected against its enemies. On utilitarian grounds too, it is not clear that freedom of thought and discussion will always promote happiness. One can readily think of cases where withholding the truth from someone may be in their best interests. For example, is it always in the best interests of someone to be told they have an incurable disease, particularly, in the case, say, of a disease such as multiple sclerosis, where the symptoms may be in abeyance for some years? Clearly, there may be cases where it is not in a person's interests to be told such news; and yet, Mill is committed to freedom of thought and discussion as a universal principle.

Much of the debate about Mill has focused on his arguments for freedom of action. Here, it is regularly argued that the distinction between self and other regarding actions is unsustainable. Surely, it is suggested, there are few, if any, actions that affect the actor alone? Others have challenged Mill's view that actions which others find offensive, but which do not cause them

Photo 5.2 In Paris in 2015 the terror attack on the staff of *Charlie Hebdo*, a magazine, raised questions around 'freedom of action'. *Shutterstock RF: conejota/Shutterstock.com*

physical harm, should be regarded as self-regarding. For instance, the British jurist Lord Devlin (1905–92)—echoing the sentiments of the eminent nineteenth-century judge James Fitzjames Stephen (1829–94)—argued that there is no such thing as private immorality, in the sense that even our private behaviour will have public consequences. Widespread drug-taking, for instance, will have effects on economic performance and on health-service resources. For Devlin (1965), then, society is held together by shared moral values, and excessive moral pluralism will be catastrophic for social stability.

We can also challenge Mill's assumption that freedom of action is conducive to happiness or well-being, as seen in the case study of smoking. **See Box 5.3**. Similarly, a utilitarian, committed

5

CASE STUDY   BOX 5.3
Smoking and Liberty

The contemporary debate about smoking illustrates the difficulty of delineating the boundaries of freedom of action. The British government's proposal for a total ban on smoking in pubs and clubs came into force in July 2007. The main philosophical justification for the ban is that smoking harms those who are forced passively to inhale the smoke of others. This is a principle associated with J. S. Mill, who would argue that smoking in private where no one else will be harmed is legitimate.

If it can be established that passive smoking is harmful, which it seems it can, then the application of Mill's other regarding principle would seem to be clear-cut. Of course, it might be argued that non-smokers choose to frequent places, such as pubs and clubs, where others smoke; but if smoking is allowed in all public places, then the choice of those who do not smoke is severely constrained. Moreover, the health risks of those who work in places where people smoke are even greater because of the amount of time they are exposed to smoke.

There are two criticisms of Mill's harm principle that do not challenge the smoking ban but rather suggest that it does not go far enough. The first is the argument that even smoking in private can, in most circumstances, harm others. This relates to the oft-stated criticism of Mill's harm principle that it is difficult to distinguish between self and other regarding actions. Thus, is it not the case that smoking, even in private, potentially harms others? If I become ill through smoking, as is likely, then this will impact upon family members who will be harmed—financially and emotionally—by my death or incapacity. Similarly, my ill health will have wider financial consequences, for the health service that has to treat me and the social benefit system that has to keep me if I am unable to work.

The second criticism is the point that, even if we can denote an action as being self-regarding, there are good grounds for suggesting that the state ought to intervene to stop individuals from harming themselves. This is the paternalistic critique of liberal-inspired freedom. Here, society and the state might step in to prevent me from engaging in an activity that they have good reason to believe will harm me. My health and well-being may, then, not be served by liberty, and indeed my happiness might be enhanced by restricting my freedom. In terms of smoking, it might be argued that the state should intervene on paternalistic grounds to ban it on the grounds that to do so will, in the long-run at least, improve the health of those who choose to smoke and thereby increase levels of happiness.

to maximizing happiness in society, would have to take into account behaviour which others find offensive (whether written, said, or acted upon) but which does not directly harm them physically or financially. Such actions would have to be weighed against the benefits of allowing them to continue. This is highly relevant in an era when there have been many cases where religious sensibilities have been injured by, for example, the publication of blasphemous caricatures of religious beliefs. This was highlighted in 2015 in the context of the terrorist attack in Paris on the staff of *Charlie Hebdo*, a French satirical weekly magazine. Very few would want to argue that the magazine's negative depiction of the prophet Muhammad justified such a brutal attack. On the other hand, it is very difficult to argue against the claim that the depiction caused great offence and upset to many people.

To be fair to Mill here, however, remember that racially motivated writing or speeches could be prohibited on the grounds that they are other regarding. This is the principle behind the prosecution in Britain of those deemed to be inciting racial hatred. This has included, most notably, the radical cleric Abu Hamza and, more recently, Mark Meecham who was found guilty of a hate crime after posting footage online of a dog performing Nazi salutes in response to the phrases 'gas the Jews' and 'Sieg Heil'. Such prosecutions were carried out not because their actions were deemed to be offensive, although they undoubtedly were, but because they were construed as an incitement for others to take racially motivated action to harm others.

Mill, Marx, and Socialism

Mill, of course, is putting forward a liberal theory of freedom, justifying limited state intervention and maximizing personal autonomy. This has been very influential in shaping the modern liberal theory of the state with its emphasis on neutrality and moral pluralism. It should be noted, however, that Mill was equally aware of the poverty and squalor evident in nineteenth-century England, and the consequences of this for the enjoyment of freedom. Indeed, he recognized the challenge and, to some extent the value, of the socialist critique of liberalism that was emerging towards the end of the century. Mill can therefore be located on the cusp between the old classical liberalism and the new liberalism emphasizing social reform that came to dominate British politics.

➔ See Chapter 2 for more on the liberal theory of the state.

➔ See Chapter 6 for a discussion of the difference between classical and new liberalism.

The socialist and, more specifically the Marxist, critique of the liberal theory of freedom centres on the impact of the inequality seen as the natural consequence of a capitalist economy. In the best-known Marxist account, Cohen (1979) points to the freedom to own property, and the resulting unequal ownership of property, as providing severe limitations on freedom for those who do not own property. In liberal capitalist regimes, the right to deprive others of the use of one's own property is a central feature. According to this approach, then, the freedom of the proletariat is necessarily constrained, and only when property is collectively owned can freedom be enhanced.

KEY POINTS

- Various reasons for valuing freedom have been put forward. These include freedom as a basic human right, freedom as a means to the end of happiness, and freedom as a means to self-development.

➔

- J. S. Mill argues for maximizing freedom, only actions which are other regarding being suitable for state or societal intervention.
- A number of problems with Mill's formulation are evident. In particular, there is a case—on the grounds of maximizing happiness, or paternalism, or the pursuit of knowledge—for limiting areas of freedom that Mill would regard as sacrosanct.
- The relationship between freedom and equality is a complex one, with those on the left arguing that equality is not necessarily a constraint on freedom.

THE MEANING OF JUSTICE

Justice is yet another one of those political concepts that is difficult to define. Very basically, justice requires us to give to others what they are due or entitled to. This contrasts with charity. It may be morally good for us to contribute to a charity, but we are under no obligation to do so. Political philosophers are most interested in justice as a distributional concept; that is, concerned with how different resources—wealth, income, educational opportunities, and so on—ought to be distributed. It is a concept, then, that implies that resources are scarce, for if we had more than enough resources to go around, there would be no need to agonize over who should have them.

A distinction can be made between procedural justice and social justice. In the former case, justice involves the following of rules, irrespective of the outcomes, whereas the latter is more concerned about outcomes. Modern theories of social or distributive justice have identified a number of criteria that we might consider as guides to distribution (Miller, 1976: 24–31). We could say that resources ought to be distributed according to *need*, or *desert* (or *merit*) or a principle of equality. It is widely thought that all theories of justice must involve equality, not in the sense that resources ought to be distributed equally, but that there ought to be consistency of treatment. This involves equality before the law and the principle that individuals ought to be treated equally. In terms of the distribution of resources, a distinction is usually draw between, on the one hand, equality of opportunity and, on the other, equality of outcome. **See Box 5.4**. Having accepted this, we may decide that some humans are not equal with others in various respects and therefore differential treatment can therefore be justified. For instance, we might decide that since some people work harder than others, or are more talented than others, they ought to have more of the resources available for distribution.

A theory of justice based on need is particularly associated with socialism, as in the slogan 'from each according to his ability, to each according to his needs'. Even in modern liberal democracies, however, the existence of a welfare state amounts to a recognition that meeting needs is just, although such societies also adopt desert as a criterion for the distribution of resources once basic needs are met.

A meritocratic theory of justice advocates distributing resources to those who display some merit and therefore deserve to be rewarded. It is associated with liberalism. Merit can include a natural talent, or it can refer to someone's propensity for hard work or a general contribution

5

The two main versions of equality as a distributive ideal are equality of opportunity and equality of outcome. The latter, as it suggests, equates justice with an equal share of resources, whatever the input made by individuals. Advocates of the former, which has a much broader level of support amongst politicians and the public, argue that account should be made of the abilities individuals have and the efforts they are willing to make, and therefore that inequality is justified not least to provide incentives. However, individuals should have a fair chance of achieving their goals, and making use of their talents, so a level playing field should be created.

Equality of outcome is particularly difficult to justify partly because it does not take enough account of the efforts individuals make and their talents. It is also consistent with levelling down where everyone ends up with less. Despite these objections, equality of outcome is defended by reference to its capacity to remove guilt and envy, and by the increase of fraternity, self-respect and even happiness it is alleged to produce (Wilkinson and Pickett, 2009). Equality of opportunity, on the other hand, can be criticised as incoherent in the sense that to achieve it arguably requires such a significant amount of redistribution that it morphs into equality of outcome, thereby rendering the notion of incentives as redundant. As Swift (2013: 108) points out: 'We start off by saying that we want people to have equal opportunities so that their outcomes reflect natural ability and choices rather than social circumstances. But in order for this to hold for their children, we end up having to deny that they be permitted to achieve unequal outcomes'.

Questions
1. Examine the case for equality of outcome.
2. Is equality of opportunity a coherent concept?

to society. A contemporary take on the desert principle can be found in the literature on luck egalitarianism (Barry, 2006). According to this position, the causes of inequality should be distinguished so that those who are unequal because of bad luck ought to be compensated, whilst those who are unequal because of their own lack of hard work or poor choices should not be.

A desert-based theory of justice, then, regards it as just to differentially reward talent and hard work. In addition, it recognizes the social advantages of encouraging the development and employment of talent through the deployment of incentives. It is linked to the principle of equal opportunity. If we intend to reward talent or hard work, it would seem unjust for an individual to start out with a structural disadvantage. It therefore would seem to demand educational and welfare opportunities for all to allow for the creation of a level playing field.

KEY POINTS

• Justice is a distributional concept. What political philosophers have mainly disagreed about is the criteria for distributing resources.

- Distributing resources based on need is problematic because it is not always clear what need consists of. In addition, it denies the importance of desert.
- Distributing resources based on desert takes account of incentives, but considerable state intervention would seem to be necessary in order to facilitate the equality of opportunity that the principle demands.

5

RAWLS'S THEORY OF JUSTICE

The meaning of justice becomes clearer if we look at a particular account. The best known is John Rawls's *A Theory of Justice*, published to much acclaim in 1971. (**See Box 5.5**.) Indeed, his lengthy book is regarded as the most important work of political philosophy published since the end of the Second World War. Rawls's account can be divided into two. First, there is the *method* he uses to arrive at his principles of justice and, second, the *principles* themselves.

Rawls (1921–2002) draws from the long-neglected social contract tradition associated with Hobbes and Locke. He seeks to devise a method for arriving at principles of justice to which everyone can consent. The problem with competing theories of justice is that they rest on judgements about values that are objectively irresolvable. Thus, how do we choose between a theory of justice emphasizing merit from one emphasizing needs? Does it not depend on pre-existing normative arguments about, for example, whether one favours a more equal society or a freer one, or one which places greater store on individual efforts and achievements?

Rawls's answer to this is to devise a hypothetical situation in which, he argues, there will be unanimous support for particular principles of justice. Imagine, he asks, a so-called original position in which individuals are asked to meet and decide how they want their society to be

SHORT BIOGRAPHY BOX 5.5
John Rawls (1921–2002)

John Rawls was an American academic who spent most of his career in the Department of Philosophy at Harvard University. Despite his retiring disposition, and his unwillingness to be involved in political debate, Rawls's major work, *A Theory of Justice* (1971), is widely regarded as one of the most influential works of political philosophy in the twentieth century, selling more than 300,000 copies in the USA alone. His rights-based theory of justice not only rejuvenated a discipline in apparent decline but also provided a major challenge to the, at the time, dominant utilitarian tradition.

Rawls's second book, *Political Liberalism* (1993) is concerned to demonstrate that his theory of justice only seeks to explore the basic political structure and not the wider area of ethics. In this wider sphere Rawls advocates the widest possible freedom for people to pursue different conceptions of the good life. This moral pluralism has become a central feature of the liberal creed.

➡ See Chapter 2 for more on the social contract tradition.

organized. In this original position, the members will be under a 'veil of ignorance'; that is, they will have no idea what their own position in society will turn out to be. They do not know if they will be rich or poor, black or white, male or female, disabled or able bodied. Rawls also assumes that individuals in the original position will be self-interested, wanting the best for themselves. Finally, he also suggests that they will desire what he calls primary goods such as wealth, good health, education, and so on.

In the second part of the theory, Rawls outlines the principles he thinks will derive from individuals in the original position. There are two (Rawls, 1971: 302):

1. Each person is to have an equal right to the most extensive total system of equal basic liberties compatible with a similar system of liberty for all.
2. Social and economic inequalities are to be arranged so that they are both:
   (a) to the greatest benefit of the least advantaged . . . and
   (b) attached to offices and positions open to all under conditions of fair equality of opportunity.

Rawls adds that (1) (the liberty principle) has priority over (2), and 2(b) (the fair opportunity principle) has priority over 2(a) (the difference principle). This means, for example, that one cannot sacrifice liberty in order to achieve economic improvement, thereby ruling out slavery, where it is conceivable that individuals could have a relatively high degree of welfare but no liberty.

A Critique of Rawls

Rawls's work has generated a huge literature (see, for instance, Daniels, 1975; Wolff, 1977; Kukathas and Pettit, 1990; Freeman, 2007). It is useful to distinguish between criticisms of his method, on the one hand, and his principles, on the other. In the former case, it has been questioned whether people in the original position would have produced the principles of justice which Rawls arrives at. His central claim is that, because they do not know where they will end up in the social strata, individuals behind the veil of ignorance will be conservative, in the sense of being unwilling to take risks.

It is not clear, however, that people in the original position would choose the kind of risk-averse strategy he suggests (Wolff, 1996: 177–86). Rawls calls it the 'maximin' strategy (maximizing the minimum) where we try to ensure that the worst possible scenario is as good as possible. It would clearly be extremely risky to adopt the other extreme (the 'maximax' strategy) whereby we seek to create a society where the rich are very rich and the poor are very poor; but, against Rawls, it can be argued that there is a middle way between these two extremes. We could, for example, opt for a society that has a great deal of inequality, but which also protects the worst-off, so they have basic protection. In this scenario, the average position in society would be considerably improved, but at the same time, if you did end up at the bottom of the social pile, it would not be totally catastrophic.

Rawls's reluctance to sanction the 'middle way' option leads some to suggest that he has merely created a method that will produce the outcomes he desires. There is some evidence for this. Rawls admits that he is not totally reliant on the heuristic device of the contract to derive his principles of justice. Rather, he adopts a procedure described as 'reflective equilibrium', whereby the principles derived from the original position are checked for consistency with our moral intuitions (Rawls, 1971: 20). Inevitably, then, the principles of justice arrived at will be, at the very least, influenced by already existing moral conventions.

This leads us to examine Rawls's principles of justice, irrespective of the method he uses to arrive at them. These principles have been criticized, from the left and the right. From the left, it has been argued that Rawls's difference principle is not as egalitarian as it seems (Wolff, 1977). Suspicions are aroused, in particular, by the priority given to liberty. Is it really the case that liberty should always be protected against any alternative? Here, Rawls's presumption of a general level of affluence is marked. The same cannot be said for many parts of the world where poverty is such a problem that liberty ought, and in many cases is, sacrificed in order to achieve a sustainable standard of living (as will be discussed).

From the right, Rawls's major critic has been the American philosopher, Robert Nozick (1938–2002). Nozick, writing from a libertarian perspective—heavily influenced by John Locke—in which the minimal state protecting property rights is the ideal, puts forward a procedural theory of justice; that is, he regards the way in which property is acquired as the key principle of justice and not the outcome of this acquisition. It is therefore a historical and not an end-state theory in which 'past circumstances or actions of people can create differential entitlements or differential deserts to things' (Nozick, 1974: 155). Provided that an individual's acquisition of property is fair, then she has a just entitlement to it. Nozick regards any attempt to redistribute property (defined in a wide sense to refer to anything possessed by an individual), even through taxation, as unjust.

Nozick therefore regards Rawls's end-state theory—that inequality is justified only when it benefits everyone, and in particular the worst-off—as illegitimate. He notes that Rawls's principles are inconsistent. How can one hold that liberty should be prioritized and, at the same time, advocate a considerable redistribution of resources? Achieving the one precludes the other. For Nozick, any attempt to enforce patterns of justice, such as an end-state principle seeking to meet need, requires enforcing, which will involve restricting liberty. Left to their own devices, people's actions will always disrupt a particular pattern.

Nozick provides two provisos to his entitlement theory. In the first place, the original acquisition to property has to have been fair, in the sense that it was gained not by force or fraud. If it was acquired in such a way, then compensation is due. As critics have pointed out, it is clearly the case that much property has, in the past, been unfairly acquired. The levels of compensation that might be required to provide redress, and the difficulty of establishing how much is due, create huge difficulties for Nozick's theory (Barry, 2000: 151). The second proviso is that acquisition must not be inimical to the essential well-being of others. This, reasonably enough, rules out someone acquiring all the water or food supplies in a community and then denying it to others.

Intuitively, one might doubt that the consequences of Nozick's principles are just. It could, for instance, result in such inequalities that the poorest members of society are at risk of starvation. His attack on taxation as a form of forced labour can be regarded as an exaggeration. Moreover, it can be argued, as we saw earlier in the chapter, that redistributing resources actually increases liberty because it increases choices for the poor (Wolff, 1996: 194–5).

KEY POINTS

- Rawls's theory of justice has been criticized for the method he uses to arrive at his principles of justice and the principles themselves.

5

- It has been argued that it is not necessarily the case that individuals in the original position will choose the principles Rawls says they will. There is a suspicion that he has manipulated the method in order to produce the outcome he desires.
- Rawls's principles of justice have been criticized from the left and the right. From the left, he is not regarded as egalitarian enough; from the right he is too egalitarian.
- Robert Nozick has provided the best-known critique of Rawls from the right. He argues that the kind of redistribution that Rawls calls for is illegitimate. Individuals should be entitled to hold the property they own without intervention from the state, provided that they have acquired it fairly.

ALTERNATIVE THEORIES OF JUSTICE

Rawls and Nozick, although different in many ways, both put forward a theory of justice based on liberal ideas and limited their terms of reference to relationships between human beings within sovereign states. It is important to note that there are alternative theories of justice that are not similarly constrained.

Cosmopolitan Theories of Justice

The growing interconnectedness in the world of peoples and sovereign states has provided a fillip for extending justice beyond national boundaries. Limiting a discussion of justice to the internal affairs of wealthy Western states seems trivial, given the staggering inequalities between different parts of the world, particularly given the oft-made claim that the rich northern states are at least partly responsible for the poverty in the South. This has led political theorists to develop theories of justice that are global in scope. (**See Box 5.6**.)

➡ See Chapter 17 for a further discussion of cosmopolitanism.

This so-called cosmopolitan approach to justice is based on the principle that our loyalties ought to be with human beings as a whole, rather than only those who happen to live within the boundaries of the state within which we reside. This idea, that human beings are equal members of a global citizenry, has a long history in political thought but the growing inequality between the North and the South in recent decades, and the greater recognition of this inequality, has made questions surrounding global justice 'one of the great moral challenges of the age' (Linklater, 2008: 555).

There is little agreement on what our moral obligations should be to those outsiders who do not belong to our community. At the extreme end, Singer (2002) puts forward the principle of unlimited obligation whereby we (in the rich North) are obliged to help others (in the poor South) even to the point of seriously eroding our own standards of living. A less extreme position is to apply Rawls's principles on a global scale, thereby justifying a greater degree of redistribution between the rich and the poor parts of the world (Beitz, 1979; Pogge, 1989). All cosmopolitan theories of justice are vulnerable to the charge, often put forward by exponents of non-ideal theory, that they are putting forward principles which are unrealizable.

5

CASE STUDY BOX 5.6
Climate Change and Justice

Photo 5.3 The Kyoto Protocol is an international treaty which commits state parties to reduce greenhouse gas emissions. *Shutterstock RF via DAM; M. Shcherbyna/Shutterstock.com*

Cosmopolitan theories of justice seek to impose a duty on individuals and states either to act positively to end injustices in the world or, at the very least, to refrain from acting so as to cause harm. Both practices feature in the politics of climate change. Cosmopolitans insist that rich industrialized countries should desist from continuing to burn fossil fuels at the rate they currently are. Equally, since these countries are held responsible for climate change, they are also obliged, it is argued, to assist those states in the developing world which have not been responsible for causing climate change, but which are least able to deal with its consequences (Caney, 2008). Despite intensive international negotiations over the past two decades or so, neither outcome has materialized to the degree that many cosmopolitan theories of justice would advocate. Having said that, in the initial treaty designed to tackle global warming—the Kyoto Protocol—no CO_2 reduction targets were set for developing countries partly as a recognition that it was the responsibility of the developed countries—because of their past responsibility for climate change—to take action, and partly because developing countries refused to accept any reduction targets. In addition, in subsequent negotiations, the developing countries have agreed to reductions in greenhouse gas emissions, but only in the context of a complex system of financial and technology transfer from the richer parts of the world to the poorer.

5

Communitarianism and Justice

An alternative to cosmopolitan theories of justice, and to liberal theories of justice in general, is provided by communitarianism. Communitarians adopt a perfectionist theory of justice whereby the state articulates and aims to bring about a particular conception of the good, or a particular way of living. They also reject the universal nature of Rawls and Nozick's theory of justice; that is, liberal theories are designed to apply in all social settings, whatever the particular historical or cultural features of that particular society. Communitarians reject this universalism in favour of culturally specific justice claims. In other words, principles of justice should take into account the particular social and cultural character of the society for which they are designed. They will differ from society to society (Walzer, 1985).

The communitarian position provides an important critique of the cosmopolitan theory of justice. Communitarians regard the cosmopolitan notion of a global citizenship as naïve since our loyalties develop, and our identities are forged, within our own particular communities (Walzer, 1994). They also see it as undesirable as it is illegitimate to impose our own, liberal, conception of distributive justice on to other cultures. Somewhat ironically, support for this position is provided by Rawls himself who, in a later work (1999), does not think that we have a duty to apply a liberal conception of justice globally. Instead, all that should be expected of us is to live in peaceful co-existence with others, including a recognition of each other's sovereignty and the principle that states do not intervene in the affairs of others unless threatened.

Green Political Thought and Justice

In recent years, there has been the development of a body of green political thought which challenges the view that justice can only be applied to currently living humans. There are a number of positions in this debate which can be put on a continuum. At the more moderate end, many philosophers have now raised the question whether justice ought to be applied to future generations of humans (see Barry, 1999). Of course, this intergenerational justice might clash with intragenerational justice. Put starkly, can we really justify cutting back on economic development for generations to come when there are so many people in the world who currently have a very low standard of living?

Some green political theorists and moral philosophers want to go further than recognizing the justice claims of only human beings. There has been a sustained attempt, for instance, to apply justice to at least some non-human animals (Garner, 2013). Some green political theorists want to go beyond humans and animals and include the whole of nature as recipients of justice. Some draw the line at living things (Taylor, 1986) whereas others want to include inanimate objects too, arguing that we can talk sensibly about applying justice to ecosystems, or biodiversity (Fox, 1984).

➡ See Chapter 7 for more on the ideology of environmentalism.

KEY POINTS

- There have been challenges to the conventional liberal view that theories of justice should apply only within states and not between states and should be applicable only to human beings.
- Cosmopolitan theories of justice argue that we have obligations towards all humans and not just those residing within our own national boundaries.
- Communitarian theories of justice insist that principles of justice depend on particular social, cultural, and historical experience and should not be regarded as universal, thereby challenging the cosmopolitan emphasis of universal global citizenship.
- Green theories of justice challenge the assumption that justice only applies to humans.

CONCLUSION

This chapter has employed the three major forms of analysis used by political philosophers. We have spent time examining the meaning of liberty and justice (semantic analysis) and have tried to assess the values central to competing theories of liberty and justice (normative analysis). In undertaking the second task, empirical arguments come into play, although never decisively. An examination of freedom and justice has revealed how interconnected political concepts are. We cannot properly evaluate freedom, for instance, without considering how it relates to conceptions of justice. Such an exercise also involves considering the respective merits of freedom and equality, which for most, if not all, are seen as conflicting objectives. What we have seen too is that the essentially contested nature of political concepts makes it difficult to go beyond an exercise in semantics.

There is no doubt that theorists of freedom and justice now have to engage with the impact of globalization. Our greater knowledge of different cultures—enabled by technological developments which now give us a clearer picture of how different societies operate, and by increasing mobility leading to the emergence of multicultural communities—makes us more circumspect about the value of freedom and what practices should be regarded as legitimate restrictions on freedom. Likewise, there are increasing calls for the principle of justice to be applied globally to address the shocking inequalities between different parts of the world. These developments provide important challenges to political philosophers, challenges with which they have only recently begun to grapple.

KEY QUESTIONS

1. What constraints exist on our freedom?
2. Are there only two types of liberty, negative and positive?
3. Is Mill's distinction between self and other regarding actions a viable principle?
4. Should we maximize freedom of thought and expression?

5. For what values, if any, would you want to limit freedom?
6. Can justice exist without freedom?
7. Is equality a justifiable objective?
8. Critically examine Rawls's theory of justice.
9. How viable is a cosmopolitan theory of justice?
10. Can justice apply to non-humans?

FURTHER READING

Berlin, I. (1969), *Four Essays on Liberty* (Oxford: Oxford University Press).
This is a celebrated defence of negative liberty.

Dobson, A. (1998), *Justice and the Environment* (Oxford: Oxford University Press).
This is a wide-ranging consideration of the relationship between justice and the environment by a leading green political theorist.

Dower, N. (1998), *World Ethics: The New Agenda* (Edinburgh: Edinburgh University Press).
This is a useful survey of the international ethics literature.

MacCallum, G. (1967), 'Negative and Positive Freedom', *Philosophical Review*, 76.
An influential article seeking to provide a universal definition of freedom.

Mill, J. S. (1972), *Utilitarianism, On Liberty, and Considerations on Representative Government* (London: Dent).
This is the classic case for individual freedom.

Rawls, J. (1971), *A Theory of Justice* (Cambridge, MA: Harvard University Press).
There is no substitute for reading this hugely important book.

Swift, A. (2014), *Political Philosophy: A Beginners Guide for Students and Politicians* (Cambridge: Polity, 3rd edn).
This contains a very accessible coverage of the main arguments relating to liberty and justice.

For additional material and resources, please visit the Online Resources at:
www.oup.com/he/garner4e

TRADITIONAL IDEOLOGIES

READER'S GUIDE

After considering the general characteristics of an ideology, a range of traditional ideologies is considered in this chapter. All of these ideologies were shaped by the Enlightenment, either, in the case of liberalism, socialism, nationalism, and anarchism, adopting its key principles, or, in the case of conservatism and fascism, railing against them. Each ideology, too, cannot be understood outside the economic, social, and political environment in which it emerged. Most of the ideologies discussed have had an extraordinary impact on the development of world politics in the last two centuries, and it is fair to say that the world would have been a very different place had they not existed.

WHAT IS AN IDEOLOGY?

This chapter and the next focus in detail on a range of political ideologies. Ideologies are central to this whole book because they help to shape the domestic and international political landscape. Many of the themes within them will be familiar because ideologies contain a collection of political ideas, many of which we have examined in previous chapters of this book. Liberalism, for instance, centres on the concept of liberty, whereas socialism centres on the concept of equality.

In this chapter, we will examine traditional ideologies associated with the school of thought known as the Enlightenment. **See Box 6.1**. Liberalism, socialism, nationalism, and anarchism emerged as embodiments of the Enlightenment, whereas conservatism and fascism sought to challenge its assumptions. In the next chapter, we will move on to examine more contemporary ideologies that challenge the claims of the traditional ideologies looked at in this chapter.

KEY CONCEPT BOX 6.1
Enlightenment

Photo 6.1 The Storming of the Bastille took place in Paris, France on July 14th 1789. This signified the start of the French Revolution. *Alamy (library image): World History Archive/Alamy Stock Photo*

A seventeenth- and eighteenth-century intellectual and cultural movement that emphasized the application of reason to knowledge in a search for human progress. It was both a cause and effect of the decline in the authority of religion. The influence of the Enlightenment was felt in many disciplines, in arts and sciences. In politics, it is associated with the attempt to model political institutions around a set of abstract rational principles. The French Revolution is often regarded as the highlight of the Enlightenment. Its chief critic within political philosophy was Edmund Burke (1729–97) who railed against the Enlightenment in his violent attack on the French Revolution.

The term 'ideology' was first used at the time of the French Revolution at the end of the eighteenth century by Antoine Destutt de Tracey (1754–1836). He used the term to denote a rationalistic science of ideas, which could be discovered in the same way as truths in the natural sciences. The normative character of ideology, however, quickly became apparent to others. For some, the word ideology has a pejorative or negative meaning. In contemporary popular usage, for instance, an ideologue is often used to denote someone with an uncompromising devotion to a set of ideas irrespective of their utility, or as simply an extremist. Marx is the best-known political thinker who defined ideology in negative terms. He used the term to mean a set of ideas that is false, deliberately designed to obscure reality in order to benefit a particular class in society. Marx's aim was to contrast ideology with the truth which his 'scientific' socialism was designed to reveal.

Others would regard Marxism itself as a classical example of an ideology. To so define Marxism, we need a more neutral or descriptive definition of the term. Here, an ideology might be defined as a set of ideas designed to provide a description of the existing political order, a vision of what the ideal political order ought to look like and a means, if necessary, to transform the former to the latter. An ideology, therefore, contains empirical, normative, and semantic elements.

Marxism is a classic case of this. Marx has often been described as the first social scientist. This is because he claimed to have discovered laws of social, political, and economic change which, he argued, enable us to predict the course of human history. Marx, therefore, described himself as a 'scientific socialist' to distinguish him from other socialists who put forward a normative case for socialism. However, Marx himself offers us both an empirical and a normative account of socialism. He seeks to tell us that socialism is desirable, it ought to happen, but he also puts forward an empirical theory which purports to predict that it will, as a matter of fact, happen.

A number of other features of ideologies are worth noting. First, ideologies are, more often than not, action-orientated in the sense that they seek to promote a particular social and political order for which they urge people to strive. Second, it is sometimes said that ideologies are less rigorous and sophisticated than 'proper' political philosophy. In reality, as Vincent (1995: 17) points out: 'ideological themes can be found on a continuum from the most banal jumbled rhetoric up to the most astute theorizing'.

Third, it is often said too that the twentieth century in particular can be regarded as the age of ideologies in the sense that regimes based on particular ideological traditions—communism and fascism—wreaked havoc during this century. However, it is more appropriate to say that the twentieth century was the age of ideologies with which liberalism—which had tended to dominate in the West up to that point—profoundly disagreed. The liberal critique of fascism and communism as ideologies is a reflection of a tendency among some liberals to regard liberalism as somehow above the ideological fray. As Goodwin (2014: 39) points out: 'Liberalism appears as a necessary truth, the basis of reality, rather than as one political ideology among many.'

Fourth, as well as containing empirical and normative elements, ideologies also seek to combine concepts that political philosophers, as we have seen, will look at individually. An attempt can be made to identify the core characteristic of a particular ideology but this is difficult, if not impossible, because all ideologies have different strands or schools, and sometimes there is considerable overlap between one ideology and another, such as when we talk about liberal versions of feminism or social democratic versions of socialism. Ideologies are, then, in the words of Festenstein and Kenny (2005: 4), 'internally pluralistic, contested, complex, and overlapping'. One way out of this problem is to adopt the approach suggested by Freeden (1996). In a major study of the concept of political ideology, Freeden recommends identifying the morphology of an ideology. By this he means it is possible to distinguish between concepts at the core of an ideology from those which are further away from the centre and those which are at the periphery.

One final general point about political ideologies is worth making in this introductory section. It is important to recognize that ideologies reflect, as well as shape, the social and historical circumstances in which they exist. To give an illustration of this, the two main ideologies since the nineteenth century have been liberalism and socialism. It was no accident that these ideologies emerged at the time of the industrial revolution and reached their zenith in the nineteenth century. In the first place, both liberalism and socialism reflected the optimism of the time, a time when it was thought that there was nothing that human beings could not understand rationally and achieve politically and economically. Human beings could be masters of all they surveyed. This optimism derived from the dominance of so-called 'Enlightenment' thinking. Second, liberalism and socialism became dominant ideologies because they were associated with new social groupings created by the industrial revolution. Liberalism was largely promoted by the industrial middle class and socialism was promoted by, or in the interests of, the industrial working class.

This chapter considers those ideologies shaped by the Enlightenment whether, as in the case of liberalism and socialism, supportive of its values or, as in the case of conservatism and fascism, opposed to them. If we turn our attention to the twentieth century and beyond, and in particular to the post-1945 period, we see that the dominance of Enlightenment ideologies has begun to wane. This new ideological climate is the subject matter of Chapter 7.

KEY POINTS

- Traditional ideologies were shaped by the Enlightenment.
- For some, ideologies have a pejorative meaning; others adopt a more neutral term.
- Ideologies are action-orientated and seek to combine concepts.
- It is usually possible to identify the core concepts of an ideology, but all ideologies have disputed meanings.
- Ideologies reflect, as well as shape, the social and historical circumstances in which they exist.

LIBERALISM

Liberalism is an important ideology because it has been the dominant political tradition in the West for many centuries. We have already encountered various facets of liberalism throughout this book, and many of the key Western political thinkers—Hobbes, Locke, Bentham, Mill, Rawls, and Nozick—are in the liberal tradition.

The Historical Development of Liberalism

Liberalism is a term that came into common usage in the nineteenth century where a party of that name emerged under the leadership of William Gladstone (1809–98), British Prime Minister on four separate occasions. Liberalism, and the values associated with it, however, has had a much longer history. The origins of liberalism are often traced to the rise of a capitalist political econo-my, and, in particular, as a defence of private property. The individualistic political philosophy of Hobbes and Locke is crucial here (Macpherson, 1962).

Liberalism is difficult to pin down, not least because of its longevity and the fact that it has gone through a variety of different formulations. The diverse character of liberalism is illustrated by the fact that it has been used to describe parties of the right, such as in Australia, and the left, such as in Canada. In some countries, it is associated with the free market whereas in others, most notably the USA, it denotes state intervention. Moreover, liberal politics has not been restricted to liberal par-ties. In Britain, for example, much of the twentieth-century political debate in Britain was couched in liberal terms with the Labour Party inheriting the Liberal Party's mantle. Indeed, much of the 'so-cial democratic' agenda promoted by the Labour Party in Britain, and many other social democrat-ic parties in Europe, has really been liberal in character, or at least a revised version of liberalism.

The liberalism associated with the social democratic left is a type known as 'new' or 'social' liberalism, which differs from the traditional classical liberalism which had its heyday in the nineteenth century. The classical tradition, drawing, in particular, on the economic theory of Adam Smith (1723–90) and the social theory of Herbert Spencer (1820–1907), emphasizes that the state's role should be limited to ensure internal and external security and to ensure that pri-vate property rights are enforced. It is partly justified on the grounds that the market is the most effective means of meeting human needs. There is also a moral dimension, in that a limited state maximizes freedom and rewards those who work hardest.

Classical liberalism began to be questioned towards the end of the nineteenth century, as the extent of poverty began to be recognized and socialist ideas emerged as an alternative. From within the liberal tradition, a new emphasis on social reform began to emerge, associated with thinkers such as T. H. Green (1836–82), L. T. Hobhouse (1864–1929), and J. A. Hobson (1858–1940). This new liberalism saw a much more positive role for the state, in correcting the inequities of the market, but it was argued that far from reducing liberty this actually increased it by creating greater opportunities for individuals to achieve their goals. It influenced the di-rection of the British Liberal Party politics, the Liberal Government, elected in 1906, carrying through a range of social reforming measures including old-age pensions.

The new liberalism came to dominate the political landscape for much of the twentieth century, although largely under the auspices of social democratic parties. In turn, however, a revised version of classical liberalism emerged to challenge it in the 1970s, under the guise of the New Right, and right-wing governments, particularly in Britain and the USA, were elected on programmes that were, in part, influenced by the classical liberal agenda. The academic ballast for this popular political move-ment was provided by thinkers such as Hayek and Nozick, whose ideas we have already touched upon in this book. Indeed, the debate between Nozick and Rawls that we encountered in Chapter 5 is an academic version of the ideological debate between the classical and new liberal traditions.

➜ See Chapter 22 for a discussion of liberal political economy.

Liberal Thought

One of the key questions about liberal ideology is the degree to which the two types of liberal-ism identified previously are compatible. Bearing this in mind, we can attempt to ascertain the core meaning of the ideology. The core meaning of liberalism can be found in the concepts of

➜ See Chapter 5 for Nozick's critique of Rawls's Theory of Justice and Chapter 1 for a considera-tion of the New Right theory of the state.

liberty, tolerance, individualism, and a particular kind of equality. Liberty is *the* concept right at the centre of liberal thought, 'the primary value in the liberal creed' as Goodwin (2014: 46) puts it. For some liberal thinkers, liberty is seen as an intrinsic good; for others, such as J. S. Mill, it is a means to an end in the sense that its value is in the possibilities for self-development it produces.

➡ See Chapter 5 for a discussion of the distinction between positive and negative liberty.

The classical liberal tradition emphasizes negative liberty. Freedom is about removing external constraints. The new liberal tradition emphasizes positive liberty, whereby the state can remove obstacles to freedom. In emphasizing the collective role of the state, the new liberalism has been accused of abandoning 'true' liberalism by relegating the role of the individual. In its defence, advocates of the new liberalism argue that liberty can only be maximized through the enabling role of the state.

A corollary of liberty is the liberal focus on the individual. As exemplified by the social contract tradition of Hobbes and Locke, the individual is prior to society. The notion of rights is prominent in liberal thought precisely because of the prominence given to individuals. Individuals ought to be protected against society and the state, as seen in J. S. Mill's classic defence of individual liberty. At its extreme level, individualism denies the state's right to intervene in any aspect of the life of the individual. As we have seen, even the classical version of liberalism sees some role for the state, and therefore extreme libertarianism is best located in anarchist thought (see the end of the chapter).

➡ See Chapter 2 for discussion of the liberal social contract tradition.

The liberal focus on the individual stems from the belief that individuals are rational, and able to determine their own best interests, which they will always pursue. Thus, in the economic realm, individuals, according to the classical liberal position at least, are best left to their own devices as consumers and producers. The 'hidden hand' of the market will then ensure that economic utility is achieved.

The prominence of the individual in liberal thought involves the downgrading of the community. The community is merely an aggregate of individuals with competing interests and values. There is no room for regarding the community as a unified entity, as in the political philosophy of those such as Hegel and Rousseau. The distinction between the community and the individual is the source of the modern debate between liberals and communitarian thinkers. Communitarians criticize the liberal social contract tradition which envisages humans in a pre-social state. For communitarians, political principles must be derived from actual existing societies which provide identity and meaning for individuals.

➡ See Chapter 2 for a discussion of communitarianism.

The liberal approach to equality is distinctive. Liberals regard individuals as of equal value, but they do not accept equality of outcome. Rather, the liberal position is characterized by equality of opportunity, whereby fairness is ensured because individuals—in theory at least—starting from the same position, are rewarded for their efforts. Of course, the free market does not allow for genuine equality of opportunity because individuals do not start out in life from the same position as some inherit advantages gained by the antecedents. It might be argued that the state intervention advocated by the new liberals actually makes equality of opportunity more of a reality. The introduction of free education and healthcare, in particular, has the effect of equalizing life chances. However, as we saw in the case of Nozick's critique of Rawls, redistributive policies can reduce the role of incentives, a central plank of the liberal emphasis on self-reliance.

➡ See Chapter 5 for a further discussion of equality.

6

SOCIALISM

The word socialism was first used in a working-class publication called the *Cooperative Magazine* in 1827. Socialism is an ideology, like liberalism, that is a child of the industrial revolution and the creation of the industrial working class. Socialism has been associated with working-class parties, but it differs from mere trade unionism in the sense that it seeks to transform society in cooperative and egalitarian directions. Somewhat ironically, indeed, many of the advocates of socialism have in fact been middle class, and they have always faced a certain degree of hostility from working-class organizations.

Historical Development

The historical development of socialism pivots around the giant figure of Karl Marx. The pre-Marxian socialists have often, following Marx himself, been described as utopian. Three thinkers—Claude-Henri Saint-Simon (1760–1825), Charles Fourier (1772–1837), and Robert Owen (1771–1858)—are usually regarded as the founders of socialism. Marx regarded these thinkers as utopian in the sense that they regarded socialism as ethically desirable but had no contextual historical analysis of the possibilities of bringing about political change. Marx, by contrast, developed what he called a 'scientific' socialism which not only argued that socialism was ethically desirable but also attempted to explain the historical conditions that would bring it about.

➡ See Chapter 2 for a discussion of Marxist ideas on the state.

Marx's ideas have had a huge impact on the development of socialism, and indeed world politics in general. Lenin and the Bolsheviks revised his ideas to suit Russia's circumstances, and after the Russian Revolution in 1917, the Soviet state, built on Marxist ideas, was created. This historical event resulted in the division of world socialism into two camps; on the one hand, communism, centring on the so-called 'Third International' of world communist organizations, and, on the other, social democracy. The roots of this division lie in the political development of the German SPD prior to 1914, where there was an intellectual debate between the revisionists and the orthodox Marxists.

The revisionists, whose leading exponent was Eduard Bernstein (1850–1932), sought to revise Marxism in light of contemporary circumstances. In most central and western European countries, this revisionist Marxism, later restyled as social democracy, predominated. Marxism had less influence in Britain where more moderate socialist organizations had always predominated. From 1917, Marxists looked to Russia for their inspiration. Originally dominated by Lenin, his mantle was passed on, first to a three-pronged leadership involving Trotsky, Stalin, and Bukharin, and then to Stalin alone.

The collapse of communism in Eastern Europe has seriously weakened the Marxist version of socialism as a practical proposition. Social democratic parties vied for power in Western European countries for much of the twentieth century. However, it is widely thought that the decline of the traditional working class and the reality of globalisation—which limits the ability of social democratic governments to initiate radical change within the borders of the nation state and necessitates competing within a neo-liberal global market—have been important factors in ushering in a decline of left-wing politics in Western Europe (Keating and McCrone, 2013). Against that negative position, however, is the point that socialism has a new lease of life as the focal point of the attack on global inequality. In addition, the prospects of left-wing parties have improved as a consequence of the effects of the financial crash in 2008, particularly in Greece and Spain, and, to a lesser extent, in the UK (Heywood, 2017: 133–5) (**see Box 6.3**).

Means and Ends in Socialist Thought

As we have seen, all ideologies are a collection of ideas and it is often difficult to pinpoint core and peripheral ideas in their morphologies. Socialism, above all ideologies, would seem to have the largest number of competing varieties. As a result, it is tempting to use the word 'socialisms' rather than 'socialism', the former being the title of a well-known book on the subject (Wright, 1996).

In order to understand the key divisions within the socialist tradition, it is useful to distinguish between *means* and *ends*; between, that is, the methods that socialists have thought appropriate to achieve their objectives and the end goals or objectives. In terms of means, the key distinction has been between revolutionary and evolutionary socialism. In the revolutionary camp we need to make a further distinction. There are those, most notably Marx, who tended towards the assumption that a revolution would be a popular uprising. On the other hand, there are those, such as Lenin, whose preference was for a coup involving a disciplined band of revolutionaries. It was Lenin's advocacy of a disciplined party—the Bolsheviks—which created the structure that after the revolution became the Communist Party, a political party that dominated the Soviet Union for decades after 1917.

Evolutionary socialism has been the main alternative to revolution. It is based on the belief that with universal suffrage, socialism can be achieved through political democracy. It assumes, therefore, that the state can be responsive to working-class interests once enfranchised. This formed a central part of the division of socialist thought after the Russian Revolution.

A key thinker here was the German socialist, Eduard Bernstein. In his book, popularly known as 'Evolutionary Socialism' (1961), Bernstein argued that capitalism had not developed in the way that Marx had predicted, and it was therefore time for Marxists to revise Marx's central ideas. The working class was not becoming more impoverished, and the move towards universal suffrage meant that a socialist party could win power through political democracy. Rather than being a historical inevitability, socialism, for Bernstein, would come about as a result of a growing perception of its desirability. It is questionable whether Bernstein can be described as a Marxist. His socialism is more akin to the social democratic tradition, and, indeed, Bernstein was heavily influenced by the British socialist organization, the Fabian Society.

Socialists, too, disagree about the ends of socialism. Two dimensions to this are most apparent. First, some socialists see a crucial role for the state in a socialist society, whereas others envisage a decentralized communal society. Again, the contrast between Marx and Lenin is apposite here. Marx suggests that once class conflict is eliminated, there will be no need for a state, since the capitalist state is merely a vehicle for the ruling class. At times, Marx's vision of a future communist society envisages the absence of any centralized administrative structure. This approaches an anarchist position (see Anarchism: p. 135). As we saw earlier in this book, this rather optimistic scenario has been questioned. Lenin did recognize the need for a state, at least for a period of time after the communist revolution. This so-called 'dictatorship of the proletariat' was designed to defeat the enemies of the revolution, a very real threat at the time. The state, of course, remained in the Soviet Union long after this. (**See Box 6.2**.)

The second dimension of socialism's ends concerns the balance between public and private ownership of the means of production. Within socialist thought there is a continuum with complete public ownership at one end of the spectrum to relatively little at the other. This debate has been central to socialist debate within the West (**see Box 6.3**). Socialists have also differed over the form that public ownership should take, with the state corporation model challenged, particularly since the 1960s, by more decentralized forms involving workers' cooperatives and even a market socialism model (Miller, 1990).

Key Socialist Principles

Behind these differences of means and ends, it is possible to identify a number of core socialist principles. The first of them is *a particular view of* human nature. Socialists tend to have an optimistic view of human nature, which, they suggest, is capable of being shaped by social, economic, and political circumstances. Liberals and conservatives tend to regard human beings as selfish, individualistic, and materialistic. Socialists, on the other hand, regard such behaviour as socially

> **KEY QUOTE** BOX 6.2
> Marx's Vision of Communism

Marx wrote very little about what a future communist society would look like. In the *Communist Manifesto*, however, he does say this:

When, in the course of development, class distinctions have disappeared, and all the production has been concentrated in the whole nation, the public power will lose its political character . . . If the proletariat during its contest with the bourgeoisie is compelled, by the force of circumstances, to organize itself as a class, if, by means of a revolution, it makes itself the ruling class, and, as such, sweeps away by force the old conditions of production, then it will, along with these conditions, have swept away the conditions for the existence of class antagonisms and of classes generally, and will thereby have abolished its own supremacy as a class. (Marx and Engels, 1976: 105)

Questions
1. Why does Marx think that classes will cease to exist under a communist regime?
2. Does this passage provide a justification for the Soviet state?
3. Can the 'public power' have a non-political character?

KEY DEBATE BOX 6.3
Socialism in the British Labour Party

Although there have been various Marxist-inspired left-wing parties and movements, socialism in Britain has been dominated by debates within the Labour Party. The Labour Party, as Ralph Miliband (1972) has emphasized, has always been committed to a parliamentary route to socialist or social democratic ends. Debate has tended to take place instead about the degree of public ownership seen as desirable. At each period of the Labour Party's existence, there have been those (the Independent Labour Party in the 1920s, the Bevanites in the 1950s, and the Bennites in the 1970s and 1980s—named, respectively, after their leading exponents Aneurin Bevan and Tony Benn) who have wanted the party to move further and faster towards greater public ownership.

The key question is, where do we draw the line? When does a particular balance between public and private ownership cease to be socialist and become something else, such as social democracy? This debate became particularly vociferous in Britain after the 1945 Labour Government had undertaken extensive nationalization. In the 1950s, while the Bevanites wanted to go further along the public ownership route, the Gaitskellites—named after the Labour leader Hugh Gaitskell (1906–63)—were prepared to settle for the mixed economy as a permanent state of affairs, with Tony Crosland's book *The Future of Socialism* (1980) providing the intellectual ballast for this so-called 'revisionist' position.

There are those who have argued that, since the 1990s, there has been a new or 'neo' revisionism within British (and European) mainstream left-wing parties, necessitated by the shrinkage of the working class—itself a product of deindustrialization—and the impact of globalization, which has diluted their social democratic credentials (Heffernan, 2000). Thus, under Blair's leadership, the Labour Party abandoned Clause IV of the Party's constitution (which committed the Party to

Photo 6.2 Jeremy Corbyn, the former Labour Party leader elected in 2015, shifted the party to the left. *Shutterstock RF: Bart Lenoir/Shutter stock.com*

→

nationalization), and Labour governments in 1997–2010 largely accepted the market, rather than the state, as the main instrument of economic policy. The effects of the financial crash in particular have reenergized the left and, since his election as leader in 2015, Jeremy Corbyn—once a staunch supporter of the left-winger Tony Benn—has shifted Labour to the left once again.

Questions
1. Is social democracy really a form of socialism?
2. What ideological characteristics must a social democratic party possess?

conditioned rather than innate. A socialist society would promote values of cooperation, fellowship, and compassion, thereby shaping the values of its citizenry.

The second core socialist principle is *equality*. For many, equality is the defining feature of socialism. Unlike liberals, socialists are more likely to advocate equality of outcome. This is partly because socialists see inequality as resulting not so much from differences of ability but in terms of an individual's location in a social structure. Educational attainment, in particular, is seen by socialists as a classic example of inequality at work since it is heavily influenced by social class. Equality of outcome is promoted by socialists, too, because they have a less pessimistic view of human nature. For liberals, inequality is necessary in order to provide incentives. For socialists, on the other hand, human nature can be moulded to the point where individuals would be willing to work for the good of society, irrespective of the lack of material incentives available.

➡ See Chapter 5 for a further discussion of the concept of equality.

The third core principle of socialism is *community and cooperation*. There is an emphasis in socialism on what humans can achieve collectively rather than individually. Therefore, there is an emphasis on the achievement of collective rather than individual goals through cooperation. Community is linked to the other two core socialist values in the sense that common ownership and equality are obvious ways in which communal values can be furthered.

Socialism, Authoritarianism, and Utopia

Many have suggested that the socialist vision is utopian. The word utopia, originally coined by Thomas More in the sixteenth century, is a play on two Greek words translated as good and nowhere. Utopian, therefore, refers to the 'good society which is nowhere', or, to put it another way, the society which is impossible of realization. This leads to the question whether socialism is similarly unrealizable.

Liberals and especially conservatives brand utopias as unrealistic and unrealizable and suggest that socialism comes into this category. According to this argument, socialists develop utopian visions of a better society in which human beings can achieve genuine emancipation and fulfilment as members of a community. The problem, however, is that such a society demands too much of its citizens. This might be acceptable if its effects are benign but, so the argument continues, to maintain such an egalitarian society inevitably results in an authoritarian state which has continually to intervene to prevent differential levels of talent and effort from eroding the socialist distribution of goods (Popper, 1962).

Such a critique is directed at the Soviet style of communism whose overbearing state was, it is argued, a direct product of socialist ideas. Whether or not this critique is justified, it is clear that the authoritarian label cannot be attached to the social democratic variety of socialism which, in any case, draws from liberalism as much as it does from Marxian varieties of socialism. Even then, as we saw in Chapter 5, there is a libertarian critique of redistributive versions of liberalism that claims that it illegitimately infringes liberty.

KEY POINTS

- Socialism is dominated by the work of Karl Marx, who described his socialism as scientific as opposed to the utopian variety of those socialists who preceded him.
- At the turn of the twentieth century, socialism divided into two camps, with the communists on one side and the revisionists (later to be social democrats) on the other.
- To classify different varieties of socialism, it is useful to distinguish between means and ends.
- Core socialist principles include an optimistic view of human nature, equality of outcome, and community and cooperation.
- Some argue that socialism is utopian and has authoritarian tendencies.

CONSERVATISM

Elements of conservative thought can be found throughout history. Indeed, the Greek philosopher Plato, in urging the maintenance of the rule of the intellectual elite—the Philosopher Kings as he called them—can be regarded as the first conservative thinker. However, conservative thought received its greatest fillip as a response to the Enlightenment tradition. Whereas liberalism and socialism bought into the progressive and rationalistic values of the Enlightenment, conservatism provides a negative response to it. The classic text here is Edmund Burke's (1729–97) vitriolic attack on the French Revolution of 1789, first published in 1790 (1968). (**See Box 6.4.**)

Conservative political movements have not been ideologically uniform. In much of Europe, for example, they have historically been anti-liberal, reactionary, and authoritarian, whereas in Britain, conservatism has been tinged with liberalism. The nineteenth-century Conservative Party was notable for the social reforming administrations of Peel and Disraeli, and later, following the creation of the post-1945 settlement by the British Labour Party, the Conservative Party largely accepted the dominance of social democratic ideas. Following the breakdown of the social democratic consensus in the 1970s, however, the Conservative Party became heavily influenced by the New Right. A similar shift to the right was noticeable in the USA with the election of President Ronald Reagan in 1980.

With its emphasis on the unconstrained free market, the New Right had more in common with classical liberalism than conservatism. Certainly, the ideological character of Thatcher's leadership was inimical to the pragmatism of conservative thought. However, the New Right also embodied a number of traditional conservative values—such as law and order, respect for authority, and the importance of traditional values—and the Thatcher governments were prepared to use the state to enforce them. This ideological mix was described by one British academic commentator as 'the free economy and the strong state' (Gamble, 1994).

➡ See Chapter 2 for a discussion of the New Right theory of the state.

SHORT BIOGRAPHY BOX 6.4
Edmund Burke (1729–97)

Burke was born in Dublin in 1729. After studying at Trinity College in Dublin, he moved to England in 1750 where he qualified as a lawyer before settling on a career in politics. He became an MP in 1776 in a rotten borough before winning a seat in Bristol in 1775. He died in 1797, a rich man with an estate of some 600 acres in Buckinghamshire.

Burke's fame emerged from his writing and speeches on important political issues of his day. He is best known for his vitriolic best-selling attack on the French Revolution, but he also wrote and spoke on the British constitution, and the relations between Britain and India and the American colonies. There is a, much discussed, apparent contradiction in Burke's writings in the sense that he opposes the French Revolution but supports the American Revolution and the Indian opposition to British colonial rule.

Some put this down to an unstated fear that the French Revolution threatened the emerging capitalist class in Britain. Others argue that there was no inconsistency since Burke was applying his political principles in a logical way. Thus, he was opposed to the French revolutionaries because they were overthrowing an established order on the grounds of abstract rational principles. On the other hand, he supported the Americans and the Indians because they were seeking to uphold long-held traditions against the encroachment of the British.

Photo 6.3 Edmund Burke was best known for his vitriolic attack on the French Revolution.

Shutterstock RF: Bart Lenoir/Shutterstock.com

In the USA, so-called 'neoconservatism' has been more successful in challenging traditional conservatism. This has combined a brand of social authoritarianism with nationalism to create a reactionary movement which has had a large impact on the direction of US domestic and foreign policy, particularly under the presidency of George W. Bush. The major intellectual adherent of neoconservatism in foreign policy has been the political thinker Leo Strauss (1899–1973). Strauss, with a Zionist background, argued that the USA should fight tyranny wherever it was found. Initially, this took the form of recommending a strong line against the Soviet Union, but since its collapse, the attention of 'neocons' has turned to the threat from religious fundamentalism, seen as a challenge to conservative values. The intervention in Iraq and Afghanistan can be seen as a product of neoconservative ideas.

Neoconservatism's relationship with the Trump presidency is complicated. Some neocons opposed Trump's election because of his opposition, during the campaign at least, to interventionist foreign policies and his apparent isolationism. However, since being elected, neocons have supported Trump's approach towards Iran and Venezuela, and his defence of Israel (the most recent, August 2019, manifestation being his sustained attacks on the new Muslim congresswomen Ilhan Omar and Rashida Tlaib who have openly condemned Israel's policy towards the Palestinians). However, neocons have opposed other aspects of Trump's foreign policy such as his withdrawal of troops from Syria and his willingness to engage in a positive manner with North Korea.

Conservative Thought

Determining the nature of conservative thought is not easy, not least because it tends to claim to be non-ideological, preferring practical principles and pragmatism over abstract reasoning. As a result, conservative thinkers have been reluctant to set out their position in a reasoned and codified fashion since to do so would be to engage in an exercise which they themselves condemn. This has been problematic, however, for taken literally, the word conservatism suggests a desire to conserve which has reactionary overtones. Conservatives, therefore, risk being accused of merely seeking to defend the status quo in order to defend existing privilege and power. This is unfortunate because conservatism can be seen as an ideology where 'certain fundamental convictions have been identified which constitute a distinct political standpoint' (Goodwin, 2014: 180).

Pride of place among these convictions is an *aversion to rationalism*. This rationalism was very much a product of the Enlightenment. It celebrated the ability of human beings to construct societies on the basis of rational principles such as—in the French Revolution—'liberty, equality, and fraternity'. There was no limit to the progress possible in human societies. For Michael Oakeshott (1901–90), a notable twentieth-century conservative, a rationalist 'stands . . . for independence of mind on all occasions, for thought free from obligation to any authority save the authority of reason' (Oakeshott, 1962: 1).

It was the rationalist temper of the French Revolution that Burke so savagely attacked. By trying to create a new society based on abstract principles, the French revolutionaries had destroyed the traditions and institutions that had evolved over the centuries. For Burke and conservatives in general, the social and political world is too complex to be susceptible of easy rational comprehension. Better then to rely on the tried and tested -traditions—what Burke describes as 'prejudices'—which contain the collective wisdom of a society gained over many generations.

A number of other conservative values derive from this attack on rationalism. In the first place, the *conservative model of society is organic rather than mechanical*. In other words, society cannot be taken apart and rearranged like the parts of a machine. Rather, society is a little-understood, complex, and interdependent organism. To change one part may have an unpredictable and undesirable impact on other parts. Burke is not saying that no change is ever permissible, but it should be gradual and moderate, taking care to preserve what is valuable in the organism. There is a much-challenged assumption here that what exists does actually have value and is functional for the well-being of society. Clearly, this is not always the case and conservatives are guilty of deriving an ought—existing traditions and institutions should be preserved—from an is—the mere existence of these traditions and institutions.

The second conservative value to derive from anti-rationalism is *human imperfection*. Conservatives are sceptical about the human capacity fully to understand their social and political environment. At the very least, collective wisdom of the past and present is preferable to the abstract reasoning of a few. We should as far as possible, therefore, stick with what we know. This scepticism about human capacities follows through into the conservative *advocacy of hierarchy*. As Plato had recognized, effective self-government is a myth. Some are innately more capable of governing than others. This is the reason behind Burke's well-known justification of MPs retaining autonomy from their constituents.

KEY POINTS

- Conservatism is a reaction to the Enlightenment tradition of political thought.
- The New Right has liberal and conservative elements.
- The underlying principles of conservatism are an aversion to rationality, an organic view of society, human imperfection, and a preference for hierarchy.

NATIONALISM

It is undoubtedly the case that the desire to organize political communities according to nationalistic principles has been of central importance in the past two centuries. Nationalism emerged in the nineteenth century, as the decline of monarchical power and authority eroded previous loyalties. People no longer regarded themselves as subjects and sought new ties and identities to organize their lives.

The search for national identity was initially a European phenomenon, centring on the striving for German and Italian unification, achieved in 1871 and 1861 respectively, and, after the end of the First World War, national self-determination as set out by the US President Woodrow Wilson in the peace settlement. After the Second World War, the centre of the striving for nationalism shifted to the colonies as countries in Africa and the Middle East, in particular, sought, and largely secured, their independence (**see Box 6.5**). In more recent times, there has been a resurgence in nationalism particularly in Eastern Europe after the collapse of the Soviet Union. Nationalism has continued to be the source of much conflict and bloodshed in countries and regions as diverse as Northern Ireland, the former Yugoslavia, Kosovo, Afghanistan, and Rwanda, and has played a large role in spawning populist parties and movements in the twenty-first century.

➜ See Chapters 7 and 15 for a discussion of populism.

Despite the fact that nationalism is an important political concept, however, there is a question mark about its ideological character, and an even bigger question mark over its normative worth. This is based partly on the belief that it is not a universal principle as not everyone can have their nationalist objectives realized. Indeed, the achievement of one person's nationalist desires (based, say, on religion) denies it to others (based, say, on language). Nationalism also lacks

> **! KEY CONCEPT** BOX 6.5
> Anti-Colonial Nationalism
>
> Anti-colonial nationalism is a phenomenon that began to emerge in the colonized world after the First World War, taking practical form in the widespread movement for decolonization in Africa, Asia, and the Pacific which followed the Second World War. Although directed against European domination, anti-colonial nationalism—which was an important factor in the collapse of European empires and national liberation—drew much of its inspiration from certain European liberal-democratic ideas about justice, human rights, and, especially, national self-determination (Neuberger, 2006: 516).
>
> States previously subject to colonial rule tend to be based on boundaries established by colonial powers bringing together many different ethnic groups in a single political unit. In some cases, such as in Indonesia, powerful national identities were forged out of the highly disparate elements that made up the colonial state (Reid, 2010: 110). In other cases, sub-state identities were created under colonial rule, some of which, as in Rwanda and Sudan, were to become highly problematic in later years (see Brown, 2000: 161).

political content. Its only concern is national identity. Unlike the other ideologies considered so far in this chapter, then, nationalism is not a set of interrelated ideas. It has nothing to say about the character of the political system within the nation-state, or what the role of political principles such as justice, rights, and liberty might be (Goodwin, 2014: 292). Also, unlike the other ideologies we have considered so far, there is a paucity of great works advocating nationalism. It is a subject area that has largely preoccupied political scientists but not many political theorists (Hoffman and Graham, 2006: 266).

At the very least, we can say that nationalism is a confused concept. It is a simple principle in that it holds that political organization ought to be based on national identity, but the bases of this identity have varied. These have included race and language (as in Germany), religion (as in Northern Ireland and the demands for Islamic states), culture, and membership of an existing state. A profitable distinction is between civic nationalism, on the one hand, and ethnic nationalism on the other, as made by the political scientist Hans Kohn (1944). More recently, anti-colonial nationalism has become equally important (**see Box 6.5**).

Civic nationalism refers to loyalty to the institutions and values of a particular political community. Ethnic nationalism, by contrast, refers to loyalty to a shared inheritance based on culture, language, or religion. Whereas the former is inclusive, open to anyone who wishes to sign up to the values and institutions of a particular community, the latter is exclusive in the sense that membership is inherited and not the product of a rational choice. Many separatist movements have been inspired by ethnic nationalism. These, most notably, have existed in Quebec in Canada, the Basque country in Spain, and Scotland and Wales within the UK.

Because of its inclusive character, civic nationalism would seem to be less of a threat to political order than the exclusivity inherent in ethnic nationalism. This distinction can be exaggerated, however, because even a political community based on loyalty to institutions and values has borders which have to be protected. Inclusion, while not based on religion or race, must be based on something and this has the potential for conflict. However, despite its negative image, nationalism need not necessarily result in division and conflict. Liberal nationalism, for instance, while for some too romantic, sees nations as the source of internal unity and envisages cooperation between nations.

Such is the negativity associated with nationalism, however, that some traditions of political thought seek to envisage a world where national identity ceases to be an organizing principle of people's lives. Liberal internationalism, for instance, promotes interdependence between nations, either through the creation of supranational institutions—such as the League of Nations and now the United Nations—or through free trade between nations. For Marx and many in the socialist tradition, class, rather than the nation, is the chief cleavage in society. Nationalism is therefore misplaced, seen as a device to distract the working class from their exploitation. The proletariat should instead look towards unity across nations if their liberation is to be achieved, and a peaceful world created.

KEY POINTS

- Nationalism has had an enormous impact on the development of world politics since the nineteenth century.
- Many argue that nationalism is not, properly speaking, an ideology and that it is of dubious normative worth.
- The bases on which nationalism has been justified vary.
- A profitable organizing distinction is between civic nationalism, ethnic nationalism and anti-colonial nationalism.

FASCISM

Unlike the other ideologies we have discussed in this chapter, fascism is a twentieth—century phenomenon. It is particularly associated with the relatively short-lived, and terrifying, regimes led by Mussolini (1883–1945) in Italy and Hitler (1889–1945) in Germany in 1925–43 and 1933–45 respectively, although there were also fascist movements in the 1930s outside of Europe and particularly in Asia (Larsen, 2001). For some commentators, fascism is regarded as a distinctly inter-war phenomenon (Trevor-Roper, 1947). Others disagree with this limitation (Kitchen, 1976) (**see Box 6.7**). More attention has been paid to the causes of the rise of fascism than its ideological character. Fascism is seen, for instance, as a product of particular political and historical circumstances, or as a product of a flawed human psychology, or of moral decay (Vincent, 1995: 145–50).

Fascism represents an extreme form of nationalism and authoritarianism. Unlike other forms of nationalism, however, fascism is accompanied by a wider set of ideas. Some of these ideas are distasteful and implausible. In addition, fascism rejects abstract intellectualizing in favour of action, instinct, and emotion and as a result there are few intellectual works on which to rely, the principal exceptions being those of the Italian fascist Giovanni Gentile (1875–1944) and Hitler's *Mein Kampf* (1926/1969), the latter being of some use in explaining the character of the ideology. An added difficulty of studying fascism is that the Italian variety is different in significant respects from the German, not least in the latter's treatment of race and its greater extremism, and there is a case, therefore, for considering Nazism as a distinct ideological phenomenon.

Despite these caveats, it would be a mistake to regard fascism as non-ideological. It is best understood in terms of its oppositional mentality. Fascism is, above all, anti-Enlightenment. It therefore opposes Enlightenment ideas such as liberalism, democracy, reason, and individualism. It is also profoundly anti-Marxist. Certain elements of fascism are similar to conservatism, in particular the focus on the organic state, but fascism is also revolutionary and, in the case of Germany at least, also racist and nationalistic. Fascism's opposition to liberalism and individualism stems from the belief that it is the community that creates individuals. Without it, they are nothing. It is therefore opposed to the liberal position that humans can be envisaged living in a pre-social state. Rather, their identity is forged through membership of a community.

Accompanying the social nature of individuals is an authoritarianism which consists of the elite view whereby some individuals are regarded as superior to others, and thereby fitter to rule than others. (**See Box 6.6**.) The masses are regarded as largely ignorant needing to be led by an elite, and particularly by one all-powerful leader, a Fuhrer or Duce. Italian fascists, in particular, were influenced by the elite theory of the state we encountered in Chapter 2. As we saw, elite thinkers such as Pareto, Mosca, and Michels regarded elite rule as inevitable. This was largely put forward as an empirical theory with limited normative overtones. What elite theory did, however, was to provide a justification for the fascist belief in the inevitability of hierarchy and the herd-like character of the masses.

 See Chapter 2 for a discussion of the elite theory of the state.

Fascism's totalitarian tendencies make it an extreme form of authoritarianism. In fascist theory, it is the state that confers meaning upon individual lives and, as a result, individuals should be subservient to it. This provides a justification for the totalitarian state, one in which the individual is subsumed in the state's greater goal, largely achieved through technological means. In Italy, in particular, the role of corporations was, theoretically at least, to provide the means whereby society—and particularly employer and employee organizations—were to be incorporated into the state.

In German fascism, in particular, this emphasis on inequality and hierarchy took on a racial character, with the German Aryan race regarded, as a result of the adoption of various pseudo-scientific theories, as superior to other racial groups, and particularly Jews and Negroes. A belief

---

! KEY CONCEPT BOX 6.6
Elitism in Political Thought

The concept of elitism has been used in the context of a number of the ideological traditions discussed in this chapter. It is important to recognize the different ways in which the concept is being used. The classical elitist theories discussed in Chapter 2, and used to buttress the claims of fascism, were putting forward an empirical theory arguing that elites will always exist, whatever the claims of democracy. They were not claiming that such a form of rule was desirable. Both fascism and conservatism, however, are using the term in a normative sense to argue that the rule of an elite is not only inevitable but is also desirable. In national socialism, if not Italian fascism, this elitism took on a racial connotation which is absent from conservatism. The idea of an elite norm derives from Plato who advocates the rule of an intellectual elite.

CASE STUDY BOX 6.7
Neo-Nazism

There has been a large number of neo-Nazi organizations and movements in the post-Second World War period, although, for obvious reasons, its adherents rarely use that term. Their goal has been to revive the ideology of national socialism, or some variant of it. The neo-Nazi phenomenon exists in many parts of the world including the USA and many European countries, including, most notably, Austria, Russia, Belgium, Croatia, and France, as well as in non-Western countries such as India, Pakistan, Taiwan, Iran, Brazil, and Costa Rica (see https://www.jewishvirtuallibrary.org/neo-nazism). It has even emerged in Germany, particularly after reunification in the 1990s, despite the extensive programme of denazification after 1945. Even Israel has not been immune, as immigrants from the former Soviet Union, some of whom do not identify as Jews, have exported extreme right-wing views.

There was little overt neo-Nazi activity in Europe until the 1960s. Since then, neo-Nazis have engaged in a number of common activities. Some have competed in elections; Holocaust denial has been common, or at least the claim that it needs to be contextualized with reference to human rights abuses of the allies; Nazi regalia has been promoted; attempts have been made to gain support in student organizations; and violence, against immigrants, Jews, and Muslims has been common and this has sometimes involved murder. While their activities are often shocking and newsworthy, the membership of neo-Nazi organizations remains small, although, particularly since the financial crash in 2008, radical right-wing parties, some of whom might be described as fascist, have had some electoral success (Schain et al., 2002; Mudde, 2007).

in the German nation or *Volk* fed into a militant, aggressive, and expansionist nationalism. The goal of nationalism was therefore to establish the 'master race' across the globe, by a process of natural selection drawn from social Darwinism, putting into servitude, or eliminating, inferior races in the process. War and conflict was seen as inherently virtuous and character-building as well as serving the goal of racial superiority.

KEY POINTS

- Fascism is anti-democratic, anti-liberal, and totalitarian
- Fascists reject abstract intellectualizing in favour of action.
- Fascism is best understood in terms of its oppositional mentality.
- Central fascist themes are the emphasis on the state's role in creating meaning for individuals, and an elitist view of humans. In Germany, the belief in the superiority of some humans took on a racial dimension.

ANARCHISM

Anarchism is the last of the traditional ideologies we will consider in this chapter. Anarchism has many similarities with the liberal and, particularly, socialist traditions and might have been considered in this chapter at an earlier point. It has been left until last, however, because, although it has an impeccable intellectual pedigree, it is extremely questionable whether anarchism has had any lasting impact, or is capable of having any impact, on the development of modern politics.

Anarchism dates back to the nineteenth century. Like a number of ideologies, anarchist thought has come in a number of varieties, although Goodwin (2014: 134) is probably right to say that the primary link is with the socialist tradition. Thus, anarchists such as Proudhon (1809–65), Bakunin (1814–76), and Kropotkin (1842–1921) were all involved in practical socialist politics within the socialist International, engaging in debate, and regularly falling out, with Marx the dominant intellectual figure within it. One of the first anarchist thinkers, William Godwin (1756–1836), was an exponent of the liberal, individualist school of anarchism, but this is particularly associated with a group of twentieth-century American thinkers, and most notably Murray Rothbard (1926–95).

Despite the many differences between anarchists, they share an abhorrence of the state, which they regard as an illegitimate, even criminal, type of organization illegitimately exercising force over individuals and society and reducing the liberty of the people. Obviously, this simple principle raises many questions. In the first place, there is a question mark over what anarchists are actually opposing. Is it just the state or is it the state, government, and any form of authority structure? Clearly, if the latter, then anarchism does rely on an optimistic view of human nature. In fact, anarchist thinkers differ here, with some holding that human nature is intrinsically good, and others holding that it is socially determined, and therefore can be shaped by the social and political environment. Whatever the exact form of the theory, anarchists all tend to argue that an anarchist society will be one in which the people will be morally correct, doing what is required of them.

Even assuming that human nature is generally good, anarchists still face problems. How are the functions of the state to be performed? One answer, suggested by some anarchists, is that the free market could take on this role. One problem here is the inequality likely to be caused if the market is responsible for providing functions such as education and health. Another is the authority deficit likely to follow from a private police force responsible for tackling crime and social deviancy. For socialist and communist anarchists, similarly, it is unlikely that their egalitarian objectives can be met without a body, such as the state, to ensure they come about. Moreover, if an authority structure is necessary to provide egalitarian outcomes, it will, of course, be counter to the anarchist argument that this will reduce freedom.

Hoffman (1975) tries to rescue anarchism. He argues that the anarchist mistake was to regard the state and the government as synonymous, whereas this is to confuse force and constraint. The state exercises force, and this is what anarchists are opposed to, but government, while inevitably requiring constraints, is not an institution exercising force. Therefore, 'to link the state and government as twin enemies of freedom is to ignore the fact that stateless societies have governments, and that even in state-centric societies, the role of government is positive and empowering'. It follows then that 'without a distinction between state and government it is impossible to move beyond the state' (Hoffman and Graham, 2006: 259). This does not entirely let anarchists off the hook, however. This is because government, without a state, relies on authority since it has no means of force to ensure its decisions are obeyed. This rather takes us back to square one; that is, how will such a society deal with those who refuse to accept the authority of the government?

Compared with the other ideologies we have considered in this chapter, anarchism would appear to have had little influence on modern politics. Strong anarchist movements existed between the 1880s and the 1930s, and anarchists briefly held power during the Spanish Civil War (Vincent, 1995: 117). Since then, there have been anarchist tendencies present in the 1960s counter-culture, the student protests, and, more recently, in the environmental and anti-globalization movements. It has remained a peripheral ideology however, tainted, however unjustly, with the charge that it is a recipe for confusion and chaos.

> **KEY POINTS**
>
> - Anarchism is primarily an offshoot of socialism.
> - Anarchists share an abhorrence of the state, but this principle raises many difficult questions which many argue anarchists cannot effectively answer.
> - Anarchism has had relatively little influence on modern politics.

CONCLUSION

In this chapter we have examined a variety of traditional ideologies. Quite clearly, they have exercised an extraordinary influence on world politics, not always in the way their adherents intended. Indeed, such has been the negative impact of at least some of the ideologies discussed previously that since the middle of the twentieth century, political thinkers have been much more circumspect about offering the kind of overarching interpretations of the world, or 'metanarratives', that ideologies traditionally offered.

Ideologies since then have been much less ambitious and much less certain. The ideologies that have emerged in this different climate—such as postmodernism and environmentalism—are discussed in the next chapter. For now, we should say that it is easy to see why these new ideologies have become more important in recent years. Unlike the nineteenth century, there is now much greater scepticism about the ability of human beings to master the world. In this sense, the influence of the Enlightenment has begun to wane. We are now much more cautious about universal ideologies which proclaim to understand the world and know how to put it right.

KEY QUESTIONS

1. What is an ideology?
2. Does new liberalism develop or depart from classical liberalism?
3. Is equality a necessary component of liberalism?
4. Is modern social democracy socialist?
5. Is socialism utopian and authoritarian?
6. To what extent can conservatism be considered an ideology?
7. Is nationalism an ideology?
8. Did fascism die with Hitler and Mussolini?
9. Assess the claim that fascism is concerned more with political action than political ideas.
10. Is anarchism naïve and unrealistic?

FURTHER READING

Bellamy, R. (2000), *Rethinking Liberalism* (London: Pinter).
This is a collection of essays on the development of liberal thought by a noted scholar.

Freeden, M. (1996), *Ideologies and Political Theory* (Oxford: Oxford University Press).
This is a monumental work that not only covers ideologies in depth but also offers an innovative way of thinking about them.

Freeden, M., Sargent, L., and Stears, M. (2015), *The Oxford Handbook of Political Ideologies* (Oxford: Oxford University Press).
A very useful account of different ideological positions.

Goodwin, B. (2014), *Using Political Ideas* (Chichester: John Wiley & Sons, 6th edn).
This is an excellent, well-established, introduction to the ideologies discussed in this chapter.

O'Sullivan, N. (1976), *Conservatism* (London: Macmillan).
This is a well-regarded account of conservative thought.

Passmore, K. (2014), *Fascism: A Very Short Introduction* (Oxford: Oxford University Press).
As its title suggests, this is a short book but it provides an authoritative sketch of fascism.

Wright, A. (1996), *Socialisms* (London: Routledge, 2nd edn).
This reflects well the diversity of socialist thought.

 For additional material and resources, please visit the Online Resources at:
www.oup.com/he/garner4e

CHALLENGES TO THE DOMINANT IDEOLOGIES

READER'S GUIDE

This chapter explores a range of more contemporary ideologies which challenge the traditional ideologies encountered in Chapter 6. They differ from traditional ideologies in a number of ways. They are, first, less optimistic about the ability of ideologies to construct an overarching explanation of the world, not surprisingly since they emerged in the aftermath of the catastrophic impact of some traditional ideologies. They also respect difference and variety. This is a product of social and economic change which has eroded the 'Fordist' economy, brought into being a number of powerful identity groups based on gender, culture, and ethnicity, and raised question marks over the environmental sustainability of current industrial practices.

A NEW KIND OF IDEOLOGY

Contemporary ideologies, explored in this chapter, should be seen in the context of growing scepticism about the utility of Enlightenment ideologies. They are much less ambitious and much less certain than the traditional ideologies discussed in Chapter 6. It is easy to see why these new ideologies—such as feminism, environmentalism, and multiculturalism—have become more important in recent years. Unlike the nineteenth century, there is now much greater scepticism about the ability of human beings to master the world. In this sense the influence of the Enlightenment has begun to wane. We are now much more cautious about universal ideologies which proclaim to understand the world and claim to know how to put it right.

➡ See Chapter 2 for a discussion of identity politics.

There are a number of other factors impacting on the character of contemporary ideologies. For instance, growing affluence, in some parts of the world at least, has made quality of life issues, such as the state of the natural environment, more pertinent. Likewise, social and economic change has reduced the homogeneity of social classes and created much more ethnically-diverse societies (**see Box 7.2**), thereby contributing to the growing importance of cultural identity as a source of division.

Postmodernism offers the most fundamental challenge to modernism. The claims of any one ideology that it is able to encompass total understanding of the social and political world are rejected. Postmodernism, therefore, celebrates difference, accepting the subjective nature of political ideologies. For postmodernists there are, in the words of Gamble (2000: 116), 'no foundations, no objective standards, no fixed points, above all no universalism and no knowledge which is not constructed and relative'. Some modern feminist thought also rejects monolithic value systems and seeks to promote the differences between men and women as politically important. The politics of difference is also explored in the context of multiculturalism, an antidote to the ethnic nationalism we discussed in Chapter 6. Another contemporary ideology, environmentalism, incorporates the growing scepticism about the human ability to master and control nature. Finally, the idea of the dominance of liberal values in the world is clearly at odds with the political and social importance of religious fundamentalism, based on a belief system very different from the largely secular Enlightenment ideologies looked at in the previous chapter.

KEY POINTS

- Contemporary ideologies challenge the metanarrative character of traditional ideologies.
- Traditional ideologies are regarded as too homogeneous and certain in their orientation.

POSTMODERNISM AND POPULISM

Postmodernism is a label given to a wide variety of theorists in a wide variety of disciplines, not just in the social sciences but in art, architecture, and cultural studies too. It is also associated with a wide variety of academics and authors, although perhaps the two with the biggest impact on political theory have been Michel Foucault (1926–84) and Jacques Derrida (1930–2004). It is difficult to provide one all-embracing definition of postmodernism as it contains so many different emphases and nuances. At the very least, the postmodern attitude points out the necessary limitations in the project to master the nature of reality. It is therefore a direct challenge to the modernist approach.

The modernist approach, influenced by the Enlightenment, is essentially a belief in the omnipotence of reason; a confidence in the ability of reason to penetrate to the essential truth of things and to achieve progress; and a foundationalist ontology which argues 'that a real world exists independently of our knowledge of it' (Stoker and Marsh, 2002: 11). We saw in the previous chapter

that, with the exception of conservatism, this confidence was present in post-Enlightenment ideologies, and principally liberalism and socialism. Postmodernism represents a challenge to this
confidence. It suggests that the search for ultimate answers is a futile exercise as the world is too
fractured and too diverse for grand explanatory schemes or theories. Instead, difference and variety are celebrated. Moreover, an anti-foundationalist ontology is promoted whereby the world
cannot be objectively observed but is socially constructed in a variety of ways. (**See Box 7.1**.)

➡ See
Chapter 18 for a
discussion of
postmodernism's
contribution to
international
relations.

For some postmodernists, the approach represents merely the description of a historical period
that comes after modernity. Therefore, it is not a normative theory as much as a signpost of the
way the world is heading in a more fractured and uncertain way. In politics, for instance, we can
note the collapse of the homogeneous Soviet bloc in Eastern Europe and its replacement by a plurality of democratic regimes. We can also point to the decline of regimented class politics in the
West altering the nature of party systems and voting behaviour. There is now room for a greater
plurality of issues, such as environmentalism and feminism, to emerge, and voting behaviour is
more individualistic, electoral choice being determined by a wider array of factors. The decline
in class politics is, in part, the product of the decline in manufacturing industry, and the rise of
a greater variety of employment patterns, so marking the end of the Fordist era. (**See Box 7.2**.)

The postmodern age is also equated with the end of a theory of knowledge; that is, postmodernists are held, by some, to adopt a relativistic attitude arguing that all knowledge claims, all
political and moral commitments, are redundant. Clearly, such a position is antithetical to much
of what we have been trying to do in the opening few chapters of this book, for a postmodernist

7

 KEY CONCEPT BOX 7.1
Ontology, Epistemology, and Foundationalism

Whereas an ontology is concerned with what there is to know about the world, epistemology
asks what can we know about what exists? A key ontological question is whether there is an
objectively observable 'real world' out there that is separate from our knowledge of it. Such
a question is not capable of being decided by empirical information. Foundationalists argue
that there is an observable real world out there and we can therefore set about trying to find
out about it epistemologically. So-called 'anti-foundationalists' argue that there is not, that the
world is socially constructed and that the key is to understand this process rather than scientif-
ically to explain the world.

KEY CONCEPT BOX 7.2
Fordism

Fordism refers to a form of large-scale mass-production that is homogeneous in both terms of
the products made and repetitive jobs that came with it. The social structure that came with this
form of mass-production consisted predominantly of unionized blue-collar workers who lived
similar lifestyles and tended to vote en bloc for left-of-centre parties. It is named after the mass
production of cars by the Ford Motor Company in the USA. We are now in a post-Fordist society
where the manual working class has declined as a more varied economic structure has emerged.

of this ilk would reject the effort to put a rational case for democracy or freedom, or to decide between the liberty claims of liberalism against the equality claims of socialism. As such, postmodernism has been criticized for being overly destructive. As Hay (2002: 217) points out, 'by confining itself to deconstruction postmodernism never risks exposing itself to a similar critique by putting something in place of that it deconstructs'. In other words, postmodernism is criticized for its oppositional nature. In Gamble's words (2000: 116), it offers 'no guidance as to what should be done about all the modernist processes which are in full flow'.

We could respond in two ways to this charge. In the first place, we could say that the deconstruction evident in postmodernism is a valid corrective to the certainties illegitimately displayed in much political analysis. It is not the postmodernist's fault that the world is not as modernists paint it to be. In addition, though, we should be careful about simplifying postmodernism. Hay (2002: 226), for instance, argues that postmodernism can be read in a more sympathetic fashion, as a position which merely questions existing beliefs in a sceptical fashion, rather than ruling them out completely. Indeed, 'postmodernism is perhaps best seen as a heightened sensitivity to the opinions and worldviews of others—a respect for others and other perspectives.'

For many, postmodernism is not an ideology so much as a critique of ideologies, or at least, particular types of ideology. Thus, some of the major textbook accounts of ideologies (for example, Vincent, 1995; Hoffman and Graham, 2006; Goodwin, 2014; Heywood, 2017) do not have separate chapters on postmodernism. Similarly, it might not be correct to describe another contemporary phenomenon—populism—as an ideology. Populism is a concept that was first used in the nineteenth century but is one which has only been commonly used in the current century. It reflects a distrust of political elites and the pitting of the people's instincts and beliefs (which are regarded as legitimate) against those of the establishment (which are not). As a political movement, therefore, it involves populist politicians making appeals directly to the 'people' over the heads of political elites who are regarded as corrupt and self-serving.

➡ See Chapter 15 for a further discussion of populism.

There is also a dispute about whether populism can be regarded as a separate and distinct ideology rather than a style of politics or type of political discourse (Mudde, 2018). Doubts about its distinctive character rest on its lack of political content, a quality it shares with nationalism. This is reflected in the fact that there are right- and left-wing varieties. It is true that right-wing xenophobic nationalistic populist movements—such as the Front National in France, the Freedom Party in Austria, the Five Star Movement in Italy, and UKIP in the UK—and right-wing populist leaders—such as Donald Trump (USA), Marine Le Pen (France), Rafael Correa (Ecuador), and Jair Bolsonaro (Brazil)—represent the dominant form of populism. However, they have been accompanied by left-wing populist movements—such as Syriza in Greece and Podemos in Spain—and a left-wing version of the doctrine has been advocated academically (see Mouffe, 2018).

➡ See Chapter 6 for a discussion of ethnic nationalism.

Both right- and left-wing versions of populism see the 'people' as a homogenous group. As a result, populism of all varieties is anti-pluralist and anti-individualistic. However, left-wing populism perceives the 'people' in class terms and sees its role as the defender of the poorest against political elites who defend the wealth and power of the privileged. It therefore sees politics in primarily economic terms. By contrast, right-wing populism also operates with a restricted characterization of the 'people' but, unlike the left, often defines it in terms of ethnicity. As a result, its major concerns are cultural—rather than economic—and it therefore focuses, most notably, on issues such as immigration and assimilation.

KEY POINTS

- Postmodernism represents a critique of particular ideologies rather than being an ideology in itself.
- The postmodern attitude points out the necessary limitations in the project of trying to master the nature of reality.
- There is a celebration of diversity and difference.
- Postmodernism has been criticized for being overly destructive without offering any guidance to action.
- Populism and postmodernism are both representative examples of post-Enlightenment ideologies, although there are doubts about whether they can be properly described as ideologies.

FEMINISM

There have been campaigns led by women, on such issues as the suffrage and temperance, since at least the nineteenth century, but feminism as a body of thought has only been a recognizable part of the political landscape since the 1960s. Feminism starts from the empirical claim that women are disadvantaged in a variety of ways. Other ideologies, such as fascism, regard the subordinate role of women as entirely natural and proper, whereas feminism is notable for its normative assertion that this subordination is wrong and ought to be overthrown. It has been common since the 1980s to divide feminism into liberal, socialist/Marxist, and radical strands, although since then feminism has further fragmented into a number of different, sometimes cross-cutting, categories. As a result, 'feminists are profoundly and at times bitterly divided, not only over political priorities and methods, but also over goals' (Bryson, 1999: 5).

➜ See Chapter 18 for coverage of feminism's contribution to international relations.

Liberal Feminism

So-called 'first wave' feminism, in the late nineteenth and early twentieth centuries, was characterized by its liberal character. The position of liberal feminism is that women ought to have the same liberal rights as men in the public sphere, where equality is demanded in the worlds of politics, education, and work. Two early key texts of liberal feminism advocating political and legal rights for women are Mary Wollstonecraft's *A Vindication of the Rights of Women*, and J. S. Mill's *The Subjection of Women*, originally published in 1792 and 1869 respectively. A modern statement of liberal feminism is provided by Betty Friedan (1963).

There is no doubt that substantial ground has been made in securing greater equality for women in the public arena. Women have legal and political rights in Western liberal democracies. Thus, after ferocious campaigning by the suffrage movement, women in Britain were granted the vote in 1918 and on the same terms as men in 1928. Other liberal democracies have followed suit. In the workplace, too, legislative initiatives against sex discrimination, such as the British Equal Pay Act, have helped to equalize male and female pay and working conditions. Marriage laws, too, are much more enlightened, women no longer being regarded as essentially the property of men.

Without doubt, too, however, greater strides are needed in both the workplace and political arena. Women's representation in the political arena, for instance, still lags far behind men. Research by the Inter-Parliamentary Union found that in 2019, women constituted only about 6% of heads of state and government, and there were only four countries—Rwanda, Cuba, Bolivia and the United Arab Emirates—where women constituted at least 50% of the representatives in lower houses of the legislature (the world average amounted to less than a quarter). In the UK, of the 650 MPs elected in the 2015 General Election, only 191 (29 per cent) were women and this increased to 208 (32 per cent) after the 2017 General Election and 220 (34 per cent) after the 2019 General Election.

Of course, there is the wider question of whether the adequate representation of women's interests requires that the legislature and executive mirrors exactly the gender composition of the wider society. On the one hand, it might be argued that the feelings and interests of women may be better understood and attended to if their interests are represented by other women (Phillips, 1995). On the other hand, it might be questioned whether women need to be represented by other women, particularly given that all politicians in liberal democracies face potential electoral defeat if it is thought they have not represented the electorate's interests. Moreover, to ensure that legislatures mirror the wider society in terms of gender composition requires a great deal of electoral engineering, such as the introduction of women-only shortlists for parliamentary seats. To do so, however, is to impose constraints on electoral choice which many would regard as undesirable.

→ See Chapter 11 for further discussion of representation in legislatures.

In the workplace, despite equal pay legislation, women's average earnings remain less than men's, not least because women do different jobs that tend to be valued less. The revelation that there is a significant gender pay gap in many major employers, including—most notably—the BBC, is testimony to this. Moreover, women remain the primary carers and are disadvantaged, and often deeply psychologically affected, by their enforced absence from work (Friedan, 1963). As a result of this continued inequality, some feminists argue for the introduction of measures such as positive discrimination (an example from the political realm would be the introduction of quotas for parliamentary candidates as mentioned previously) designed to redress the unfair competition between men and women.

Liberal feminists, however, still regard the state as the 'proper and indeed the only legitimate authority for enforcing justice in general and women's rights in particular' (Jaggar, 1983: 200). This will be achieved, they argue, through the elimination of sexist attitudes in society, through education, and pressure on the state applied through interest representation and political parties.

Radical Feminism

The 'second wave' of feminism, dating back to the 1960s, has been characterized by its radical strand. There are a variety of different interpretations of radical feminism, but they all share the position that the exploitation of women is more central and universal than liberal feminists think and is not merely a product of inequality in the public realm. The crucial point is the identification of a 'patriarchal' basis to society, not just, or most importantly, in the public realm but also in private family life and in relationships between men and women at all levels of society. (**See Box 7.3**.) Patriarchy means literally 'rule by the father'. For radical feminists, men's oppression of women, therefore, is all-pervading (Millett, 1971). Radicals argue, therefore, that 'it is not equality that women should want, but liberation' (Hoffman and Graham, 2006: 329).

> ## KEY QUOTE BOX 7.3
> ### Kate Millett on Patriarchy
>
> What goes largely unexamined, often even unacknowledged . . . in our social order, is the birth right priority whereby males rule females . . . It is one which tends moreover to be sturdier than any form of segregation, and more rigorous than class stratification . . . However muted its present appearance may be, sexual dominion obtains nevertheless as perhaps the most pervasive ideology of our culture and provides its most fundamental concept of power.
> (Millett, 1971: 25)

There are two important points to be made about radical feminism's denial of the public/private divide. In the first place, the importance that radical feminists attach to power relationships within the private sphere clearly puts it at odds with liberal feminism. From a liberal perspective, the state's role ought to be limited to the public sphere, whereas the private sphere remains a sphere of personal choice and individual freedom. For radical feminists, such an ideology leaves the source of men's power untouched. Thus, the focus on the state by political theorists has been heavily criticized by feminists. Pateman (1988), for example, argues that the social contract justification for the state (which we encountered in Chapter 3) assumes a sexual contract in the private sphere in which women contract with their husbands to protect them in return for accepting the rule of men in the family.

Second, as we saw in the Introduction, the fact that radical feminists operate with a broad definition of the boundaries of the political, raises question marks against the distinctiveness of the discipline of political studies. At the very least, it means that the topics political scientists ought to engage with are much more wide-ranging than has traditionally been the case.

Some radical feminists emphasize the sexual repression of women under patriarchy, that women have been effectively 'castrated' by the patriarchal culture which demands that they be passive and submissive creatures. This was the theme of Germaine Greer's book, *The Female Eunuch*, published in 1970. Women have also suffered death and physical mutilation at the hands of a patriarchal society, not least in the practice of female infanticide in China and India and female genital mutilation which is still widespread in many parts of the world. Unlike Marxist feminists (to be discussed later in this chapter), radical feminists regard patriarchy as an independent explanatory variable rooted in biology, and not therefore a product of the organization of economic classes in the capitalist system. This gender-based sphere of domination, radical feminists argue, is largely ignored by conventional political theory's focus on the state. As Pateman (1989: 3) points out, 'the public sphere', in conventional political theory 'is assumed to be capable of being understood on its own, as if it existed *sui generis*, independently of private sexual relations and domestic life'. By upholding patriarchal domination in families and civil society, the state therefore contributes to gender-based oppression. MacKinnon (1989: 80) puts this eloquently when she writes that: 'However autonomous of class the liberal state may appear, it is not autonomous of sex. Male power is systemic. Coercive, legitimized, and epistemic, it *is* the regime.' The feminist project, therefore, is for this form of oppression to be understood and eliminated. Only then can the state be feminized.

Race, Class, and Feminism

A number of feminist criticisms have been made of this radical strand. One is that by politicizing all aspects of our lives, feminism has totalitarian tendencies where 'feminists are to be held accountable to their "sisters" for every aspect of their behaviour' (Bryson, 1999: 28). Another is that it, falsely, creates an image of women as helpless victims, and men as the enemy, thus undervaluing what women have achieved and reducing the possibility of utilizing men as supporters of feminism.

Perhaps the most important critique is that radical feminism has a tendency to ignore the oppression of women based on race and class. In terms of the former, it has been argued that feminism has universalized the experiences of white (usually middle-class) women, thereby neglecting the specific oppression that women of colour have been subject to. There needs, therefore, to be a greater recognition of the particular experiences of black women whose life experiences cannot be merely subsumed under one all-encompassing feminist critique.

In terms of class, Marxist and socialist feminists put a different slant on women's exploitation (Mitchell, 1971; Barrett, 1988). The reality of capitalism is that, for both men and women, working life is equally exploitative, particularly for working-class women whom, they argue, feminists often ignore. For both men and women, therefore, socialist feminists argue for a transformation of society so that working lives become more amenable and domestic lives cease to have an economic function.

→ See Chapter 3 for an exploration of Marxist ideas on power and the state.

Marxist feminists, in particular, are much less sanguine than the liberal strand about the possibilities of women's position improving through focusing on the state. Here, elements of the Marxist theory of the state are utilized to explain the woman's position. In one influential version of this theory, women's domestic role, where they are subservient to men, is regarded as functional for the smooth running of the capitalist economy, freeing men to work. Thus, the capitalist state has an interest in maintaining women's inferior role (McIntosh, 1978). Crucially, here, however, the main battle lines are not the state, because the state is merely doing the bidding of the dominant class. This functionalist analysis raises some important questions, common to this type of Marxist analysis. Most notably, what propels the state to act so as to maintain the patriarchal family? What is clear is that both black and socialist feminists emphasize the intersectionality of race, capitalism, and gender, and their capacity to produce and perpetuate systems of oppression and class domination (Crenshaw, 1989).

The divisions caused by competing perceptions of the link between gender, race and class is well illustrated in the conflict that has occurred within the women's movement in the United States. For example, some of the organizers of the so-called Women's March Inc. have been accused (by others in the women's movement as well as by outsiders) of siding with the Nation of Islam and of making anti-Semitic statements. This reflects a wider debate about intersectionality with supporters of the national Women's March Inc. arguing that, as the most oppressed, the interests of women of colour ought to be prioritized with others (such as the organizers of the much smaller New York-based Women's March Alliance) arguing that all women should be united in a shared set of goals (Lang, 2019).

The Fragmentation of Feminism

In recent years there has been enormous fragmentation within feminist thought. Disputes have occurred, for instance, over the significance of biological differences, with some (Firestone, 1972) regarding these differences as the source of women's oppression, while others (Pateman, 1989) denying this, some seeking to recapture the importance of motherhood from a feminist viewpoint, and others seeking to emphasize the importance for women to be able to choose not to be mothers. Some feminists have violently opposed pornography (Dworkin, 1981), while other, liberal feminists, have sought to reclaim it for women (McElroy, 1995). Feminists have also differed over the character of political structures, with some wanting separatist, non-hierarchical political structures while others reject this oppositional stance and seek to build alliances with other social groups and participate in conventional political structures even though they are male dominated.

Feminism has also had to come to terms with the recent emergence of the trans movement which emphasizes gender fluidity and the importance of gender self-identification. Some feminists, particularly in the early days of trans activism, opposed strongly this rejection of a binary conception of gender regarding trans activism as damaging to the central feminist link between gender and the oppression of women (Jeffreys, 2013). More recently, buoyed by the work of feminist scholars such as Judith Butler in a book originally published in 1990 (2007), so-called transfeminism has sought to build links between feminist and trans activism.

Some feminists have sought to make alliances with postmodernism. Postmodernism, superficially at least, would seem to be a strange bedfellow of feminism, as the former would reject the latter's attempt to universalize a theory which explains the subordination of women. As a result, some prefer to see feminist thought as an offshoot of Enlightenment modernism. However, postmodernism does offer something of value to feminists. In the first place, it emphasizes difference and variety, which suits feminism's attempt to shift attention away from the public to the private realm. Similarly, postmodernism facilitates celebration of the differences between men and women, allowing women's separate roles, and values, to be regarded as equally important. It also allows an appreciation of the differences among women based on their class, race, and culture. A postmodern feminism, therefore, recognizes the difficulty of developing one approach with which to challenge a patriarchal society.

Feminism, Equality, and Difference

The nature of the cross-cutting fragmentation within feminist thought is illustrated well by the debate over goals. Liberal, socialist, and radical feminists all put forward an egalitarian position, but they differ over what kind of equality is most significant, with liberal feminists advocating legal and political equality for women, socialist feminists advocating economic equality, and radical feminists advocating social equality for women in the private sphere. All, though, seek equality for women. So-called difference feminists, a small but significant group, on the other hand, challenge this goal of equality. Women should not try to be like men but should seek to change, or feminize, society.

Central to difference feminism is the essentialist claim that differences between men and women do have political and social importance. Much of the impetus for this position derives from the work of Carol Gilligan (1982) whose research on male and female values led her to posit a dualism, based on gender, between a masculine focus on rights, justice, and autonomy, and a feminine tendency to focus on caring, responsibility, and interaction with others. Women and men, therefore, have different moral 'voices'. Difference feminists suggest that it is misguided for women to seek to mimic masculine values—of greed, competitiveness, aggression, and hierarchy. Rather, women ought to promote female values such as caring, compassion, and consensus.

Much of the impact of the so-called care ethic espoused by difference feminists has been felt within the disciplines of environmental and animal ethics (Donovan and Adams, 2007). There have been attempts, however, to assess the impact of introducing an ethic of care to public policy in general (Tronto, 1993). There have also been, as we will explore in Chapter 18, attempts by feminist scholars in international relations to examine the impact of 'male' values in global politics, and possible alternatives.

Taken to its extremes, the implications of difference feminism have been too much for many feminists to stomach. For if differences between the sexes are natural and immutable then there is no point in trying to change men. Men, then, are the enemy, and feminists should not seek to involve them politically. This leads inexorably towards political separatism which, for some, has meant political lesbianism (Brownmiller, 1975).

Current Position

As indicated, the utility of feminism has been damaged by internal ideological debates and general fragmentation. Further problems have been caused by the hostile political environment feminists have had to operate in since the 1980s. Some have argued, in the light of gains made by women, that radical feminism seeks to go too far. As a result, there has been a backlash against the women's movement (Faludi, 1991). More recently, feminism has benefitted from the growing importance of identity politics—the #MeToo movement being a particularly powerful example of its impact.

➡ See Chapter 2 for an account of identity politics.

Political and economic inequalities based on gender are still widespread in Western liberal democracies. Moreover, in other parts of the world, cultural practices damaging to women—female genital mutilation, infanticide, forced marriages, and punishments for being the victim of sexual attacks, to name but a few—are commonplace. Feminism, therefore, clearly still has an important role to play while inequality and subordination based on gender still persists.

KEY POINTS

- Feminism starts from the assumption that women are unequal to men, subject to subordination, at best, and oppression, at worst.
- Feminism is best divided into liberal, socialist, and radical strands.
- Liberal feminism seeks to achieve the same rights for women as possessed by men in the public sphere.
- Significant progress has been made in the securing of liberal rights for women, although this should not be exaggerated.
- Socialist feminists insist that more attention should be placed on working-class women whose plight is inextricably linked to the existence of the capitalist system.
- Radical feminism seeks to focus attention on patriarchal relationships in the private sphere.
- Feminist thought has undergone a great deal of fragmentation with differences evident over motherhood, pornography, political strategy, and the value of postmodernism.

ENVIRONMENTALISM

Concern for the natural environment is not a new phenomenon. Legislation designed to control pollution, for instance, dates back to the nineteenth century and there are probably earlier examples than this. As a distinctive issue, however, the environment did not really exist until the 1970s, and it did not become a mainstream issue for another decade. The rise of environmentalism is partly a consequence of the existence of severe objective environmental problems: the effects of air pollution, the use of pesticides in agriculture, the depletion of non-renewable resources, the extinction of many species of plants and animals, and the more recent problems of ozone depletion and climate change. A number of international gatherings—those at Stockholm in 1972 and the Earth Summit at Rio twenty years later being the most symbolic—helped to establish the state of the environment as a key issue of our time, albeit one that rarely has an impact on national elections.

Ideologically, environmental thought can be divided into two main categories. On the one hand is the reformist approach (sometimes described as light green or shallow environmentalism). On the other is the radical (dark green or deep) approach. For some political philosophers, only the latter can be properly described as an ideology (Dobson, 2007). To distinguish the two, one might refer to the former as environmentalism and the latter as ecologism. Environmentalism can be seen, then, as a single-issue concern not necessarily inconsistent with a range of ideologies, whereas ecologism is a separate ideology with a set of distinct ideas. The differences between the two can be illustrated if we examine their major characteristics.

→ See Chapter 18 for coverage of environmentalism in the context of international relations.

Photo 7.1 Climate change protesters march through the streets of London. *John Gomez/Shutter stock.com*

The Economic Realm

One major distinction between reformist and radical accounts is their approach to economic growth. Radical greens see economic growth as incompatible with environmental protection. The aversion to economic growth is partly a normative claim, that individuals will lead much more fulfilled and happy lives in a non-materialistic society (Jackson, 2009). It is primarily, however, an empirical claim that there are natural limits to growth, and unless production and consumption levels and population size are reduced to sustainable levels, then economic and political collapse will be the result.

This empirical claim received its impetus from a report by a group of American scientists published as *The Limits to Growth* (Meadows, 1972). The report was based on a series of computer runs which factored in potential solutions to a range of environmental problems while growth in the other variables stayed the same. At each step, the authors argued, the solution did not solve the need for a cut in economic growth to forestall environmental degradation. Their conclusion was that if we failed to cut economic activity, then the point of no return would be reached not far into the current (twenty-first) century.

There have been many criticisms of the *Limits to Growth* report (Martell, 1994: 33–40). Not least, it has been suggested that there is no necessary trade-off between economic growth and environmental protection. This reformist challenge is based on the assertion that, provided growth is sustainable, then it is permissible from an environmental perspective. Sustainable development is therefore the centrepiece of a reformist alternative. There have been numerous definitions of sustainable development, the best known defining it as development that 'meets the needs of the present generation without compromising the ability of future generations to meet their own needs' (World Commission on Environment and Development, 1987).

Sustainable development is notoriously vague, or at least lacking in detail. A more precise formulation is the principle known as ecological modernization (Hajer, 1997) which suggests a number of ways in which growth can be sustainable. First, growth need not necessarily occur through the use of non-renewable resources such as coal and gas. The use of renewable energy, such as wind and wave power (and even nuclear power), coupled with energy conservation, can ensure that growth remains sustainable. Second, the production of environmental goods—such as, for example, catalytic converters for cars or scrubs removing the pollution from power stations—can itself be a source of economic growth. Finally, it is argued that environmental damage is not cost-free economically, so that protecting the environment can be consistent with economic growth. This was the major finding of a 2006 British government report—chaired by Sir Nicholas Stern—on climate change. Stern estimates that if temperatures rise by 5°C, up to 10 per cent of global output could be lost, and the poorest countries would lose more than 10 per cent of their output.

The Moral Philosophy Realm

Reformists (like all of the ideologies we have encountered in this chapter and the last) adopt an anthropocentric view of the world. This ethic is human-centred. Humans are regarded as having intrinsic value and non-humans have only extrinsic value. Anthropocentrism is challenged by those who want to include non-human animals as morally considerable because of their sentience, and also by ecocentric thinkers who regard the whole of nature as worthy of moral standing. For exponents of anthropocentrism, the value of non-human nature is extrinsic to us. We protect the environment, in other words, because it is in our interests to do so and not because we think that nature has any worthwhile interests of its own. Some radical greens, on the other hand, adopt what has been called an ecocentric ethic (Leopold, 1949; Eckersley, 1992; Fox, 1995). This position accords intrinsic value to both humans and to non-human parts of nature. In other words, nature has moral worth independently of human beings. Two observations about this distinction in environmental ethics are, first, that it has resonance in practical environmental politics (**see Box 7.4**) and, second, that, philosophically, an ecocentric ethic is difficult to justify (**see Box 7.5**).

The Political Realm

There is now a considerable body of green political thought (Dobson, 2007; Gabrielson et al., 2016; Garner, 2019). We have seen earlier in this book, for instance, that green thinking has influenced our consideration about concepts such as justice and democracy. For reformists, environmental solutions can coexist with existing political structures. By contrast, radicals argue that in order for environmental objectives to be achieved it is necessary for far-reaching social and political change. There is a division of opinion, however, on what change is necessary. In the so-called

7

CASE STUDY BOX 7.4
Whaling and Environmental Ethics

The issue of whaling provides an interesting case study of environmental ethics in action. In 1946, the International Whaling Commission (IWC) was set up by the whaling nations (most notably Japan, Norway, and Iceland) in order to regulate whaling. The aim was to protect whale stocks so that they could continue to be hunted. The motivation behind this move, then, was clearly anthropocentric. Whales were regarded as a human resource and their value was merely extrinsic to the humans who benefited from products that derived from their capture. Such was the scale of hunting that in 1986 a moratorium on commercial whaling was introduced to try to prevent a number of whale species from becoming extinct.

   Protecting the whale became an important part of the environmental movement in the 1970s. The symbol of Greenpeace activists risking their lives by sailing close to whaling ships in order to obtain documentary evidence had a significant impact on Western public opinion. By the 1980s, the whaling nations were becoming outnumbered in the deliberations of the IWC and repeated attempts to restart commercial whaling since then have been resisted. The whaling nations, quite consistently with their ethical position, have argued that since whale stocks have recovered, they should be allowed to resume commercial whaling. The nations opposing this adopt a very different ethic. With the backing of public opinion, they object to whaling, not primarily because it is unsustainable, but because the practice is cruel and infringes the interests of whales. In other words, they regard whales as having intrinsic value that ought to be taken into account. As a result, the debate is unlikely to be resolved amicably because the two sides are arguing past each other.

KEY DEBATE BOX 7.5
Justifying an Ecocentric Ethic

The difficulties of justifying philosophically an ecocentric ethic are considerable. For many philosophers, sentience—or the capacity to experience pain and pleasure—is the key benchmark for moral standing. It is easy to see why damaging the interests of a human or an animal matters to her, but it is more difficult to see why damaging a tree matters to the tree. We can clearly negatively affect a tree's interests but, following Frey (1983: 154–5), it does not seem sensible to talk about wronging the tree. Thus, polluting a river is to harm it but since the river only has extrinsic value for those sentient beings who benefit from it, it is only they who can be wronged by polluting the river.

Responses to the critique of ecocentrism have focused on themes such as the moral significance of intuition and the possession, by living things, of the property of autopoiesis—the capacity of self-renewal (Garner, 2019: 60–1). Given the difficulty of establishing an ecocentric ethic, though, the key question would seem to be whether establishing an ecocentric ethic is an essential ingredient for protecting the environment. Increasingly, green thinkers argue that there are sufficient prudential grounds for protecting nature (Barry, 1999). To give an example, we should protect forests not because forests have intrinsic value but because it is in our interests to do so, not least because they provide crucial sinks for carbon dioxide and therefore help to control rises in the temperature of the planet.

Questions

1. What is a non-anthropocentric ethic?
2. Why should we protect the environment?

'survivalist' literature, principally from the 1970s, there is an authoritarian strain. Most famous here is the work of Garrett Hardin (1968). Hardin argued that, left to their own devices, people will always despoil the environment through greed and naivety. Humans, therefore, need to be directed by a strong state, not least in reproduction habits. This authoritarian strain (seen also in the writings of Ophuls, 1973, and Heilbroner, 1974) raises question marks about the utility of democracy for environmentalism.

Most radical greens now advocate decentralized small-scale, self-sufficient anarchist-type communities linked together by loose authority structures, a model which draws from the work of such luminaries as Bookchin (1971) and Schumacher (1973). Despite their ability to reduce or eliminate large-scale industrial production, to enable people to be closer to nature, and to facilitate political participation and social cohesion, the environmental utility of these loose alliances has been questioned by some green thinkers (Goodin, 1992). At a time when international agreements are seen as essential for effective environmental protection, and yet difficult to achieve in the existing state system, the ability of a diverse range of small, self-governing communities to ensure effective coordination is, at the very least, problematic. Partly as a result of this, attempts have been made to bring the state back in as a vehicle for environmental protection (**see Box 7.6**).

Finally, in the political realm, the question of agency has been raised. Which social class or grouping is most likely to act as the harbinger of change? A variety of candidates have been suggested, ranging from the middle class (Porritt, 1984) to the unemployed (Gorz, 1985). The

➡ See
Chapters 4 and 5
respectively for
an exploration of
the relationship
between
environmentalism
and democracy
and justice.

KEY DEBATE BOX 7.6
The State and the Environment

Environmentalists have tended to be sceptical about the state's capacity to solve environmental problems. The preferred option for Radical Greens is a decentralized political structure which is anarchistic in character. As many have commented, however, this solution is counter-intuitive given the global character of environmental problems. It has long been appreciated that pollution is no respecter of national boundaries and requires cooperation between states to deal with it. More recently, the international dimension of environmentalism has become more prominent because of the identification of genuinely global problems, such as climate change and ozone depletion. Only global cooperation can hope to solve these problems.

One approach seeks to re-establish the role of the state as a major player in the environmental debate. The most concerted attempt to develop a normative model for a green state has been provided by Eckersley (2004). She recognizes that hers is a revisionist account given the distaste for the state that exists in much green political thought. The justification for bringing the state back in is, at least in part, a product of the pragmatic recognition that the state remains the most important form of political organization. According to Eckersley, a green state must:

- facilitate a green public sphere to create greater ecological consciousness;
- be outward-looking seeking to cooperate with other states to tackle environmental problems;
- be impeccably democratic, encouraging participation, entrenching environmental rights, and incorporating the interests of non-human nature.

On a more practical note, one increasingly popular programme to 'green' the state is the so-called Green New Deal (GND). First mooted in 2006 in the United States, the GND was so named to draw parallels with the economic stimulus package introduced by president Roosevelt in the 1930s. It argues, in contrast to the Limits to Growth school, that an emphasis on environmental initiatives—such as renewable energy and a sustainable transport infrastructure—can be compatible with economic growth. It is also allayed with a programme of policies aimed at reducing economic inequality. Since the 2018 Congressional elections, the idea of a GND has gained ground within the environmental movement as well as the Democratic Party, particularly amongst the new intake of left-leaning Democrats within the House of Representatives. A similar programme has also been endorsed by the British activist group Extinction Rebellion and by the British Labour Party in the 2019 General Election.

issue of agency is linked to questions of justice, since those worst affected by environmental degradation are the very same people one might expect to campaign for action to deal with it. This is the rationale of the environmental justice movement which exists, in particular, in the USA.

A Distinct Ideology?

One key question is how far radical environmentalism or ecologism represents a distinct ideology, separate from the other ideologies we have considered. A quick glance at the literature reveals that a number of traditional ideological positions have sought to claim environmentalism for themselves. Thus, there are works of eco-socialism (Pepper, 1993), eco-liberalism (Wissenburg,

1993), and eco-feminism (Mellor, 1997). There is even an attempt to claim the green label for fascism (Bramwell, 1989).

On the other hand, the existence of separate green political parties throughout the world suggests that ecologists regard their position as distinct. Clearly, the limits to growth position adds an extra dimension to political thinking. In particular, it challenges the shared optimistic vision that liberals, socialists, and Marxists have about the ability of humans to master their environment for their own infinite economic ends. Similarly distinct is the ecocentric ethic adopted by some radical greens. All traditional ideologies are incorruptibly anthropocentric in orientation, regarding the natural world as a resource for humans to exploit.

Distinct it may be, but one critique of ecocentrism emphasized by exponents of eco-feminists and eco-socialists in particular, is that, while not wrong in itself, ecocentrism is a position in moral philosophy and therefore lacks a political dimension. That is, it says nothing about power relations and political agency. It does not, that is, tell us how exploitative power relations result in environmental degradation. From an eco-feminist and eco-socialist perspective, on the other hand, such an account is given, with gender and class, respectively, regarded as the source of environmental problems (rather than anthropocentrism per se). These alternative ideologies, therefore—unlike ecocentrism—offer a *political* programme to solve the environmental crisis.

Ecology is less distinct in its political orientation. Here, it borrows from other traditions of thought—from the authoritarian implications of Hobbes's *Leviathan* to the participatory democracy of Rousseau, and the lack of hierarchy advocated by anarchism. In so far as these political positions are recommended for the achievement of environmental objectives there is a case for saying that they are being used in distinctive ways, but, as we have seen, there is no one favoured political position for ecologists.

KEY POINTS

- The rise of environmentalism has been, partly at least, the product of severe environmental problems.
- Environmental thinkers can be divided into radical and reformist camps.
- In economic terms, the radicals support a limit to growth while the reformists advocate a version of sustainable development.
- In philosophic terms, the radicals hold an ecocentric ethic while the reformists hold an anthropocentric ethic.
- In political terms, radicals advocate far-reaching change while the reformist position can coexist with a variety of ideological positions.
- In its economic and philosophical/ethical guises there is a case for saying that environmentalism is a distinct ideology, but this is less clear-cut in terms of political structures.

MULTICULTURALISM

Multiculturalism has emerged as a direct challenge to those nationalists who desire to create distinct states based on ethnicity, and the traditional model of citizenship, associated above all with the work of T. H. Marshall (1950) which emphasized the need to 'promote a . . . common national identity among citizens' (Kymlicka, 2002: 327). By contrast, multiculturalism seeks to advocate pluralistic states based on many different religious, cultural, and ethnic identities. It has become a particularly pressing issue, in theory and practice, precisely because modern societies have become increasingly multicultural in a factual sense, as a result of globalization and increased migration. The term multiculturalism was first used as recently as the 1960s in Canada, as a result, in particular, of growing demands among the French-speaking community in Quebec who reject the Anglophone domination of the Canadian state. By the 1970s, multiculturalism had become official government policy (Tierney, 2007). The two key questions we will consider here are, first, what is the correct ideological location for multiculturalism, and, second, is it a positive or negative phenomenon?

Multiculturalism and Ideology

Initially, before the 1990s, multiculturalism was seen by political theorists as particularly aligned with communitarianism. As we saw in Chapter 2, communitarianism, by focusing on group rights and community cohesion and identity, is a direct challenge to the liberal focus on the autonomous individual. As Kymlicka (2002: 337) points out 'Communitarians . . . view multiculturalism as an appropriate way of protecting communities from the eroding effects of individual autonomy, and of affirming the value of community'. To this end, Kymlicka (1995) sought to develop a theory of group rights. These include rights of self-governance—for national, territorially concentrated, minority populations such as the Inuit in Canada—'polyethnic' rights to allow minority groups to preserve their distinctive ways of life, and representative rights to correct the underrepresentation of minority or disadvantaged groups in education and public and political life.

➡ See Chapter 2 for a discussion of communitarianism.

This opposition between multiculturalism and liberalism might strike the reader as somewhat odd. After all, the liberal emphasis on the neutral state, the reluctance of liberals to countenance interfering in competing conceptions of the good (seen most notably in the later political philosophy of John Rawls), and the liberal focus on the protection of minority rights, would seem to suggest that liberalism is the most appropriate ideological location for multiculturalism. This is particularly the case when one considers that liberalism emerged as a defence of religious toleration. It is not surprising, therefore, that, since the 1980s, liberals have sought to accommodate multiculturalism.

However, this accommodation presents problems for liberals. There is a potential conflict between liberal values and the upholding of minority cultural rights when the latter involves the infringing of individual rights. It would be odd, for instance, for liberals to sanction illiberal practices such as forced marriages, confining women to the home, and, even worse, female genital mutilation, all issues which have troubled feminists, as well as removing children from public education and apostasy (the practice of preventing individuals from rejecting a particular faith). Moreover, the use of a group right against behaviour from others that might offend can conflict with freedom of expression, a central canon of liberalism.

One way out of this dilemma for liberals is to offer limited support for multiculturalism, affirming it only when it does not involve the infringement of individual rights (Kymlicka, 2002: 340–1). Rawls (1993) essentially does this by arguing that liberals can only accept a 'reasonable pluralism', thereby not forcing it into a position where it is has to accept the moral legitimacy, say, of slavery. Kymlicka (1995) wants to go further than Rawls in a multicultural direction by arguing that the degree to which we should expect different cultures to assimilate depends upon how the minority group's position is established. Thus, refugees, and those who have chosen to emigrate, should be prepared to assimilate, whereas in the case of indigenous national minorities who have not chosen to be cultural minorities, such as the Australian Aborigines and the American Indian tribes, more effort should be made to permit differentiated rights, even when they conflict with liberal principles.

While we may think that Kymlicka's principle has a great deal of validity, it is somewhat arbitrary, and it is debatable how far it remains consistent with liberal values. Others either reject multiculturalism or reject liberalism. The best example of the former is the political theorist Brian Barry (2001), who has doubts about the value of multiculturalism because it is a threat to liberal values. On the other hand, some political theorists argue that a convincing multiculturalism must go beyond the liberal objection to the infringement of individual rights, since the liberal multiculturalism of those such as Rawls and Kymlicka is too heavily weighted towards liberalism. Parekh (2000), for instance, argues that we should adopt a much more pluralistic morality and be prepared to jettison liberalism when it conflicts with multiculturalism. This has the effect of offering a separate ideological status for multiculturalism, separate from liberalism and communitarianism.

Is Multiculturalism a Good Thing?

A related question is whether multiculturalism is a positive principle that we ought to adopt. This has become an issue of some political saliency, particularly in the context of 9/11, and the Islamic terrorism in Europe carried out by home-grown citizens. Multiculturalism has been challenged primarily because of a concern for social unity, and a feeling that it is 'corrosive of long-term political unity and social stability' (Kymlicka, 2002: 366). It has therefore been seen as part of the explanation for the emergence of identity politics which, as we saw in Chapter 2, has been criticized for its tendency to promote the differences people have and not what binds them together (Fukuyama, 2018: 111). It is for this reason that France, among European states, practises the most insistent policy of assimilation, which has caused particular controversy in the case of the wearing of religious dress. In addition, as we have indicated, the danger of moral pluralism is that it allows for the potential infringement of individual rights.

➡ See Chapter 2 for an account of identity politics.

In defence of multiculturalism, it offers a solution to the inevitable cultural diversity present in modern societies. In addition, there is 'remarkably little evidence' that multiculturalism leads to social conflict. Indeed, it might be regarded as a force for social inclusion since allowing minority cultural groups to practise their differences is more likely to make them feel positive towards, and included within, the society in which they live (Kymlicka, 2002: 367). Moreover, cultural diversity brings a richness to otherwise homogeneous lives, encourages toleration of difference, and allows individuals to generate a sense of belonging. Rejecting different approaches to life, as some liberals would seem to be doing, also suggests an arrogance and infallibility which many argue is not justified.

KEY POINTS

- Multiculturalism seeks to promote pluralistic states based on many different religious, cultural, and ethnic identities.
- Multiculturalism was initially aligned with communitarianism but was later adopted by liberals.
- The liberal advocacy of multiculturalism is problematic because of the need to sanction practices within minority cultures that are illiberal.

→

- Some liberals seek to reject multiculturalism on the grounds that it can be illiberal, others seek to qualify their support, while others, writing from outside the liberal tradition, argue that liberalism ought to be sacrificed in favour of multiculturalism.

- Multiculturalism has been attacked for its divisive nature and the potential for the infringement of liberal principles. Others defend it as one means of accommodating diversity and the richness diversity brings.

RELIGIOUS FUNDAMENTALISM

Religion is not ideological insofar as it remains a private concern among individuals and groups. It becomes ideological if it seeks to organize political principles along religious lines and seeks political influence or power in order to achieve it. There are, of course, many instances in world history of religion playing a political role, not least the European conflicts between Catholics and Protestants in the sixteenth and seventeenth centuries.

Since then, however, many societies, influenced by the Lockean principle of religious toleration, have separated the church from the state, not least in the USA, where this is enshrined in the Constitution. In these secular regimes, religion becomes a private pursuit not impinging on the public realm, and the state remains neutral between competing faiths, providing that the practices of any one of them do not infringe the rights of any citizen, and even then, there may be exceptions. Secularism is therefore a distinct feature of Enlightenment political ideologies. Despite this, there are many contemporary examples of conflicts centring on religion, such as Northern Ireland (between Protestants and Catholics), particularly in the 1970s, Iraq (between Sunni and Shia Muslims, a strand of the former which morphed into Islamic State of Iraq and al-Sham (ISIS), the so-called Islamic State of Iraq and Syria), and Darfur in the Sudan (between Muslims and Christians). As Goodwin (2014: 445) states, 'religious differences have, for millennia, led to a waste of human life and to the undermining of the imperatives of human toleration'.

The fundamentalist religious strands, which became current in the twentieth century, are ideological precisely because they do seek to enter the political realm. To be a fundamentalist is to be convinced of the truth of the doctrine one is professing (in the case of religious fundamentalism based on an interpretation of a sacred text), and to seek to ensure that these truths are adopted by the state, even by the use of force and violence. Such is the publicity given to it, and its impact, that when we think of religious fundamentalism, the Islamic variety comes easily to mind. Indeed, the scholar Samuel Huntington (1996) argued, in a controversial study, that we are now faced by a 'clash of civilizations' in which societies upholding Western values are under attack from non-Western civilizations, and particularly those dominated by Islam.

A number of important caveats need to be made about fundamentalism in general, and religious fundamentalism in particular. First, most Muslims, Christians, and Jews are tolerant and peaceable and are content to allow for religion to remain separate from politics. In Turkey, for instance, the Islamic government has tried to combine Islam with a secular political framework. Second, all religions—Christianity, Islam, Judaism, Hinduism, Sikhism, and even Buddhism—have their fundamentalist elements, although, by and large, they remain in

➡ See Chapter 19 for more on ISIS and the security situation in Iraq and Syria.

a minority. Therefore, it is preferable, as one critique of Huntington has suggested, to talk about a clash between fundamentalist Muslims and fundamentalist Christians rather than a 'clash of civilizations' (Ali, 2002). It might also be argued that fundamentalism is not limited to religion; that all ideologies have their fundamentalist elements. The obvious candidates here would be the Stalinist version of communism and fascism in inter-war Germany and Italy; but even liberalism can be said to be fundamentalist about its belief in the value of liberty, something which must be protected at all costs.

It is possible, then, to draw a distinction between Islam as a faith, and radical Islamism as a political movement that seeks to create a particular type of state. This is a very simplistic distinction, however, and there is a great deal of controversy about the relationship between Islam and Islamism (see Heywood, 2017: 304–7). Huntingdon (1996), for one, for instance, argues that the roots of the latter lies within the anti-pluralism of the former. At the very least, some versions of Islam, whilst eschewing violence as a strategy, do hold very socially conservative values which are ideologically significant.

The characteristic of Islamic fundamentalism (or Islamism) is its desire to create a theocracy (a state based on religious principles) which follows Islamic (Sharia) Law, or—to be more precise— a particular interpretation of Islamic Law. It is undoubtedly a potent religious force, particularly in Africa and the Middle East, receiving a fillip when the Shah of Iran was deposed by an Islamic fundamentalist regime led by Ayatollah Khomeini in 1979. Following on from the Muslim Brotherhood, formed in Egypt in 1928, a number of new militant Islamic groups have emerged, most notably ISIS, and Boko Haram in Nigeria, to add to Al-Qaeda (literally 'the base') formed by Osama bin Laden in Afghanistan in 1988, and held responsible for the attacks on the Twin Towers in New York and the Pentagon in Washington on 11 September 2001.

In some senses Islamic fundamentalism is opposed to modernity. Thus, it is virulently anti-democrat and morally conservative, regarding modern Western values as corrupt and licentious. Moreover, militant Islam is associated with the use of violence as a strategy in pursuit of jihad, meaning the struggle. Whilst opposed to modernity, Islamism is 'best described . . . as a modern movement opposed to modernity' (Hoffman and Graham, 2006: 397). This is because Islamic fundamentalists (and those of the Christian variety too) have not been slow in using modern communication devices, such as the internet, to propagate their cause and mobilize support. It is noticeable, too, that an Islamic regime such as Iran is fully prepared to use the benefits of scientific research, as in the case of nuclear weapons' technology, to defend itself against perceived threats from the West.

As with all fundamentalist groups, the certainty of belief of Islamic fundamentalist groups is infectious and is therefore prone to lead to the mobilization of activists, although it is also true that its strength derives from social and economic circumstances, often coupled with the mistakes of existing non-fundamentalist elites. Thus, rightly or wrongly, it has been claimed that the Islamic terrorist threat has been largely provoked by the response of the USA, itself influenced by its own fundamentalism, hence the label the clash of fundamentalisms.

Given that Christianity is the world's biggest religion, it would be surprising if it did not have a fundamentalist element. Christian fundamentalism is particularly associated with the Christian New Right that emerged in the USA in the 1970s. There is a range of loosely attached groupings, perhaps the best known being the Moral Majority, led by the Reverend Jerry Falwell. There has been no attempt to establish a theocracy. Instead, the Christian New Right has sought to campaign for conservative moral values—particularly against the rights given to particular social groups, such as blacks, feminists, and the gay rights movement—and against abortion.

Christian fundamentalists have sometimes resorted to violence, particularly against the staff and clients of abortion clinics, and sometimes against the intrusion of the public sector in general, such as in the Oklahoma bombing in 1995. More usually, however, Christian fundamentalists have sought to influence Republican politicians, usually through the financing of campaigns. Major progress was made by the election of Ronald Reagan in 1980 and—after the secular presidencies of George Bush Senior and Bill Clinton—George Bush Junior who is, himself, a born-again Christian.

KEY POINTS

- Religion becomes ideological if it becomes embroiled in politics.
- Religious fundamentalism can be characterized by its intention of organizing politics along religious lines.
- Not all Muslims are fundamentalists, and fundamentalism occurs in all religions and, arguably, in all ideologies.
- Religious fundamentalists, of the Muslim and Christian varieties, are anti-modernist in the sense of being morally conservative and, in the case of the former, anti-democratic too, but they are also modernist in the sense that they utilize modern communication media and campaigning strategies.

CONCLUSION

Whereas the ideologies we discussed in Chapter 6 were focused on the state, the ideologies in this chapter represent a challenge to the state. This is seen first in the greater emphasis on the supranational dimension observed, in particular, in environmentalism, multiculturalism, and religious fundamentalism (Hoffman and Graham, 2006: 317–18). All have been impacted on by the phenomenon of globalization, a central theme of this book. The new ideologies are also a product of social and economic change, centring in particular on the decline of class as a major fault line in world politics. Finally, environmentalism is a product of the objectively deteriorating state of the natural environment coupled with rising affluence. All of this has resulted in an ideological world which, while more dynamic and pluralistic, is less sure of itself and more open to change.

The final point to make is that the traditional ideologies considered in Chapter 5 have responded to the challenges presented by those examined in this chapter. We have seen, for instance, how liberalism and socialism have contributed to the debate about feminism, environmentalism, and multiculturalism. Indeed, it is not clear, in the case of the latter two at least, how far they exist as distinct ideologies, rather than as particular issues to which the traditional ideologies have responded. All of this suggests that the modernist project, while not in rude health, has some life left in it.

KEY QUESTIONS

1. Account for the emergence of challenges to the traditional ideologies.
2. What has been the impact of postmodernism on ideologies?
3. Has feminism achieved its objectives?
4. Does feminism have a theory of the state?
5. Is there a distinct ideology of environmentalism?
6. How justifiable is a non-anthropocentric ethic?
7. Is multiculturalism consistent with liberalism?
8. What are the strengths and weaknesses of multiculturalism?
9. Under what circumstances does religion become ideological?
10. Is modernism dead?

7

FURTHER READING

Bryson, V. (2003), *Feminist Political Theory: An Introduction* (Basingstoke: Palgrave, 2nd edn).
This is an excellent introduction.

Garner, R. (2019), *Environmental Political Thought: Interests, Values and Inclusion* (London: Red Globe Press).
A comprehensive, and up to date, account of the major debates in the discipline.

Gray, J. (2003), *Al Qaeda and What it Means to be Modern* (London: Faber & Faber).
This is a typically incisive account of religious fundamentalism by a key thinker.

Heywood, A. (2017), *Political ideologies: An Introduction* (London: Palgrave, 6th edn).
An up to date edition of a well-known and highly regarded account of political ideologies.

Kymlicka, W. (2002), *Contemporary Political Philosophy* (Oxford: Oxford University Press, 2nd edn), ch. 8.

Lang, M. (2019), 'What's in a Name? Women's March groups spar over who owns the name and the movement', *Washington Post*, 14 January https://www.washingtonpost.com/local/whats-in-a-name-womens-march-groups-spar-over-who-owns-the-name-and-the-movement/2019/01/14/354df744-15c3-11e9-b6ad-9cfd62dbb0a8_story.html
This covers, in summary form, the multicultural debate in which the author is a key participant.

Moussalli, A. (ed.) (1998), *Islamic Fundamentalism* (Reading, NY: Ithaca Press).
This is a good collection of articles by leading experts in the field.

 For additional material and resources, please visit the Online Resources at:
www.oup.com/he/garner4e

PART 2

comparative
POLITICS

by Peter Ferdinand

INSTITUTIONS AND STATES

READER'S GUIDE

This is the first in a series of chapters that change the focus of analysis to domestic institutions. Political scientists spend a great deal of time analysing the behaviour of institutions and theorizing about them. All the social sciences do. This chapter will first introduce you to the concept of institutions and then different factors that structure political behaviour. Then it will present the multi-faceted concept of the state. After that will come a brief historical account of the ways that the European type of state and the European state system spread around the world between the seventeenth and twentieth centuries. This will lead on to a discussion of the modern state, and some of the differences between them—strong states and weak states—before offering a conclusion.

INSTITUTIONS

Institutions are essentially regular patterns of behaviour that provide stability and predictability to social life. Some are informal in that they have no formally laid down rules—the family, social classes, kinship groups, and such. Individuals internalize 'codes of behaviour' from them as a result of socialization, by example or out of conviction. Others are more formalized, having codified rules and organization—governments, parties, bureaucracies, legislatures, constitutions, and law courts. Institutions structure the behaviour of individuals and groups. In that sense they are constraints. On the other hand, they serve as resources for the knowledgeable who navigate their way through them to achieve desired outcomes. Thus, institutions are both constraints and resources.

→ See Chapter 12 for a discussion of Duverger's Law.

Students of politics tend to concentrate more upon formal institutions, which form political systems. This is especially true of those who work on Western political systems, where such institutions dominate political life. They try to identify the regular processes of change that are intrinsic to the system itself or to parts of it. Sometimes they claim to have identified regularities that can be elevated to the level of 'laws', as in the natural sciences. One example, to which we shall return in Chapter 12, concerns **Duverger's Law**. This stated that first-past-the-post electoral systems produce two-party systems. At the same time, however, political studies also focus on the environment in which these systems are situated. Any political system may be buffeted by pressures arising either in the society surrounding it, or in the international arena. This may lead to disruption or even breakdown, in the form of revolutions; but in most cases, states adapt to these challenges. Political scientists attempt to identify regular patterns of adaptation as a way of generalizing more widely about the behaviour of political institutions.

As Steinmo put it: 'Institutions define the rules of the political game and as such they define who can play and how they play. Consequently, they ultimately can shape who wins and who loses' (2001: 7555).

It is, however, important also to grasp the relationship between political institutions and the surrounding environment of other political, social, and economic forces. We will use a simplified version of structuration theory, originally formulated by Giddens, to clarify these relationships. He distinguished between 'system', 'structure', and 'structuration' (Giddens, 1979: 66). We will adapt the term 'system' to mean 'political system'. We will use the term 'structure' to mean 'political institution'. And **structuration** will refer to the complex of factors that both constrain and also provide resources for changes in the operation of institutions and the system as a whole. These can range from levels of economic development, through regional or class group activity, to the behaviour of individual political actors. In studies of politics, as in the social sciences more generally, it is rarely the case that big events or changes can be attributed to a single factor. Most political decisions are the product of the interaction of several factors. It is the relative weight of these factors that determines the specific outcome. Thus, explanation of causation is a matter of judgement.

→ See Chapter 22 for an exploration of the relationship between the state and economic institutions.

At this point it is important to introduce another basic distinction from the categories used in studies of politics to explain political events: 'structure' versus 'agency'. Here, what is meant by 'structure' is the impact of the particular configuration of institutions. To what extent did they determine the outcome, or at least predispose a particular outcome? Sometimes this is presented in terms of 'path-determined' outcomes. The contrast is with 'agency', i.e. the effect of choices and actions by one or more agents, whether individuals or groups of them. Since politics is a social activity, it is very rarely the case that a particular political outcome was absolutely determined by structure alone. Nor is it the case that agents have complete freedom. Their options are always constrained by structures of one kind or another.

KEY POINTS

- Institutions play a vital role in structuring political behaviour.
- Political, economic, and social factors all provide structuration in political life and determine particular outcomes.
- 'Structure' and 'agency' perform complementary and contrasting functions in determining outcomes.

STATES

Chapter 2 outlined the concept of the state, as well as some of its ambiguities. Let us recall the definition that was given there: 'the state is sovereign, its institutions are public, it is based upon being legitimate, it is in the business of domination, and it covers a particular territorial area'. To this let us add one other characteristic that will be elaborated more in Chapter 10. In addition to their monopoly on the means of violence, states, especially modern states, also claim a monopoly on law-making. Pre-modern societies evolved binding rules for their members through a variety of means: edicts of rulers, clan or family traditions, religious prescriptions, and so on. They also often allowed a variety of agencies to enforce them. Modern states, however, claim the sole right to formulate laws and they insist that state courts enforce them.

At its most general, the state becomes a synonym for the structure of rule and authority within a particular geographical area. It is abstract. 'In some important senses, the state is more an idea held in common by a group of people, than it is a physical organism' (Buzan, 1991: 63). We talk of the nation-state, the welfare state, and so on.

Yet there is another, more limited and more concrete use of the term. This is used to designate the apparatus of institutions and individuals who are responsible for managing public affairs. It includes executives, legislatures, courts of justice, the armed forces, and central and local officials. This apparatus also collects revenue to pay for the services that it provides, whether through taxes or other forms of contributions. This use of the term is easier to grasp, but the overlap between the two levels of meaning of the term 'state' complicates the individual's relationship with the state. As Edelman wrote over fifty years ago: 'The state benefits and it threatens. Now it is "us" and often it is "them". It is an abstraction, but in its name men are jailed or made rich…, or killed in wars' (Edelman, 1964: 1). Commentators may alternate between the two and it is important always to keep this in mind. Most of this chapter will concentrate on the more organizational features of the state, although you should not forget the broader usage of the term. The rest of this chapter will focus first on the rise of the European state and then its proliferation across the world with the spread of the European state system. After that will follow a discussion of the modern state, and then of strong and weak states.

In more distant times, there was a much greater variety of forms of rule in tribes and small communities around the world. The antecedents for European ideas on government are to be found in writings from classical Greece and Rome, including the idea of democracy, and they were revived during the Renaissance after centuries of oblivion. However, the modern European state emerged gradually between the seventeenth and nineteenth centuries. And then, as we shall see, it spread to other parts of the world. Although there certainly were alternative forms of rule in other parts of the world that preceded it, such as the imperial system of classical China, modern states in other parts of the world display key features that make them more similar to the European model than their own historical predecessors.

KEY POINTS

- The term 'the state' is used in a great variety of ways, some concrete and some abstract. This makes detailed analysis difficult and contentious.

THE RISE OF THE EUROPEAN STATE

The first thing to note is the growth of state capacity over the last three centuries—a key fact that has already been mentioned in Chapter 2 and to which we will return again in Chapter 22. In Chapter 2, we introduced you to the theoretical concept of the state. Here, we will focus more upon its historical evolution. As Tilly put it, over the last 1,000 years, the European state has evolved from being a wasp to being a locomotive (Tilly, 1990: 96). By this he meant that the state has evolved from a small inconvenience to the people that it ruled into becoming a powerful driver of social and economic development. As we will show in more detail in Chapter 15, the origins of the modern state are to be found in Europe as it emerged between the seventeenth and the nineteenth centuries. Up until then, it was impossible to separate the personality of the state from the personality of the ruler. The ruler used personal appointees as officials to run the affairs of state. The ruler was also responsible for paying them and although some states did impose taxes, a great deal of the upkeep of officials came from the ruler's own property and income. A salaried bureaucracy began to emerge, and one of its most important functions was to collect and administer taxes. Gradually what emerged was a system for extracting taxes from broader sections of property owners, especially to pay for the most expensive state activity, which was warfare. Protracted wars risked bankrupting a monarch. As Tilly put it: 'War made the state and the state made war' (Tilly, 1975: 42). Time and again the need to raise funds for fighting drove further governments to devise new ways of raising money. The USA, for instance, introduced income tax in 1861 to pay for the effort of the civil war. Gradually this capacity, allied with access to a modernizing and industrializing commercial economy and a large rural population, enabled some states to dominate others (Tilly, 1990: 15). They in turn became the models with which others had to deal and, if possible, surpass.

The French Revolution transformed the powers of the state, as it introduced a level form of taxation for all its citizens and the principle of the modern mass army. This enabled the French for a while to dominate continental Europe. Britain was forced to emulate it so as to resist it. By the beginning of the nineteenth century, as Hegel recognized, the bureaucracy itself had become the state, elevating itself high above and separate from the rest of society (van Creveld, 1999: 143). This was a decisive development. First, what was expected from state officials was a primary loyalty to the state and the public good, rather than to any individual monarch or section of society. Then, second, they evolved rules and patterns of administration that further separated them

➡ See Chapter 2 for an exploration of different theoretical conceptions of the state.

➡ See Chapter 22 for an exploration of states in a globalizing world.

8

from the rest of society. Later, Weber publicized the importance of the new bureaucratic form of public administration: impersonal, rule-based, goal-oriented activity, with promotion of officials exclusively based on merit and performance. He made it into an ideal type of social organization, which he identified, not without misgivings, as part of a process of ever-growing rationalization of social life. He emphasized the technical superiority of bureaucratic over any other form of organization. Subsequent commentators have coined the term 'Weberian' public administration to denote this type of organization.

➡ See Chapter 16 for a more detailed discussion of the rise of the modern state system.

In addition, in the eighteenth and nineteenth centuries, the economic and military might of the dominant European powers, reinforced by superior technology, enabled them to develop empires overseas. This spread the European type of state to other continents through colonies, albeit in a cut-down version. Sometimes a private agency took over public functions. In India, for example, individual behaviour was traditionally regulated by caste associations rather than by the state. And the state had little power to levy taxes. 'Politics was thus consigned to the realm of spectacle and ceremony. No concept of a state, an impersonal public authority with a continuous identity, emerged: kings represented only themselves, not enduring states' (Khilnani, 2004: 20). Therefore, when the British arrived, the East India Company could start raising its own funds for public services without competing with the existing state authorities. In Burma, what made the colonial state different was also the concern of the new rulers with the growth of trade, something the traditional rulers had ignored (Taylor, 2009: 70). Administration in colonies was always more rudimentary than in the metropolitan countries, but even if it was a pale shadow of the original, it was still a recognizable copy.

➡ See Chapter 13 for a discussion of theories of bureaucratic policy-making.

The power of the model can be seen in the response of a state such as Japan. While the imperial European powers imposed their systems on the peoples that they colonized, not all territories became colonies, although most did. Japan was an exception. It had cut itself off from the outside world for 300 years when, in 1854, the American Commodore Perry led a number of warships into Tokyo Bay and demanded that Japan open up to international trade. The Japanese had no ships that could challenge the Americans and they were forced to agree. This set in train a whole series of transformations of Japanese society and the state as the Japanese sought to modernize, so that they could compete with the West and make Japan 'rich and strong'. This led to the imposition at first of a more authoritarian system of rule with the restoration to more effective power of the Meiji Emperor in 1868. The government swelled into a much larger civilian bureaucracy that could develop resources for the state. It sent representatives abroad to learn more about the political, legal, and technological strengths of the West, so that the best could be transplanted to Japan. The traditional class of independent warriors—the samurai—were forced to serve the state, either by becoming officials or officers in the new national army. In 1890 the first Japanese constitution came into force, which set limits (albeit ambiguous ones) on the powers of the Emperor. This also established a parliament and an independent judiciary. All of these reforms transformed Japan. From a backward and introverted nation it gradually became a recognizably modern state that by 1895 was able to defeat its biggest regional rival, China, and by 1904–5 was the first non-European state to win a war against a European imperial power—Russia. Japan then developed its own empire. Within a few decades, Japan had exploited the new state to expand its national might in a process that had taken European nations centuries.

Turkey is another of the few examples of the territories that did not become a Western colony but which adopted Western forms of rule so as to compete with the West. By the nineteenth century, the Ottoman Empire was in decline, and significantly, it was the military that took the lead in looking to the West for ideas and models of reform so that Turkey could compete. It was military considerations that drove increasingly radical reforms of the state in the nineteenth and twentieth centuries. This culminated in the rise of Ataturk as president of a secular republic in 1923, who pushed through a full separation of state and religion that was modelled primarily upon principles of laicism borrowed from France (Starr, 1992: 8–15).

After independence, the former colonies took over these state apparatuses and also the institutions that they had established. Whether it was the former Spanish colonies in Latin America during the nineteenth century, or the former British, French, German, and Italian colonies in the twentieth century, the newly independent states largely adopted the same basic attributes of rule, the same apparatus of institutions, even though they also in other respects usually expressed a forthrightly anti-imperialist ideology. Most importantly, they also adopted and often developed the bureaucratic machine that extracted resources from the people to pay for government. In some cases the innovation of the separation between ruler and officials that had earlier marked the rise of the modern state was now reversed. In what have been called patrimonial states, some rulers came to use the state to extract resources from the rest of society for their own benefit. This practice has been associated with African states, although it is not exclusive to that region.

As the European states grew stronger, gradually new institutions were devised to try to prevent them from becoming too despotic. Legal principles were established that would also constrain rulers, particularly through constitutions. Finer emphasized two events that were crucial in this respect: the American Revolution and the French Revolution. For him:

> the transcendent importance of the American Revolution is that it demonstrated for ever that quality of the Western European government we have called 'law-boundedness'. Here is a government which draws its powers from and can only act within a framework of fundamental law—the Constitution—which is itself interpreted by judges in the ordinary courts of the country. Could law-boundedness go further, could it receive a more striking affirmation?   (Finer, 1997: 1485)

From this followed six innovations, as can be seen from **Box 8.1**.

It was the American constitution that introduced the formal principle of 'separation of powers'. To some extent this evolved from practice in Britain, which had had a constitutional monarchy since 1689, and which had been extolled by Montesquieu (1689–1755) in his work *On the Spirit of Laws* of 1748, a strong influence upon many of the framers of the American Constitution.

BOX 8.1
The Governmental Innovations of the American Revolution

1. The deliberate formulation of a new frame of government by way of a popular convention.
2. A written constitution.
3. A bill of rights enshrined within it.
4. Guaranteed protection for these rights through judicial review.
5. The separation of powers along functional lines.
6. The division of powers between the national and the state governments.

(Finer, 1997: 1485)

Photo 8.1 The US Constitution/Bill of Rights. *Shutterstock RF: Pamela Au/Shutterstock.com*

However, whereas in Britain, and in other states in continental Europe, the basis for the different houses of parliament was social class—e.g. the House of Lords and the House of Commons—the distinction in the American Constitution was entirely abstract and functional—the House of Representatives and the senate. It was a more democratic form of institutionalization, which assumed that all citizens were equal and subject to the same laws.

At the time, the combination of new institutions and principles was an experiment. No one knew whether they would all work together. However, the American constitution has proved a model and a starting point for all subsequent writers of constitutions.

Then, only just over a decade later, another revolution further transformed the theory and practice of government: the French Revolution.

> **The French Revolution is the most important single event in the entire history of government. The American Revolution pales beside it. It was an earthquake. It razed and effaced all the ancient institutions of France, undermined the foundations of the other European states, and is still sending its shock-waves throughout the rest of the world.**   (Finer, 1997: 1517)

The governmental legacy of the French Revolution can be summarized in four main points. (**See Box 8.2.**)

As can be seen from this list, not all of the points can be reconciled with each other. The French Revolution celebrated the Rights of Man making all men equal, and at the same time inaugurated an era of populist dictatorship. Although the revolution had a universal appeal, France became

BOX 8.2
The Governmental Legacy of the French Revolution

1. The Declaration of The Natural Rights of Man and the Citizen established the legal basis for the sovereignty of the democratic state, based upon the General Will.
2. Nationalism—it laid down the national unity of all French citizens, and their primary obligation of loyalty to it. The Napoleonic wars spread the doctrine throughout Europe and provoked a matching response from the peoples of other nations.
3. Citizen armies—in the defence of the Revolution the French state mobilized far more citizens to fight on its behalf than had ever been seen in Europe, which forced its enemies to compete.
4. Neo-absolutism—the rise of the Committee of Public Safety followed by the Napoleonic dictatorship.

(Finer, 1997: 1538–66)

the prototype nation-state, with nationalism as its core political ideology and it provoked a backlash among other peoples, especially in the German states, that led to the creation of nation-states throughout Europe in the nineteenth century. And although it preached universal harmony, it also devised a new form of military organization—the mass citizen army—that became the model for military organization throughout Europe. Yet in their different ways, these diverse elements became the precursors for various forms of modern government not just in Europe, but also throughout the world. Both modern democracies and dictatorships, rule by law and by force, were prefigured by the French Revolution. Thus, although the French Revolution began as an attempt to create checks upon the absolutist monarchy, it instituted new forms of state activity that led to far greater intrusion in the lives of ordinary people than ever before. In that sense, as Finer puts it: 'all four [of these elements] are still alive, working like a leaven throughout the globe. In that sense the revolution is a Permanent Revolution. Nothing was ever like it before and nothing foreseeable will turn this Revolution back' (Finer, 1997: 1566).

KEY POINTS

- A crucial importance in the development of the European state was the separation of state officials from personal servants of the ruler.
- Another crucial development was the separation of the state from the rest of society through institutionalization and bureaucratization.
- Warfare was a catalyst for increasing the raising of funds for the state from society and increasing the state's reach.
- The American and French revolutions developed modern principles of government.
- This led to the invention of institutions to check the power of the state.

THE SPREAD OF THE EUROPEAN STATE SYSTEM

States today have two sets of roles or functions. The first consists of functions that they exercise towards their own populations. The second is those that they perform towards other states. States 'recognize' each other and by doing so confer an additional degree of legitimacy.

➜ See Chapter 16 for a more detailed discussion of the globalization of the modern state system.

The rise of the European state also transformed the international system. We will briefly outline it here because it explains the spread of the European type of state across the world. We will then return to it a more detailed discussion of the state and the international system in Chapter 16.

The modern European state system is normally taken to have resulted from the treaties that established the Peace of Westphalia in 1648 and ended the Thirty Years War. This led to the paradigm of a

> European state . . . [that] was a sovereign, territorially delimited political unit, facing other similar units, each striving for supremacy but never achieving it owing to their rapidly adopted skill of forming combinations that would defeat such a purpose, that is, the techniques of the 'balance of power' first developed by the Italian city-states in the fourteenth and fifteenth centuries.   (Finer, 1997: 1306)

In subsequent centuries Europeans spread their patterns of inter-state behaviour around the world as they built up empires, first in South America, then North America, Africa, and Asia. Western concepts of state sovereignty, originating with Bodin (see Chapter 16), differed from traditions in other parts of the world in two respects. First, they were based upon formal legal principles. Second, they insisted upon the sovereignty of a state running uniformly throughout territory within prescribed boundaries. In Africa, by contrast, authority and rule were more fluid. According to Clapham:

➜ See Chapter 16 for discussion of state sovereignty.

> African [states] formed islands of relatively settled government beyond which stretched deserts, forests or zones of progressively impoverished savannah which a strong ruler would seek to control but from which a weak one would retreat. Dissident or defeated groups could strike out into the borderlands to conquer or establish kingdoms of their own.   (Clapham, 1996: 29)

Likewise in South-East Asia, traditional understandings of state sovereignty focused more upon the mystical power of the ruler at the centre of the state which radiated outwards, like a force-field or like a cone of reflected light. Thus, the power was weaker the further that one went from the centre, until it ran up against a stronger force field from another state (Suwannathat–Pian, 1988: 29). In both continents states were defined by their capitals rather than by their perimeters. Therefore, traditional rulers concentrated more upon maintaining and strengthening the power at the centre and they paid less attention to what was happening on the periphery (Anderson, 1990: 21–36).

Western states imposed stronger boundaries on their territories and insisted upon undivided sovereignty right up to those borders. They drew much firmer borders, imposing them, often arbitrarily, upon peoples that they colonized. This was particularly true of South America and sub-Saharan Africa. The consequences of this for state legitimacy and viability are still with us today. When these colonies became independent, they usually took over the existing legal framework and these borders, reasserting the latter's inviolability. After independence they then tried to build modern nation-states, attempting to forge nations out of citizens on the European model. Thus, in many parts of the world it has been the state that has created the nation, whereas in Europe it has often been the nation that has created the state.

KEY POINTS

- The European type of state spread to lands on other continents.
- War and colonial expansion were the key elements in doing so.
- This also led to the emergence of a European-type system of states around the world.

THE MODERN STATE

Today the state has become the universal form of political organization around the world. Currently, 193 states are members of the United Nations, ranging in size from China with a population of over 1.3 billion to Tuvalu with a population estimated at 12,000. In area, they range from Russia with over 17 million sq. km to Monaco with an area of 2 sq. km. A third set of functions performed by a state relates to its relations with other states. States have to manage relations with each other through diplomacy and they have to devise defence policies to protect their territory and their people against attacks from outside. Equally importantly, states recognize each other as legitimate rulers over defined areas of territory and in this way they reduce the anarchy that exists, at least potentially, at the global level because of the lack of a global government. This diplomatic recognition provides reassurance against attack, although it is not an infallible guarantee. On the other hand, it also means that states expect their counterparts to interact with them in familiar and predictable ways. Bureaucratic agencies in one state that deal with the outside world—and in an era of globalization this is increasingly the case—expect to find equivalent agencies in other states. This strengthening international society contributes to the proliferation of government agencies in individual states.

There is no doubt about the national importance of state apparatuses—given the growing share of state expenditure in individual countries' GDP, as can be seen from **Table 8.1**.

This charts their growth, particularly since the end of the Second World War. Figures on the size of government bureaucracies tell the same story, as seen in **Table 8.3**, even though there are great differences between the practices of countries over whom they count as state officials. Some states have been proportionately much bigger than these three.

How, then, do we generalize what states are and what they do? One way is to focus upon their origins and sources of legitimation. Stepan has proposed a distinction between what he terms 'nation states' (e.g. France, Sweden, Japan, and Portugal) and 'state nations' (e.g. Belgium, Canada, India, Spain, and Ukraine) (see **Table 8.2**). The differences between them are explained in **Box 8.3**. But it is worthwhile considering a third type of state which does not otherwise fit easily into this typology, namely Islamic states. So the key debate also presents a synopsis of key features of such states.

Table 8.1 Growth of general government expenditure in selected countries, 1870–2016 (% of GDP)

General government for all years	About 1870	1913	1920	1937	1960	1980	1990	1995	2006	2016 (*2015)
Australia	18.3	16.5	19.3	14.8	21.2	34.1	34.9	37.4	34.9	37.2*
Austria	10.5	17	14.7	20.6	35.7	48.1	38.6	56.3	49.4	51.1
Canada			16.7	25	28.6	38.8	46	48.5	39.3	41.6
France	12.6	17	27.6	29	34.6	46.1	49.8	54.4	52.7	56.5
Germany	10	14.8	25	34.1	32.4	47.9	45.1	54.8	45.3	44.3
Italy	13.7	17.1	30.1	31.1	30.1	42.1	53.4	52.5	49.9	49.6
Ireland			18.8	25.5		48.9	41.2	41.1	33.8	28.1
Japan	8.8	8.3	14.8	25.4	17.5	32	31.3		36	39.4*
New Zealand			24.6	25.3	26.9	38.1	41.3	41.4	39.9	39.5*
Norway	5.9	9.3	16	11.8	29.9	43.8	54.9	50.9	40.5	51.1
Sweden		10.4	10.9	16.5	31	60.1	59.1	65.1	54.3	50
Switzerland	16.5	14	17	24.1	17.2	32.8		35	33.7	33.9*
United Kingdom	9.4	12.7	26.2	30	32.2		39.9	43.9	44.2	42.1
United States	7.3	7.5	12.1	19.7	27	31.4	32.8	37	36.4	37.7*
Average	10.8	13.1	19.6	23.8	28	41.9	43		42.1	43.8*

Source: Tanzi and Schuknecht (2000: 6–7); OECD *Government at a Glance 2009* (https://read.oecd-ilibrary.org/governance/government-at-a-glance-2009/general-government-expenditures-as-a-percentage-of-gdp-1995-2006_9789264075061-graph4_1-en#page1); OECD *Government at a Glance 2017* (https://stats.oecd.org/viewhtml.aspx?datasetcode=GOV_2017&lang=en).

A second approach to analysing and comparing states is functionalist. This focuses upon the different types of functions that they perform. Gill has suggested that there are three basic types of internal roles performed by the modern state. The first is that of the state as partisan. In other words, the state operates on the basis of, and pursues, its own interests. This is reinforced by a Weberian state bureaucracy with its own structure and procedures that resist pressures from the rest of society. This would be typical of authoritarian regimes.

The second role is that of the state as guardian. Here the state stabilizes and where necessary rebalances society in a way of which society itself is incapable. Therefore, the state is essential for social stability. This could be because of fundamental conflict in society which threatens to tear it apart. Examples of this would be federal or consociational political systems which have been designed to counter fundamental cleavages in society and to which we shall return in more detail in Chapter 10. Or it could take the form of a developmental state already mentioned in Chapter 2, as in East Asia, where the state directs the development of society and the economy in what it regards as a path of development that is in the national interest, e.g. industrialization and economic modernization.

➡ See Chapter 2 for a description of the developmental state.

KEY DEBATE BOX 8.3
Nation-States, State-Nations, and Islamic States

'Nation-state policies stand for a political-institutional approach that attempts to match the political boundaries of the state with the presumed cultural boundaries of the nation . . . By contrast state-nation policies stand for a political-institutional approach that respects and protects multiple but complementary sociocultural identities . . . State-nation policies involve crafting a sense of belonging (or "we-feeling") with respect to the state-wide political community, while simultaneously creating institutional safeguards for respecting and protecting politically salient sociocultural diversities.'

Table 8.2 Ideal Types of Nation-states and State-nations

	Nation-state	State-nation
Pre-existing conditions: sense of belonging/'we-feeling'	Attachment to one major cultural civilizational tradition, which largely corresponds to existing state boundaries	Attachment to more than one cultural civilizational tradition within existing boundaries, possibly of an existing state
State policy: cultural policies	Unity in oneness: homogenizing cultural identity, especially one official language	Unity in diversity: recognition and support for more than one cultural identity, including more than one official language, within one state
Institutions: territorial division of power	Unitary states or symmetrical federations	Federal or asymmetrical unitary states, accepting state multilingual areas
Politics: ethno-cultural or territorial cleavages	Not very salient	Salient, recognized, and democratically managed
Politics: autonomous or secessionist parties	Autonomist parties are normally excluded from coalitions. Secessionist parties are outlawed or marginalized	Autonomist parties can be included in coalitions at the centre and govern in federal units. Non-violent secessionist parties can participate in the democratic process
Citizen orientation: political identity	Single identity in state and cultural nation	Multiple but complementary identities
Citizen orientation: obedience/loyalty	Obedience to state and loyalty to nation	Multiple state identity and identification with multiple institutions

Source: Stepan, Linz, and Yadav (2011: 4–5, 8).

Islamic States

Islamic states, or states with predominantly Muslim populations, amalgamate many features of these two types. They accept diversity of cultural and linguistic policies, and historically they have recognized the need for special administrative arrangements for religious and ethnic minorities, but they are suspicious of secessionism. They have practised tolerance rather than toleration (Krämer, 2015: 179–84). The state expects loyalty and obedience. It bans the conversion of Muslims to other religions, while encouraging the conversion of other believers to Islam. Even though numerous separate states have been created in the Middle East, their legitimacy has been periodically challenged by the supranational values of Islamic religion and of the aspiration for a global community of believers, the *umma*. From this perspective, sovereignty belongs only to God (Allah), rather than to people, or any group of them. Legitimacy comes ultimately from divine sources rather than from any particular territory. 'Islamic government draws its principles, laws, and practices from the shari'a' (Shahin, 2015: 72). As a consequence, Islamic states always make an explicit claim to practise (divine-inspired) morality (Hallaq, 2014), and their legitimacy should be assessed according to the extent to which they do so (Rauf, 2015) Other kinds of states do not admit to behaving immorally, but they do not typically make an explicit claim to epitomize morality.

This marks a basic difference from both nation-states and state-nations in the rest of the world. Both of these other types are fundamentally contested in the Islamic world. In Islamic political thought, 'the state is never considered in terms of a territorialized nation-state: the ideal is to have a power that would rule over the entirety of the *umma*, the community of the faithful, while actual power is exercised over a segment of the *umma*, whose borders are contingent, provisional, and incomplete' (Roy, 1994: 13). The long-term ambition is to restore the concept of a 'caliphate' as both precedent and future ideal, a single Islamic state ruled by a caliph (i.e. a 'deputy of God') for all Muslims, as originally existed in the Islamic world immediately after the death of the Prophet. Radical movements to create new Islamic states, such as the Muslim Brotherhood, ISIS (Islamic State in Syria, Iraq, and the Levant), and Hezbollah aim to merge existing states (e.g. Syria, Iraq, and Lebanon) and destroy the state boundaries imposed by colonial powers in the early twentieth century as a step towards one overarching caliphate. Such an enterprise is, however, bedevilled by the fundamental division in the Islamic world between Sunnis and Shi'as (Muslim Brotherhood and IS are predominantly Sunni, while Hezbollah is Shi'a), by persisting ethnic and other divisions, and by the need at least for now to interact with other states. Attempts to establish Islamic states have ended in failure, but according to Roy (1994), the ideal of an Islamic caliphate does not die either.

Based on: Roy (1994); Hallaq (2014); Krämer (2015); Shahin (2015); Rauf (2015).

Questions

1. Are nation-states only to be found in the developed world?
2. Are state-nations only to be found in the developing world?
3. Are there any examples of state-nations becoming nation-states?
4. How different are explicitly Islamic states such as Iran from other types of states?

8

Table 8.3 Size of government bureaucracies, selected years

	1821	1985*
Germany	23,000**	855,000
UK	27,000	1,065,000
USA	8,000	3,797,000

*Central government civil servants only

**Prussia only

Source: Finer (1997: 1624). From Catherine Jones Finer, 'The New Social Policy in Britain', *Social Policy & Administration*, 17 December 2002. John Wiley and Sons. © John Wiley & Sons Ltd.

The third type of role is the state as instrument. Here the state operates primarily as a tool in the hands of some group or groups in society at large. This could take the form of a genuine liberal democracy, where the people are in control of the state's actions. Alternatively it could be a state that is controlled by a particular section of society, e.g. a particular ethnic group or 'big business'; or it could even be a patrimonial state, where political actors take advantage of state power to enrich themselves and their clients. Here the state is just a tool.

In practice, any modern state performs a combination of all three roles. Most state bureaucracies operate to some extent on the basis of their own codified procedures and institutions that are intended to resist outside turbulence. Most states do develop some perspective on the desirable path of development for that society and attempt to mobilize resources to achieve it, and most states are to some extent responsive to groups outside themselves. Dictators such as former President Suharto of Indonesia favour 'loyal' businessmen who do their bidding and in return enjoy special favours. Thus, what is important is the balance between these three types of roles in particular states. Are they *predominantly* partisans, guardians, or instruments?

KEY POINTS

- The state in the West today is larger than at any time in history.
- A basic ideal-type distinction is between 'nation-states' and 'state-nations'.
- States with large Islamic populations amalgamate the two types, and are also overshadowed by the traditional ideal of a single Islamic caliphate.
- The modern state can act predominantly either as partisan, as a guardian, or as an instrument.

STRONG STATES AND WEAK STATES

This list of state functions, internal and external, suggests that the modern state has become more powerful than at any time in its history. According to the historian A. J. P. Taylor (1965: 1), 'Until August 1914, a sensible, law-abiding Englishman could pass through life and hardly notice the existence of the state, beyond the post office and the policeman.' All this was changed by the First World War. There is no doubt that the twentieth century witnessed the most extreme manifestations of state power that the world has ever seen, in the form of what some analysts characterized as totalitarian systems, such as Hitler's Germany and Stalin's Russia. Even though state control was never as completely total as the term might imply and there still remained pockets of resistance, there was no doubt about the aspiration of their leaders for total control, or the spread of institutions to try to achieve it. Now that the archives of some of these states are open, it is possible to gain a clearer perspective on the size of such states. For example, at the time of its collapse in 1989, the German Democratic Republic had what has been described as a 'honeycomb' state, in which perhaps one-sixth of the adult population were involved in one way or another in the state's 'micro-systems of power'. Over 91,000 were full-time employees of the secret police alone by the time the state collapsed, a ratio of one to every 180 people in the population and the highest for any former communist state (Fulbrook, 2005: 236, 241). Yet, however strong and all-powerful they looked, most of these regimes have now collapsed.

These were extreme versions of the modern state. As the powers of the state have increased in the twentieth century, so too have been the expectations of what it can perform. Rotberg has provided a long list of the political goods or functions that a modern state might be expected to provide its citizens. Typically the most important are:

1. human security;
2. predictable, recognizable, systematized methods of adjudicating disputes, and regulating both the norms and the prevailing mores of a particular society or polity;
3. freedom to participate in politics and compete for office, respect, and support for national and regional political institutions, such as legislatures and courts, tolerance of dissent and difference, and fundamental civil and human rights.

However, there are many others also expected by citizens: medical and healthcare, schools and educational institutions, roads, railways, harbours and other elements of physical infrastructure, communication networks, money and a banking system with a national currency, a beneficent fiscal and institutional environment within which citizens can pursue personal entrepreneurial goals and potentially prosper, space for the flowering of civil society, and methods of regulating the sharing of the environmental commons (Rotberg, 2004: 2–3). If we look at states in the developed world, we can usually find that they perform these functions to the satisfaction of their citizens, even if not perfectly. They are 'strong' or 'robust' states.

However, it is important to remember that not all states today are like that. There are many that are clearly weak. Most are to be found in the developing world. Chabal and Daloz have argued that the state in Africa is 'not just weak, but essentially vacuous, with virtually none meeting the Weberian criteria' (Chabal and Daloz, 1999: 1). Bayart amplified this by saying that in most states of sub-Saharan Africa:

> The frontiers of the state are transgressed, the informal sector is a canker on the official economy, taxes are not collected, poaching and undisciplined exploitation of mineral resources becomes endemic, weapons circulate, resettled villages split up, the people appropriate the legitimate use of force to themselves and deliver summary justice, delinquency spreads, businesses suffer from languor induced by underproductivity, delays and absences.   (Bayart, 1993: 258)

Table 8.4 contains a list of the twenty 'weakest' states according to the *Foreign Policy* magazine in 2007 and 2013.

Table 8.4 Ranked list of the twenty weakest states in 2007 and 2019

Rank	Country 2007	Country 2019
1.	Sudan	Yemen
2.	Iraq	Somalia
3.	Somalia	South Sudan
4.	Zimbabwe	Syria
5.	Chad	Democratic Republic of Congo
6.	Ivory Coast	Central African Republic
7.	Democratic Republic of the Congo	Chad
8.	Afghanistan	Sudan
9.	Guinea	Afghanistan
10.	Central African Republic	Zimbabwe
11.	Haiti	Guinea
12.	Pakistan	Haiti
13.	North Korea	Iraq
14.	Burma	Nigeria
15.	Uganda	Burundi
16.	Bangladesh	Cameroon
17.	Nigeria	Eritrea
18.	Ethiopia	Niger
19.	Burundi	Guinea Bissau
20.	East Timor	Uganda

Source: Fund For Peace (http://fsi.fundforpeace.org/rankings-2007-sortable) and (https://fundforpeace.org/2019/04/10/fragile-states-index-2019/).

The case study presents the story of Somalia which has been effectively a territory without a central state since 1991. (**See Box 8.4**.) This makes it the territory with the longest such experience in modern times. How did this happen? As Hobbes was quoted as saying in Chapter 2, this should be a region where life is 'solitary, poor, nasty, brutish and short': is this actually the case?

Thus, even though the structures of modern states are fairly similar, they vary considerably according to their capacities. This raises the question of what makes a state strong, and conversely, what makes it weak. It is possible to identify a series of factors.

Clearly, one is size. Although China enjoys the same international legal status as Monaco, in practice there is an enormous difference in their respective capacity to pursue their goals in the world.

Another factor is the strength of the economy. As the largest economy in the world, the USA possesses the capacity to finance a high level of domestic public services and respond to the

➡ See Chapter 2 for more on Hobbes and the social contract tradition.

CASE STUDY BOX 8.4
Somalia as a Failed State

Unlike many postcolonial states, especially in sub-Saharan Africa, Somalia does not suffer particularly from ethnic heterogeneity. Nor are most of its boundaries much disputed, though Somalis have also traditionally resided in what are now Ethiopia, Kenya, and Djibouti. Occupying territory as large as France, it has a population estimated in 2007 at 9.1 million, i.e. only roughly 15 per cent of the French. However, all Somalis believe they are descended from a common ancestor. The main divisions between Somalis are based upon clans and sub-clans rather than separate ethnicity. In addition, some commentators on Somalia have also stressed the strong-minded individualism of nomadic herdsmen who view authority with suspicion. The colonial and postcolonial states have all been suspended above the rest of society, only partially integrated into it.

In 1960 the post-independence state was formed from former British and Italian colonies. In 1969 power was seized by General Siad Barre after the assassination of the last civilian president. Barre attempted to create a modern state by suppressing traditional clan ties, but gradually the army fragmented along clan lines. Barre's regime became notoriously corrupt and its domestic support shrank to his own clan.

In 1991 he was overthrown by his former intelligence chief, Mohamed Farah Aidid, which then provoked a bloody civil war between rival militias. Initially the conflict was confined within the country, but hundreds of thousands of people died either from the ferocious fighting or

Photo 8.2 The 1st July 1960 marked the unification of former British and Italian colonies in Somalia. *hikrcn/Shutterstock*

➔

subsequent starvation. In 1993 the UN, and primarily the USA, attempted to impose a peace which would mark a new role in peace-making in the post-Cold War era with Operation Restore Hope. They were initially welcomed into the capital, Mogadishu, but after a few months their unsuccessful attempts to arrest the most prominent warlord, Aidid, led to widespread civilian casualties and united Somalis against outsiders. Even the Red Cross had to be protected. Mogadishu was devastated by withering American firepower and retaliation (Peterson, 2000). The deaths and mutilation of American servicemen in the events popularized in the film *Blackhawk Down* turned American popular opinion against the intervention, and the UN later withdrew. Since then, Somalis have largely been left to their own devices.

There is no central authority in Somalia. In 2003 Kenya took the lead in organizing a conference that established a Transitional Federal Government, but little progress has been made in its national legitimacy. In late 2006, forces from Ethiopia intervened to frustrate a movement for unity on the basis of Islamic courts.

Menkhaus (2007: 86-7) writes of 'a loose constellation of commercial city-states and villages separated by long stretches of pastoral statelessness'. *De facto*, one part of the country (Puntland) has declared autonomy, while another (Somaliland) in the north is effectively independent. The only effective administrations are at the local level, and public services (education, healthcare, welfare) have collapsed. Clans and sub-clans defend their interests using traditional customary interclan practices of recompense for injuries or damage received by their members instead of relying upon state justice, but heavily armed militias can still demand resources largely with impunity. Yet average life expectancy is estimated in the CIA's *World Factbook* at fifty-two years (though no statistics are very reliable)—higher than in many other African countries and about the same as in Nigeria. Somaliland is supposedly as safe as anywhere in the Horn of Africa. It has even established a rudimentary democratic system with elections and political parties. Insecurity is certainly a major problem in the country—perhaps 500,000 people have been killed and there are estimates of 2 million Somali refugees abroad, one-fifth of the population. Sporadic civil war continues, driving refugees abroad and periodically emptying the capital, Mogadishu.

The traditional economy of trade in herds of cattle is flourishing as compared with the pre-1991 period, since the state cannot extract usurious taxes (Little, 2003). Private enterprise has found ways of providing services such as the transfer of money within and outside the country despite the lack of banks. Businessmen also buy off militiamen to provide security for their trade, so there is no state monopoly on the means of violence. Mobile phone companies prosper, while the landline service decays. The private sector has taken over the supply of public services where quick profits are possible, e.g. running ports, airports, electricity supply, but not public sanitation. Transnational corporations such as Total and GM have found ways of doing business in the country despite the lack of a stable institutional and legal system. Somalis abroad remit back home anywhere between US$500 million and US $1 billion per year, which bolsters the domestic economy, especially in the cities.

Somalis have found ways of coping with the lack of a state, which they regard as 'an instrument of accumulation and domination, enriching and empowering those who control it and exploiting and harassing the rest of the population' (Menkhaus, 2007: 86-7). Yet they are disadvantaged because they cannot protect their maritime resources, having no navy, and they cannot defend their businesses against foreign discrimination. Saudi Arabia, previously the largest importer of Somali cattle, banned them because the country could no longer provide a veterinary service to prevent the spread of disease. The insecurity in urban areas has prevented any significant investment in infrastructure or industry. The lack of a normally functioning state has also facilitated intrusion by outside forces, whether Islamic groups such as the Islamic Courts Union which for a while occupied part of the country, and then were pushed back external peace-keeping forces from Ethiopia and Kenya.

preferences of its people. By contrast, a poor state such as Burma is much less capable of providing a wide range of adequate services for its people.

A third factor is military might. Again, the USA as the only remaining military superpower can do far more than other states to protect its people and territory, as well as pursue foreign policy goals, although its failures in Iraq suggest that there are more limits to this power than were previously supposed.

So far, we have looked primarily at external factors in estimating the strength of states, but equally important are domestic ones. First, there is the issue of legitimacy. If a state lacks the consent to rule on the part of its people, then it is bound to be potentially weak, because it will need to rely more upon force to achieve acquiescence. This could be the result of dissension over its borders. Many postcolonial states have international frontiers that were imposed more or less arbitrarily, with the frequent consequence that ethnic or tribal communities straddle borders and refuse to think of themselves as citizens of at least one of the states where they are found and wish to establish their own homeland; or it could be the result of challenges to the dominant ideology of the state. Ultimately what brought down the regimes in Eastern Europe and the former Soviet Union was the lack of support for the official ideology of communism. And some states are bedevilled by the legacies of overlapping layers of different historical colonizers. Syria, for example, was a much larger entity in the Ottoman Empire, but then had its current borders fixed by the British and the French after the First World War. Syrian leaders never fully accepted the change and now the country has sunk into murderous civil war. Without that shared sense of popular legitimacy and accepted borders, states are brittle, however superficially strong they may look. They are vulnerable to new challenges because they lack flexibility and are slow to adapt.

A second crucial factor in the strength of states is the robustness of the state institutions themselves. To what extent can they withstand turbulence from the rest of society? Bayart, Chabal, and Daloz repeatedly emphasize the weakness of many African states as the result of the interpenetration of state, society, and the economy. Individual African politicians expect to use the state to become rich as a way of impressing others and redistributing resources to their 'clients'. 'Rich men are powerful and powerful men are rich' (Chabal and Daloz, 1999: 52). Ethnic and tribal communities expect 'their' representatives, whether democratically elected or even lowly officials in the government bureaucracy, to channel resources to them, because if they do not do so, no one will. Thus, state institutions in Africa are far less robust than in the West, because they do not stand above or apart from society in the same way. The structuration provided by the rest of the society outweighs the capacity for autonomous, rule-based behaviour on the part of the bureaucracy. The institutions are not really institutionalized, and the African state is more easily penetrated by outside forces as a result—at least for the moment. The emergence of robust African states may in part be simply a matter of time—the time that it takes for political ideas and political behaviour to adjust to the still relatively new state units. Van Creveld (1999: 306) reminds us that in the nineteenth century newly independent states in South America suffered similar fragility. Colombia had thirty civil wars, Venezuela had fifty revolutions, and Bolivia sixty. According to Coronil on Venezuela, at the beginning of the twentieth century:

> [T]he state was so weak and precarious as a national institution that its stability and legitimacy were constantly at risk. Without a national army or an effective bureaucracy, in an indebted country that lacked a national road network or an effective system of communication, the state appeared as an unfulfilled project whose institutional form remained limited to localized sites of power with but partial dominion over the nation's territory and sway over its citizens.   (Coronil, 1997: 76)

We shall see in Chapter 11 that it does not look like this now. From this, it might be argued that maybe in time African states will also acquire greater robustness.

To some extent, this section has identified fundamental disparities between the state in the developed world and the state in the developing one today. In general, European states and the USA are strong, while those in the developing world are weaker. All of the weak states listed in **Table 8.4** are former Western colonies. General theorizing about the state by Western political scientists has tended to focus on the issues associated with the strong. Recently, however, the problems of weakening states in the developed world have begun to attract more attention. Increasing globalization is beginning, but still only just beginning, to recast this debate. States in the developed world are now increasingly exercised by the erosion of their sovereignty, for example by multinational corporations and other transnational actors and forces (Marsh et al., 2006: 176). The erosion has not yet reached anything like the same level as in the developing world. Nevertheless, there seems to be a spreading slow decline in the autonomy of the state in different parts of the world. To that extent the vectors of state capabilities in different parts of the world are beginning to converge again. This is an issue to which we shall return in Chapter 21.

➡ See Chapter 11 for a case study on Venezuela.

➡ See Chapter 21 for an exploration of the impact of globalization on the study of politics.

KEY POINTS

- There is an enormous range in the capabilities of states in different regions of the world.
- Some states are at best 'quasi' states (Jackson, 1990).
- States need legitimacy and robust institutions to be strong.
- Globalization has a growing impact on limiting state capabilities around the world.

CONCLUSION

This chapter has set the framework for the next seven chapters. These will explore various dimensions of the state, whether as organization or as structures of authority. It has also illustrated the great disparity in capabilities between some states and others. The next chapter will expand the focus to cover political culture, and introduce themes of the way that peoples outside the West think about politics.

KEY QUESTIONS

1. What is a nation-state? Does it matter whether the nation or the state came first?

2. Does the state require moral authority to enjoy domestic legitimacy?

3. Is state capacity simply a function of the level of economic development? Or is it simply a function of longevity and habituation (compare Latin America with sub-Saharan Africa)?

4. How far can theories of the modern Western state (see Hay et al.) be applied to states in the developing world?

5. Is the UK now a nation-state or a state-nation? What about Canada?

6. Did internal dissension or external destabilization play a bigger role in destroying the Somalian state?

7. How would you try to strengthen a weak state in the developing world? Would democracy help?

8. Is Pakistan a failed state (see Lieven)? Can the outside world do anything about it?

9. Are some states simply too weak and/or too arbitrarily constructed to justify continued international recognition? Should the international community simply let them disintegrate? What would be the consequences?

10. Is the state entering a period of decline? How would you measure its effectiveness compared with earlier periods?

FURTHER READING

Buzan, B. (1991), *People, States and Fear* (London: Harvester International, 2nd edn), esp. ch. 2.
A much-read study that considers both the internal and external roles of the state.

Chabal, P. and Daloz, J.-P. (1999), *Africa Works: Disorder as Political Instrument* (Oxford: International Africa Institute in association with James Currey).
This is a vivid account of the distinctive features of states in Africa.

Feldman, N. (2008), *The Fall and Rise of the Islamic State* (Princeton: Princeton University Press).
A sophisticated introduction to the history of the Islamic state and its contemporary evolution.

Fergusson, J. (2013), *The World's Most Dangerous Place* (Boston, MA: Da Capo Press).
A journalist's account of life in Somalia.

Fukuyama, F. (2011), *The Origins of Political Order: From Prehuman Times to the French Revolution* (London: Profile Books)

Fukuyama, F. (2014), *Political Order and Political Decay: From the Industrial Revolution to the Globalization of Democracy* (London: Profile Books)
A magisterial account of the origins of states in various continents.

Gill, G. (2003), *The Nature and Development of the Modern State* (Basingstoke: Palgrave).
This is a good survey of theories of the state in the aftermath of the collapse of communism.

Hay, C., Lister, M., and Marsh, D. (eds) (2006), *The State: Theories and Issues* (Basingstoke: Palgrave).

This is a collection of articles that discuss contemporary issues in theories of the Western state.

Kaviraj, S. (2011), 'On the enchantment of the state: Indian thought on the role of the state in the narrative of modernity', in Akhil Gupta and K. Sivaramakrishnan (eds), *The State in India After Liberalization: Interdisciplinary Perspectives* (London and New York: Routledge), 31–48.

An excellent outline of the evolution of Indian thinking on the state over centuries, which also sketches the different type of rule in pre-colonial times.

Leftwich, A. (2004), 'Theorizing the State', in Peter Burnell and Vicky Randall (eds), *Politics in the Developing World* (Oxford: Oxford University Press), 139–54.

This is an attempt to extend theories of the state to the developing world.

Lieven, A. (2011), *Pakistan: A Hard Country* (New York: Public Affairs).

A sympathetic and well-informed analysis of a troubled state whose fate is often linked to security in the West.

Van Creveld, M. (1999), *The Rise and Decline of the State* (Cambridge: Cambridge University Press).

This is a sweeping historical survey of the rise and spread of the Western state.

 For additional material and resources, please visit the Online Resources at: **www.oup.com/he/garner4e**

POLITICAL CULTURE AND NON-WESTERN POLITICAL IDEAS

READER'S GUIDE

Chapter 8 emphasized the crucial importance of **institutions** in structuring political behaviour, whatever the form of government. Yet, at the same time, states with basically similar political structures operate in different ways. One of the main causes of this is the political culture of a particular country.

This chapter will begin by presenting the concept of political culture. Then it will turn to examining non-Western political ideas. Finally it will look at the differing ways in which 'liberalism' has been understood in different states and regions as a way of illustrating the complexity of the ways in which political ideologies may be understood today in different parts of the world.

POLITICAL CULTURE

Political culture is 'the totality of ideas and attitudes towards authority, discipline, governmental responsibilities and entitlements, and associated patterns of cultural transmissions such as the education system and family life' (Robertson, 1993: 382). Pye (1968: 218) adds that it is 'the product of both the collective history of a political system and the life histories of the members of that system, and thus it is rooted equally in public events and private experiences.' This makes it both a substantial factor in any nation's politics and a very elusive one to analyse.

One of the pioneers of this approach to politics was Alexis de Tocqueville, who was trying to explain the differences between politics in the US and in continental Europe in the mid-nineteenth century. He argued that American family relations and social life were quite different from the aristocratic societies with which he was familiar in Europe and that this produced a different kind of politics.

The World Values Surveys have produced a cultural map based upon their findings over the period 1981–2015 which has identified nine groupings of countries whose social values over a whole range of issues, not just politics, tend to make them more similar. These are (in no order of importance): Protestant Europe, English-speaking, Catholic Europe, Latin American, Orthodox, Baltic, South Asian, African-Islamic, and Confucian (World Values Survey, 2019). Whilst they argue that there is a long-term continuity to these groupings, it is also clear that the boundaries of these groupings can shift over time, and if so, it reinforces the point made in Chapter 8 about factors such as political culture 'structuring' political behaviour rather than determining it. Insofar as this is true, it qualifies the emphasis that de Tocqueville placed upon political culture as the fundamental determinant of political life.

Yet, at the same time, another differentiating factor is the degree of interest in politics among a nation's citizens. The most recent World Values Survey (2010–15) demonstrated this with the following results, but these too may fluctuate over time, often depending upon political events

Photo 9.1 Alexis de Tocqueville. *Library of Congress*

or trends within them. For example, the high degree of interest in politics claimed in Thailand in **Table 9.1** can at least in part be attributed to waves of protests over democracy and the lack of it that were flowing over the country at that time. The same is true for the figures for Egypt, which was then in the aftermath of the 'Arab Spring'. For the previous survey (2005–9), only 9.1 per cent

➡ See Chapter 4 for a discussion of deliberative democracy.

> ## KEY QUOTE BOX 9.1
> ### Alexis de Tocqueville (1805–59)
>
> It is therefore particularly mores (i.e. habits and opinions) that render the Americans of the United States . . . capable of supporting the empire of democracy, and it is again [mores] that make the various Anglo-American democracies more or less regulated and prosperous . . . I am convinced that the happiest situation and the best laws cannot maintain a constitution despite mores, whereas the latter turn even the most unfavourable positions and the worst laws to good account. The importance of mores is a common truth to which study and experience constantly lead back. It seems to me that I have it placed it in my mind as a central point; I perceive it as the end of all my ideas. (Tocqueville, 2000: 295)

9

Table 9.1 Intensity of interest in politics in selected countries: Proportion of responses to question 'How important is politics in your life?' (%)

Country	Very important	Rather important	Not very	Not at all
Brazil	12.5	28.8	29.6	28.4
China	10.4	28.3	46.5	7.2
Egypt	31	44	14	11
Germany	10.1	34.2	42.5	13.1
India	17	26.2	26.8	25.9
Japan	23.5	42.6	23.9	2.7
Kuwait	31.2	27.6	20.6	14.7
Mexico	17	28	31.8	23.3
Nigeria	21	28.1	33.4	17.4
Russia	6.9	20.2	40.1	30.3
South Africa	21.4	24.2	28.9	23.7
Spain	5.9	15.8	41	36.5
Thailand	32	41	19.8	5.2
Turkey	16.1	31.3	32.3	19.2
US	11.2	41.8	34.9	11

Source: Inglehart et al. (2014).

of respondents claimed to be 'very interested' in politics, whilst 62.5 per cent admitted that politics was either 'not very important' or 'not at all important' in their lives, almost the reverse of the later findings.

The significance of political culture and the weight that it places on politics can be seen in the difficulties that states and leaders have in trying to change it, or even completely remake it. A good example comes from China and the attempts of Mao to transform Chinese social attitudes during the Cultural Revolution, **see Box 9.2**.

CASE STUDY BOX 9.2
The Attempted Chinese Cultural Revolution

In China the state has traditionally been obsessed with its history. 'Chinese governments have, for at least 2,000 years, taken history much too seriously to allow the future to make its own unguided judgements about them . . . Historical myth-making has so far been remarkably effective, not just in inventing a single Han Chinese ethnicity but also—and this is a far bigger triumph—in winning acceptance of it . . . The religion of the Chinese ruling classes is the Chinese state, and it is through history that the object of devotion is to be understood' (Jenner, 1992: 3–4).

When the Chinese Communist Party came to power in 1949, it did so contrary to orthodox Marxist predictions and scepticism from Stalin, and in the face of apparently overwhelming military opposition. The Chinese communist leaders were euphoric, and none more so than Mao. Although they were well aware of China's economic backwardness, they believed that the success of the revolution had shown the fundamental revolutionary spirit of the Chinese people and their aspiration to break out of a century of Chinese decline and humiliation. This would mean turning their backs on the old history.

In 1958 Mao launched the Great Leap Forward (GLF), his attempt to get China to catch up and overtake the developed capitalist nations of the West through the introduction of socialist forms of management. He argued that the Chinese people were ambitious for revolution and 'poor and blank' like a sheet of paper, on which the regime could paint beautiful and inspiring pictures. It was an audacious attempt to transform and politicize popular attitudes. At its core was the creation of communes, would-be self-sufficient communities of anywhere up to 100,000 people in both the countryside and urban areas, which would satisfy the needs of their inhabitants for agricultural and industrial goods and would supplant the traditional family with a new socialist community.

The GLF proved a disaster. Anywhere up to 45 million people died in the resulting famine (Dikötter, 2010). Mao was forced to retreat—for a while. At the end of 1965 he launched what came to be known as the Great People's Cultural Revolution, which was intended to revive the people's revolutionary spirit by stigmatizing the forces of reaction that were holding the country back—the 'four olds', i.e. old ideas, old customs, old habits, and old culture. One of the targets of the Cultural Revolution was Confucius, whose precepts on social organization were presented as 'reactionary'. For at least three years the country was wracked by political turmoil, with frequent campaigns to mobilize young people to instil new revolutionary ideas throughout the people, which often degenerated into factional conflicts (Dikötter, 2017).

→

Although the Cultural Revolution subsided from 1969 onwards, Mao never recanted its goals. After his death in 1976 his successors gradually abandoned the open revolutionary disruption of society and implemented economic reforms, which have made China into the second largest economy in the world. And from the early 1990s the Chinese communist leadership has restored Confucius to a place of legitimate national honour, albeit presenting his teachings along the lines of a twenty-first century more meritocratic society rather than those of a 'feudal', hierarchical one (Bell, 2008; Yu, 2009). It has even established a network of Confucius Centres around the world to spread foreign understanding of China and its culture, and to promote China's image and soft power as a state with an ancient and still relevant civilization, although his status remains contentious in some quarters. In 2011 a statue of Confucius was formally unveiled on Tiananmen Square in Beijing, only for it to be mysteriously removed a few months later.

This case study has illustrated the persisting grip of a nation's political culture on the minds of its people, even in the face of the enormous power of a communist regime. It has also suggested that political culture tends to hold back other kinds of social change, as people filter new ideas through the prism of their sense of the legitimacy of the existing political and social order.

It is certainly the case that political actors sometimes reject new ideas on the grounds that they are out of keeping with existing social and political norms. They blame political culture for why (new) things don't happen, or why governments fail to deliver. General de Gaulle once whimsically remarked on the difficulties of governing an individualistic country like France with 246 cheeses (and now the 'Guide to Raw Milk Cheeses' in France lists over 1,500) (*So Cheese*, 2012).

Perceptions of political culture sometimes translate into policies. During the Brexit debate in the UK one of the reasons advanced by Leavers was the argument that Britain's 800-year distinctive parliamentary and common law systems set it apart from other EU members. This meant that the UK had always had to adjust to the principles and practices of the EU more than any other state. Since, they implied, this would never change, it would be better to leave (Hannan, 2016).

Political culture can often be cited as a reason for something *not* happening. And yet, such claims, however plausible, can also sometimes go badly wrong. In 1985 Lucian Pye, one of the pioneers of the concept of political culture and an expert on Asian politics in general, wrote a magisterial book, *Asian Power and Politics*, which claimed that democracy would not spread to Asia because it conflicted with the traditional hierarchical values of Asian societies as exemplified by Confucianism. Yet, in 1987, Taiwan and South Korea—states with long Confucian traditions—became the first East Asian ones since Japan to introduce democracy, and they have since been followed by other states in the region.

The substantive, and yet also malleable, nature of 'political culture' can be illustrated by the way it has been applied to Russia. One long-lasting theme of Russian politics and the Russian state over recent centuries has been the dilemmas over its identity and its place in the world. Does Russia belong in the East or the West? Should it? The standard dichotomy of debates in Russia over its future course in the nineteenth century revolved around the terms 'Westernizers' versus 'Slavophiles'. Should Russia seek to develop in the company of, and following, Western Europe? Or should it seek its own path, resting on the values of (Orthodox) Slavdom (Billington,

9

2004)? The victory of the Bolsheviks in 1917 inaugurated an era of pursuing its own road, but the collapse of the communist regime in 1991 reopened the question. For the rest of that decade it seemed as though Russia had opted decisively for a Western or European future. Polls in 1991/2 showed that three-quarters of respondents had a positive view of the US and Europe. And even when President Putin replaced President Yeltsin, this orientation initially seemed to persist, as he raised again the question of Russia's future membership of the North Atlantic Treaty Organization (NATO) and the EU. But gradually disagreements between Russia and the West, principally the US, over a widening range of international issues led Russia to reassert its difference, even its unique path. Instead of Slavophilism, the Russian regime now identified itself as a 'Eurasian' state, where its unique geographical position and geostrategic history meant that its interests and priorities necessarily diverged from those of the West.

Then, to strengthen the acceptability of such claims, the Kremlin began to advance interpretations of Russian political culture as being determined by Russia's long history—Putin is an avid reader of Russian history (Hill and Gaddy, 2012). It stressed the importance of the traditional value of *sobornost*, i.e. the spiritual community of Orthodox believers, which was counterposed to the individualism of the West. Khomiakov (2018: 158–9) proposed this as a basic principle of a new state ideology, along with the notion of the Russian people as one big family. These changes coincided with a gradual enhancement of the Russian Orthodox Church in public life and even foreign policy, though this anti-individualism and familialism are also more akin to principles of order in Asian societies, as we shall see later in this chapter. Putin's 'ideologist', Vladislav Surkov in a rare public lecture rationalized this change, **see Box 9.3**.

More recently, he has argued in a slightly eccentric way: 'Russia's epic westward quest is finally over. Repeated and invariably abortive attempts to become part and parcel of the Western civilization, to get into the "good family" of European nations have ground to a final halt . . . we are destined to a hundred years (or possibly two hundred or three hundred) of geopolitical loneliness . . . Russia is a Western-Eastern half-breed nation. With its double-headed statehood, hybrid mentality, intercontinental territory, and bipolar history, it is charismatic, talented, beautiful and lonely' (Surkov, 2018).

Over the past two decades the West has lost attraction in Russian public opinion, although not to the same extent as governmental relations, as can be seen from the figures from the Levada Centre for public opinion. But, what **Table 9.2** also illustrates is significant fluctuations in the overall trend of greater disenchantment with the West.

The Russian experience demonstrates the fluidity of political culture. Like a river, it flows through and around the political consciousness and behaviour of a nation or community, sometimes changing course on its own, sometimes forced to do so by state actions. It is an oversimplification to claim, as Surkov did, that 'culture is fate'. It is not so deterministic, but skilful political

KEY QUOTE BOX 9.3
Surkov on Russian Political Culture

[C]ulture is fate. God ordered us to be Russians . . . We can take pride in our political culture.
(Surkov, 2007)

Table 9.2 Changes in Russian public opinion towards the West, 2003–18 (%)

Towards	Dec. 2003	Dec. 2007	Nov. 2011	Nov. 2015	Feb. 2019
EU positive	72	64	71	29	42
EU negative	11	21	14	60	45
US positive	59	47	64	21	34
US negative	30	42	23	70	56

Source: Levada-Center (2019) (https://www.levada.ru/en/ratings/).

entrepreneurs can devise plausible and attractive narratives that resonate and win support. Even if political culture in Russia has fluctuated more widely than Surkov would admit, the figures from **Table 9.2** suggest that the Kremlin has succeeded in fostering a shift away from the West.

The Rise of 'Civilization States'

Over the past decade, both Russia and China have led the way in cultivating an image as 'civilization-states' (Coker, 2019). This is based upon claims of achievements in building culture and civilization in earlier centuries. Such an appeal is oriented towards both their own populations and the wider international community. For a domestic audience this is intended to encourage pride in the nation and confidence that it is capable of great things in the future. For the international community (and primarily the West) it is intended to evoke 'respect'. Both Russia and China have based such claims upon a deliberately cultivated sense of domestic grievance over past unjust treatment by the West. China has organized large-scale 'patriotic education' campaigns about past injustices to demand better, fairer treatment for China in the future (Wang, 2012; Zhang, 2012; Wang and Wang, 2013). President Xi Jinping launched his leadership of the country in 2012 with the appeal to 'The Chinese Dream', which amounted to an aspiration to restore China's traditional pre-eminence in the world, predating the 'century of humiliations' by the West between 1839 and 1949, by rejuvenating the nation (Ferdinand, 2015). 'The Chinese nation has an unbroken history of more than 5,000 years of civilization. It has created a rich and profound culture and has made an unforgettable contribution to the progress of human civilization . . .' (Xi, 2014). And, in the case of Russia, the perceived plunder of national resources under West-approved economic reforms in the 1990s has been interpreted as yet one more example of centuries-long misery and exploitation at the hands of the West. In response Russians should rediscover their distinctive sense of spiritual community and follow their own road (Viktorov, 2009; Platonov, 2016).

These initiatives are part of a wider attempt around the world to turn away from Western models and paths of development. In Turkey political elites, especially those associated with the ruling AKP party of President Erdogan, have also presented it as a civilization state with a glorious past and future (Yeşiltaş, 2014; Davutoglu, 2014). India, under Prime Minister Modi, has been doing the same thing (Mohan, 2015).

> **KEY POINTS**
>
> - Political culture is the totality of group and individual attitudes towards politics in a given community.
> - It is extremely difficult to assess objectively.
> - It has substance and it structures rather than determines the behaviour of both individuals and groups within a given community.
> - At the same time political entrepreneurs sometimes reshape it with alternative narratives of its content.
> - It can be quite malleable, and governments may try to change it radically, but public attitudes may shift more slowly, even in the face of extreme pressure.
> - It can be used to synthesize a nation's (self-)identity.
> - It may change significantly in response to specific events and it may fluctuate considerably.
> - It tends more often to be interpreted as an obstacle to political change, but sometimes change takes place despite apparent strong countervailing pressure from political culture.
> - Political leaders may make important decisions based upon their perceptions of the way things 'normally' seem to get done in their country or another one.
> - Recently some non-Western states have begun to identify themselves as 'civilization states', i.e. states with a long and proud civilizational history of their own, which differentiates them from Western forms of modernization and modernity.

NON-WESTERN POLITICAL IDEAS

Chapter 8 emphasized the way that Western (primarily European) notions of the state gradually spread around the world from the sixteenth century onwards. This has also meant that political theory has tended to congeal around issues associated with the modern state, predominantly by Western political thinkers. Parekh has noted that despite South Asia's long tradition of civilizational development:

> Indian scholars tend to look to the West for recognition and approval, and they can obviously secure it only by writing on themes acceptable to the Western intellectual establishment. There is a rarely articulated but nonetheless unmistakable Western view of what 'serious' Third World scholars should think and write about, how they should study Western or their own societies, along what lines they may criticize either, and so on. While Indian political thought remains a poor cousin, all politics departments [in India] teach Western political thought at the undergraduate level, but it too is centred around mainly modern and somewhat badly-selected individual thinkers. (Parekh, 2010: 27)

It is only in the most recent decades that serious academic analysis has moved towards more sustained engagement with India's own intellectual history. And to some extent this has diverted attention towards other types of issues and other ways of conceptualizing the good society.

In particular Chatterjee (2010) has emphasized the significance of and prioritization of community in Asian societies, as compared with the greater stress upon individualism in Western ones. And this also has structured Asian thinking on the subject.

Generally speaking the alternative approaches towards political ideas that come from non-Western societies stem from dissatisfaction with, even complaints about, Western societies. There have been four themes in this. The first is rejection of perceived impersonal, individualistic Western societies. The second is the stigmatizing of the perceived immoral, or at least amoral, Western civilization with its lack of attention to upholding a moral order. The third is the condemnation of imposed Western values and institutions, principally through colonialism, which diverted non-Western societies from their own more 'natural' roots. And the fourth is rejection of Western approaches to the bases of order in Western societies. In turn this las led to four counter-streams of thinking to at least enrich the principles of political rule in non-Western societies and even possibly to replace them.

More 'Organic' Communities

In the 1990s and 2000s there was a movement to promote 'Asian values' in the global community as an alternative to more mechanistic and less altruistic 'Western' ones. This also reflected East Asia's increasing economic success and reflected a widespread belief in the region that the future of the planet was Asian (Cauquelin et al., 1998; Mahbubani, 2008).

As Chatterjee puts it:

> What is ignored is the underside of modern individualism—the callous impersonality and massification of market-driven societies that destroy age-old institutions of sociability and community living without putting anything in their place. Contrary to the beliefs of modernizers, traditional community structures are not simple and inflexible: primordialities are multi-layered, the self is open-ended, adjustment and compromise are ethical norms. (Chatterjee: 290)

Asian societies have typically been seen as warmer, more humane, more generous communities than individualistic Western societies—the word 'society' in Japanese (*shakai*) was originally devised in the nineteenth century to capture a Western concept and then transferred to China as *shehui*. Lebra (1976) characterized traditional culture in Japan as being based upon 'belongingness', i.e. group cooperation, though not on belonging to a whole national community. 'The outcome of these practices [of encouraging group solidarity] is that "society" is not abstraction, but a very tangible, distinctive, largely face-to-face entity with clear boundaries, norms and customs' (Rohlen, 1989: 28).

Traditionally, this sense of group orientation has been bolstered by a fundamental fear of disharmony in relations with others. Bogart (1998: 160) has expressed this clearly for Thailand:

> Thai society is essentially a conflict-avoidance society. Everything is done to maintain harmony. Avoidance of conflict is the governing principle of every aspect of life . . . In the face of frustration or anger, it is better to stay calm . . . Calm coupled with respect and politeness is appropriate behaviour.

Confrontation in politics, society, or personal life was discouraged.

Asian societies were traditionally often presented as being more 'human' than Western ones on two grounds. The first was the universal practice of gift-giving to establish more humane relations than in the impersonal West. How can individuals and how can society as a whole achieve cooperation? How can the selfish pursuit of self-interest be overcome?

'Gift-giving' at the beginning of and throughout a relationship is intended to encourage the other party to behave more sympathetically. It resonates with Keohane's concept of 'diffuse reciprocity' in the field of international relations. Keohane (1986) proposed this as a way of achieving cooperation between international actors. It means giving a gift not with the purpose of achieving a particular objective in return (i.e. specific reciprocity), but rather with the purpose of winning general goodwill and cooperation (diffuse reciprocity). But it can also be applied within individual societies. In China this practice of exchanging gifts for the sake of winning cooperation is linked to the practice of developing 'relations' (*guanxi*), and there it can be elevated to a high degree of sophistication (*guanxixue*). Of course, it can lead to corruption. But the more sympathetic interpretation is that, when practised properly, it encourages generosity rather than selfishness, cooperation rather confrontation. Indeed it is supposedly what makes society 'humane' (Bian, 2018). In Chinese one word for a gift—*renqing*—also means 'human feelings'.

The second way in which Asian societies have been presented as more 'humane' than Western ones is the traditional stress on familialism—the principle of putting the family first, making it the centre of social and political organization. In Asia the most developed expression of this principle came in Japan with the notion of the 'family-state' (*kazoku-kokka*) which lasted from the latter part of the nineteenth century to 1945. This portrayed the emperor as the 'father' of the nation and compared the relationship between him and his subjects with that between the head of the patriarchal family and its members. In each case the head was owed obedience and deference, encapsulated in the term 'filial piety'. Gluck (1985: 78) described the role of the emperor: 'As the patriarch of a family-state he [the Emperor] became the symbolic representation of harmony, and as the descendant of the sun goddess, the deified evidence of the ancestral ethnicity of the Japanese.'

Actually, this equating of the roles of head of family and head of state was typical of the Chinese empire too. For imperial China the family was a crucial institution in linking the individual with the rest of society and maintaining order. This is what Confucius advocated. In the West, by contrast, it could be argued, the state has been used to remedy weaknesses and fractures in society by imposing order. Hobbes is the thinker who is most associated with thinking on the use of state power to establish social order, or at any rate re-establish it after the chaos of the English Civil War. Their views are contrasted in **Box 9.4**.

But, in Japan, the principle was taken even further. Other organizations in society were structured on analogous lines. Troupes of geishas and actors had 'mothers', 'fathers', 'daughters', 'sons'. Companies, schools, and offices were run on familial (critics said paternalistic) lines. Even criminal gangs—the *yakuza*—had (and still have) 'fathers', 'brothers', and 'sons'. The whole of Japan was structured on the basis of real or fictive households (Japanese for household is *ie*). As Kumagai (1996: 13) put it: 'It is the deep-rooted traditions inherent in Japan's hierarchical family system that go furthest in explaining the meaning of contemporary Japanese society.'

Nor was it restricted to North-East Asia. The Indonesian constitution still maintains the 'family principle' (*kekeluargaan*) as one of its principles. This drew upon largely inter-war European theories of society as a harmonious organic whole where everyone had a supposed specific function,

Hobbes argued in *The Elements of Law* that man in the state of nature is prone to violence—a state of war. The English Civil War had demonstrated only too clearly how disastrous that might be. As a result, they needed a 'Leviathan'—a state much more powerful than any other group of men—to awe them into submission for the common good. 'The central point Hobbes makes . . . is that political authority is the most effective means of providing protection and security . . . The problem with the family in matters of security is that it is small' (Chapman, 1975: 78). Families, like individuals continually vie with each other for power in the state of nature. All families were prey to other families. His picture of the family is certainly authoritarian, and probably patriarchal, but 'what is unique about Hobbes is that he sees the family logically as a small version of the state' (Chapman, 1975: 90). However strong the authority of the family patriarch, without a strong state there would only be anarchy. Thus public order and social stability depended upon the maintenance and exercise of strong state power.

Confucius did not deny the importance of emperors. They were vitally important in keeping society in balance with the cosmic order—they enjoyed the 'mandate of heaven'—and it was vital that emperors performed all the rites that were required to maintain that order. It was also vital that emperors did not oppress the people or demand unreasonable, extortionate taxes. But he argued that social order depended more upon two things: firstly the importance of the family as the basic institution within society. In a patriarchal family its head would keep a check on the behaviour of all its members and prevent misdeeds. If he (and it was always a 'he') failed to do this, he would suffer as serious punishment for any crimes committed as the actual perpetrator. And secondly social health depended upon members of society knowing and carrying out their expected roles. These roles were based upon their relations within the family. Similar roles in broader society were patterned upon those of the family. Fundamentally there were five of them: 1) ruler and ruled; 2) father and son; 3) husband and wife; 4) elder brother and younger brother; 5) friend and friend. If everyone was aware of their appropriate role in every social situation and carried it out, the result would be a harmonious social order.

In general, he reversed the hierarchy of the relationship between the family and the state as compared with Hobbes: 'To put the world in order, we must first put the nation in order; to put the nation in order, we must put the family in order; to put the family in order, we must cultivate our personal life; and to cultivate our personal life, we must first set our hearts right.' Thus, Confucius inverts Hobbes' hierarchy of the agents establishing order in society. Instead of order being imposed from the top down, it rises from the bottom.

as well as ideas disseminated during Japan's brief occupation of Indonesia in the Second World War, and was intended to symbolize the spirit of cooperation and harmony rather than individual rights. Although it borrowed from Japanese ways of thinking, it was also taken as exemplifying the Indonesian traditions of cooperation and harmony that had been upset by Western colonialism and the intrusion of individualism (Bourchier, 2015). At least until the downfall of President Suharto in 1998, units of public administration—schools, military units, and so forth—presented themselves as 'families' for their members (Shiraishi, 1997: 11). And Mulder (2003: 193)

Photo 9.2 A statue of Confucius. *Shutterstock RF via DAM*

has written more generally about the stress on the family in the education systems of Thailand, the Philippines, and Indonesia, **see Box 9.5**.

According to him, 'the image of the nation-state as family is ubiquitous' (Mulder, 1996: 171).

The anthropologist Margery Wolf (1968: 23) has very persuasively evoked the warm human nature—and obligations—of the traditional Taiwanese family, and implicitly throughout the Confucian world:

> The interaction of the Taiwanese villager with his friends and neighbors is like the spice in his soup, savory, but of little sustenance. It is with his family, his parents and grandparents, his children and grandchildren, that he takes the measure of his life. His relations with his parents may be strained, with his wife distant, and with his children formal, but without those people he would be an object of pity and of no

 KEY QUOTE BOX 9.5
Family Values and Social Order in Southeast Asia

The prevailing social imagination seems to be inspired by family ideals. Not only that individuals are seen as integrated parts of family, group, and community. There they have tasks and duties. They functionally depend upon each other. Such an imagination does not allow for conflicts. It allows for moral solutions to differences. The social responsibility it places on the shoulders of individuals is to watch themselves and to toe the line. Otherwise, peaceful social life will be disturbed.

small amount of suspicion. He would be pitied because he had no parents to 'help' him and no children to support him in his old age. For the same reasons he would be an object of suspicion. A man not thoroughly imbedded in a network of kinship cannot be completely trusted because he cannot be dealt with in the normal way. If he behaves improperly, one cannot discuss his behaviour with his brother or seek redress from his parents. If one wants to approach him about a delicate matter, one cannot use his uncle as a go-between to prepare the way. Wealth cannot make up for this deficiency any more than it can make up for the loss of arms and legs. Money has no past, no future, and no obligations. Relatives do.

For Lee Kuan Yew, the founding prime minister of Singapore, the peoples of Asia should evolve different forms of government from those in the US and Europe which would be based more explicitly upon ethical values and on the social importance of the family (Zakaria, 1994: 118–9). And in the Islamic world as well, the family has been seen as the bedrock of society, a 'microcosm of the moral order' (Eickelman and Piscatori, 2018: 83).

KEY POINTS

- Even in non-Western academia it is still difficult to get proper recognition of indigenous ideas and thinkers
- Asian thinking on politics tends to promote the idea of natural 'organic', humane communities rather than impersonal Westernized ones
- Families have traditionally been said to play a greater role in the stability and decision-making of Asian societies than in the West
- There is a long and deep tradition in Asia of linking the family, the state and public order

---

THE PRINCIPLE OF LIBERATION

A second theme in non-Western political ideas is that of liberation and emancipation. This is not surprising since so many non-Western states are former colonies. The instinct for liberation came naturally, though the specific forms that it took varied from one country to another. We will give five examples of this theme: (i) the extension of the Marxist category of proletarian class to peasants (in China) and race (in South Africa); (ii) the Gandhian concept of *swaraj* in India; (iii) Fanon's elevation of violence as both liberation and emancipation in the anti-colonial struggle; (iv) *jihad* in the Islamic world; (v) liberation theology in South America.

Peasants and Races as 'Proletarians'

In the twentieth century, Marxism was revised to serve the struggle against colonialism and imperialism, which involved redirecting the classic principles of Marxist ideology to facilitate or legitimize revolution in largely non-industrial former colonies of Western states. Marx's main objective had been to bring about a socialist revolution, but what attracted great attention at the time was his claim to have established a 'scientific' explanation for the process by which socialism and communism would replace capitalism, i.e. through a workers' revolution in the most advanced capitalist countries. Subsequent revisions have expanded the emancipatory power of Marxism at the expense of Marx's more deterministic predictions.

Chapter 6 explained that the Bolsheviks under Lenin revised Marxism to legitimize their revolution in a much less industrialized, still predominantly agricultural, economy. Even though many peasants took part in the revolution, Bolshevik doctrine laid down that they did so under leadership of the proletariat, i.e. the workers, albeit with many of their leaders themselves coming from the intelligentsia. But at least when considered from the global perspective, Russia could be said then to be among the most industrialized capitalist economies, even if it was much less developed than Britain, Germany, and France. And Lenin had developed a theory of imperialism which claimed that since capitalism had become a global phenomenon ('imperialism—the highest stage of capitalism'), it was legitimate to try to break it at its weakest link, i.e. as it turned out, Russia, and not necessarily in Germany or Britain.

After the victory of the Bolsheviks but the failure of world revolution, the Soviet Union and the Communist International began to try to spread revolution to the colonies. As it turned out, the most successful place was China, although this was mainly because of the efforts of the Chinese communists themselves rather than because of leadership from Moscow. But how was it possible to legitimize a 'Marxist' revolution in an overwhelmingly agricultural society where most of the revolutionaries were peasants? It was Mao who was most associated with the further revision of Marxism to take account of this. Obviously, part of the explanation was an extension of the theory of imperialism. But what Mao did was to redefine, or at any rate reconstrue, the concept of the 'proletariat'. Previously the term had been understood as designating the industrial workforce, and this was as true of the Bolsheviks as it was of west European Marxists. But, in Chinese, the term for proletariat was translated as 'propertyless class' (*wuchan jieji*). It had no intrinsic connotation of industrial workers, although it did also cover industrial workers in cities like Shanghai. Mao used the Chinese version of the term to include poor peasants as well, since in China they were so poor, and protection for any property rights was so ineffective, that they effectively lacked property in land.

This sympathy for the peasants remained with Mao for the rest of his life, and in the Cultural Revolution Chinese students were urged to leave urban areas and go to live among the peasants so as to rediscover and learn from the authentic people. When, after 1949, he demanded that people should 'emancipate their minds', he meant that they should learn to think more like peasants, i.e. like more authentic people—a call that would have been anathema to Marx and even Lenin.

Later, when independence movements sprang up in African colonies, Marxism went through a further reformulation. Once again, an industrial working class was lacking. Now a lot of revolutionary inspiration focused on ethnic or racial protest. How could this be reconciled with Marxism, which famously made an absolute value of class conflict? The answer was '*racial* proletarianization' (Halisi, 1999; emphasis added). Colonizers had taken the land from natives and so turned them into a racially-based 'propertyless class'. A temporary Dutch administrator graphically described the process in South Africa at the beginning of the nineteenth century:

> [T]he colonists hounded down these timid wretches, destroyed their Kraals and villages, stole their cattle, seized the men and boys and reduced them to a state of subjection and slavery, drove others in fear of their lives, to seek shelter to the depths of wild caves and forests and callously allowed them to sink into a state of utter barbarism.   (Halisi, 1999: 28)

Some became slaves. And, later on, some of the impoverished natives were recruited as wage labourers (proletarians) in the industries of the newly created cities. All this generated a demand for liberation and still persists in demands for full emancipation in the South Africa of the African National Congress, meaning both returning land to its 'original' owners, and also overcoming persisting inequalities between races.

Gandhi and *Swaraj*

In India the notion of liberation and emancipation was encapsulated in the term *swaraj* (self-rule) that was launched by Mahatma Gandhi as part of the struggle for independence, **see Box 9.6**.

Obviously, at one level, this was directed at Britain—the title of one of Gandhi's earliest political writings was *Hind Swaraj* (1909), i.e. Indian self-rule. But it also advocated a particular strategy for practising self-rule, not just democracy, but one based as far as possible upon *local* self-government. It has continued to serve as a spur for demands for decentralization of government (Kejriwal, 2015) It is also associated with the school of 'subaltern studies' in India, which is dedicated to uncovering the persisting tendency of state officials to behave as they did in the old colonial system, i.e. pursuing their own interests whilst ignoring the concerns of ordinary citizens, and which aims at giving voice to people at the bottom of society (Prakash, 2010). It has thus become an important strand of modern Indian political culture, associated with postcolonial critiques of (predominantly Eurocentric) power. But even more broadly it is associated with the spirit of individual self-rule, and therefore of self-emancipation and self-control. 'Swaraj, for Gandhi, existed in oceanic circles of village republics ensconced in organic proximity to nature. It was a civilization that abhorred coercive power and functioned through moral persuasion. It was true home rule manifesting the people's world' (Roy, 2011). Gandhi advocated a return to simple life on the land as being most likely to realize these goals.

Fanon and Violence in Liberation

Gandhi was implacably opposed to (British) colonial rule but advocated its overthrow mainly by non-violent means. Frantz Fanon was equally implacably hostile to colonialism, but much more explicitly urged its violent overthrow, **see Box 9.7 and Box 9.8**.

His most famous work—*The Wretched of the Earth*—appeared in 1961 at the height of the independence struggle in Algeria, at a time of mounting atrocities on both sides. The book takes

KEY THINKER BOX 9.6
Mahatma Gandhi

Mahatma Gandhi (1869–1948) was one of the great figures of the Indian independence movement. A trained barrister, he devised many key concepts that gave intellectual credibility and substance to the movement by reinterpreting and updating classical Sanskrit notions. He advocated a return to the simplicity and traditional values of the Indian peasant and village as the basis for an independent India. His political activism was based upon the principle of non-violence, and he was imprisoned many times for his organization of resistance. A believer in a pluralistic India that accepted Muslims and other believers as the equals of Hindus, he was assassinated by a Hindu extremist soon after independence.

KEY THINKER BOX 9.7
Frantz Fanon (1925–61)

Born in Martinique, Fanon studied medicine and psychiatry. While working in a hospital in Algeria he observed the horrors of the decolonization struggle at first hand and became an unsparing supporter with an international reputation as an activist. He was an early writer on colonialism and racism. In 1961 he was diagnosed with leukaemia and just managed to complete his best-known work *The Wretched of the Earth*, although he died in hospital in the US before it was published. He was buried in Algeria.

KEY QUOTE BOX 9.8
Fanon on Violence in Decolonization . . .

[D]ecolonization is always a violent phenomenon . . . The naked truth of decolonization evokes for us the searing bullets and bloodstained knives which emanate from it. For if the last shall be first, this will only come to pass after a murderous and decisive struggle between the two protagonists. . . . [Because, he argued, colonization had been forced upon peoples, decolonization could only succeed by force—] . . . the agents of government speak the language of pure force . . . [C]olonialism . . . is violence in its natural state, and it will only yield when confronted with greater violence . . . The colonized man finds his freedom in and through violence.
(Fanon, 2001: 27, 28, 29, 48, 68)

on the issue of violence from the beginning. The first chapter is entitled 'Concerning violence' andthe key quote in Box 9.8 shows how it begins.

Critics of Fanon alleged that he glorified violence: 'At the level of individuals violence is a cleansing force. It frees the native from his inferiority complex and from his despair and inaction; it makes him fearless and restores his self-respect' (Fanon, 2001: 74). Defenders emphasize that Fanon himself was not personally a violent man. 'We can speak, therefore, of a liberating violence, but not of the purifying violence that has been attributed to Fanon by many of his interpreters. What is at stake here is not purity but humanity, the possibility of coming up with a new way of being' (Cherki, 2006: 172, 183). It is certainly true that his main concern was to show that nothing less than the destruction of colonialism by any means would be required to liberate not only former colonized peoples, but also former colonialists, since it would lead to a global socialist transformation and peace. He was primarily obsessed with structural transformation. Nevertheless it is easy to see how he could be perceived as an apologist, even an advocate, for violence. Hansen refers to Fanon's 'loose' use of the word violence: 'He has in mind acts of physical and psychological injury, or force, or coercion. On the whole he does not make any distinction between force, violence, power and coercion' (Hansen, 1977: 84). Fanon was also deeply interested in psychiatry, and the last section of the book presents individual cases of psychiatric disorders that were caused by colonialism. Under those circumstances, violence might well be thought to be individually liberating. And Sartre's Preface reinforced this impression: 'The native cures himself of colonial neurosis by thrusting out the settler through force of arms. When his rage boils over, he rediscovers his lost innocence and he comes to know himself in that he himself creates his self' (Fanon, 2001: 18). It was, in any case, a very different conclusion from that of Gandhi.

Jihad

Liberation as a political concept also figures among thinkers with a religious goal. In recent years the notion of *jihad* has attracted enormous attention both inside and outside the Islamic world. It has come to be widely associated with armed struggle by Muslims against non-believers or believers in other religions. It is extremely controversial—**see Box 9.9**.

Thus it is associated not only with the goal of liberation of territory from control and oppression by unbelievers, but also with personal emancipation, however hard, from everything that prevents a Muslim from following the path to God, **see Box 9.10**.

So, classical scholars would speak of the '*jihad* of the self' to strive against personal vices, the '*jihad* of speech' for preaching and telling truth to power, the '*jihad* of the pen' for scholarship and research into Islamic science, the '*jihad* of wealth' for charitable giving, as well as of the '*jihad* of force'. Austere teachers for whom the *jihad* of the self was the most important principle would talk of 'doing the *jihad*' to pursue a saintly life. One of the most famous modern interpreters of

9

KEY DEBATE BOX 9.9
Esposito versus Cook on *Jihad*

The term *jihad* has a number of meanings which include the effort to lead a good life, to make society more moral and just, and to spread Islam through preaching, teaching, or armed struggle. Muslim jurists distinguished ways 'in which the duty might be fulfilled, by the heart, by the tongue, by the hands and by the sword'.

In its most generic meaning, 'jihad' signifies the battle against evil and the devil, the self-discipline (common to the three Abrahamic faiths) in which believers seek to follow God's will, to be better Muslims. It is the lifelong struggle to be virtuous, to be true to the straight path of God. This is the primary way in which the observant Muslim gives witness to or actualizes the truth of the first pillar of Islam in everyday life. The spread of Islam through 'tongue' and 'hands' refers to the Quranically prescribed obligation of the Muslim community 'to enjoin good and forbid evil' . . . Finally, 'jihad' means the struggle to spread and to defend Islam.
(Esposito, 1999: 30–1)

This definition has virtually no validity in Islam and is derived almost entirely from the apologetic works of nineteenth- and twentieth-century Muslim modernists. To maintain that *jihad* means 'the effort to lead a good life' is bathetic and laughable in any case. In all the literature concerning jihad—whether militant or internal jihad—the fundamental idea is to disconnect oneself from the world, to die to the world, whether bodily (as in battle) or spiritually (as in the internal jihad) . . . .

Again, Esposito apparently deliberately spiritualizes what is an unambiguously concrete and militant doctrine, without a shred of evidence from the Qur'an or any of the classical sources, in which the jihad and fighting is against real human enemies, and not the devil.
(Cook, 2005: 42)

> ## KEY QUOTE BOX 9.10
> ### Sheikh on *Jihad* . . .
>
> The word jihad . . . is found in a total of thirty-five times in the Quranic text. In thirty-one of these instances, the term bears no relation to acts of combat. Indeed, in the Meccan period of the Revelation, during which the nascent community of faith was under instruction not to resist violence with violence, even in the course of self-defense, ample verses of the Quran exhort the believers to practice jihad, carrying the aforementioned meaning of righteous self-exertion. In the four instances in which the term itself is used in martial contexts, the text itself never uses jihad as a synonym for armed combat (*qitāl*), but rather as reiterations of what may be referred to as more generic 'will to serve' that is to permeate all acts of devotion by sincere believers. At this initial, non-securitized stage of the intellectual history of jihad, it retains no conclusive predisposition for armed violence; rather it purports to act merely in a transformative capacity—an aspect that lends itself to a variety of uses. (Sheikh 2015: 289–90)

Islam and the founder of the Muslim Brotherhood (a clandestine Islamic organization that sought to infiltrate centres of power first under colonialism and then after independence), Sayyid Qutb, advocated violent *jihad* but also saw it as a 'universal desire for freedom from the servitude of others' (Browers, 2013: 232.) In fact Qutb also mentioned the need for 'the complete liberation' of the soul from 'the inner shackles' of pleasures and passions, ambitions and desires (Shepard, 1996: 53), in a way reminiscent of Gandhi's goal of (self-)liberation. Nevertheless, according to Kelsay (2015: 86), 'early in the development of Islam *jihad* came to be associated with fighting or making war "in the path of God".'

Thus there is an enormous literature on debates associated with *jihad* and the notion of liberation in an Islamic context, e.g. should it be only defensive, or should it be offensive too, with a very wide range of views, both inside and outside the Muslim world. But whilst there is widespread Muslim acclaim for those who fight for Islam and especially for martyrs in the cause, there is no sense of violence itself being psychologically liberating for individuals, as there is in some interpretations of Fanon. The purpose of violence here is to sweep away obstacles to the path to God.

Liberation Theology

Liberation theology among Catholic thinkers presents another version of religion-based thinking on emancipation. It emerged in Latin America at the end of the 1960s as a response to the increasing inequality in society across the region and also as a reaction against authoritarian rule. The seminal work is usually taken to be *A Theology of Liberation* by a Peruvian priest, Gustavo Gutierrez (**see Box 9.11**).

POLITICAL ORDER

The second recurring theme of non-Western political thinking is order: how to establish it and maintain it. To some extent this contrasts with Western priorities. According to Raskin (2004: 69): 'The American system, in a cultural sense, denies the principle of Order, for social openness and empty spaces allow for and create barely contained disorder.' People who for whatever reason

KEY THINKER BOX 9.11
Gustavo Gutierrez (1928–)

Gutierrez was born in Peru in 1928. After starting to train as a doctor and then extended graduate theological study in Europe, he returned to a shanty town in Lima as a parish priest. His experience there of the life of the poor persuaded him that the Catholic church needed to concentrate upon their needs and social change, rather than religious contemplation and the status quo. He also encouraged the formation of 'base communities' within the church, informal small gatherings of believers who linked Bible study in the church with social action. Particularly prominent during widespread authoritarian rule in the 1970s and 1980s, the movement ebbed as democracy returned to various countries in South America. But, the continuing high levels of inequality mean that the underlying issues have not gone away, and the current Pope, the Argentinian Francis I, the first from Latin America, after initial scepticism, has become more sympathetic to the Liberationist approach than his predecessors.

Gutierrez argued that the church needed to return to the simplicities of its life in the first centuries after Christ, with less pomp and more humility. He took as the starting point the message of Christ the Liberator. He reinterpreted the Gospel message in three respects. Firstly, he rejected poverty as something to be endured by virtuous believers who should be more concerned with their spiritual life and argued that it should always be opposed. Secondly, he regarded poverty as caused not by individual laziness or bad luck, but as something that required structural remedies. And, thirdly, he encouraged the poor to organize themselves so as to bring about change in this life, rather than waiting for reward in the next. He fiercely rejected any suggestion that the poor should feel guilt or responsibility for their plight.

All this was a profound challenge to both political and religious leaders. It led to accusations of crypto-Marxism, whilst the Catholic hierarchy condemned what they regarded as the prioritization of temporal and political issues over religious ones. But the message spread widely among Catholics in the developing world, and the innovation of 'base communities' of believers even penetrated the United States. It strengthened the international reputation of the Catholic Church as a progressive political force. And the underlying principles have also attracted sympathizers in other world religions. (De La Torre, 2008)

9

disapproved of or challenged the existing social order could always go West or go South and 'emigrate' through the open frontiers that lasted until the twentieth century.

Elsewhere in the world, the priority of the concern with 'order' is much greater. One of the underlying constants of Chinese political culture, for example, has often been said to be the fear of chaos (*luan*)—and this is said to apply to the Overseas Chinese as well. Cheek (2006) has argued for example that avoiding *luan* (especially the chaos of the Cultural Revolution) was the single most important priority for the PRC under Deng Xiaoping. Rosen highlights the same concern under Islam: 'Chaos (*fitna*) is the greatest threat; if there is chaos, there is no justice' (Rosen, 2010: 79). This need to establish order was particularly acute for newly independent ex-colonies in the second half of the twentieth century in a world where national sovereignty and borders had become more important than they had ever been before. Obviously one solution was to try to construct an effective Western-type state with an efficient Weberian bureaucracy (see Chapter 13). But we will focus upon two alternatives: (i) the Islamic ambition to build a state based upon the principle of 'justice'; (ii) the (re)discovery of alternative traditional forms of rule and statehood that preceded the colonial era and could be adapted to modern conditions.

Justice and Order in the Islamic World

In the Islamic world, a great deal of thought has been devoted to the principle of justice as the foundation of a legitimate social and political order. 'If "rights" is the language of discourse in the United States, and "liberty" or "freedom" or "solidarity" for other nations and times, "justice" is undoubtedly the watchword for Muslims when issues of their place in the political and moral order are at issue (sic). It is the term that suffuses every element of Islamic thought from the Qur'an to the most commonsensical of aphorisms' (Rosen, 2010: 69). Globally, 'justice' has become 'the cornerstone' of Muslim identity (Lo, 2019). But, what does it mean? In fact it is quite complex with various overlapping connotations.

In Arabic there are several words which are translated as 'justice', but the most common is *adl*. According to Kamali (2002): 'Literally, 'adl means placing something in its rightful place; it also means according equal treatment to others or reaching a state of equilibrium in transactions with them.' Khadduri (1984: 8) expresses it somewhat similarly: 'The literal meaning of 'adl in classical Arabic is thus a combination of moral and social values denoting fairness, balance, temperance and straightforwardness.' A *fatwa* from a North American Muslim cleric concluded that justice 'means to maintain the balance and to give everyone and everything its proper due' (Rosen, 2010: 72). It is, therefore, rather different from and broader than the more legally-oriented and more abstract definition of 'justice' in English, although it obviously is also used in Islamic law. It is also distinct from the related, but still different, Arabic term *al-qist* (fairness), which denotes receiving the entitlements associated with stipulated rights. 'It ['adl] takes on both the qualities of the particular Muslim cultures in which it is found and calls forth the implications of its entire worldview and universal faith' (Rosen, 2010: 70). And the connotation of 'equilibrium in transactions with others', i.e. reciprocity, is reminiscent of the Chinese usage and practice of *guanxi* mentioned previously. 'Face-to-face relationships are required for justice', as in China. And, as in China, there is an 'emphasis on negotiation, reciprocity, manoeuvrability, and access to multiple bases for building indebtedness' (Rosen, 2010: 78).

Of course, a tradition of reciprocity can be very conservative. It can attempt to hold back change. But *adl* (and diffuse reciprocity) allows for change and evolution with the principle of equivalence. A favour can be regarded as returned with something that both parties regard as being equivalent, if not precisely equal, depending on the context. 'Equality is simply not a central aspect of Islamic conceptions of justice' (Rosen, 2000: 166).

Ultimately, a well-ordered Muslim society may be taken to be one where everyone knows their place (although that place may change over time) within a divinely prescribed framework of laws, obligations, and roles, though the practise of them is (or should be) subject to face-to-face negotiation. This makes freedom a lesser concern than in Western political thinking, at least in the sense of political and legal freedom—'justice trumps freedom' (Rosen, 2010: 79). Muslim thinking is more concerned with freedom from impure thinking and with removing anything that might obstruct truly following God. Lo (2019) has extrapolated from this basic polarity an argument about the fundamental global clash between the West and Islam revolving around the different priorities of freedom (the West) versus justice (Islam).

Traditional Pre-Western Bases of Rule

A second strategy of building a stable new state was to uncover, rediscover, or invent alternative principles of state legitimacy and statecraft that had existed or were imagined to have existed in earlier, pre-colonial time. This presupposed that those principles had enjoyed (greater) acceptance in the past, which might be contentious. But for political leaders who had made their careers out of condemning the horrors and injustices of Western colonialism, it was plausible to assume that an alternative non-Western form of rule might enjoy greater popular acceptance. It would make colonialism an enforced divergence from a more natural, longer-term trajectory of non-Western (or not necessarily Western) national development, to which nations could now revert.

This may help to explain the surprising rediscovery of Confucianism in China by the Chinese Communist Party (CCP) leadership from the early 1990s onwards, which ran entirely counter to the enormous drive of Mao's Cultural Revolution to get rid of all the 'four olds'. Since Confucianism had been the official doctrine of the imperial Chinese state for well over a thousand years, it could easily be said to have demonstrated some kind of staying power, even if the state itself had been subject to major ups and downs, and even if it had ultimately failed to protect China from the incursions of the West in the nineteenth century. The basic principles are outlined in **Box 9.1**. As China has experienced breakneck economic growth and resulting social turmoil since the 1980s, it is understandable that the regime should try to find ways of shoring up its authority, even if this particular turn was unexpected. In general the CCP has attempted to strengthen its authority by inserting its history into a longer narrative of Chinese traditions, e.g. restoring traditional lunar festivals and holidays (Ai, 2015).

India, since independence, has not undergone the same thorough-going assault on its traditions as in China, so many principles of traditional state rule and social order have persisted. Before colonialism arrived, social order in most of the princedoms depended less upon rulers than upon the caste system, and in particular upon the monopoly of literacy vested in the highest caste, the Brahmins.

> The Brahminic order in India was certainly an oppressive system of economic production, and it enforced degrading rules about purity and pollution. But its capacity to endure and retain its grip over a wide geographical area flowed from its severely selective distribution of literacy . . . By renouncing political power, the Brahminic order created a self-coercing, self-disciplining society founded on a vision of a moral order.   (Khilnani, 1999: 19–20)

It proved remarkably enduring. Kaviraj (2012: 84) notes the lack of challenge from the lower orders, given that '[t]raditional Indian culture was deeply aristocratic, repressive and massively violent towards the oppressed.'

After Independence the Indian constitution laid down equal rights for all under the law, but the government also sought to provide redress for past discrimination against the lower castes by establishing special group rights to favour them, e.g. in jobs with public employers. Whilst this was intended as a temporary measure, it has survived to the present day—as much because of the self-interest of these civil society groups and the political entrepreneurs that they spawn. This often means that group interests prevail over those of individuals. Whether this is primarily a result of a still prevalent tradition of support for group values over individual ones in Asian societies, or of constitutional inconsistency, or of obsessive politicking by interest groups is more debatable. No doubt they all contribute.

Another way in which Indians have sought to enhance the authority of public institutions is by rediscovering pre-colonial practitioners of statecraft, e.g. the 'rediscovery' in recent years of Kautilya (**see Box 9.12**).

It might have been expected that nationalists would have eagerly grasped the opportunity to identify pre-colonial masters whose ideas could redirect India back towards a distinctive long-term trajectory of development of its own. In fact, however, Kautilya has remained on the margins of university courses in India, and well outside them elsewhere, even though major political figures such as Nehru have testified to the influence that he exerted on their own thinking (Liebig, 2013).

The problem of simply rediscovering earlier national thinkers and then talking up their significance for politics today is that the construction of the colonial/post-colonial bureaucratic state has fundamentally and irrevocably transformed the practice of politics everywhere. Pre-colonial societies maintained order in various ways and through various social mechanisms, e.g. castes and their own separate associations, that presumed a restricted role for the state. Now the state everywhere simply is much more important, as was shown in Chapter 8. So too is the principle of popular involvement in, even control over, public decision-making. In pre-colonial India ruling was the preserve of the king and his advisers. It was not and should not be the concern of people in other groups and castes (Kaviraj, 2013). And in China *The Analects* of Confucius assert: 'He who holds no ranking in a State does not discuss its policies . . . When the Way prevails under Heaven, commoners do not discuss public affairs' (Confucius, 1938: 135, 204). There is no way of resurrecting the whole pre-colonial order. So issues of public policy now involve the state far more than before. Rediscovering the ideas of indigenous thinkers from pre-modern times is of lesser relevance today, unless they can be adapted to modern circumstances. That is what has happened in India with the caste system. The Indian state has become a much more important arbiter of and actor in inter-caste thinking and disputes than ever before. Similarly in modern-day China, Confucianism and the principles of order that it embodies have to fit around CCP control. In that sense the state cannot be kept out.

KEY THINKER BOX 9.12
Kautilya

Kautilya (also known as Chanakya) lived 320–275 BC. A Brahmin from northern India, he was a statesman, adviser, and prime minister of Emperor Chandragupta. His work *Arthashastra* is regarded as a classic of Hindu civilization and was praised by Weber as a classic exposition of statecraft that preceded Machiavelli by over a thousand years. It ranges widely over political philosophy and theory, public administration, economics, diplomacy, intelligence, and international relations.

But more generally this explains why a great deal of non-Western political thinking is not based upon completely indigenous, pre-colonial, non-Western ideas, but upon rethinking ideas and ideologies that can be found elsewhere, including in the West, and adapting them to local conditions and modern circumstances. This can be seen in terms such as African socialism, Mexican liberalism, Asian conservatism, etc. **Box 9.13** will demonstrate this with reference to African socialism.

The next section will illustrate this issue of ideologies with a global life more fully with a survey of the different ways in which liberalism has been perceived and received in different parts of the world.

At the same time the conflicting priorities of emancipation and order pose a challenge to non-Western states, and indeed to states more generally. These priorities may easily contradict each other, and they may stimulate unpredictable responses from the public. One obvious way in which this might happen is the association of emancipation with equality for all. Traditional societies were not at all egalitarian. Trying to (re)impose traditional thinking that assumed hierarchical behaviour on to a modern society which has been touched by the spirit of the French revolution may be equally destabilizing, however much the traditional ideas may be touted as 'ours' rather those of the colonists. In China the regime has attempted to solve this problem by having Confucius reinterpreted for the modern era (Bell, 2006). It does not do away with the basic instinct for hierarchy in Confucius, but it reinterprets it as hierarchy based upon meritocratic opportunity for all through education, which was only true to a very limited extent in imperial China, where familial power was much more pervasive and constricting, and literacy was much less common. And in India, maintenance of order through the activities of the castes—traditionally even more hierarchical than the family-based order of imperial China—has been tempered by state interventions to try and make it (somewhat) less unfair for those at the bottom of the hierarchy and therefore more compatible with the evolving demands of a developing economy. As Corbridge, Harriss, and Jeffrey (2012) argue, caste still matters in Indian politics, but not in the traditional way.

KEY POINTS

- Two key themes in non-Western political thinking are liberation and emancipation, and the establishment and maintenance of public order
- The adaptation of Marxist ideas to non-European societies has increased their emancipatory dimension at the expense of the more deterministic ones
- Gandhi's concept of *swaraj* has acquired a life of its own in the thinking of post-independence India
- Liberation theology has played an important part in the politics of South America in recent decades. It has spread to other regions of the world, and may now be winning greater sympathy within the Catholic Church again
- One approach to the problem of establishing and maintaining order in non-Western states has been to rediscover pre-colonial ideas of statecraft and patterns of social organization
- But their relevance depends upon them being adapted to conditions within modern, much more powerful state apparatuses
- It is difficult to reconcile these two themes, but one strategy that has so far enjoyed some success has been through the open toleration of older principles of social hierarchy, albeit tempered or modified by state policy

CASE STUDY BOX 9.13
Ujamaa and the New Village Project in Tanzania

In newly independent Tanzania in the 1960s, President Nyerere launched a nationwide campaign for socialist development. This was, however, a type of African socialism, based upon the principle of *ujamaa*, i.e. the traditional extended family. It represented an attempt to synthesize socialist principles with traditional African values and institutions. 'It harmonized a spirit of mutual assistance with an ethos of individual responsibility and drew on available resources instead of seeking outside assistance.' In that sense it was simultaneously 'transformative and restorative' (Lal, 2015: 27). In many ways it paralleled the concerns and objectives of Mao's GLF, although where one of Mao's goals was to replace the traditional family, Nyerere's was to transform it and make it fit for a modern world.

At the core was a project to move people from traditional to newly built modern villages. One success was a significant increase in literacy across the country as the new villages made the widespread provision of education much easier. Health care also became much more accessible. But the campaign proved too expensive for the Tanzanian economy, as commodity prices fell in the 1970s and the country became embroiled in a war with Uganda. It did not lead to the same economic catastrophe as the GLF, but in 1985 President Nyerere decided to stand down as president and the project was formally abandoned, although it has left an enduring mark upon rural Tanzanian society.

Photo 9.3 President Nyerere of Tanzania. *National Archives of the Netherlands Photo Collection 917-6721*

THE PROTEAN FACES AND UNEVEN RECEPTION OF LIBERALISM AROUND THE WORLD

Chapter 8 emphasized the importance of the Western, European-type state spreading around the world. It has transformed the way that 'politics' is conducted, and public policies are formulated. The consequence is that many of the issues surrounding political institutions, the way that decisions are taken in one country and the ideas surrounding them are often more similar to those in another, even possibly in another region of the world, rather than to similar processes and institutions in pre-'modern' times. In the same way, ideologies that were originally formulated in Europe have spread to other regions of the world and taken on a life of their own—the preceding section already introduced this notion with the various emancipatory revisions of Marxism. This section will focus upon the differential reception and understanding of liberalism to illustrate this point more fully. It will also caution against an over-simplified (mis)understanding of differences between 'Western' and 'non-Western' political thinking and encourage more fine-grained analysis.

Liberalism, like socialism, has spread around the world. The Liberal International is an organization that aims to provide international links and support between political parties that subscribe in general to liberal principles. Its website provides a succinct summary of what those parties are supposed to stand for, **see Box 9.14**.

Yet, within this overall framework of progressive, high-minded virtue, individual parties have different priorities, and these vary from one region of the world to another.

This distinction was important because it illuminates the nature of liberalism in Central and South America. There the former colonies of Spain and Portugal had independence thrust upon them at the beginning of the nineteenth century by the Napoleonic wars. The French broke the communications between the colonial powers and their colonies, which declared independence. But there was no liberation struggle, as occurred later in British and French colonies in the twentieth century. This meant that political and economic power continued to be exercised as before by local, now ex-colonial agents. This has meant that the identity and societies of South

> **KEY QUOTE** BOX 9.14
> The Liberal International on Liberalism . . .

Liberals are committed to build and safeguard free, fair and open societies, in which they seek to balance the fundamental values of liberty, equality and community, and in which no-one is enslaved by poverty, ignorance or conformity. Liberalism champions the freedom, dignity and well-being of individuals. Liberalism acknowledges and respects the right to freedom of conscience and the right of everyone to develop their talents to the full. Liberalism aims to disperse power, to foster diversity and to nurture creativity. The freedom to be creative and innovative can only be sustained by a market economy, but it must be a market that offers people real choices. This means that Liberals want neither a market where freedom is limited by monopolies or an economy disassociated from the interests of the poor and of the community as a whole. Liberals are optimistic at heart and trust the people while recognizing the need to be always vigilant of those in power. (*Liberal International*, 2019)

American states for a long time continued to resemble that of Spain and Portugal. Though not part of Europe, they could be seen, and many of their peoples did see themselves, as 'another Europe', with a different tradition from that of the Anglophone world (Morse, 1999). 'Latin America's political tradition draws from Aristotle, Plato, Roman law, Augustine, Thomas Aquinas, Spanish medievalism, sixteenth-century neoscholastics such as Suárez, Rousseau, Comte, Rodó, Hispanismo, and corporatism. And instead of liberty, equality, individualism, and pluralism, most of these writers tend to emphasize order, discipline, hierarchy, authority, non-equality, integralism, organicism, and the group or communal basis of society . . . [I]t is an alternative tradition within Western thought' (Wiarda, 2001: 345). Until around 1870 the old centres of power staunchly resisted change, but gradually liberals and liberalism took over as the ideology of modernity and the future, one of (self-)liberation from the remnants of colonial power. The main preoccupations were the establishment of a rule of law and of individual rights, and the strengthening of the state to control the dominance of the Catholic Church, rather than promoting free trade—the same sorts of issues as preoccupied liberals in Catholic Europe in the nineteenth century. 'Liberalism' evoked progress, modernity, secularism, man's control over nature.

> As perceived by the contemporary elites of Latin America, the two decades following 1870 represented the fulfilment of liberalism . . . The earlier American phenomenon of 'barbarous' caudillos finally yielded to a 'civilized' and uniform regime of law . . . The liberal struggle to establish the secular state had been won . . . What appeared the fulfilment of liberalism was in fact its transformation from an ideology in conflict with the inherited colonial order of institutions and social patterns into a unifying myth.   (Hale, 1996: 134)

Reyes Heroles (1974), for example, has presented liberalism as the dominant ideology in Mexican politics throughout the last quarter of the nineteenth century and the first half of the twentieth, even though for most of that period Mexico was ruled by the Institutional Revolutionary Party (PRI) in which he was a leading official. This had finally taken power in 1929 after nearly twenty years of chaos following the peasant-led revolution of 1910–11 and joined the Socialist International. But he also stressed that Mexican liberalism should be viewed as 'social liberalism', i.e. defending the interests of workers and peasants against the havoc wrought by uncontrolled market forces. In the countryside the revolution introduced rural cooperatives to prevent peasant immiseration.

According to Tosto (2005), liberalism in Brazil had a somewhat different evolution. In Europe liberalism was associated with the rise of the new middle classes who sought to push aside the old aristocracy. In Brazil, however, 'during the nineteenth century, liberalism held aristocratic connotations, as Brazilian state-builders sought to create a European-style aristocracy in order both to institutionalize a market economy based on slave labor and to protect the country's integrity from fragmentation' (Tosto, 2005: 173). But later these aristocratic connotations came to be a hindrance as the country underwent rapid change, with the abolition of slavery and large-scale immigration of people from Europe who felt no sense of deference towards aristocrats. Gradually liberalism in Brazil began to seem out of place. Its appeal as a unifying myth faded.

If we turn to Asia, liberals there were definitely represented in the debates that took place in India and China over national emancipation and self-strengthening during the first half of the twentieth century. In China in the first decades 'it was identified with anti-Confucianism, science, democracy, liberty, progress and the vernacular movement (i.e. rejecting the use of classical Mandarin). Also, it was associated with Westernized radicalism' (Fung, 2010: 133). Rather than concentrating upon the establishment of legal and representative political institutions as in South America, even though all the old institutions of China were crumbling away, it was associated with the spirit of emancipation—and the word for liberalism in Chinese (*ziyouzhuyi*) can also mean the principle of 'free-ness' or even 'license', though most Chinese liberals regarded liberty as an important, but not the supreme, value. So the term embodied the contradictory notions of 'control' through science and modernity and the lack of (self-)control. 'Few [Chinese liberals] showed an interest in Locke, Smith, Montesquieu, and other eighteenth-century liberal thinkers. Instead they were interested primarily in the modern or state liberalism of nineteenth-century Europe, then in the New Liberalism of early twentieth-century England, before embracing the social democratic ideology of Western Europe. Chinese liberalism rose in reaction to, and as a critique of, modern capitalism' (Fung, 2010: 134). But China was confronted by such powerful challenges in the 1920s and 1930s, both internal and external, that liberals were not strong enough to organize solutions. In the end the more radical enemies of capitalism—the communists—won. More recently the gradual opening up of China after the death of Mao in 1976 provided opportunities for more open debates over possible paths of reform, and liberal ideas did spread, especially among intellectuals and even some officials—former Prime Minister Wen Jiabao told a press conference of foreign journalists of his support for democracy, and he claimed that he took a copy of Mill's *The Theory of Moral Sentiments* with him on trips abroad (Li, 2015: 25, 23). But, when liberals published Charter 08 ('Charter 08', 2008), a kind of manifesto for political, legal, and economic reforms in 2008, the regime suppressed it. Since then political pressure has increased and liberalism as such has not spread widely outside intellectual circles.

In India, too, liberals were involved in the debates over the struggle for independence. In fact there were Indian liberal writers already in the early nineteenth century, and their preoccupations were not very dissimilar from those of European liberals of the time. But gradually these diverged. On the one hand Indian liberals became disenchanted with British liberals who prioritized human progress as led by Britain over respect for different social values in their colonies. Their liberalism smacked of superiority. And on the other hand communitarianism—the prioritizing of community over individual rights—gradually infiltrated into Indian liberalism as the struggle for independence gathered momentum (Bayly, 2007). In turn this handicapped liberalism's appeal to potential supporters, who felt greater sympathy for other anti-imperial ideologies such as socialism. So whilst liberalism did and does continue to leave its mark on Indian politics, it never became a 'unifying myth' for post-independence India in the way that it had done in South America. 'Liberalism in India had never been as devoted to individualism or the market as its Anglo-Saxon equivalent. Instead it had tended to be polarised between statist and communitarian versions of liberalism . . . Few politicians or public men now lay claim to this tradition directly, but it continues centrally to inform Indian politics and social life' (Bayly, 2012: 354, 357). For it to recover influence, according to Alagappa (2016: 64), 'it must be replaced with a philosophy that eschews the moral high ground that liberals seem to think is their exclusive property and instead cultivate the ability to see themselves, and the world, from the eyes of their enemy, and acknowledge the view as something that was formulated as an equal.' This notion of the perceived sense of moral superiority of liberalism and liberals is not confined to India and is one to which we shall return.

In Africa the association of liberalism with imperial rule also disadvantaged it as compared with other ideologies, such as socialism and communism. Even in post-apartheid South Africa, which had the most developed economy and also an incipient black middle class, which might have been expected to sympathize with liberalism, the then President of the South African Institute of Race Relations, could ask the question: why are there so few black liberals? His answer was the continuing salience of racial issues in South African politics. On the one hand, he surmised, liberalism as an attitude to life is quite widespread among black Africans. But liberalism as a political doctrine is much less attractive because 'South African politics are overwhelmingly racial, though not necessarily racist. Black South Africans emotionally and traditionally identify with something that has the name "African" or "Black" in it' (Sono, 1998: 302). There had been a Liberal Party under apartheid, which was dominated by whites, and although it was suppressed by the apartheid regime, 'African critics detected the "hypocrisy"—or what they called the "great pretence"—of white liberals on this issue of racial exclusivity. They saw the Liberal Party talking tall principle, but walking short roads of insincerity' (Sono, 1998: 298). Thus liberalism's failure to deal satisfactorily with the racial issue has restricted its appeal.

But it is in the Muslim world that liberalism has become divisive rather than unifying. This is because of its association with secularism. Classical liberalism in Europe connoted a belief in progress and modernity. That included a belief in a secular, rational world, that contrasted particularly with the conservatism of the Catholic church. In the Muslim world modernization in the twentieth century for a long time was also associated with secularism because religion was blamed for the region's backwardness. In Turkey, the nationalist reformer Ataturk imposed a draconian form of it in the 1920s, which separated religion and state. Religious organizations were banned from political activity, even though the majority of the population remained Muslims. The state was made resolutely 'laïc' (secular) on the French model. The ruling Republican People's Party exercised tight control over the government for decades, and Muslim believers could be imprisoned for even minor public political 'crimes', e.g. singing Muslim songs at political party meetings. Even though liberals disapproved of draconian punishments, they did not mount serious organized resistance. And secular liberals often sympathized with the intolerance with which laicism was imposed. To Muslims, these liberals appeared intolerant.

More recently, the Muslim Justice and Development Party (AKP) led by now President Erdogan was able to take control of the state in 2002, and part of its appeal at that time was a kind of liberalism, in that it claimed to speak for the majority of the population who were Muslim and wished their religious beliefs to count in the formulation of public policy. Though its fundamental ethos was conservative (Hale and Ozbudun, 2011), its appeals also resonated with a kind of liberalism, in the sense of tolerance and equality for all (Tuğal, 2016) but without the secularist overtones. For a while the AKP managed to win support from liberals (Denli, 2018), though without formally endorsing 'liberalism' as such, but subsequently it has turned away again and become much more authoritarian, as we shall mention in Chapter 14.

More widely in the Muslim world, liberalism as a doctrine has been associated with Enlightenment, rationalist philosophy, and Western colonial domination. It has therefore been treated with suspicion by Muslim believers. This does not mean that states with Muslim majorities cannot practise toleration or democracy, but that they are likely to reject the term 'Liberal'.

Menchik captures this point in the subtitle title of his book about possibly the most democratic state in the Muslim world, *Islam and Democracy in Indonesia: Tolerance without Liberalism*.

Lastly, let us turn to Russia for another illustration of ways in which Liberalism can be divisive rather than unifying. Liberalism there is also associated with radical modernization. Liberals in nineteenth century Russia were all Westernizers, urging radical reform of serfdom and then later constitutional government to make Russia a modern European state. But it was always a minority view in Russia, and the liberals were eclipsed by more radical reformers, ultimately the Bolsheviks.

Then, when the USSR collapsed in 1991 and Russia seemed to be embarking upon renewed Western-oriented development, there were high hopes for a liberal path as well. After all, very little bloodshed had been involved in the collapse. There was a substantial intellectual middle stratum of society who were attracted by modern European values. And there was the prospect of substantial Western assistance to guide the transition. Yet, the take-off never occurred. Partly this can be explained by mistakes made by liberal political groups (Hale, 2004). But it was also a reaction against the type of liberalism that seemed to be most strikingly on offer in Russia at that time, i.e. neoliberal market fundamentalism. The Russian government, with strong Western support, had embarked upon a radical programme of privatization, partly to prevent a return of the communists, but also to integrate the economy into the global one. No programme on this scale had been attempted before and the international financial institutions anticipated certain pain at first but optimistically rapid recovery. In fact, the ensuing economic recession wiped out the savings of almost everyone, including any putative potential middle class, lasted longer than anyone had predicted, and favoured the rise of a group of 'oligarchs' who took control of whole swathes of the Russian economy and became fabulously rich, sometimes by force, more often by corruption and the breaking of (admittedly opaque and sometimes contradictory) laws. Meanwhile, all social programmes, e.g. pensions, were eviscerated. It was the antithesis of social liberalism. (Neo)liberalism seemed to have led to chaos and anarchy rather than a modern liberal order. Despite its aura of modern moral superiority, it had facilitated the 'license' and decay that had worried Chinese critics of liberalism decades earlier.

The backlash persists to this day. In addition, the Putin regime has more recently promoted the rise of the Orthodox church in public life as a way of stimulating nationalism, and this has led to the stigmatizing of European liberal causes such as equality for homosexuals and same-sex marriages as manifestations of decadent, non-Russian, atheistic values (Platonov, 2016). The conservative commentator Khomiakov claims that 10–15 per cent of the population are liberally minded (although he believes them to be particularly concentrated among the ruling elite), roughly 30 per cent are left-inclined, whilst the remainder are conservative-minded (Khomiakov, 2018: 84). In 2010, the leading liberal reformer Igor Iurgens reluctantly concurred, lamenting the fact that it was the Russians who were preventing the modernization of Russia, because they were too stuck in their old way (*Russkaia Narodnaia Liniia*, 2010). Even though public opinion may be less hostile than the government might wish, it nevertheless is the case that instead of liberalism becoming a unifying myth in Russia, it is *anti*-liberalism that has become a unifying myth in the hands of government propaganda there today. And in June 2019 Putin told *The Financial Times* that liberalism had become 'obsolete' (*FT*, 2019).

> **KEY POINTS**
>
> - A lot of political thinking in non-Western societies consists in reinterpreting concepts that originated elsewhere
> - Liberalism has enjoyed a very mixed response around the world
> - Though there are common themes in liberalism, there are different emphases in different countries and regions of the world

CONCLUSION

The previous section has demonstrated the importance of Halisi's point that when considering political ideologies, it is important to analyse not only their content, but also how they are received in a particular community. 'The very essence of Eurocentric thought is the failure or refusal to take seriously the intellectual development and extension of Western political ideas in non-Western contexts. Therefore, at times, liberalism and socialism are more usefully viewed through the optic of black political thought' (Halisi, 1999: 54). In other words it is important to make fine-grained analysis of ideas and their contexts to do them full justice.

This chapter has stressed the importance of political culture in national politics and the ways that it can vary around the world. It has illustrated different principles of political and social order in various regions of the world.

The practice of comparing political thought, as opposed to political institutions, is relatively recent and still lacks a robust methodology (Freeden and Vincent, 2013). It is still very rare to find comparisons of political ideas across non-Western countries (Liebig and Mishra, 2017). Very often, individual commentators may construct their own over-simplified or tendentious account of what 'some people' think in one part of the world, to contrast it with an alternative, in their eyes often superior, formulation of how 'some other people' think about the same issue. Sometimes this is simply a natural result of the difficulty of comprehending the complexity of all the issues. For example, one point made earlier in the chapter concerned the widespread belief in 'Asia' about the importance of family values as the basis of social order there. This has often been contrasted with supposed individualism in 'the West'. If people in Asia think family values are crucial, then they will behave in a way that makes that a reality. But it is an oversimplification to regard this as a set of values that are uniquely or especially characteristic of the region, or that they are ignored in 'the West'. Others report the importance of family values and familialism in (at least some) countries in Europe, namely those with strong Catholic societies in southern Europe, i.e. Italy, Spain, Portugal, France, and also Ireland. Goody remarked: 'The West has tended to misunderstand even itself in drawing too sharp a contrast between *our* individualism, our rationality, our nuclear family, and *their* collectivism, their extended families. These differences are matters of degree rather than of kind' (Goody, 1996: 246; emphasis in original). In any case, the most recent World Values Survey reported that in all the countries surveyed around the world at least 95 per cent of respondents rated their family as either important or very important to them.

Sometimes essentializing is done by politicians and governments for the sake of making a political point. This is particularly glaring in the case of Russia, where the regime's overall orientation towards the West changed so radically over 10–15 years—and yet Surkov claimed that the current line of looking away from Europe is in keeping with centuries of tradition because 'culture is fate'. We must recognize that perceptions of other countries or regions do sometimes shape national and regional identities. The political culture and identities of individual nations and communities are partly built upon a sense of difference from others.

Still, it is important to try to be fair-minded in analysing them. In 1978 Edward Said first published a very influential book entitled *Orientalism*, which condemned past Western thinkers and commentators who had painted oversimplified and condescending portraits of Asians, often for the sake of manipulating and controlling them. In turn, others have identified the opposite temptation on the part of Asians—Occidentalism—for the sake of justifying 'Asian Values'. Sometimes oversimplification may be inevitable. Doing justice to every idea or value with a completely objective appreciation of the context is challenging. But that does not mean that you shouldn't try.

KEY QUESTIONS

1. How plausible is it for the World Values Survey to identify five different 'worlds' with distinct values in Europe, only two in Asia, and only one for the whole of Africa?

2. Do claims of the superiority of Asian values and the importance of subaltern studies suffer from Occidentalism?

3. Would a more prominent place for families in the maintenance of public order in any state create a more 'humane' society? Would it be more moral? Would it be compatible with economic development and 'globalization'?

4. Is the recent form of Confucius' ideas popularized in China really true to the original? How far does the CCP rely upon it?

5. How compatible is the caste system in India with modernity? Should the state do more to dislodge it? Would it be democratic to do so?

6. What are the differences between liberalism and tolerance?

7. How relevant is *swaraj* to political life outside India?

8. Where do the goals of *swaraj* and liberalism coincide, and where do they diverge?

9. Compare and contrast the thinking of Gandhi and Fanon on emancipation and political violence.

10. Compare and contrast the approaches of *jihad* and liberation theology to emancipation in this world.

11. Compare and contrast the social political order inherent in the principles of *guanxi* and *adl*.

12. Where, to whom, why and how is liberalism still a radical philosophy? To whom isn't it, and why?

13. Is religious liberalism feasible, or a contradiction in terms?

14. Is genuine liberalism compatible with a sense of moral superiority?

15. How can/should liberalism treat race-based issues?

16. What more do we learn about liberalism as a political ideology from studying how it has been received and understood in different regions of the world?

17. What are the key problems with Orientalism? And Occidentalism? How would you avoid them?

FURTHER READING

Bell, D. A. (2008), *China's New Confucianism: Politics and Everyday Life in a Changing Society* (Princeton and Oxford: Princeton University Press).

A very informative analysis of the revival of Confucianism in modern China. Chapter 1 focuses on the changing political discourses, as well as the potential challenge for Western liberal democracies.

Bell, D. (2014), 'What is liberalism?', *Political Theory* 24(6): 682–715.

A very good introduction to different versions of liberalism, primarily in Anglo-American literature.

Bell, D. (2016), *Reordering the World: Essays on Liberalism and Empire* (Princeton and Oxford: Princeton University Press).

A careful examination of the ways in which liberalism in Europe came to be associated with imperial ambition.

Buruma, I. and Margalit, A. (2004), *Occidentalism: A Short History of Anti-Westernism.* (London: Atlantic Books).

A response to Said, censuring Asian thinkers who 'essentialize' and oversimplify Western thinking.

Coker, C. (2019), *The Rise of the Civilizational State* (Cambridge: Polity).

Presents a re-emerging trend of states linking nationalism with historical civilizational greatness and longevity.

Corbridge, S., Harriss, J., and Jeffrey, C. (2012), *India Today: Economy, Politics and Society* (Cambridge: Polity).

An excellent introduction. Chapter 12 discusses the question: Does caste still matter?

Deneen, P. (2018), *Why Liberalism Failed* (New Haven and London: Yale University Press)

A recent powerful critique of liberalism in America.

A response to Said, censuring Asian thinkers who 'essentialize' and oversimplify Western thinking.

Ferdinand, P. (2012), *Governance in Pacific Asia: Political Economy and Development from Japan to Burma* (NY: Continuum).

Chapter 3 contains a fuller survey of political culture and the ideas underpinning them across the region.

Franon, F. (2001), *The Wretched of the Earth* (London: Penguin Classics).

A classic from the anticolonial struggle, especially Chapter 1 'Concerning Violence'. It was dashed off as the writer was dying from leukaemia. The introduction by Sartre attracted almost as much attention.

Johnson, R. W. and Welsh, D. (1998), *Ironic Victory: Liberalism in Post-liberation South Africa* (Cape Town and Oxford: Oxford University Press).

A still relevant collection of articles on the difficulties of practising liberalism in Africa's economically most developed country.

Kaehne, A. (2007), *Political and Social Thought in Post-Communist Russia* (London and New York: Routledge).

A stimulating account of the evolution of political thinking in Russia since the collapse of communism, as well as an analysis of why 'Western' concepts misfire when applied to Russia.

Kautilya (1992), *The Arthashastra* (Gurgaon: Penguin Random House).

A monumental work, the introduction by Rangarajan includes a survey of 'The Kautilyan State and Society' (pp. 27–77).

9

Lacorne, D. (2019), *The Limits of Tolerance* (New York: Columbia University Press).

A timely enquiry into the meaning and practices of tolerance.

Liebig, M. (2013), 'Kautilya's relevance for India today', *India Quarterly* 69(2): 99–116.

An enlightening attempt to show why a great pre-modern Indian thinker is still relevant to modern Indian politics and international affairs, despite his neglect in the dominant Anglo-American canon of the discipline of International Relations.

Löwy, M. (1996), *The War of Gods: Religion and Politics in Latin America* (London: Verso).

A concise introduction to the issues surrounding Liberation theology there.

Martin, G. (2012), *African Political Thought* (Basingstoke: Palgrave).

A good introduction to the main themes of African political thinking.

Massad, J. A. (2016), *Islam in Liberalism* (Chicago and London: Chicago University Press).

A provocative examination of the reasons why Muslims are suspicious of 'liberalism' and 'liberals'.

Peters, R. (2016), *Jihad: A History in Documents* (Princeton, NJ: Markus Wiener, 3rd edn).

Contains both analysis and translations of basic original documents. Chapters 8 and 10 examine more modern interpretations.

Rosen, L. (2010), 'Islamic Concepts of Justice', in Akbar S. Ahmed and Tamara Sonn (eds), *The Sage Handbook of Islamic Studies* (London: Sage), pp. 69–82.

A very good introduction to the complexities and subtleties of the term.

Roy, H. (2010), 'Gandhi: Swaraj and Satyagraha', in Mahendra Prasad Singh and Himanshu Roy (eds) (2011), *Indian Political Thought: Themes and Thinkers* (Delhi, Chennai, Chandigarh: Pearson).

A clear introduction to two key ideas of Mahatma Gandhi.

Said, E. (2003), *Orientalism* (Harmondsworth: Penguin).

A very influential critique of Western thinkers' attempts to 'essentialize' Eastern thinking as a way of achieving and maintaining colonial control.

Wiarda, H. L. (2014), *Political Culture, Political Science, and Identity Politics: An Uneasy Alliance* (Farnham and Burlington, VT: Ashgate).

An illuminating account of the evolution of the discipline of political culture, as well as an enthusiastic defence of its importance.

Yu, D. (2009), *Confucius from the Heart: Ancient Wisdom for Today's World* (London: Macmillan).

Widely-read in China, a popular interpretation of Confucian ideas for life there in the twenty-first century.

 For additional material and resources, please visit the Online Resources at:
www.oup.com/he/garner4e

9

10

LAW, CONSTITUTIONS, AND FEDERALISM

READER'S GUIDE

This chapter will first discuss the importance of constitutions in determining the basic structure of the state and the fundamental rights of citizens that they establish. It will raise the question of whether the Universal Declaration of Human Rights is Western-centric. Then, as a reminder that the rule of law may not always be interpreted uniformly, we shall explore different ways in which states may attempt to realize justice in applying the law, focusing in particular on differences between Islamic and Western practice. Next, we shall consider the importance of constitutional courts. After that we shall turn to the institution of federalism as a way of containing the powers of the state and of managing diverse societies. Then we will look at consociationalism as an alternative approach to managing such diversity. We will conclude with a brief discussion of the increasing legalization of political life.

LAW AND POLITICS

Chapter 8 emphasized the power of the modern state and attempts to control it. According to Finer, one of the main Western innovations in the theory of the state was the introduction of the 'law-bounded state', although Bonnett (2004: 5) argues that it was only towards the late nineteenth century that the idea of the West being a law-governed society came to be widely accepted. In other words, the decisions of the ruler(s) had to be codified and published so as to impose limits on the exercise of arbitrary power and to provide predictability in public affairs. Zakaria (1997: 27) concurs: 'For much of modern history, what characterized governments in Europe and North America and differentiated them from those around the world, was not democracy but constitutional liberalism. The "Western model" is best symbolized not by the mass plebiscite but the impartial judge'.

The spread of Western conceptions of law around the world is a consequence of the spread of Western ideas of the state. Previously, in traditional societies in other parts of the world, authoritative rule-making was not seen as the exclusive domain of political rulers. Binding rules on human conduct could emerge from a variety of sources, e.g. clans or tribes, and religious authorities. Although these rules may not have been specifically called 'laws', they had the same force. Because there was no single source of authority for these rules, there existed a kind of norm-creating pluralism. Moreover, traditional societies in Africa and Asia were inclined to prefer to achieve order through internalized harmony and self-regulation, rather than formal legal adjudication (Menski, 2006: 547).

Gradually, however, Western states arrogated to themselves exclusive responsibility for issuing such rules as laws, and they also codified them for the sake of consistency of application. Then, as legislatures became more common, law-making became their primary function. Gradually these

Photo 10.1 Statue of Justice. *Shutterstock RF via DAM*

practices spread around the world as Western states did. It was associated with the 'civilizing mission' that Western states set for themselves. This monopoly on legislative activity is another essential feature of the modern state. A further refinement is that states often claim as well that the legitimacy of binding rules for society depends upon approval by the legislature. Sometimes this is described as legal-positivism, i.e. law is what the state says it is. Other types of rule lack this legitimacy, and so lack the same degree of authority. It has become widely accepted as normal in Western states. As Twining (2000: 232) put it:

> [O]ver 200 years Western legal theory has been dominated by conceptions of law that tend to be monist (one internally coherent legal system), statist (the state has a monopoly of law within its territory), and positivist (what is not created or recognised as law by the state is not law).

It is perhaps best exemplified in the principle of secularism in France where the civil state authorities assert their precedence over all competing sources of rule-making authority, especially religious ones. Ataturk was heavily influenced by this example in the reforms that he introduced in the 1920s which asserted Turkish state supremacy over Islamic religious authorities. There, the state's Directorate of Religious Affairs controls the mosques by employing all Muslim clerics on salaries and subjecting them to an administrative hierarchy, which supervises their pronouncements. The most striking demonstration of the state's claim to authority was the announcement in 2008 that it would seek to establish which of the Prophet's sayings or *hadith* were genuine.

The extent to which this claim to legal monism has become accepted can be seen in the UK in the heated opposition to the Archbishop of Canterbury's lecture in 2008 which raised the possibility of the state accepting principles of shariah law in regulating family life of Muslims in the UK. He did not actually propose that a system of parallel law should be established, merely that some principles of shariah law might be incorporated into state law. Nevertheless, it was widely taken as challenging the dominant assumption of the primacy of state-approved and state-codified law. In fact, states in other parts of the world do allow greater legal pluralism. India, Pakistan, and Bangladesh, for example, do allow different religious communities the right to establish their own rules to regulate matters of faith and family rules; so legal pluralism does exist, and it may spread further in the future as a result of globalization. For the moment, Western states still claim a monopoly on the making of law. Lieven (2011), however, explains why the state legal system in Pakistan still attracts widespread discontent, because it is more unwieldy, more bureaucratic, and more expensive than traditional and religious legal systems.

There is a close connection between legal and political systems. It can be said of the law, as it was for politics in Chapter 2, that its primary concern is the 'authoritative allocation of values in society'. Creating laws to regulate human conduct, i.e. legislation, has been one of the most basic functions performed by states since earliest times. This is 'rule by law'. For laws to be legitimate, i.e. to be accepted by citizens, states have established rules of procedure, which are themselves legitimate and have to be followed. They have to be approved in legislatures, a subject to which we shall return in Chapter 11. Almost all states have legislatures, although their powers and procedures may vary widely.

There is a second function performed by law. It determines what is criminal behaviour, it prescribes punishments for criminals, and it provides impartial rules for binding adjudication in disputes. This is often encapsulated, especially in the West, in the concept of the rule of law, although Ajani (2019: 17) points out that the term carries different connotations when translated into other languages: '[C]ontinental terminology … still does not possess a fitting term to translate and express the notion of rule of law. All the translations which include the term "state" (*Rechtsstaat, Etat de droit, stato di diritto, pravovoe gosudarstvo*) are inappropriate in that they misconstrue the essence of the rule of law. The English term is more abstract and more neutral with regard to the role of the state. Nevertheless they all converge on the same principle, which goes further than rule by law. It means that everyone in a society, whether ruler, minister, or ordinary citizen, is expected to obey the law. At least in theory, everyone is equal before it.' Bingham (2011) identified eight elements in the rule of law. (**See Box 10.1**.)

As enshrined in the American constitution and repeated widely in other constitutions since then, the legal system is a check upon the exercise of power by the executive. One essential prerequisite for it to perform that function is independence from the state, in the sense that the state accepts that judges are free to determine the merits of legal cases irrespective of the consequences for state administration. Although an impartial legal system is a check upon the freedom of manoeuvre of legislators and therefore of the majority in a democracy, the rule of law is one of the essential elements of what Western states call good governance, a topic to which we shall return in Chapter 13. It is certainly an integral feature of liberal democracy. We shall return to the adjudication function of legal systems and their relationship with political systems towards the end of this chapter.

➡ See Chapter 13 for a discussion of good governance.

CONSTITUTIONS

The term 'constitution' can be used in two different ways, one general and one more narrow. In the broad sense it denotes the overall structure of a state's political system. King provided a broad definition. (**See Box 10.2**.)

This can also be expanded even wider to cover a nation's political culture, as when people talk about a particular decision being contrary to the nation's 'constitution', i.e. it may infringe the 'spirit' of the constitution rather than its precise terms.

The second, narrower use of the term constitution refers to a specific document that lays down the basic institutions of state and procedures for changing them, as well as the basic

> **BOX** 10.1
> List of Requirements for the Rule of Law
>
> a) The law must be accessible, intelligible, clear, and predictable.
> b) The laws should apply equally to all.
> c) Public officials should exercise their functions fairly, not unreasonably, and for the purpose originally intended.
> d) The law must adequately protect fundamental human rights.
> e) Means must be provided to settle civil disputes without prohibitive cost or inordinate delay.
> f) Trial procedures should be fair.
> g) States must comply with international legal obligations.
>
> (Bingham, 2011)

> **❝ KEY QUOTE** BOX 10.2
> King on Constitutions

[T]he set of the most important rules and common understandings in any given country that regulate the relations among that country's governing institutions and also the relations between that country's governing institutions and the people of that country. (King, 2007: 3)

rights and obligations of its citizens. It also serves as the basic source of national law, so that individual laws and legal codes are expected to conform to it. It is, or should be, the core of the legal system. For most states this is a demanding requirement, which requires continual monitoring and, usually, a special constitutional court that can adjudicate whenever there seems to be a conflict. Islamic states in addition require the harmonization of divinely inspired, avowedly universal shariah law with national, civil, more secular codes. For an example of an attempt to devise an Islamic constitution, see Moten (1996: appendix B). For the more practical difficulties of a constitutional court (in this case in Egypt) trying to cope with these problems, see Lombardi (1998). This could be contrasted with the existing constitutions of Iran and Saudi Arabia.

In practice, the difference between the two uses of the term constitution is not nearly as wide as it used to be. Only three states—the UK, New Zealand, and Israel—now do not have a specific constitution. In Britain's case the advantage of an unwritten constitution is said to be the greater flexibility that it offers for resolving new political disputes with constitutional implications that emerge within a democracy. It offers greater adaptability—the decision to devolve some decision-making powers away from Whitehall to Scotland and Wales in 1997 was accomplished much more easily than would have been the case if Britain had a written constitution. The turmoil over Britain's departure from the EU has brought to the fore, however, the disadvantages. 'The British Constitution is a state of mind', says Peter Hennessy, a historian who calls this the 'good chap' theory of government. 'It requires a sense of restraint all round to make it work.' Yet, amid Britain's current crisis, 'such restraint has been lacking' (*The Economist*, 2018). When key political decisions depend upon the interpretation of precedents from arcane rules of parliamentary procedure dating back up to 500 years, few understand, including MPs and even government ministers. It does nothing for transparency in democracy. More substantively, the relative powers of parliament and the executive in a supposedly parliamentary democracy have been disputed—can the government ultimately suspend (prorogue) parliament to ensure leaving (as Prime Minister Johnson has claimed), whether or not this was backed by a referendum? What is the constitutional force of a referendum in a representative parliamentary democracy? If referendums become a more common feature of political life, should a majority of 50.01 per cent be sufficient to change policy, however fundamental it might be, or should it need to be a 'super-majority' of some kind? And can a part of the UK (Scotland) be taken out of the EU despite a majority of its voters opting to stay and despite devolution? The muddle surrounding all these issues has revived arguments over the need for at least a thorough-going constitutional review once the Brexit process is over (*Prospect* magazine, 2019; Bogdanor, 2019), although some still oppose a written constitution (Sumption, 2019).

The last twenty years have seen an enormous surge of constitution writing around the world. At least eighty-one states introduced new constitutions, while a further thirty-three carried out major constitutional reform. In many cases this was a consequence of the collapse of communism and the independence of many states in the former Soviet Union and former Yugoslavia: but it also included Saudi Arabia which adopted a constitution in 1992, Algeria (1989, amended 1996), and Morocco (1996). Therefore, legitimate patterns of political behaviour became both more transparent and also more regularized. Still, as King (2007) reminds us, no state includes all of even the most fundamental elements of the political system in a single written document. For example, virtually no state establishes a particular electoral system in its constitution, yet this is a vital element in determining how power can change hands.

In addition to the details of specific constitutions, you should also bear in mind the related notion of constitutionalism. This can mean two things. It can encapsulate a normative outlook on the political values embodied in a particular country's constitution, i.e. doing things according to its 'spirit'; or it can mean a broader normative standpoint: making the observance of constitutions the most fundamental principle of political life. At its most extreme, this could mean that constitutions, once codified, should remain inviolate. In practice no state makes this an absolute principle. Constitutions do change. They are amended or even replaced. However, states generally make it very difficult by insisting upon special procedures for changing them so that such change takes place without haste and after due reflection. This notion of the special status of constitutions in general is part of constitutionalism. Respect for the primacy of the constitution remains a core element of the American political system. The same is true of continental Europe, where the memory of disastrous dictatorships accentuated the attractiveness of a robust constitutional order. Western advice on good governance to developing countries regularly stresses the importance of constitutionalism and the rule of law.

KEY POINTS

- Common usage of the term 'constitution' is ambiguous. It can mean either a legal document and/or a pattern of rule.
- Constitutions may embody aspirations for future patterns of rule, as well as regulating how that rule should be exercised now.
- Constitutionalism is a normative doctrine giving high priority to the observance of a constitution's provisions and making it effective.

FUNDAMENTAL RIGHTS

One of the basic features of constitutions is that they usually contain a list of fundamental rights of citizens. The first lists of civil rights were contained in the American constitution and the list of the Rights of Man from the French Revolution. Though more recently the UN adopted in 1948 a Universal Declaration of Human Rights, the fact that the notion of human rights first emerged in Western countries has led rulers of non-Western states to claim that it is inappropriate for non-Western societies, particularly when they are criticized by Western governments for failing to respect them. This is illustrated by **Box 10.3**.

KEY DEBATE BOX 10.3
Are Human Rights a 'Western' Construct?

In the aftermath of the Second World War, the newly created United Nations attempted to establish a better world that would never revert to the injustice and conflict of the past. It adopted the Universal Declaration of Human Rights in 1948, which declared in Article 1 that 'all human beings are born free and equal in dignity and rights'. Article 2 goes on to add that everyone without exception is entitled to these freedoms and rights (for more details, **see Box 10.4**). However, Article 29(2) clarifies that limitations on the exercise of these rights can only be tolerated 'for the purpose of securing due recognition and respect for the rights and freedoms of others and of meeting the just requirements of morality, public order and the general welfare *in a democratic society*' (emphasis added). In other words, even though not all founding states of the UN were democracies in the Western sense, e.g. the USSR, most were, and the Universal Declaration of Human Rights does assume the standards and perspective of (predominantly Western) democracy.

Subsequently that perspective has been challenged by newly independent colonies and state socialist regimes, e.g. China, which all instinctively mistrust Western pretensions to establish the basic standards of international political morality. But more recently Islamic states and peoples have also begun more openly to assert alternative principles of international morality. For their perspective on human rights let us consider the Cairo Declaration on Human Rights in Islam (1990) and the Arab Charter on Human Rights (updated 2008), which are more coloured by their distinctive religious traditions and national experiences of colonization from the West. The first ten articles of the Cairo Declaration are devoted to the principles of religious morality underlying human life. The first article declares that all human beings are united by submission to God and that 'all men are equal in terms of basic human dignity and basic obligations and responsibilities, without any discrimination on the grounds of race, colour, language, sex, religious belief, political affiliation, social status or other considerations'. Article 6 specifies that 'woman is equal to man in human dignity and has rights to enjoy as well as duties to perform; she has her own civil entity and financial independence, and the right to retain her name and lineage'. However, it adds that 'the husband is responsible for the support and welfare of the family'. Article 10 prohibits attempts to convert people to another religion or atheism. Article 11 prohibits slavery, humiliation, oppression, and exploitation, and specifically prohibits colonialism as 'one of the most evil forms of enslavement'. The rest of the articles specify rights to free movement, work, property, a clean environment, medical and social care, and privacy. According to the Cairo Declaration, all individuals are equal before the law, but the shariah is the sole source of authority over what constitutes crime and punishment. The declaration ends with three articles that specify the shariah as the basic framework for interpreting all these rights and emphasizes that everyone has the freedom to express opinions provided they are not contrary to its principles.

The Arab Charter on Human Rights repeats most of these rights, but without specifying the shariah as the basic framework for interpreting them. It also adds (Article 24) that individuals have the right to take part in political activity, to stand for election, to freedom of association and peaceful assembly, provided this is compatible with restrictions 'necessary in a democratic society in the interests of national security or public safety, public health or morals, or the

→

protection of the rights and freedoms of others'. It draws no distinction between the rights of men and women. In that respect it traces a more moderate line in-between the two previous positions, appealing to secular as well as religious Arab states. It converges more with the UN Declaration and accepts the perspective of democracy. It repeats the caveat of possible restrictions on the enjoyment of those rights for the sake of national security, public order, and public morality. But redress for citizens who allege violation of human rights may still be more tricky than in the West, especially in explicitly Islamic states that incline more towards the Cairo Declaration. The enjoyment of human rights greatly depends upon the operation of a state's legal system and how it understands the rule of law.

In the twentieth century, constitutions have often gone beyond purely 'political' rights to include broader social rights. These additions usually relate to welfare provisions, but they may also specify other conditions as well. For example, many states (especially those with Catholic or Islamic societies) lay particular emphasis upon the family as the basic unit of society and assign it a privileged position. The Universal Declaration of Human Rights was an early exemplar of this trend of establishing social rights. It includes additional specific political rights that were not mentioned in the Rights of Man. It lays down that every individual has the right to freedom of thought, conscience, and religion, including the right to change them (Article 18); the right to freedom of opinion and expression, including the freedom to receive and impart information and ideas through any media and regardless of frontiers (Article 19); and the right to freedom of peaceful assembly and association (Article 20). In addition, it lays down a number of social rights as well. Everyone has the right to social security (Article 21), to work and equal pay for equal work (Article 23), to rest and leisure with reasonable limits on working hours (Article 24), to a standard of living 'adequate for the health and well-being of himself and of his family' (Article 25), to education (Article 26), and to participation in the cultural life of the community (Article 27). In theory, all states that have accepted the Universal Declaration of Human Rights have also committed themselves to observing it, whether or not its provisions are specifically incorporated into their constitutions.

At least in principle, these rights are 'justiciable' within individual states, i.e. a citizen should be entitled to go to law to seek redress if they feel that any of these rights are being infringed by their government. This depends upon the willingness, and the resources, of individual citizens to pursue their own claims in the courts. More recently a further trend has emerged, especially in the USA and Catholic states, which is support for the 'right to life'. In other words, citizens can take up the right of someone else, in this case the unborn, and so prevent abortions.

What is clear from this extension of rights is that they leave a great deal of room for judicial interpretation. The various welfare and cultural rights do not lend themselves to simple yes or no adjudication. They leave open the question of amount or degree. Is a citizen of a developing country entitled to the same degree of welfare as one in Europe? What level of healthcare? Of education? It leaves open the question of the relative priorities of every sovereign government. Should the courts become involved in determining the levels of welfare spending as opposed to other claims on the budget? This is a particularly sensitive issue in democracies. Even in the case of the more 'political' rights, such as freedom of expression and association, where a yes/no adjudication by the courts is more likely, recent experience has shown that these too may increasingly have to be balanced against other public priorities. For example, the right to freedom of expression may have to be weighed against the 'right' to public security, as in the examples of government restrictions to prevent incitement of hatred or terrorism.

In addition Sumption (2019) argues that the European Court of Human Rights (ECHR) has interpreted Article 8 of the European Convention on Human Rights, which protects the right to respect for an individual's private and family life, into a much broader principle of respect for an individual's privacy, **see Box 10.4**.

This has then opened the way for it to rule on all sorts of things that might impinge upon an individual's personal autonomy, including things which involve political choices and on which there may be no consensus, as can be seen from the Guide that the ECHR provides (European Court of Human Rights, 2019).

Although the twentieth century has seen a dramatic expansion in the range of rights to which citizens are supposedly entitled, there is still scope for individual legal systems to come up with a great variety of interpretations. All of this explains why, in democracies, perhaps even more than in authoritarian regimes, the court system is increasingly limiting the freedom of manoeuvre of elected governments. This is true even of Britain, which did not have a Charter of Human Rights of its own, but since 1998 has subscribed to the European Convention on Human Rights as laid down in the Human Rights Act. The new Conservative Government in 2015 announced an intention to withdraw from this Convention to replace the European Court of Justice with the British Supreme Court as the supreme arbiter of human rights in the UK, but it also claimed that this will not in any way diminish the protection now afforded to those rights.

Increasingly, constitutions of nation-states contain not only provisions regulating the operation of specific institutions. They also include aspirations about the direction in which their respective political systems are expected to develop. This has always been a feature of constitutions of states in Latin America, but it is increasingly prominent in Europe and also in Islamic societies. In so far as they contain provisions that are not yet realized, then they also allow greater scope for the courts to contribute to the realization of those aspirations. In that sense they allow for greater legalization of the political process. In fact they will contribute to it.

> **KEY QUOTE** BOX 10.4
> Article 8 of the European Human Rights Convention

Right to respect for private and family life
1. Everyone has the right to respect for his private and family life, his home and his correspondence.
2. There shall be no interference by a public authority with the exercise of this right except such as is in accordance with the law and is necessary in a democratic society in the interests of national security, public safety or the economic well-being of the country, for the prevention of disorder or crime, for the protection of health or morals, or for the protection of the rights and freedoms of others.

> **KEY POINTS**
>
> - Over the last two centuries there has been an increasing number of universal rights.
> - They have expanded from political freedoms to rights to welfare, cultural protection, and cultural respect.
> - There is a potential clash between the enforcement of rights by courts and the sovereignty of parliament.

CONSTITUTIONAL COURTS AND JUDICIAL REVIEW

Chiefly because of the sensitivity of the issues that they are called upon to determine, all states have a constitutional court of some kind. As we shall see, this is particularly true of federal states where constitutional guarantees to subnational units are a crucial reassurance that their interests will not be repressed. Some courts may be called by that name specifically. Others may assume that role as part of a wider range of judicial functions. In most countries those who serve on these courts are either trained and experienced lawyers, or academic lawyers. France is something of an exception, however, in that its Conseil Constitutionnel has more limited powers. It can only pass comment on a law in the short period of time between its approval in parliament and its promulgation. Once promulgated, a law in France cannot be changed, except by parliament; and it is not required that a member of the conseil be a lawyer—sometimes they are distinguished politicians. At present, out of ten members, one is a former president of the republic, three more are politicians, and two are former civil servants. Only four are lawyers, although others have studied law.

One trend that has become more evident in recent years has been the readiness of courts in the USA and the UK to challenge government decisions through judicial review, on the grounds that fundamental rights have been infringed, or that administrators have failed to observe due process. In the US, this has stemmed from Constitutional Amendment 14, which can be found in Key Quote, **Box 10.5**.

The Supreme Court has used this to expand its remit to cover potentially any decision of the executive that might impinge upon personal autonomy and privacy, which has become effectively an additional right. It has been adduced in a very wide range of rulings, ranging from the legality of trade unions to abortion (Sumption, 2019). While such interventions have often been regarded as at the very least embarrassing or irritating for governments, the courts have justified this intrusion by the need to ensure that human rights have been duly observed, even those of condemned criminals. Although this appears to be a tendency that is spreading to other countries, France again is an exception. There the state takes the view that challenges to the constitutionality of potential

 KEY QUOTE BOX 10.5
US Constitutional Amendment 14

No State shall make or enforce any law which shall abridge the privileges or immunities of citizens of the United States; nor shall any State deprive any person of life, liberty, or property, without due process of law; nor deny to any person within its jurisdiction the equal protection of the laws.

human rights abuses are better raised in parliament, which has the duty of holding the government to account, than by the courts. British judges used to share this view until the 1970s, but no longer (King, 2007: 115–49), in part because of the higher authority conferred on the ECHR in Strasbourg since Britain adopted the Human Rights Act in 1998. On balance, Sumption (2019) would wish to resurrect the earlier approach by withdrawing from the ECHR and instead imposing a British Human Rights Act. To support his case, he cites the 'obvious irony' of the ECHR concluding in 2012, in the name of democratic legitimacy, that the British parliament had no power to deprive prisoners in jail of the right to vote, because that was a question of human rights established by law (Sumption. 2019: 69). He argues that the strength of the democratic political process is that it reconciles conflicting interests, however messily. 'Litigation can rarely mediate differences. It is a zero sum game. The winners carry off the prize, and the losers pay. Law is rational. Law is coherent … Opacity, inconsistency, and fudge may be intellectually impure, which is why lawyers do not like them. But, they are often inseparable from the kind of compromises that we have to make as a society if we are to live together in peace' (Sumption, 2019: 41–2).

KEY POINTS

- States establish special courts, or legal arrangements, to safeguard constitutions.
- There is an increasing tendency to appeal for executive policy-making to be subject to standards laid down by judicial review.

LEGAL ADJUDICATION OF POLITICAL PROBLEMS

As these examples show, within the general trend of creeping legalization of political life, there remains considerable scope for variation in the interpretation and implementation of even universal human rights by the courts of different nations. This is not only because of the interests, or self-interest, of particular nation-states, but also because of different approaches to the ultimate objective of the justice that legal systems are expected to dispense. Approaches to the function and purpose of law also vary from one country to another. As Montada (2001) put it, the concern for justice seems an anthropological universal, but it takes many faces, because there are divergent views on what is meant by the term and how it is realized in particular legal jurisdictions. Let us outline four basic differences, and they revolve around different interpretations of the meaning of 'justice' in a stricter legal sense—Chapter 9 has already identified a different Islamic approach to the notion of 'justice' in a broader sense.

The first can be summarized as a kind of legal positivism. The law of a particular country is neither more nor less than the sum of the laws which it has established. It can be summed up by a common phrase used by French lawyers: *La loi est la loi.* This means that the wording of each individual law as approved by parliament, as well as the whole legal code, is sacrosanct. It is inappropriate for judges to seek to enquire whether any particular law is phrased inadequately. Their task is simply to enforce it.

This approach to constitutional issues is replicated in France's former colonies, but it resonates more widely too. In pre-modern China there was a school of legal thinking called the Legalists.

Their main concern was to ensure that the Chinese obeyed the law. As long as they did, this would ensure order and harmony in society and prevent anarchy. The Legalists were not especially interested in 'justice' except in so far as an orderly society was also a just one. It was order and harmony that was just, not necessarily any particular law. They wanted to deter law-breaking, as that would be unjust. To this end, extreme punishments were 'just', however brutal for the individual law-breaker, as they would ensure justice for the rest of society. This was rule by law, but it was aimed at making people fear rulers and officials. It was law for deterrence.

A second approach to the social function of law was typified by communist states. Here the function of law was subordinated to some higher, non-legal goal: communism itself. Universal human rights were of lesser concern, except in the indefinite future, even if such states' constitutions specifically upheld them. Judges had to be members of the Communist Party, which meant that they had to defer to the party leadership. So appeals to the courts to defend the human rights of political dissenters were bound to fail. And still in China today officials of the Communist Party can only be prosecuted for criminal offences after the party leadership has agreed. Thus, although in China there is increasing talk of 'rule of law' replacing 'rule by men', there is still a long way to go, at least by Western standards.

A third approach to law and society can be seen in Islamic states. In general there is no doubt about the traditional importance of justice and the law there, as has already been indicated in Chapter 9. According to Hallaq (2005: 193), 'if ever there was any pre-modern legal and political culture that maintained the principle of the rule of law so well, it was the culture of Islam'. However, in so far as this rule of law existed, it was more because of practice, rather than because of the explicit separation of the powers of rulers and judges as in the West: it was because both rulers and judges were supposed to defer to the revealed law of the shariah. In general, rulers appointed and could dismiss judges. There was no notion of ordinary people having rights vis-à-vis their rulers, unless the latter broke divine law.

On the other hand, the state did not claim the same monopoly over law-giving as Western states do. Laws were mainly formulated by legal scholars, not by rulers; and there are four equally respected schools of legal scholarship to which Sunni judges could belong (the Hanafi, Maliki, Shafi'i, and Hanbali). The traditions of these schools could lead to different decisions in particular cases, especially commercial ones. People could choose their lawyers according to the type of decision they would be likely to make in a particular dispute. Moreover, there was not the same insistence upon consistency between the decisions of judges and upon binding precedents. Judges much more frankly tried to do justice according to the particular circumstances of an individual case, rather than forcing the facts to fit a set of orthodox decisions. There was no systematic codification of legal precedents. Therefore, traditionally in Islamic societies there was a tendency for political monism but legal pluralism, whereas in the West we find the obverse: a greater tendency towards political pluralism and legal monism, with legal systems expected to deliver consistent authoritative verdicts.

By contrast, the fourth approach to legal justice—what we can loosely term the Western approach—places greater stress upon procedural justice. This means making sure that verdicts are similar and more consistent in similar sets of circumstances. It requires a greater legal bureaucracy to ensure consistency of verdicts, with one or two higher layers of appeal courts, as well as ministries of justice to administer them. It also risks delivering verdicts that are less well tailored to individual circumstances. However, it does provide greater predictability about likely outcomes to court cases. Gradually the Western approach spread more widely around the world in the nineteenth and twentieth centuries. It was part of the spread of the Western state that was described in Chapter 8, and it also contributed to it, because the state took the responsibility of codifying laws and creating the judicial apparatus to achieve this. Again one of the best examples is Japan. As the Japanese state sought to respond to challenges from the West in the second half of the nineteenth century, it sent scholars to Europe to study alternative national legal systems, particularly Britain, Germany, and France, and present comparative reports on the respective merits of different legal codes. In the end Japan turned to the principles of German administrative law to provide the basis of its new code of administrative law, while it looked to Germany and France for the principles of commercial law. Turkey responded in similar ways as it sought to withstand the challenge to its own empire from Europe. From the 1870s onwards, Turkey too began to produce legal codes that grafted Western legal principles and the organization of justice onto its own well-established forms of jurisprudence and courts, and these were then spread throughout its empire in the Middle East. Civil courts assumed greater authority over religious ones. Gradually the state assumed control of the legal process as it embarked on Western-style modernization.

➡ See Chapter 8 for a discussion of the rise of the Western-type state.

Although the Western legal practices and norms have spread around the world, this does not mean that they have become universal and fully consistent. The decision in 2007 of President Musharraf of Pakistan to 'correct' the Supreme Court by dismissing most of the judges and replacing them with more pliant ones was a striking example of persisting differences. In 2017 President Erdogan dismissed over 3,000 judges following a failed military coup.

In addition we should also remember that other elements in the context of national legal systems may also have a significant bearing on the way law is practised. Epp, for instance, has shown how the pursuit of civil rights in a number of states with quite similar legal frameworks—the USA, India, the UK, and Canada—has varied considerably according to the legal infrastructure of individual countries. In particular, what matters is the availability of public resources to help poorer litigants pursue cases. Litigants in the USA and Canada find this much easier than in the UK or India. The consequence is that there has been a much stronger movement to pursue rights-related cases in North America, with Canada in particular undergoing what Epp describes as 'a vibrant rights revolution' since 1960. He explains this in part by the adoption in 1982 of the Charter of Rights and Freedoms, but also in part by a growing support structure for legal mobilization (advocacy organizations, government aid for litigants, lawyers, and legal scholars who changed the previous prevailing conservative mindset of the legal system) (Epp, 1998: 156, 195–6). The availability of resources for litigation has an important impact upon the pursuit of rights. What this shows is that there is a close connection between a country's legal system and the evolution of its political system. The two interact with and impact each other.

Even the simple fact of the number of lawyers that are qualified in a country will have a big impact on the place of law in a nation's public life and therefore on citizens' ability to have recourse to law. The USA has almost 1 million qualified lawyers, which represents about 0.3 per cent of the population. This reflects a society that is prone to litigation but the availability of lawyers no doubt also contributes to it. The UK has half that proportion, Germany has a quarter, France an eighth, while Japan and India have only roughly one-twenty-fifth. No doubt this also played a part in the limited pursuit of rights in India that Epp mentioned previously. These figures explain the widespread perception that the Japanese are very reluctant to go to law and to the courts when they have a problem. They try to find alternative ways of resolving disputes. Yet they would all be said to practise the rule of law.

This section has argued that a whole range of factors contribute to a variety of interpretations of the rule of law in the practice of legal systems in different regions of the world.

KEY POINTS

- Orientations on appropriate functions for legal systems have traditionally varied from country to country, and this can lead to variation in the practice of the 'rule of law'.
- This can lead to different interpretations of even universal rights.
- There is a distinctive emphasis in Western jurisprudence on realizing procedural justice through greater consistency and bureaucratic organization.

FEDERALISM, CONSOCIATIONAL DEMOCRACY, AND ASYMMETRICAL DECENTRALIZATION

The American Constitution was explicitly designed to restrain the power of the state. One way, as we have seen, was through the establishment of checks and balances, with the threefold division of power between executive, legislature, and judiciary. There was, however, a second way. This was through the establishment of a federal system. The territorial decentralization of power, it was hoped, would further obstruct any possible oppression. Ever since then, federalism has been touted as a solution to the risks of potential dictatorship. The importance of this idea can be seen in the federal constitution that was imposed upon West Germany after the Second World War. It was intended to undermine the remaining roots of Nazi dictatorship and it has justified the hopes that were placed upon it. These institutions have taken root in the German political system and have made Germany a reliable democratic partner in the heart of Europe.

In general, what is federalism? According to Robertson (1993: 184):

> Federalism' is now used to describe such a form of government, in which power is constitutionally divided between different authorities in such a way that each exercises responsibility for a particular set of functions and maintains its own institutions to discharge those functions. In a federal system each authority therefore has sovereignty within its own sphere of responsibilities, because the powers which it exercises are not delegated to it by some other authority.

What this definition emphasizes is the constitutionally backed equality between the national government and the federal units for responsibility for performing particular functions. It reassures the federal units or states that their decisions cannot be overridden by some higher authority. It is a protection against a domineering centre or worse.

To provide substance for that protection, federal systems usually establish two institutions. First, there is normally a two-chamber parliament, with the upper chamber composed of representatives from the states. The latter are given specific powers to ensure that their constitutional prerogatives cannot be legislated away without their consent. Second, there is usually a constitutional court to rule upon the constitutionality of legislative proposals, again aimed at reassuring the states that they cannot be coerced into submission.

Generally, however, since the American Revolution, federalism has been called upon to provide a constitutional framework for states facing two other challenges. The first is simply territorial size. Most federal states occupy a large area. As can be seen from **Table 10.1**, seven of the ten largest states in the world by area are federations. Of course, many of them are heterogeneous in terms of population, but size is also an important issue. Here, Australia is the paradigmatic example. The federation there was originally created in 1900 to allow significant devolution of power to individual states because of the difficulties of trying to run the whole country from Canberra, given the communication technologies that were available at that time. Diversity of population was not a significant factor in the decision.

In most cases, however, federalism has been proposed to provide guarantees for minority communities—usually ethnically based—that they will be able to preserve their particular way of life, their culture, their language, their religion, etc. Or, at any rate, that there will be no political challenge to them. Because of this, as can be seen from **Table 10.2**, federations vary considerably in size, some being very small indeed.

The experience of federations is of course not always positive. There is quite a long list of those that have disintegrated, some disastrously. The collapse of the USSR has been described by President Putin as one of the greatest disasters of the twentieth century, while that of the former Yugoslavia unleashed the greatest conflict in Europe since the Second World War. (**See Box 10.6**). Even where federations have survived, some have still gone through bloody civil wars, e.g. Nigeria in the 1960s, or the USA in the 1860s. The experience of Belgium, which in 2007 went for over 150 days without a national government and for a further 589 days in 2010–11, also suggests that they are not always capable of decisive national decision-making. So federations are not automatically capable by their very existence of preventing violent conflict and/or dissolution, or of providing effective government. Yet it can be argued that a prime cause of the collapse of the USSR and

Table 10.1 Federalism among the ten largest states in the world by territory

State	Federal/Unitary
Russia	F
Canada	F
USA	F
China	U
Brazil	F
Australia	F
India	F
Argentina	F
Kazakhstan	U
Sudan	U (but decentralized)

Table 10.2 List of federations

Argentina	Germany	Russia
Australia	India	St Kitts & Nevis
Austria	Iraq	Switzerland
Belgium	Malaysia	
Bosnia and Herzegovina	Mexico	United Arab Emirates
Brazil	Micronesia	USA
Canada	Nepal	Venezuela
Comoros	Nigeria	
Ethiopia	Pakistan	

Yugoslavia was the lack of the legal support and the rule of law without which constitutional provisions of any kind are more vulnerable. It was not the constitutional provisions themselves. On the positive side Stepan (2004: 441) declared: 'Every single long-standing democracy in a territorially based multilingual and multinational polity is a federal state.' And Rotimi has maintained that, despite the civil war, 'federalism has long been recognized as the indispensable basis for Nigeria's identity and survival' (2004: 328).

Yet, in the 1970s, the idea that federalism was the naturally most appropriate solution to the problems of division in deeply divided societies was challenged by the theory of consociationalism, which was initially introduced in Chapter 4. This was based upon the experience of a few small states with deep multi-ethnic and multi-confessional cleavages, largely in Europe, that had achieved intercommunal harmony and cooperation without a formal federal system. The first example of this to be cited was the Netherlands. The key to its success was attributed not to formal constitutional arrangements or legalism, but rather to iterated patterns of cooperation between elites in sharing power which generated and reinforced mutual trust. According to Lijphart (1977), there are four main characteristics of consociational democracies. (**See Box 10.6**.)

➡ See Chapter 3 for an introduction to consociational democracy.

 CASE STUDY BOX 10.6
The Collapse of the Former Yugoslavia

Yugoslavia was created at the end of the First World War as a state for South Slavs to prevent the return of imperial powers to treat them as colonies. However, between the wars it was bedevilled by enduring enmity between the two largest ethnic communities, the Serbs and Croats. In the Second World War it was dismembered under Axis control and hundreds of thousands were killed in fratricidal conflict.

After Liberation, largely by the communist partisans under Tito, the Yugoslav state was restored, this time as a federation. Even the ruling Yugoslav Communist Party was divided into separate federal units. The six federal republics (Serbia, Croatia, Slovenia, Bosnia–Herzegovina,

Macedonia, and Montenegro) had equal representation in the federal government, and after 1974, the two autonomous regions of Kosovo and Vojvodina in Serbia were granted only slightly less. Yugoslavia was by far the most genuinely federal communist state. In 1963 it created the only constitutional court in the communist world. For a long time the memory of the blood-letting during the war, a political culture that exalted the shared heroism of the partisan resist-ance, the pride in a Yugoslav road to socialism based upon workers' self-management, the threat of foreign intervention, as well as Tito's own robust leadership, all helped to preserve national unity. Despite occasional challenges to the leadership (in 1968 a new generation of Croat lead-ers tried to introduce a more liberal set of policies but were rejected by Tito), Yugoslavia stayed united and prosperous until he died in 1981.

Afterwards, however, the state ran into increasing difficulties. There was no cohesion in the national leadership. Tito had avoided naming a successor and he had created a federal system with a collective presidency, where the leader of each of the federal republics acted as head of state for just one year in rotation. He had emphasized the need for national decision-making on the basis of 'consensus', i.e. unanimity. After he was gone, all the republic leaders put the inter-ests of their own republic above that of the state as a whole. The national economy fragment-ed increasingly into republic units. Inter-republic trade actually declined. Inflation continued to increase throughout the 1980s. The national leadership agreed remedies in Belgrade and then refused to implement them when the leaders returned to their republic capitals. No one was prepared to make sacrifices for the good of the country as a whole. Popular dissatisfaction grew. All the nationalities, even the Serbs, the largest one, felt that they were the losers of the Federation. Trust disintegrated across the country.

Then in 1987 the heir apparent to the Serbian leadership, Slobodan Milošević, made a speech at an event commemorating the 600th anniversary of the defeat of the Serbs at the hands of the Ottoman Turks in Kosovo. He made an unexpected appeal for Serbs to stand up for their rights and vowed that Belgrade would back them. This provoked an emotional response across Serbia, which he then tried to turn into a movement to restore decisive national government under his leadership. Large numbers of Serbs were mobilized to march on Montenegro and then Slovenia to bring them to heel. In turn this provoked apprehension in the other republics about resurgent Serbian chauvinism. The constitutional court proved ineffective. The collapse of the communist regimes in Eastern Europe exacerbated the sense of crisis. Partly to forestall similar developments in Yugoslavia, and partly to keep Milošević at bay, the leaders of the communist parties in Croatia and Slovenia began to call for multi-party elections.

In turn this provoked Milošević to send the federal army into Slovenia and Croatia to try to bring them to heel or, if that failed, to establish a greater Serbia which could protect all Serbs against a repeat of the genocide that they had suffered in the Second World War. With that he launched a civil war that became the biggest conflict in Europe since the Second World War and destroyed the state of Yugoslavia.

(For a discussion of various explanations for the collapse of the former Yugoslavia, see Ramet, 2005.)

In fact, some of the other states that were later adduced as examples of the same practice ran into serious problems. Consociationalism, no more than federalism, is no automatic guarantee of social harmony. Not all of these difficulties were domestically caused. Lebanon, for instance, was destabilized by conflict between Israel and the Palestinians living in Lebanon. Cyprus was destabilized by Turkish invasion. Nevertheless, since this model was usually applied to small states in general, this made them more vulnerable in the case of outside intervention. In fact most sets of consociational arrangement have proved relatively short-lived, and not just because of external intervention. Only the Netherlands has remained faithful to the model. This has suggested that the model may be more appropriate as a temporary solution to societies that have recently suffered from major division or conflict. It can help to stabilize the state through increased trust between communities, before some transition to a more permanent set of arrangements (**see Box 10.7**).

One last development should be noted. This concerns new state practices in managing their centre–periphery relations around the world. This is a greater willingness to consider flexibility in arrangements between some states or provinces and the centre which is not offered to all those units. States no longer feel that they have to make an exclusive choice between either unitary or federal systems. They sometimes devise hybrid combinations. This can be called asymmetric decentralization or asymmetric federalism, and the general principle can be found in both federal and unitary states. A particularly striking example is Spain, which has granted much more extensive self-governing powers to some of the regions or 'autonomous communities', such as Catalonia, the Basque country, Galicia, and Andalusia, than to the other thirteen, although the Catalan political scientist Colomer still called the Spanish state 'the clearest case of failure ... to build a large nation-state in Europe' (Colomer, 2007: 80). The same principle has been applied in the UK, with varying powers granted to the Scottish, Welsh, and Northern Irish assemblies. More recently the Scottish Nationalist Party has advanced the quasi-federal argument that the UK should not be able to leave the EU without majorities in favour in all four constituent parts of the kingdom. France, where the state has traditionally been very preoccupied with constitutional equality and the dominance of Paris, has granted greater autonomy to Corsica than to other *départements*. All of these are still formally unitary states. Federal states display the same tendency for hybridity. The Soviet Union for decades distinguished between federal republics, autonomous republics,

BOX 10.7
Features of Consociationalism

- Government by grand coalition, i.e. governments included deputies from the parties representing all of the main communities, which usually required that they held far more than a bare majority of seats in parliament.
- Segmental or subcultural autonomy, i.e. each ethnic or confessional community was responsible for administering policies in specific policy areas that affected them.
- Proportional representation in the electoral system, which made simple majoritarian rule very unlikely, and proportionate representation in the distribution of posts in government bureaucracies, the distribution of public funds, and so on.
- Agreement on minority vetoes for certain types of legislation.

autonomous regions, and autonomous districts, all of which had different sets of powers from the more 'orthodox' provinces. Pakistan allows greater self-rule to the north-west frontier region and the federally administered tribal areas as compared with Punjab or Sindh. This means that other states that are confronted by challenges of great ethnic or religious cleavages can draw upon a much wider range of possible precedents to demonstrate flexibility. In many ways the old distinction between federal and unitary states has disappeared, as similar kinds of asymmetrical relationships are introduced into both of them.

KEY POINTS

- Federalism has a dual role: as a check on centralized government, and as a way of managing profound social diversity.
- Federations may collapse without appropriate legal structures or widespread popular support.
- Consociationalism is an alternative approach to handling social diversity, relying on elite cooperation rather than legal formalism.
- Consociationalism may be understood more broadly as a more consensual form of rule than majoritarianism.
- There is an increasing use of asymmetric arrangements to handle diversity in both federal and unitary political systems, which erodes the differences between them.

CONCLUSION: GROWING LEGALIZATION OF POLITICAL LIFE

This chapter has highlighted four things. The first is the importance of constitutions as fundamental institutions that structure political systems. By establishing the basic principles for political life, they channel the political behaviour of all the inhabitants of a state in various directions and, equally importantly, prevent some other forms of political behaviour; and they help to provide greater transparency about the ways that public decisions are made.

Second, constitutions need a developed legal system to give life to the provisions that they contain. Without some kind of accompanying rule of law, constitutions may be flouted by government, or they may be undermined, as the example of Yugoslavia shows.

Third, this still allows for different approaches by which legal systems attempt to achieve justice. Emphases vary from one state to another, and this will also mean that interpretations of universal human rights will to some extent vary from one country to another.

Fourth, federalism as a form of government does help to prevent excessive concentration of powers in a nation's capital. It can also help to provide reassurance to some minorities that their interests will not be overridden by larger communities. It can promote harmony in heterogeneous states marked by deep cleavages. However, it is not the only structure that can achieve this. Consociationalism offers an alternative approach to the same challenge, although it has tended to succeed only in smaller states, and then over a more limited period of time. More recently, unitary states have shown greater flexibility in devising new forms of decentralization which take account of the regional differences and vary the rights that they offer to particular communities. In this way the boundaries between federal and unitary states are becoming more blurred.

Last, there is a trend underlying the argument of this chapter. This is the expanding role played by law in social life. The extent to which law plays a central role in the political process varies considerably from one state to another. It is certainly more pronounced in the developed world, especially the USA. However, the trend is much more widely evident. Pakistan is but one example. The attempt by President Musharraf in 2007 to curtail the independence of the Supreme Court provoked concerted resistance from lawyers as a whole, with widespread popular support.

There are two dimensions to this trend. It encompasses first a growing tendency to devise legal frameworks to regulate and impose conformity upon an increasing number of dimensions of social behaviour within individual states (Sumption, 2019), and second an expansion of international legal activity to support globalization (Lieberman, 2001; Buxbaum, 2004). We have already mentioned the increased use of judicial review in the USA and most European states. The change in the growing salience of law and legal processes is striking in the case of a state such as China, which at the beginning of its reforms in the early 1980s had only 200 lawyers and now has around 230,000. The increase in the number of trained lawyers certainly marks a change in the direction of the rule of law, even if China is still a long way from practising it in the same way that the West does. This trend does make for greater checks upon the power of the state and the executive branch of government; but it also makes politics more complicated, more difficult for non-lawyers to understand. Dahl has remarked that the American system 'is among the most opaque, confusing, and difficult to understand' among Western democracies (Dahl, 2001: 115). At roughly the same time in a survey of public opinion in the Trilateral countries (the USA, Japan, and Western Europe), King concluded:

> The American people have lost confidence in their government because they have ceased to understand it ... The American political system was probably hard for most ordinary people to understand when it was first designed in the 1780s ... it has become even more complicated since then.   (King, 2001: 91–3)

The checks on the power of the state may be greater, but is politics becoming more opaque and more esoteric, increasingly confined to a more limited political 'class'? This is an issue to which we shall return in Chapters 11 and 12.

KEY QUESTIONS

1. Go to http://confinder.richmond.edu/ and find the longest and shortest constitutions in the world. What would you expect to be the consequences for the operation of the political systems of these two states? How different are they likely to be?

2. What is the most absurd constitutional provision that you have come across? Does it deserve the special status?

3. Compare these three documents. How significant are the differences?

4. Is there any sense in which the rights enshrined in the Universal Declaration of Human Rights are less complete than those in either of the other two documents?

5. Is there a significant Western bias in the Universal Declaration of Human Rights?

6. If accepted, what difference would the Archbishop of Canterbury's proposals on the adoption of shariah legal principles make to the relationship between the state and law in the UK?

7. Britain has no formal constitution. What difference does that make as compared with the political arrangements and practices of any other state with which you are familiar? Has the Brexit debate increased the need for one?

8. Are the French right to resist the expansion of judicial review in political life and leave constitutional challenges largely to parliament?

9. Assess Dahl's arguments about the weaknesses of the American Constitution. Is there any likelihood of them being remedied?

10. What are the main differences between federalism in Canada and the USA?

11. If federalism does indeed weaken the power of the government, does it make weaker states in the developing world too weak? What is the evidence from Nigeria, India, Brazil, and/or Pakistan?

12. Do the autonomous communities of Catalonia and the Basque country in unitary Spain have greater powers for self-government than the federal Länder in Germany?

13. Are federalism or consociationalism viable solutions to the internal conflict in Iraq?

14. If the rule of law is a good thing, does that mean that the more laws a state has, the better?

FURTHER READING

Amoretti, U. M. and Bermeo, N. (eds) (2004), *Federalism and Territorial Cleavages* (Baltimore: Johns Hopkins University Press).
This is an account of the ways in which federalism can manage territorial divisions within states.

Bingham, T. (2011), *The Rule of Law* (London: Penguin).
A readable account of the principles inherent in the rule of law from Britain's former senior Law Lord.

Bogdanor, V. (2019), *Beyond Brexit: Towards a British Constitution* (London: I.B. Tauris).
An in-depth analysis of the reasons why the issue of a written constitution for the UK has become pressing.

Burgess, M. (2006), *Comparative Federalism: Theory and Practice* (London: Routledge).
This is a recent account of the theory of federalism.

Dahl, R. A. (2001), *How DeUUmocratic is the American Constitution?* (New Haven, CN: Yale University Press).
This is a study of weaknesses of the American Constitution, including the great difficulty of changing it.

King, A. (2007), *The British Constitution* (Oxford: Oxford University Press).
This is a recent authoritative study of the British 'constitution' in the broad sense.

Lane, J.-E. (1996), *Constitutions and Political Theory* (Manchester: Manchester University Press).
This is an examination of the relationship between constitutions and political theory.

10

Lieven, A. (2011), *Pakistan: A Hard Country* (New York: Public Affairs).

Chapter 3 contains an insightful account of the reasons for popular preferences for non-state legal adjudication.

Lijphart, A. (1999), *Patterns of Democracy: Government Forms and Performance in Thirty-Six Countries* (New Haven, CN: Yale University Press).

This states the case in favour of big coalition government, including consociationalism, as a more consensual and ultimately more effective form of rule.

Prospect magazine (2019), 'Does Britain need a proper constitution?' (https://www.prospectmagazine.co.uk/magazine/does-britain-need-constitution-debate-sionaidh-douglas-scott-adam-tomkins).

Two academic lawyers debate the advantages and disadvantages of a written constitution for the UK.

Sumption, J. (2019), *Trials of the State: Law and the Decline of Politics* (London: Profile).

The enlarged version of the 2019 BBC Reith Lectures by a former UK Supreme Court Justice questioning the apparently ever-increasing intrusion of law into democratic political life.

For additional material and resources, please visit the Online Resources at:
www.oup.com/he/garner4e

10

VOTES, ELECTIONS, LEGISLATURES, AND LEGISLATORS

11

READER'S GUIDE

This chapter will first explain some of the basic issues involved in assessing the operation of voting and electoral systems. Then it will survey the functions of legislatures. It will also discuss the growing practice of measures to establish quotas to increase gender equality in legislative recruitment. It will present a classification of legislatures based upon their capability to stand up to the executive branch of government. After that comes a basic introduction to the internal structure of legislatures: the choice of single or double chambers, and the role of parliamentary committees. Then it will deal with trends in the backgrounds of members of parliament (MPs) in various countries, specifically focusing upon the criticism that they constitute a 'political class'. Finally, it will introduce some themes from recent new thinking on institutional ways of remedying this.

THE VOTING PARADOX

Voting is a mechanism for making collective decisions. It is also intended to be a means for en-suring that the majority preference for a candidate or a policy is reflected in the ultimate decision. It is possibly the most basic element of any democracy. Yet it is subject to two basic paradoxes. The first is that the huge number of citizens in any modern state means that no individual's vote is likely to make the difference between two or more choices. This makes it potentially 'irrational' for any individual to bother to vote at all. Yet without votes, democracy—or at any rate represent-ative democracy—is not possible. This helps to explain why, although we shall argue in Chapter 16 that democracy is associated with values of freedom and liberation and although voter turnout in national democratic elections generally remains quite high, some states make it compulsory, e.g. Argentina, Australia, Brazil, Cyprus, and Singapore.

The second paradox concerns the difficulty of relying upon votes to determine the objective preferences of the public. This is due to the mathematical problem known as the Arrow impossi-bility theorem, which asserts that when a group of people are asked to make one choice as their preference between three or more alternatives, it is impossible to conclude that one particular out-come is the one 'most preferred' unless over 50 per cent all vote for it. Let us see an example from **Table 11.1** that illustrates this, where people are choosing between three alternatives (A, B, C).

None of the three alternatives wins a majority of first choices, but if we just count first choices, then C wins with ten votes out of twenty-two. If the first two choices are counted equally, then B wins, with eighteen votes out of forty-four. However, it might be fairer to give extra weight to first choices over second ones, since that would reflect more genuine strength of preference. Suppose first choices are given two points, and second choices are given one. In that case, A wins with twenty-four points out of a possible sixty-six.

We can see that all three possibilities could win, depending on the counting system used, without the actual votes changing at all. None of the options ever achieved a majority of the total votes or points available, whichever system was being used, so it would be impossible to conclude that the general preference was 'clearly' in favour of one particular option. As you can easily imagine, this problem gets worse with a greater number of alternative choices, whether they are candidates or policy options. This means that the determination of preferences depends upon the particular procedure chosen for assessing the votes. Any procedure chosen is a compromise between theory and practicality. It also explains why referendums are usually reduced to a choice between two possible alternatives. In that way, even though it might seem artificially to constrain the choices that are being voted upon, it will result in an unambiguous outcome.

Table 11.1 Hypothetical distribution of votes

No. of voters	1st choice	2nd choice	3rd choice
8	A	B	C
4	B	A	C
6	C	B	A
4	C	A	B

Therefore, the choice of method for assessing votes is crucial and really can alter the outcome. To give one famous example, Riker showed that when Lincoln won the presidential election in 1860 against three rivals, different methods of assessing the votes which are used in various parts of the world today could easily have led to either of two others winning equally well (Riker, 1982: 227–32). If that had happened, then the American Civil War might never have occurred, and world history might have developed along quite different lines.

More recently, votes have been used to estimate the strength of commitment of voters to particular public policy choices. How strongly do people prefer one option as compared with another? Public choice theory has developed a whole range of techniques derived from microeconomic theory for estimating likely public preferences. These all rest on the same assumption as has dominated economics, i.e. that voters, like economic actors, are fundamentally rational beings who base their vote upon calculation of the likely benefits and costs to them of any particular decision that they have to approve. It is an assumption that offers the prospect of predictability in politics. The majority of voters will support proposals that bring them greater benefit than losses, so political leaders need to formulate proposals that will appeal to those interests. From that perspective, political success is about devising a winning calculus of benefits.

Yet it is not clear that voters exclusively behave in ways that maximize their self-interest. Caplan (2007) has written of the 'rational irrationality' of politics. He argues that voters generally fail to appreciate how their economic interests are most likely to be served, because their instincts conflict with the rational recommendations of economic theory. His conclusion is that economists should stress even more the importance of preferring markets to provide goods, public goods included, over government provision, in the hope that public understanding will follow.

And a third set of perspectives focuses upon ethnographic analysis of actual voter behaviour. These illuminate the fact that people often vote for reasons of self-expression rather than self-interest. Even though in any large polity no individual's vote is likely to be the one that makes the crucial difference between two policy choices, and so it might be thought irrational for individuals to bother to vote, they do so because it strengthens their sense of being citizens equal with one another and reminding public officials of their obligations of democratic accountability. This is true even in India, the largest democratic polity in the world.

The contrasting positions are exemplified in **Box 11.1**.

> **KEY POINTS**
>
> • The method chosen for assessing votes plays a crucial part in determining the outcome.
> • Votes can be used to calculate the strength of voters' rational preferences.
> • The act of voting may also express emotional commitment and a sense of self-worth.

ELECTIONS

Elections are methods of assessing preferences through votes. They are vital to democracy. According to Article 12 of the Universal Declaration on Democracy adopted by the Inter-Parliamentary Union in 1997: 'The key element in the exercise of democracy is the holding of free and fair elections at regular intervals enabling the people's will to be expressed' (Inter-Parliamentary Union, 1997).

KEY DEBATE BOX 11.1
Can Voter Behaviour be Explained on the Basis of Rationality?

Downs (1957: 36–7) on rational voting:

> In order to plan its policies so as to gain votes, the government must discover some relationship between what it does and how citizens vote. In our model, the relationship is derived from the axiom that citizens act rationally in politics. This action implies that each citizen casts his vote for the party he believes will provide him with more benefits than any other . . .
>
> Given several mutually exclusive alternatives, a rational man always takes the one which yields him the highest utility *ceteris paribus*, i.e., he acts to his own greatest benefit.

Caplan (2007: 195) on irrational voting:

> The optimal mix between markets and government depends not on the absolute virtues of markets, but on their virtues compared to those of government. No matter how well you think markets work, it makes sense to rely on markets *more* when you grow pessimistic about democracy . . .
>
> Above all, I emphasize that voters are irrational. But I also accept two views common among democratic enthusiasts. That voters are largely unselfish, and politicians usually comply with public opinion . . .
>
> Thus, when the public systematically misunderstands how to maximize social welfare—as it often does—it ignites a quick-burning fuse attached to correspondingly misguided policies. This should make almost anyone more pessimistic about democracy.
>
> The striking implication is that even economists, widely charged with market fundamentalism, should be more pro-market than they already are. What economists currently see as the optimal balance between markets and government *rests upon an overestimation of the virtues of democracy*. In many case, economists should embrace the free market in spite of its defects, because it still outshines the democratic alternative [emphasis in the original].

Banerjee (2014: 144–68) on the reasons Indian citizens give for voting:

> Indian citizens have plenty of reasons to be dissatisfied with the performance of governments and they do not hold politicians in great esteem either. Why then do they bother to vote? And why do poor people vote more than middle-class ones? And why does 80 per cent of the population prefer a democratic albeit inefficient system to an authoritarian one?

An ethnographic survey identified a wide spread of motivations: resignation or inertia, instrumentality, loyalty, protest vote, affectivity or emotional commitment, peer pressure, voting for citizenship, and voting for recognition.

> Indian citizens, especially those who otherwise felt ignored by the state, were clearly motivated to vote to remind the state of the importance of the sovereignty of ordinary people in a democratic country. As some put it, politicians might hold power for five

years at a time, but for the 15 days of campaigning, the voter was the king. Often people remarked that they felt important during the elections, because the powerful people who were usually remote and inaccessible had to come to them during a campaign, shake their hand and ask them how they were doing . . . For those members of society who belonged to the lowest sections . . . this momentary glimpse of being valued was hugely important. (Banerjee 2014: 144–68)

This debate demonstrates that the notion of rational voting behaviour, while a plausible hypothesis, is difficult to operationalize and subject to various interpretations, because voters have a wide range of interests and differing rationales for their ways of assessing them.

For electoral systems, there are two basic alternative principles underlying them, although there are several subvariants. These are summarized in **Box 11.2**.

The first basic type is the simple plurality, first-past-the-post majority system. This has the advantage of simplicity. At least in theory, it allows voters to choose individual candidates rather than party representatives. It also tends to be biased in favour of producing governments with larger majorities, at the expense of more representative reflections of public opinion. This can allow governments to be more decisive. It can also facilitate a strong opposition, and broadly based parties. It disadvantages extremist parties. On the other hand it can exclude minorities, and it can have the effect of restricting the number of women representatives. Also, in many constituencies it can lead to a large number of 'wasted' votes for a candidate who has no realistic chance of being elected, thereby discouraging those voters from voting at all (Reynolds, Reilly, and Allis 2007: 36–7). The figures from the last three British general elections are striking. In 2005, the Labour Party won the election with 35.2 per cent of the vote and 356 MPs. In 2010, the Conservative Party gained 36.1 per cent of votes but only 306 MPs, i.e. more votes and fewer seats. In 2015, the Conservatives gained 36.9 per cent of votes and 331 seats, i.e. even more votes than Labour in 2005 but still twenty-five fewer seats. Similarly, in the Indian general election of 2014, the Hindu nationalist Bharatiya Janata Party (BJP) Party won an outright majority with only 30 per cent of the votes. (**See Box 11.3**.)

BOX 11.2
Types of Electoral System

1. Majoritarian systems (first-past-the-post)
   - single member plurality systems (UK, USA, India)
   - two-round system (France)
   - alternative vote (Australia)
   - block vote (Singapore, Syria)
2. Proportional representation (PR)
   - party list (Netherlands, Israel, Brazil)
   - single transferable vote (Ireland)
3. Hybrids (Germany, Russia, Japan, Scottish parliament, Welsh Assembly)

CASE STUDY BOX 11.3
The Indian General Election 2014

The Indian general election in 2014 marked a turning point in Indian politics. Prior to the election, widespread expert expectations were that national politics would continue to suffer from paralysis caused by an 'inevitable' coalition government, with thirty-five parties contesting seats in the lower house of parliament, the Lok Sabha. However, with widespread voting on the basis of caste or regional identity rather than policies, the nationalist BJP under Narendra Modi won a stunning victory. For the first time since 1984, a party in India won an outright majority, gaining 282 seats out of 543. It also evidenced the possibility of first-past-the-post systems delivering majorities on a minority vote—the BJP won 52.9 per cent of seats with only 31.3 per cent of the vote. This was also the first time that the BJP had ever won more votes than the main opposition Congress Party. Allied parties gained a further sixty-one seats. Their previous total combined with the BJP was 159 seats. Voter turnout was also very high at 66 per cent, with voting spread over five weeks in different parts of the country.

In its electoral campaign, the BJP exploited widespread dissatisfaction with the ineffectiveness of the outgoing Congress Party-led coalition, especially in its handling of the economy. The party also made effective use of social media to popularize the image of its leader, Narendra Modi (Wyatt, 2015).

The BJP still faces considerable challenges in getting its legislation passed. It is in the minority in the Indian Upper House, and in 2015 it suffered a staggering reverse in elections in New Delhi, where the anti-corruption Aam Aadmi Party won nine-tenths of the seats in state elections. Nevertheless in the 2019 general election, with turnout slightly higher than in 2014, it pushed its share of the vote up to 37 per cent, which translated into 303 seats, or 55 per cent. The triumph of the BJP serves as a reminder of the way that free elections, however imperfect, can bring about radical change in government without provoking the overthrow of the system.

11

Photo 11.1 An Indian voting mark. *Shutterstock RF via DAM: Saikat Paul/Shutter stock.com*

Variants of this system can include multi-member constituencies, where voters either have as many votes as the required number of successful candidates, in which case this can produce even stronger majorities if people vote consistently for the same party, or they have only one vote, in which case candidates can be elected with as little as 20 per cent of the vote, undermining their legitimacy (an up-to-date list of countries practising these and all of the other alternative systems mentioned for their national legislatures can be found at www.idea.int/esd/world.cfm).

The alternative principle is proportional representation, where the priority is to ensure an adequate representation of the range of public opinion, irrespective of whether it strengthens or weakens the cohesion of government that results from it. This can be important for new democracies in creating a wide sense of ownership of the system. It reduces the number of 'wasted' votes, favours minorities, but also encourages parties to spread their appeal beyond their core districts. It may contribute to greater stability of policy and make coalition agreements more visible, as argued by Lijphart. On the other hand, it is more likely to lead to coalition governments and to fragmentation of the party system, with small parties able to negotiate a disproportionate say in policy-making—see the scathing condemnation of the effects of proportional representation in Israel by Asa-El later in this chapter. Holding coalition governments to account for individual decisions is more difficult under proportional representation (Reynolds, Reilly, and Allis 2007: 58–9).

→ See Chapter 10 for more on Lijphart and consociational democracy.

Since first-past-the-post and proportional representation systems tend to produce different kinds of outcome, each of which has much to commend them, a more recent trend has been for countries to adopt hybrids such as the alternative member model, with some seats elected on the basis of a simple majority and some on the basis of proportional representation. Germany, Japan, New Zealand, and Russia, for example, have all gone down this route, though a British referendum rejected it in 2011.

One alternative intermediate system is to hold two rounds of elections in constituencies where the first round does not produce an absolute majority. In the second round the candidates are reduced to the two most successful alternatives, which prevents strategic voting and ensures that there is no doubt about the preference of the majority. France does this, as do many of its former African colonies, as well as Iran and several former republics of the Soviet Union.

Altogether, of the main types of electoral system, seventy states in the world have proportional representation, forty-seven have first-past-the-post (plus twenty-two with two-round elections), and there are twenty-one hybrids (Reynolds, Reilly, and Allis 2007: 32).

Colomer has argued that electoral change around the world has tended to take place in the direction of increasingly inclusive formulas, leading to fewer risks for the parties involved. This has meant a much greater tendency for electoral reform to move from majoritarian to mixed or proportional systems, rather than the reverse. His explanation is party self-interest: when threatened by challenges from newcomers, parties prefer to minimize the risk of complete extinction, which would be far greater under majoritarianism than by agreeing to a more proportional representation-based system. This would offer greater opportunities for survival, albeit in somewhat reduced numbers of representatives elected (Colomer, 2004: 4, 58; Farrell, 2001: chs. 7, 8). Dunleavy (2005) has argued that this process is now under way in Britain. The 2010 election showed that hung parliaments could happen in Britain, in part because increasing numbers of parties are winning seats. However, the referendum in 2011 on the voting system reconfirmed popular preference for the majoritarian system.

> **KEY POINTS**
>
> - The two main alternative voting systems widely used are first-past-the-post and proportional representation.
> - Their outcomes tend to have different virtues: stronger government versus more representative government.
> - There are hybrid or intermediate alternatives that attempt to mitigate the disadvantages of theoretically purer systems.
> - Voting systems have a big impact upon party systems.

FUNCTIONS OF LEGISLATURES

Norton (2013: 4) has pointed out a fundamental paradox about legislatures in the modern world. 'On the one hand, legislatures are in decline, yet on the other they are ubiquitous.' At present there are 263 parliamentary chambers in 189 countries. This means that a little under one-third of countries have two chambers. If we bear in mind the subnational elected bodies that determine policies for more restricted areas, there are thousands of elected bodies around the world. It is no wonder that legislative studies is one of the oldest branches of political science. Within this potential diversity, there is a paradox about the main object of the studies. Gamm and Huber (2002: 313) present it clearly: 'The scholarly world of legislative studies is, overwhelmingly, a world that studies the US Congress. And the study of Congress tends to be the study of the post-war House of Representatives.' Yet, this chapter will illustrate much of the diversity from around the world, not just the USA.

Legislatures are crucial institutions in any political system, but above all in democracies. A democracy would be inconceivable without a parliament. They are vital elements in the structures of power within the state and they usually, though to varying degrees, act as checks upon the freedom of manoeuvre of the state executive. Without legislatures power in the modern state would be highly concentrated and potentially oppressive. They are essential in upholding constitutions because they can publicize attempts to subvert them and they can support the courts if the executive attempts to undermine or suspend them.

There are two ways of presenting a comparative overview of legislatures, as indeed is the case for most political institutions. One way is to focus upon the functions that they perform. In that sense they or the actors who devised them are responding to a perceived need in the political system. The second way is to concentrate upon institutional arrangements that are common so as to show their similarities and differences: in this case debating chambers, standing committees, how members of staff run their offices and handle links with constituents, and so on. We shall largely concentrate on the former type of exposition—the functional—but in Chapter 12 we will examine one particular institutional issue: the differences between parliamentary and presidential political systems and their respective merits.

The functions of parliaments can be divided into three broad groupings. First, there are the representational functions, where parliaments represent either the views of citizens, or are representative of particular groups in society. Second, there are governmental functions: legislatures

➜ See Chapter 12 for a discussion of political systems.

11

contribute to forming governments, formulating policy, ensuring the accountability of government for its actions, and enhancing government communication with citizens. Third, there are procedural functions that determine the procedures under which legislatures do their work (Olson, 1994).

Representation

The original function of parliaments in Europe was to provide a forum where different classes in society could express their views to the monarch on matters of public concern. Their role was purely consultative. There was no sense that parliaments could decide policy, let alone impose their will on monarchs. Gradually, however, they acquired greater authority as rulers saw fit to consult them when needing to raise taxes for public works, most importantly for raising armies. Thus, not only did the European state grow in response to the needs of war, as suggested in Chapter 8, parliaments did so as a means of constraining the ability of monarchs to make war.

→ See Chapter 8 for a discussion of the rise of the European state system.

Inherent in parliaments, therefore, is the notion that they are representative of wider society. To be legitimate they have to 'represent' the people. However, over time different dimensions of possible representativeness have been proposed. In practice these are difficult to reconcile, not least because the composition of parliaments is also inevitably intertwined with the electoral system on which they are based. So states with different histories and different national priorities may arrive at different institutional solutions to the same problem.

Does representation mean that deputies should be numerically representative of particular sections of society, as were originally the Lords and Commons in the UK? Should the numbers of female representatives roughly correspond to the number of women in the population as a whole? What about ethnic minorities? One perspective on this is offered by Jacobson (1997: 207). He points out that in the US Congress, blacks and Hispanics are under-represented, though the disparity between share of population and share of representatives is not as great as in the case of women; but he condones this with a different slant on representation. 'Congress is probably quite representative of the kinds of people who achieve positions of leadership in the great majority of American institutions. What it does produce is a sample of local elites from a remarkably diverse nation.' Election to Congress is certainly an elite achievement, and so it would be both more appropriate and realistic for members of Congress to be representative of elites rather than the population as a whole. This was not, however, an explicit objective of the Founding Fathers. Rather it is a rationalization.

A more recent trend has been actively to seek to make the composition of legislators correspond more exactly to the basic structure of the population as a whole. Most obviously this has concerned the proportion of women in parliaments.

In that respect, communist regimes were more 'representative' than states in the West because members of their parliaments were statistically fairly representative of broad sections of society. However, in recent years there has been an active movement around the world to increase the proportion of women in national legislatures in democracies. There are now at least forty countries that have introduced quotas for female representatives in legislatures, while in a further fifty countries, political parties have adopted quotas for female candidates for election (Dahlerup, 2005: 145). At present, there is still a long way to go before such quotas will be achieved, for reasons that Matland (2005) and Dahlerup (2005) have discussed. Nevertheless, it is likely to increase pressure for measures to be adopted to raise the recruitment of people from other groups in society that are also regularly under-represented. In that case, at least in democracies, legislatures will undergo major transformation in the coming decades.

Or should 'representation' rather refer, as suggested in Chapter 4, to the role of deputies in expressing the views of their constituents? In that case, the personal characteristics of individual deputies are less important. Representation is then taken to be an expressive function. Whoever is an MP expresses views on behalf of others. They are understood to be a channel of communication to those in authority. This leaves open the question as to how far a representative is obliged simply to express the views of a larger community of citizens, and how far they have the freedom to express personal opinions or come to individual judgements. As we have seen in Chapter 4, the view that they are positively entitled to exercise their individual judgement is associated in the UK with Edmund Burke and with the practice of the House of Commons. (**See Box 11.4**). However, it resurfaced with particular force during the Brexit process for MPs who took the opposite position to the majority of voters in their constituency in the referendum. In practice, representatives usually have some latitude, but on this issue several MPs were deselected by their local party association as passions escalated.

➡ See Chapter 4 for a discussion of representative democracy.

Some other parliamentary systems adopt a more restrictive view and enshrine the principle of recall, whereby electors can 'recall' their representatives, or rather delegates, either to be replaced or to face re-election for failure adequately to represent the views of their constituents. This is a principle instituted by French National Assembly after the Revolution. It subsequently became part of the socialist tradition, so that deputies in communist and some socialist states such as China and Cuba are liable to recall if a significant number of their electors conclude that the deputy has failed to carry out the mandate. Such a provision would guard against deputies elected on a one-party ticket subsequently moving to another party without resubmitting themselves to the electorate for approval.

> **KEY QUOTE** BOX 11.4
> Burke on the Relationship between an MP and His Constituents

Certainly, Gentlemen, it ought to be the happiness and glory of a Representative, to live in the strictest union, the closest correspondence, and the most unreserved communication with his constituents . . . But, his unbiased opinion, his mature judgement, his enlightened conscience, he ought not to sacrifice to you; to any man, or to any set of men living Your Representative owes you, not his industry only, but his judgement; and he betrays, instead of serving you, if he sacrifices it to your opinion.

Parliament is not a *Congress* of Ambassadors from different and hostile interests; which interests each must maintain, as an Agent and Advocate, against other Agents and Advocates; but Parliament is a *deliberative* Assembly of *one* Nation, with one Interest, that of the whole; where, not local Purposes, not local Prejudices ought to guide, but the general Good, resulting from the general Reason of the whole. You chose a Member indeed; but when you have chosen him, he is not Member of Bristol, but he is a Member of *Parliament*.

(Burke, 1996: 68–9; italics in original)

On the other hand, many states enshrine the principle of parliamentary immunity to protect the right of deputies to speak out without fear of prosecution or threat of libel proceedings for what they may say in parliament. This also means that occasionally, individuals will seek election as a way of preventing, or at any rate postponing, prosecution for some criminal act. In the 2014 Indian general elections, for example, one-third of all deputies elected to the Lok Sabha had criminal records or pending prosecutions, and for one-fifth this involved serious crimes such as murder, kidnapping, and robbery.

The Burkean position is normally regarded as a core element of British representative democracy and is assumed to be widely respected. Yet during the turmoil over Brexit a YouGov poll in August 2019 asked the question: 'Are MPs elected to exercise their own judgement or do their constituents' bidding?' It found that 60 per cent of MPs surveyed thought they were elected to exercise their own judgement, whilst 63 per cent of the general public disagreed (YouGov, 2014). This is a valuable reminder that generalizations about a nation's political culture need to be tempered by an awareness of significant sectional variations.

Another key question is: who are a particular deputy's electors? In general, most parliaments enshrine the principle of a direct link between an elected representative and a particular district within the country. There are a few exceptions, e.g. Israel, Peru, and the Netherlands, where voters in a single national constituency choose between the lists of candidates offered by different parties, so that those elected accurately represent the national preferences of the people. This ensures that MPs are proportionately representative. On the other hand, critics of the Israeli system have alleged that this proportionality has exacerbated the difficulties of forming a government, since it concedes excessive power to small parties, which makes executive policy-making extremely fraught. According to Amotz Asa-El (2008), a former editor of the *Jerusalem Post*:

> Israel maintains the most extreme model of the proportional electoral system and the results are nothing short of disastrous. This system has been depleting Israel's political energies for decades: it radicalised the territorial debate, debilitated the economy, obstructed long-term planning, derailed government action, distracted cabinets, diverted budgets, weakened prime ministers, destabilised governments, enabled anonymous and often incompetent people to achieve positions of great influence and responsibility and blurred the distinctions between the executive and legislative branches of government. Perhaps most crucially, it has led talented, accomplished, moral and charismatic people to abandon the political arena.

We have already discussed the relative merits of plurality versus proportional representation systems. What is important to note here is the effect of the combination of a solely national constituency, proportional representation, and a low threshold for parties to be allowed to take up seats—they only need to win 2 per cent of votes to do so in Israel, though it should be remembered that the Netherlands has the lowest threshold in the world of 0.67 per cent, and the same fragmentation and polarization does not seem to occur there. According to Asa-El, an essential element in reform will be the linking of at least some Knesset seats with specific constituencies within the country. This will increase the incentives for representatives to focus on local issues that are of concern to voters. At present its members allegedly pay scant attention to the type of local issues that are the staple of constituency politics in other countries. On the other hand, in Israel a wide range of minority views are represented in parliament. If nothing else, this does avoid the risk of neglecting the views of minorities that are not geographically concentrated in a few places so that their local representatives have to listen to them.

For most states the connection between an individual representative and the people that they represent in a territorial constituency is regarded as an essential contribution to the legitimacy of parliament. This is held to be so, even though it may lead to other distortions in the way that the people's overall views are represented. However, this raises another set of questions. Is there an optimal size for a constituency? How similar in size should they be? Further, who should be responsible for redrawing constituency boundaries as population concentrations change? Most European states assign this responsibility to public officials, but in the USA the boundaries of districts for the House of Representatives are determined by incumbents. This no doubt contributes to the fact that between 80 and 90 per cent of House races are won by incumbents. This fact has led Princeton University to set up a project to overturn gerrymandering and establish a robust objective framework for delineating constituency boundaries in each state (http://gerrymander. princeton.edu/).

The size of constituencies, and the redrawing of their boundaries to reflect demographic changes in their population so as to ensure rough parity between different constituencies is always a highly contentious issue. In England the maximum disparity in size between parliamentary constituencies is roughly two to one—largely because of the unique size of the Isle of Wight (Boundary Commission for England, 2007: 482–3). Otherwise, it would be a great deal more even. In Wales there is only a disparity of one-and-a-half times, but in Scotland it is three-and-a-half times, because of a special requirement that the Orkney and the Shetland Islands which have smaller numbers of inhabitants form distinct constituencies. The effect of this is to create even greater disparity within Britain as a whole. The disparity between the Isle of Wight and Na h-Eileanan an Iar (a constituency in the Outer Hebrides) is roughly five to one. To reduce it, the new Conservative government in 2015 announced its intention to cut the number of constituencies from 650 to 600.

In Japan, by the end of the 1970s, urban areas had nearly four times as many eligible voters as rural areas in elections to the lower house of the parliament, the Diet. Since then the disparity has been halved by redrawing boundaries, to roughly the same level as England. But for the upper house, the House of Councillors, there is still a disparity of over five times between different prefectures (Stockwin, 1999: 128–9).

One of the most extreme manifestations of this problem is in the US Senate, where there is an even greater disparity between states over the number of eligible voters, though there is greater equality between House districts. The US constitution grants two senators to each state of the union, irrespective of size. The consequence is that now Wyoming, the state with the smallest population, has the same number of senators as California, the state with the largest population, even though California's population is seventy-two times larger. Even though the cumulative effect of this principle is that smaller (often more rural) states have a disproportionate impact on Senate voting, because together they can mobilize a much greater proportion of votes there than their combined populations would warrant, there is no prospect of this being changed because to do so would require a constitutional amendment, and the smaller states can muster enough votes to prevent it.

KEY POINTS

- MPs represent wider society, most often through the means of territorial districts.
- Part of their legitimacy is based upon the assumption that they are also representative of society.
- The extent and ways to which they are 'representative', however, is contentious and varies from one state to another.
- The introduction of quotas to increase recruitment of women in parliament may lead to measures to do the same for other groups under-represented there.

Apart from the responsibility of forming governments, parliaments have three other functions: formulating legislation, ensuring governmental accountability, and forming public opinion.

Legislation

An alternative term for parliament is legislature, i.e. the supreme law-giver in society. It is the national legislature that determines the final shape of laws, although as we saw in Chapter 10, in most states this is now qualified by the need to respect international legal conventions and in many by the practice of judicial review. To some extent, this legal function also helps to explain the relative frequency with which elected representatives have been trained as lawyers. In the USA, which reserves a very prominent role for the law in public affairs (as we saw in Chapter 10), roughly 40 per cent of House members were lawyers in the mid-1990s, while the equivalent figure for senators was 54 per cent (Jacobson, 1997: 207). In 2015, 14 per cent of British MPs were lawyers. This represents a slight increase in the average of 11–12 per cent elected over the previous thirty years, but in 1979 and 1983 roughly 15 per cent were lawyers (McGuinness, 2010; Hunter and Holden, 2015).

In practice, however, it is the executive that is the chief initiator of legislation. According to Olson, there is a common experience around the world that 90 per cent of new legislation originates in the executive rather than in parliament, and that 90 per cent of that is adopted (Olson, 1994: 134). This is true even of the USA, where the executive cannot on its own introduce proposed new legislation into Congress: it needs to find sympathetic members of the House or Senate to do so. The picture is more complicated for members of the European Union (EU), where member states have to introduce national legislation to give force to decisions agreed in Brussels. According to a report from the House of Commons Library (2010), roughly 6.8 per cent of all statutes and 14.1 per cent of all statutory instruments passed by the UK parliament had a role in implementing European obligations, but the proportion rose to around 50 per cent for legislation 'with a significant economic impact', above all in agriculture. It also commented that, for other EU members, the proportion ranged from 6.3 per cent to 84 per cent, though directly comparable statistics were not available. All of this means that today national legislatures primarily respond to initiatives that originate elsewhere.

11

➡ See the discussion in Chapter 10 on the growing legalization of political life.

➡ See the discussion in Chapter 10 of legal adjudication in political life.

Ensuring Accountability

Parliaments, especially in democracies, hold the government to account for its actions. This is particularly important as a way of ensuring that governments honour the commitments that they made to the public when seeking election. It strengthens the incentive for credible commitments and hence increases the chances of a government being replaced at the next election for failure to keep its promises. But even in authoritarian regimes where this is unlikely, parliaments can hold executives to account. According to Olson (1994: 143–4), even under authoritarianism it is difficult for the executive always to control the legislature. He cites as examples the growing activism of the Brazilian Congress under military rule in the 1970s and 1980s, and of the Sejm under martial law in Poland in the 1980s. Another example is China. There, the National People's Congress only meets for two weeks per year and thus performs more of a symbolic function as far as legislation is concerned. However, in recent years, it has become an increasingly vocal critic of the policies of individual ministries, while refraining from criticizing the government, and therefore the regime, as a whole. In particular it has cast votes condemning inadequate government action to deal with issues such as corruption and crime. Thus simply having parliaments can strengthen trends toward democracy over time.

It should be noted, however, that parliaments are not the only institutions that hold the executive to account. In most states the media also perform this role, whether or not it is explicitly recognized by the state. Also, within the executive there are institutions that keep a check on what other executive agencies do—what O'Donnell (2003) called 'horizontal accountability', which he contrasted with the 'vertical accountability' performed by parliaments. Examples of such agencies are audit offices, such as the National Audit Office in the UK, which check on government spending. In practice all of these institutions contribute to the accountability of government and they often cooperate with each other.

Formation of Public Attitudes

A fourth function of legislatures is to contribute to the formation of public opinion and often to set the agenda for public debate. This is an expansion of the role of representing the views of the people to government. Here, parliaments take the lead in forming public opinion as well as providing a forum. Obviously, in an era of mass communications where the media play such a role in informing the public about issues of the day, the role of parliaments in this respect is more circumscribed than it was in the nineteenth century, when debates in parliament were reckoned to set the agenda for public debate. Nevertheless, there are issues, for example, moral ones such as abortion or environmental ones such as genetically modified foods, where parliamentary debates play a key role in forming public opinion, although the line between parliament forming public opinion and representing it becomes fuzzy. Debates in parliament and in parliamentary committees are regularly reported in the media. In North America the C-Span and CPAC cable networks are devoted full-time to coverage of the US Congress and Canadian parliament. Some parliaments, such as the Bundestag, the Dutch and Scottish parliaments, have attempted to take advantage of the new communications technologies such as the Internet to stimulate public debate over current affairs. This was an attempt to develop a more reflexive approach to policy-making in society at large—the sort of deliberative democracy discussed in Chapter 4—although it seems to have had only limited success.

➡ See Chapter 4 for a discussion of deliberative democracy.

Another way in which parliaments can stimulate public debate in politics can be observed in Sweden. There MPs regularly meet with advisory commissions to formulate legislative proposals. This acts as a constraint on both the executive and the sovereignty of parliament, but it does help to ensure a wider range of views are involved in the legislative process, which should lead to better legislation (Olson, 1994: 135).

KEY POINTS

- Today, parliaments mostly respond to initiatives for policy that originate from elsewhere in the political system, primarily the executive.
- Parliaments provide a means for holding governments to account for their election promises.
- Parliaments also provide a forum for national debate.

Procedural

There are also three procedural functions that legislatures perform.

Ritualizing Conflict

Parliamentary activities help to ritualize conflict. They function on the basis of debate, i.e. the expression of differing views. To that extent they legitimize diversity of views and its expression. In the Iranian parliament, for instance, though access to it is restricted to religious parties as secular ones are banned, what would otherwise be in danger of being condemned as factionalism conducted by dissident groups acquires greater respectability or legitimacy (Baktiari, 1996). Critics of democracy sometimes allege that parliaments exacerbate divisions in society by providing opportunities for dissenting opinions to be expressed. It is true that Westminster-type parliaments formalize the role of official opposition to the government. This often, it is alleged, forces the parties not in government into excessive confrontation, further exacerbated by the seating arrangements that have the government and opposition facing each other at a distance of a little over two swords' lengths. In some states such as Taiwan, national legislators exploit the media coverage of their debates to establish a partisan image that will help their chances of re-election, for example, occasionally throwing lunch boxes at each other to dramatize the differences between them and their opponents and to attract TV attention.

A response to this is that all societies have a plurality of opinions on any issue and parliament only reflects that. As far as seating arrangements are concerned, a more common arrangement is for the MPs to be arrayed in a semi-circle facing the speaker in a debate, as in European parliaments and the US Congress. Where dissension is particularly extreme, parliaments can help to resolve disputes which might otherwise take a more violent turn. In that sense they 'routinize' conflict, and even though MPs sometimes use parliamentary debate to rouse public opinion in pursuit of extremist goals, it does not mean that parliaments by nature manufacture conflict. Often, they can tame its excesses.

Partisanship

Although it occasionally happens that independent members are elected to parliament, in the overwhelming majority of cases legislators represent political parties as well as territorial constituencies. Even in the Chinese National People's Congress, where roughly two-thirds of deputies are members of the Chinese Communist Party (CPP), the remaining third have to be approved by the CCP and are expected to support the regime. Unlike the judiciary, MPs are expected to hold partisan ideologies that structure their overall views on political issues and priorities. This fact reinforces the role of parliaments as debating chambers out of which better legislation emerges.

Transparency

Parliaments are generally committed to openness, to publicizing issues and policies. A parliament that kept secret its deliberations would make no sense—as was the case with the Supreme Soviet in Stalin's time. It would have purely symbolic value. Although debates in parliaments in authoritarian regimes may publish only edited versions of debates rather than full transcripts, they still to some extent contribute to the publicizing of important issues. They make policy-making somewhat more open. The publication of verbatim transcripts of all their deliberations obviously does this even more. All this contributes to the more open resolution of disagreements in society and thus to its stability. However, this is a problem in societies that are most accustomed to more traditional, possibly more consensual styles of decision-making. It certainly comes as a shock to politicians who are more used only to negotiating deals behind the scenes. The greater openness can be used to embarrass politicians. It upsets and changes political culture, as any Chinese or Arab leader will acknowledge.

> **KEY POINTS**
>
> - Parliaments assume diversity of opinions and ritualize political disputes.
> - They assume that legislators have partisan opinions.
> - They also contribute to open policy-making and dispute resolution.

TYPES OF LEGISLATURES

As will be obvious, legislatures vary considerably not only in their powers, but also in their relations with the surrounding political and societal structures. Mezey (1990) produced an influential typology of legislatures to try to identify the range of their possible operations. He proposed a fivefold classification based upon the principle of the capacity of a legislature to stand up to the executive: (i) active legislatures; (ii) reactive legislatures; (iii) vulnerable legislatures; (iv) marginal legislatures; (v) minimal legislatures.

More recently, Fish, and Koenig (2011) have offered a quantitative comparison of the relative powers of parliaments around the world, based upon their formal powers vis-à-vis the rest of the political system. The strongest and weakest parliaments are listed in **Table 11.2**—but note that these scores were calculated before more recent major political changes in Libya, Myanmar, and Turkey.

Table 11.2 The strongest and weakest parliaments around the world

Strongest		Weakest	
Germany	0.84	Bhutan	0.22
Italy	0.84	Chad	0.22
Mongolia	0.84	Jordan	0.22
Czech Republic	0.81	Qatar	0.22
Macedonia	0.81	Bahrain	0.19
Bulgaria	0.78	Oman	0.16
Croatia	0.78	North Korea	0.13
Denmark	0.78	Libya	0.13
Latvia	0.78	Saudi Arabia	0.09
Lithuania	0.78	Turkmenistan	0.06
Netherlands	0.78	UAE	0.06
Turkey	0.78	Myanmar	0
UK	0.78	Somalia	0

Note: 1 = all-powerful; 0 = powerless.

Source: Fish and Kroenig (2011: 756–71).

11

In general they show that the most powerful parliaments tend to be found in Europe, while the least powerful ones are in the Middle East.

Lastly, we should mention a parliament of a special type—namely, the European parliament. This is an institution in evolution, just as the EU itself is. Originally a mainly consultative institution composed of delegates from the parliaments of the member states, it has developed a life of its own, with members elected directly from each member state. In general, it has equal powers of legislation with the European Council of Ministers, who represent the individual member states (though there are some areas where one or the other has primacy). In that sense, the two institutions could be seen as a special kind of bicameral. And, under the Lisbon Treaty, the European parliament approves the composition of the European Commission and can dismiss it with a vote of no-confidence. However, this power is relatively limited, in that the Commission is also responsible to the individual member states, who ultimately have to agree upon its overall finances.

The president of the parliament is a member of the *troika* of officials who represent the EU to outsiders, along with the presidents of the Commission and Council of Ministers. Its members in general want to expand its powers vis-à-vis the Commission, but the Commission is not accountable to the parliament in the way that executives are in national democracies, though the parliament can certainly embarrass the Commission by publicizing issues where it disagrees. It has been suggested that one way forward for the EU would be to see the parliament as part of a tricameral European legislature, where the other two chambers would be the Council of Ministers and the parliaments of the member states (Cooper, 2013), though this would be an extremely complex and potentially cumbersome body. Others speculate about the evolution of the EU into a more conventional presidential or parliamentary system (Marschall, 2015), but either is still a very distant prospect.

KEY POINTS

- Legislatures can be classified according to the extent to which they can impose their will upon the executive.
- The factors that contribute to this capability derive both from internal factors and the broader political and social context.
- The European parliament is a special kind of transnational legislature, the functions and powers of which are slowly evolving.

STRUCTURE OF LEGISLATURES

Now let us turn to two structural features of the way that parliaments work.

Unicameral/Bicameral

As mentioned at the beginning of this chapter, roughly one-third of parliaments around the world have two chambers. Thus, one major issue in establishing a parliament concerns whether to have one (unicameralism) or two (bicameralism) chambers. In practice there is an enormous variety in the arrangements that individual nations make to order the relations between two chambers where this occurs. As of the late 1990s, out of sixty-one second chambers, only nineteen were composed exclusively of directly elected members. Fifteen were hybrids, with mixed member-ships of the directly elected and the nominated, while the remaining twenty-seven contained no directly elected members (including the House of Lords). Within these three subcategories, there is still room for enormous variety in the ways in which the second chambers are constituted—for details, see Patterson and Mughan (1999: 6–7). Within this variety it is possible to identify three sorts of factors underlying them. The first is tradition. In the past, two chambers allowed for the separate representation of different sections of society, usually the aristocrats in one and the ordinary people in the other. They have generally survived even in the context of a modernizing society, though Denmark took the decision to abolish its upper chamber in 1953 and Sweden did the same in 1959.

The second reason for an upper house often has to do with federalism. The places in it are set aside for representatives from the next lower level of government. This serves as a guarantee to them that their wishes will not be ignored by the national government. It reassures them that they do not need to contemplate leaving the union.

➡ See Chapter 10 for a discussion of federalism.

The third reason is the expectation that it will lead to better legislation (Tsebelis and Money, 1997). This is explained in two ways. On the one hand, there is the rationale of efficiency in terms of legislation. The need for legislation to be scrutinized in two chambers rather than one should lead to it being better fit for purpose—what Patterson and Mughan (1999: 12–16) call the principle of 'redundancy'. It allows for a second opinion on the best form of a particular law. The other reason for expecting better legislation is that the need for legislation to satisfy two chambers increases the likelihood that the final outcome will better approximate to the wishes of the population at large (which may be difficult to determine definitively given the problems of establishing societal preferences, as suggested by the Arrow impossibility theorem, as discussed earlier in this chapter), especially if the two chambers have been elected or selected according to different principles or at different times. Both principles resonate with the concern expressed by Madison in *Federalist Papers 62* about the need to prevent overhasty, too subjective legislation.

According to Tsebelis and Money (1997: 4–5), the existence of one or two chambers of parliament makes little difference to the relations between the legislature and the executive, but it obviously does affect the legislative process. This largely depends on the specific powers of the two chambers and the rules that they adopt for regulating the process by which they achieve agreements. Most constitutions give greater powers to one chamber than to the other, especially where control of the government budget is concerned. This obviously determines the way in which the two houses achieve compromise in cases of disagreement. Italy is the exception that proves the rule: there the Senate and the Chamber of Deputies have coequal powers. This obviously complicates the negotiation of agreements, adding to the paralysis of Italian government, although it has been successful in preventing the return of a fascist dictatorship, as it was intended to do. In 2016 the government proposed sweeping reforms that, amongst other things, would have made the Chamber of Deputies ultimately more powerful than the Senate, but almost 60 per cent of electors rejected it in a referendum.

But even where one chamber is more powerful than the other, the need to find compromises still regularly affects the final version of laws. Even if one chamber lacks the power to veto proposals (as in the case of the House of Lords at present), the process of trying to achieve compromise will affect at least some legislative outcomes. The mechanism used to achieve this compromise will also affect the outcome: is it a joint committee of both houses, or does a bill have to be considered by full sessions of each chamber, and in both cases what kind of majority is needed? All this makes a difference.

Committees

In practice, legislators spend most of their time working in committees rather than in full sessions of the parliament. This is because most of the detailed consideration of proposed legislation is carried out in ad hoc committees convened to consider particular bills. In addition, most parliaments also establish permanent committees to effect regular scrutiny of the workings of individual ministries. They often interrogate ministers and senior officials, and sometimes they hold inquiries into particular issues of policy that the members think worthy of consideration or reconsideration. As some of the committee members may have long experience of parliament and government, they may be very knowledgeable about particular policy areas, in which case they can embarrass ministers or even the government as a whole. For legislators from parties not in government, this can be a very useful way of weakening the popularity of the party or parties in power, and thereby establishing their own credibility as alternatives. It is also another way of parliament fulfilling its functions of the formation of public opinion and the visibility of policy-making. However, beyond that, parliaments differ considerably in their committee arrangements. Some parliaments, such as the German and Swedish, allow these parliamentary committees to propose legislation to the house as a whole, whereas this cannot happen at Westminster. In France there are a few, large, permanent committees that divide into ad hoc committees to consider specific bills.

KEY POINTS

- Bicameralism may offer the prospect of better legislation that corresponds more closely to the preferences of the population, but it is more time-consuming.
- The procedures for resolving disagreements between two chambers will affect the particular legislative outcomes.
- Most parliamentary work is done in committees of the legislature.

LEGISLATORS

Now let us turn to some common features of those securing election as legislators. In democracies, as has been explained previously, there is a presumption that MPs are representative of the population at large. This is true in only the most general terms, for most people obviously do not stand for election to parliament. In general, legislators tend to be male, better educated than the average citizen, and to come from the middle class (even if they represent socialist parties).

In fact, commentators have remarked on a growing tendency in Western states for the emergence of a political 'class'. The term was originally coined at the end of the nineteenth century by Gaetano Mosca, the Italian political scientist who was mentioned in Chapter 2. By this he meant, as Oborne (2007: 24) explains, a group that is 'self-interested, self-aware and dependent for its economic and moral status on the resources of the state'. However, according to Oborne, it did not fit the reality of that time very well, because there were significant external checks upon political figures and because the resources of the state were not so easily bent to serve them. Now, however, he argues: 'The Political Class has won its battle to control Britain . . . In an unannounced takeover of power, the public domain has been seized by the Political Class' (Oborne, 2007: 310). Nor is this argument made about Britain alone. Rizzo and Stella (2007) have made much the same claim about Italian politics, where they stigmatize 'an oligarchy of insatiable Brahmins'. 'Anti' politicians have sought to exploit the term as a way of discrediting rivals. The leader of the UK Independence Party, Nigel Farage, regularly rails about the British and European 'political class', though, as they sometimes riposte, he has been a member of the European parliament since 1999.

Academics as well as journalists have begun to make use of the same concept. Borchert (2003: 6), for instance, introduced the term in a study of most Organisation for Economic Co-ordination and Development (OECD) countries and explained it as meaning the political class that 'lives off politics' and acts as a 'class for itself'. Actually, as Borchert emphasizes (2003: 16), the concept is bound to be fuzzy at the edges when applied to individual countries. It is clear that it includes legislators and elected members of lower-level public councils, as well as employees of political parties; but should it apply to judges who are publicly elected, as in the USA and Germany? Also, what about party nominees on the boards of state-owned companies in many states of Europe? Clearly, therefore, it will be difficult to achieve full comparability.

Nevertheless, this term has analytical utility and potentially much wider comparative application. As we have already seen in Chapter 8, accounts of politics in African states also typically emphasize the widespread pursuit of politics for the purposes of making money (Bayart, 1993; Chabal and Daloz, 1999). So the term could be used as the basis for wider comparative studies. What Borchert and his colleagues also highlighted is a more recent phenomenon specific to OECD democracies, namely the emergence of a category of political professionals who are skilled in the arts of winning elections, whether as candidates or working for candidates, and who have never had another career. In earlier periods MPs included a much higher proportion of people for whom politics was their second or third career, people who had had a wider experience of life, which they then brought to their legislative activity. This is no longer so common, and it is now often regarded as a defect.

➔ See the discussion in Chapter 8 on strong states and weak states.

This trend is not uniform, and it has national specifics in the way that it operates. In Japan and Ireland, for instance, a surprisingly high proportion of members of the national parliament are the children of older legislators who used to hold the same constituency. In Japan the figure had risen to 28 per cent of deputies to the Lower House of the Diet in 2003 (Usui and Colignon, 2004: 408–9), while in Ireland the figure remained fairly constant between 22 and 25 per cent between 1992 and 2002, and the proportion of candidates from 'political families' went up for the principal parties in the 2011 election (Gallagher et al., 2003: 114; Gallagher and Marsh, 2011: 65). This certainly suggests class-like characteristics but does not seem to be replicated in other countries, though there certainly are individual cases of parliamentary seats passing from father to child in other countries. The income of political professionals varies considerably from one country to another. To some extent that reflects different degrees of self-interest on the part of politicians in different countries.

On the other hand, Hardman (2018) has identified various problems that deter many would-be politicians. A career in democratic politics requires many sacrifices in terms of time, personal finances and family life. Voters as a whole are cynical about politicians' motives. At least in Britain they expect politicians to live on modest salaries whilst always 'going the extra mile' in trying to help with personal problems, whatever those might be and irrespective of whether a legislator is the most appropriate person to provide help. Journalists can be even more cynical and dismissive of any politician who claims to be motivated by public service. Yet, a political career can be extremely precarious. The chances of being elected or re-elected more often depend upon voters' assessments of parties' performance as a whole, than on the work of an individual MP or candidate. It can end without warning—and the options for alternative work for recently rejected representatives are often limited at best. And now politicians can find themselves trolled and their reputations trashed on social media for an incautious word. All this is in addition to the normal politician's role of trying to reconcile (often passionately expressed) conflicts between contending interests. It is no surprise that such a career does not attract a lot of people. It is easy to see why representatives do not turn out to be typical of the population as a whole and why this supply problem contributes to the image of politicians as people apart.

Finally, let us consider the regard in which parliaments are held by their citizenry. It might be expected that parliaments elected by the people would enjoy broad popular support, especially in democracies with free and fair elections; yet the World Values Surveys suggest differently. To some extent citizens in democracies and developed countries have less trust in their representatives, which can be seen from the most recent round carried out in sixty countries in 2010–14, as reported in **Table 11.3**:

11

Table 11.3 Confidence in parliaments

Uzbekistan	85	Turkey	54
Qatar	85	Germany	44
China	77	Japan	20
Singapore	76	USA	20
Bahrain	72	Romania	15
Malaysia	69	Peru	12
Kazakhstan	67	Poland	11
Rwanda	65	Slovenia	6
Azerbaijan	64	Average	38
Philippines	60		

Note: Proportion of respondents in various countries answering, 'a great deal of confidence' or 'quite a lot of confidence' to the question: 'How much confidence do you have in parliament?'.

Source: http://www.worldvaluessurvey.org/WVSOnline.jsp V117 (accessed 28 May 2015).

The World Values Surveys also asked questions about confidence in other institutions. Overall the average around the world for those with confidence in parliament was lower than that for national governments (46 per cent), the press (43 per cent), but more than political parties (29 per cent).

Nevertheless, when people criticize parliaments, they are often in reality complaining about something else. Mainwaring concluded from a series of studies on the legislatures in the five Andean states of Bolivia, Colombia, Ecuador, Peru, and Venezuela that lack of trust there was primarily the result of popular perceptions of broader deficiencies in the political system as a whole. The economies had failed to develop and so had standards of living. There were also serious problems with corruption. Thus, the popular lack of confidence in legislatures reflected a deeper dissatisfaction with the failure of the political system as a whole to deliver a better quality of life to the people. 'Better state performance is key to promoting greater confidence in the institutions of representative democracy and greater satisfaction with democracy' (Mainwaring, 2006: 331).

KEY POINTS

- There is an increasing trend of professionalization of political representatives.
- Some have alleged that this has already led to the emergence of a 'political class'.
- A political career is often precarious and that discourages many people from standing for public office.

Alternative Forms of Public Decision-Making: Sortition and Citizen Assemblies

Given all these problems of trust in legislatures and legislators, does this mean that the notion of representation is itself coming under greater strain? Should alternative or additional channels of

Photo 11.2 Voting in a Citizens' Assembly. *Q4PR: Citizens' Assembly / Maxwell's*

11

public decision-making be sought to revivify democracy through deepening deliberation? This has stimulated theoretical rethinking (Floridia, 2018), as well as an increasing number of experiments around the world (Bächtiger et al. 2018).

One possibility that receives more attention now than it used to is sortition, i.e. the selection of public representatives by lot or lottery rather than election. If there is a problem with an increasingly distinct political class losing contact with the rest of society, would this be remedied by selecting representatives at random and for fixed, non-extendable terms of office? Such a procedure was practised in Athens and also in parts of late medieval Italy, so it does have a tradition.

Delannoi and Dowlen (2017: 500) identify four possible benefits: (i) impartiality—it would do away with string-pulling and corruption, at least where election is concerned (though, as they admit, someone selected at random might still then abuse their position, especially if they know that their time in office is limited); (ii) simplicity of procedures and the saving of the costs associated with getting elected; (iii) the sense of integration—everyone has an equal chance of being selected; (iv) the 'serenity effect', i.e. no-one can feel offended by failing to get selected. Of course such a model does assume that all members of society would be equally willing to take part in this process and selflessly to devote themselves to making it work if selected. And whilst it may have worked in small communities in centuries past, it is difficult to see how it could realistically be implemented in large modern nation states, though the German-speaking community in Belgium has voted to introduce an assembly to represent them with randomly selected members.

A second possibility is related to this, but more modest: citizens' juries (Smith and Wales, 2000; Sutherland, 2004). This is a more modest institution. These would have an advisory rather than a decision-making role—they would be adjuncts to existing representative institutions. They would normally be time-limited and issue-specific, thus reducing the demands made upon participants. They would be chosen by lottery or at random, trying to ensure coverage of as widespread a range of views as possible. They would hear evidence from a range of experts. And then they would try to come to a consensus on what the policy in that area should be. They would not be able to make decisions themselves, but they could put pressure on elected representatives to follow their advice by publicizing their conclusions and the reasons for them. This is one of the ways in which a Citizens' Assembly in Ireland helped break years of political deadlock, which led to the referendum result in 2018 that overturned the previous ban on abortion that had been heavily supported by the Catholic Church and also by many pro-life groups in the US (Palese, 2018). Such assemblies could also launch citizen initiatives to change public policy. And their potential effectiveness can be seen in institutional innovations such as direct citizen participation in key policy areas such as setting the overall budget in Porto Alegre in Brazil (Baiocchi, 2005).

KEY POINTS

- Choosing representatives as in a lottery might prevent a 'class' of (professional) politicians;
- But it might impose unacceptable burdens upon citizens selected in that way.
- Consultative assemblies might contribute to the same result and be chosen in the same way.

CONCLUSION

As this chapter has indicated, there is a burgeoning field of new thinking on ways of supplementing, or even possibly replacing, representative democracy with institutional innovations, more often at the local level. These usually reflect a greater involvement for civil society in public decision-making—and we shall analyse the notion of civil society more fully in Chapter 14. Nevertheless there is no doubt about the fact of widespread declining public trust in elected representatives in many countries. Even though it is true that some of the dissatisfaction can be attributed to the failure of particular systems to deliver a better life for all or most citizens, and therefore not to more specific failings of representative institutions as such, all of this is part of a broader phenomenon of questioning democratic politics as it has been practised in recent decades. It is associated with the rise of populism in many countries, and it is an issue to which we shall return in Chapter 15.

11

KEY QUESTIONS

1. What are the relative strengths and weaknesses of the various alternative means of assessing votes—e.g. simple plurality, Borda count, Condorcet count, and approval voting? (See Saari, 2001.)
2. Do you intend to vote in the next national election? What about other students in your class? Why, or why not? And what considerations would determine your vote?
3. Should voting in national elections be made compulsory? What about in local elections?
4. Should we expect the same considerations to structure voting behaviour in the USA and India?
5. How typical are Indian election practices to those held in democracies around the world?
6. How threatening for democracy is the emergence of a 'class' of 'professional' politicians in the UK? Can anything be done to prevent it?

7. How useful is the term 'political class' in comparing the politics of different states?

8. What should be the powers and functions of a reformed House of Lords as a second chamber? Why has producing a long-term replacement for the old House of Lords proved so difficult?

9. Does a second chamber of parliament make it more likely that laws better reflect the preferences of the whole population? Are there any circumstances in which it might not?

10. How representative should a legislature be of the citizens of a given country? In what ways?

11. Would you be willing to stand for election as a representative? Why, or why not?

12. Assess the arguments in favour of special measures to increase gender equality among MPs. Should the same arguments be applied to other groups in society currently under-represented?

13. How far does it matter if there is great disparity in the size of constituencies electing representatives to the same legislature? Why?

14. Are citizens in democracies more critical of their representatives? Why?

15. How far should parliaments seek to lead public opinion, and how far should they simply follow and represent it?

16. How do you explain the greater public confidence in legislatures in many authoritarian regimes than in democracies?

17. Is it realistic to apply the principle of sortition, and if so, how and where should it be done?

18. What would be the benefits and disadvantages of selecting public officials by lottery? Do you think the benefits would outweigh the disadvantages?

FURTHER READING

Baiocchi, G. (2005), *Militants and Citizens: The Politics of Participatory Democracy in Porto Alegre* (Stanford, CA: Stanford University Press).
An in-depth study of an early and influential experiment in citizen involvement in local decision-making.

Ballington, J. and Kazam, A. (eds) (2005), *Women in Parliament: Beyond Numbers* (Stockholm: International IDEA, revised edn), www.idea.int/publications/wip2/index.cfm#toc.
An international discussion of ways in which the number of female legislators could be increased.

Banerjee, M. (2014), *Why India Votes?* (New Delhi: Routledge).
Based on recent ethnographic fieldwork on how elections are conducted in the world's largest democracy.

Cowley, P. and Ford, R. (eds) (2014), *Sex, Lies and the Ballot Box: 50 Things That You Need to Know About British Elections* (London: Biteback).
A fascinating collection of summarized academic articles on what election analyses tell us about the practice of British politics.

Crewe, E. (2015), *The House of Commons: An Anthropology of British MPs at Work* (London: Bloomsbury).
An ethnographic study of what it is like to be a British MP today.

Delannoi, G. and Dowden, O. (2017), 'Sortition, direct democracy and indirect democracy', in Laurence Morel and Matt Qvortrup (eds), *The Routledge Handbook to Referendums and Direct Democracy* (London: Routledge).

Farrell, D. M. (2011), *Electoral Systems: A Comparative Introduction* (Basingstoke: Palgrave, 2nd edn).
This is a very approachable introduction to the various types of electoral systems.

Jacobson, G. C. (2012), *The Politics of Congressional Elections* (New York: Longmans, 8th edn).
An authoritative account of the evolution of election issues in the USA.

Mehra Ajay, K. and Kueck, G. W. (eds) (2003), *The Indian Parliament: A Comparative Perspective* (Delhi: Konark Publishers).
This presents aspects of politics and procedure in the Indian parliament from a European perspective.

Mosca, G. (1939), *The Ruling Class* (New York: McGraw-Hill).
This is a classic of political analysis.

Norton, P. (ed.) (1998), *Parliaments and Governments in Western Europe* (London: Cass, two vols).
This is an authoritative compendium of material on various European legislatures.

Oborne, P. (2007), *The Triumph of the Political Class* (London: Simon & Schuster).
This is a political columnist's indictment of the political class in Britain.

Reynolds, A., Reilly, B., and Allis, A. (2007), *Electoral System Design* (Stockholm: International IDEA).
This details the considerations that should underlie the choice of electoral system, especially for regimes in transition to democracy.

Smith, G. and Wales, C. (2000), 'Citizens' juries and deliberative democracy', *Political Studies*, 48(1): 51–65
An early article advocating citizens' juries.

Sutherland, K. (2004), *The Party's Over: Blueprint for a Very English Revolution* (Exeter: Imprint Academic).
A radical proposal for the random selection of MPs.

Tsebelis, G. and Money, J. (1997), *Bicameralism* (Cambridge: Cambridge University Press).
This presents the issue of two chambers from an academic perspective.

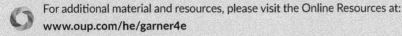

For additional material and resources, please visit the Online Resources at:
www.oup.com/he/garner4e

POLITICAL PARTIES

READER'S GUIDE

This chapter will look at political parties: why they emerged, how they can be classified, what functions they perform, how they interact, and finally what are the challenges facing them today.

PARTIES

One of the paradoxes about democracies is that on the one hand there is near unanimity on the indispensability of political parties. They are almost ubiquitous, even in authoritarian regimes. The Universal Declaration on Democracy included in Article 12 'the right to organize political parties and carry out political activities' as one of the 'essential civil and political rights' (Inter-Parliamentary Union, 1997); yet a strict public choice approach to politics would question the logic of their existence. From this perspective, individuals only rationally form groups to pursue their interests when they can be sure that the benefits that they are likely to obtain are greater than the costs of membership. This is only likely to be the case for small groups where the share of benefits that any individual member can obtain in the case of success will be larger. For big organizations such as political parties, especially at the national level, the benefits that any individual member is likely to gain are bound to be minuscule, while the costs of membership are still significant. Thus it is irrational for people to join parties. They should only form (small) interest groups.

Then, too, criticism is often levelled at parties because they allegedly create and exacerbate divisions in society rather than help to mitigate them. This is particularly the case where political parties exclusively represent specific ethnic communities. As we shall see from **Box 12.3** this underlay the attempt in Uganda to do without parties after years of ethnically based civil war. The same argument is repeated by the leaders of the People's Republic of China to justify the leading role of the Communist Party (CCP).

Carothers (2006: 4) expands on what he terms the 'standard lament' about political parties in various countries where he has done research:

1. Parties are corrupt, self-interested organizations dominated by power-hungry elites who only pursue their own interests or those of their rich financial backers, not those of ordinary citizens.
2. Parties do not stand for anything: there are no real differences among them. Their ideologies are symbolic at best and their platforms vague or insubstantial.
3. Parties waste too much time and energy squabbling with each other over petty issues for the sake of meaningless political advantages rather than trying to solve the country's problems in a constructive, cooperative way.
4. Parties only become active at election time when they come looking for your vote; the rest of the time you never hear from them.
5. Parties are ill-prepared for governing the country and do a bad job of it when they do manage to take power or gain places in the national legislature.

12

KEY POINTS

- Parties are a vital element in modern political systems, especially democracies.
- Despite this, the rationality of party membership can be questioned.
- Parties generally suffer from low public esteem and are often associated with corruption.

EMERGENCE OF PARTIES

Historically, there were two phases in the development of political parties. Originally, they emerged within the parliaments of the first democracies as groups of independently elected representatives who needed to find ways of cooperating in passing legislation. These were caucus parties, loose organizations of like-minded representatives. Then, later, parties became involved in the process of trying to structure the vote in popular elections. For most countries these two stages were combined, because the model of parties was imported from abroad at the same time as parliaments. For them, parties had to structure both the popular vote and also the workings of parliament, but in the case of party pioneers, such as Britain and the USA, it is possible to separate the two stages.

There is an alternative way of theorizing the emergence of parties that goes beyond the purely chronological. This concentrates on the previously unfulfilled functions that parties emerged to perform. In this approach, historical description and more abstract logic are intertwined. It seeks to explain the systemic needs that parties had to fill. This approach is most common in the USA, so let us consider how it is used to explain the emergence of parties there.

Why did parties initially emerge in Congress? This was because the task of finding a new coalition each time a proposed bill was being considered for legislation was extremely time-consuming, especially if it involved sounding out the views of each representative afresh. Forming blocs of relatively like-minded representatives simplified the negotiating process and also enlarged the influence of individual members over legislation. It was easier for groups of members to have an impact because together they were more likely to have the casting vote over a particular bill than would individual members. They could extract greater concessions in the terms of the bill, or alternatively, they could more effectively trade concessions over one bill for advantages over another—what in the USA is called 'log-rolling'. Because legislation is a repetitive process, group commitments encouraged greater confidence that commitments would be honoured than those of individuals. It was easier to hold groups of legislators to their word than it was for individuals, and thus to penalize those who broke it. Relatively coherent groups of legislators provided greater predictability for other legislators or groups of them as negotiators. This crucial role of parties in structuring and facilitating the business of parliaments should always be remembered, because, as we shall see, even if today there seems greater reluctance on the part of individuals to become committed rank-and-file party members, thus provoking doubt about the future role of parties in society, their function in structuring the work of parliaments is unlikely to disappear.

The importance of this point can be seen in the very fact that they emerged in the new American Congress after Independence, when the American Founding Fathers had a distinct antipathy to any kind of party or faction, which they regarded as incompatible with real democracy. In *Federalist Paper No. 10*, Madison attacked 'factions', because they could oppress or exploit the people as a whole. He defined 'faction' as follows:

> [A] number of citizens, whether amounting to a majority or a minority of the whole, who are united and actuated by some common impulse of passion, or of interest, adverse to the rights of other citizens, or to the permanent and aggregate interests of the community.

By the Third Congress (1793–4), like-minded legislators had begun to form groups to smooth the passage of bills. Even in the circumstances where Congress only met for one or two months per year, and therefore had a tiny legislative load compared with today, so that the problems of log-rolling were small, this predictability was still a key benefit (Aldrich, 1995: 68–96).

Later, parties began to form outside Congress as a way of mobilizing support for candidates in first presidential and then local elections. Aldrich argues that the first time that this happened was in 1828 with the emergence of the Democratic Party of supporters for General Andrew Jackson. The effectiveness of the party was first shown in the fact that he won this election, where he had lost in 1824. Moreover, he did so on the basis of a turnout that increased from 30 per cent of the electorate to over 50 per cent, so party organization motivated supporters to vote. Then, when opponents followed suit by organizing the Whig Party (though it only lasted for about twenty-five years), the combined effect of these two parties could be seen in a turnout rate of over 78 per cent in 1840. The emergence of mass parties both changed the course of elections and also stimulated greater interest in politics in general, at least as measured by turnout. Thus they strengthened democracy (Aldrich, 1995: 97–125).

Since then, political parties have gone through several mutations. The next was the emergence of mass parties between the second half of the nineteenth and the first half of the twentieth centuries. The effectiveness of the American parties, as well as the lessons of growing party democracy in Britain, made political parties a vital element in the extension of democracy elsewhere in Europe and later further afield. In addition, industrialization overturned traditional patterns of authority relations and drove increasing numbers of people into growing urban areas, where parties could more easily mobilize support. All the political issues associated with industrialization provided the matter for a new, more popular democracy where mass parties became the norm and where the franchise was extended to include all men and then all women. This was the era when party membership was highest. This period also entrenched a key social divide as the basis for a great deal of political activity, i.e. that between capital and labour. While not all party systems revolved around this division, many did.

To cope with this at times exponential increase in party members, and to ensure greater coordination both in their activities and also those of party elected representatives, the number of full-time party officials increased. While it brought greater professionalism to the internal workings of political parties, it also complicated the practice of democracy in internal decision-making in parties. How much weight should be given to the views of ordinary party members as opposed to those of party officials? Should they all be treated as equal? Could they be?

Since the Second World War, parties in Europe have evolved further towards what have been termed 'catch-all' parties, i.e. parties that devote less attention to ideology and more to strategies to win over the median voter, who would make the crucial difference in a general election, even though it might mean appealing to voters who would instinctively support a different party. The consequence of this change has been to strengthen the hand of the party leadership that would be needed to make these strategic decisions. An early indication of the change came in West Germany in 1959 when the Social Democratic Party renounced Marxist ideology and committed itself to a market economy and liberal pluralism.

More recently, European and American parties have, it has been argued, undergone a further mutation as they turned into cartel parties that seek to exploit their access to state resources to solidify their pre-eminence and discourage newcomers (Katz and Mair, 1995, 2009). (**See Box 12.1**.) They are also often seen by critics as contributing to the emergence of a political class.

➜ See Chapter 11 for a discussion of the emergence of a 'political class'.

12

KEY DEBATE BOX 12.1
Modern 'Catch-All' versus Cartel Parties

Democracies need parties, yet today parties in Western democracies are losing members and generally finding it increasingly difficult to attract adequate resources to operate (see also Chapter 15). Should they operate as 'catch-all' parties that continue to rely solely on voluntary contributions from citizens, although in practice this may involve disproportionate obeisance to wealthy individuals and large corporations, who expect policy favours in return? Or should they seek funds for their public service from the state as a kind of cartel? Either choice could be interpreted as a form of, or at any rate a tendency towards, corruption. This could also be presented as a choice between 'American' and 'European' party practices, and judgement in part also depends upon your view of the state: does it embody a higher moral character (the predominant European view) or is it no different from other large organizations that pursue their interests at the expense of the rest of society (a view prevalent in American political culture)

(see also Chapter 8)? Is state-funding of political parties a necessary evil in the modern era, or the beginning of a slide towards the alienation of politicians from the public, and potentially to the downfall of democracy itself?

The implications for modern party behaviour and party leadership are sketched in Table 12.1, particularly the two right-hand columns. Which type would you favour?

Table 12.1 Katz and Mair on different types of party

Characteristics	Mass party	Catch-all party	Cartel party
Time period	1880–1960	1945–	1970–
Principal goals of politics	For or against social reform	Social amelioration	Politics as profession
Basis of party competition	Representative capacity	Policy effectiveness	Managerial skills, efficiency
Pattern of electoral competition	Mobilization	Competitive	Contained
Nature of party work and campaigning	Labour intensive	Labour- and capital-intensive	Capital intensive
Main source of party's resources	Members' contributions	Wide variety of contributions	State subventions
Relations between ordinary members and party elite	Bottom up: elite accountable to members	Top down: members are cheerleaders for elite	Stratarchy, i.e. mutual autonomy
Character of membership	Large and homogeneous; actively recruited on basis of class identity; emphasis on rights and obligations	Membership open to all; rights emphasized, but not obligations; membership marginal to individual's identity	Members as individuals valued for contributing to legitimizing myth; blurred distinction between members and non-members
Party channels of communication	Party had its own	Party competes for access to non-party channels of communication	Party gains access to state-regulated channels of communication
Position of party between civil society and state	Party represents sections of civil society	Party is broker between civil society and state	Party becomes part of state
Representative style	Delegate	Entrepreneur	Agent of state

Source: Taken from: Katz and Mair (1995: 18). Richard S. Katz, Peter Mair, 'Changing Models of Party Organization and Party Democracy', *Party Politics: The International Journal for the Study of Political Parties and Political Organizations*, 1 January 1995. © 1995 SAGE Publications.

12

As party membership has declined, this has strengthened the authority of the party machine, which in turn has become increasingly professional in its handling of all the media alternatives for putting its message across. Aldrich has particularly focused on this evolution in the case of the two American parties since the 1960s. Where previously the parties were dominated by local party machines such as that of Mayor Daley in the Democratic Party in Chicago and careers of elective office holders were made through the party machine, now parties have turned into organizations of media-savvy professionals ready to serve the needs of whichever candidates emerge to prominence. Thus, the parties have become candidate-centred rather than machine-centred (Aldrich, 1995).

This historical outline of the emergence of the modern party suggests that analysis of any modern party can usefully be divided between its activities in three arenas: (i) the party-in-government (including parliament); (ii) the party-in-the-electorate (i.e. its strategies for winning popular support and votes); and (iii) the party's internal organization (Aldrich, 1995). All parties that seek election have to establish their own synthesis of these three roles, but the political system in which they operate, the policy goals that they set themselves, and the attitudes of ordinary citizens towards them all provide structuration for the particular synthesis that they evolve. All of this determines their particular interpretation of intraparty democracy.

KEY POINTS

- The first parties emerged to structure the work of legislatures.
- Later phases of development were mass parties to structure the votes of electors, catch-all parties to win more votes irrespective of ideological appeal, and cartel parties more dominated by party professionals.
- All parties seeking electoral success have to balance three sets of roles: vis-à-vis government, the electorate, and their own internal professionals.

FUNCTIONS OF PARTIES

Modern political parties are protean organizations performing an extremely wide range of functions in the pursuit of political power. Ware has provided the following definition: 'A political party is an institution that (a) seeks influence in a state, often by attempting to occupy positions in government, and (b) usually consists of more than a single interest in the society and so to some degree attempts to "aggregate interests" ' (Ware, 1996: 5).

In general they perform seven functions, irrespective of whether they operate in democracies or authoritarian regimes. These are listed in **Box 12.2**.

The balance between these functions varies according to the type of state. Not all parties perform all of these functions. In democracies, parties have a more prominent role in providing choice between individual political actors and between policies—indeed, in performing most of the last six functions. Authoritarian regimes place more emphasis upon the second function—though their interpretation of integration and mobilization implies more of a top-down rather than bottom-up process—and functions five to seven. For example, Greene (2007) has shown how the Revolutionary Institutional Party (PRI) in Mexico used its control over state resources to hamstring potential rival parties, making it one of the longest-lived ruling parties in the world.

BOX 12.2
Functions of Political Parties

- Legitimation of the political system
- Integration and mobilization of citizens
- Representation
- Structuring the popular vote
- Aggregation of diverse interests
- Recruitment of leaders for public office, thus facilitating (normally) non-violent choice between individuals
- Formulation of public policy, facilitating choice between policy options

Meanwhile, the CPP, with over 80 million members, continues to allocate members to key positions throughout the state (Shambaugh, 2008; McGregor, 2010). However, while it may be almost unthinkable for democracies to exist without political parties (for an exception that proves the rule, see the example of Uganda in **Box 12.3**), what is striking is the wide variety of states than contain them. Most states today, not just democracies, contain political parties. The only significant

CASE STUDY BOX 12.3
Uganda as a No-Party State

Uganda is a rare example of a state that has attempted to practise democracy without political parties.

Since independence in 1962, Uganda has gone through civil war, genocide, and revolution. It was originally put together as a colony by Britain from a variety of former tribal kingdoms and principalities. There was no tradition of democracy, and in the less than seventy years of colonial rule, Britain only began to introduce it in the last few years. Milton Obote was elected the first president, but democratic values did not develop among the newly elected parties. Uganda effectively became a one-party state from 1964, but Obote was overthrown by Idi Amin in 1971, who declared himself president for life. Gradually, the country slid into tyranny, chaos, violence, and economic collapse. In 1979, he was overthrown and Obote was reinstalled as president. This time he attempted to restore a multiparty system, but the party leaders refused to cooperate with each other, and violence returned. Between 1971 and 1986, an estimated 1 million people died.

When the National Resistance Movement under Yoweri Museveni took over the country, he declared that the country needed a fresh political start. Political parties would be banned because they institutionalized division and antagonism in the country, as shown by the experience of 1979–86, where what was needed was unity. The new regime would try to inculcate the spirit of unity, mutual tolerance, and democracy through the dissemination of the principles that had underlain the practice of the resistance movement. This would also be better in keeping with African traditions of tribal consultation.

→

The constitution adopted in 1995, after nearly a decade of military and transitional rule, allowed for either a multiparty political system or a democratic 'movement political system', but although political parties were not banned, the regime prevented them from organizing openly. Party representatives had to stand for election to parliament as individuals. Instead, the regime focused its efforts at democratization on local resistance councils. However, armed groups in the north still challenge the authority and the democracy of the government in Kampala.

The constitution laid down a limit of two five-year terms on any president. As Museveni's second term drew towards its close, the regime began to float the idea of a third term. This provoked unease both at home and among foreign governments that gave aid. In the end a referendum was held which approved the change to a multiparty democracy. Thus the reintroduction of open political parties was a response to both domestic and external pressure. However, in the general election called in early 2006 Museveni won a clear majority, despite opposition allegations of electoral irregularities. The Supreme Court upheld the outcome by a vote of four to three. Critics alleged that little changed in the way the country is ruled. As of 2015, twenty-nine political parties were registered with the Ugandan Electoral Commission. President Museveni is still in power.

group of exceptions has been many Islamic states, although even Iran has political parties. Even communist regimes, which never tolerated challenges to the leading role of the communist party, organized regular elections at all levels of the state as a way of re-engaging the commitment of their citizens to the goals of the regime and also of demonstrating claims to popular legitimacy to the rest of the world. Authoritarian regimes too, such as South Korea's between the 1960s and the end of the 1980s, have devoted considerable resources to holding regular elections and mobilizing support for the ruling parties, even though there was never a realistic possibility of political alternatives winning power.

Thus legitimation of the political system, whatever its basic structure, remains the single most common function of political parties. The only exceptions are parties that seek to overthrow the existing political system, especially those that seek violent revolution rather than change through the ballot box.

The ways in which parties perform these roles depend upon three things: (1) the constitutional framework within which they operate; (2) the particular national system of elections; and (3) the technologies of communication available to them.

1. As we have already seen in Chapter 10 from the constitutional distinction between federal and non-federal regimes, the degree of central authority in a state has a key impact upon the organization of political parties. The relative powers of a party's central apparatus and local organizations to some extent reflect the relative powers of the corresponding government authorities.

2. Countries with primaries to select candidates for election to major offices have to organize their activities to a different timetable from that of other countries.

3. As television and advertising have become more powerful, parties have turned to them increasingly to get their messages across rather than relying upon more personalized direct contact with party activists, even though this has greatly inflated their costs. Now the rise of the Internet is beginning to offer new possibilities for much more personalized canvassing, with candidates contacting voters individually to respond to their particular concerns.

12

→ See Chapter 10 for a discussion of federalism.

→ See Chapter 14 for a discussion of the impact of the media on politics.

KEY POINTS

- Parties perform an extremely wide range of functions in political systems.
- These are structured by the constitutional framework of the political system, the national system of elections, and the technologies available to them for communicating with voters.

TYPOLOGIES OF POLITICAL PARTIES

Political scientists develop typologies of political parties to try to think more systematically about their activities and to make more meaningful comparisons. **Table 12.2** presents the typology of Gunther and Diamond which they explicitly formulated to take account of political parties in various regions of the world. It is based primarily upon the ways in which and the extent to which parties organize themselves. This means that the lower down the table we go, the more organized they are.

TYPES OF PARTY OUTSIDE THE WEST

DeSouza and Sridharan (2006) accepted the Gunther and Diamond typology to provide the basic structure for their analysis of Indian political parties, although ideologies also play a role in Indian politics. Varshney (2002: 55) has identified three 'master narratives' underlying Indian

Table 12.2 Typology of political parties

Basic category	Variants	Sub-variants
Elite-based	Traditional local notables (esp. 19th cent.)	
	Clientelistic	
Electoralist	Personalistic	
	Catch-all	
	Programmatic	
Movement	Left-libertarian	
	Post-industrial extreme right	
Ethnicity-based	Exclusive ethnic	
	Congress/coalition movement	
Mass-based	Religious	Denominational
		Fundamentalist
	Nationalist	Pluralist
		Ultranationalist
	Socialist	Class/mass based
		Leninist

Source: Gunther and Diamond (2003: 173). Richard Gunther, Larry Diamond, 'Species of Political Parties', *Party Politics: The International Journal for the Study of Political Parties and Political Organizations*, 3 January 2003. © 2003 SAGE Publications.

politics in the twentieth century, which also differentiate political parties: (i) secular nationalism; (ii) religious nationalism; and (iii) relations and struggles between caste groups in Hinduism. Vaishnav (2017: 136–7) expands on the way this operates:

> While ideology of a programmatic sort is virtually absent, it is present in a very different (non-economic) sense. Across political parties, caste, religion, and language all represent cleavages in society that have acquired ideological import over time. In diverse societies, the practice of ethnic politics revolves around concepts like 'dignity', 'honor', 'justice', and 'inclusion'. Although they do not operate on a conventional left-right spectrum, these notions do contain substantive content.

Yet, Vaishanav (2017: 136) also argues that, in practice, 'ideology is largely an afterthought in Indian politics.' While political activists marshal ideas to win support, more pragmatic considerations govern their actions and those of potential supporters. So whilst the Hindu Bharatiya Janata Party (BJP) party defeated the secularist Indian National Congress (INC) in 2014 and even more decisively in 2019, winning an absolute majority, which certainly had a strong ideological dimension, this had as much to do with the dynamic leadership of Narendra Modi of the BJP contrasting with the lacklustre campaigning of the latest scion of the Nehru-Gandhi-dominated INC, Rahul. The BJP seemed to offer the prospect of more benefits for more people because of its more business-friendly policies. Money matters at least as much in Indian politics as it does in the US. Parties there are vehicles for winning power and getting access to mechanisms for redistributing resources, so they engage in all sorts of activities, including (not very covert) corruption to win votes. Criminal prosecutions are no bar to public office either. A fifth of the deputies elected to the Lok Sabha in 2014 declared that they were the object of serious criminal prosecutions and, if convicted, would be liable to lengthy jail time (Vaishnav, 2017: x).

One other feature of the Indian party system should also be noted: the proliferation of parties, as their backers seek to win power at the local level, even if they are ineffective as national parties. This is a strengthening trend. During the first two decades after independence, the INC dominated electoral politics at the national, as well as the state, levels, although the toleration in Delhi of local party bosses meant it was a fairly decentralized organization. But, in recent decades, political fragmentation has gathered momentum. In 2015, 1,866 political parties were registered with the Electoral Commission and 464 parties contested the 2014 general election. Of these, thirty-four actually won seats in the Lok Sabha.

On the face of it, this is a puzzle, since India has a first-past-the-post electoral system, and Duverger's Law (see Chapter 11) suggests that this should encourage two-party national politics, not fragmentation. But Sridharan (2010) explains that the key intervening variable is the fact of India's federal system. There is indeed a discernible tendency towards bi-party outcomes in most of the states of India, but the two main parties differ from one state to another. In many cases, these are parties concentrated in one state. Consequently, at the federal level, coalitions involving regional parties have become a regular feature of national politics—at least until 2014. And though it has a majority on its own in parliament, the BJP government under Modi has included a few non-BJP ministers as a way of preserving relations with partners in certain localities.

The phenomenon of party proliferation and political fragmentation is fairly common, especially in large states with diverse populations. In Brazil, a state with twenty-six federal units, there are thirty-five registered parties and twenty-two of them held seats in the lower house of parliament in 2016. Yet in Mexico, another federal state with thirty-one units, where democracy has become consolidated since 2000 when the candidate of the National Action Party (PAN), Vicente Fox, became the first president from outside the Institutional Revolutionary Party (PRI) since 1929, politics continues to be dominated by the three parties that were established well before 2000—the two just mentioned and the Party of the Democratic Revolution (PRD). So, while general explanations can be offered for party fragmentation around the world, there are always exceptions.

Elischer (2013: 26–42) also accepts the Gunther and Diamond typology as the starting point for his analysis of African political parties but amends it so as to make it less Eurocentric and more appropriate for comparative research across other regions of the world. He argues that the differentiation between two different types of elite-based party which are based upon different historical periods in which parties emerged makes no sense in the context of twenty-first African politics. The same is true for the two 'movement'-based party variants, since they are based upon post-industrial values, which are premature for an Africa that is largely still to industrialize. He proposes replacing the congress/coalition variants of ethnicity-based parties with 'multi-ethnic alliance' and 'multi-ethnic catch-all' variants (which also replaces the catch-all variant of electoralist parties, since, in his view, all African parties are, to some extent, ethnically based). And he also dismisses the pluralist and ultra-nationalist sub-variants of movement-based parties, since they are more or less identical to the exclusive-ethnic and multi-ethnic categories, see **Table 12.3**.

At the same time, Booysen's (2011) detailed study of the African National Congress (ANC), in power since 1994, can serve as a reminder of the difficulty of locating many parties precisely within such frameworks in general. This is partly because of the wide range of functions that a long-time ruling party comes to perform and partly because its activities evolve with different leaders. The party sees itself as a multi-ethnic alliance, representing all the citizens of South Africa. At the same time, to use Gunther and Diamond's categories, its leadership tries to maintain the tradition of the disciplined Leninist style of organization that it had to develop to survive in the struggle against apartheid. As a programmatically socialist party, it prides itself on its ties to 'the masses'—and it still wins large majorities in general elections and it is the only national mass party in South Africa. It could be seen as 'personalistic' in that its appeal has been heavily buttressed by the personal leadership of Nelson Mandela, Thabo Mbeki, Jacob Zuma, and Cyril Ramaphosa—although that attraction has been gradually declining, in large part because it has also become more 'clientelistic' and corrupt, especially under Zuma. Booysen herself identifies

Table 12.3 Typology of African political parties

Party type
Mono-ethnic
Ethnic alliance
Ethnic catch-all
Programmatic
Personalistic

Source: Elischer (2013: 391).

its most basic identity as a 'party-movement' rather than a ruling party. All of this is a reminder of the provisional nature of such classificatory assessments.

KEY POINTS

- Typologies facilitate more systematic comparison between party activities.
- They vary according to the primacy accorded to different basic features.

More research needs to be done in overcoming Eurocentric categories in establishing valid typologies for parties across different regions of the world.

Giving due weight to all the dimensions of a party's activities, so as to synthesize them and fit it into a general typology is a matter of fine judgement.

PARTY SYSTEMS

Any state with more than one political party also has a party system. Sartori defined these as 'the system[s] of interactions resulting from interparty competition' (Sartori, 1976: 44). These interactions are affected by (1) the nature of the political system as a whole; (2) the pattern of basic cleavages in society which underlie the differentiation between parties; and (3) the channels open for competition between the parties, i.e. primarily the electoral system, though not exclusively: for example, uneven availability of campaign funding to individual parties can also significantly affect electoral outcomes.

12

1. Clearly, the constitutional nature of the state has a fundamental impact upon the competition between parties, as parties have to operate according to its rules. Parties have to operate rather differently in liberal democratic regimes, where electoral success does lead to changes of government, from more authoritarian regimes where the rulers will not contemplate electoral overthrow and where opposition parties, if tolerated, have to be much more circumspect in their criticisms. It also matters whether a regime is presidential or parliamentarian.

2. The pattern of relations between political parties is in part determined by the fundamental cleavages in society. These are based on social history. The original version of this as it applied to politics in Europe was formulated by Lipset and Rokkan. They concluded that there were four fundamental cleavages that had structured the rise of the new mass parties in Europe either towards the end of the nineteenth century or in the first quarter of the twentieth. Since then these 'frozen' cleavages have remained the basis of West European party systems. These cleavages were: (i) centre versus periphery: this meant the competing claims of different communities within the same state for power both at the centre and in regional authorities (sometimes these were also based upon different linguistic communities, but not necessarily); (ii) state versus church: this was particularly important in Catholic states where a significant part of the challenge to the Church's temporal powers was mounted by anticlerical liberals and radicals; (iii) land versus industry: the growth of industrialization and of industrial capitalists posed a challenge to more traditional rural elites; and (iv) owner versus worker: the rise of capitalism also pitted the interests of the new industrial workers against those of their employers (Lipset and Rokkan, 1967). All West European states were

affected to varying degrees by these divisions, but the outcome differed in terms of actual party representation.

3. The electoral system also affects the system of political parties. A political science classic, Duverger's *Political Parties* argued that first-past-the-post electoral systems tend to produce two-party systems—what later became known as Duverger's Law. By contrast, he argued, proportional representation tends to produce multiparty systems (Duverger, 1964). While these are more generalizations than uniform 'laws' (in the past, e.g., Venezuela had proportional representation and also a two-party system), there is no doubt about the logic of the argument.

Given these structuring factors, most typologies of party systems focus upon the number of parties contained in them. One version gives the following fourfold classification (Ware, 1996: 159):

1. Predominant party systems, where one party occupies a dominant place in the national legislature. It is rare in developed democracies, but it has emerged in Russia because of official backing, and this situation is very common in sub-Saharan Africa, where non-ruling parties are short of resources (Doorenspleet, 2003: 205). Some authoritarian regimes, e.g. Indonesia under former President Suharto, have explicitly supported the primacy of one party on the grounds that it provides opportunities for representation of different interests and groups within the constraints of a single party where unprincipled party competition would jeopardize social cohesion (Reeve, 1985).

2. Two-party systems, e.g. the USA.

3. Systems with three to five parties, e.g. France, Germany, and the UK.

4. Systems with more than five parties, e.g. Belgium, Denmark, and Italy.

What is striking is that, once established, especially in liberal democracies, party systems tend to change very slowly—as in Lipset and Rokkan's 'frozen' party systems of Western Europe. They can play a big part in the successful operation of a democracy, such as a two-party system, and they can also frustrate it; for example, with a highly fragmented party system with many small parties, as in Italy since the Second World War; yet it is almost impossible to design and impose a particular system when voters' choices are genuinely free. Then, party systems just emerge and acquire a life of their own. They are not easily changed even when reformers set out to do so because of perceived and unpopular weaknesses in them. Take the case of Japan. The Liberal Democratic Party (LDP) was in government from 1955, with the brief exception of a period in 1993–4, until 2009. In the 1990s, however, the LDP became unpopular because of its association with corruption and money politics. Apart from the general need of parties for money, this corruption was attributed to the particular electoral system of multi-member constituencies, where several candidates from the same party could compete with each other as well as with other parties. To try to break this, the electoral system was reformed with more first-past-the-post voting so as to try to facilitate a more genuine two-party system. It was thought that this would reduce the incentive for escalating campaign expenses and also, as Duverger's Law would predict, favour a two-party system by strengthening opposition to the LDP (Rosenbluth and Ramseyer, 1993). Yet, despite the reforms, the LDP upset these calculations, adapted to the new circumstances, and continued to win a majority of seats in the key lower house of the Diet (parliament) until 2009 and again since 2012. Nor has campaign spending been noticeably reduced. It is a reminder of a more general warning made by Gambetta and Warner after reviewing electoral reform in Italy: 'Several of the effects of introducing new electoral systems are seldom predictable' (Gambetta and Warner, 2004: 249).

KEY POINTS

- Party systems are the product of sociological and institutional interactions.
- They cannot be designed in genuine democracies.
- Once formed, they are very durable and, again in democracies, difficult successfully to reform so that they realize different objectives.

PROBLEMS FACING PARTIES

As ever, serious problems now confront political parties, although they vary in nature from one region of the world to another. In Western Europe the traditional main parties themselves and the party systems still survive. There, the problem is one of declining party membership. In general, the mass parties that were typical of the inter-war and post-war eras are a thing of the past. Although parties do not always maintain scrupulous records of members, in part because of the need to appear strong to outside observers, the trend seems clear throughout Europe, as can be seen from **Table 12.4**. In the case of Spain, one of the two exceptions to this general trend, it should be noted that the base year of 1980 was only five years after the death of the dictator Franco and only two years after the promulgation of a new constitution.

This means that by the end of the 1990s, the average share of European populations who are party members was around 5.7 per cent, only around a third of what it had been thirty years earlier (Mair, 2005: 15). By coincidence, this figure is almost exactly the same as the share of CCP members in the Chinese population by 2007—though the CCP is still, at least nominally, deliberately more selective in its membership; and yet membership of the CCP is going up, while that of parties in the West is declining.

Table 12.4 Trends in changing membership in European parties, 1980–2009

Country	Period	Change in numbers	% change in original membership
France	1978–2009	−923,788	−53.17
Italy	1980–2007	−1,450,623	−35.61
UK	1980–2008	−1,158,492	−68.42
Norway	1980–2008	−288,554	−62.60
Austria	1980–2008	−422,661	−28.61
Sweden	1980–2008	−241,130	−47.46
Germany	1980–2007	−531,856	−27.20
Greece	1980–2008	+ 335,000	+ 148.49
Spain	1980–2008	+ 1,208,258	+ 374.60

Source: van Biezen, Mair, and Poguntke (2011).

12

Much thought has been devoted to the reasons for this increasing apparent reluctance for party activism in Europe. In Britain, one of the objectives of the Power Inquiry held between 2004 and 2006 was to remedy this. It recommended a number of measures, including calls for 'a responsive electoral system—which offers voters a greater choice and diversity of parties and candidates—to replace the first-past-the-post system', a minimum voting age of 16 and state funding for parties through vouchers assigned by voters at a general election (Power Inquiry, 2006). This last principle of state funding for political parties has become much more common around the world in recent years, as a way of boosting funds for the vital functions that parties perform in democracies and also as a way of trying to reduce their dependence on corporate sponsors.

Critics, however, warn of the need to ensure that this does not protect parties from new challengers and prevent newcomers from winning seats in parliament, as did happen in Venezuela (**see Box 12.4**) (International IDEA, 2003). State funding can encourage party fragmentation rather than consolidation, opening the possibility of funds for dissident factions to set themselves up as new parties, as happened in Japan in the 1990s. Other critics argue that the cause of the indifference is the sense that individuals can make no impact upon government or party decisions—a variant of the public choice argument about the 'irrationality' of membership for the party rank-and-file mentioned previously. From this perspective, the only solution is to change the process of political decision-making to make it more 'relevant'. Once this had happened, people would flock back to parties.

 12

CASE STUDY BOX 12.4
Venezuela and the Downfall of Liberal Democracy

From the time when democracy was re-established in 1958, Venezuela had the reputation of the most stable and most liberal democracy in South America. Yet, recent years have seen this system pushed aside by President Chavez in favour of a more populist democracy. It is a reminder that while liberal democracy may have been presented by Fukuyama as 'the end of history', this type of regime may be vulnerable too. How did it get into this situation?

In 1958, former dictator Pérez Jiménez was overthrown in a military coup that led to the reintroduction of democracy. In October the leaders of the three main parties signed a pact at Punto Fijo that committed them to observing the same basic rules of the political game for the sake of preserving democracy. Subsequently this underlay the evolution of Venezuela into a state with effectively two parties: Acción Democrática (AD) and Comitida de Organización Política Electoral (COPEI). The concept of 'pacted democracy' was later cited by commentators as a model for how to establish a successful democracy, especially in Latin America, and for many years it underpinned US policy for promoting transitions to democracy there.

The two parties extended their reach into a wide range of other organizations: professional associations, peasant federations, state enterprises . . . which helped both to strengthen their control and also to increase their membership. On the one hand the two parties exercised very strict control over their members. On the other hand they sought consensus between themselves wherever possible, though this did not prevent energetic competition for power, with the presidency changing hands regularly.

Photo 12.1 Juan Guaidó. *Shutterstock RF: Regulo Gomez/Shutterstock.com*

This system worked well for nearly two decades, reinforced by prosperity based upon oil wealth. From the mid-1970s, however, the economy began to stagnate and decline. This was partly caused by falls in the international price of oil, but partly also by corruption and waste. Popular dissatisfaction grew and the parties did not reform. They became more isolated from the public.

In 1998, former Lt Colonel Hugo Chávez won a presidential election as an outsider. He promised a 'Bolivarian' revolution, appealing to the example of the nineteenth-century liberator from Spanish rule, Simon Bolívar, though the latter had traditionally been seen more as a liberal and an admirer of the American Revolution. Chávez aimed at sweeping away corruption and redistributing wealth towards the ordinary people. He attacked the 'partocracy' (*partidocratia*) that kept all power in the hands of the two parties and their state funding was abolished. What gradually emerged was a populist regime that promoted social polarization rather than consensus. Chávez introduced a new constitution that removed many of the checks upon the powers of the president. Attempts to overthrow him through a putsch and by holding an election to recall him from office on the grounds of misusing his position both failed. The old party system fragmented, to be replaced by a multiparty system with numerous small parties. They are overshadowed, however, by Chávez's dominant Fifth Republic Movement (now the United Socialist Party of Venezuela).

Aided by the additional wealth that came from increasing world oil prices, despite a more polarized society, Chávez won a second term of office in January 2007. Chavez pushed on with his Bolivarian socialist revolution, as did his successor Nicolas Maduro after Chavez's sudden death in 2013. But the political polarization that this provoked, exacerbated by the collapse in world oil prices after 2014, which hit the Venezuelan economy hard, led to increasingly fractious politics. In 2016, the economy fell 10–15 per cent and annual inflation reached 800 per cent. Poverty soared, with widespread shortages of basic medicines. In 2017, Maduro called a national referendum on a Constituent Assembly to establish a more 'popular' form of rule to replace he constitution that Chavez himself had introduced. The opposition boycotted it. Maduro claimed victory after winning all 545 seats. Street demonstrations increasingly turned violent. In 2019 the President of the National Assembly, Juan Guaidó declared himself the acting president of the country and was recognized by the US and the UK. Maduro hinted darkly that he should take a heed to his safety. In May 2019 the annual inflation rate reached almost 1 million per cent. GDP had halved since 2013. Nevertheless the regime-imposed restrictions on trade, including food, with countries whose governments criticized it. The UNHCR (United Nations High Commissioner for Refugees) announced that 4 million Venezuelans had become refugees abroad. The country had moved very far from the pacted consensus of 1958.
(Coppedge, 2002; McCoy and Myers, 2004; Gott, 2005; Corrales and Penfold, 2007)

12

In the USA, there is an analogous problem, though it is not one of resources. In the 2004 presidential election, the two parties declared combined expenditure of US$880 million. In 2008, this amount more than doubled to US $1.82 billion, over ten times more than in 1980, in large part due to the Obama campaign's success in using the Internet to mobilize small sums from large numbers of supporters. In 2012, it swelled even further to over US $2.6 billion, with the two candidates alone spending US $1.2 billion (Open secrets, 2012). In 2016 the amount raised directly by the candidates swelled to US $1.5 billion, though Hillary Clinton outspent Donald Trump almost two to one and still lost (Open secrets, 2016). At least the same amount is spent every two years on elections to Congress and state legislatures. An enormous amount of this goes on media campaigning, but there is no shortage of volunteers who help on campaigns without pay. Nevertheless, here too we find a trend towards declining party membership. Individuals can be motivated to join and help with the campaigns of particular candidates whom they support, but they are more fickle in their allegiance. Here too, the party professionals play a bigger role in determining party image and appeals to the electorate. This can risk the parties losing contact with the rest of society, as happened in Venezuela.

For new democracies there is no problem in forming new political parties. As of 2004, Russia, for example, still had forty-four political parties registered with the government; yet as Hale has described, Russia's parties have failed to become dominant institutions (Hale, 2006). In Latin America, parties and party systems are still often weaker and less institutionalized, with the consequence that, as in Peru at the end of the 1990s, an elected authoritarian leader such as Fujimori can break them down (Levitsky and Cameron, 2003). The problem for these regimes is that political parties find it difficult to become the equivalent to the national institutions that they are in established democracies. If parties in the latter are seeing an erosion of their membership, when these parties have an established image and can adapt to changing electoral circumstances, the problem of membership is much worse in new democracies, where it is extremely difficult to grow to an effective size. For them an added complication is the lack of obvious fundamental social cleavages that can underpin a party system. With the Cold War over, socialist parties on the defensive, and the emergence of post-industrial economies where social identities are more fluid, the old divisions between capital and labour no longer underpin fundamental party divides (Biezen, 2003: 37–8). It may be the case that the issue of Brexit will catalyse a reordering of support for British parties, with support for both the Conservative and Labour parties at a historic low in early 2019.

Taiwan is an exception that proves the rule. Since 1987, Taiwan has become one of the most successful new democracies. It has a stable party system, with two main parties and one or two minor ones. The two main parties—the Nationalist Party (KMT) and the Democratic Progressive Party (DPP)—do indeed confront each other over a vital basic political issue, but this is not one of the four traditional divides that Lipset and Rokkan identified. It is unique to Taiwan: the issue of independence from mainland China. The DPP would prefer formal independence; the KMT opposes it. In fact, there is disagreement within both parties over the best way to frame policies to achieve either of these goals, so there is not complete unanimity. Both parties have a wider range of policies to appeal to voters, some of which overlap and cut across the basic cleavage, preventing the antagonism from becoming irreconcilable. This is the fundamental difference between the core images of the two parties. It structures the party system. But other new democracies do not have the same fundamental cleavage, or an analogous one, so their party systems are more volatile.

Although there are many differences between the parties in the established democracies of Western Europe and the USA, and those in the newer democracies in other parts of the world, there does seem one trend of convergence. This is the enhanced importance now of party professionals in determining party 'brand' and policies to appeal to the electorate. This is the result of a combination of factors. On the one hand, it is a consequence of the reduction in rank-and-file members of previously mass parties. On the other, it results from the growing importance of state funds in financing party activities. While the two main American parties do not suffer from the same problems of financial stringency, Aldrich has argued that the same change has taken place there. Since the 1960s the Democratic and Republican parties have both changed from mass parties to ones that are candidate-centred with party professionals at their service (Aldrich, 1995: 254). This convergence also makes it likely that parties in various parts of the world will seek to derive lessons from the American experience on ways of winning elections, even if the electoral systems are quite different, especially where those parties also mutate into candidate-centred organizations, as in Peru.

There is a growing divide between party professionals and the party rank-and-file. According to Mair, parties in Europe 'have reduced their presence in the wider society and have become part of the state'. They are less concerned with playing the function of opposition and more concerned with preparing for government. 'Within politics . . . the parties are either all governing or waiting to govern' (Mair, 2005: 20).

The corollary of this is that the fundamental difference between rank-and-file party members and ordinary citizens in the internal life of parties is eroding. Some attempts to revive interest in politics may exacerbate the problem. For example, theories of deliberative democracy advocate new ways of consulting public opinion in policy-making by involving representative groups of ordinary citizens—as suggested in Chapter 11. At the same time, parties in various countries have experimented with open primaries, where potential candidates are selected by voters in the given constituency, irrespective of their own allegiances, as a response to criticisms about parties becoming apart from society. This privileges the decision-making role of ordinary citizens over that of both party professionals and party rank-and-file in a key area of party activity. It erodes the boundaries separating parties from the rest of society.

➡ Also see the discussion on electronic decision-making in Chapter 14.

> **KEY POINTS**
>
> - Political parties are facing a range of new challenges.
> - In various parts of the world the balance between rank-and-file party members and party professionals is tipping towards the latter.
> - Despite the lack of esteem for them, parties remain vital for the formulation and legitimation of public policies.

CONCLUSION

As ever, parties and party systems are in transition and their future shape is not clear. Across Europe and in the US they are increasingly challenged by the rise of populist movements—an issue to which we shall return in Chapter 15. Yet even in Italy—the country with perhaps the most populist political system—a poll in 2013 showed that 57 per cent of respondents still agreed that there could be no democracy without parties (Biorcio, 2015: 106). And Levitsky, Loxton, and van Dyck (2016: 3; emphasis in original) have shown how political parties have succeeded in Latin America:

> Robust parties emerge not from stable democratic competition, but rather from *extraordinary conflict*—periods of intense polarization accompanied by large-scale popular mobilization and, in many cases, violence or repression. Episodes of intense conflict such as social revolution, civil war, authoritarian repression, and sustained popular mobilization generate the kinds of partisan attachments, grassroots organizations, and internal cohesion that facilitate successful party-building.

There seems little chance that the old mass parties will return; but parties will continue to play an important role in the way that policy choices are presented to citizens for approval. Indeed, where significant resources are at their disposal, they will have an increasing impact on the presentation of policies, managing a widening variety of media strategies. They will also continue to play important roles in structuring the work of parliaments. They will act as recruitment channels for ministerial positions, and they will certainly continue to legitimize, or be used for the purposes of legitimizing, political regimes. Although parties often suffer from a bad press, and they are sometimes accused of exacerbating social divisions rather than finding ways of reconciling them, attempts to devise alternative forms or organization such as 'movements' have failed to supplant them for long. Political parties are not a guaranteed solution to problems of political instability. They structure the formulation of public policies, but their leaders still have to make choices about priorities, and they can change them. They make mistakes, antagonize people, and seem self-interested; but without them a politics dominated by narrower interest groups would be even less attractive (Fiorina, 2002: 541). It remains difficult to envisage the formulation and legitimation of public policies without parties.

Yet Savoie (2010) also stresses the importance of personal leadership in parties and in democracies in general—it always has been crucial in authoritarian regimes. 'Personalism is now the key to understanding where both power and influence are located and who has it' (2010: 214). Presidents Obama, Chavez, and Erdogan all exemplify this trend. Donald Trump was elected as much against the Republican (as well as the Democratic) Party as with its support. According to Savoie, the same is true of Canada. In general, he declares: 'Power today is more fluid and transient than at any time in the past' (2010: 227).

KEY QUESTIONS

1. How stable is the party system in any country with which you are familiar? What might upset it?

2. The land area of the Indian state is roughly one-third of that of the US. The American population is roughly a quarter of that of India. Both are consolidated federal democracies. How do you explain the fact that two main parties contested the last presidential election in the US, while over fifty parties contested the 2019 Indian election?

3. Are Chinese leaders right to fear that political parties divide societies more than they integrate them? Are these lessons from the Indian experience? Or the Mexican?

4. Do you take an active part in the life of a political party? How do you justify this? How rational is it?

5. Has the Labour Party in Britain managed to reverse the long-term trend of declining party membership across Europe? How and why?

6. How appropriate is state funding of political parties? How valid are the objections?

7. How far do American parties conform to the model of cartel parties?

8. Are parties' programmes becoming more difficult to distinguish from each other? Are they becoming less 'ideological'?

9. Are parties in other parts of the world becoming more 'American'? If so, in what ways? Does it matter?

10. How well does the typology of party systems fit the political systems of countries with which you are familiar?

FURTHER READING

Aldrich, J. H. (2011), *Why Parties? A Second Look* (Chicago: Chicago University Press).
This is a theoretically informed history of the rise of parties in the USA.

Dalton, R. J., Farrell, D. M., and McAllister, I. (2011), *Political Parties and Democratic Linkage: How Parties Organize Democracy* (Oxford: Oxford University Press).
A wide-ranging survey of the practice of parties in democracies.

Elischer, S. (2013), *Political Parties in Africa* (Cambridge: Cambridge University Press).
A very good introduction to party systems in several African states.

Gallagher, M., Laver, M., and Mair, P. (2011), *Representative Government in Modern Europe: Institutions, Parties and Governments* (Boston: McGraw Hill, 5th edn), chs. 7–10.
This is a survey of parties in various European states.

Greene, K. J. (2007), *Why Dominant Parties Lose: Mexico's Democratization in Comparative Perspective* (Cambridge: Cambridge University Press).
This is a sophisticated analysis of how one of the most durable ruling parties stayed in power for seventy years and then lost it.

Katz, R. S. and Crotty, W. (eds) (2006), *Handbook of Party Politics* (London: Sage).
This is a compendium of information on many features of political parties.

Katz, R. S. and Mair, P. (1995), 'Changing models of party organization and party democracy: The Emergence of the Cartel Party', *Party Politics* 1(1): 5–28.
A widely cited analysis of recent changes in the organization and role of parties, especially in Europe.

Levitsky, S. and Cameron, M. A. (2003), 'Democracy without parties? Political Parties and regime change in Fujimori's Peru', *Latin American Politics and Society*, 45(3): 1–33.
This is a study of a political system whose president attempted to rule without parties—complements the case study on Uganda.

Levitsky, S. and Cameron, M. A. (2005), *Parliamentary Affairs* 58(3), special issue on 'The Future of Parties'.
This is a collection of articles on the challenges to political parties.

Mainwaring, S. (ed.) (2018), *Party Systems in Latin America: Institutionalization, Decay, and Collapse* (Cambridge and New York: Cambridge University Press).
This presents party systems in Latin America.

Mair, P. (1997), *Party System Change* (Oxford: Oxford University Press).
This is a theoretical discussion of how modern parties change.

McGregor, R. (2010), *The Party: the Secret World of China's Communist Rulers* (London: Allen Lane).
A journalist's eye-opening account of the internal life of the world's largest party.

Reeve, D. (1985), *Golkar of Indonesia: An Alternative to the Party System* (Singapore: Oxford University Press).
This presents the Indonesian justification for an authoritarian ruling party as a substitute for democracy.

Ware, A. (1996), *Political Parties and Party Systems* (Oxford: Oxford University Press).
This is a thorough survey of the relationship between parties and party systems.

 For additional material and resources, please visit the Online Resources at:
www.oup.com/he/garner4e

13

EXECUTIVES, BUREAUCRACIES, POLICY STUDIES, AND GOVERNANCE

READER'S GUIDE

This chapter will first set the general framework of legislature–executive relations, focusing mainly on the competing claims of parliamentary versus presidential systems. Then it will introduce the subject of the civil service and its traditional role in building up the effective power of the state. It will suggest that embedded autonomy is an appropriate way to characterize its relationship with the rest of society, using examples from economic policy-making. Then it will introduce theories of bureaucratic policy-making, and in particular the problem of facilitating policy innovation. It will take the basic issue of relations between principals and agents as the starting point. This leads on to the more recent proliferation of agencies in government set up to implement policies devised by the political leadership but operating at arm's length from the structures of ministries.

→

This expands the scope of study from governments to governance and, in the case of the developing world, the related subject of good governance. The domain of policy-making spreads beyond state officials or civil servants to issue networks and policy communities. Finally, the conclusion addresses the emergence of a 'network state', what that might mean, and the implications for civil servants.

LEGISLATURES AND EXECUTIVES

Parliaments and political parties are intimately connected with the executive branch of government. There are two overlapping meanings for the term **executive**. In the broader sense, it denotes one of the three main branches of government, alongside the legislature and the judiciary. In the narrower sense, it denotes the more explicitly 'political' elements of a government. Both legislature and executive are responsible for formulating government policy, and the executive is responsible to parliament for its implementation in democratic systems and most non-democratic ones. There are two distinct alternative principles underpinning their relationship: parliamentarianism and presidentialism, though there are an increasing number of hybrid systems that combine features of both.

Presidentialism versus Parliamentarianism

In a parliamentary system, the head of the government is almost always decided by the parliament. Thus **parliamentarianism** denotes the principle that parliament is the final arbiter in the choice of the head of the government. The UK is one of the best-known examples. The alternative principle is **presidentialism**, which means that the head of state, whether elected or not, either determines the choice of prime minister, if there is one as in France, or is personally the head of the executive branch of government, as in the USA. In the latter case, the direct election of the president by the whole nation confers a powerful mandate. If there is a separate prime minister, the parliament can offer advice and ratify the decision, but it does not have the power to make the decision itself. In practice the implication of this distinction determines the primary direction of loyalty of members of the executive. Ministers and officials are either primarily responsible for policy to the prime minister or to the president.

   In parliamentary systems the normal practice is that the prime minister is chosen because they can command a majority in the parliament. Where a single party has a majority of the seats in parliament, the choice is usually easy. Where no single party has a majority, this usually involves negotiations between several parties who try to form a coalition government, as happened recently in the UK and Australia. If that fails, then sometimes minority governments are formed which hold only a significant proportion of the seats in parliament, but not a majority. In that case, the government is obviously more vulnerable to defeat if the opposition can unite against it, but sometimes minority governments can survive for quite a long time by careful selection of policies.

13

These general structures of course hide wide variations in the ways that particular presidential and parliamentary executives operate. In the US, for example, presidents Johnson and Carter ran their administrations in quite different ways, even though they came from the same party. Among democracies there are widespread variations in the power of prime ministers relative to the rest of the cabinet. For example, while there is recurring comment upon the 'imperial' tendencies of British prime ministers, Japanese prime ministers still hold office on average for only one to two years, and often recently even less.

Linz (1992) argued that parliamentarianism is more advantageous for democracy because it leads to greater stability, whereas presidentialism is more fragile. (**See Box 13.1**.) He based most of his case upon the experience of Latin America, which has experienced a high degree of political instability, and where almost all regimes have been presidential. Linz identified one fundamental problem that caused this. Presidential democratic rule assumes a powerful executive based upon

KEY DEBATE BOX 13.1
Presidential versus Parliamentary Systems

New democracies are confronted by a fundamental immediate choice: should they opt for a presidential or a parliamentary system? It is not a simple choice. There are numerous examples of both types in the world. Each has strengths and weaknesses. There are also more and less successful versions of each. But whichever choice is made then structures other key characteristics of the system. Linz and Cheibub outline some of the key contrasting considerations.

> Perhaps the best way to summarize the basic differences between presidential and parliamentary systems is to say that while parliamentarianism imparts flexibility to the political process, presidentialism makes it rather rigid . . . [W]hile the need for authority and predictability would seem to favour presidentialism, there are unexpected developments—ranging from the death of the incumbent to serious errors in judgement committed under the pressure of unruly circumstances—that make presidential rule less predictable and often weaker than that of a prime minister.
>
> Presidentialism is ineluctably problematic because it operates according to the rule of 'winner-take-all'—an arrangement that tends to make democratic politics a zero-sum game, with all the potential for conflict such games portend . . . [Parliamentary elections] more often give representation to a number of parties. Power-sharing and coalition-forming are fairly common . . . By contrast, the conviction that he possesses independent authority and a popular mandate is likely to imbue a president with a sense of power and mission, even if the plurality that elected him is a slender one. Given such assumptions about his standing and role, he will find the inevitable opposition to his policies far more irksome and demoralizing than would a prime minister, who knows himself to be but the spokesman for a temporary governing coalition rather than the voice of the nation or the tribune of the people. (Linz, 1992: 122–3)
>
> True, presidential democracies are more unstable than parliamentary ones, but this instability is not caused by the incentives generated by presidentialism itself. Presidential

13

> democracies die not because the institutions are such that they compel actors to seek extra-constitutional solutions to their conflicts. The conflicts themselves should take some of the blame, since they are probably hard to reconcile under any institutional framework . . . One of the advantages of presidentialism is that it provides for one office with a national government. (Cheibub, 2007: 165, 168)

a mandate from the whole people, while at the same time legislators lay claim to popular mandates. Therefore, president and parliament are driven by their respective senses of equal public legitimacy into clashes over policy, even where they agree over the basic direction in which they would like government policy to go. It makes for a 'zero-sum' approach to policy-making, with each side striving for a winner-takes-all outcome.

By contrast, Linz (1992) argued, parliamentary systems tend to be inherently more flexible. They encourage actors holding different political positions to negotiate compromises because they have to reconcile their own individual mandates with the potential national mandate for government. They can also keep tighter discipline among their members in parliament because they can offer the prospect of promotion to ministerial posts as an incentive to avoid challenging government policies. He found confirmation of his argument in the very successful transition to parliamentary democracy that was achieved in post-Franco Spain. This differed strikingly from the experience of many less successful transitions to democracy in Latin America.

On the other hand, Persson and Tabellini (2007) have argued that presidential regimes have smaller governments and lower welfare expenditures than parliamentary ones. And Cheibub (2007) has argued that even if presidential systems appear less stable than parliamentary ones, the reason lies not in the different forms of government themselves, but in the political contexts in which they have to operate. He claimed that in Latin America, there is a tendency for military authoritarian regimes to be replaced by democratic presidential ones, and if the transitions break down, then it is because of a more fundamental crisis of authority than because of the type of system adopted. Thus, the balance of advantages of parliamentary systems as compared with presidential ones may be less clear-cut.

King (2015: 283) has remarked that the British system is an exception to Linz's argument. While being parliamentary, it hoards power at the centre rather than sharing it. 'The government of the UK is still meant to govern—full stop. It is not meant to, and does not, share power with others, certainly not with opposition parties. On almost every issue that arises, the government of the day is expected to take the initiative. The government of the day acts. Others react. Ministers decide. No-one else does. The political parties in coalition governments certainly share power between or among themselves, but they do not share it with anyone else.'

In any case, in practice there are hybrid versions that synthesize these two principles. One form of this is the increasing practice of parties choosing their leader through elections that involve their wider membership rather than simply their own parliamentary members. The main British parties now involve all of their membership in the selection of their leaders. Parties in some states, for example, Canada and Germany, have their prospective candidates for leader in parliament and therefore also for becoming prime ministers, elected by conventions of all party members rather than just the representatives of those parties in parliament. As both are federal states, this allows for the possibility of a national prime-ministerial candidate being chosen who holds a post in one of the state governments rather than from the national parliament. If this happens, then the same party has to find a way of enabling that person to become a member of the national parliament. In general, these reforms have the effect of strengthening the role of party members in selecting their leader, thereby weakening the power of their parliamentary colleagues.

Another hybrid system was devised in France, and has subsequently been copied in other states, including Russia. Here, the president is responsible for nominating the prime minister, but the prime minister must enjoy the confidence of parliament. If the parliament passes a vote of no confidence in the prime minister, then general elections have to be called. The original reasoning behind this system was to make the position of the prime minister quite strong and avoid the endless wrangling between small parties that was characteristic of the Fourth Republic up until 1958. On the other hand, it can also make for rivalry between president and prime minister that can divide the government, especially when the latter has ambitions to become president later and uses the post to advance those ambitions. For many years, the problem was further complicated by having different terms of office for the president and the prime minister. It was not uncommon for the president and the prime minister to come from different parties because they were elected at different times, when the relative popularity of parties had changed. This led to uneasy periods of cohabitation, when the rivalry between the two became much more intense and often paralysed decision-making. The same effect can be observed in other states where the terms of office of directly elected heads of state and of parliaments have diverged, sometimes leading to different parties controlling the two institutions, e.g. Taiwan and South Korea. The USA has often suffered from a similar problem since the Second World War. The Democrats dominated the House of Representatives between 1954 and 1994, but the Republicans controlled the presidency for more of that time, which led to frequent 'gridlock' in Washington. Even though elected presidents have constitutionally greater powers than prime ministers, and therefore ought to be able to overrule them, the fact that both can claim a mandate from the people and usually take advantage of that to appeal to public opinion to support their views means that the struggle is often quite tangled and intense. Principally for that reason, the French constitution was amended in 2000 so that both president and prime minister now hold office for identical five-year terms. The same happened in Taiwan in 2008.

13

KEY POINTS

- Parliaments perform a number of 'governmental' functions.
- They usually play an important role in the choice of head of government in presidential systems, and in parliamentary ones their role is decisive.
- Parliamentary and presidential systems may have different effects on the stability of democratic regimes.
- There are a number of hybrid systems that attempt to synthesize these two different forms of government.
- Cohabitation of an executive head of state and a prime minister from different parties can easily paralyse government decision-making.

CIVIL SERVICE

If you remember from Chapter 8 the share of GDP taken by the state in modern Western societies, you will appreciate the immense significance of ensuring that all that money is well spent, i.e. allocated to the highest priority projects and managed so as to ensure successful outcomes. Misguided or mismanaged projects have wasted billions of pounds in the UK alone over the last thirty years (King and Crewe, 2013). Probably no other branch of political science offers the possibility of saving large sums of money for taxpayers as policy-making studies.

➡ See Chapter 8, Table 8.1 for figures on general government expenditure.

In Chapter 8, we saw how the Western-type state spread across the globe in the nineteenth and twentieth centuries. One important factor in this was that state's bureaucratic mode of operation. Weber emphasized the impact of the innovation of the large modern bureaucracy, which transformed economic organizations such as companies, but did the same for government too through the greater consistency, impartiality, and effectiveness that it brought to policy-making. (**See Box 13.2**.)

The qualitative change that it brought is associated with what came to be known as the civil service in Britain. It was the Northcote–Trevelyan Report of 1854 that laid the basis for it. This recommended the establishment of a government service divided between those responsible for routine tasks and an administrative class responsible for policy formulation. It also recommended replacement of the previous system of recruitment of officials by personal recommendation to one based upon competitive examination. In principle, under the reform civil servants could move from one ministry to another without losing any of their entitlements, although in practice this did not happen so often. It served as a model for other states later setting up their own systems of administration and it eliminated corruption from the recruitment process. It survived more or less unchanged for a century.

➡ See Chapter 8 for a discussion of the rise of the modern state.

It was also an important innovation in the development of a democratic state. Officials were supposed to be politically neutral. They were no longer serving at the whim of the monarch, except in the most formal sense. In return for abstaining from active political commitment, officials were assured of protection against malicious or capricious dismissal. They were guaranteed tenure as professionals. Whichever party was in power was entitled to the best impartial advice on policy and how to implement it. Officials could and should offer this even if it was unpalatable to their political masters. This objectivity reinforced the ability of democratically elected leaders to translate their ideas into the most appropriate and most effective policy.

The British version of the impartiality of the civil service laid particular stress upon the impartiality of officials even at the highest levels. However, there can be problems for leaders who wish to

13

> **KEY QUOTE** BOX 13.2
> Max Weber on the Efficiency of Modern Bureaucratic Organization

The decisive reason for the advance of bureaucratic organization has always been its purely *technical* superiority over any other form of organization. The fully developed bureaucratic apparatus compares with other organizations exactly as does the machine with the non-mechanical modes of production. Precision, speed, unambiguity, knowledge of the files, continuity, discretion, unity, strict subordination, reduction of friction and of material and personal costs—these are raised to the optimum point in the strictly bureaucratic administration.
(Weber, 1968: 973)

introduce radical changes in policy, especially after a change of government, when they feel that the officials through whom they have to work are still committed to the old policies because they have implemented them as effectively as they could in the past. Other states have been more ready to allow political appointees to hold senior administrative posts. The French system of administration allows for political appointees to hold posts in the office of ministers, including and especially the *chef de cabinet*, i.e. the head of a minister's office. The USA still operates a 'spoils system' (i.e. to the victor, the spoils), which allows newly elected political leaders at various levels of government to fire and hire large numbers of officials, although their ability to do so was much curtailed in the twentieth century. Currently, every incoming president has around 9,000 positions as listed in the *US Government Policy and Support Positions* (the 'Plum Book') to which they can appoint supporters. This is a tiny proportion of the total number of federal employees which stands currently at 2.75 million, but it does represent all the most senior and politically sensitive posts. In continental Europe, political leaders can also appoint supporters to top posts in state corporations, which can include public broadcasting organizations—part of what is now called *lottizzazione* ('parcelling out') in Italy. In Britain, the Thatcher government also began down this road, introducing the possibility of ministers appointing political advisers who worked in the minister's private office—though not always harmoniously, if *Yes, Minister* is to be believed. During the Major government there were around thirty-five special advisers in Whitehall. The Blair government doubled that to around eighty (Richards, 2008: 180), and it rose to just over one hundred in the coalition government. Under Mrs May the figure fell to eighty-three in December 2016, thirty-two of whom worked for her (Adam, 2017).

Thus, European states developed forms of state administration that emerged from their own particular political, legal, and historical context, with the British version of the civil service operating the most stringent separation of civil servants from political roles. In general, in continental Europe they placed greater stress upon the role of law in establishing the relationship between the state and the bureaucracy, as law had played a greater role than in the UK in curbing the powers of autocratic regimes (Lynn, 2006: 58–9). It was associated with the German concept of the *Rechtsstaat*, i.e. a law-based state. According to Ginsborg (2001: 217), this is most evident in the case of Italy. An official Italian government report on administrative reform in 1993 estimated that, whereas in France there were 7,325 laws in force and in Germany 5,587 passed by the central government, in Italy there were 90,000 laws or regulations with legal status. Even though a later report by the Italian parliament put the figure closer to 40,000, this was still a significant excess. The effect is to place much greater constraints on the freedom of initiative of Italian civil servants and it still did not necessarily lead to a more impartial civil service. Italian officials found ways of favouring clientelistic or familial connections. Over a fifteen-year period in the 1980s and early 1990s, 60 per cent of the hirings of state officials were initially made on the basis of 'temporary' or 'precarious' contracts, which were not subject to the same strict regulations as permanent ones, but later these were converted into permanent employment (Ginsborg, 2001: 218).

There was also a greater tendency for administrative, political, and business elites to overlap. This is most evident in the case of France, where the École Nationale d'Administration has trained generations of administrators, some of whom have gone on to glittering careers in the state administration, others have gone into politics with four (Giscard d'Estaing, Chirac, Hollande, and Macron) later becoming president, while others have become top businessmen (though in 2019 Macron announced a plan to close it).

The colonial powers also transferred these forms of administration to their colonies. After independence the new states took them over for their inaugural administration. The difference that this could make can be seen in the different experiences of India and Nigeria before and after independence. In India the merit system of appointment by examination was introduced in 1853, i.e. slightly earlier than in Britain itself, and the Indian Civil Service (ICS) continued to attract high-quality applicants from Britain until independence nearly a century later. It was quite small—around the 1930s the colonial state employed nearly a million people to administer a population of 353 million, but the ICS itself only employed around 1,000 and by then half of the new recruits were already Indian rather than British. This relative paucity meant that its presence was uneven around the country. Nevertheless, according to Kohli (2004: 237–40), it made long-term contributions to Indian state formation for three reasons. First, it resisted provincialism and ensured consistent all-India administration. It ensured a unity that nationalists were happy to harness later. Second, its competence and efficiency enabled limited, good government. Third, it exemplified the idea that a modern state can put the public interest above private ones. All of this justified the praise that Weber had heaped upon modern bureaucratic administration.

The experience of the colonial state in Nigeria was quite different. 'In stark contrast to India, the civil service the British created in Nigeria reflected the minimal goals of British colonialism in that country and therefore was not very good. The numbers were relatively small; they were not well trained; and very few Nigerians were incorporated' (Kohli, 2004: 306). In fact the numbers of British officials were proportionately much greater in Nigeria than in India. In the latter there was one British official to every 353,000 in the population in the 1930s, while in Nigeria there was one to every 20,000. But the quality of the civil service in Nigeria was much lower. Recruitment continued to be on the basis of personal recommendation rather than competitive exam. Few Nigerians were recruited to the administrative service. Equally, much less emphasis was placed upon consistency of administration across the country as a whole, which meant lower resistance to division after independence (Kohli, 2004: 306–7).

13

> **KEY POINTS**
>
> - The creation of an impartial civil service developed first the effective power of the state and then later the stability of democracy.
> - European states developed different variants of the civil service and national traditions of administration.
> - Colonial powers transferred these forms of government organization to their colonies, with varying long-term success.

'EMBEDDED AUTONOMY' AND ECONOMIC POLICY-MAKING

The notion of a civil service closed off from the rest of society is, however, an over-simplification. Rather it would be more appropriate to borrow from developmental political economy and describe the role of the civil service with the term embedded autonomy. In other words, civil servants are insulated from pressures from the rest of society, but not completely isolated. Their position is embedded in a set of official regulations that guarantee it, but it also grows into a habit of mind, a form of political culture. Let us see how this emerged.

The term comes in particular from the successful development of East Asian states that is transforming the world economy. Nowadays there is fairly widespread agreement about the contribution that the developmental state, as introduced in Chapter 2 has made to those achievements. The success of the first of these, Japan, was subsequently attributed to the coordinating role of the Ministry of International Trade and Industry (MITI) from the 1960s (Johnson, 1982). Later accounts have challenged the leading role that Johnson attributed to MITI, arguing instead that MITI provided more of a coordinating role for major actors in the economy, while ideas on the desirable direction of policy emerged from industry representatives (Calder, 1993). Nevertheless, there is a consensus that MITI played an active role in the process.

➜ See Chapter 2 for a description of the developmental state.

Subsequently, the lessons of the state as autonomous actor in economic policy-making were learnt by other states in the region. South Korea, Taiwan, and Singapore all achieved economic breakthroughs. Evans (1995) then generalized from this some lessons about the reasons for their success. In particular he explained the prolonged economic success of South Korea in terms of the embedded autonomy that state economic decision-makers enjoyed vis-à-vis other economic actors. By this he meant that they were insulated, but not completely divorced, from pressures from various economic actors. If they had been completely divorced from the rest of society, then all of their plans would have risked unreality. They had to be aware of society's current needs and priorities. They also needed some detachment to determine what was in the public interest and follow it.

Nor is the term 'embedded autonomy' only relevant to developing economies. In their path-breaking study of economic systems in Europe and the USA, Hall and Soskice (2001) identified two distinct categories. On the one hand there is the Anglo-American 'liberal' model, which does indeed prescribe a more autonomous role for both the market and the state, as private capitalist actors determine how to interact with each other on the basis of expected comparative advantage. The contrast is with the coordinated market economies (CMEs) of continental Europe, particularly France and Germany. Here governments play a more active role in directing the economy through a substantial number of state-owned enterprises, in regulating competition (possibly making hostile takeovers more difficult), in managing labour relations, and in providing technical and professional education and training. In general, there is a more sceptical attitude in CMEs towards what Landier and Thesmar (2007) have characterized as 'the big, bad market'.

13

Yet such typologies are at best illustrative simplifications of reality. Even the category of the Anglo-American 'liberal' model is less homogeneous than this theory might suggest. Though the British and American governments often share similar perspectives on financial capital markets, this does not apply to welfare arrangements. Their respective policies have diverged as a result of different national political traditions and culture. Nowhere is this more evident than in policies governing the provision of health services, as can be seen from **Box 13.3**.

The importance of bureaucracies in government policy-making in all states has generated a whole range of theories to explain how they operate.

CASE STUDY BOX 13.3
Healthcare Provision in the UK and the USA

Photo 13.1 The National Health Service logo. *Shutterstock RF: Barry Barnes/Shutterstock.com*

In Britain, there is very widely shared support for a government-run National Health Service (NHS) which does not charge for most treatments at the point where it is delivered. Originally founded after the Second World War, the Labour Party still proclaims that this is one of its greatest achievements, and the NHS has been said to enjoy quasi-religious devotion in a secular age. According to a report from the Commonwealth Fund of New York (2013), in 2011 spending on the NHS in England accounted for 9.4 per cent of GDP, which was nearly the lowest among other European states, but it provided universal coverage. The same report showed that healthcare arrangements in Britain enjoyed the highest approval rating of eleven Organisation for Economic Co-ordination and Development (OECD) countries. In the USA, on the other hand, traditional political suspicion of 'big government' and socialism, added to lobbying from private insurance companies, means there is much greater support for private provision of healthcare, even though millions of Americans cannot afford serious medical procedures that would save their lives, or even basic insurance. According to the Commonwealth Fund, in 2011, 50 million Americans lacked health insurance, and a further 30 million were underinsured. Yet, the USA spent almost twice as much as the UK on healthcare, i.e. 17.7 per cent of GDP, and the Commonwealth Fund report showed that Americans had the second lowest approval rating for their system among the OECD countries, after Australia.

In practice, neither system is as internally homogeneous as the rhetoric would suggest. In the UK, adult patients are expected to contribute to prescriptions for medication, to dental care, and eye care. The state will sometimes pay for medical treatment in private hospitals if public ones are full. In the USA, the state provides basic healthcare for the very poor and the elderly through Medicaid and Medicare. In addition, healthcare in both countries is facing the same looming challenge of rising costs as populations age. In the UK, this has led both Labour and Conservative governments to experiment with reforms that are intended to achieve greater value for money, some of them involving quasi-market incentives. In the USA, the fact that tens of millions of Americans are unable to afford either expensive medical procedures or basic insurance led the Obama administration to introduce the Affordable Care Act in 2010, which was intended to expand government-backed health insurance and reduce costs.

Such innovations might suggest gradual convergence. Both systems are facing increasingly daunting challenges. Neither can afford not to change and adapt. No country will be able to afford ever-increasing resources, for healthcare as for anything else. Yet governments in both countries continue to provoke fury from opponents who allege that 'their' government is planning to adopt the system of the other. In the UK, Labour and Conservative governments have found themselves repeatedly forced to deny any intention of 'privatizing' the NHS or any part of it. In the USA, even though the Supreme Court ultimately accepted its constitutionality, 'Obamacare' continues to provoke implacable hostility from many Republicans, though left-wing politicians have again become more vociferous advocates of a state-run system. In both systems there is a wide spectrum of views on possible reforms, involving various combinations of private and public providers. Yet the healthcare care arena remains a striking manifestation of the way that ideology and national political culture can still dominate debates over public policy and drown out practical alternatives.

13

KEY POINTS

- The civil service needs a degree of embedded autonomy if it is to pursue the public interest, but it may realize this autonomy in different ways.
- Some policies, such as healthcare, attract considerable controversy based upon ideology and national political culture.

THEORIES OF BUREAUCRATIC POLICY-MAKING

Theories of bureaucratic policy-making have always revolved around what are now often termed principal–agent issues. This is a set of situations found in micro-economic game theory where the actions of two or more actors need to be harmonized but their interests do not necessarily converge. A set of incentives and/or rules needs to be devised so that they do converge, and activity is coordinated. In the case of a civil service this takes the form of one person (minister, 'the principal') or one group giving instructions to others ('agents') on what to do. This always involves a hierarchical relationship. Civil services (agents) are subordinated to the decisions of political leaders (principals). Of course, within the civil service, there are further nested hierarchies, with varying levels of principals having the authority to issue instructions for implementation by agents below them. Theories of bureaucratic policy-making have always sought to do two things: (i) clarify how bureaucracies actually implement decisions and (ii) identify ways that will enable principals better to ensure that policy outcomes conform to the original policy objectives.

Over time, theories of bureaucratic policy-making have evolved. Allison (1971) wrote a very influential work on the Cuban missile crisis which attempted to theorize the ways that the executives in both the USA, but especially the USSR, formulated policies and interacted. He identified three competing paradigms. The first hypothesized that government as a whole, and individual ministries, operated as a single rational actor, where outcomes corresponded to the original objectives. Research quickly showed, however, that this did not seem to be the practice, at least not uniformly. It left many uncertainties about key developments during the crisis which could not be easily explained or understood on this basis.

The second paradigm was what Allison called 'organizational process'. This hypothesized that, rather than government agencies designing new structures and practices to implement new policies, they adapted wherever possible existing structures and practices to the new circumstances. In other words, a great deal of policy-making consists of what Allison termed 'standard operating procedures' (SOPs). Of course, outsiders trying to decipher policies from outcomes without knowing the underlying procedures would have great difficulty in identifying the SOPs—as sometimes happened to the Americans when puzzling over Soviet moves that needed an urgent response. It is often the case that outsiders will not be able to penetrate the rules of the civil service, so that they will not be able to decide whether particular policy outcomes are the result of SOPs. Determining how large a part this plays in the overall picture of policy-making is bound to be problematic. However, it clearly cannot be the case that all policy-making is the product of SOPs. Hence, Allison formulated his third paradigm.

This focused instead on bureaucratic politics, i.e. the ways in which particular institutions interacted with each other that led to specific policy outcomes. This is a self-evidently reasonable thing to do, but reliably identifying this process is also as difficult for outsiders to penetrate as SOPs.

The Problem of Policy Innovation

To some extent, Allison's third paradigm became an orthodoxy for analysts of bureaucratic politics, but at the same time it exacerbated frustrations about the responsiveness of bureaucratic institutions to the decisions of their political masters. It seemed not merely to explain but also to legitimize the different agendas of public servants from ministers. Put together with the size of government bureaucracies and their reputation for Weberian efficiency, it seemed to pose an enormous problem for public policy innovation in general. *All* public administration seemed to be 'embedded autonomy'. How could it be reduced?

A great deal of analysis has been devoted to clarifying the extent to which policy innovation does occur. Kingdon (1995), for example, showed that there were 'windows of opportunity' for it to take place. Baumgartner and Jones (1993) introduced the notion of 'punctuated equilibrium' in US politics, i.e. periods of policy continuity interrupted by bouts of change. Innovation could be the product of activity by alternative policy-makers, media pressure, or simply changing circumstances. But if one wanted to theorize ways of making change happen, how could one go about it?

One of the most influential approaches was emphasis upon the principal–agent relationship, at a time when economic game theory was becoming more influential in the social sciences. It stressed the need for clear specification of objectives by principals for agents, and an appropriate selection of incentives and sanctions to elicit the desired response. As it happened, the broader context of policy-making was also changing then. This too changed perspectives on policy-making and what it could be expected to achieve. Serious economic crises in the 1970s and 1980s concentrated the minds of Western governments on reducing their expenditure and getting better value for money. Neo-liberal ideas on economic reform gradually spread from the USA and displaced Keynesian approaches to policy-making. Then the collapse of communism opened the way for initiatives for government restructuring in new parts of the world.

What emerged was what came to be known as the New Public Management (NPM). This new paradigm of managerialism explicitly emphasized incentives, competition, and performance instead of the traditional values of rule-based hierarchies. 'The mantra has grown in volume: the bureaucratic paradigm is dead; long-live quasi-markets and quangos, flattened hierarchies and continuous improvement, competitive tendering and subsidiarity' (Lynn, 2006: 2). As will be obvious from this terminology, a lot of the ideas for reform came from economics and from business management.

For some critics this was fundamentally mistaken. It was based upon a confusion over the different purposes of public and private institutions. NPM implies that 'the public sector is not distinctive from the private sector' and that its practitioners are 'self-interested, utility maximizing administrators' like corporate executives (Olsen, 2003: 511, 522). It challenged the traditional notion of the impartial, public-spirited civil service.

➡ See the discussion of the modern state in Chapter 8.

Nevertheless, it has been an extremely influential approach to public sector reform. Toonen (2001: 186) has identified six features, as can be seen from **Box 13.4**.

There is a paradox about these reforms, however. The wave has spread from the more developed countries and international aid agencies now encourage developing countries to learn lessons from it. As Ourzik (2000: 44), a Moroccan professor of administration, said in an address to the African Training and Research Centre in Administration for Development:

> The role of the State has been shaped by a trend which is today universal, that of a State as an enabler rather than a doer, a State that regulates instead of manages. Like a genuine orchestra conductor of social and economic activities, the State is required to promote private initiative without stifling or restricting it. A State that is at once modest and ambitious, since the population still expects much of it: it must, while ensuring that overall balances are maintained, protect the environment, ensure proper land-use management, put in place new infrastructures, provide health and education services, etc.

Yet the context in which these ideas were originally formulated was countries where civil services were relatively well established with traditions of impartiality and incorruptibility. In the developing world these traditions are not always so strong. True, the Indian Administrative Service retained the elite ethos of its colonial predecessor and until the 1990s maintained a firm grip upon the country and its strong public sector of the economy. Indeed, there were regular complaints about the extent of the stifling 'licence raj' of permits that they imposed upon the economy. The

> **BOX** 13.4
> The Features of New Public Management

- A business-oriented approach to government;
- 'a quality- and performance-oriented approach to public management';
- an emphasis on improved public service delivery and functional responsiveness;
- an institutional separation of public demand functions (councils, citizens' charters), public provision (public management boards), and public service production functions (back offices, outsourcing, agencification, privatization);
- a linkage of public demand provision, and supply units by transactional devices (performance management, internal contract management, corporatization, intergovernmental covenanting and contracting, contracting out), and quality management; and
- wherever possible, the retreat of bureaucratic institutions in favour of an intelligent use of markets and commercial market enterprises (deregulation, privatization, commercialization, and marketization) or virtual markets (internal competition, benchmarking, competitive tendering).

challenge of NPM was particularly appropriate there, as the state moved towards deregulation of the economy after an economic crisis in 1991.

In Africa, however, there were many problems. On the one hand, by the early 1990s many African states were confronted with the need to reduce what had become bloated state bureaucracies. International financial institutions such as the World Bank were advocating NPM as a coherent way of doing this (Adamolekun, 2007). On the other hand, these states were also suffering from widespread official corruption. NPM did not explicitly foster an official ethic of incorruptibility. Rather, it assumed that this had already been inculcated. Nigeria can be taken as a serious, but not untypical example. As reported by Salisu (2003: 171–2), there are problems with the internal organization of the Nigerian civil service: overstaffing and poor remuneration of employees, poor assessment of labour needs, inadequate training, and lack of qualified technical support. In addition there has been considerable political interference in personnel administration, which has bred apathy, idleness, and corruption. Although there have been several attempts to reorganize the structure and operation of the service so that incentives and performance are better aligned, the problem of eradicating corruption remains huge, so there is a real danger in seeking to transfer NPM here that, by treating civil servants as if they were business executives, it will undo previous efforts to inculcate an ethic of incorruptibility.

KEY POINTS

- Policy innovation in government bureaucracies is extremely complex and often unpredictable.
- Theories of public administration have always revolved around principal–agent relations.
- NPM borrowed its basic principles from business studies and economics.
- It may undermine efforts to eradicate corruption in public administration in developing countries.

EMERGENCE OF AGENCIES

One key element of the NPM reforms has been the hiving off of government departments and functions to newly created separate agencies—which is encapsulated in the ugly term 'agencification'. In the UK this saw the emergence of institutions such as the Child Support Agency and the Driver and Vehicle Licensing Agency. The underlying rationale was on the one hand to simplify the tasks of government administration, and on the other more clearly to establish incentives for good performance which could lead to greater rewards for those who deliver it. In one sense it merely extended a well-established principle of public administration which is to separate 'policy' from 'implementation'. However, what was new was the proliferation of 'outside' agencies that were not directly under the control of those who made the policy. Most were hived off from existing administrative structures, though the extent to which some 'new' agencies were really separate from ministries was sometimes opaque. Implementation was to be the responsibility of a different principal, who established distinct rules and procedures for its own agents. This undermined the homogeneity of a civil service with common standards and operating procedures. The control over the performance of the agencies was often to be framed in the form of targets for desirable outcomes. Achievement of them was the standard by which the agencies would be judged. Thus, the setting of targets became an expanding feature of administrative leadership.

Talbot (2004: 6) has concluded that there are really three dimensions to the idea of 'agency':

- structural disaggregation and/or the creation of 'task-specific' organizations;
- performance 'contracting'—some form of performance target setting, monitoring, and reporting; and
- deregulation (or more properly reregulation) of controls over personnel, finance, and other management matters.

It represented a move towards what Rhodes (1997: 87–111) has called the 'hollowing out' of the state, and what Bevir and Rhodes (2006: 74–86) have termed the 'decentring' of governance. This reflected a trend of devolving both decision-making authority to Scotland, Wales, and Northern Ireland, and also implementation authority to agencies outside Whitehall. For them it reflected a gradual change towards more autonomous steering of society by actors outside the government. This would mean greater policy-making from, if not below, at least lower down in the system. Governance meant steering society rather than guiding it, and now there would be more hands on the steering wheel.

One type of reform that was introduced involved the creation of public-private partnerships between government agencies and private companies to provide services or infrastructure, such as hospitals. Under such arrangements, private-sector institutions would provide the finance for new projects in return for contracts ensuring profits for years ahead. This was touted as a way of expanding infrastructure without having to raise taxes or for the state to borrow more. But critics alleged that it provided an opportunity for nimble and devious entrepreneurs to extract excess profits by running rings around less agile, trusting government administrators, or worse, for corruption through collusion. **Box 13.5** illustrates some of the attractions and drawbacks of public-private partnerships.

13

➡ Also see Chapter 2 for a discussion of the 'hollowing out' thesis.

CASE STUDY BOX 13.5
The Costly Shambles of the Public-Private Partnership
for the London Underground

Photo 13.2 A London Underground tube sign. *Shutterstock RF via DAM: Tupungato/*
Shutterstock.com

13

When New Labour won the general election in 1997, the London Underground was in a dreadful mess. In their manifesto, both the Conservative and Labour parties had promised radical reform. The Conservatives had proposed full-scale privatization. New Labour wanted to demonstrate policy originality. It also wanted to show it was business-friendly and it believed that the private sector was often more efficient than the public—certainly the management of the Tube was, in Labour's eyes, incompetent. It wanted to rebut allegations it was a high-tax party. Secretly, New Labour leaders were afraid that the party's likely candidate in the forthcoming elections for mayor of London—Ken Livingstone—would want to lavish public money on the network and they wanted to pre-empt him, in case it prejudiced their attempts to demonstrate that Labour was not obsessed by old-fashioned high-spending public ownership. The solution was the idea of a public-private partnership—a new way for private enterprise and the state to cooperate without pushing up public spending. The London Underground became a flagship project for New Labour's Third Way—between traditional capitalism and socialism. It met a whole range of policy objectives.

The idea was to sell the infrastructure rights for individual Tube lines (individual stations, etc.) to three consortia of companies, who would operate them for up to thirty years. The companies would commit to investing in infrastructure and service them in return for a guaranteed rate of profit. If they made losses, the companies would bear the cost. In theory, it should have ensured more stable funding than when the Tube was financed out of the overall local government budget, where its share could fluctuate wildly from one year to the next (Wolmar, 2002: 106).

Implementation, however, became a nightmare. Because of the novelty of the idea, lots of (expensive) consultants had to be hired to flesh out the details. The companies required detailed legal contracts to guarantee their rights, which involved large numbers of (expensive) City lawyers. The contracts totalled 28,000 pages. Again, because of the novelty and importance of the project for New Labour, several ministers and politicians wanted to keep their hands on the steering wheel. It was far removed from the NPM ideal of clear and simple principal-agent relations. Accountability was far too diffuse to be effective. There was a high turnover of administrators, so expertise was constantly being undermined. The companies in the consortia, having agreed on their original bid, failed to agree on much else afterwards. When they failed to deliver to contract, they blamed each other, or factors 'beyond their control'. They claimed compensation from the government and, even though they were contractually liable for losses, the government found that the reputation of the project was so bad, no-one else was willing to bid to replace the operators, so the government had to compensate them for fear of the worse nightmare of the Tube having to close.

In the end, the arrangements collapsed in 2007 and the public entity Transport for London took control. The cost to the public is difficult to quantify, but King and Crewe (2013: 221) put it anywhere between £2.5 billion and £30 billion, which makes it one of the most expensive failures in recent years.

It was a disaster that was hushed up. No minister lost their job. The Labour government was re-elected in 2001 and 2005. As one of the top people involved put it to King and Crewe (2013: 221): 'You couldn't make it up. You couldn't make it up.'
(Based on King and Crewe, 2013: 201–21; Wolmar, 2002)

13

As this case study shows, it certainly enabled greater policy autonomy and hindered parliamentary scrutiny and accountability. Governance meant steering society rather than guiding it and now there would be more hands on the steering wheel.

On the other hand, reformers touted an additional potential benefit of the reforms, namely. a greater priority for the delivery of services as an activity in its own right. 'Delivery' became a mantra during the later years of the Blair government. Barber (2007) was the Director of the Number 10 Delivery Unit and he has produced a very insightful insider's account of the procedures that were adopted and the lessons that could be learnt for further reforms. For him, better implementation is essential if the huge sums of money spent on public services are to be politically sustainable (Barber, 2007: 294), especially as, according to King and Crewe (2013), misguided or mismanaged projects have wasted billions of pounds in the UK alone over the last thirty years. However, for the reforms to become permanent, civil servants would have to internalize them and make them the basis of their official behaviour. Blair believed this could only be achieved if the prime minister's office acquired greater power to supervise the implementation processes. Savoie (2010) suggests that this centralization of power is common in modern democracies.

However, the separation of policy-making from implementation added to problems of accountability—as we have seen in **Box 13.5**. Though an elaborate array of techniques came to be developed to clarify ways in which implementation agencies could be made accountable to the policy principals (Lynn, 2006: 139–40), accountability of policy-makers to parliament was more difficult to enforce. If particular targets were not met, was it the fault of principals who had set unrealistic ones? Was it due to lack of commitment on the part of the 'agents', i.e. the officials? Or were the targets contradictory or incompatible? If so, whose fault would it be, and who would decide? And when (given that the flaws in large-scale projects may take several years to become clear, by which time all the decision-makers may have moved on)? Also, the greater the incentives for meeting targets, and also the penalties for failure to do so, the greater the danger of neglect of other work where targets were more difficult to devise, but which might still be regarded as important. It could lead to perverse effects. The whole process reduced the salience of politics in policy-making and made the whole policy process more technocratic. It attenuated the whole notion of ministerial responsibility.

KEY POINTS

- The emergence of agencies charged with implementation of policies formulated elsewhere facilitated concentration upon delivery.
- In Britain the prime minister's office became more directly involved in pushing through the reforms.
- There was a heavy reliance upon targets as performance indicators.
- This complicated the problems of ministerial accountability.

GOVERNANCE AND GOOD GOVERNANCE

As will be clear from the previous discussion, an increasing trend in political science is to blur the old distinction between state and society. Instead of focusing upon government, now there is greater stress upon governance. However, there are a variety of interpretations of its meaning. Pierre and Peters (2000: 1) use the term to focus on 'the capacity of government to make and implement policy—in other words, to steer society'. They emphasize, however, that sometimes the term is used to describe the structure of decision-making. From this perspective, people conceptualize it as hierarchies, or as markets, or as networks, or as communities, or as combinations of these. Sometimes it is used to concentrate on processes of steering and coordinating. And sometimes it is used rather as an analytical approach, which questions the normally accepted meaning of terms such as 'government' and 'power', as well as the distinction between state and society. These diverse uses in themselves cause confusion (Pierre and Peters, 2000: 14–27).

By contrast, the UN Economic and Social Commission for Asia and the Pacific (UNESCAP) has defined governance simply as 'the process of decision-making and the process by which decisions are implemented (or not implemented)' (UNESCAP, 2009). Actually, the term does not have to be used in a political context at all. For example, it is also used in the term 'corporate governance', i.e. the processes by which companies make decisions. However, when involving the state, it stretches to cover non-governmental participants in the decision-making and implementing processes. Indeed, it can include circumstances when non-state actors may take the lead in formulating policies in a particular issue area, or even in their implementation. An example of the latter would be private security organizations that are hired to protect government offices or to provide protection for a country's nationals abroad, such as in Iraq. Because of their importance for the implementation process, this also gives them the freedom to make greater inputs into the policy that they are supposed to be implementing.

A related term that is now much used in international politics is good governance. Governments in the developing world are often encouraged to practise this, sometimes as a condition for foreign aid. Again, it emphasizes the importance of non-state actors as well as government in decision-making. UNESCAP has identified eight features of this term. (See **Box 13.6**.)

UNESCAP accepts that few states meet all of these criteria, but emphasizes that without progress in most of them, real sustainable development is not possible.

Kayizzi-Mugerwa (2003: 17) presents the concept of good governance in more concrete terms, focusing more explicitly on institutions. According to him it includes:

1. An effective state, that enables economic growth and equitable distribution;
2. Civil societies and communities that are represented in the policy-making process, with the state facilitating political and social interaction and promoting societal cohesion and stability; and
3. A private sector that plays an independent and productive role in the economy.

This summary recapitulates the principle underlying the more general concept of governance, namely that it involves wider sections of society. The steering of society implicit in the term governance, and even more so in *good* governance, cannot be successfully performed without the active involvement of civil society and the private sector.

13

BOX 13.6
The Elements of Good Governance

- Participation, i.e. encouragement for the involvement of a wide range of actors in making and implementing decisions. It would contribute to, but does not actually require, democracy.
- Rule of law, i.e. clear, legal frameworks that are enforced impartially. It implies respect for human rights, an independent judiciary, and incorruptible police.
- Transparency, i.e. open decision-making procedures.
- Responsiveness, i.e. policies that are formulated and implemented in ways that respond to social needs.
- Consensus-oriented, i.e. decision-making through mediation between different interests.
- Equity and inclusiveness, i.e. opportunities for all, especially the most vulnerable, to improve the conditions under which they live.
- Effectiveness and efficiency, i.e. good policies to make the best use of available resources and protect the environment.
- Accountability, i.e. decision-makers, both public and private, must be responsible for all their decisions to society as a whole, and there must be procedures for making sure that this happens.

> **KEY POINTS**
>
> • This change of focus reflected a broader perspective of focusing upon governance rather than just government.
>
> • This blurs or ignores the distinction between state and society.
>
> • Developing states are encouraged to introduce and practise good governance, which also downplays the state–society distinction.
>
> • Good governance presumes wide societal involvement in the formulation and implementation of policies, as well as accountability to the people for their outcomes.

POLICY COMMUNITIES, 'IRON TRIANGLES', AND ISSUE NETWORKS

The focus of this chapter has gradually expanded from the civil service to the totality of policy-making and steering processes. One other concept that links the two together is that of policy communities. This is an analytical concept drawn from elitist understandings of politics, which originated in the study of British politics in the 1970s (Thatcher, 2001: 7940). It was based upon the assumption that policy-making in a particular area emerged out of the interaction of officials responsible for policy in a certain area and interest groups. It argued that out of this regular interaction the views of officials and interest groups gradually converged. They tended to see issues and solutions to problems in congruent ways. Thus, the policies that emerged were likely to enjoy greater legitimacy and have greater effectiveness because of this convergence of perspectives.

➡ See Chapter 3 for an exploration of elitism.

13

Another version of the same idea emerged from the study of US politics at about the same time. This was the notion of iron triangles. These are groups of officials, politicians, and outside experts who together formulate a set of policies towards a particular issue area. The difference from policy communities is the more explicit inclusion of politicians in them. A long-established feature of politics on Capitol Hill is the lobbying of members of Congress by business organizations, and sometimes the lobbying of some members of Congress by others. This process of lobbying helps to establish a commonality of views on policy.

A variant of this process can be found in Japan, which reflects the greater organizational power of parties. There, the Liberal Democratic Party (LDP) has been in power almost continuously since 1955. Over the years it established powerful policy committees that meet regularly with civil service counterparts to devise new policies. This has created what have been termed policy 'tribes' (*zoku*), that have had a distinctive impact upon Japanese policies because of the LDP's long hold on power. The LDP created committees for specific areas of public policy, e.g. welfare, construction, and agriculture, that met regularly with representatives from the sector concerned and with ministry officials to discuss the operation of existing policies and the formulation of new ones. Traditionally they have had great opportunities to set the parameters for policy in a given area and also resist changes that were proposed from outside or above. These 'tribes' have had a great impact on policies, often obstructing change that the prime minister would wish to introduce (Kim, 2006).

There is a problem, however, about these theories. In the urge to identify the commonality of views that emerges through close interaction, their proponents sometimes exaggerated the degree of this closeness as compared with other kinds of groupings in the political system, e.g. political parties, or more formalized structures of policy-making. Also, they did not necessarily allow for change taking place. The tighter the implied connections, the more difficult it was to identify spaces through which new or alternative ideas might penetrate. Once again it raised the issue of how to achieve public-interest policy innovation. Clearly, policy alternatives do periodically emerge in every issue area, so there developed instead the looser concept of issue networks. As Thatcher (2001: 7940) describes it:

> An issue network consists of a large number of issue-skilled 'policy activists' drawn from conventional interest groups and sections of the government, together with academia and certain professions but also comprising expert individuals regardless of formal training. Participants are constantly changing, and their degree of mutual commitment and interdependence varies, although any direct material interest is often secondary to emotional or intellectual commitment.

Building on this insight, subsequent theorizing attempted to identify typologies of networks to identify different types and to show how they interact in the overall policy process.

One of the best-known examples of such a typology was proposed by Rhodes (1997: 38). It had five elements that represented a continuum of organizational strength, running from weak (issue networks, sharing only common ideas) to strong (policy communities that share both ideas and organization):

1. Issue networks, which tend to be unstable, with large numbers of members and limited vertical interdependence;
2. Producer networks, most often sharing economic interests, which tend to have fluctuating membership, limited vertical interdependence, and to serve the interests of producers;
3. Intergovernmental networks, which tend to have limited membership, limited vertical interdependence, and extensive horizontal articulation;
4. Professional networks, which are more stable, with highly restricted membership, vertical interdependence, limited horizontal articulation, and serve the interests of the profession; and
5. Policy or territorial communities, which are much more stable, with highly restricted membership, vertical interdependence, and limited horizontal articulation.

In general, issue networks tend to be larger, covering a wide range of interests, with fluctuating contacts between members, with regular disagreements between members, with only limited resources as a group, and with uneven powers, resources, and access. By contrast, policy communities have much more limited membership, are more focused on economic or professional issues, have frequent, high-quality interaction of members, who share basic values and have access to common resources, and have a hierarchical leadership that can deliver support from members to government (Rhodes, 1997: 44).

KEY POINT

- Where officials and non-governmental actors are jointly involved in policy-formulation and implementation, the nature of their relations can be located somewhere on a continuum stretching from issue networks to policy communities.

CONCLUSION: TOWARDS A NETWORK STATE?

The focus of this chapter has widened from an initial concern with civil administration to the broader context in which policy is formulated. In previous decades civil services brought efficiencies and effectiveness to governmental policy-making, especially in Western Europe and the USA. More recently, their role has come to be more questioned by people both inside and outside government, as governments have sought to reduce their own size and increase efficiency. In Africa, issues of reforming governance became a higher priority for three not dissimilar reasons. First, there was a recognition that weaknesses in governance were limiting the pay-offs to economic reform. Second, the collapse of communism deprived some African states of aid. Third, Western donors could become more demanding in the conditions that they expected recipients to observe, because there were no longer any rivals in the East (Kayizzi-Mugerwa, 2003: 20).

The result has been a widening of the focus in studies devoted to policy-making. They now devote much more attention to non-governmental actors, both individuals and groups. There is a changed awareness about the primacy of the state in many areas of policy, and this in turn has weakened the emphasis upon the authority of the state to impose its will and expect compliance. How far this change can be reconciled with the persistent need to establish effective and clean administration where this does not already exist in developing countries remains to be seen.

Nevertheless, as was indicated in Chapter 2, there is a growing literature that envisages a hollowing out of the nation-state as a response to globalization. Though some, such as Weiss (1998), would contest the inevitability of such changes, we have seen in this chapter the emergence of converging approaches to administrative reform in various parts of the world that might further contribute to this process. The stress upon both governance and good governance implies a re-balancing of relationships between state and society in favour of the latter. Various commentators have looked forward to a state of the future that will look more like a market-based network than a traditional Weberian bureaucratic hierarchy (Bobbitt, 2002). Castells (1998) visualizes the European Union as a network state of the future.

Kamarck has gone so far as to claim that we are witnessing the end of government as we have known it, at least in the USA, and the emergence of a new kind of state. She looks forward to two things: (i) 'government by network'; and (ii) 'government by market'. 'Government by network' she interprets as follows:

> The state makes a conscious decision to implement policy by creating a network of nongovernmental organizations through its power to contract, fund or coerce. In government by network, the state itself decides to create, activate, or empower a network for the purpose of implementing a policy. Thus the network is a self-conscious creation of a policymaker or a group of policymakers rather than a naturally occurring part of the greater society. (Kamarck, 2007: 100–1)

As for government by market, here she means something broader than a government or state that just relies upon markets to run the economy, though that is subsumed in it. As she explains it: 'In . . . government by market, the work of government involves few, if any, public employees and no public money . . . the government uses state power to create a market that fulfils a public purpose' (2007: 127). Here her examples are drawn from environmental policy, where the state creates markets so as to achieve publicly desired ends, e.g. trading in carbon emissions and reducing pollution. It could also include the creation of markets in schooling, so as to put pressure on failing schools, or it could be used to stimulate the provision of welfare services without relying upon state providers.

This is an imaginative sketch of a future state that is very far removed from the Weberian-type bureaucracy, though Rhodes (1996) already indicated the difficulties such network organization would pose for integrated public policy. How far can networks provide structuration for policies as compared with more organized institutions? Not only does it mean more hands on the steering wheel of the state, but also it means multiple steering wheels. Clearly, networks do not have the same capacity to impose or implement policies except by persuasion. And Savoie (2010) has remarked on the lowered prestige and morale of civil servants that has resulted from the reforms. How far the traditional features of civil services such as hierarchies will survive remains to be seen, as do the ways in which they interact with the new networks that they have helped to create. Certainly, the legal basis of state administration in continental Europe will not be easily eroded.

However, it is a strong reminder of the significance of groups and organizations outside the state and civil service in determining the way that governance operates. The next chapter will deal with the roles of interest groups and the media.

KEY QUESTIONS

1. If you were establishing a new democratic system, which type would you prefer and why?
2. If presidential democracies are more prone to collapse, how do you explain the longevity of the American presidential system?
3. If parliamentary democracies are more stable, why did Italy have fifty-six governments between 1945 and 2000?
4. Can a valid distinction be drawn between the values and motivations of public administration and business management?
5. How would you set about trying to reform the healthcare system of the country where you live so that it can cope with the various multiple challenges?
6. Is it unrealistic to expect civil servants to be politically impartial?
7. Should state security functions be devolved to private contractors? What are the dangers?
8. How can civil services be made incorruptible? Will NPM help?
9. Is good governance a Western imposition on the developing world? Did the West have it at similar levels of development? Did it matter then?
10. What are the advantages and disadvantages of the 'spoils' system in the USA?
11. How can agencies and officials be made accountable under the NPM?
12. What would a network state look like? In what ways would it differ from more traditional states?

FURTHER READING

Barber, M. (2007), *Instruction to Deliver* (London: Politico's).

This is a fascinating insider's account of the Blair government's Delivery Unit, illuminated by comparisons of the administrative load of the prime minister today with earlier periods.

Barber, M. (2015), *How to Run a Government so that Citizens Benefit and Taxpayers Don't Go Crazy* (London: Allen Lane).

An update on general principles of 'deliverology'.

Kamarck, E. C. (2007), *The End of Government . . . as We Know it: Making Public Policy Work* (Boulder, CO: Lynne Rienner).

This details the prospects for state administration transformed by new technology.

King, A. and Crewe, I. (2013). *The Blunders of our Governments* (London: Oneworld)

A salutary collection of case studies that show how even policies devised with the best of intentions can go spectacularly wrong in implementation.

Lijphart, A. (ed.) (1992), *Parliamentary versus Presidential Government* (Oxford: Oxford University Press).

The argument in favour of a parliamentary system.

Lynn, L. E., Jr (2006), *Public Management: Old and New* (London: Routledge).

This is an account of changing approaches to public management.

Pierre, J. and Peters, B. G. (2000), *Governance, Politics and the State* (Basingstoke: Palgrave).

This is a good introduction to the concept of governance and its implications.

Rhodes, R. A. W. (2000), 'The Governance Narrative: Key Findings and Lessons from the ESRC's Whitehall Programme', *Public Administration*, 78(2): 345–63.

A summary of the findings of a very influential research programme on reforming public administration in the UK.

Savoie, D. J. (2010), *Power: Where is it?* (Montreal and Kingston: McGill-Queen's UP).

A critical analysis of increasing difficulty in ensuring the accountability of public officials in Canada and elsewhere stemming in part from the NPM reforms.

13

 For additional material and resources, please visit the Online Resources at: **www.oup.com/he/garner4e**

CIVIL SOCIETY, INTEREST GROUPS, AND THE MEDIA

READER'S GUIDE

This chapter will cover a selection of dimensions of political life outside the state and political parties. First, it will look at the very popular and broad concept of 'civil society', which encompasses the activity of apparently non-political actors, certainly not 'politically' organized actors, in pursuing their goals. After that it will present interest groups and also corporatism. Next will come an introduction to 'infrapolitics', i.e. politics from below, as presented by political anthropologists, particularly with regard to politics in the developing world. Then we will turn to the role of the media in political life and democracy. Finally, we will consider the impact of new communications technologies on political life, and the extent to which they are transforming its practices or may do so in the future.

CIVIL SOCIETY

This term was originally mentioned in the Introduction. Robertson (1993: 69) defined it as follows:

> Civil society is the framework within which those without political authority live their lives—economic relationships, family and kinship structures, religious institutions and so on. It is a purely analytic concept because civil society does not exist independently of political authority, nor vice versa, and, it is generally believed, neither could long continue without the other; therefore, no very clear boundary can be drawn between the two.

A term originally formulated in the eighteenth century, civil society became much more widely used at the end of the 1980s when a number of regimes were overturned by tides of apparently unorganized, previously non-political forces. Some of these took place in the Far East. In 1986, the authoritarian President Ferdinand Marcos of the Philippines was overthrown by waves of 'people power' demonstrations in Manila supporting Corazon Aquino, the widow of one of his most famous victims, Benigno Aquino. In 1987, demonstrations in Seoul destabilized the plans for an orderly handover of power by South Korean President Chun Doo Hwan to his chosen successor, General Roh Tae Woo. This set in train a sequence of events which led to the reintroduction of democracy. In spring 1989, a demonstration in Beijing by thousands of students mourning the death of the Chinese Communist Party's former General Secretary, Hu Yaobang, turned into a massive challenge to the nation's leaders on Tiananmen Square and in many other cities of China that drew in hundreds of thousands of protestors and was only put down on 4 June with the loss of thousands of lives.

The biggest demonstration of the potential power of civil society, however, came in the autumn of that year in Eastern Europe. It was civil society that brought down the communist regimes there and hastened the end of the Soviet Union in 1991. This was despite the fact that those regimes had had decades to organize the repression of opponents and to establish very powerful secret police forces. They had brutally suppressed demonstrations in Hungary in 1956 and Czechoslovakia in 1968, which served as enduring lessons. The victory of the demonstrators in Eastern Europe was achieved with minimal casualties. It was a striking affirmation of the potential political power of civil society, if roused.

They had achieved this despite—or more likely because—other more 'regular' political groupings such as parties had been relentlessly repressed. The communist regimes had devoted enormous resources to identifying, dispersing, and punishing organized opposition, and yet it had all been in vain. The more amorphous civil society had overcome it—for more details, **see Box 14.1**.

After this, civil society became the focus of intense attention, as it seemed to offer the promise of an alternative, more consensual, non-coercive democratic politics. For some it acquired a normative status. It became a metaphor for the good society. (**See Box 14.2**.)

Would-be reformers started looking at other authoritarian regimes to try to identify analogous groupings to those in Eastern Europe in the hope that they could achieve similar results. It did not matter whether these groups were well organized or agreed on their long-term goals. They contained the germ of freedom, if only some way could be found to incubate it. Policy-makers in Western governments and international charities had become disenchanted with giving aid to governments in the developing world which had failed to reduce poverty and, in particular, they

➡ See Chapter 15, Box 15.1 for more discussion of the fall of communism in Poland.

CASE STUDY BOX 14.1
Civil Society and the Collapse of Communism

Photo 14.1 The fall of the Berlin wall. *Alamy: Agencja Fotograficzna Caro/Alamy Stock Photo*

By 1989, the communist regimes in Eastern Europe were beset by mounting difficulties. Their leaderships were ageing and the economies were stagnating. The regimes themselves had been imposed by the USSR after the Second World War and lacked popular legitimacy. Attempts by individual states to extricate themselves from Soviet tutelage had provoked brutal repression in Hungary in 1956 and Czechoslovakia in 1968. All attempts at organized political opposition were crushed.

However, the Soviet Union was descending into turmoil after four years of *perestroika*, which was failing to deliver the promised economic revival. The new Soviet leader, Gorbachev, no longer seemed to offer the same unconditional support for East European leaders in return for political loyalty as Brezhnev had done. He started pressuring them to reform their systems as he had done.

The crisis first broke out in Poland, where the regime was among those most beset by economic and political problems. There the independent trade union, Solidarity, which had been challenging the regime throughout the decade despite martial law, forced the government into round-the-table negotiations over reforms. As the price for agreeing to participate in what were expected to be rigged elections, it extracted an agreement for its own legalization. However, contrary to everyone's expectations, including its own, it won all but one of the seats that it

→

could contest in the elections in June. This fatally undermined the legitimacy of the communist rulers and, by September, Solidarity had become the dominant actor in a new government.

The ferment of expectation and resistance spread to other states. East Germans tried to flee to the West by travelling to Hungary and seeking asylum in the West German embassy. The Hungarian authorities were reluctant to suppress them, when Moscow would not commit itself unequivocally to support such action. Their indecision was noted and spread to other capitals. It further encouraged hopes of change. The aged East German leader, Honecker, was deposed, and his successors began also to make conciliatory noises. Demonstrations started taking place and, when they were not repressed, involved masses of people. By November the demonstrations had spread to Prague, and there the authorities quickly capitulated with virtually no loss of life in what came to be known as the 'Velvet Revolution'. Change was remarkably peaceful and amicable. Also in November, the new East German leadership abandoned rather feeble attempts to keep the Berlin Wall closed. With the Wall open, it was no longer possible to prevent people crossing to the West. After that, resistance in most East European regimes crumbled. The last to do so was Romania in mid-December, although it was accompanied by street fighting and the filmed execution of the former dictator Ceausescu and his wife.

The regimes collapsed remarkably easily after over forty years of repression. Through a combination of circumstances, they had become sclerotic, brittle, and weak. However, it had taken the courage and heroism of tens of thousands of demonstrators in all the states to reveal this by challenging the authorities. Although largely not organized beforehand, they quickly found ways of cooperating decisively. It was a time and movement of joyous good humour or, as one account put it, 'a carnival of revolution' (Kenney, 2002). The legend of the power of civil society was born.

KEY QUOTE BOX 14.2
Edwards on Civil Society

It is a truism that civil society is what we as active citizens make it, but it is also true that 'social energy', or 'willed action', is the spark that ignites civil society as a force for positive social change. The determination to do something because it is the right thing to do, not because we are told to do it by governments or enticed to do it by the market, is what makes associational life a force for good, provides fuel for change in the practices of states and business, and motivates people to raise their voices in the public sphere . . . Against the background of weak democracies, strong bureaucracies, corporate power, legalism and nationalism resurgent, civil society, as both concept and reality, is essential to the prospects for a peaceful and prosperous world order in the twenty-first century . . . Warts and all, the idea of civil society remains compelling, not because it provides the tidiest of explanations but because it speaks to the best in us, and calls on the best in us to respond in kind. (Edwards, 2004: 111–12)

were exasperated by official corruption, so they fastened on civil society and the voluntary sector as instruments to spread good governance and democracy. Aid money was liberally dispensed to non-governmental organizations (NGOs) in the developing world in the hope that they would spread their enthusiasm and experience among fellow citizens. They had the advantage of large numbers and, unlike political parties in dictatorships, they operated at the grass roots. Even existing democracies such as Japan began to pay more attention to their NGOs as potential political actors, or at any rate as institutions with legitimate political inputs to make. The 1990s was a heroic decade for civil society. It became one of the top items on the international agenda. It was this heroic aspect of civil society that many people found so inspiring. It seemed to symbolize the possibility of the downtrodden rising up and overthrowing their oppressors.

In addition, there was the economic appeal of voluntary associations for helping with welfare in developing world countries where a welfare state would be beyond their means. This was attractive for aid donors because it provided them with opportunities to ensure that their aid actually reached the grass roots, and because often they involved women, who had previously been excluded from this. It was attractive for the governments because it helped to reduce the pressure on them to provide welfare, and it was attractive for the recipients too because it provided them with opportunities to organize and stand up more for their rights. Left-inclined local authorities in developing countries occasionally experimented with ways of drawing selected groups of citizens into active participation in the compiling of budgets; for example, in Porto Alegre in Brazil (Baiocchi, 2005) and Kerala in India. This was blurring the distinction between civil society and elected representatives.

Of course, problems quickly emerged in trying to spread it around the world. On the one hand, the policy became a victim of its own success. Many NGOs in the developing world became dependent upon foreign funding for their activities. This meant that their leaders had to spend as much time, if not more, on devising projects that would attract foreign funding rather than ones that they themselves felt their communities needed most urgently. On the other hand, dictatorships were quickly alerted to the potential political threat from civil society and moved to hem it in. Authoritarian regimes also sought to restrict the flows of foreign aid that might be channelled their way, sometimes, like Russia, playing the nationalist card and complaining about unjustified foreign interference from organizations like the Carnegie Foundation for International Peace. Many started organizing alternative, pliant, civil society organizations. This led to a plethora of new acronyms, such as GONGOs (Government Organized Non-Governmental Organizations). In Indonesia in 1990, for instance, one of President Suharto's ministers (and later successor as president), B. J. Habibie, created the Ikatan Cendekiawan Muslim se-Indonesia (or Indonesian Association of Muslim Intellectuals; ICMI), an organization of Islamic intellectuals close to the regime, so that it could have an impact upon the authoritarian political decision-making system. They were expected to act as a think tank for new ideas on furthering Islam while promoting education. By 1994 it claimed to have 20,000 members.

On the other hand, one of the strengths of the concept for the study of comparative politics was that it could open the way to integrating regimes that lacked many of the political institutions of the developed world. It brought the study of informal social politics back in, as well as political activity at the margins of institutions. Jenkins (2005: 280–1) has explained that in India there is a long-standing tradition of political parties, especially the Congress Party, fostering associations that were part of the independence movement. This relationship has continued into the

14

post-independence era, so a clear-cut division between the state and civil society would preclude consideration of important elements of Indian politics. The term certainly attracted a great deal of interest among students of Middle Eastern politics. Social institutions such as the salons in the Gulf states, where all sorts of subjects could be discussed including politics, or the informal 'circles' in Iranian society were known to play a significant part in political life (Eickelman, 1996: pp. x–xi). Now there was a framework that could integrate them into broader comparisons with informal politics elsewhere in the world. Traditionally, the state had played a more limited role in the lives of Muslims, and non-state actors, e.g. charitable foundations, had provided a great deal of public services such as education and water supplies. Although their role has become more limited, it is still important. So too is the role of professional organizations of doctors, engineers, teachers, and such like (Ibrahim, 1995). They embody the principle of a self-organizing society separate from the state. So the concept of civil society could accommodate their activities too (Hoexter, 2002).

Not surprisingly, given the enormous interest that was generated in it, the concept of civil society remained subject to great contradictions and misunderstandings. For one thing there was disagreement over whether it was primarily an analytical term or a normative one. The concept of 'civil society' itself was subjected to quite disparate interpretations. Did it mean that all the groups shared some kind of common perspective when they pursued political goals? In particular, was it committed to an altruistic advocacy of policies that were judged to be in the public interest? Or at least were they committed to some kind of 'civility', which meant excluding from consideration groups that pursued non-civil goals? Could it include the advocacy of interest groups? Could it include clientelistic networks, mafia organizations, fundamentalist religious sects, and extreme right-wing nationalist groups? Or is it a bulwark against the **anarchy** of weak or failed states (Chabal and Daloz, 1999: 17–18)? Does some form of civil society keep Somalia together after the collapse of the state outlined in Chapter 8? Or is it simply a collective noun that designates all the activities of a wide variety of groups and organizations that are not part of the state or of political society? Finally, civil society is vulnerable to existing inequalities in society, which may privilege some groups and disadvantage or even silence others and which inhibits its normative potential.

➡ See Chapter 8, Box 8.4 for the case study on Somalia.

14

Beyond this, there was difficulty in translating the term into foreign languages because of extra connotations that attached to the term in English and which could imply some new version of Westernization. Right-wing critics of Japanese democracy such as Saeki (1997) stigmatize 'civil society' as a (harmful) Western implant. Islamic societies were also suspicious about the term. Some of them were unhappy about the derivation of the term from nineteenth-century European philosophy, which they associated with an Enlightenment, i.e. secular, project. They condemned it as part of an intolerant Westernizing project. They wanted instead a term that was more compatible with Islamic traditions and goals, one that focused more upon organizations of the *ulama*, the body of Islamic scholars.

Analysts of African politics also complained that the term had been inappropriately transferred from a quite different European context.

> In Africa, as in other places, 'civil society' evokes otherwise inchoate—as yet unnamed and unamiable—popular aspirations, moral concerns, sites and spaces of practice; likewise it bespeaks a scholarly effort to recalibrate worn-out methodological tools, and to find a positive politics, amid conceptual confusion.   (Comaroff and Comaroff, 1999: 2–3)

Kaviraj (2001: 287) indicated that this was part of a wider problem: 'To understand political modernity in the non-Western world is impossible without Western social theory; it is equally impossible entirely within the terms of that tradition.' Western concepts need at least to be adapted to non-Western circumstances.

Not only is there ambiguity over the meaning of the concept. There is also ambiguity over the boundaries of the phenomena that it is supposed to encompass. In simple terms it seemed to indicate the space for social activity between the state on one hand and private individuals on the other. We have already seen from Chapter 8 that the boundaries of the state are also fuzzy, which then makes the boundaries of civil society equally fuzzy. As Chabal and Daloz put it (1999: 17), the fundamental problem in trying to apply the concept of civil society is that there is no clear division between the state and society. Instead there is constant interpenetration. Chandhoke (2003: 10) emphasizes that civil society is impossible without a robust legal system that can protect civil rights. On the other side, it was not always clear—or at any rate made clear—where the boundaries of 'the private' began. Did it only apply to individuals? Or did 'the private' include the family too, as has usually been the case in the West since Aristotle (Swanson, 1992)? If it did, then it would seem to exclude the very important dimension of family-based social activity which is typical of Middle Eastern, African, and Asian societies (as well as Southern European; see Ginsborg, 2001). Hahm (2004: 454–7), for instance, has argued that the traditional Confucian view could either not accommodate the public/private distinction or made it a fluctuating one. This was because Confucian doctrine began with the development of virtue in the individual and then gradually widened its horizon to encompass the whole of society. The goal of a virtuous society was impossible without virtuous individual members of it, and individuals could not be virtuous unless they performed the necessary familial roles and rites. So distinctions between family and society were positively detrimental.

➡ See Chapter 8 for a discussion of the modern state.

➡ See Chapter 9 for a discussion of Confucianism.

Lastly, the subsequent evolution of the civil society groups in Eastern Europe after 1989 weakened enthusiasm for it as a model for the future. In Eastern Europe itself, the euphoria that surrounded the unbelievable success of groups such as the independent trade union Solidarity in Poland quickly evaporated. The hopes that such groups might form the basis for a new kind of consensual rule were quickly dashed, despite all the encouragement and approval from outside. The need to make radical changes and take drastic decisions in the face of mounting economic crises quickly revealed the difficulty for civil society organizations to maintain their cohesion. They lacked ideologies and organization forged in earlier years that would keep their members together. The crises polarized them rather than uniting them. Solidarity—the largest such organization and the one with the longest and most distinguished history of struggle against the communist authorities—quickly fragmented. Instead new political parties began to appear like mushrooms—further confirmation of their importance for democracy, however difficult the circumstances. By 1992, only three years after the collapse of the communist regime, 222 parties had been registered in Poland, although not all of them had candidates standing at elections.

All of these uncertainties have made the use of the term problematic, and the unhappy experience of the 'Arab Spring' since 2011 has also challenged the belief in the natural emancipatory power of civil society. What began as a series of unorganized protests in several Arab countries and initially led to the downfall of several dictators has subsequently regressed into revived authoritarianism in Egypt, a failed state in Libya, and protracted bloody civil war in Syria. These contrasting perspectives are illustrated in **Box 14.3**.

14

Photo 14.2 The Arab Spring. *Shutterstock RF*

The rapid spread of the Arab Spring initially brought hopes of a repeat of the emancipatory Velvet Revolution in Eastern Europe. However, in some places popular movements fell into chaos. In others, authoritarian opponents fought back. Perspectives and interpretations of those events have varied greatly.

Filiu on emancipation and the Arab Spring:

> Arabs have been fighting for their rights as citizens for more than a generation, but cultural prejudices and political bias prevented to grasp the extent of this disaffection . . . [T]he real Arab exception is the speed with which the democratic protests sweep the regimes away . . .
>
> If there is an Arab exception, it is an exceptionally young population: the median age in the Arab world is twenty-two in 2009 . . . Their anger is their power and their rage could be the energy of the future. And they all echo the militant message from Tahrir [Square]: tomorrow is yours if you fight for it . . .
>
> Social networks . . . were crucial in nurturing a community feeling of shared grief and aspirations, mainly among the educated and urban youth. By exposing the lies and crimes of the ruling regime, they helped to bring down the wall of fear. Once this was done, their real importance in the revolutionary process became secondary . . .

> Leaderless movements . . . were able to topple entrenched dictatorships through peaceful protests, before a combination of street pressure, labour unrest and freedom activists paved the way for a democratic transition coupled with constitutional change. (Filiu, 2011: 16, 32, 42, 56, 72)

Stacher (2015) on the aftermath of the Arab Spring:

> While the cases [i.e. regimes] travel diverse paths, the overwhelming majority have brought with them increased state violence that has militarized the governing apparatus. This is not a transitional moment of uncertainty. It is deliberate political engineering by elites who are directing violence against their citizens in order to maintain some part of the existing regime or create a new regime on the ashes of the older order . . .
>
> Elites are deploying state violence against those pushing for more freedoms, better economic prospects and more social justice. This popular mobilization may still one day result in democratization but for now scholarly efforts are better directed at developing more concise theories of militarizing state violence if we are to accurately portray contemporary Arab politics. (Stacher, 2015: 269)

The Arab Spring has renewed questioning of the theoretical and practical utility of the term 'civil society' (Cavatorta, 2012; Härdig, 2014).

Yet 'civil society' has now acquired such widespread usage that it is impossible to abandon it. After all their criticisms, Comaroff and Comaroff (1999: 33) conclude: 'Civil society may be deeply flawed as an analytic construct . . . But it still serves, almost alone in the age of neoliberal capital, to give shape to reformist even utopian visions.' Edwards (2004) advocates positively embracing its diversity. If you use the term, you should specify clearly what you understand by it, and what you do not. Remember, as Chandhoke (2003: 33) reminds us: 'civil society is not a given; it is what its practitioners make of it'. It is as much a project to be created as a concept to be applied. Like politics more generally, it is an arena of great contestation.

Now let us turn to a subset of institutions that are often included within the notion of civil society, i.e. interest groups.

14

KEY POINTS

- Civil society is an ambiguous term subject to a wide variety of interpretations.
- It acquired a heroic aura because of its association with the protests that brought down communist regimes in Eastern Europe.
- Subsequently, it was appropriated by policy-making elites in the West as the targets for aid that they wished to distribute to grass-roots organizations in the developing world.
- There is a big disagreement over whether it can be applied in a non-European environment, and if so, how.

INTEREST GROUPS

Interest groups represent a big component of civil society. They are an essential element of democracy—it is impossible to think of a democracy without interest groups and to a limited extent they may raise or enhance the level of democratic participation, especially in polities where 'cartel' political parties have become more integrated into the state (see Chapter 11). Interest groups also attract normative comment. For some writers they exert a baleful influence on democracy, because they may disproportionately privilege some interests at the expense of others, or of the public interest as a whole. This was the kind of attitude expressed by Madison about 'factions' that was mentioned in Chapter 10. For others they are entirely desirable because they facilitate the input of new ideas into the political process. According to this view, they are a key element in the pluralism which is an essential feature of (liberal) democracy. For rational choice theorists such as Olson (1971), interest groups are the most rational form of political activity for ordinary citizens, because they are smaller than parties and offer a greater likelihood of return on effort. On the other hand, group interests are not just confined to democracies. All societies are prone to them, including dictatorships, even though the opportunities for expressing them may be more restricted in the latter.

➡ See the discussion in Chapter 11 on the emergence of parties.

➡ See Chapter 1 for a discussion of pluralism.

Interest groups have attracted an enormous amount of comment and analysis, both in general and with respect to particular political systems, and they still do. There is also a long-standing argument about the term itself. What counts as a 'group'? Does it have to be a self-consciously cohesive group, like Friends of the Earth? For groups of this kind, an alternative term is pressure group, although it is less widely used. Or could it denote a disparate group of people who share common interests but do not act in a cohesive manner, e.g. corporations or social classes? There is no definitive answer to this, and analysts differ over which version to employ. But generally interest groups are conceived as more organized elements of civil society.

According to Robertson (1993: 240), interest groups are 'associations formed to promote a sectional interest in the political system'. They differ from political parties in that they do not seek to present themselves as candidates for government. Instead they focus on a narrower range of issues than a government does, although it does happen that interest groups turn into political parties, as environmental groups have done. One distinction often made is between insider and outsider interest groups. Insiders concentrate upon winning support through lobbying, personal contacts, etc. Outsiders rely more upon winning over public opinion through campaigning, the media, etc. While some groups may be permanently oriented towards insider or outsider roles because of their membership, the difference between the roles may also be determined by the nature of the government. For example, conservative governments are typically more inclined to treat employers' associations as insiders, giving greater attention to their views in formulating policy, while labour or socialist governments typically treat trade unions more as insiders.

Puhle (2001: 7703–4) divided interest groups into eight types: (i) professional associations; (ii) groups of business, commerce, and industry; (iii) trade unions; (iv) agricultural organizations; (v) single-interest groups, such as the National Rifle Association in the USA; (vi) ideological interest groups, such as the British Humanist Association, or religious groups; (vii) public interest groups, such as Amnesty International; and (viii) welfare associations, such as the Royal National Institute for the Blind.

14

Interest groups operate in a great many ways, but in so far as they pursue political goals, they will adapt themselves to the structure of the institutions that they wish to influence. If they want to influence the national government, then they will turn most of their attention to the capital, appealing to public opinion, lobbying ministers, officials, and members of parliament. In federal systems they will devote much attention to winning support in individual states. In more administratively dominant communities, interest groups will concentrate most of their efforts on lobbying officials, as happens in Brussels with the European Union. Schlozman (2001) suggests that the strong centralized French political system leads to weak interest groups. On the other hand, the traditions of 1789 continue to endorse a greater inclination towards direct action by interest groups, such as farmers, in France than is normal in other European states. Given the enormous range and diversity of interest group activity around the world, it is very difficult to generalize about it with overarching theories. It is the basic features of individual political systems that structure what interest groups do and how they do it.

KEY POINTS

- There is an ambiguity in the term interest group
- It can refer to consciously organized groups promoting interests or concerns, in which case it is an essential element in any democracy.
- Or it can refer to groups of interests in society which some actors may promote, in which case it can be found in any state.
- In either case, they are adapted to the institutional framework of a particular regime to maximize their effect.

14

Corporatism

One variant of interest group theory is called corporatism, which was also discussed in Chapter 12. As mentioned previously, governments do not treat all interest groups equally. They will be more inclined to listen to some, i.e. 'insiders', than to others. In this model, though, the state is still responding to ideas or pressure from outside, but some states do more to formalize this relationship. They set up arrangements for regular consultation of key interest groups that represent the views of sections of society that are politically or economically strategic—what have been termed 'peak' associations, as in Britain the Confederation of British Industry and the Trades Union Congress. They do this for the sake of better policy-making, which they recognize requires regular consultation. It resonates with the tendency to focus on governance rather than government as the most appropriate framework for national decision-making, as was outlined in Chapter 13. Because this role is rather different from that of more conventional interest groups that concentrate on expressing views to the government, Schmitter (1980) coined instead the notion of 'interest intermediation'. In other words, this more select group of organizations acts as channels for exchanging views between their members and the government, rather than necessarily promoting a set view.

➡ See Chapter 2 for a discussion of corporatism.

➡ See Chapter 13 for a discussion on governance.

Schmitter also identified two distinct patterns of establishing these relationships. One, which he termed the 'societal' variant of corporatism, emerged out of pressure from below, i.e. from society or economic actors. As a consequence the choice of which of these actors the state recognizes depends partly on these pressures from below. In the alternative variant, which he termed 'state' corporatism, it was the state that took the lead in designating its preferred partners.

Lehmbruch (2001) suggests that corporatism has been more prominent at certain periods of history and in certain groups of countries than others. The practices of corporatism were particularly important at times of Keynesian economic management in the 1960s and 1970s, when government, employers, and trade unions regularly consulted over policies that made a trade-off between levels of unemployment, wage rates, and inflation rates. Although several European countries later turned away from these methods, they remain influential in others. The Nordic countries, Germany, and France all practise variants of 'organized' or 'concerted' capitalism, as indicated in Chapter 13, which still allow significant scope for negotiations between national partners as opposed to impersonal market forces in determining socio-economic policies.

➔ See Chapter 13 for a discussion of co-ordinated market economies.

KEY POINTS

- Corporatism privileges certain national 'peak' organizations as negotiating partners for the state in determining socio-economic policies.
- There are two variants: society-led or state-led.
- It is still a common approach to governance in countries in continental Europe.

INFRAPOLITICS AND SUBALTERN STUDIES: THE STATE VIEWED FROM BELOW

The preceding sections of this chapter have focused on ways in which civil society responds to state actors and tries to manoeuvre them into cooperation. This is politics from below. It is important to realize that politics can be viewed through this lens, as well as through a lens focused on national governments and state leaders. Another manifestation of this comes from political anthropology. It is important to appreciate this because it is an important dimension of the study of politics, especially in the developing world, although their insights are not just confined to developing states.

One of the key concerns of political anthropologists is power and its disguises, to use the title of a book by Gledhill (1994). They focus on the ways in which ordinary people relate to political systems: how they view rulers, defer to them, and also manipulate the system for their own ends. One very influential work was Scott's 1990 book, *Domination and the Arts of Resistance*. What attracted his attention was the ways in which peasants among whom he had done fieldwork talked differently among themselves from the way that they talked to their social superiors. It alerted him to the existence of a whole world that he designated as 'infrapolitics', i.e. the subtle ways in which the powerless subvert or undermine the authority of the powerful. Most often, it depended on ambiguity rather than direct expression of opinions. Individuals needed to avoid retribution. 'Infrapolitics is the realm of informal leadership and nonelites, of conversation and oral discourse, and of surreptitious resistance.' Because of this ambiguity, he argued, it had often been missed, or misunderstood, by outside observers. In fact, social historians such as Hobsbawm had written about such phenomena, but it was much less commonly noted by political scientists. Infrapolitics could take the form of covert resistance such as poaching, squatting on land, desertion (of slaves),

➔ See Chapter 8 for a discussion on the spread of the Western state.

14

evasion, and foot-dragging. It could lead to dissident subcultures of resistance: millenarian religions, folk myths of social banditry, and class heroes, e.g. Robin Hood (Scott, 1990: 200, 198). Holston (2008: 34) conveys the disconcerting effect of seeing political institutions in Brazil from this perspective with his notion of 'insurgent citizenship':

> [I]nsurgence describes a process that is an acting counter, a counterpolitics, that destabilizes the present and renders it fragile, defamiliarizing the coherence with which it usually presents itself. Insurgence is not a top-down imposition of an already scripted future. It bubbles up from the past in places where present circumstances seem propitious for an eruption. In this view, the present is like a bog: leaky, full of holes, gaps, contradictions, and misunderstandings. These exist just beneath all the taken-for-granted assumptions that give the present its apparent consistency.

Banerjee (2014) has remarked that this sounds a lot like politics in India.

➜ See Chapter 16 for a more detailed discussion on the rise and spread of the state system.

One particular recent approach in political anthropology has been to try to see the politics and institutions of other regions of the world in their own context and in their own right, not in the shadow of Europe. Given the way in which the European state spread around the world, as outlined in Chapters 8 and 16, this is an understandable reaction. There has emerged a school of 'subaltern' studies, especially among academics in and studying South Asia. This approach too began with social history. Again, the concern is with the underdogs in society and their relationship with lower-level officials, the 'subalterns'. As Gupta (2006) explained, there is relatively little ethnographic evidence of what lower-level officials do in the name of the state and how this impacts on the lives of ordinary citizens. These officials are differentially positioned in hierarchical networks of power, which means that they behave differently whether they are turned towards their administrative superiors or towards ordinary citizens. The consequence is, he argued, that there is no such thing as a single state. Instead there are multiple variants of the state within the same nation, with different groups having different experiences of it.

Another concern of the subaltern school is 'decentring' or 'provincializing' Europe, i.e. examining politics and society in other parts of the world in their own right and on their own terms, not as seen through a European lens (Chatterjee, 2001: 15240). Apart from trying to give a voice to the previously underprivileged in society, it also aims at challenging those who would recommend a Western path to modernity—an issue to which we shall return in the Conclusion. They want equality of respect with and from the West. They recommend the search for an alternative path to modernity which is not necessarily the same as in the West and is more in tune with local circumstances.

14

KEY POINTS

- Political anthropology examines the connections between political attitudes and political behaviour and their cultural contexts, especially at the grass roots.
- Subaltern studies emphasize the multiplicity of ways in which the state is perceived by people because of the disparate ways in which they are treated by local officials.
- Subaltern studies also demand consideration for development strategies that are not borrowed from the West and are better adapted to local (non-Western) conditions.

THE MEDIA AND POLITICS

We have now moved on to considering the ways in which politics and the state are perceived by citizens. One crucial set of actors that determines this is the media. It is difficult to exaggerate the extent to which the media structure perceptions of politics among citizens in a particular country. According to a former head of the British civil service, Lord Richard Wilson (2013: 23): 'Communication is a central activity of the state in the modern age. It is the bread and butter of everyday life in government.' In addition, democracies recognize the importance of the media in upholding freedom of speech. The First Amendment to the US Constitution in 1789 established the principle of freedom of speech as an essential element of democracy. Since then this principle has increasingly figured in other states' definitions of a democracy. This also established the importance of the media in ensuring an informed democratic citizenry.

As journalist Andrew Marr (2004: 63–4, 60) puts it:

> Suppose in an average week you are aware of a dozen news stories. It is probably many more than that, but take twelve as the number you think about, even briefly. These stories, 600 in a year—though since stories intermingle and repeat themselves, let's cut it a bit—affect you. They colour your attitude to the world, and often condition how you take specific decisions., from holiday plans, to saving or spending, to how you look at a possible mugger . . . Your world view is altered by the news you get.

At the same time, he reminds us:

> 'News' is not 'facts'. News is based on fact. We have to believe, at least for a while, that what is said to have happened did happen. But our interest comes from how effectively we can use these facts to make sense of the world and our place in it. News is a source of emotion, belonging, even morality.   (Marr, 2004: 62)

Journalists 'make' news out of facts, just as chefs make meals out of ingredients. They (primarily editors) choose the stories that they are going to cover and then construct narratives to make them interesting ('newsworthy') to the public that they wish to reach. According to the former editor of the *Sunday Times*, Harold Evans: 'Facts may be sacred—but which facts? The media are not a neutral looking glass: we select what we mirror' (Davies, 2009: 112). At the same time things that they do not report may never reach the public's consciousness or provoke the public debate they may deserve. Journalists cannot report everything, and even if they did, we would not have time to read or watch it. In that sense they have traditionally acted as default 'gatekeepers' of public debate, sometimes deliberately, sometimes inadvertently—to the chagrin of many politicians. They certainly structure, but do not determine, what their publics think about politics, although we should not forget that other things affect views of politics and political issues too. Dramas, films, novels can also make a political impact. *Yes, Minister* had an iconic status in presenting to the public the relationship between politicians and civil servants, whether or not it was always accurate. *Spitting Image* fictionalized life in Mrs Thatcher's cabinet in a way that seemed more realistic than real life. In the US *The West Wing* attracted a wide following as, for some, it revolved around the best Democratic president the country never had. President Putin told the newly appointed defense minister Shoigu that, if he wanted to understand American politics, he should watch *House of Cards* (Zygar, 2016: 332). Audiences do not neatly separate political entertainment from factual news—and conversely political reporters have learnt tricks from entertainment as they try to reach bigger audiences. Bailey (2011) has suggested that fiction might help us to understand the 'true' nature of 'real' politics, since politics seems to be about drama and the clashes of alternative choices. Or is it that reporting often presents politics in this way because the public likes it and believes it must at bottom be true?

Of course, journalists generally subscribe to a code of accuracy in reporting. Factual accuracy is fundamental. Boris Johnson's career as a journalist at *The Times* ended quickly when he was found to have invented a quotation from his godfather and fabricated two stories (*iNews*, 2018). In general terms, Harrison (2006: 2–3) characterizes core news journalism as a 'disposition towards truthfulness'—that is, not an absolute commitment to it—but only since, as she puts it, 'truth is impossible to attain in anything other than a forensic or scientific setting, although even here it is not guaranteed'.

But journalists are also expected to make stories 'interesting', so as to attract viewers or readers. Sometimes 'stories' are printed because they are *felt* to be true, or at least credible or amusing. 'Freddie Starr Ate My Hamster' (1986) is one of *The Sun*'s most iconic headlines and though there was no truth to it, no-one lost their job. Readers gulped, laughed, and moved on. TV news bulletins have to entertain, as well as to inform. They need to have variety to keep viewers watching. Personalities, especially 'celebrities', are more gripping than lengthy dissections of policies, let alone party manifestoes. And a common device is to present political issues in democracies in terms of horse races for political office between rivals, because all the competitors can be presented in the same way without having to go into details of the merits of their different policy proposals (Patterson, 2017). A journalist acts like a storyteller to provide overall meaning to readers. The art of the journalist is not so dissimilar from that of the novelist, dramatist, or film director.

Simplicity is definitely a prized journalistic virtue. Marr (2004: 267) recounts the advice he was given when he moved to BBC television:

> **Your job is to take an often confusing or complicated situation or series of events and make sense of it for the viewer . . . If your story needs to be seen more than once before it can be understood (and too many do), then it will have totally failed . . . You are distilling information, not packing it in. Get to the point, stick to it, know when it's finished, then end it.**

14

Tabloid newspapers are generally most blamed for populist political reporting, oversimplification, and 'dumbing down' politics. But are the practices of 'quality' publications always so different? For example, an editor of *The Economist* famously urged his journalists in writing articles, first of all to simplify (distil), and then to exaggerate (Henry, 2007). While this house style certainly makes for a clear perspective—a trait valued by readers with busy schedules—it can oversimplify complex issues. When this happens, at what point does simplification and exaggeration turn into oversimplification, distortion, or even falsehood?

It should also be remembered that the standards and expectations of journalism do vary around the world. The Worlds of Journalism project has shown that journalists in the developing world tend to adopt a more positive framework in reporting national development policy and a less confrontational attitude towards domestic politics than their counterparts in the developed world (Kalyango et al., 2017). The diversity is particularly true of the print media, where different national traditions of newspaper ownership persist. Hallin and Mancini (2004) identified three distinct newspaper systems in the West: (i) the Mediterranean or 'polarized pluralism' model, typically found in southern Europe, where newspapers are more partisan and where journalists are expected to be more committed to a particular party view than 'objectively' professional; (ii) the northern European or democratic corporatist model, with traditions of state intervention and state subsidies, but strong professionalism and institutionalized self-regulation; and (iii) the North American or liberal model, in the US and the UK, with strong professionalization, non-institutionalized self-regulation, and market regulation, apart from public broadcasting in the UK. When they extended this analysis, they concluded that other regions of the world tended to come closer to the 'polarized pluralist' model than to liberal America (Hallin and Mancini, 2012). All this affects the way journalism impacts political life.

Theorizing the Media and Democracy

It is very difficult to envisage democracy without freedom of the press. This is illustrated by **Table 14.1**, which shows the 2019 ranking of the states with the greatest press freedom, as compiled by Reporters Without Borders. All would be termed democracies.

Historically the rise of democracy has been associated with the emergence of a space for debating politics and government policy—what Habermas termed 'the public sphere', which was distinct from the broader overlapping realm of civil society that also encompassed private interests and the market. He believed it was an essential precondition for genuine democracy. The term has become very influential and is used widely in the field. Garnham's definition (2001: 12586) is in **Box 14.4**.

According to Habermas (1989: 182) journalists and publishers had played a key role in becoming 'the carriers and leaders of public opinion'. Schudson (2008) has enlarged upon this by identifying seven important functions performed by the media, that are listed in **Box 14.5**.

14

Table 14.1 Press Freedom Index 2019

Rank	Country	Rank	Country
1	Norway	2	Finland
3	Sweden	4	Netherlands
5	Denmark	6	Switzerland
7	New Zealand	8	Jamaica
9	Belgium	10	Costa Rica
11	Estonia	12	Portugal
13	Germany	14	Iceland
15	Ireland	16	Austria
17	Luxemburg	18	Canada
19	Uruguay	20	Surinam
33	UK	48	US

Source: Reporters Without Borders (2019) (https://rsf.org/en/ranking).

KEY QUOTE BOX 14.4
Garnham on the Public Sphere

The public sphere was both a set of institutional spaces—newspapers, lecture halls, coffee houses, etc.—and a set of discursive rules . . . a site within which the formation of public opinion, and the political will stemming from and legitimized by such opinion, is subject to the disciplines of a discourse, or communicative ethics, by which all views are subjected to the critical reasoning of others. At the same time, a democratically legitimate public sphere requires that access to it is open to both all citizens and all views equally, provided only that all participants are governed by the search for general agreement. (Garnham 2001: 12586)

KEY QUOTE BOX 14.5
Schudson's Seven Key Functions that the Media Perform for Democracy

1. information: the news media can provide fair and full information so citizens can make sound political choices;
2. investigation: the news media can investigate concentrated sources of power, particularly governmental power;
3. analysis: the news media can provide coherent frameworks of interpretation to help citizens comprehend a complex world;
4. social empathy: journalists can tell people about others in their society and their world so that they can come to appreciate the viewpoints and lives of other people, especially those less advantaged than themselves;
5. public forum: journalists can provide a forum for dialogue among citizens and serve as a common carrier of the perspectives of varied groups in society;
6. mobilization: the news media can serve as advocates for political programs and perspectives and mobilize people to act in support of those programs;
7. publicizing representative democracy: journalists [should] cover more carefully some institutions and relationships that today they take for granted or ignore. (Schudson, 2008: 12, 23–4)

14

Hart and LaVally (2017: 109) have argued that political journalism now 'more closely resembles a Second Legislature of debaters than a Fourth Estate of onlookers.' In other words journalists have become much more powerful in the political process. Sometimes they challenge and sometimes they bolster official authorities by spreading the official line, just as legislatures do. Exactly how powerful they are is a matter for passionate debate, and the evidence is mixed—it is difficult to demonstrate the media clearly causing political or policy outcomes. Nevertheless according to Marr, a former newspaper editor (2004: 186): 'There is a strong sense that the power to set the agenda and initiate the terms of national debate has passed from ministers to journalists.' They certainly play an important role in holding politicians and officials to account—a vital element in Keane's (2009) notion of present-day democracy as 'monitory democracy'.

As a consequence, their status and power has itself become more challenged in the UK and the US. Misdeeds and hacking of private phones by the media provoked the British government into setting up the Leveson enquiry which recommended more statutory regulation of press behaviour (though the government has shied away from implementing it). And in the US popular frustration over press 'elitism' and their perceived bias in selecting and covering the news was an important precondition for the rise of the grassroots Tea Party organization, which in turn laid the foundation for the populist rise of Donald Trump. The founder of Breitbart News, a website devoted to countering the alleged bias of the mainstream news organizations, declared:

> The Left is the media . . . I'm at war with the mainstream media because they portray themselves as objective observers of reality when they're no such thing – they're partisan 'critical theory' hacks who think they can destroy everything America stands for by standing on the sidelines and sniping at patriotic Americans with all their favorite slurs . . . The Democrats have the Big Three Networks and major news dailies as their offensive line, and a starting backfield of Hollywood celebrities and academia . . . Everyone is disillusioned about the media. Nobody is fooled into believing that most reporters are objective, straight-down-the-middle truth-seekers. (Breitbart, 2012: 3, 58, 210, 222)

And his successor as head of Breitbart, Steve Bannon, became for a while Donald Trump's chief strategist, leading his campaigns against 'fake news'.

Schudson's 2008 book was entitled: *Why Democracies Need an Unlovable Press*. It has never been more apposite.

KEY POINTS

- Traditionally the media, especially the press, have been seen as an essential element of liberal democracy and a check on the power of the executive.
- Politicians and the media are by turns adversaries and accomplices.
- More recently the media have been condemned for dumbing down the coverage of politics, while politicians have been criticized for 'spinning' their activities.
- An assessment of the power of the media needs to take into account the way politics is presented in all the formats where it appears and not just in current affairs programmes.
- The way 'the power of the press' operates is extremely difficult to pin down.
- The press perform an important function in making politicians and governments accountable, but they are not always loved for it.

THE CHALLENGE OF NEW TECHNOLOGIES

In recent years new communications technologies have begun to revolutionize the role of the media in politics again. Indeed, it can be argued that they may have a bigger impact than newspapers and TV did in the past, not least because they provide additional opportunities for ordinary citizens to take advantage of the new public space to make an impact on politics. They can provide civil society with new arenas for activity. There are three reasons for this. First, the Internet and mobile phones have transformed the ability of ordinary citizens to organize themselves in groups even when confronted with repression from their authorities. Second, they have widened the possibilities for people outside the media world to report news and make influential comment on events. In that sense they have democratized access to the media. Third, they offer the future possibility of transforming decision-making institutions as well, e.g. voting and referendums. We will consider these three dimensions in turn. Finally we will look at some new challenges to democracy that stem from more recent developments in the use of the new technologies.

Promoting Horizontal Communication

Previously, communications channels within states were mainly vertical ones. The most influential media outlets tended to congregate in national capitals. That was especially true of TV stations. Political parties and interest groups achieved results by concentrating their efforts there. The opportunities for other groups to make themselves into significant forces were constrained by the difficulties of contacting people through landline telephones and the mail. Now, however, there are much greater opportunities for would-be political actors to mobilize support using horizontal communications—mobile phones (including SMS texting) and the Internet.

In the early years of the Internet there was optimism about the possibilities that the new media offered for organizing political parties. In the USA, in particular, the enormous cost of standing for office made it very difficult for outsiders to be elected. Much was made of the success of a former wrestler, Jesse Ventura, in winning election against all expectations as Governor of Minnesota in 1998 as a third-party candidate. He made widespread use of the Internet as a cheap means to get his message across. This seemed to open the way for other outsiders to follow his example. However, the established parties quickly took note of the threat and started throwing money at their Internet strategies. They have refined the techniques of using the Internet for candidates to communicate directly with individual voters and target specific messages to their various concerns. Once again, they have outflanked the challengers. As was mentioned in Chapter 12, American political parties have profited from the Internet by mobilizing far more campaign contributions than ever before.

➡ See Chapter 12 for a discussion on the swelling cost of political campaigns in the USA.

On the other hand, the new technologies can empower groups to organize protests, as they can mobilize supporters much more quickly and unexpectedly in real time. This can still be very effective. The Philippines saw an important example at the end of 2000, with an explosion of SMS texting making a decisive contribution to the overthrow of the democratically elected President Estrada. Social networking sites such as Facebook, MySpace, and Twitter all contributed to the Arab Spring.

These new possibilities for self-organization will impact both democratic and authoritarian states, although in different ways. More open systems are vulnerable to the activities of what Rheingold (2002) has termed 'smart mobs'. These are technologically sophisticated groups who use their skills to organize group protests that the authorities find difficult to prevent, even if they are aware of what is planned, because of the short warning that they are given. It can be a kind of political blackmail. It certainly challenges the ability of the state to satisfy demands without alienating the rest of society that did not take part. Obviously, authoritarian regimes place more emphasis on controlling the freedom to organize in this way because any such protest is fundamentally more threatening. (**See Box 14.6**).

> ## KEY QUOTE BOX 14.6
> ### *Rolling Stone* on the Internet and Authoritarian States

The Internet is the censor's biggest challenge and the tyrant's worst nightmare . . . Unbeknown to their governments, people in China, Iraq and Iran, among other countries, are freely communicating with people all over the world. (*Rolling Stone*, 1995: see www.fas.org/cp/swett.html)

China, in particular, has devoted enormous efforts to surveillance of the Internet. It has erected a firewall to limit the access of its own citizens to politically sensitive material abroad. It also has a large number of censors (nicknamed 'Internet mamas') supervising electronic message boards and requiring that politically or socially undesirable materials are deleted (Griffiths, 2019). However, technologically sophisticated netizens use mirror servers to obtain sensitive information from abroad and outwit the censors. The danger for these sorts of regimes is that they can control the Internet in normal times, but that the new technologies will exacerbate any serious crisis if and when it occurs. In the absence of legitimate democratic institutions to channel protests in a constructive direction, these technologies may increase the opportunities for protest if and when people become very dissatisfied. But it is a cat-and-mouse game, and 'the cat' (i.e. the Chinese state) has been getting stronger, as it applies facial recognition technology to monitor citizen behaviour in more detail, as well as increasing pressure for people to go online and demonstrate that they are 'good citizens' by the material that they post.

Of course, not all the groups that use the new technologies to aid organization are benign. The Internet can be extremely useful to small extremist groups for attracting adherents, which they would have found much more difficult to do relying on the older methods of personal contacts, public meetings, pamphlets, and posters. The challenge of combating groups bent on violence or terrorism has been made more serious for all governments, whether democratic or authoritarian.

Everyone a Blogger, Everyone a Journalist

→ See the discussion in Chapter 12 on problems facing parties.

The new media have also made it much easier for non-journalists to publish comments and views in blogs on politics. Some have become more influential than established commentators and are quoted by journalists, especially at times of elections. Politicians, whether elected or standing for election, now increasingly publish blogs to connect with voters, though this further strengthens the trend mentioned in Chapter 12, whereby the personal image of candidates is enhanced at the expense of their parties.

Equally, individuals can now report breaking news as quickly as news agencies if they happen to be in the right place at the right time. They can also publish alternative versions of events if official government sources are perceived to be putting their own (inaccurate) spin on what happened. Despite the controls, this has already begun to happen in China, as the regime has been forced to reconsider and apologize for initial official explanations of disasters or major accidents that local people thought were mistaken.

In both these ways, the new media have begun to change the traditional media landscape creating more hybrid forms (Chadwick, 2013) and potentially also the structure of authority in society. Gradually, they are giving voices to Scott's 'infrapolitics' and to Habermas' notion of the public space. But it has meant that the public space has become even more of an abstract concept (actually the original German term—*Öffentlichkeit*—was abstract and contained no implication of a specific 'place'), since comments on public affairs can appear anywhere on the Web, not just in predetermined sites for public debate and engagement.

Electronic Decision-Making

Evangelists for the new media have also suggested that they can be used to bring public decision-making much closer to the people than ever before. Barber (1998, 1984), for instance, has looked forward to the new technology inaugurating a new era of 'strong' democracy, i.e. a modern equivalent of the democracy of ancient Athens. However, for the moment, actual proposals have focused more on two alternative strategies. The first is based on local government, the other on greater use of referendums.

The local government option has been based on the model of town meetings in the USA, i.e. meetings of citizens in a local community to debate and decide policy. The electronic variant is to arrange for citizens to be connected through cable so that they can debate and decide online (Becker and Slaton, 2000). The expectation was that this would enable a richer form of democracy to take root locally and then gradually spread throughout the nation. It assumed that the electronic meetings would themselves propose and decide on policy. The alternative was to organize regular electronic consultation of citizens about proposals that initially emerged either from representatives or from administrators. The model would be based more on the referendums regularly organized in Switzerland (Budge, 1996). This latter variant is clearly a 'weaker' form of democracy than the former, though the one might lead to the other. Neither variant has yet made a great deal of progress. The same is true of research on electronic voting in Europe.

There is an important issue hanging over all such proposals. How reliable is the technology, especially for voting? An American report reminded us that there are a great many potential dangers (*Asking the Right Questions about Electronic Voting*, 2005). These dangers are likely to be less great when the voting is confined to localities. Once voting is aggregated at higher levels, there is a serious danger of the integrity of the voting process being compromised. Votes could be secretly stolen or redirected or simply dumped. The whole process could be disrupted by viruses. Even though the existing American system of voting in many states ran into serious criticism after the shambles of the 2000 presidential election recounts, there are still good reasons for waiting until a really secure voting system can be devised. Until that happens, the more ambitious hopes for e-democracy will have to be delayed.

But although these are daunting challenges, they are not the only ones that stand in the way of politics being transformed by e-democracy. As McLean (1989) pointed out, there are other fundamental difficulties in aggregating preferences of citizens in some direct democracy. They relate to the difficulty of coming to a definitive view of the wishes of large numbers of people expressing preferences for a range of alternative policy proposals which they rank in quite different ways. This is another manifestation of the problem identified by the Arrow impossibility theorem mentioned in Chapter 11. This problem becomes even more intractable if any of the possible choices are dependent upon conditions resulting from other choices, as is almost always the case where spending priorities are involved. Thus the problems of e-democracy transforming traditional problems of democracy are not likely to be resolved in the near future.

➡ See Chapter 11 for a discussion of the Arrow impossibility theorem.

14

Subverting Democracy, 'Fake News', and the Facebook Challenge

As the previous *Rolling Stone* quote claimed, twenty years ago there was confidence in the West that the new communication technologies would work in the West's favour. They would undermine authoritarianism and promote democracy. More recently, authoritarian governments have been fighting back. What has attracted the most attention have been the accusations of interference in election campaigns in the US and France from Russia. It has been alleged that computer hackers there, posing as Americans or Frenchmen, spread rumours intended to undermine either support for particular candidates or even confidence in the political system as a whole, as a way of weakening the West's ability to stand up to Russian foreign policy pressure. And sometimes these hackers then created automated computerized robots that multiplied messages online, as if from real people, to strengthen the appearance of popular appeal. But China has also been marketing its online control tools to other countries that are interested in controlling the subversive potential of the Internet.

This has spread doubts about the robustness and reliability of the political process in democracies. The turmoil was also exacerbated by populist campaigns against political establishments. These were not only limited to online channels, but social media certainly gave them greater opportunities to post arguments or claims online that would never have appeared in the traditional mainstream media. Donald Trump was its most artful exponent:

See Chapter 17 for a discussion of populism.

> He exploited Twitter's ability to express raw sentiment instantly, without nuance or subtext, and its ability to blur, even extinguish, the boundary between sentiment and fact . . . He made enemies, pursued feuds and communicated a sense of apocalyptic

Photo 14.3 45th President of the United States, Donald J. Trump. *Alamy (library image)*

doom. He was very funny and often acute . . . Trump told lies, smeared and fabricated in order to destroy opponents. If the facts proved what he was saying to be untrue, Trump didn't care. He constructed a personal epistemology. His truth claims were purely instrumental. He made assertions about his own honesty—and the lies of his enemies—in order to gain power and win arguments . . . He viscerally understood the power of this new medium to simplify complex ideas, to remove nuance and subtext and, above all, to remove any boundary between assertion and fact. Donald Trump was the first modern politician . . . to create a world impervious to reality. He understood that politics was entertainment. Hence the name-calling, the bullying, the public humiliation, the relish to combat.   (Oborne and Roberts, 2017: xi, xxvii)

Trump was relentless in his allegations of 'fake news' from the media. In addition, his campaign allegedly mobilized artificial intelligence to spread its own news and fake news through endless automated linked 'bots' to create the sense of mass support (Anderson and Horvath, 2017). In turn this also exploited changes in the way people accessed news. Where previously they would have turned to the media, now their smart phones were dominated by retweets of titbits of 'interesting' information. Increasing numbers have come to rely upon sources like Twitter and Facebook for information and news. They click 'like' and send it to their friends. This then creates what Sunstein (2017: 109) has called 'cybercascades', when 'large numbers of people end up believing something—whether or not it is true—simply because other people whom they like seem to believe it is true' (Cheeseman and Klaas, 2018). A study from MIT found: 'Fake news and false rumors reach more people, penetrate deeper into the social network, and spread much faster than accurate stories' (*The Atlantic*, 2018). Fake news is often remembered because it appears more striking or novel than real news, and because it provokes an emotional response.

The strategy proved immensely successful. Despite all the efforts by various organizations to check facts and refute falsehoods, Trump won, against all expectations. Others have already imitated it. In the Brexit referendum, the Leave campaign took a leaf out of Trump's book. One of the organizers, Aaron Banks afterwards explained: 'The Remain campaign featured fact, fact, fact, fact. It just doesn't work. You've got to connect with people emotionally. It's the Trump success' (d'Ancona, 2017: 15).

As if this wasn't challenging enough for representative democracies, a subsequent development is even more worrying. This was the discovery that social media platforms such as Facebook and Twitter had been harvesting data from users and exploiting it to predict likes and preferences of individuals and groups without their consent, using increasingly sophisticated algorithms. The original motivation for this was commercial—to enable these platforms' corporate clients better to satisfy consumer tastes. But as Susskind (2018) pointed out, this could also transform the way politics is conducted in the future, in democracies and authoritarian regimes alike. If governments can work out with a high degree of reliability what 'the public' wants, what is the need for representatives? Would there even be a need for voting, if it simply confirmed that the algorithms were right? It would open the way to 'direct democracy', but of an intuitive and potentially authoritarian kind. It would certainly undermine any meaningful place for 'infrapolitics'. This is one of the many challenges that the new technologies are throwing up for the practice of politics.

14

KEY POINTS

- New communications technologies have aroused great hopes for transforming citizen involvement in politics, by enabling outsiders and new ideas to penetrate established political systems.
- They can also enable 'smart mobs' to disrupt government and hold the public to ransom.
- Their effect may be greater in states with less established or less legitimate political institutions, especially at times of crisis.
- They also allow non-journalists to publish news stories and influential blogs.
- They may enable greater participation in local decision-making.
- Electronic voting is still subject to great risks about the integrity of the technology.
- But authoritarian regimes are beginning to retaliate by using the Internet to interfere in the politics of states that are critical of them and spreading 'fake' news.
- Political debate in democracies is also becoming infected with disputes over genuine and fake news.
- A further potential challenge in the future is the possibility for governments to use artificial intelligence to predict citizens' policy preferences and remove the need for elected representatives or even voting.

CONCLUSION

This chapter has concentrated on views of the state from below and attempts to influence it. It has also discussed the concept of civil society and the great impact it has had on policies of the developed world towards the developing world since the 1980s; yet, as we have seen, it also suffers from great ambiguities and contradictions, which make it another essentially contested concept. The final section focused on the impact of new communications technologies on political life. Although we are only at the beginning of the revolution in political behaviour that they herald, it is clear that they may make the concept of civil society even more unwieldy. At the same time, they will force us to rethink the way politics is and should be conducted. Not only do they enable citizens within states to organize for the pursuit of political goals more easily than ever before, but they also further blur the boundaries between national and foreign politics. Neither the Internet nor mobile phones are great respecters of national frontiers. Like-minded groups can organize much more freely across them. This was already seen in the demonstrations that disrupted the 1999 World Trade Organisation (WTO) summit in Seattle, which brought together protest groups from around the world. Since then WTO and the annual Group of Eight (G8) summits have tended to attract similar swarms of protesters, although not with the same degree of violence. What is clear is that these new possibilities for group self-organization are not only transforming civil society within individual states, but they are also beginning to promote what can be described as international civil society, i.e. a global community of political activists and organizations that demand a greater say in the running of international politics. The new technologies are not merely promoting alternative views of the state from below. They are also promoting alternative views of the international order from below. Castells (1996) has written of the emergence of the 'network society'. It may also be the beginning of the 'network world'.

KEY QUESTIONS

1. What are the problems involved in applying the concept of civil society to analyse the Arab Spring? Is the term any less valid there than it was during the collapse of the communist regimes in Eastern Europe?

2. What makes political blogs interesting and are they different from the output of commentators in newspapers or on TV? Do they have more credibility?

3. Do TV series such as *The West Wing* and *Yes, Minister* do more to shape political opinions than 'straight' political reporting? How would you measure the impact?

4. Is there any point in trying to preserve public broadcasting as something distinct in an era when broadcasting possibilities are expanding almost exponentially on the Internet?

5. What needs to be done to make electronic democracy work?

6. How do media outlets create the sense of credibility in their coverage of politics? Do they use the same techniques for fictionalized accounts of politics as for straight political reporting?

7. Is the rise of single-issue interest groups good for democracy?

8. Why is there not a single model of a successful interest group that others could follow?

9. Identify some of the 'weapons of the weak' with which you are familiar. How can you tell whether they are subversive of the existing order?

10. Can 'fake news' be combatted? How?

14

FURTHER READING

Cavatorta, F. (2012), 'Arab Spring: the Awakening of Civil Society. A General Overview' (Barcelona: IEMed) (http://www.iemed.org/observatori-en/arees-danalisi/arxius-adjunts/anuari/med.2012/Cavatorta_en.pdf).
This article, and the one by Härdig, are interesting attempts to apply the concept of civil society to the Arab Spring.

Chadwick, A. (2013), *The Hybrid Media System: Politics and Power* (Oxford: Oxford University Press).
This is a wide-ranging account of the impact of the new technologies on the media and politics.

Coleman, S. and Blumler, J. G. (2009), *The Internet and Democratic Citizenship: Theory, Practice and Policy* (Cambridge: Cambridge University Press).
This is a stimulating contribution to the debate over the impact of the Internet on democracy, focusing on the beneficial potential.

Edwards, M. (2004), *Civil Society* (Cambridge: Polity Press).
Here, we have committed advocacy of the potential for civil society to transform politics by the Director of the Ford Foundation's Governance and Civil Society Program.

Griffiths, J. (2019), *The Great Firewall of China: How to Build and Control an Alternative Version of the Internet* (London: Zed books).

An up-to-date analysis of the way the Chinese government tries to tame the Internet

Härdig, A. C. (2014), 'Beyond the Arab revolts: conceptualizing civil society in the Middle East and North Africa', *Democratization* (DOI: 10.1080/13510347.2014.917626).

Read together with Cavatorta's article.

Jordan, G. and Moloney, W. A. (2007), *Democracy and Interest Groups: Enhancing Participation?* (Basingstoke: Palgrave).

This is an enquiry into the ways in which participation in interest groups enhances democracy.

Kaviraj, S. (2001), 'In search of civil society', in Sudipta Kaviraj and Sunil Khilnani (eds), *Civil Society: History and Possibilities* (Cambridge: Cambridge University Press), pp. 287–323.

A carefully nuanced analysis of the origins of the term and of its partial relevance to politics in the global South, especially India

Moore, M. (2019), *Democracy Hacked: How Technology is Destabilising Global Politics* (London: Oneworld).

An up-to-date analysis of the various challenges that new technologies are posing to political systems and practices, especially democracies

Savoie, D. J. (2010), *Power: Where is it?* (Montreal and Kingston: McGill-Queen's UP).

Chapter 4 contains an eloquent account of the increasing domination of democratic political life by the media and by political consultants.

Scott, J. C. (1990), *Domination and the Arts of Resistance: Hidden Transcripts* (New Haven, CT: Yale University Press).

This is an influential examination of the ways in which ordinary people get around authoritarian rulers.

Street, J. (2010), *Mass Media, Politics and Democracy* (Basingstoke: Palgrave, 2nd edn).

This is a very good analysis of the relationship between the media and democratic politics.

Wilson, G. K. (1990), *Interest Groups* (Oxford: Blackwell).

This is a well-regarded analysis of interest groups.

 For additional material and resources, please visit the Online Resources at:
www.oup.com/he/garner4e

14

DEMOCRACIES, DEMOCRATIZATION, AND AUTHORITARIAN REGIMES

READER'S GUIDE

Democracy and democratization have long been among the most widely researched and most hotly contested topics in comparative politics. More recently there has been a resurgence in interest in authoritarian systems, as many have survived the wave of democratization that took place in the 1980s and 1990s. This chapter will first outline the main approaches to analysing democratization. It will then consider different analytical models of democracy and indexes to measure democracy. Then it will survey the more recent literature on authoritarian systems and why they persist. The final part of this chapter will discuss the challenges that confront democracy in the face of this authoritarian revival, including that of populism.

THE SPREAD OF DEMOCRACY

According to Freedom House in the USA, there were 122 electoral democracies in the world in 2013, which represented 63 per cent of the 195 countries and territories surveyed. This is an enormous increase compared with the end of the 1980s, when just 41 per cent of 167 states were democracies. The first time that a majority of states in the world were democratic was 1992–3 (Freedom House, 2015). Clearly, the collapse of communist regimes in Eastern Europe and the former Soviet Union (FSU) was the most important factor in this change, but it was not the only one. Replacement of authoritarian regimes by democracies had already started in the 1970s. According to Huntington (1991), the 'third wave' of democratization began in 1974 with the demise of the long-standing authoritarian regime in Portugal, followed by the end of Franco's dictatorship in neighbouring Spain the following year—**see Table 15.1** for the three waves of democratization.

The World Values survey in 2000 showed that at least 63 per cent of the respondents in seventy-nine out of eighty countries agreed with the proposition that 'democracy may have its problems but it's better than any other form of government'. Nigeria was the sole exception with only 45 per cent agreeing (Inglehart et al., 2004: table E123). All of this suggests that democracy has become the predominant legitimate form of state organization around the world.

➡ For a discussion of why democracy is regarded as special, see Chapter 5.

DEMOCRATIZATION

Why do people embrace democracy? According to an important recent study by Welzel (2013), World Values Surveys over more than twenty years show that the aspiration for democracy is part of a more general syndrome of emancipative values—the aspiration to be free from external domination and dependency.

Table 15.1 The three waves of democratization

1828–1926	1943–62	1974–
US	Uruguay	Portugal
UK	Brazil	Spain
France	Argentina	Argentina
Switzerland	Colombia	Brazil
Italy	Peru	Philippines
Argentina	Venezuela	Taiwan
	W. Germany	S. Korea
	Italy	Pakistan
	Japan	E. Europe
	India	FSU
	Sri Lanka	Mexico
	Philippines	Nigeria
	Israel	S. Africa

Source: Huntington (1991: 16–26).

Democracy is conventionally held to have originated in ancient Athens in the fifth century BC. Certainly, the term itself came from classical Greek, designating a different form of rule from that of aristocracy or dictatorship. However, Keane has argued in his magisterial history of democracy (2009) that the practice of communities running their affairs through assemblies is much older—up to two millennia earlier—and can be traced back at least to Persia, India, and the Phoenician Empire. The term 'democracy' may be Western, but the practice has never been exclusively Western.

➜ See Chapter 4 for a further discussion of democracy.

Political science has generated an enormous literature to analyse the global rise of democracy over the last thirty years. Basically, it divides into two types of analysis: first, long-term trends of modernization that create preconditions for democracy and opportunities for democratic entrepreneurs; and, second, the sequences of more short-term events and actions of key actors at moments of national crisis that have precipitated a democratic transition—what has sometimes been dubbed 'transitology'. Let us consider these two alternative approaches in turn.

Long-Term Structural Trends (I): Economic Development

One constantly recurring claim has been that the emergence of democracy is part of a broader pattern of modernization. An influential early example of this approach was Lerner's *The Passing of Traditional Society* (1958), which focused mainly on the Middle East. It suggested that modernization led to increasing convergence of social, economic, and political structures as well as ways of life. 'Modern' people around the world had more in common with each other than they did with the remaining 'tradition-oriented' sections of their separate societies. And what had driven this transformation, according to Lerner? Primarily, it was economic change.

This sparked one of the most heatedly debated trends in the study of democratization which continues to the present day: the possible connection between economic development and democratic change. Lipset (1959) argued that the more prosperous a nation, the greater its ability to sustain democracy. Over the last fifty years, this claim has provoked a veritable flood of analyses of evidence for and against. According to Huntington (1991), historical evidence showed that states with a per capita income of at least US$3,000 (in contemporary nominal, not Purchasing Power Parity, terms) were very unlikely to see a successful military overthrow of a democratically elected, civilian government. While this did not explicitly equate to a claim that democracy was assured in states with that level of per capita income, it was very suggestive.

Subsequently, Przeworski et al. (2000) qualified the argument by distinguishing between the role of economic development in launching democratization and its role in strengthening democracy once it had been established. They claimed that there was no persuasive evidence of economic development bringing about democratization, only of it strengthening democracy once established. Soon afterwards, however, Boix and Stokes (2003) rebutted this argument with equally weighty statistical evidence to claim that it did bring about democratization. In any case, whichever was true, no-one could claim there were no exceptions. India is regularly cited as a counterfactual example to both theories, since it has been a functioning democracy almost continuously since independence in 1947, despite the fact that even now its per capita income, at around US$2,000, is still below the level predicted to bring democratic stability. On the other hand, Singapore, with a per capita income estimated by the World Bank in 2018 at US$64,582, still is not a democracy. Even if either explanation could claim validation from the trajectories of most democracies in the world, the most that either of them could demonstrate is correlation, not causation. This raises the question of why economic development should lead to democratic change.

15

Long-Term Structural Trends (II): The Rise of the Middle Class

Again, it was Lipset (1960) who suggested the first and most influential hypothesis. Economic development depended on the emergence of a middle class, whose interests and ambitions led them to challenge traditional elites and demand a share in national affairs, which could only be satisfied by democracy. This was what the history of Western Europe showed. This too has led to a welter of studies that seek to identify and theorize the political aspirations and activities of middle classes in states around the world. For Barrington Moore (1966: 418), the converse also applied in the past to Russia and China: why had they not democratized? As he put it, 'no bourgeois, no democracy'. Historically, he argued, authoritarian rule there had prevented the emergence of an independent-minded bourgeoisie.

Until the 'third wave' of democracy, this supposition seemed generally plausible. To some extent, Huntington's analysis could be said to have updated this approach, since a higher level of development might be assumed to require a more developed middle class too. It still applies. For example, one of the key factors that led to the refashioning of democracy in Turkey under the Justice and Democracy Party (Adalet ve Kalkinma Partisi—AKP) since 2002 has been the material support and encouragement of Muslim small businessmen in the Anatolian heartland (Bugre and SavasKan, 2014).

But Huntington's analysis is not universally valid. It is difficult to argue that the middle classes played the key role in the downfall of the communist regimes of Eastern Europe and the FSU, or in the 'Arab Spring'. Also, in 'developmental states' (identified in Chapter 3) outside the West, the state has dominated the middle class in directing development. Businessmen there tend to be more dependent on the state for finance, contracts, and favours, so they are more cautious about advocating political and economic liberalization for fear of being penalized by government. For example, in China, where even though per capita income in 2018 was calculated by the International Monetary Fund (IMF) and the World Bank at US\$9,771, which puts it at the top end of the range when a transition to democracy might be expected, the state continues to dominate the economy and resist democratization ('Building of democracy in China', 2005; Nathan, 2013; Chen, 2013).

So analysis of the path to democratization in any particular country requires consideration of a wider range of factors.

Short-Term Explanations: 'Transitology'

Other attempts to theorize the reasons for the relative success or failure of democratization have focused on more immediate, short-term factors. The collapse of communist regimes and the rising wave of democratization in the 1990s sparked academic and policy-oriented analysis, which is sometimes called 'transitology'. This sought to identify and disseminate lessons of successful democratic transition after events of a national crisis. Part of its attraction lay in the fact that it offered the hope not only of a smoother, less painful transition for the latecomers to democratization, but also of engineering a successful transition even in states that might lack many of the obvious 'prerequisites' for democracy. In this sense, it was the reverse of the Barrington Moore approach outlined above. Where Moore had suggested that some states were fated to fail at democratization because they had followed the 'wrong' path to modernization, transitology suggested that skilful political statecraft might lead to the triumph of democracy even in the most unfavourable context. Both of these approaches of course suffered from over-simplification. Any radical political change is bound to be messy and difficult to control. However, the proliferation of democratic experiments in the 1990s led some to offer a more sophisticated conceptual framework to structure successful transitions to democracy.

The best-known example of this approach is the so-called 'pacted' path to democratization (Karl, 1990). According to this principle, once democratic change is accepted on to the national agenda, all the major political players need to agree on the ground rules for that transition, preferably in the shape of a formal pact. Either implicitly or explicitly, they are also to agree to abide by those rules, even if the final outcome does not favour them. This pact establishes democracy as the only game in town. The prototype for this approach occurred during the transition to democracy in Venezuela in 1958, when the leaders of the three main parties signed the Pact of Punto Fijo committing them to respect the outcome of the forthcoming general election. This inaugurated forty years of democracy for Venezuela. As it is located in a region not noted for the longevity of democratic regimes, it often came to be presented as a model for successful democratic transition in general.

It is true that the essentiality of a 'pact' in ensuring a successful democratic transition can be exaggerated. Democratization has certainly taken place in surprising places without pacts in place; for example, in Indonesia after the fall of President Suharto in 1998. Yet successful transitions have taken place in unpropitious circumstances where pacts were in place, while the lack of a 'pact' has scuppered successful democratic transitions. As we can see from **Box 15.1**, pacts are easier to recommend in theory than to agree in the midst of a chaotic systemic crisis, with extremists on all sides trying to derail the whole process.

➡ For the later downfall of liberal democracy in Venezuela, see Chapter 12.

CASE STUDY BOX 15.1
Pacts and Democratic Transitions

For successful 'pact'-based democratic transitions, consider Poland and South Africa.

Poland

By the end of the 1980s, many felt that no regime in Eastern Europe had less legitimacy than Poland. The military government of President Jaruzelski had ruled since 1981, pre-empting the alternative of a likely Soviet invasion, but it had repressed Solidarność (Solidarity, a Polish trade union), it was despised by most of the population, it was shunned by the West, and the country was effectively bankrupt. In 1989, the regime and Solidarity finally embarked upon difficult, public, round-table negotiations to try to formulate a way out. This lasted three months and eventually they agreed a formula that would allow Solidarity to stand for election to the parliament for the first time, with some seats reserved for it in a (relatively) free and fair election. Until then the ruling Polish United Workers Party (PUWP) had insisted upon approving all candidates for seats in parliament and took most of them themselves. The PUWP had again reserved 65 per cent of the seats for themselves, but to everyone's surprise Solidarity won all the remaining seats that were contested. Even the Solidarity leaders had not expected this result, let alone the regime. Yet they all accepted the outcome. The PUWP faded away and was dissolved in 1990. Since then, Poland has gone through political reconciliation and gradual transformation that has turned it into one of the most successful democratizers, despite the initial economic trauma of

15

→

 For more
discussion on the
fall of
Communism in
Poland, see
Chapter 13.

radical 'shock therapy' through radical market reforms and privatization of state-owned indus-try. Afterwards, even former communists could find a way back into politics. In 1995, the former communist, Kwasniewski, outpolled the iconic Lech Walesa to become the second president of free Poland. Since it is the largest state in Eastern Europe, Poland's significance for the eventual success of the quiet revolutions in the rest of the region cannot be overstated.

South Africa after the end of apartheid

By the end of the 1980s, few believed in a bright future for South Africa. A pariah racist state shunned by the rest of the world, with increasing violence perpetrated by the regime upon its enemies and vice versa, it seemed destined for a bloodbath. Yet from the late 1980s, the Boer regime had begun secret talks with representatives of the African National Congress, which led to Nelson Mandela's release from prison in 1990. From then on, the official regime and the black opposition engaged in protracted public negotiations over transition to majority rule. These lasted for three years and were periodically interrupted by brutal violence and murders, with extremists on both sides trying to disrupt the negotiations and harm their enemies. But in the end, an agreement was reached on a transition that involved an agreement over power-sharing that came into force in 1994. Since then, despite many economic problems, South Africa has been one of the most successful democracies in Africa.

Russia: A failed and 'pact'-less tradition

There, early optimism over democracy in the 1990s has given way to an increasingly authoritari-an regime since 2000. Though commentators have offered various explanations, such as the lack of a democratic tradition in Russia and a persisting political culture of deference to a strong state, it can equally well be argued that the failure results from decisions made by the Yeltsin regime during the transition to democracy. The collapse of the communist regime in December 1991

15

Photo 15.1 Nelson Mandela. *Alamy (discount): Alexander Caminada/Alamy Stock Photo*

raised hopes abroad that Russia might make as successful a transition to democracy as the states in Eastern Europe. However, in Russia there was no pact between the key political actors over what should replace communism. President Yeltsin did not believe that the failure of the coup in August 1991 signalled the definitive defeat of the communist opposition. The Communist Party remained by far the strongest political organization in Russia and all the military high command had been party members before 1991. To guard against a communist-military coup, Yeltsin refused to hold new elections to the national parliament in case the democrats lost. This led to two years of wrangling between Yeltsin and the opposition in the existing Supreme Soviet, culminating in Yeltsin's own 'coup' in 1993, when loyal troops shelled the parliament to get the opposition out. Until he resigned in 1999, Yeltsin seemed much more preoccupied either with dismantling the power bases of the communists or with undermining potential rivals than with building robust new democratic institutions. Instead of trying to agree on ground rules with the opposition, he polarized and stigmatized any opposing views. Russia failed to build a democratic system that enjoyed widespread legitimacy. At the same time, he introduced radical 'shock therapy' economic reforms that savagely cut the standard of living of most of the population. Given these circumstances, the lack of support for democracy among Russians seemed understandable. In the World Values Survey held at the end of the 1990s, Russia recorded the lowest level of satisfaction with the way that democracy was developing in their country, with only 7 per cent of respondents declaring themselves 'very' or 'rather satisfied' (Inglehart et al., 2004: E110). Many Russians in turn believed that things would only get better with President Putin in charge.

After a decade, however, the democratization wave of the 1990s began to subside. With it subsided confidence in devising recipes for successful transitions. In 2002, Carothers wrote a provocative critique: 'The End of the Transition Paradigm'. In it, he remarked that devotees of transitology had applied the formula too simplistically. They had assumed that states in transition were necessarily moving towards democracy, while this was not necessarily the case. External advice needed to be tailored to specific local conditions and to be sensitive to national traditions; for example, in some cases, insisting on early elections might cause greater division than cooperation between social groups.

In January 2014, the issue acquired a new lease of life, at least in part as a response to the worsening situation in the Middle East, where the early optimism over the Arab Spring turned into bafflement as one country after another descended into murderous chaos. Instead of a pact, all too often what came to the fore was resentment, recrimination, and revenge over past repression, rather than cooperation for a better future. The same happened in Iraq after 2003 despite, or because of, the Anglo-American invasion. Nor was this fate restricted to the Middle East. The earlier 'colour revolutions' in Ukraine and Kyrgyzstan also failed to establish a stable democratic order.

This series of failures testifies to both the complexity of post-authoritarian transitions and potential benefit of getting them right. While accepting all of Carothers' scepticism about the objectivity of 'transitology' mentioned above, the fate of these regimes demonstrates the costs of failed transitions, human even more than financial. The opportunity for freedom is not in itself enough to ensure democratic success.

These two sections have demonstrated the difficulty in identifying a predominant or set route to democracy. The combination of long- and short-term causes and effects in the democratization of any given country requires sensitive analysis. Any adequate analysis generally requires consideration of both.

KEY POINTS

- The aspiration for democracy is part of a broader aspiration for freedom.
- There are two basic approaches to explanations for democratization, focusing on long-term socio-economic change, or on the short-term interplay of key political actors at moments of crisis.
- Democratization has long been correlated with economic development and with the rise of the middle class, especially in the West, although there are many exceptions.
- In developmental states, social groups beyond the middle class may be more active in pushing for democracy.
- There is no 'science' of transitions, but evidence suggests skilful statecraft can facilitate success.
- The most desirable element in a transition is a 'pact' between the key political actors over the ground rules for the new system that all respect.
- However, there is still no guarantee that the collapse of an authoritarian system will lead to democracy.

TYPES OF DEMOCRACY

15

One of the strengths of democracy has been its flexibility—its ability to adapt to a wide range of different circumstances. Athenian democracy was based on direct, regular involvement of the public in all key public decisions, if only involving male citizens. Subsequently, as states got bigger, direct decision-making came to be replaced by representation.

➡ See Chapter 4 for a discussion of representation.

Today, it is difficult to settle on a set of core institutions common to all states that call themselves 'democracies'. In part this is because of the increasing number of states that claim to be democratic, but different from the liberal West (Zakaria, 1997), such as Iran, Pakistan, Turkey, and, now, Russia. Even North Korea claims to be a democracy. In part, it is because the term is used in an enormous variety of ways (Paley, 2002) and, in part, it is because academic analysts disagree widely over which systems can meaningfully be classed as democracies—leading to wrangles over 'democracy with adjectives', as Collier and Levitsky (1997) put it (e.g. liberal democracy, representative democracy, multi-party democracy, populist democracy, etc.).

Keane (2009) has proposed another version of democracy with an adjective, i.e. 'monitory democracy'. By this, he means that the key common principle is not how decisions are made, nor ensuring choice between candidates for public office (although elections are crucial too), but rather holding officials and governments accountable for their actions—as he puts it, 'putting politicians, parties and elected governments permanently on their toes'. This makes it for him 'the most complex form of democracy yet' (Keane, 2009: 689). He also commends it as the closest to a universal form in the modern era. Yet, insofar as consultative authoritarian regimes also organize elections and hold officials to account, this approach can blur the distinction between democracies and authoritarian regimes.

An earlier and very influential model of democracy in modern Western industrial societies is Dahl's 'polyarchy'. Extrapolating from his analysis of how local government operated in 1960s New Haven, Connecticut, this focuses on the activity of members of a range of elites who represent wider sections of the population. It aimed to update the traditional notion of representative democracy so that it better reflected the realities of political power in the large states of the late twentieth century. For details, **see Box 15.2**.

A more widely used term, however, is liberal democracy. There is no complete consensus on the key elements of liberal democracies, but Diamond has provided a useful list of the common features. (**See Box 15.3**.)

Whether one prefers the term polyarchy or liberal democracy—and there is evidently a lot of overlap—there is no doubt about the need for some kind of analytical distinction between at least two different types of democracy: a minimalist one that consists essentially of just elections, and another, more elaborate version, that displays many more dimensions of popular involvement in public decision-making. More recently, Møller and Skaaning (2013) have gone further and proposed a simple four-stage analytical typology of different types of democracy. This is reproduced in **Table 15.2**. For them, the key difference between polyarchy and liberal democracy is that the latter explicitly requires the rule of law.

KEY QUOTE BOX 15.2
Polyarchy

Polyarchy is a political order distinguished by the presence of seven institutions, all of which must exist for a government to be classified as a polyarchy:

1. Elected officials. Control over government decisions about policy is constitutionally vested in elected officials.
2. Free and fair elections. Elected officials are chosen in frequent and fairly conducted elections in which coercion is comparatively uncommon.
3. Inclusive suffrage. Practically all adults have the right to vote in the election of officials.
4. Right to run for office. Practically all adults have the right to run for elective offices in the government, though age limits may be higher for holding office than for the suffrage.
5. Freedom of expression. Citizens have a right to express themselves without the danger of severe punishment on political matters broadly defined, including criticism of officials, the government, the regime, the socio-economic order, and the prevailing ideology.
6. Alternative information. Citizens have a right to seek out alternative sources of information. Moreover, alternative sources of information exist and are protected by laws.
7. Associational autonomy. To achieve their various rights, including those listed above, citizens also have a right to form relatively independent associations or organizations, including independent political parties and interest groups.

(Dahl, 1989: 221)

15

> **KEY QUOTE** BOX 15.3
> Liberal Democracy

The deeper level of liberal democracy requires the following:

- Freedom of belief, expression, organization, demonstration, and other civil liberties, including protection from political terror and unjustified imprisonment.
- A rule of law, under which all citizens are treated equally and due process is secure.
- Political independence and neutrality of the judiciary and of other institutions of 'horizontal accountability' that check the abuse of power, such as electoral administration, the audit, and the central bank.
- An open, pluralistic civil society, which affords citizens multiple, ongoing channels for expression and representation of their interests and values, in independent associations and movements and in the mass media as well.
- Freedom of cultural, religious, ethnic, and other minorities to speak their languages, practice their cultures, and express their identities.
- Civilian control over the military.

(Diamond, 2002: 213)

The merit of this typology is that it provides a clear and relatively simple framework for assessing the extent of a particular system's democracy. It also embodies an implicit sequencing of stages for deepening democracy. But the next question then is how to 'measure' a country's democracy. How might individual dimensions of democracy be assessed? Can this data be synthesized into an overall assessment? And if this can be done, should it be?

KEY POINTS

- Numerous different models of democracy have been proposed.
- Often, these use Western experiences as a reference point.
- It makes analytical sense to differentiate between different levels of democracy.
- The two most widely used models of developed democracy are polyarchy and liberal democracy.

Table 15.2 Typology of democratic regimes

	Competitive Elections	Inclusive Elections with High Integrity	Civil Liberties	Rule of Law
Minimalist democracy	+			
Electoral democracy	+	+		
Polyarchy	+	+	+	
Liberal democracy	+	+	+	+

Source: Møller and Skaaning (2013).

MEASURING DEMOCRACY

There are two common strategies to measure democracy. The first is to assess a particular system along a set of dimensions that constitute what it means to be democratic and then synthesize them into a single score. The best-known example of this is the Freedom House Index, based in the USA. This ranking assesses the extent of freedom (rather than primarily democracy) in a country along two fundamental dimensions: political rights and civil liberties. These are then synthesized into an overall assessment.

It is the most comprehensive survey of its kind, now covering 195 countries and fourteen territories. It is repeated every year, and as a result perhaps its greatest strength is the way it charts changes over time. Its data are often used in quantitative academic research to search for correlations with other dimensions of social and economic development.

It is not, however, the only such index. Other similar, albeit less comprehensive, indexes include the Bertelsmann Foundation's Transformation Index, the Economist Intelligence Unit's Democracy Index, and the Polity IV database of political regimes.

Since the focus of each of these indexes is slightly different, and since each depends on judgements by analysts, they may come to different assessments of individual countries. Freedom House, for instance, classifies France as fully free, and Pakistan as partly free, while Polity IV classifies both as democracies, but not 'complete democracies', unlike, for example, the USA, the UK, Germany, Italy, and Spain.

There is a further problem: all these institutions are based in the West. They can create the impression of being superior teachers, marking the 'grades' of non-Western states like pupils. Freedom House is not a politically neutral institution—it deliberately aims to promote democracy—and chiefly American-style democracy—around the world. This, in itself, can antagonize citizens, not to mention governments, of developing countries, who resent the perceived condescension.

Koelble and LiPuma (2008) have forcefully urged the 'democratization of democracy', arguing that the democratizing trajectory of postcolonial states is bound to be different from that of developed countries (though, of course, the USA was itself originally a colony). They rejected the possibility of an ahistorical, value-neutral, scientific measurement of democracy, since the starting point for ex-colonies—inequality and entrenched discrimination between ethnic or other communities—still hangs over them, in a way that former metropolitan states have never had to confront.

The International Institute for Democracy and Electoral Assistance (IDEA), an institution which promotes democracy internationally, has responded to this line of criticism. It produced a handbook of a myriad possible proposals for democratization (Beetham et al., 2002). However, the expectation was that citizens wanting to promote democracy in their country would carry out a 'democratic audit' of their system, identify the most obvious obstacles to democracy, and then set out the most urgent and important recommendations appropriate for reform for them. IDEA has been criticized for not providing a methodologically consistent, sequenced programme for democratization (though it has compiled a great deal of useful comparative data on aspects of democracy around the world). Rather, its main objective was to inspire democracy activists in the field to action. Even if this led to conflicting priorities between countries, it would not matter, since IDEA accepts different trajectories to democracy.

15

> **KEY POINTS**
>
> - There are two diverging approaches to devising a methodology for measuring a country's democracy.
> - The first—and most common—is to compile a standard list of indicators, devise an analytical framework for assessing them, and form a group of experts in one centre to apply the methodology consistently.
> - The alternative is to encourage democracy activists in individual countries to come up with their own list of the most urgent areas for democratic or democratization reform, possibly providing them with a checklist of all the things that they might wish to include.
> - 'Liberal democracy' as a term is too suggestive of Western democracy.
> - It cannot be assumed that developed democracies have to be 'liberal'.

VARIETY IN DEMOCRACY

An early article in the *Journal of Democracy* made a point that is often overlooked in the hunt for quantitative assessment. It is possible for states to be 'differently democratic' (Schmitter and Karl, 1991: 77), even those with consolidated democracies. Møller and Skaaning have proposed 'liberal democracy' for the most developed form, but the use of the term inevitably carries overtones of Western superiority, since the typical models of liberal democracy tend to be found in the West. The term is not value-free. It can imply that as democracies develop around the world, they will inevitably converge with those in the West. In the very long run this scenario may indeed prove correct, but for now it seems premature and contentious.

One country that epitomizes this issue is India, as we shall see in **Box 15.4**.

Scepticism about the appropriateness of the term 'liberal' for India and other democracies is not to question the extent or the depth of their democracy. Rather it is to question the

15

CASE STUDY BOX 15.4
Indian Democracy: Consolidated—But Liberal?

India is unquestionably a consolidated democracy with a well-established legal system and it embodies all four characteristics of liberal democracy listed in **Table 15.1**, though to varying degrees. In 2014, 1,766 national or local political parties were registered with the Indian Electoral Commission, so there is no doubt about competitive elections. In the 2019 general election, over 600 million people voted, a turnout of 67.1 per cent. Though there are always allegations of vote-buying, the legitimacy of this outcome was not seriously challenged. There are substantial legal protections for civil rights. The courts are active and authoritative, if overworked. In 2019, Freedom House classed India as free, but gave it an overall score of 2.5—the lowest possible composite figure for a state in the 'fully free' category. India is unquestionably a consolidated democracy, but is it a liberal one?

Photo 15.2 A city in India. *Shutterstock RF via DAM: sladkozaponi/Shutterstock*

There are two problem areas. The first concerns Indian political culture, i.e. the framework of shared understandings within which Indian democracy operates. Implicit in the term 'liberal democracy' are three connotations more associated with the West: equality between individuals, toleration based on individualism, and free-market economics—the sorts of ideas associated with thinkers like John Stuart Mill and Adam Smith. Indian writers such as Chatterjee (2010: 297) have sought to emphasize the deep differences in social values between India and the West: 'community has a very tenuous place in the Western liberal theory of civil society and state; in the new political societies of the East, communities are some of the most active agents of political practice'.

While Chatterjee is advocating tolerance in the West for non-Western social values, this could also have darker implications. For example, it could lead to condoning group discrimination and violence. Indian politics, like Indian society, continues to be heavily impacted by local or regional hierarchical caste systems, legitimated by Hindu religious traditions, which segment people into different hereditary groups. 'Discrimination, degradation and violence were written into customary norms of caste relations' (Varshney, 2013: 214). Economic development and democracy have profoundly affected inter-caste relations. Yet violence is still often perpetrated against couples who try to marry across caste-lines, as well as against non-Hindus, such as Muslims.

According to Varshney (2013: 114), 'politics since Nehru [the first Indian prime minister] has paid even less ideological attention to the principles of pluralism and tolerance'. For Mohanty (2004: 117), the ethic that has taken over (not surprisingly in a former colony) is *swarajatantra*,

→

i.e. self-rule and liberation. A bewildering array of groups—whether ethnic, religious, or regional—pursue their own liberation against others more or less as a zero-sum game, often violently. It does not make for liberal toleration.

And as for economic liberalism, the first leaders after independence wanted to develop rapidly without the capitalism of their former colonial masters. So they established a developmental state that would direct development for the national good. Even though some liberalization has taken place more recently, Varshney (2013: 39) notes: 'India still has not witnessed a national-level politician who can make a *political* claim on behalf of markets and integrate it as part of an election campaign' (emphasis in original).

The second problem is a consequence of the first. While all Indian citizens are constitutionally equal before the law, not all enjoy equal treatment. To overcome caste discrimination, the constitution lays down special rights for particular groups of citizens, particularly those from the Scheduled Castes, the Scheduled Tribes, and the Other Backward Classes. This grants them special privileges in terms of state employment and standing for elected office. Even though significant progress has been made in reducing traditional inequality, castes have become interest groups with a kind of veto power to prevent dilution of these rights, so there is unlikely to be much change soon.

Thus, on both these counts, it is difficult to apply the term liberal democracy to India.

→ See Chapter 9 for a discussion of liberalism in India and Turkey.

appropriateness of the label itself. A more neutral term would seem preferable that allowed for countries to be 'differently democratic', such as consolidated or stable democracy. Bell (2006) has expressed similar scepticism about the relevance of 'liberal democracy' in East Asia for potential democracies such as Singapore and China, as we shall see in **Box 15.5**. And no doubt the same would be argued about Turkey. Though the ruling AKP presents itself as more liberal than its opponents, it is still conservative rather than liberal in its attitudes towards social values (Axiarlis, 2014). According to White (2003, 2013), liberalism as a doctrine is contentious in Turkey because for many it is associated with (aggressive) Western-style secularism, even if imposed by Turkey's own rulers.

The Resurgence of Populism

This has acquired a particular resonance recently, especially in the West. Populism was widespread in Africa after decolonization, and also in Latin America after the Second World War until the 1990s. But it seemed to have faded away, especially in Latin America, with the 'third wave' of democratization, as a result of policy failures and protests over human rights abuses. Now it is coming back. The most striking examples are the victory of Donald Trump in the US and the vote to Leave in the UK Brexit referendum. Now populist parties regularly win 15–20 per cent of the vote in European countries. Marine Le Pen from the Front National came second in the presidential election in France in 2017. The Syriza party ran the government in Greece between 2015 and 2019. And Viktor Orban has been President of Hungary since 2010. These are all populists, but perhaps the biggest change has taken place in Italy, where it can be argued that

KEY DEBATE BOX 15.5
Equality versus Elitism in Democracy

de Tocqueville on the primacy of equality in democracies:

> Democratic institutions awaken and foster a passion for equality which they can never
> entirely satisfy . . . It has been supposed that the secret instinct which leads the lower
> orders to remove their superiors as much as possible from the direction of public af-
> fairs is peculiar to France. This is an error, however; the instinct to which I allude is not
> French, it is democratic . . .
>
> I think that democratic communities have a natural taste for freedom . . . But for
> equality their passion is ardent, insatiable, incessant, invincible; they call for equali-
> ty in freedom; and if they cannot obtain that, they still call for equality in slavery.
> de Tocqueville (1994: i, 201–2; ii, 97)

Bell on the need to take elitism seriously in designing democracy for East Asia:

> Few, if any, Western liberal democratic theorists in the post-World War II era have
> sought to learn from the traditions and experiences of East Asian societies . . . Western
> liberal democratic theory stands out by its apparent imperviousness to developments
> in East Asia and elsewhere in the non-Western world . . .
>
> In the eyes of Singapore elder statesman Lee Kuan Yew, a 'Confucianist view of or-
> der between subject and ruler helps in the rapid transformation of society . . . in other
> words, you fit yourself into society—the exact opposite of the American rights of the
> individual.' A modern Confucian society ruled by wise and virtuous elites, that is, can
> provide the benefits of rapid economic growth and social peace, but it must sacrifice the
> democratic political rights that make government so difficult in the West . . .
>
> Confucian political culture places great emphasis on the quality of political rulers.
> The main task of the educational system is to identify and empower the wise and
> public-spirited elite, and the common people are not presumed to possess the capabili-
> ties necessary for substantial political participation . . .
>
> A modern-day 'Confucian democrat' is therefore confronted with the dilemma that
> while Western-style democratic institutions do not fully accommodate concerns for
> the 'rule of the wise', the 'Parliament of Scholar-Officials' idea goes too far in the elitist
> direction by failing to incorporate any form of political decision-making by the people.
> The compromise solution may seem obvious at this point: a bicameral legislature, with
> a democratically elected lower house and a 'Confucian' upper house composed of rep-
> resentatives selected on the basis of competitive examinations.
> Bell (2006: 4, 8, 152, 165–6)

15

the whole political system has come to be dominated by populists—see **Box 15.6**. And outside
Western Europe, there has been the transformation of Turkey under President Erdogan from an
apparently fairly tolerant, if not liberal, regime, into a much more personalistic, authoritarian one
(Temelkuran, 2019).

CASE STUDY BOX 15.6
The Rise of Populist Movements in Italy

At the beginning of the 1990s the Italian political system was convulsed by two seismic events. In 1991 the collapse of the Soviet Union led to the dissolution of the Italian Communist Party, hitherto the core of the Italian Left since the Second World War. In 1994 the Christian Democrat Party (DC), hitherto the dominant party on the right, was dissolved in the wake of judicial investigation into corruption (the 'Tangentopoli' scandal) and connections with the mafia. This created an entirely new playing field for politics, especially as other parties also disappeared in the wake of these events. At the same time the years of Italy's economic boom had ended, being replaced by increasing problems of deindustrialization and unemployment, which made the public more apprehensive and suspicious of technocratic politicians. By 2013 less than a third of voters declared that they felt 'very close' or 'quite close' to any political party.

The result has been the emergence over time of four distinct populist groupings, which have all risen to take part in government, although their paths to power have been markedly different. They exploited three essential factors: (i) the delegitimation of traditional parties and politicians; (ii) the appeal over their heads to 'ordinary people'; (iii) the coupling of problems (e.g. unemployment) with popular fears (e.g. immigration).

The first major newcomer was the Forza Italia party on the right, led by the media magnate Silvio Berlusconi. This aimed at basically the same public as had previously voted for the DC, but its core was Berlusconi himself, who exploited his media background and TV stations to build a direct relationship with the Italian public. He offered business-friendly programmes of low taxes. He also repeatedly warned against the possible return of 'the communists'. Both his programmes and methods of winning support were reminiscent of the US—he offered a personal 'Contract with Italy' promising a commitment to bring about change, echoing Newt Gingrich's 'Contract with America'. Forza Italia was really Berlusconi's electoral committee, which he ran like a company. For a while he renamed his party 'the House of Liberty', alluding to his antipathy for both communists and a high-tax state. He presented himself as a successful businessman who could achieve for the Italian people what he had achieved for himself—'a million new jobs'. He claimed to be an outsider and railed against the 'puppet shows' of national politics. He did serve as prime minister, but the performance of his governments disappointed, his private life became notorious, he was subjected to various prosecutions for tax fraud over his previous business career (some of which succeeded), and he was gradually supplanted by other populist leaders.

The second populist movement was the Lega Nord (Northern League), which had emerged in the north of the country in the 1980s as a grassroots protest against the large-scale subsidies that were sent to the poorer southern part of the country, but for which it blamed the 'thieving Rome' (*Roma ladrona*), i.e. the national government and its political elite, alleging large-scale corruption (which was later justified by Tangentopoli). For many years it flirted with appeals for independence for its region—which it called Padania—which limited its appeal for the rest of the country, but it did sometimes participate in a fractious coalition with Berlusconi. Its own founder, Umberto Bossi, later got caught up himself in a corruption scandal involving his son, but his successor, Matteo Salvini, has turned it into a national force, dropping the reference to the north in the name, with campaigns against immigrants and the interfering and tightfisted European Union.

The third populist movement, the 5-Star movement, was founded in 2007 by a comedian, Beppe Grillo, who had been satirizing Italian politicians for decades, and a web designer,

15

Gianroberto Casaleggio, who had a vision of how the Internet could be exploited to create a new political party. Unlike movements on the right, it explicitly wanted to encourage mass political participation and support for public goods—education, the environment, etc. It began as an online protest community, but Grillo skilfully used his entertainment and media contacts to organize real-life 'events' that brought supporters, especially young ones, together as much for fun and entertainment as for political action. These grew into national campaigns, such as the V-Day demonstrations ('V' standing for 'b*****-off in Italian, i.e. what the elites should do), when carnivals of protest took to the streets in various cities simultaneously. Gradually this movement turned into a potent left-of-centre political force, although Grillo disclaimed any ambition in politics for himself—he professed to be just 'the megaphone of the people'. So in 2017 the movement selected Luigi Di Maio as its candidate for prime minister in the forthcoming general elections. In those elections the 5-Star movement and the Lega Nord won the largest share of the votes and so their two leaders agreed to form an unlikely coalition of the left and right, with the two leaders serving as deputy prime ministers and a law professor, Giuseppe Conte, as prime minister. Since then the two leaders have engaged in a fiery partnership, both appealing to their popular bases through the media.

The fourth populist leader is Matteo Renzi, the youthful former leader of the Democratic Party. He was no outsider—he came from a well-to-do background, and then joined the newly created Democratic Party, which combined elements from earlier left-wing political parties. He was soon elected Mayor of Florence and then became leader of the party, which he wanted to transform into a much more American-style, open party. Although this was not originally a populist party, Renzi turned himself into a populist leader, not merely with a strongly personal style, but also offering to 'scrap' institutions that were holding Italy back, and using the same kind of brutal political language against 'elites' (the Lega then matched this by putting an excavator on its publicity material). His campaign revolved around the simple theme: 'it can be done' (*si può fare*), which recalled Obama's 'yes, we can'. He was elected the youngest ever prime minister in 2014, but his proposals for radical reform of the constitution (in temporary alliance with Berlusconi) were rejected in a referendum in 2016, and he resigned. However, he has remained a very vocal politician and critic of his successors.

The result has been that populism has come to dominate politics of both the Left and the Right (though their leaders, like Renzi, reject the terms and they all claim that they represent the centre). Casaleggio and Grillo (2011) declared 'war' on the other parties. The aggression of the populists in general has squeezed the rest, as well as the space for other ways of appealing to the public, In summer 2019 the aggressivity produced new instability. The leader of the League, Salvini, ran a very aggressive public campaign against migrants to win support from the South of the country, which has been most impacted by the waves of migrants coming across the Mediterranean and where the League has been weak, and to undermine their coalition partner, the 5-Star movement, which was stronger in the South. This culminated in August 2019 in their withdrawal from government to try to provoke a general election, where Salvini expected to do well. However, to everyone's surprise, the 5-Stars negotiated a deal to form a new coalition with their previous bitter opponents, the Democratic Party (now under a new leader, Nicola Zingaretti), which forced the League into opposition.   (Based on Biorcio, 2014, and Biorcio, 2015)

15

What is Populism?

Fundamentally **populism** challenges liberal democracy. According to Mudde and Kaltwasser (2017: 9–19), there are three basic principles that underpin it: (i) 'the people', though it can receive varying emphases, for example the people as sovereign, the 'common people', or the nation; (ii) an elite or establishment, who actually manipulate power to their advantage and who should be confronted: and (iii) the 'general will' of the people, which should be absolute, as expressed through direct consultation or referendums, but which can be appropriated by individual leaders who instinctively 'know' what it is.

Beyond that, populism is a 'thin' ideology which is usually combined with another, 'thicker' one which proposes more general and specific objectives, e.g. nationalism, socialism, religious belief, or secularism. But these combinations make it more difficult to disentangle populism from its 'host'. Often, the stress upon 'the (ordinary) people' in populism is more likely to prize the virtues and values of local communities over those of allegedly self-interested transnational elites, which is why it is often associated with nationalism. It always implies a (nearby) 'we' opposed to a (distant) 'they'.

Because populist movements view politics from below, they tend to be led by outsiders, or at any rate by people who present themselves as authentic 'men of the people' (and they are almost always men)—in their views, in their speech, in their tastes, in the way they dress, etc. President Fujimori of Peru in the 1990s stressed his poor Japanese immigrant forebears. President Morales in Bolivia stresses his indigenous, pre-Spanish roots, a role that he 'performs' on a daily basis by wearing a traditional sweater. But that does not mean that populists can only come from below. They only have to claim, plausibly, that they are 'outsiders'. President Trump is the most obvious example. Despite his wealthy father and the millions that he himself made from business, he has always regarded himself as an 'outsider' vis-à-vis the comfortable liberal New York establishment, and now the even more comfortable and liberal Washington establishment.

Populists always represent a challenge to the existing order, a protest that things are not working as they should. Eatwell and Goodwin (2018) structure their analysis of populism along the axes of the 'four Ds': distrust, destruction, deprivation, and de-alignment. They often break with the practices of 'conventional' politics. In that sense they could be said to be democratizing it, in that they open new ways of doing politics. But in general they can attempt to win power through three pathways: (i) by taking over an existing political party, as with Jörg Haider and the Austrian Freedom Party in the 1990s, or Matteo Renzi in Italy; (ii) by grassroots civil activism, e.g. the Tea Party in the US, or the Lega Nord in Italy; (iii) by creating a new movement, as did Berlusconi and Grillo in Italy. In practice, the third is the most common because it exemplifies the claim to be creating a new kind of politics. But this also means that leaders may be reluctant to stand down from leadership of the party or movement that they originally created (viz. President Museveni of Uganda mentioned in Chapter 12). Equally, movements may fail because they remain overshadowed by their founder. Venezuela exemplifies the problem. After the death of President Chávez in 2013, his successor. President Maduro, has struggled to maintain the momentum of the 'Bolivarian' socialist transformation of society in the face of mounting economic chaos and protests on the streets. However much he stigmatizes the opposition as 'them', i.e. the elites opposed to the poor who have 'sold out' to American neo-liberalism, his support from the 'real' people shrinks as economic difficulties and physical violence increase, and his challenger, Juan Guaidó, in turn claims to speak on behalf of 'the people'.

15

Populist leaders want a direct and immediate link between decisions and their implementation—see the YouTube video of Chávez excoriating officials to their face for failures. They pride themselves on a direct relationship with 'their people'. As Chávez told a mass demonstration in Caracas: 'I am not an individual, I am the people. It's my duty to demand respect for the people' (*Sydney Morning Herald*, 2010). They would like to talk directly to the people, wherever possible. Chávez held regular and interminable phone-ins under the rubric 'Alo Presidente'. Though populists usually demonstrate great concern about control over traditional media, they will become alive to the possibilities of the Internet and social media for talking directly to the people—viz. the rise of the 5-Star movement in Italy and the victory of Trump.

In general, populists can accept some kinds of political institutions—and often they introduce new constitutions after coming to power, but they are uneasy about institutions in general, even 'democratic' ones, which might be used to frustrate 'the will of the people'. They do not respect an independent judiciary or the rule of law. They certainly are wary of any constitutional 'checks and balances' that might limit the will, President Trump included (Lewis, 2018). The conflicting pressures were exemplified in the name of the populist party that ruled Mexico after its revolution between 1929 and 2000—the Institutional Revolutionary Party (PRI). And because of this suspicion about institutions, they succeed more often in contexts where existing institutions are rather weak, e.g. in newly established democracies such as Eastern Europe, or ones that have already undergone serious institutional upheaval, such as Italy in the 1990s.

The aftermath of the 2008 global financial crisis and popular reactions to austerity have opened the way for populist parties in Europe—Spain, Italy, Greece, etc. They have flourished because the crisis discredited the previous elite consensus on the need for neo-liberal economic policies to spread prosperity, which had downplayed the importance of fairness in distributing the rewards. Grievances have been intensified by the failings of the cartelized political party systems that were explored in Chapter 12, with its tendency to encourage cooperation between party elites (the 'caste') at the expense of ordinary citizens. The populist parties can be said to have remedied democracy by opening the way for new ideas to infiltrate politics. On the other hand, their aggressivity has polarized debate. Marietta and Barker (2019) have vividly shown how liberals and conservatives in the US no longer debate whilst listening to the other side. Instead each side simply doubles down on its own assertions and view of the world. Worryingly, the authors admit they can see no way out of the problem.

This means that populism is not likely to go away in the near future. In any case, according to Canovan (2002: 25), there is a deeper and more long-lasting reason why populism will never go away completely: 'the paradox is that democratic politics does not and cannot make sense to most of the people it aims to empower. The most inclusive and accessible form of politics ever achieved is also the most opaque.' In Chapter 10 we have already seen King remark on the difficulty any American has in understanding the constitution. In Europe the difficulty is magnified by the added layer of complexity provided by the existence of the EU. Ideologies help dispel the mist and 'help' ordinary people understand what 'really' happens. Populism, however 'thin-centred', can be enlisted to do this. It can offer a simpler and apparently more satisfying explanation for events than is offered by regular coverage in the traditional media: basically, that the elite(s) are abusing their position to hoodwink and exploit 'ordinary working people'. The bottom this claim rests upon the principle of the sovereignty of the people, which is also a foundation of democracy. That is why it can never be made to disappear for good.

15

THE PERSISTENCE OF AUTHORITARIAN REGIMES

While the 1990s saw widespread democratization, the period since then has seen a revival of authoritarianism; for example, in Egypt and Venezuela. The number of democracies worldwide continued to creep slowly upwards, but many authoritarian regimes that had seemed 'ripe' for democratization stabilized. Kurlantzik (2013) has written of democracy globally 'in retreat'. Wike and Fetterolf (2018) have written of liberal democracy's 'crisis of confidence'. A third of states in the world remain authoritarian. Others have regressed. Many of their leaders have recovered their self-confidence.

Apart from failed transitions, e.g. in Libya, Syria, Iraq, and Afghanistan, not to mention Russia, two other factors have contributed to this authoritarian revival. The first is the greater level of sophistication of some authoritarian regimes. Shambaugh (2008) has documented the enormous efforts that the Chinese Communist Party (CCP) put into studying the reasons for the collapse of the other communist regimes and learning lessons to aid their survival.

The second factor is the growing internationalization of the confrontation between democratic and authoritarian regimes. This has been marked by the readiness of some authoritarian regimes to intervene in the internal affairs of others, paralleling the efforts of Western governments to spread democracy. Saudi Arabia, the Gulf States, Venezuela, and Russia have all done this (Vanderhill, 2013).

Over the past ten to fifteen years, political scientists have begun to pay more attention to authoritarian regimes. This can encompass a wide variety of regimes: monarchies, personal dictatorships, military regimes, theocratic regimes, racially or ethnically polarized regimes, and one-party dominant regimes. What defines them is what they are *not*, rather than what they are— they are *not* democracies (however that may be defined). Devising a single definition for this very heterogeneous group has thus far proved impossible.

Nevertheless, they do have things in common. After reviewing the literature on authoritarianism, Frantz and Ezrow (2011: 85) point out that regularities appear in different policy outcomes from democracies. Autocracies tend to spend less on social programmes, wages, and environmental policies than democracies. They also tend to attract less foreign direct investment (FDI), perhaps because they also tend to be weaker on enforcing property rights. Perhaps not surprisingly, they also offer the greatest opportunities for corruption. Most strikingly, according to Przeworski et al. (2000: 230), dictatorships tend to have higher death rates (but also higher birth rates) than democracies, whatever the level of development. A graphic example of this was in North Korea in the late 1990s, when anywhere between 240,000 and 3.5 million people died of starvation out of a total population of 22 million. Nobel Prize-winning economist Amartya Sen (1999: 7–8) points to the contrast: 'no substantial famine has ever occurred in any democratic and independent country with a relatively free press'. Furthermore, according to Geddes et al. (2014), it is possible to distinguish different trends in periods of longevity and different patterns of collapse according to whether the regime was monarchical, personalistic, dominated by a military junta, or controlled by a ruling party.

The research on authoritarian regimes has tended to focus on two distinct but overlapping themes of legitimation: (i) how do authoritarian regimes structure their institutions of rule; and (ii) why do ordinary people not challenge authoritarian regimes more?

15

Authoritarian Institutions

Sometimes, authoritarian regimes hold elections to demonstrate their legitimacy, but then one of the puzzles is why people bother to vote when there is no likelihood of it changing the way the country is run. Magaloni (2006) examined the record of the PRI in Mexico which held power from 1929 to 2000, which made it one of the longest-lived ruling parties in the world—almost as long as the Soviet Communist Party. It achieved this without resorting to terror. Instead, it held regular national elections and people regularly voted for it because it offered patronage (jobs working for the government or state corporations, such as the national oil corporation PEMEX), 'pork' (i.e. state largesse for localities that voted for the PRI), and (limited) influence over specific government policies to their supporters (Schedler, 2006: 12–13). So, voters could vote to secure benefits, even if they could not change their rulers.

As for how authoritarian systems structure their rule, Gandhi and Przeworski (2007) have argued that those that hold regular elections last longer than those that do not. And, in general, Gandhi (2008) has shown that dictators have an incentive to create institutions to share in policy-making, both as a way of co-opting support, whether from 'insiders' in the regime or from key elite groups outside it, and also as a Machiavellian way of exposing real or potential opposition. But the recent experience of Turkey illustrates the risks. It can backfire. In March 2019 the AKP narrowly lost the mayoral election for Istanbul, the largest city and hitherto a stronghold. The AKP had been very confident—President Erdogan is himself a former mayor there. It contested the result because of 'procedural irregularities' and forced a rerun. But then in June 2019, the challenger, Ekrem Imamoglu, won a much more decisive victory from an electorate that was scornful of the AKP's machinations. This gave new heart to the opposition.

Authoritarian regimes sometimes adopt institutions more often associated with democracies to stay in power. In Russia, the Kremlin has created a moderate opposition party, A Just Russia (as well as the ruling party United Russia), and a 'social chamber' (in addition to the national parliament) for non-governmental organizations, ostensibly as part of a policy of 'guided democracy' to encourage moderate and constructive new ideas for policy-making and to pre-empt radical opposition. Meanwhile, China has begun experimenting at the local level with its own forms of deliberative democracy (explained in Chapter 4) which were originally devised to strengthen established democracies, as we can see in **Box 15.7**.

In turn, such tendencies complicate the previous categorical distinction between democracies and authoritarian regimes, leading to more hybrid regimes.

15

➡ See Chapter 4 for a discussion of deliberative democracy.

Popular Acceptance of Authoritarianism

It is obvious that terror can subdue peoples, especially if it seems as though any individual, high or low, can be targeted. Frantz and Ezrow (2011: 72) recount the story of Saddam Hussein inviting ministers to contribute ideas on ending the Iran–Iraq War (1980–8) when it was going badly. The minister of health suggested that Saddam should step down temporarily from power to ease negotiations with Iran. For this, he was arrested and executed. 'Insecurity, unpredictability, and fear of the unknown . . . all . . . permeated Iraq' (Sassoon, 2012: 128).

However, most authoritarian regimes do not rely exclusively on terror to maintain their rule because it always risks provoking opposition out of despair and even a counter coup. Even dictators

CASE STUDY BOX 15.7
China as a Hybrid Authoritarian System

China is a striking example of a hybrid authoritarian system. The Chinese Communist Party CCP has ruled since 1949 and does not allow serious political competition. It brutally suppressed opponents, particularly during the Great Leap Forward (1958–60) and the Cultural Revolution (1966–9). Since the death of Mao in 1976, it has gradually moved from personal domination by a single leader towards more institutionalized leadership with no official constitutionally allowed to hold the same leading position for more than ten years. There is significant market freedom and the regime allows private enterprise. Limited competitive elections take place between approved candidates in many villages and townships, and a number of seats in the National People's Congress are reserved for elected representatives from eight 'democratic' parties, though they cannot challenge the leading role of the CCP. However, the regime still controls all key positions in the state apparatus and armed forces, and its members are above the law—they cannot be prosecuted by the legal system unless this has been approved by higher party officials.

According to the World Bank, China is now an upper-middle income country with a per capita income of around US$9,770 in 2018, which puts it well within the range where a transition to democracy might take place. Chinese citizens are economically more free than at any point since 1949. There is now a substantial middle class—according to McKinsey, it amounted to around 475 million people in 2012 ('Mapping China's middle class', 2010). Moreover, the explosion of the Internet and social media users—in June 2014 there were 802 million reported Internet users in China (Forbes, 2018)—gives citizens much greater opportunities to express views publicly than at any time since 1949, even though the state organizes widespread surveillance of online activity and bans Western search engines and social media sites.

However, widespread demonstrations in favour of democracy were brutally suppressed across the country in June 1989 and the current leader, President Xi Jinping, has reversed the relatively relaxed policies of his predecessor by increasing restrictions on freedom of speech—reportedly Western democracy is now a taboo subject in Chinese universities ('Western values forbidden', 2015). The 2019 Press Freedom Index of the organization Reporters Without Borders ranked China 177 out of 180 countries ('World Press Freedom Index', 2019). Instead, the CCP has mounted an increasingly draconian campaign against official corruption, using language of popular accountability akin to that associated with Keane's 'monitory democracy'. It harps on the need for social stability and is very wary of an untutored civil society.

At the same time, officials respond to proposals and criticisms from civil society groups to develop better policies, and they use the social media to stimulate citizen responses to individual policy initiatives. In this way, it practises a consultative authoritarianism that encourages and exploits popular support for social stability and sustained improvements in the standard of living (Teets, 2014). This combination of rapid economic growth and stable elite leadership elicits positive responses elsewhere in East Asia (Welsh and Chang, 2015), and in the West too.
(Berggruen and Gardels, 2013)

15

need legitimation, including Saddam Hussein. According to Sassoon on Iraq (2012: 193): 'Fear played a major role in sustaining the Ba'ath regime for more than three decades, but the party's control of the population was not based only on fear. An elaborate system of rewards and punishments provided a robust framework for the Ba'ath Party's domination.'

Divide and rule—privileging some groups over others—is a technique that has supported dictatorships and empires since at least Roman times. This may involve the use of brutality—for example, the military government in Myanmar continued to exploit civil war with minorities in various parts of the country to legitimize its rule with the majority Burmese (Callahan, 2003), as has happened in Syria.

KEY POINTS

- The term 'authoritarian regime' can be applied to a very disparate group of states.
- Authoritarian rule can rest on terror, threats, and coercion.
- Authoritarian rulers are also concerned to legitimize their rule.
- The more skilful authoritarian rulers devise institutions to give at least the appearance of involving people outside the core leadership in policy-making, if not of sharing power.
- This can lead to hybrid regimes that have at least some features of democracy.

CONCLUSION: SMARTER DEMOCRACY, DEEPER DEMOCRACY, OR TOWARDS DEMOCRATIC-AUTHORITARIAN HYBRIDITY?

As authoritarianism has revived, satisfaction with democracy in the West has declined. As the Norwegian sociologist Ringen put it: 'At the moment in history when the standing of democracy in the world is stronger than ever, its standing in the eyes of citizens is weak and probably weakening' (Ringen, 2007: 41). He wrote this before the global financial and the Eurozone crises which have further shaken confidence in Western governments. Della Porta (2013) has raised the question of whether democracy (at least traditional liberal representative democracy) can be saved at all.

Critical questions and challenges multiply. Are democracies too prone to concentrate on short-term issues? Can they devise policies to tackle big long-term challenges, such as climate change (Burnell, 2012)? What about preserving intergenerational equality between older and younger generations over paying for social services? Berggruen and Gardels (2013: 9), for instance, have suggested that more intelligent public governance for the twenty-first century would synthesize, as they put it, Western 'consumer democracy' and Chinese 'meritocratic Confucianism' into 'knowledgeable democracy' with 'accountable meritocracy'.

Runciman (2013) agrees with some of these criticisms in his survey of crises that have challenged Western democracies since the early twentieth century. Democracies do find it difficult to take the long view. The time horizon of (most) elected legislators is no longer than the date for their re-election. Yet, while democracies may find it difficult to devise long-term plans, and

15

even more difficult to stick to them, he also concludes that democracies are better at coping with complex social and economic changes and adapting to them because they are more pragmatic. Incremental change is what democracies do best. But because they have surmounted difficulties in the past, people in democracies also suffer from what he terms the 'confidence trap', i.e. a refusal to address serious problems until almost too late, believing that they will muddle through again somehow, as they (almost) always have. Casual democratic optimism brings costs, even within established democracies.

As Ringen (2007) suggests, in the end democracy will survive and thrive if its citizens believe that they enjoy a strong sense of freedom and control. In other words, democracy needs to sustain the sense of emancipation that was mentioned at the beginning of this chapter. In general, people do not choose to live under authoritarianism if given a real choice, though they may put up with it for the sake of other compensations. As the World Values Surveys show, there is near-universal majority support for the principle of democracy, but the ways in which that principle is implemented vary considerably, and that variety is only likely to increase. It certainly is no longer the case that the traditional Western model of liberal, representative, parliamentary democracy inspires deference at home or abroad. New forms of democracy and/or new political actors are needed to revive it. Already more than a decade ago the Council of Europe (2004) came up with a list of reforms to restore confidence of citizens in their democracies in Europe (though few have been implemented). Democratic reformers will try to learn lessons from the experiences of other countries, and not just in the West. Local experiments in participatory budgeting in Brazil and India have inspired imitation in Western Europe (Rocke, 2014). Conversely, authoritarian regimes will also sometimes borrow lessons to try to increase their legitimacy without, they hope, losing control. Populism can be either democratic or authoritarian. Whether or not that leads to hybrid regimes, these trends will complicate attempts to differentiate between democratic and authoritarian regimes. So rigorous thinking and consistent use of concepts will be more vital than ever for meaningful analysis and debate.

KEY QUESTIONS

1. How useful is the term 'monitory democracy' in characterizing modern democracies?

2. Is there any point in trying to measure democracy and, if so, who should do it?

3. What are the limits within which states can be deemed to be 'differently democratic' while still remaining democracies?

4. Do the citizens of a liberal democracy have to practise liberal toleration towards each other?

5. Will China and Russia become democracies? If so, why and how?

6. Will India ever be a liberal democracy? What about Turkey?

7. Why was there no 'pact' between all the main political actors in Iraq after 2003, and how far does that explain the recurring political chaos there?

8. Is there any future in trying to synthesize 'knowledgeable democracy' and 'accountable meritocracy'?

9. If they were implemented, how effective would the Council of Europe recommendations be in reviving confidence in democracy?

10. Can rivals only defeat populists by beating them at their own game, i.e. developing a populist persona of their own? Why?

11. How persuasive are Mudde and Kaltwasser's (2017) suggestions on ways to combat populism and populists?

12. How does the intensified populism of Prime Minister Modi affect your assessment of Indian democracy?

13. Has Donald Trump installed authoritarian populism in the White House?

14. Are there any lessons from the way earlier populist regimes ended for the future of current populist regimes and movements?

FURTHER READING

Bell, D. A. (2015), *The China Model: Political Meritocracy and the Limits of Democracy* (Princeton, NJ: Princeton University Press).
Raises the question of whether China enables better leaders to rise to the top than Western democracies.

Berggruen, N. and Gardels, N. (2013), *Intelligent Governance for the 21st Century: A Middle Way Between East and West* (Cambridge: Polity).
Chapter 5 presents a thought-provoking template for a more intelligent system of governance attempting to synthesize liberal democracy, deliberative democracy, and meritocratic bureaucracy.

Brooker, P. (2014), *Non-Democratic Regimes* (London: Palgrave, 3rd edn).
A reliable introduction to the wide range of authoritarian regimes.

Council of Europe (2004), *The Future of Democracy in Europe: Trends, Analyses and Reforms* (Strasbourg).
Includes a list of proposed reforms to restore citizens' confidence in democracy in Europe that are still valid today.

Dahl, R. A. (1989), *Democracy and Its Critics* (New Haven, CT, and London: Yale University Press).
A classic work of debates about the strengths and weaknesses of democracy.

Diamond, L. (2008), *The Spirit of Democracy: The Struggle to Build Free Societies Throughout the World* (New York: Henry Holt).
The sub-title conveys the basic message of this work by one of the USA's leading analysts of democracy.

Dobson, W. J. (2012), *The Dictator's Learning Curve: Inside the Global Battle for Democracy* (New York: Doubleday).
An American journalist interviews democratization activists in several authoritarian regimes on their experiences.

Eatwell, R. and Goodwin, M. (2018), *National Populism: The Revolt Against Liberal Democracy* (London: Pelican).
An excellent survey.

15

Keane, J. (2009), *The Life and Death of Democracy* (London and New York: Simon & Schuster).
A magisterial account of the evolution of the democratic idea.

Koelble, T. A. and LiPuma, E. (2008), 'Democratizing democracy: A postcolonial critique of conventional approaches to the "Measurement of Democracy"', *Democratization*, 15(1): 1–28.
A fundamental critique of Western attempts to measure democracy around the world and effectively a response to Diamond.

Møller, J. and Skaaning, S.-E. (2013), 'Regime types and democratic Sequencing', *Journal of Democracy*, 24(1): 142–55.
Presents a clear and well-argued framework for comparative analysis of democratic systems.

Paley, J. (2002), Towards an anthropology of democracy', *Annual Review of Anthropology*, 31: 469–96.
An introduction to the enormous variety of ways in which the term 'democracy' is understood and used around the world.

Ringen, S. (2013), *Nation of Devils: Democratic Leadership and the Problem of Obedience* (New Haven and London: Yale University Press).
Chapters 8 and 9 contain hard-hitting criticisms of British and American democracy.

Saich, T. (2011), *Governance and Politics in China* (London and New York: Palgrave Macmillan, 3rd edn).
A clear introduction to the Chinese political system and its evolution.

Sassoon, J. (2012), *Saddam Hussein's Ba'ath Party: Inside an Authoritarian Regime* (Cambridge: Cambridge University Press).
Provides an eye-opening picture of Saddam Hussein's rule based on many documents discovered after his death.

Schmitter, P. C. and Karl, T. L. (1991), 'What democracy is . . . and is not', *Journal of Democracy*, 2(3): 75–88.
An early and still very relevant discussion of the ways to go about comparative research on democracy.

Varshney, A. (2013), *Battles Half Won: India's Improbable Democracy* (New Delhi and London: Penguin/Viking).
A very insightful analysis of one of the oldest democracies outside the West: the first three chapters concentrate on an assessment of Indian democracy.

Wike, R. and Fetterolf, J. (2018), 'Liberal democracy's crisis of confidence', *Journal of Democracy*, 29:4, 136–50
An up-to-date analysis of problems facing liberal democracies

15

 For additional material and resources, please visit the Online Resources at:
www.oup.com/he/garner4e

global
POLITICS

by Stephanie Lawson

16

INTRODUCING GLOBAL POLITICS

READER'S GUIDE

Global politics has become a specialized field of study within the broader discipline of politics, although it should never be considered as a self-contained sphere, entirely separate from the study of national or domestic politics or from history, law, economics, and other social sciences. This chapter first presents a broad overview of the field along with the phenomenon of globalization. We then consider, in broad historical context, what is usually taken to be the central institution, not only of domestic political order, but international or global order as well—the state. At the same time we examine another form of international political order that has actually been far more common throughout history, and that is empire. In the contemporary period, however, global or international order has been underpinned by the modern sovereign state system rather than a system of empires, although the two are not altogether unrelated. The modern state and state system, along with ideas about sovereignty and nationalism, first arose in Europe and were effectively globalized through the practices of modern imperialism and colonialism. The latter are therefore implicated directly in the production of contemporary global order. In the final section we return to the more general phenomenon of globalization which, ironically, is often seen as undermining key aspects of the very order created by the internationalization of the European state system.

POLITICS IN A GLOBALIZING WORLD

If politics in the national sphere is a multifaceted activity that resists easy definition, this is no less the case in the global sphere. But at the very least we can say that global politics involves the distribution and utilization of power and resources on a worldwide basis, often accompanied by questions of what is right or wrong, just or unjust, in this distribution. Such questions frequently generate disagreement and conflict. This may not always lead to political violence or warfare. Indeed, the history of our species points to an enormous capacity for cooperation and peaceful negotiation within and between communities as well as the ability to deploy political power to achieve positive goods. Even so, the tendency to violence and the abuse of power seems an ever-present danger, constituting a central concern for individuals and communities.

A major challenge for politics is to work out ways of resolving or managing conflict and disagreement without resort to violence. In the global sphere, unlike the national or domestic sphere, this must be done in the absence of a sovereign authority capable of enforcing laws and punishing transgressors. We shall see later that the United Nations, while constituting the prime organ of global govern*ance*, is not a world govern*ment* in the sense that it possesses sovereign authority and capabilities. Because there is no world government, the global sphere is generally described as anarchic (a term that means, literally, 'no ruler'). This does not mean that it is chaotic by any means—people can institute order in the absence of formal government—but it does have implications for global order and security.

Here we should note that the term 'global politics' has been used increasingly as a replacement for the more conventional term 'international relations' (IR). This is partly because the latter is seen as denoting an overly narrow concern with the relations between sovereign states in an international system of states. Although the study of states and their interactions remains a major focus for the study of global politics, non-state actors and the dynamics they generate are equally important. One obvious example is the fact that the actions of relatively small but resourceful and determined non-state actors in the form of Al-Qaeda, Boko Haram, Al-Shabab, and (despite its name) Islamic State (IS) have reverberated throughout the global system, triggering both major warfare and insurgencies as well as a plethora of changes in the securitization of international travel, financial processes, and in other areas. Other important non-state global actors include transnational corporations (TNCs) as well as a myriad non-government organizations (NGOs), not to mention criminal organizations of all kinds.

The activities of all these groups tend to transcend state boundaries, contributing to a highly pluralistic global system characterized by multiple overlapping interactions and dynamics. These factors also contribute to the phenomenon of globalization which, as a historic phenomenon, may be seen as occurring over a very long period. But it really only received concerted attention after the end of the Cold War. At this time, global politics underwent a major transformation with the collapse of bipolarity and the emergence of new ideas about the shape of global order for the future. The defeat of communism was also accompanied by a renewed faith in the power of capitalism and liberal democracy and, in this context, globalization very quickly became a prominent theme in public discourses about a new paradigm for global order (**Box 16.1**).

An important aspect of globalization is increased public awareness of developments on a global scale, facilitated by technological developments such as the proliferation of the internet (a massive global networking infrastructure), the World Wide Web (a system of websites and pages that uses

➡ See Chapters 1 and 2 for more on the phenomenon of globalization.

16

! **KEY CONCEPT** BOX 16.1
Globalization

Numerous definitions of globalization appear in the literature, but common themes include the compression of time and space and an observable increase in interdependence, integration, and interconnectedness on a global scale which also signals the development of some kind of 'global culture'. The material aspects of globalization include flows of trade, capital, and people. These are facilitated by communications, transport, and financial infrastructure (Lawson, 2011). Thus globalization is a process rather than a fixed 'thing', and one that appears to be ongoing. The very term 'global' also implies not just the crossing of borders but their transcendence or possibly even their erasure. This contrasts with conventional ideas about the concept of the 'international' which denotes a world separated into discrete bounded entities—namely sovereign states or nation-states—with political interaction occurring primarily between those entities. 'Transnationalism' is a closely related term used in reference to a variety of 'cross-border relationships, patterns of exchange, affiliations and social formations spanning nation-states' (Vertovec, 2009: 2). But whereas the term 'transnationalism' references the existence of bounded national entities, globalization transcends them and, in stronger versions, even erases them.

the internet to navigate and connect with different sites), and with online social media and global news networks playing an increasingly prominent role. This has enabled the emergence of a global consciousness simply not possible in previous periods where information could take days, weeks, and even months to circulate. Global awareness is also an important factor in the extension of moral concerns beyond the borders of one's own political community and social networks. Images of humanitarian disasters around the globe, for example, whether wrought by natural causes or induced by human activity, invariably bring responses in the form of both state-sponsored and private aid and relief efforts to victims of floods, fires, earthquakes, tsunamis, epidemics, social and political violence, and outright warfare wherever these may occur. This extension of moral concerns to all people, regardless of national boundaries, is often referred to as 'cosmopolitanism'. This does not mean that national communities have no importance, or that cultural and other differences should be erased, but rather that they should not be seen as barriers. Philosopher Kwame Anthony Appiah (2015: 7) says that cosmopolitanism, which 'begins with the simple idea that in the human community, as in national communities, we need to develop habits of coexistence', emphasizes what humans have in common rather than what makes them different.

Another point to note about globalization is that the phenomenon is not simply an objective process that can be described in mechanical terms. Globalization—or more especially global*ism*—is also an ideology or is at least implicated in the formation of ideologies, and very powerful ones at that (**Box 16.2**). The ideological aspects of globalization in the contemporary period have been linked closely to a neo-liberal agenda in the economic realm (see Guillén, 2010: 4–5). Indeed, globalization is frequently associated very closely with global capitalism. Certainly, the increasing power of capital and the institutions through which it operates (corporations, banks, and other financial institutions) at a global level appears to be a very tangible phenomenon, and one which has tended to dominate discussions of globalization and the global economy. We consider these issues further in Chapter 22.

16

> ### KEY QUOTE BOX 16.2
> Globalization

[G]lobalization contains important *ideological* aspects in the form of politically charged narratives that put before the public a particular agenda of topics for discussion, questions to ask, claims to make . . . The social forces behind . . . competing accounts of globalization seek to endow this concept with norms, values, and meanings that not only legitimate and advance specific power interests, but also shape the personal and collective identities of billions of people.
(Steger, 2010: p. vii)

Globalization has also been discussed extensively in terms of its impact on the cultural dimensions of social and national life, although this is not unrelated to its economic aspects. The spread of certain products—Coca Cola, Levi's, McDonald's, Starbucks, Nike—and various chain stores which seem to have a presence in modern shopping malls right around the globe, along with the dominance of 'culture industries' such as the Hollywood movie machine and the American pop music industry, have given rise to images of a homogenizing (and largely US-dominated) global culture, linked in turn to the machinery of global capitalist production, which is set to obliterate a myriad local cultural practices.

Is this a genuine possibility, or a grossly exaggerated scenario? Even if we concede that some sort of 'global culture' is developing, is it necessarily the case that the principal vehicle will be American or 'Western' popular culture? And is it possible to think of 'culture' in other ways, and not just in terms of the commodification of certain goods that can be manufactured, packaged, sold, and consumed? There is certainly more to culture than this. We can envisage, for example, the development of global cultural norms which are supportive of human rights, including the rights of women and minority groups. Here some may argue that contemporary norms associated with human rights are also a product of 'Western culture' and simply another imposition on non-Western people who may have very different values. On the other hand, while we may concede that many of the norms associated with human rights have their origins in the West, they do seem to have strong resonance elsewhere.

The discussion of human rights in terms of culture also highlights the fact that 'culture' is not a 'thing' to be bought, sold, or used. Nor is it associated simply with music, art, clothing, food, language, religion, and so on, although it may encompass any or all of these things. Culture is, more than anything else, a *process* through which people organize their group lives, establishing rules and norms of behaviour as well as ways of dealing with the environment in which they find themselves. At the same time, culture as a process involves not just discrete groups and interactions within such groups—it is also essential to inter-group relations (see Lawson, 2006). If we consider that almost all human groups on the planet are now connected in one way or another, it is clear that a global web of interaction has formed and is still forming. This is essentially a cultural process and a key aspect of globalization.

We now turn to the question of the state vis-à-vis the power of non-state actors, especially in the economic sphere, and the extent to which the traditional sovereign state and its capacities may be compromised or undermined by these actors in a globalizing world. Some 'hyper-globalists' have gone so far as to suggest that the sovereign state is already largely dysfunctional and will eventually become redundant. This raises a further question: if states as political communities, and as a major basis for national and global political organization, cease to fulfil these functions, what could replace them? Others seriously question the wisdom of dismissing the importance of the state, and relations between states, both now and in the foreseeable future. States remain very powerful actors and, in many ways, still dominate the global system.

Whether the modern state is a 'good thing' is another question. The capacity of states, or at least those in command of states, to utilize their resources to prosecute large-scale international warfare as well as mass murder of their own citizens was demonstrated only too clearly during the twentieth century. Indeed, the unprecedented scale of the violence in the First World War gave a significant impetus to the formal study of politics in the international sphere. The early focus was largely on relations between states and the maintenance of a state-based international order which the early practitioners believed ought to be studied as a specialized field in its own right, apart from the study of political institutions within states. In the US, especially in the aftermath of the Second World War and the early years of the Cold War, there were renewed calls to promote the study of politics in the international sphere in a specialized discipline which became more commonly known as IR.

As we have seen, however, the idea of *global* politics is much more multi-faceted than one which seems focused almost exclusively on relations between sovereign states in an international system of states. Certainly, many scholars have come to believe that the sphere of global politics cannot be neatly demarcated from other spheres of politics. Domestic political and indeed social, cultural, economic, and other concerns interact constantly with the international sphere and vice versa. The idea of a 'global environment', for example, is often used to emphasize the transcendence of state boundaries in relation to such issues as pollution, global warming, and climate change, rather than an 'international environment' which seems to make less sense.

A further consideration for this introductory section concerns the concept of a 'global IR'. This has been developed in response to concerns about the highly ethnocentric nature of the discipline, given its origins in Europe and North America and other parts of the entity known as 'the West'. As we shall see throughout much of the discussion of global politics, this entity often appears as hegemonic, dominating not just the political sphere but also social, cultural, and economic spheres. The issues raised by the promotion of global IR—along with the West/non-West or Global North/South—are highly relevant to the field of postcolonial theory and the 'decolonization of the curriculum' discussed in more detail in Chapter 18. For the moment, we should note that global IR 'seeks to ensure the transformation of the discipline into something that actually captures and explains the relationships among states and societies in all parts of the world: East, West, North, South.' In so doing, it does not seek to displace existing theories, but rather 'challenges them to broaden their horizons and acknowledge the place and role of the non-Western world' (Acharya, 2017). As another commentator has noted, 'to focus on the historical story of contested and multiple traditions and patterns of thought and practice; and to explore how ideas that emerge from different historical, developmental, and cultural contexts can have more general, even global, relevance, and application' (Hurrell, 2016, 151). In summary, the project of global IR promises to deliver a much richer set of perspectives on a whole range of problems and issues in the study of global politics, not to mention more relevant knowledge in the practical application of global policy measures.

16

> ### KEY POINTS
>
> - Global politics as a field of study encompasses the traditional concerns of IR with how states interact under conditions of anarchy but places more emphasis on the role of non-state actors and processes in a globalizing world.
> - Globalization became a prominent concept after the end of the Cold War. Although it is a contested concept, it generally denotes the compression of time and space together with the transcending of traditional political, economic, and cultural boundaries.
> - Conventional approaches to the study of global politics or IR have generally been dominated by Western perspectives, thus limiting the relevance and applicability of its insights.

STATES AND NATIONS IN CONTEMPORARY GLOBAL POLITICS

The terms 'state' and 'nation' are often used synonymously or joined together to produce 'nation-state', but they refer to two quite distinct entities. You will find that the 'state' by itself is given several different dictionary meanings. But for present purposes, the 'state' refers to a distinctive political community with its own set of rules and practices and which is more or less separate from other such communities. As we saw in Chapter 8, the state is virtually synonymous with the structure of rule and authority, and the institutions which regulate these, within a particular geographical space. In the global sphere, 'the state' refers specifically to the modern sovereign state which is recognized as possessing certain rights and duties. This kind of state is

Photo 16.1 Though the terms 'state' and 'nation' are often used together, they are actually quite distinct entities. *Shutterstock RF via DAM: Artistic Photo/ Shutterstock*

16

distinct from the states that generally make up a federal system, such as the individual states of which the United *States* of America is composed—or of India, Malaysia, Nigeria, South Africa, Germany, Russia, Canada, or Australia, and others which are also federal systems.

The sovereign state has been given a clear legal definition by the 1933 Montevideo Convention on the Rights and Duties of States. Of the sixteen articles adopted in this convention, the most important are the first eleven, and of these, Article 1 provides the most succinct understanding of the criteria for a modern sovereign state, namely: *a permanent population; a defined territory and a government capable of maintaining effective control over its territory and of conducting international relations with other states*. Thus the state in global politics is envisaged as a *formally constituted, sovereign political structure encompassing people, territory, and institutions*. As such, a state interacts with similarly constituted structures in an international system of states which, ideally, is characterized by peaceful, non-coercive relations, thus establishing a similarly peaceful international order conducive to the prosperity of all. One might well say, if only it were so! The last century saw horrific manifestations of large-scale inter-state war, putting paid to the notion that a sovereign state system could guarantee peace. On the other hand, inter-state warfare has been on the decline with most large-scale violent conflicts now taking the form of civil wars. The latter, however, very often involve other states as well. A notable example in the present period is the Syrian civil war in which Russia and Iran have supported the government of Syrian president Bashar al-Assad while the US and various other state actors including Turkey, France, and Saudi Arabia have intervened as well, although mainly in areas where IS forces had taken over.

We look in more detail at the historic emergence of the state shortly, but for now let us consider the nation, a term which refers specifically to 'a people' rather than a formal, territorial entity. There is no widely agreed definition of what constitutes 'a people' beyond the fact that it denotes a species of collective identity grounded in a notion of shared history and culture and which often lays claim to some kind of political recognition as well as to a specific territory. We have seen in Chapter 6 that nationalism as an ideology holds that political organization ought to be based on a 'national identity'. Nationalist ideology in general therefore supports the claims that each nation is entitled, in principle, to a state of its own. Since the early twentieth century, this has generally been based on the apparently democratic principle of national self-determination.

➡ See Chapter 6 for a discussion of nationalism.

Nationalism, at least in the more extreme right-wing versions, may also seek the exclusion of 'alien' elements from an existing state to safeguard the 'authenticity' of its national character. Nationalism as an ideology is therefore often implicated in debates about immigration and border protection and also stands opposed to some of the principle elements of globalization which favour more open borders and free trade. These issues have been especially prominent in debates about Brexit as well as President Trump's policies in the US.

However defined, 'nations' are assumed to populate sovereign states and are very often described in singular terms; that is, one state may be assumed to contain one nation. The state of France, for example, is occupied by the 'French nation', Japan by the 'Japanese nation', Turkey by the 'Turkish nation', and so on. These examples indicate the commonly accepted conflation of state and people that produces the familiar term 'nation-state' which, again, reflects the principle of national self-determination. However, only a moment's critical reflection is needed to recognize that the matching of state and nation is seldom so neat. Rather, it is an ideal that has rarely, if ever, been achieved. There is virtually no state in the world encompassing a single, homogeneous nation. Japan is often described as a 'pure' nation-state but it has an indigenous minority—the

Ainu—and also encompasses the people of Okinawa who consider themselves as distinct. Turkey has other minorities—the Kurds for example—who, along with Kurds in other parts of the region, consider themselves a nation in their own right.

Many states are made up of two or more 'nations'. The contemporary British state, for example, is comprised of recognized substate national entities: the Welsh, Scots, English, and Northern Irish. In 2014, the Scottish 'nation' voted on whether or not to establish Scotland as a sovereign state, failing by just under 6 per cent. But all the national sub-groups within the UK are multilayered, especially since immigration over the centuries has brought dozens of different 'nationalities' to the British Isles, thereby producing the 'multicultural' and indeed 'multinational' Britain of the contemporary period. A close inspection of other national entities in Europe will show similar stories. And what started out as British settler colonies, which are a legacy of modern empire and of mass migration—both aspects of globalization—are now among the most 'multinational' in the world today—the USA, Canada, Australia, and New Zealand in particular.

If we look to places like Nigeria, India, and China, however, it is also evident that these states are made up of many different groups speaking different local languages and possessing different cultural practices. Even relatively small states can be incredibly diverse. Papua New Guinea, for example, has a population of just over 6 million, yet there are more than 850 different languages spoken and each language group could theoretically consider itself to be 'a nation'. It is often because of such diversity that states like Papua New Guinea are seen to be 'weak states' or 'fragile states'. On the other hand, Somalia, often considered a classic example of a 'failed state', is relatively culturally homogeneous. But social order in Somalia, to the extent that it exists, has been extremely fractious.

Although most states are acknowledged as containing many more than one 'nation', the identity of the state will to some extent be equated with a dominant majority. Thus in the USA, Canada, and Australia, for example, a dominant white English-speaking majority constitutes a mainstream. Another interesting case is China where the category of 'Han Chinese' constitutes more than 90 per cent of the population, although these speak numerous different dialects and are therefore scarcely homogeneous. China also encompasses Tibet and the Tibetans, who are clearly distinct from the dominant majority, as are the Uigar people of the north-western Xinjiang region who are largely Muslim. Both areas have given rise to secessionist or independence movements.

In other cases, secession movements, usually based on a claim by a minority to a distinct nationhood that can be properly accommodated only by the establishment of a sovereign state of their own, have led to civil war. Although such conflicts are technically *intra*state, they invariably have significant repercussions in the global sphere, from the generation of large numbers of asylum seekers to the fuelling of illicit trade in weapons.

This brief discussion of the basic distinctions between 'state' and 'nation'—and some of the political dynamics associated with the relationship between the two entities—provides some indication of how simple terms attempt to capture complex realities. It also highlights how modern sovereign states are often seen as constituted through and by a 'nation'. Sometimes these nations claim a very long and continuous history, usually in association with a particular territory. Other nations have been much more recently 'constructed' and are sometimes described as 'artificial' for that reason. The contemporary 'Australian nation', for example, may be seen as a construct with its origins in the relatively recent past; that is, from the beginning of British settlement in 1788, although it also encompasses indigenous Australians whose ancestors have occupied the land for up to 60,000 years as well as more recent immigrants from all around the world. The 'South African nation', another product of European colonialism, is also incredibly diverse as reflected in the fact that there are eleven official languages.

Whatever their historic status and the manner of their formation, nations are seen as integral to, and indeed constitutive of, the modern state. The term 'nation-state' is therefore likely to endure as a category in global political order for the foreseeable future, even though the constitution of particular nations and the political claims made in their name remain deeply contested.

KEY POINTS

- The terms 'state' and 'nation' tend to be used synonymously but are distinct entities.
- The 'nation' in a 'nation-state' is often assumed to be homogeneous in terms of culture or ethnicity but this is rarely the case.
- The relationship between 'state' and 'nation' is complex and often gives rise to deep political contestation.

STATES AND EMPIRES IN GLOBAL HISTORY

In this section we consider the variation in state forms and the phenomenon of empire throughout history. This illustrates that international systems are highly variable and that the sovereign state system with which we are familiar today may very well be replaced by a different kind of system at some point in the future. Certainly, proponents of 'globalism' believe that a transformation is under way in which state boundaries and controls will become increasingly meaningless. Others have identified a new era of empire, although there are differing views as to where its principal centre of power may lie and whether it constitutes a genuine form of imperialism. Yet others seek to reinforce the existing state system and its boundaries, emphasizing the importance of 'the nation' as the prime constituent element of the sovereign state, its integrity, and indeed its security. This has been especially noticeable in recent debates about immigration in Britain, the USA, and Australia where conservative politicians and their supporters have tended to portray migrants as a security threat. But it is also evident in other settings where minority communities are sometimes considered not part of the legitimate or authentic nation. A prime example is the minority community of Rohingya people in Myanmar where the government denies that they are indigenous to their area in Rakhine state, rather suggesting that they are 'illegal immigrants' from Bangladesh.

Note that, in this section, I use the term *international* system when referring to phenomena that are not truly global. For example, empires throughout history may be described as a form of 'international' system in the sense that they encompass different states (and/or nations), but empires are not generally 'global' in the sense that they gather in all such entities around the world under a single centre of power. Whether a true 'global empire' is ever likely to come about is another question.

Let us begin with the concept of the state understood simply as a political community. The earliest of these date more or less from the time that human groups first developed settled agricultural

Photo 16.2 The Ancient Greek word 'Polis' translates to 'city state'. *Shutterstock RF via DAM: Sergio Bertino/Shutterstock*

and/or animal husbandry practices. These required an ongoing association with a particular part of the earth's surface as well as a way of organizing the people and their resources and generally protecting themselves. As we have seen, the definition of the modern state includes a relationship between a permanent population and a certain defined territory. This part of the definition can therefore be extended back in time to cover numerous historic cases without running too much risk of anachronism. Having said that, there have also been 'stateless communities' throughout history—typically those with a nomadic lifestyle which have therefore lacked the same fixed attachment to, or control over, a particular territory. One author says that modern humans lived in small hunter-gatherer-forager societies for more than 50,000 years and that this lifestyle was the most successful adaptation made in the history of our species (Stanish, 2017: p. x). The subsequent formation of states has also given rise to 'state systems' or 'international orders' which denote the ways in which political communities have systematically organized their relations with other such communities either in their immediate geographical area or further afield.

Since the study of global politics is, by and large, based on a discipline that has developed largely in 'the West', it is scarcely surprising that the historical antecedents of statehood and international orders have been sought in the 'cradle of Western civilization'; that is, the eastern Mediterranean region where the ancient Greek and Roman civilizations flourished. These, however, had close connections with the civilizations of northern Africa and the Near East, and both

Greece and Rome drew on the rich sources of knowledge and aspects of cultural practices from both regions. In turn, the communities of northern Africa and the Near East were connected to other communities, and so processes of cross-cultural learning, including political practices, were transmitted from much further afield as well.

The 'state' of the ancient Greeks was the *polis*, often translated as 'city-state' although that is not its exact, literal meaning. The *polis* was also a body of citizens along with its customs and laws—the political community—and consisted of both an urban centre (city) as well as the surrounding rural or agricultural territory. The largest and best known was the Athenian *polis*—often referred to as the archetypal model of classical democracy. The political philosophy of certain leading thinkers who gathered in Athens—many of whom, as noted in Chapter 4, did not actually favour democracy—has also underpinned much subsequent political theory concerning the nature and purposes of the state. Aristotle, for example, saw the *polis* or state as the *natural* habitat for humans rather than an artificial construct separating them *from* nature. When he famously described 'man' as a *zōon politikon* (political animal) he did not mean that humans were naturally scheming, devious creatures, as the term is often taken to imply. Rather, he meant that the human is a creature designed *by nature* to live in a *polis* (Aristotle, *Politics* 3).

Athens for a time also headed another important form of political organization, an empire, although the best known of these in the ancient world is undoubtedly the Roman Empire. Developments in Rome are important to the historical growth of the West especially in relation to theories of republicanism as well as the legal system of parts of Europe. It is also partly due to the Roman Empire that Christianity became firmly established in Europe, a development with significant consequences for the subsequent development of political ideas and practices.

In considering empire as a form of international system, it is important to note that, like states, empires have existed at various times throughout most of the world and have taken different forms. What they tend to share in common is the fact that they are relatively large-scale political entities made up of a number of smaller political communities (generally states) with a central controlling power and are usually held together by force. While some states may also be held together by little more than force, it is more characteristic of empires. And although empires constitute a kind of international order, this is quite different from the current international state system, underpinned as it is by a theory of sovereign equality among its constituent members. In contrast, empires are characterized by hierarchical relations of domination and subordination. The brief tour of historical empires set out next also gives a better sense of the diversity of our world and the fact that not everything of historical significance happened in Europe.

The earliest known empires were situated around the river systems of the Tigris, Euphrates, and the Nile, their geographical location suggesting a certain correlation between the conditions required for successful agriculture and the establishment of settled political communities with extensive networks of relations between them. This broad region saw the rise of the Sumerian, Egyptian, Babylonian, Assyrian, and Persian Empires between about 4,000 BC and 400 BC. The methods of domination used by the controlling powers of these empires varied from direct control over smaller, subject communities to more indirect methods which allowed some autonomy to local groups provided that regular tributes were forthcoming (Stern, 2000: 57; Lawson, 2012: ch. 2).

Africa also produced a number of empires, spanning ancient, medieval, and modern periods. These include the Ghana, Mali, and Songhay empires in West Africa which thrived between about

16

the sixth and sixteenth centuries AD. The most significant city within both the Mali and Songhay empires was Timbuktu which became a significant centre for learning as well as trade and commerce, and is still famed for its precious ancient manuscripts. The Ottoman Empire, with its capital in Istanbul, emerged in the fourteenth century and lasted until the early 1920s giving it a life span of around 600 years. At its height in the sixteenth and seventeenth centuries the Ottoman Empire ruled over some 14 million people and stretched from the deserts of central Asia to parts of central Europe, northern Africa, and southern Spain (see, generally, Duducu, 2018).

Further east, the ancient kingdoms of the Indus Valley formed a broad civilizational entity, with Hinduism and Sanskrit providing some basic cultural cohesion over much of the region. Even so, political communities within the region evinced much variety, with both oligarchies and republics in evidence. The region's best-known empire was established in the north in 300 BC. Although it lasted less than a century, its reputation was assured largely because one of its leading figures, Kautilya, produced a highly sophisticated text on statecraft, the *Artha'sastra*, which set out the ways and means of acquiring territory, keeping it, and reaping prosperity from it. It is comparable to Machiavelli's writings on statecraft, although some see it as presenting a far harsher picture of the struggle for domination (Boesche, 2002: 253–76). The Islamic Mughal empire also emerged in the Indian subcontinent and held sway over most of the region until its decline in the later fifteenth and early sixteenth century. More generally, the legacy of Islamic empires—cultural, political, and military—remains today in significant parts of Africa, Central Asia, South Asia, and South East Asia (especially present-day Malaysia, Indonesia, Brunei, and parts of Thailand and the Philippines), as well as sizeable parts of Eastern Europe.

In the Americas, the Aztec, Mayan, and Inca civilizations which flourished before the advent of Europeans were virtually synonymous with imperial power. The Aztec and Inca empires emerged from a period of political fragmentation and military conflict in the thirteenth and fourteenth centuries, which ended with the establishing of strong centres of power with control over significant territories and peoples (see Lockard, 2008: 347). These, however, collapsed in the face of other imperial incursions, namely those of the Spanish who soon overwhelmed the local empires through military power as well as the spread of diseases to which the indigenous people had no immunity. This was to be a fate endured by many indigenous people around the world.

One of the most extensive and durable empires of all was the Chinese, which lasted from the time of the Shang dynasty in the eighteenth century BC, until the early twentieth century, although there was a substantial interlude during which time it disintegrated into a number of warring states. It was during a period of chaos and violence that the ancient philosophy of Confucius, which is largely concerned with setting out the political and social arrangements conducive to good order under strong leadership and authority, is thought to have developed (see Lawson, 2006: 155). This is comparable to the conditions under which European theorists of sovereignty, which is ultimately concerned with the same problems, were to develop their ideas. There are numerous other examples of empire throughout the world, from ancient through to modern times, showing just how common this form of international system has been. Indeed, they have been far more common than state systems.

While most historical empires have left important legacies of one kind or another, those which have had the most profound impact on the structure of the present international system and the nature of contemporary global order are the modern European empires. The largest and most powerful of these was the British Empire, although it had other rivals in Europe. France,

Spain, Portugal, Holland, Denmark, Belgium, Italy, and Germany were all colonizing powers at one time or another, but none acquired the same power and influence as the British. Given the extent to which imperialism and colonialism facilitates cultural spread, it is scarcely surprising that British—or more particularly English—culture gained significant ground around the world. This is partly manifest in the fact that English now prevails as the major international language although French and Spanish are also widely spoken—the latter in Central and South America in particular. Cultural spread, however, goes both ways and contemporary Britain, and significant parts of Europe, have absorbed cultural influences in turn.

More generally, the history of empire, which encompasses exploration, trade, proselytization, and migration as well as other more explicitly political aspects, is also part of the history of globalization. The networks and movements of people prompted by the global reach of the modern European empires, in particular, along with technological innovations and the development of financial and economic systems that accompanied these, established much of the basis on which contemporary global interdependence rests (**see Box 16.3**).

KEY DEBATE BOX 16.3
Globalization and the New Imperialism

The phenomenon of globalization has been linked to a new form of empire which, it is argued, is replacing the traditional form of state sovereignty with a different kind of sovereignty. This is said to rely neither on a territorial centre of power nor on fixed boundaries or barriers. Nor does the USA occupy a singularly privileged position in this new imperial configuration, simply taking up where the old European empires left off. Rather, the new imperial order is characterized by the power of TNCs or multinational corporations (MNCs), and forms of production owing no allegiance to territorial entities and which in fact seek to supplant their sovereignty (see Negri and Hardt, 2000: pp. xi–xiv). By the turn of the twenty-first century, it was noted that the 300 largest TNCs owned or controlled around a quarter of productive assets around the entire globe, while their total annual sales were the comparable to, or greater than, the GDP of most countries. Sales by Itochu Corporation, based in Japan, exceeded the GDP of Austria, while those of Royal Dutch/Shell equalled Iran's (Greer and Singh, 2000). Much of the focus of critique has been on Western (i.e. European or US-based corporations) but, as the example just mentioned shows, Japanese corporations have been equally prominent.

More recently, there has been a significant growth in Chinese corporations operating in Africa and the Pacific. One highly critical opinion piece says of this new 'Chinese imperialism' that:

Chinese corporations are all over Africa. In June 2017 a McKinsey & Company report estimated that there are more than 10,000 Chinese-owned firms operating in Africa. . . . The reason Chinese corporations are in Africa is simple; to exploit the people and take their resources. It's the same thing European colonists did during mercantile times, except worse. The Chinese corporations are trying to turn Africa into another Chinese continent [and] squeezing Africa for everything it is worth. (Mourdaukoutas, 2018)

Some may see this version of 'empire' as a grossly exaggerated scenario, but at the very least its proponents provide a basis for critical reflection on key aspects of the phenomenon of globalization and the growing power of deterritorialized corporations, both Western and non-Western, as non-state actors. Some other recent commentators *do* regard the USA as exercising genuine imperial control at a global level, although its political leaders reject any such connection. In his analysis of US hegemony, Niall Ferguson quotes prominent US politicians as emphatically denying that the global role of the USA today is an imperial project. George W. Bush claimed in 2000 that 'America has never been an empire . . . We may be the only great power in history that had the chance, and refused'. He continued with this theme when declaring a victory in Iraq in May 2003 over the forces of Saddam Hussein, insisting that while other nations had 'fought in foreign lands and remained to occupy and exploit', Americans in contrast, 'wanted nothing more than to return home' (Ferguson, 2003a). Ferguson concludes another major book on the subject of the British Empire with the observation that Americans have taken on the global role formerly played by Britain, yet without facing the fact that an empire comes with it. In short, the USA is 'an empire in denial' (Ferguson, 2003b: 370).

A contrary argument has been put by Paul Schroeder who says that much of the hype about an American empire is based on a misleading and unhistorical understanding of the term which ignores crucial distinctions between empire and other forms of power and order in the international system. A *real* empire, he says, requires effective final authority whereas the power of the USA is more correctly understood as hegemony. The latter, he says, consists of acknowledged leadership and dominant influence by one unit within a community of units which do not come under a single authority, whereas an imperial power actually rules over subordinates in a formalized hierarchical system (Schroeder, 2003). Similarly, hegemony in the context of global politics has been defined as 'the ability of an actor with overwhelming capability to shape the international system through both coercive and non-coercive means'. Examples include the UK in the nineteenth century and the US in the twentieth and twenty-first centuries as well as 'a cohesive political community with external decision-making, such as the European Union.' Furthermore, under a hegemony rule is sustained through influence over other states 'rather than by controlling them or their territory' (Norrlof, 2015).

Another commentator says that the contemporary world has some very large political units which, although technically sovereign states, or composed of sovereign states, may be usefully analysed in terms of empire. In addition to the USA, these include the EU, Russia, and China. This further suggests an expansive understanding of empire and the fact that they can be democratic, authoritarian, or mixed in character. In view of this, he says, it is time bring the concept of empire back in to the study of politics (Colomer, 2017).

Questions
1. What is the difference between hegemony and empire?
2. Is the USA an imperial power in the contemporary period?

> **KEY POINTS**
>
> - States as political communities have existed for thousands of years and have taken a wide range of forms in terms of size and institutional features.
> - Empires have existed as a form of hierarchical international order in ancient, pre-modern, and modern periods and throughout different parts of the world.
> - The rise of TNCs under conditions of globalization; the current position of the USA in global politics; and the expansion of the EU have all prompted fresh speculation as to the nature of empire as a form of international or global system.

MODERNITY AND THE STATE SYSTEM

Empires have clearly been a dominant form of international system throughout history, often encompassing states in a wider system of order characterized by hierarchy. With the exception of the imperial state, other states in such systems have generally been subordinate entities, lacking a certain integrity and capacity. The modern sovereign state and state system, however, appear to have a very different character. We now examine the historical emergence of the sovereign state and state system in Europe against the background condition known as 'modernity'. This is a complex phenomenon associated with the rise in Europe of science and technology leading to industrialization, increased military power, and, with it, enormous political and social change, including diminishing religious authority. However, the rise of modernity in Europe did not occur in isolation from other influences. Stern (2000: 72) notes that not only were important ideas and inventions transmitted from China and Arabia, but that significant aspects of Greek and Roman learning were recovered through the work of Islamic scholars. The 'discovery' of new worlds in the Americas and the Pacific also served to acquaint Europeans with a seemingly endless array of widely varying states and societies, all of which prompted new comparisons and questions for the study of politics and society (Lawson, 2006: 60).

In the year 1500—conventionally taken to mark the beginning of the modern age—the historian Paul Kennedy says that it was scarcely apparent to anyone that a cluster of rather insignificant states in Western Europe 'was poised to dominate much of the rest of the earth' (Kennedy, 1989: 3). Chinese civilization at the time seemed vastly superior to any other. Technological innovation, including moveable type printing, gunpowder, paper money, and massive ironworks had contributed to an expansion of trade and industry further stimulated by an extensive programme of canal building. China also possessed an army of over a million. All this, together with an efficient hierarchical administration run by an educated Confucian bureaucracy, made Chinese society 'the envy of foreign visitors' (Kennedy, 1989: 5). More generally, as we have seen, empires elsewhere were thriving and so there were many other important centres of power at the beginning of the modern period.

There had been no political organization of Europe as a whole in the Renaissance or early modern periods to match the Chinese or Ottoman empires. Rather, medieval Europe consisted of a rather chaotic patchwork of overlapping jurisdictions and fragmented authorities, scarcely resembling a coherent state system or international order. The only institution providing any sort of unity was the Christian (Catholic) Church based in Rome, from where it imposed some religious

16

authority on the rest of the continent. The Protestant Reformation, however, would challenge the supremacy of the established church, triggering a massive theological and political fallout.

Key aspects of the development of European states and the state system, especially with respect to their capacity, have been covered in Chapter 8. Here we should emphasize that a devastating struggle between Catholic and Protestant forces, which ended with the Peace of Westphalia in 1648, is conventionally understood to have brought about the consolidation of certain characteristics of the modern state that are central to aspects of IR theory. The current sovereign state system is therefore often referred to as the 'Westphalian system'. The characteristics of the system included not only the principle of religious coexistence, but also the monopoly claims by the state over such matters as declarations of war and the negotiation of peace, diplomatic representation, and the authority to make treaties with foreign powers (Boucher, 1998: 224). For these reasons, Westphalia was long regarded as the founding moment of the modern *sovereign* state. One scholar has said that 'Most scholars . . . see the seventeenth century, and particularly the Peace of Westphalia . . . as the best historical reference point for symbolizing that fundamental turn in European political life' (Jackson, 2018: 44). That assessment, however, has come under challenge and some regard it as little more than a 'foundation myth' with the principle driver of the rise of the modern state being best located in capitalist development in England in particular (see Teschke, 2003; see also Clark, 2005). Although the finer points of that particular debate are beyond the scope of an introductory text, it is nonetheless important to look at what the idea of the 'Westphalian moment' is based on, given that it was to become such a key reference point for the emergence of the modern sovereign state and cannot be dismissed entirely as a factor in its historical development (**see Box 16.4**).

> ### CASE STUDY BOX 16.4
> ### The Peace of Westphalia
>
> The Thirty Years Wars between Catholic and Protestant forces in Europe ended in 1648 with the Peace of Westphalia. This was achieved through complex diplomatic negotiations over a period of five years, ending with the Treaties of Osnabrück and Münster which together comprised the final 'peace'. Some of the principles enshrined at Westphalia, such as the authority of rulers to determine the religious affiliations of their subject, were very similar to an earlier agreement, the Peace of Augsburg of 1555, so the ideas underpinning the 1648 treaty were not entirely new. However, Westphalia was infused with emergent ideas about a kind of international law which could transcend religious differences and therefore be applied universally—i.e. to Catholic and Protestant states alike. The foremost thinker along these lines was the Dutch jurist Hugo Grotius (1583–1645) whose influential work, *De Jure Belli et Pacis* (*Laws of War and Peace*) confronted the problem of conflicting moralities and the need for toleration as well as setting out minimum standards for conduct. Most importantly for the development of the state system and international order, it granted co-equal juridical status to states.
>
> Westphalia has been described as the first, and perhaps the greatest, of the modern European peace treaties, and is also considered to have established the legal foundations of modern
>
>

statehood (see Fassbender, 2011). Its principal feature in this latter respect concerns the right of rulers to conduct their affairs within their own territories free from outside interference, thus establishing the principle of autonomous political authority which underpinned the development of the doctrine of sovereignty. The articulation of principles and doctrines, however, does not mean that practice always accords with their intent. There has been little to prevent violations of both the letter and spirit of the Westphalian Peace, as the subsequent history of Europe itself shows only too clearly. The Westphalian model, whether one regards it as a 'foundation myth' or not, has nonetheless provided a benchmark for both critics and supporters of the sovereign state system as well as for those who predict its eventual demise due to the irresistible state-transcending forces of globalization.

For realist thinkers, the principle of sovereignty came to be regarded as effectively enclosing states within a 'hard shell', with the shell corresponding to the territorial borders. It was meant to guarantee non-intervention in the internal governmental arrangements or any other domestic affairs of a state. The theory possessed an attractive simplicity. Rulers within states could follow the religious, political, and moral principles of their choice, and could also require their subjects to conform. The protective shell of sovereignty guaranteed the complete independence of each state—or rather the ruling elements within each state—to arrange their domestic affairs as it suited them, regardless of what any external actor might think and no matter the relative standing of the state in terms of size, power, and capacity. As pointed out in Chapter 1, the Introduction to this book, the state is sovereign in the sense that it is the supreme law-making body within a particular territory with the ultimate power of life and death over individuals. The juridical sovereignty possessed by individual states remains a basic principle of international law today.

While admirable in its theoretical simplicity, the principles of state sovereignty in the international sphere have been far less straightforward in practice. This has been demonstrated in part by the fact that Europe appears to have been no less prone to warfare among its constituent states for much of the 300-year period following Westphalia. The extent to which this can be attributed to the rise of nationalism along with the modern state system has been much debated. Whatever the historical reasons for war, it is really only in the post-Second World War period that Europeans seem finally to have struck on a formula for peaceful relations. That this was achieved via a regional suprastate framework in the form of the EU, is something of an irony, because although the principle of state sovereignty was initially formulated to prevent warfare, it seems that a more lasting peace has only been acquired through significant modification of its basic elements.

Another factor to be considered here is the moral conundrum raised by the actions of states with respect to the treatment of their own citizens or any others within their borders, whether visitors, migrants, or refugees. A strict interpretation of the theory of state sovereignty prohibits any action by actors outside the state even in cases of genocide or other forms of human rights abuses. In the present period, however, there has been much discussion of an assumed right of humanitarian intervention, a nascent doctrine which seeks to trump the sovereign rights of states—or rather their rulers—to do as they please within their own borders. This accords with another recently promoted notion—that the possession of sovereignty by a

16

state confers on it the *responsibility to protect* its inhabitants. The Libyan intervention in 2011, authorized by the UN Security Council, reflects the failure of the Libyan regime to safeguard unarmed civilians during the uprising. The 'responsibility to protect' in this instance shifted to the international community. But this has not happened to date with respect to the Syrian crisis, largely because of the politics of the UN Security Council, which we consider in Chapter 19. Even so, the international community does assume major responsibility for the millions of displaced persons or refugees generated by such conflicts, even if this often seems inadequate in execution.

Here we should note that the theory of state sovereignty faces two ways, possessing both external and internal dimensions. As Evans and Newnham (1998: 504) put it, the doctrine makes a double claim: 'autonomy in foreign policy and exclusive competence in internal affairs'. The latter depends on there being an ultimate authority within the state that is entitled to make decisions and settle disputes. Thus 'the sovereign', who may be either a person (such as a monarch) or a collective (such as a parliament representing the sovereignty of the people) is the highest and final power in the state's political system and cannot be subject to any other agent, domestic *or* foreign (Miller, 1987: 492–3). As far as the external or international sphere goes, this produces, somewhat paradoxically, a condition of anarchy—which means, literally, 'without a ruler'. For if all states are sovereign, and therefore the final arbiters of their own destinies, there can be no higher authority placed outside and above the individual states in an international system of states (see Evans and Newnham, 1998: 504).

Another important development accompanying the rise of the modern European state system is the ideology of nationalism. We noted earlier the assumption implicit in the principle of self-determination that each 'nation' is entitled to a state of its own, which is highly problematic given that there are thousands of groups around the world that could make some credible claim to constituting a nation. Despite the practical difficulties, the idea that nations and states go together seems very persuasive. But like the sovereign state itself, the idea of the nation is a relatively recent one. Indeed, its origins lie in the same state-building dynamics that arose in seventeenth and eighteenth-century Europe as well as in emergent ideas about democracy, especially through the French Revolution of 1789 which required a distinct body of people—citizens—to constitute a *sovereign people* and which came to be conceptualized as 'the nation'. Although the record of democratic development in Europe remained very patchy until quite recent times, the idea of the nation caught on very rapidly, and the subsequent development of the modern state and state system brought together the three prime characteristics of the modern state—*sovereignty, territoriality*, and *nationality*.

Another significant development came in the wake of the Napoleonic Wars. This was the 'Concert of Europe', a term designating a series of irregular conferences focused on resolving diplomatic crises between states. Beginning with the Congress of Vienna in 1815, it lasted until the mid-1850s and although the meetings were eventually discontinued, the art of diplomacy within Europe matured to a significant extent and became an important instrument of the state system. At the beginning of the nineteenth century, however, the modern European state system still existed more in theory than in practice, and it was still far from being regarded as a 'nation-state' system. But the *national* idea was becoming more prominent in the rhetoric of state-making movements throughout the century which saw the emergence of new 'national' states in Greece (1830), Belgium (1831), Italy (1961), Germany (1871), and Romania, Serbia, and Montenegro (1878).

By the beginning of the twentieth century, the modern state system with its principles of sovereignty, nationality, and territoriality was reasonably well entrenched in Europe, as well as in much of the Americas. But it scarcely existed in other parts of the world. This brings us to the subject of European colonization and decolonization, for it is largely due to the legacy of empire that the European state system became effectively globalized in the twentieth century, thus giving rise to the present global system. Here we should also note that although the discipline of IR is ethnocentric, or more specifically Eurocentric when it comes to its focus on the modern state system and its history, this makes sense 'for there is no doubt that the existing international system, forged over the preceding few centuries, has its origins in Europe and must be understood with reference to a specifically European history' (Seth, 2013: 17).

KEY POINTS

- 'Modernity' is a phenomenon associated with social, political, intellectual, and technological developments in Europe which brought significant changes to the political landscape.
- The Peace of Westphalia has been regarded, at least conventionally as the founding moment of the doctrine of state sovereignty and therefore of the modern state and state system in Europe, although this understanding has been challenged by scholars who regard the 'Westphalian moment' as a myth.
- Nationalism as a form of political/cultural identity is also closely associated with the rise of the modern sovereign state and state system.

THE GLOBALIZATION OF THE STATE SYSTEM

We have seen that numerous empires existed in ancient times and in many different parts of the world. The modern period did not spell the end of empires and, if anything, imperialism and colonialism not only continued with the rise of the sovereign state in Europe, but also thrived under it. Furthermore, it is through the European empires that the sovereign state system was effectively transported to the rest of the world. Early Spanish, Portuguese, and Dutch explorers and traders were followed by the British, French, Belgians, and Germans. Shipping routes and trading posts encircled the world, the latter providing a base for subsequent colonization. It was not long before almost the entire world came under the direct control of one or other of the European powers. After the Second World War, however, there was significant normative change concerning the legitimacy of colonial rule. The principle of self-determination, originally developed as a political principle in relation to Europeans in the aftermath of the First World War, was now invoked as a right of colonized people and drove a decolonization movement which saw almost all former European colonies achieve independence by the end of the twentieth century.

The establishment of colonial states with their relatively clear boundaries, their administrative centres, and more or less permanent, settled populations mimicked the structure of European states. When decolonization came, the transition from colonial state to sovereign state, in an international system of similarly structured states, seemed relatively simple from a technical point of view. Sovereignty was, for the most part, simply transferred from the colonizing power to an indigenous elite. In the decades following the end of the Second World War, most of the former

16

colonial states from the Atlantic and Africa through to Asia and the Pacific acquired sovereign statehood on the basis of existing boundaries and with structures of governance—parliaments, electorates, a civil service, etc.—reflecting European practices.

Virtually all former colonies therefore became part of an international system of states based largely on the European state system, a development which effectively ensured the globalization of that system. Even those states which had not been colonized, such as Japan and Turkey as well as Thailand and Tonga, adopted the European state format. But independent sovereign statehood has not been an outstanding success for a number of countries, and some would suggest that the poorest countries of the global South are sovereign in name only. While few postcolonial states have actually collapsed altogether, a number have experienced major difficulties in maintaining the basic elements of effective statehood (as noted in Chapter 9). These problems bring into question both the assumed benefits of the globalization of the European state system and its long-term prospects as an effective system of international order. Furthermore, the deepening and widening of the EU, as a project in regionalization that at once incorporates as well as transcends sovereign states, raises questions about the future of the traditional sovereign state in its original heartland. Conversely, the resurgence of nationalism in parts of Europe in recent years—as manifest in anti-EU parties in Italy, Germany, France, the Netherlands, Austria, Poland, and Hungary, not to mention Brexit—indicates a trend in the opposite direction (see Judis, 2018).

➡ For a discussion of statehood, see Chapter 9.

KEY POINTS

* It is largely due to the global reach of the European empires and their political legacies that the European state system became the basis for the current international state system and international order.

* Formal sovereign statehood has not always delivered significant benefits, especially in the Global South where a number of weak or failing states provide little in the way of benefits to their citizens.

16

CONCLUSION

This chapter has provided a broad introductory overview of key aspects of global politics with an emphasis on the evolution of the global system, including the formation of states and empires, from the earliest times through to the modern period and the present era of globalization. The various developments explored here have also introduced concepts such as hierarchy, hegemony, and sovereignty, all of which are essential to the analysis of international or global systems. Important too are historic ideas such as the nation and the ideology of nationalism. Setting the rise of the contemporary global order against this background helps to illustrate not only the variety of state forms and international systems in history, but also the fact that while some systems have achieved an impressive longevity, no system has ever achieved permanence. It would therefore be mistaken to assume that the present system, based largely on sovereign states, will necessarily remain as it is over the longer term. This is especially so given the challenges of globalization—however the phenomenon is conceived—and the various pressures it exerts on all aspects of sovereign statehood.

KEY QUESTIONS

1. How would you conceptualize the sphere of 'global politics' and how does it differ from the more conventional concept of 'the international'?
2. What are the key features of globalization?
3. To what extent is globalization a cultural process?
4. What are the key features of empires?
5. How does the concept of hegemony differ from that of empire?
6. Under what circumstances is the idea of sovereign statehood often assumed to have arisen in Europe?
7. What are the distinguishing features of the modern state?
8. What is the relationship between states and nations?
9. How did the European state system become globalized?
10. What are non-state actors how important are they in the global system?

FURTHER READING

Axford, B. (2013), *Theories of Globalization* (Cambridge: Polity Press).
   Provides a wide-ranging, critical introduction to a complex topic from a variety of disciplinary perspectives as well as raising issues and themes such as governance, democracy, intervention, and empire.

Bremmer, I. (2018), *Us vs Them: The Failure of Globalism* (London: Penguin).
   Deals with the recent rise of populist nationalism around the world and the challenges it poses for the values of international cooperation, free trade, and democracy itself.

Erikson, T. H. (2014), *Globalization: The Key Concepts* (London: Bloomsbury Academic, 2nd edn).
   Outlines the principal debates and controversies surrounding globalization, providing an anthropological perspective on the subject matter, which looks at the phenomenon both 'from above' as well as 'from below'.

Holslag, J. (2018), *A Political History of the World: Three Thousand Years of War and Peace* (London: Penguin).
   Offers a very broad overview of the various factors underlying the causes of war and the quest for peace. Examples range from ancient Egypt and Rome to China, the Middle East, the USA, and Europe.

Lamb, P. and Robertson-Snape, F. (2017), *Historical Dictionary of International Relations* (Lanham, MD: Rowman & Littlefield).
   Provides a general guide to theory and practice in relations between states, and between states and other actors on the world stage. A number of key thinkers are also discussed.

Lechner, F. J. (2009), *Globalization: The Making of World Society* (Chichester: Wiley-Blackwell).
   A comprehensive guide to the main themes and issues involved in debates on globalization with an emphasis on how a 'world society' is being forged.

 Test your knowledge and understanding further by trying this chapter's Multiple Choice Questions.
   www.oup.com/he/orsini1e

16

17

TRADITIONAL THEORIES IN GLOBAL POLITICS

READER'S GUIDE

Theory is a way of organizing the basic elements of our thinking about the world around us, and we can neither explain nor understand that world without some kind of theoretical framework in which the 'facts' of global politics are made sense of. Two major bodies of theory—liberalism and realism—constitute the theoretical terrain of traditional studies in the field. Each has offered competing explanations and solutions addressing the causes of war and the conditions for peace. From the start, we should note that traditional theories, while proffering universally valid explanations of political behaviour, have been developed largely in 'the West' and therefore draw mainly on European and North American experiences. They also developed in a milieu in which racist and imperial ideas were widespread. Indeed, it has often been pointed out that the theorists most often singled out as key figures in the development of IR theory (and political and social theory more generally) throughout much of the twentieth century, and studied on that basis, were virtually all white, and all male, and so their ideas have developed on the basis of a relatively limited, and privileged world view. It must also be noted that the more conventional term 'international politics' is used frequently in this chapter because traditional theorists conceived of their work as largely addressing relations between states and rarely conceptualized it as 'global' in the more diffuse sense in which the term is used now. An exception is the later generation of liberals whose theories have informed contemporary discourses of globalization.

EARLY LIBERAL APPROACHES

It has often been assumed that the formal academic study of international politics emerged in the wake of the World War One, for although scholars had frequently focused on political issues in the international sphere before that time, they had tended to do so from within disciplines such as history and law rather than political science. But as with the notion that Westphalia produced the modern sovereign state system, the idea that IR as a discipline suddenly appeared after this war has been branded as another foundational 'myth'. An alternative viewpoint regards 'thinking about international relations' as having become a primary academic activity only after 1945, and even later than that in the Third World (Acharya and Buzan, 2019: 6), while other see it as really dating only from the 1980s (Ashworth, 2018). Again, the details of this debate are beyond the scope of an introductory text. Whatever the 'real' origins of the discipline, it is certainly the case that the unprecedented scale of what became known as the 'Great War' prompted an urgent search for a new, more stable international order providing for lasting peace and security. Under the influence of certain key figures, including US President Woodrow Wilson (1856–1924), this was to be an essentially liberal order and the cluster of ideas supporting it became known as 'liberal internationalism' or 'liberal institutionalism', the latter reflecting the key role of institutions in underpinning international order (**Box 17.1**).

SHORT BIOGRAPHY BOX 17.1
Woodrow Wilson (1856–1924)

Thomas Woodrow Wilson was born in Staunton, Virginia, just five years before the start of the Civil War in which his father served as a pastor on the Confederate side. Wilson showed little early promise, failing to learn to read before ten or eleven years of age and experiencing difficulties all his life due, probably, to dyslexia. His later achievements as both a scholar and a politician, becoming first a Professor at Princeton University and then US President for two terms from 1913–21, therefore stand out as representing a triumph over personal adversity.

As a Democrat, Wilson gained a reputation for promoting an expanded role for government and pursued progressive liberal policies on a number of fronts, reflecting the abandonment of nineteenth-century laissez-faire dogma. Reforms included the abolition of child labour, the introduction of an eight-hour day in the private sector, a graduated income tax, and the establishment of the Federal Reserve to steer the economy. Other innovations saw regular press briefings—previously unheard of in US presidential politics. Wilson was also the first Southerner to be elected president since the Civil War. Unfortunately, he proved to be very much a product of his time and place when it came to race issues, supporting segregation and other regressive policies within the US administration which amounted to white supremacism.

Internationally, Wilson is best known for his role in bringing the US into World War One in 1917, 'to make the world safe for democracy' and, later, for his efforts at the Paris Peace Conference of 1919, held in the Palace of Versailles, and in bringing the League of Nations into being. He is also credited with articulating the general principle of the right to self-determination, although this was to be exercised initially within Europe rather than extended to the still colonised

17

Photo 17.1 Wilson: Woodrow Wilson gained a reputation for promoting an expanded role for government and pursued progressive liberal policies. *Library of Congress*

world. The latter reflected not only Wilson's attitudes to non-white peoples, but those prevailing among European leaders of the time more generally when ideas of racial superiority were rife.

Despite failing to persuade an isolationist US Congress to join the new international institution, in which hopes for a more stable and peaceful world order were invested, he was nonetheless awarded the Nobel Peace Prize in 1919 in recognition of his leading role in promoting world political organization. In the same year the first academic chair of international politics was established at University of Wales, Aberystwyth, and named in honour of Wilson.

Liberal international theorists of the early twentieth century did not produce an entirely new theoretical schema but drew on a pre-existing body of philosophy in constructing their notion of order. Ancient philosophers had emphasized the capacity of individual human reason for delineating the 'good life' and arranging institutions accordingly. They had also advanced ideas about cosmopolitanism which, as we saw in the last chapter, is a world view embracing the notion of a common human community and shared morality. Although often considered a Western idea with its roots in the thought of ancient Greece and Rome, cosmopolitanism has parallels in Chinese as expressed in the concept of *tianxia* (all under heaven), and the notion that a harmonious world order may be created within a benign Chinese cosmopolitan space (Chun, 2009: 29). Contemporary cosmopolitan thinking in communist China has also extended, at least in some formulations, to the notion that 'the proletariat knows no national boundaries' and that China should therefore be interested in the 'world proletariat' (Qin, 2011: 231).

Modern liberal thinkers advocated concrete political action in achieving reform when the existing order was found wanting. Early contributors to ideas about international order were Hugo Grotius

(1583–1645) and Samuel Pufendorf (1632–94), both of whom experienced the Thirty Years War discussed in Chapter 16. Grotius had argued for the possibility of universal moral standards against which the legitimacy of actions in pursuit of self-preservation could be judged. This has featured in liberal international thought ever since. He also formulated some of the earliest ideas in the modern period about the 'sociability' of the international sphere which were highly influential in the development of later ideas about international society (Dunne, 1998: 138–9). Pufendorf incorporated a basic natural law of self-preservation in his work on universal jurisprudence and the law of nations. He, too, promoted the essential sociability of humans which served to counter ideas about excessive self-interestedness. Another major figure is Immanuel Kant (1724–1804) whose seminal work, *Perpetual Peace*, was published in 1795. In order to secure lasting peace among states, he devised a set of propositions for a law of nations founded on a federation of free states, ideas which have remained highly influential in peace theory (see Kant in Brown et al., 2002: 432–4).

Kant further proposed that, under republican forms of government, the individual concern for self-preservation which was an entirely rational concern would ensure that citizens effectively vetoed warmongering. This is one of the rationales behind the influential democratic peace thesis. Woodrow Wilson also endorsed the idea that democracies are inherently peaceful, both within themselves and in their relations with each other, and believed that if all countries were governed democratically, then warfare would be virtually eliminated. He certainly believed that, if all European countries had been democracies in 1914, war would have been avoided.

A major theme uniting many liberal thinkers from Grotius onwards, and which helps to distinguish liberal from realist thought, includes a *relatively* more optimistic view of the possibilities for peaceful relations. This derives from a more positive view of human nature, at least to the extent that people can learn from their mistakes, some of which are undoubtedly dreadful. Beyond this, liberals generally believe that rationally chosen, self-regarding courses of action by individuals tend to lead to better outcomes for all, or at least for a majority. Thus over time humans can *progress* towards a better state of existence as individuals within their political communities and in the relations between communities. But none of this comes about by itself. People (agents) need to make it happen. So just as human rationality *and* agency are required to build a satisfactory social and political order within a state, so they are required just as much, if not more, in the construction of international institutions designed specifically to overcome the negative effects of anarchy and to contain tendencies to war. This style of thinking contributed to developments in the immediate aftermath of the First World War.

President Wilson had led his country into war in the belief that, once the forces responsible for the war were defeated, a strong international organization dedicated to preserving international peace and security could flourish. He proposed a general association of nation-states to make mutual guarantees concerning economic and political independence and territorial integrity, regardless of each state's size or capacity. This was operationalized through the 1919 Treaty of Versailles which embodied the Covenant of the League of Nations. However, the Treaty also imposed harsh reparations on Germany for loss and damage caused by the war. We consider further aspects of the League in Chapter 20, but for present purposes it provides a useful case study of how theory and practice are interwoven (**Box 17.2**).

Another important aspect of liberal international theory promoted by Wilson and others in the wake of the First World War was the principle of self-determination, a term which has several nuances. First, it can refer to the right of states freely to pursue their own policies and practices

It is often said that the League of Nations was a failure because it did not prevent the outbreak of the Second World War. And the liberal internationalism which underpinned it was derided, at least by realists, as a form of utopianism bound to fail when faced with the 'realities' of power politics in an anarchical international sphere. But is this to mistake cause and effect? Although some provisions allowed too much leeway in the application of sanctions, the institutional design of the League itself was workable enough, and the United Nations (UN) is still based on many of these. As the first major attempt to set up a mechanism for collective security on such an extensive international scale it must been hailed as a considerable achievement. Other factors were far more important in undermining its chances for success. Thus when the League, and the principles of liberal internationalism on which it was based, stand accused of failing to check the aggression of Germany, Italy, and Japan, we must remember the failure of the US to join, the refusal to allow communist Russia to join, the aggression of France itself when it invaded a German industrial area with Belgium in an attempt to exact reparation dues, the failure of Britain to condemn this violation of League rules, all combined with the vengeful nature of the Treaty's reparations provisions. A humiliated Germany was ripe for the rabid, right-wing nationalism that Hitler came to espouse while the geopolitical landscape of swathes of Eastern Europe was highly vulnerable to the aggression of a remilitarized Germany. The question then is: did the League of Nations fail; or did state leaders fail the League of Nations?

and nurture their own distinctive political culture. Second, it can refer to the right of citizens to determine their own government and therefore a preferred set of policy options—a defining characteristic of liberal democracy. And third, it can refer to the quest of a nationalist movement to secure political autonomy, which can include an act of secession to form a new sovereign state. This right to *national* self-determination further strengthens the legitimacy of the nation-state idea discussed in Chapters 6 and 16.

Historically, the principle of the self-determination of 'peoples' (understood as 'nations') was not extended to include the colonized world until after 1945, as noted previously. Indeed, the League entrenched European colonial domination through its mandate system which was designed to ensure that 'advanced nations' would continue to administer 'peoples not yet able to stand by themselves under the strenuous conditions of the modern world', on the principle that the well-being and development of such peoples was a 'sacred trust of civilization' (Pederson, 2015: 1). When the doctrine of self-determination was applied to the colonial world after 1945 by the newly established United Nations, it became a powerful ideology underpinning the entire decolonization movement.

One country that provided an exception to the general treatment of non-Western countries was Japan which had attended the Versailles conference as one of five great powers, having supported the alliance of forces opposing Germany. Japan had taken possession of Germany's former colonial territories in Micronesia (located in the northern Pacific Ocean) and continued to hold these under a League mandate. Japan had also initiated a 'racial equality proposal' at Versailles which was intended to apply, not to all non-Western people, but only to members of the League. In other words, it was designed to give Japan (and Japanese people) equal 'racial status' with Europeans. The proposal was vigorously opposed by the US and Australia—the latter having adopted an explicit 'White Australia Policy' to prevent Asian immigration. It was in fact Australia which most strongly opposed Japan's proposal and ensured its defeat even though most European countries were sympathetic to Japan's position (see, generally, Imamoto, 2018). Japan's failure to have the proposal adopted served to weaken its attachment to the League and was perhaps a factor in its subsequent strategic choices leading up to the Second World War.

In the meantime, liberal international theory reached a high point in the inter-war years. Among the prominent liberal scholars of the time was Norman Angell, awarded the 1933 Nobel Peace Prize on the basis of his extensive writings on the futility of war. It is also notable that thinkers such as Angell, although believing that humans could change for the better, were scarcely blind to their follies and self-destructive behaviour, for if humans were so inherently good and peaceful, he said, devices such as the League of Nations would hardly be necessary (Angell quoted in Sylvest, 2004: 424).

Subsequent developments saw liberal ideas overshadowed as realism rose to prominence and its proponents denounced the idealism implicit in liberal international theory and the perceived ineffectiveness of international institutions in the face of the realities of power politics. As we shall see, liberalism was to make something of a comeback in the latter part of the twentieth century and remains highly influential in international theory. In practical terms, its precepts underpin an extensive system of international law as well as the principal political institutions of contemporary international governance embodied in the UN system. In other words, liberalism underpins the theory and practice of a rules-based international order **(Box 17.3)**.

➡ See Chapters 4 and 15 for discussions of liberal democracy.

➡ See Chapter 8 for a discussion of the nation-state.

Threats to that order are said to have increased in recent years with countries like Russia and China appearing to operate unilaterally and with little regard for rules negotiated over many years. Russia's annexation of the Crimea in 2014, its backing of separatist forces in eastern Ukraine, and its alleged involvement in the poisoning of a former Russian double agent and his daughter in the UK in 2018, which violated both British sovereignty and the UN's Chemical Weapons Convention, have been major concerns. China has been accused of violations over its territorial claims in the South China Sea which include building a substantial military base on reefs in a contested area and threatening freedom of navigation under the UN's Convention on the Law of the Sea. The US and its allies, however, have also stood accused of violating the UN's most basic rules and principles by invading Iraq in 2003. More recently, President Trump has rejected key multilateral policies concerning global warming and nuclear issues in Iran while his protectionism is

17

KEY CONCEPT BOX 17.3
The Rules-Based International Order

The idea of a rules-based international order has been described 'as a shared commitment by all countries to conduct their activities in accordance with agreed rules that evolve over time, such as international law, regional security arrangements, trade agreements, immigration protocols, and cultural arrangements. . . . [It] is the only alternative to international coercion by competing great powers, spheres of influence, client states and terrorist organisations' (UNAA, 2017).

considered to be a threat to multilateralism in world trade. A recent report from the UK's House of Lords highlighted some broad trends, including problems posed not only by China and Russia but the USA as well.

> We are living through a time of worldwide disruption and change. Trends including populism, identity politics, nationalism, isolationism, protectionism and mass movements of people are putting considerable pressure on states and traditional structures of government. At the same time, the global balance of power is shifting and fragmenting in a way not experienced since the Second World War, undermining the rules-based international order. We have sought not only to look at needed responses but to understand from our many witnesses the roots of this upheaval in world affairs. . . . [The] UK's 'bedrock' relationship with its key ally of past decades, the US, is under disturbing pressure. The US Administration has taken a number of unilateral foreign policy decisions on high-profile issues, such as the Iran nuclear deal and trade policy, which undermine the UK's interests. The UK has struggled to influence the Administration, which is, in part, a reflection of a broader shift in the US towards a more inward-looking 'America First' stance, with less focus on the transatlantic alliance or multilateralism. In future the Government will need to place less reliance on reaching a common US/UK approach to the main issues of the day than has often been the case in the past.
> (UK, House of Lords, 2018: 3)

One critic of the current 'liberal world order' argues that it is neither liberal nor democratic and that Western elites, who make and break rules as it suits them, have been reaping benefits in the form of both power and profits. At the same time, they have created a world of inequality and social fragmentation in which intolerance has thrived. This has driven a kind of 'culture war' between populist nationalists and globalists with both sides adopting rigid, angry postures (Pabst, 2019). The same author has elsewhere argued for an EU built not on the pursuit of liberal values but on a Christian synthesis of ancient virtues promoting trust and cooperation—which in fact underpins Europe's common culture. Writing just before the Brexit vote, he further suggested that 'Brexit would leave the rest of the EU exposed to a German hegemony that Germany does not want and everybody else fears' (Pabst, 2016). How this scenario plays out of course remains to be seen, as does the fallout from the rise of populist nationalism, the Trump presidency, and other challenges to liberal internationalism.

17

KEY POINTS

- A significant impetus for liberal international theorists of the early twentieth century was the devastation wrought by the First World War and a determination to identify the causes of war and the conditions for peace.

- Liberal international theory accepts that sovereign states are the key actors in international affairs but proposes that their behaviour, even under conditions of anarchy, can be modified through international institutions and a strong rules-based international order.

- Liberal internationalism is also generally supportive of the trends underpinning globalization while standing opposed to such ideologies as populist nationalism and trade protectionism.

CLASSICAL REALISM

The Treaty of Versailles not only failed to resolve a number of Europe's political problems, but also exacerbated others. New states had been created in Eastern Europe partly in an attempt to apply the principle of national self-determination. Strategically, they were also supposed to serve as 'buffer states' between Western Europe and the emergent communist empire further east. The USSR's own brand of internationalism at the time was committed to the overthrow of a capitalist economic order by means of worldwide revolution. Throughout the 1920s, however, relative peace was the order of the day and even Germany had joined the League of Nations. But none of this was to prevent the rise of Adolf Hitler who set about building the Third Reich on an ultra-nationalist basis.

Developments in other parts of the world were significant too, especially the rise of Japan which had achieved extraordinary industrial growth over the previous half-century. Japan had been a member of the League of Nations and some Japanese remained committed to internationalism. But aggressive militarism and imperialism succeeded in a period where the effects of the Depression enhanced the influence of ultra-nationalists, as in Italy and Germany. The German invasion of Poland in 1939 led the world into its second large-scale war. Japan had already invaded China, but it was not until 1940 that Japan became part of the Axis Alliance with Italy and Germany and, in the following year, brought the USA into the war by attacking Pearl Harbor.

Over the period 1939–45, at least 50 million people were killed as a direct result of the Second World War—more than five times the number killed in the previous world war. The death camps of Nazi Germany, in which some 6 million people were murdered, also highlighted the consequences of racialist nationalism gone mad. The Holocaust, which refers primarily to the mass murder of Jews in this war, stands as the most notorious act of genocide in human history. Given that the study of international politics had been founded by people dedicated to the prevention of war, and the death, destruction, and suffering it caused, this war must be seen as a devastating setback. Here is where realism enters the picture as a theory designed to explain how the world *really* is, rather than how it *ought* to be.

While there is no single, concise theory that goes under the name of 'realism', virtually all realist approaches take the struggle for power and security by sovereign states in the anarchic sphere of international politics as their central focus. And although it emerged as an explicit theory of international politics only in the twentieth century, many of its proponents claim that they are part of a much longer tradition. The treatment of the Peloponnesian War between the ancient city-states of Athens and Sparta by the historian Thucydides contains a dialogue commonly taken to illustrate two cardinal principles of political realism. The 'Melian Dialogue' suggests, first, that power politics is the name of the game in relations between states, and second, that issues of morality are irrelevant in the sphere of power politics. This sphere is therefore *amoral* in the sense that no moral rules can be applied, rather than *immoral* which indicates the transgression of an existing moral rule (**Box 17.4**).

Another significant figure is Niccolò Machiavelli (1467–1527) who developed a pragmatic approach to politics, eschewing idealist imaginaries and moralizing. A particularly important idea, often traced to Machiavelli, is *raison d'état* (reason of state), which is reflected in the more common contemporary phrase national interest. Although Machiavelli did not use the precise term 'reason of state', he urged that, where the safety of the country is at stake, a ruler ought not to

Photo 17.2 Niccolò Machiavelli became infamous for his disregard for idealist imaginaries and moralizing. *Shutterstock RF via DAM: Everett Historical/Shutterstock.com*

HISTORY BOX 17.4
The Melian Dialogue

The inhabitants of the island of Melos were neutral in the war between Athens and Sparta and would not submit to Athens. The Athenians first sent envoys with terms for a Melian surrender and Thucydides records the dialogue:

> Athenians: [We will] not go out of our way to prove at length that we have a right to rule . . . But you and we should say what we really think, and aim only at what is possible, for we both alike know that into the discussion of human affairs the question of justice only enters where the pressure of necessity is equal, and that the powerful exact what they can, and the weak grant what they must.
>
> Melians: But must we be your enemies? Will you not receive us as friends if we are neutral and remain at peace with you?
>
> Athenians: No, your enmity is not half so mischievous to us as your friendship; for the one is in the eyes of our subjects an argument of our power, the other of our weakness . . .
>
> Melians: But do you not recognize another danger? For . . . since you drive us from the plea of justice and press upon us your doctrine of expediency, we must show you what is for our interest, and, if it be for yours also, may hope to convince you: Will you not be making enemies of all who are now neutrals? . . .
>
> Athenians: . . . you are not fighting against equals to whom you cannot yield without disgrace, but you are taking counsel whether or no you shall resist an overwhelming force. The question is not one of honour but of prudence . . .
>
> Melians: We know only too well how hard the struggle must be against your power, and against fortune . . . Nevertheless we do not despair of fortune; . . . because we are righteous, and you against whom we contend are unrighteous.

→

→

> Athenians: . . . of men we know, that by a law of their nature wherever they can rule they will. This law was not made by us, and we are not the first who have acted upon it; we did but inherit it, and shall bequeath it to all time, and we know that you and all mankind, if you were as strong as we are, would do as we do . . . the path of expediency is safe, whereas justice and honour involve danger in practice . . . [and] . . . what encourages men who are invited to join in a conflict is clearly not the good-will of those who summon them to their side, but a decided superiority in real power . . .
> (Thucydides, 5: 84–109)
>
> Thucydides further records that the Melians refused to surrender. The Athenians laid siege to the city and eventually forced a surrender whereupon they put to death all males of military age and enslaved the women and children.

consider what is just or unjust, merciful or cruel, but rather what will secure 'the life of the country and maintain its liberty' (Machiavelli, 3: 41).

Perhaps the most important figure claimed for the realist tradition is Thomas Hobbes (1588–1679) (see Chapters 2 and 8). Hobbes starts by positing a state of nature as well as a certain human nature, both assumed to be universal; that is, *constant for all times and all places*. Hobbes's state of nature is devoid of all that is necessary for the good life. It lacks security, justice, and any sort of morality. And it lacks these elements precisely because there is no sovereign power to enforce them. The essential characteristic of this condition is anarchy. Fear and insecurity dominate people's consciousness, driving individuals to seek the means of their own preservation above all else. And since domination is the only viable means of achieving one's preservation, the inevitable result is the war of each against all. This scenario prompted Hobbes to pen his most famous line; namely, that life in the anarchic state of nature is solitary, poor, nasty, brutish, and short!

To dispel anarchy and escape this scenario into a realm of peace and security, individuals must contract together to live under a single, indisputable political authority—a sovereign power—who can enforce order and obedience to a set of laws. People retain only a fundamental right to self-preservation, since it is for this purpose that they submit to the sovereign authority in the first place. Political communities for Hobbes are therefore artificial constructs devised to alleviate the miserable, insecure conditions of the state of nature. As for relations between states, exactly the same conditions apply as for individuals in the state of nature. Since no overarching sovereign authority holds sway in the international sphere, states are condemned to exist in a realm of perpetual anarchy where survival is the name of the game—and this is achieved only through domination and the pursuit of pure self-interest. As for justice and morality, these simply have no place in such an environment (Lawson, 2015: 33–5).

Some may ask whether the insights of Thucydides are still relevant after almost 2,500 years. Apparently, advisors in the Trump administration have thought so. It was reported in 2017 that a prominent foreign affairs figure had been invited to the White House to brief the National Security Council on the implications of Thucydides' insights for the rivalry between the US and China. He first cited Thucydides on what triggered warfare in his time: 'What made war inevitable was the growth of Athenian power and the fear which this caused in Sparta' and warned that 'the same dynamic could drive this century's rising empire, China, and the United States into a war neither wants' (quoted in Crowley, 2017).

17

Thucydides, Machiavelli, and Hobbes are just some among a longer list of key figures who are generally included in the 'classical realist canon' and are, for all intents and purposes, considered European (although it is somewhat anachronistic to call Thucydides 'European'). But because classical realism aspires to provide a universally valid theory of international politics, it has also looked outside the usual European line-up to substantiate its credentials as a transhistorical and transcultural canon of reasoned political thought, and has claimed at least two non-European figures as part of the canon: the ancient Chinese strategist Sun Tzu (c.545–470 BC) and Kautilya, an ancient Indian commentator on statecraft whose treatise, the Arthashastra, has often been compared to Machiavelli's writings. Sun Tzu's *The Art of War* gives sage advice to rulers on how power should be used to ensure their own interests and survival (Tzu, 2017). Kautilya's work, authored sometime in the first millennium BC (but impossible to date accurately), deals with similar themes, but is also more extensive in its treatment of political themes, including political economy (Kautilya, 2016). Both advise that war should be avoided wherever possible, and that a clever leader is one who can win without fighting. This accords with the approach taken by most twentieth century IR realists who, far from being warmongers, generally argue that use of force is a last resort.

These are some of the basic ideas on which theories of *classical* realism in international politics developed from the 1930s up until about the late 1960s. Also central to this development was a critique of liberalism. Indeed, at least in its classic formulation, realism is essentially a conservative response to liberal international thought (see Chapter 6). One of the most prominent critics, E. H. Carr, is often described as a disillusioned liberal who believed the peace settlement following the First World War to be a fiasco. He regarded the principal defect of liberalism as an almost complete blindness to the power factor in politics which he likened to a law of nature, rather like Hobbes. One of Carr's principal arguments holds, first, that no political society, whether national or international, can exist unless people submit to certain rules of conduct. In this respect, he is in accord with liberal principles. But he further asserts the primacy of politics over ethics, arguing that as a matter of logic rulers rule because of superior strength, and the ruled submit because they are weaker. Political obligation thus derives from the recognition that 'might is right'. This accords with the logic of Thucydides' Athenian generals noted in **Box 17.4**. In preparing the ground for a theory of realism, Carr also asserts that this theory is in fact a reaction to utopianism and cites Machiavelli as initiating a revolt against utopianism in political thought in his own time (Carr, 1948: ch. 4). (**See Box 17.5**.)

Carr's broader view of politics, however, does not concede the entire ground to realism. He was also concerned to point out that when realism is attacked with its own weapons, it is just as likely to be found lacking the cold objectivity claimed for it by its proponents as any other way of thinking (Carr, 1948: 89). This led him to conclude that sound political thinking must be based on

KEY QUOTE BOX 17.5
Machiavelli on the 'Real' versus the 'Ideal'

. . . it appears to me more appropriate to follow up the real truth of a matter than the imagination of it; for many have pictured republics and principalities which in fact have never been seen and known, because how one lives is so far distant from how one ought to live that he who neglects what is done for what ought to be done sooner effects his ruin than his preservation. (Machiavelli quoted in Carr, 1948: 63)

17

elements of both utopia and reality, for when utopianism 'has become a hollow and intolerable sham, which serves merely as a disguise for the interests of the privileged, the realist performs an indispensable service in unmasking it'. Pure realism, on the other hand, offers 'nothing but a naked struggle for power which makes any kind of international society impossible' (Carr, 1948: 93). As we shall see later in this chapter, the idea of international society was to become a central theme in the English School's contribution to theory.

After the Second World War, and with the onset of the Cold War, the study of international politics developed rapidly in the USA and acquired a distinctive realist tone. The principle figure in post-war American theorizing was Hans Morgenthau whose ideas have been compared with those of Thucydides by contemporary authors. Richard Ned Lebow (2007: 52–70), for example, says that both Thucydides and Morgenthau see politics, in any time and any place, as subject to a basic human instinct revolving around power. Realism, like conservatism, therefore, claims *not* to be an 'ideology'. This epithet is reserved for doctrines such as liberalism and socialism, which are grounded in idealist suppositions. Realism, on the other hand, claims to provide an account of how things 'really are', and thus asserts an essential objectivity.

Realism also sees politics in the domestic sphere as much the same as politics in the international sphere in so far as it is driven by power politics. The crucial difference is of course the fact that a sovereign authority resides within states and therefore makes domestic order possible. Some order is possible in the anarchic international sphere, but this is achieved only through rather fragile mechanisms. These mechanisms include, first and foremost, a balance of power among constituent elements of an international system. In realist theory, this balance of power has a deterrence effect so long as states behave in a rational manner and do not allow greed and ambition to cloud their judgement. More sophisticated versions of realism allow for the possibility of a deterrence effect to also arise from certain elements of sociability in an international system. In other words, if a group of states acknowledges a 'community of interests' or is otherwise bound by some common elements of culture, conventions, personal ties, and so on, then competition for power is greatly modified and less likely to generate warfare. Some states, however, aggressively pursue what they perceive to be their own interests regardless. Thus certain states, such as Athens during the period of the Peloponnesian War, or leaders like Napoleon and Hitler in later times, cannot be deterred. Lebow further quotes Morgenthau's wry observation that a balance of power 'works best when needed least' (Lebow, 2007: 58). **(See Box 17.6.)**

17

KEY QUOTE BOX 17.6
Hans J. Morgenthau on Power Politics

International politics, like all politics, is a struggle for power. Whatever the ultimate aims of international politics, power is always the immediate aim. Statesmen and peoples may ultimately seek freedom, security, prosperity, or power itself. They may define their goals in terms of a religious, philosophic, economic, or social ideal. They may hope that this ideal will materialize through its own inner force, through divine intervention, or through the natural development of human affairs. But whenever they strive to realize their goal by means of international politics, they do so by striving for power. (Morgenthau, 1948: 13)

KEY POINTS

- 'Realism' as an approach to the study of politics purports to analyse things as they *really are*, rather than as they *ought to be*.

- Realism comes in different forms, but virtually all realist international theory takes the struggle for power and security of sovereign states in conditions of international anarchy as their central focus.

- Classical realists emphasize the problem of human nature and its tendencies to conflict and violence.

THE ENGLISH SCHOOL AND INTERNATIONAL SOCIETY

While Morgenthau's version of classical realism was making its mark, especially in the USA, another group of scholars developed a different approach on the other side of the Atlantic. This group first gathered in London in 1959, constituting themselves as the 'British Committee' (later known as the English School), for the purpose of probing fundamental questions of international theory (Dunne, 1998: p. xi). One member, Martin Wight, thought the entire field of international politics was theoretically underdeveloped compared with the study of domestic politics. He proposed that, just as political theory asks fundamental questions about the state, so international theory must ask fundamental questions about the international sphere which they conceived as constituting a 'society of states' (Wight, 1966: 18).

As suggested in Wight's remarks, much of their theorizing revolved around the concept of international society articulated earlier by Grotius. This was understood as a society of sovereign states formed under conditions of anarchy. While English School theorists agreed that such conditions are inherently less stable than those in the domestic sphere, their emphasis was on the extent to which a stable order can nonetheless be achieved. A prominent member of the school, Hedley Bull, while accepting the basic premises of realism, proposed that state behaviour could be significantly modified through the adoption of rules and institutions. These generated an international environment and process of socialization in which norms, values, and common interests came to play an important role in influencing state behaviour. (**See Box 17.7.**)

The EU may be analysed in terms of a regionally-based international society. It declares values that are common to member countries which have come together to create 'a society in which inclusion, tolerance, justice, solidarity and non-discrimination prevail' and which are 'an integral

KEY QUOTE BOX 17.7
Hedley Bull on the Society of States

[A] society of states (or international society) exists when a group of states, conscious of certain common interests and common values, form a society in the sense that they conceive themselves to be bound by a common set of rules in their relations with one another and share in the working of common institutions. (Bull, 1997: 13)

part of our European way of life' (EU, 2018). Other regional bodies such as the African Union (AU), the Association of Southeast Asian Nations (ASEAN) and the Arab League (AL) also share characteristics of a regional international society—often declaring values held in common. But they tend to hold much more strongly to the doctrine of state sovereignty than EU members, and come nowhere close to allowing comparable levels of freedom of movement, trade, harmonization of laws, and so on. Even so, the development of regional organizations around most parts of the world along the lines of what we might call 'sub-global' international societies has become a feature of the broader global political sphere.

Despite general agreement among the early English School theorists on the basic principles of international society at a global level, there were diverging views on the extent to which a common core of norms could be established among all states. Bull, Wight, and others were living in an era of decolonization, and states very different from those of Europe were emerging around the world (**see Box 17.8**). Could a theory as Eurocentric as theirs apply universally? Could the norms of a society of European states really be exported to the rest of the world? These questions highlighted the issue of cultural difference in world politics and the fact that much theorizing to date had been characterized by ethnocentricity.

KEY DEBATE BOX 17.8
Pluralism versus Solidarism in the English School

Within the English School, opinion became divided over the extent to which norms, especially with respect to human rights and notions of justice, could be simply be exported. Some, including Bull, adopted pluralism as the basis of their approach. This recognized that different people (understood in terms of different 'cultures') invariably have different norms and values and, therefore, different standards of justice. If each state is a repository of those standards of justice, one must conclude that there can be no universal yardstick against which standards can be evaluated.

This argument tends strongly towards a notion of ethical relativism based on the idea that individual states not only have no legitimate sovereign power over them, but no moral authority over them either. The absence of a universal standard for 'right conduct' does not preclude the formation of an international society, but it does mean that it is fairly minimalist. International society is therefore held together simply by agreement on the importance of international order itself, and a normative commitment to supporting the goal of peaceful *coexistence* (Dunne, 1998: 100). This position accords more or less with communitarianism, discussed in Chapters 2 and 5. According to this approach, morality arises within particular communities and basically holds good only for those communities. In the sphere of global politics, such moral communities are, in effect, states.

Others, however, adopted a 'solidarist' approach which recognizes the inherent plurality of values among states in the international sphere, but seeks a more robust commitment to shared norms of both domestic and international behaviour, especially when it comes to human rights. Solidarism therefore reflects not simply a solidarity among states making a commitment to forming a peaceful international society bound by a commitment to non-intervention, but a broader commitment to the solidarity of humankind itself. So while a norm of non-intervention may be taken as a standard feature of the society of states in the ordinary course of events, a solidarist position allows, in principle, for this norm to be overtaken by an *extra*ordinary turn of events, such as when a population group within a state becomes a target for genocide.

Solidarism therefore shares some common ground with cosmopolitanism which contemplates the transcendence of state boundaries. For pluralists, however, the solidarist position with its cosmopolitan leanings moves too far away from an international society, understood as a socie-ty *of* states, towards something of a world or global society which de-emphasizes state bounda-ries and indeed the notion of a state system as such (Buzan, 2004: esp. 139–60).

Questions
1. Are values and norms always confined within the boundaries of particular cultures?
2. If so, what are the implications for universal human rights?

English School theory has experienced a significant revival in recent years. As two prominent authors have remarked, the importance of the English School's concern with the relationship between international order and human justice is at the heart of current debates about the rela-tionship between state sovereignty, human rights, and pressures for humanitarian intervention, as well as the phenomenon of failing states. Questions of clashing world views in a multicultural international society—a concern for some of the early theorists—also seem more urgent than ever in the 'post-9/11' world. Furthermore, ideas of international society as articulated by earlier English School theorists are seen as highly relevant for the analysis of regional integration pro-jects, problems of the international environment, and aspects of international political economy (Linklater and Suganami, 2006: 2).

Another study of legitimacy in international politics argues that, apart from underscoring the very existence of international society, questions of legitimacy have become increasingly urgent in the present period. Bodies such as the UN are seen as an essential repository of much legitima-cy in the international sphere, especially in relation to intervention, humanitarian or otherwise (see Clark, 2005). In addition, important aspects of English School theorizing resonate with emer-gent theories of social constructivism which have become especially prominent in the present period and which we explore further in the next chapter.

17

KEY POINTS

- The English School, while accommodating both realist and liberal perspectives, promotes the idea of a society of states underpinned by a set of common norms and values.
- Two main approaches developed, one 'pluralist' which seeks to accommodate varying norms, values, and standards of justice of different states within a framework of coexistence based on respect for sovereignty. 'Solidarism', in contrast, promotes a common set of norms and standards including respect for human rights and, in exceptional circumstances, a right of humanitarian intervention.

NEOLIBERALISM AND NEOREALISM

Further developments in the post-war period saw revisions of both liberalism and realism, resulting in the two 'neos'. Neorealism also goes by the name of 'structural' realism because it focuses on the structure of the international system itself. Neoliberalism, on the other hand, is sometimes referred to as pluralism for its much broader focus on the multiple forces at play in that system (Little, 1996: 66). The use of the term 'pluralism' here, incidentally, is not identical with the way in which it is used by English School theorists. Both usages invoke a concept of diversity, but whereas the English School usage was more concerned with the diversity of culture and values embodied within states, neoliberal pluralism refers to a plurality of actors and institutions in the international system. Here we should note also that *economic* neoliberalism, which is the focus of much contemporary discussion of globalization, refers to an approach emphasizing the role of global markets and free trade together with the minimization of state intervention, and so focuses on different issues.

Liberalism's period of renewal occurred after the Second World War when the international sphere underwent significant changes, especially with the founding of the UN as another attempt at creating an international institution capable of regulating global order and of keeping a check on aggressive power politics. The UN incorporated many of the League's features, including a general assembly and a secretariat presided over by a secretary-general, a court of justice, and an executive council. In addition, specialized agencies were formed to assist in the task of building a global order with a strong economic and social framework.

➡ Economic neoliberalism is discussed further in Chapter 22.

The period after 1945 also saw substantial formal decolonization in Africa, the Middle East, and the Asia-Pacific, thus 'internationalizing' the liberal idea of self-determination and, as we have seen, the sovereign state system itself as a vehicle for self-determination. As a result, the UN's membership base was much more extensive than the old League. Now, virtually every state in the world is a member and so it has become truly global. All these developments may be seen as underpinned by liberal institutionalist ideas and the aspiration to make the world a better place.

In terms of intellectual development, the renewal of liberalism in the post-war period challenged what was seen as realism's simplistic approach to the nature of the international system. Like realism, liberalism accepted the anarchic character of the international sphere as well as the central role played by sovereign states. Unlike realists, liberals not only accorded international institutions (such as the UN) a crucially important role in ameliorating the negative effects of anarchy and power politics, but also came to regard the role of non-state actors as important. These include organizations ranging from transnational corporations to NGOs such as the Red Cross/Red Crescent, the International Chamber of Commerce, the World Council of Churches, and so on. These bodies are said to constitute a form of global civil society which operates alongside the state system and the set of regional and international institutions based on that system.

In addition to its attention to the plurality of actors in the international system, neoliberalism also applied a finer-grained analysis to sovereign states. Whereas realists tended to regard states as unitary actors in the international sphere, neoliberals acknowledged a variety of state characteristics and modes of behaviour which were often influenced by domestic political constraints. Some of the earliest neoliberal ideas were formulated by Robert O. Keohane and Joseph S. Nye (1977) in terms of a new 'interdependence model' of international relations which highlighted linkages between various actors as well as their sensitivities to the effects of actions by others in

➡ For further discussion of global civil society see Chapter 21

17

the system, both state and non-state. This had important implications for global political economy and discourses of globalization, and so these liberals went beyond traditional security concerns.

While it could be argued that the idea of interdependence advances very little on older ideas about alliances, interdependence is generally seen as much more complicated than the relations generated by mere security alliances, especially since the processes of industrialization, and modernization, and globalization, more generally, have produced many more dynamics than can be accommodated in realist theory. Thus neoliberals began to talk of 'complex interdependence' to describe the principle characteristic of a modern international system with its multiple actors, agencies, and forces. Nye said a different kind of world from that depicted by realists could be imagined simply by reversing their key postulates. Thus we can see a world where states are not the only significant actors but operate alongside many others; where force is only one instrument among others, which include economic manipulation; and where the dominant goal is not security but welfare (Nye, 2005: 207).

As we have seen, liberalism has also been closely associated with ideas about creating positive conditions for peace. The link between theory and practice here occurs not just in the construction of institutions but also in the work of the peace movement more generally. Further intellectual support has also been developed in specialist peace studies programmes in universities and other institutions throughout the world, from the home of the Nobel Peace Prize (established in 1901) in Sweden to Japan, where peace activism, peace museums, and peace studies have had a strong profile since World War Two.

With neoliberalism providing a plausible alternative account of the international system, *neorealism* in turn restated the prime importance of power in an anarchical international sphere while modifying certain assumptions of classical realism. In refining the latter's ideas, neorealism also sought to produce a more *parsimonious* theory of international politics—that is, a theory stripped down to the essentials. This was meant to provide testable hypotheses in accordance with a more scientific approach. Critics would argue that this came at the expense of gross over-simplification.

The key neorealist figure in the 1970s was Kenneth Waltz whose major work, *Theory of International Politics* (1979), was highly influential in establishing the *structure* of the international state system as determining the behaviour of individual states, and not the other way around. Thus although states remained the principle actors, it was the structural attributes of the system as a whole that determined how states interacted with each other and therefore how the dynamics of the international political sphere worked. And if structure is the determinant of state behaviour, individual agents have little impact. Furthermore, this structure remains essentially anarchic regardless of how many international institutions and rules attempt to modify its effects.

In an earlier work, Waltz (1959) had already laid some of the groundwork for the neorealist/ structural realist enterprise through his delineation of three distinct spheres or 'images' of politics: (1) individuals, (2) the state, and (3) the international system of states. In the first image, warfare among individuals is driven by negative aspects of human nature—greed, stupidity, and misdirected aggression. In the second image, conflict is mediated by the internal (domestic) organization of states. The third image takes anarchy as the essential attribute of the structure of the international system, one which makes warfare much more likely to occur because of the absence of restraints under conditions of anarchy. For Waltz, the third image provides the exclusive subject matter for international politics while political activity within the first or second image exerts little influence on the international sphere because it does not affect its essential structure.

In addition to strengthening the dividing line between the domestic and the international, this move effectively eliminates the influence of human nature on international politics. Instead, the struggle for power is determined by the structure of the system itself.

A leading contemporary realist, John Mearsheimer, says that the anarchic international system, in which no higher authority sits above the great powers, and in which there is no guarantee that one will not attack another, means that each state is moved by good sense to acquire sufficient power to protect itself: 'In essence, great powers are trapped in an iron cage where they have little choice but to compete with each other for power if they hope to survive' (Mearsheimer, 2013: 78). However, the action of one state to enhance its security vis-à-vis other states in the international sphere, for example, by building up its military forces, invariably provokes other states to enhance their military capabilities in turn, thus making them more dangerous than they were before. This is, effectively, a feedback loop which results in a security dilemma, a concept developed much earlier in the Cold War period when the arms race was a prominent feature of power politics (see Herz, 1950). It also illustrates the key realist concept of the balance of power in so far as each state strives to adjust its capabilities to balance any change in the capabilities of other states, or at least those states considered relevant to the equation.

Waltz's ideas do not exhaust the range of 'neorealisms'. Other influential writers include Joseph Grieco (1988) who has elaborated on the idea of relative and absolute gains among states in terms of power and influence. Whereas liberals believe that states are content to make an absolute gain (measured against their own existing capacities rather than relative to other states), realists hold that states always seek both absolute and relative gains. Furthermore, states may well cooperate to enhance their overall position within the state system, but realists believe that states will engage in cheating behaviour if they think this will yield greater power or if continued cooperation appears likely to weaken their position.

Yet another branch of structural realism distinguishes defensive and offensive varieties and relates these to the concept of hegemony—a situation in which there is a dominant centre of power. Offensive realism holds that states constantly seek to enhance their power vis-à-vis others in the system, which is a perfectly rational means of guaranteeing survival. A state that acquires hegemonic status enjoys the greatest measure of security precisely because of its superior power. Defensive realism, on the other hand, views hegemonic ambitions in terms of the security dilemma because the pursuit of hegemony by one state will invariably provoke a reaction in others. Moreover, the combined power of other states may well be greater than that of the aspiring hegemon, leading ultimately to its defeat. However, realists of all varieties can see the dangers of expansionism and other ill-advised adventures abroad. Mearsheimer notes that almost every realist opposed the Iraq War of 2003 which turned into a strategic disaster for the US and the UK (Mearsheimer, 2013: 91).

In reflecting on developments over almost three decades since the end of the Cold War, when liberalism appeared to be in the ascendance, Mearsheimer has recently identified a cluster of problems which he associates with 'liberal hegemony'—a state of affairs which he says runs contrary to the core logic of structural realism as well as the insuperable ideology of nationalism. In the end, realism and nationalism will always trump liberalism, and any worthwhile foreign policy must recognise this. At the same time, he argues that those who pursue a militarist liberal foreign policy abroad must be aware of the threats this poses for the very values it seeks to promote at home (see **Box 17.9**).

> ❝ **KEY QUOTE** BOX 17.9
> John Mearsheimer on Liberal Hegemony

Liberal hegemony is an ambitious strategy in which a state aims to turn as many countries as possible into liberal democracies like itself while also promoting an open international economy and building international institutions. In essence, the liberal state seeks to spread its own values far and wide. . . . Liberal states have a crusader mentality hardwired into them that is hard to restrain. . . . The liberal state is likely to end up fighting endless wars, which will increase rather than reduce the level of conflict in international politics . . . Moreover, the state's militaristic behaviour is almost certain to end up threatening its own liberal values. Liberalism abroad leads to illiberalism at home. (Mearsheimer, 2018: 1–3)

Ideas about absolute and relative gains, offensive realism and defensive realism, are just some of the variations on the neorealist theme. Certain of these ideas may appear as abstract elements of an over-simplified theory of politics in the global sphere, limited in its ability to ask deeper questions about the state of the world and what the future might hold. Critics of neorealism also hold that it has little to say about a range of pressing problems which go beyond the concerns of military security, from the state of the global environment to imbalances in resource allocation and consumption around the world. Neorealism certainly says nothing about questions of global justice. There is now an emergent school of *neo*classical realism which seeks to broaden the scope of realist theory to once again attempt a more comprehensive theorization and analysis of the mass of variables which contribute to the dynamics of the global sphere (see Rose, 1998: 144–72; Lobell et al., 2009; Ross-Smith, 2018). We may well see another variety of realism develop more fully along these lines in the future.

Finally, we may ask whether the theories arising from both realist and liberal ideas, developed largely in the West, have found resonance in other parts of the world. One author says that, in China, where there has been keen interest in IR theory since the late 1970s when China began a reform process which included 'opening up' to the world of global politics, academics have drawn heavily on Western IR thought with liberal and realist views featuring in two particular approaches. These are associated with the practical implications of China's rise as a global power. One key question revolves around whether can China's rise can be achieved peacefully, or whether it is inevitable that it will provoke violence, with liberal approaches supporting the former and realism the latter. These debates raise another fundamental question, and that is how China's identity vis-à-vis international society, which shapes both China's definition of its own interests as well as its behaviour in the international sphere (Qin, 2001: 201, 231–57). The question of identity and the way in which this relates to the formulation of interests and how a state behaves in global politics, relates more specifically to constructivist approaches, as discussed in Chapter 18.

Others have drawn attention to the fact that neorealism and neoliberalism, in particular, have based their assumptions almost exclusively on the dynamics generated by 'great powers', thus relegating less powerful states—which includes almost all of the global South—to virtual irrelevance in the wider scheme of things. With specific reference to Africa, it has been pointed out that theorists of both the 'neos' have located Africa on the margins of global politics, and portrayed

African actors as possessing little agency of their own. In the case of neoliberalism, for example, it has been assumed that because African states lacks 'hegemonic power' they cannot be included in great power theorizing, except to the extent that the continent generally 'suffers the whims of the stronger global players.' And when attention has been directed to the continent, thinking has been dominated by 'development theories aimed at reproducing Western economic, political and cultural ideals' (Dunn, 2001: 3).

KEY POINTS

- Important neoliberal ideas include 'complex interdependence' which recognizes multiple actors, agencies and forces at work in the international system and more porous boundaries between domestic and international spheres—conditions favourable to globalization. States remain significant actors, but they operate alongside many others while economic power is just as significant as force.

- Neorealism takes *structure* as the prime determinant of behaviour in the international sphere which is quite separate from the state's domestic sphere of and must be studied in its own terms. The 'three images' of politics also eliminates human nature and individual agency as relevant factors, narrowing the scope of international politics and producing a more parsimonious theory which its proponents say can generate testable hypotheses. Neorealism has now split into a variety of approaches as well as being contested by neoclassical realism.

- While IR in China has drawn from both 'neo' approaches, others have highlighted their highly Eurocentric focus and the assumption that only 'great power politics' matters. This leaves much of the global South out of the picture altogether.

CONCLUSION

All academic disciplines are underpinned by bodies of theory formulated in response to particular problems and issues arising from their particular subject matter. Theorizing is clearly a mental process or ideational activity, but it is intimately related to practice. In the social sciences, of which the study of global politics is a part, it attempts to make sense of complex actions, events or phenomena. The chapter began with a survey of the circumstances under which two major competing bodies of international theory developed to provide a substantial framework for the discipline. It has also shown that although much of the explicit theorizing about international politics did not begin until the twentieth century, both liberalism and realism drew on existing ideas in the history of political thought—albeit mainly the history of Western political thought—to address basic problems of international order. Each has been modified over the years with competing strands developing within them, so neither can be taken as a single body of theory. At the same time, both liberalism and realism assume that certain propositions are universally valid—the 'fact' of international anarchy being a prime example. But neither school of thought has taken serious account of non-Western perspectives, and so present only a partial account of politics in the global sphere. These and other shortcomings have been challenged by some of the more recent bodies of theory which we consider in the next chapter.

17

KEY QUESTIONS

1. How do norms and methods inform the development of theory?

2. What were the major factors behind the rise of liberal international theory in the early twentieth century and what did early theorists hope to achieve?

3. In what way does the right to national self-determination strengthen the legitimacy of the nation-state idea?

4. Why did E. H. Carr describe early liberals as utopians, and was this description fair?

5. What are the distinguishing features of classical realist thought?

6. How does the idea of 'international society' contribute to our understanding of global politics?

7. How could the English School accommodate both realism and liberalism and remain coherent?

8. In what ways does neorealism differ from classical realism?

9. What is 'pluralist' about neoliberalism and how does pluralism relate to the concept of complex interdependence?

10. Is neorealism's parsimony a strength or a weakness?

11. Do liberal states really have a 'crusader mentality'?

FURTHER READING

Angell, N. (1934), *The Great Illusion* (London: W. Heinemann).
Originally published in 1910, this book is an early, influential statement of idealism which argues against the notion that national prosperity depends on a preponderance of military power. A sample of the text is available at http://net.lib.byu.edu/~rdh7/wwi/1914m/illusion.html

Bell, D. (ed.) (2008), *Political Thought and International Relations: Variations on a Realist Theme* (Oxford: Oxford University Press).
Examines the complexities of realist theory in international thought and the ebb and flow of its appeal to scholars. It rejects assessments of realism that portray it as little more than a form of crude *realpolitik*.

Brown, C. and Eckersley, R. (eds) (2018), *The Oxford Handbook of International Political Theory* (Oxford: Oxford University Press).
Provides a substantial and sophisticated collection of essays by leading scholars on all aspects of theory in the field of global or international politics.

Buzan, B. and Schouenborg, L. (2018), *Global International Society: A New Framework for Analysis* (Cambridge: Cambridge University Press).
Adopts a novel framework for analysing 'global international society' drawing on classical sociology, liberalism, constructivism and postcolonialism.

Moses, J. (2014), *Sovereignty and Responsibility: Power, Norms and Intervention in International Relations* (Basingstoke: Palgrave Macmillan).
Provides an in-depth analysis, supported by case studies of the notion of sovereignty as responsibility as well as sovereignty as the expression of power.

17

Sleat, M. (ed.) (2018), *Politics Recovered: Realist Thought in Theory and Practice* (New York: Columbia University Press).

A collection of scholarly commentaries covering various aspects of the quest to study politics 'realistically' while also looking at the role played by morals, values and emotions as well as facts.

Special issue of *International Studies Review* (2016), 'Advancing Global IR: Challenges, Contentions and Contributions' (ISA Presidential Special Issue), 18 (1): 1–169.

The various contributions to this collection illustrate how the notion of a 'Global IR' could provide a framework for both scholarly debate as well as for empirical research and analysis.

 For additional material and resources, please visit the Online Resources at:
www.oup.com/he/garner4e

17

CRITICAL APPROACHES
TO GLOBAL POLITICS

18

CHAPTER CONTENTS

READER'S GUIDE

While liberal and realist theorists probe each other's ideas for faults and weaknesses, both operate within the same paradigm—an international order composed of sovereign states engaging each other under conditions of anarchy. Neither have challenged capitalism and its implications for the global economy. Apart from Marxism, which developed from the mid-nineteenth century, the main challenges to traditional IR were not often discussed in the discipline of IR until around the 1970s. These latter challenges were subsequently given considerable impetus by the end of the Cold War, an event which prompted new questions about global politics and the assumptions on which traditional theories rested. In addition to the place of Marxism in IR and some important critiques of capitalism, modernization, and colonialism inspired by it, this chapter considers broad developments—critical theory, constructivism, feminism, postmodernism/poststructuralism, postcolonial theory, and green theory. Aspects of these approaches have been discussed in previous chapters, especially Chapter 3 with respect to Marxism and power, and Chapter 7 with respect to feminism and postmodernism. Here, of course, the focus is once again on the implications

→

for the study of politics in the global political sphere. It must also be pointed out, and it should become obvious to anyone working through this chapter, that what is offered here is only a very brief and therefore an unavoidably superficial account of critical approaches which (like many other topics covered in this general text) will need to be supplemented by more specialized readings to gain a more adequate appreciation of their contribution to the analysis of global politics.

MARXISM

Neither Karl Marx (1818–83) nor his close collaborator, Friedrich Engels (1820–95), wrote extensively on global politics but one of their best-known works, *The Manifesto of the Communist Party* (most often called simply the *Communist Manifesto*) sketches in broad outline the implications for global order of the rise of capitalism and the role of the bourgeoisie as controllers of capital. (**See Box 18.1**.) Their ideas have had a major influence on critical approaches to virtually all aspects of politics whether in the domestic or global sphere. Over the years, however, competing interpretations and diverging pathways have been generated and some theories, while influenced by Marxist thought, cannot now be classified as strictly Marxist. In this section we examine several major strands of Marxist-influenced theory of direct relevance to global politics including dependency theory and world-system theory. Other Marxist-inspired schools of thought include Gramscian theory (after its founding theorist, Antonio Gramsci) and Frankfurt School theory, both of which have had a major impact on contemporary critical theory. The strands discussed here are all variants of 'Western Marxism' which distinguishes the legacy of Marx and Engels from the way it has been theorized in authoritarian communist regimes, especially in China and the former USSR where it underpinned distinctive revolutionary traditions (see Chan, 2003; Marik, 2008).

➡ See Chapter 3 for a discussion of Marxist theory.

Photo 18.1 The Manifesto of the Communist Party was the founding work of 'Marxism', established by Karl Marx and Friedrich Engels
INTERFOTO/Alamy Stock Photo

18

> ## KEY QUOTE BOX 18.1
> Marx and Engels on Capitalism and Colonialism

The discovery of America, the rounding of the Cape, opened up fresh ground for the rising bourgeoisie. The East-Indian and Chinese markets, the colonisation of America, trade with the colonies, the increase in the means of exchange and in commodities generally, gave to commerce, to navigation, to industry, an impulse never before known, and thereby, to the revolutionary element in the tottering feudal society, a rapid development . . . Modern industry has established the world market, for which the discovery of America paved the way. This market has given an immense development to commerce, to navigation, to communication by land . . . The need of a constantly expanding market for its products chases the bourgeoisie over the entire surface of the globe. It must nestle everywhere, settle everywhere, establish connexions everywhere . . ..
(Marx and Engels, 1848/1976)

Another key figure in the Marxist tradition is Rosa Luxemburg (1871–1919), both an activist and a philosopher. She was notable, among other things, for her sharp criticism of fellow socialists who were willing to adopt policies that constrained individual freedom. She wrote extensively on political theory, social history, sociology, cultural theory, and ethnography, contributing to a range of issues from feminism to nationalism and the idea of self-determination (Nettl, 2019: ix–xi). With respect to the latter, Luxemburg argued that the 'formula of the right of nations' is a cliché which failed to take into account 'the wide range of historical conditions (place and time) existing in each given case' as well as 'the general current of the development of global conditions.' In addition, she said, it takes 'nations' to be homogeneous socio-political entities when they are clearly no such thing. Quite apart from the highly diverse ethnic heritage of most 'nations', Luxemburg argued that within each nation, there exist 'classes with antagonist interests and "rights"' which undermines any case for conceiving them as a 'consolidated "national" entity' (Luxemburg, 1976: 135).

As both a theorist and an activist, she was concerned always to bring matters 'down from the clouds of abstraction to the firm ground of concrete conditions' (ibid.: 141), and wrote in detail on these issues within the Russian empire of her time as well as the experiences of European states and the general implications for the colonized world which she saw as operating as 'supply depots' for capitalist European nation-states. Furthermore, if the latter were the only ones considered as eligible entities for self-determination, then 'national self-determination' becomes 'a theory of the ruling races and betrays clearly its origin in the ideologies of bourgeois liberalism together with its "European" cretinism' (ibid.). In summary, Luxemburg believed that nations and nationalism were invented for the sole purpose of capitalist exploitation (see Worth, 2012: 144).

Chapter 3 introduced the theme of power in Marxist theory, explaining ideology, hegemony, and the way in which ruling classes maintain control and promote the legitimacy of capitalism. Marx's notion of ideology as 'false consciousness' (Chapter 6) is especially important in analysing how the interests of any ruling class are presented as natural, inevitable, and desirable, even for subject classes. This masks the deeper 'truth' about domination and subordination. Here we should also note the Marxist emphasis on the role of the bourgeoisie, generally defined as a merchant and/or propertied class wielding essential economic power. The opening passages of the *Communist Manifesto* (Marx and Engels, 1848/1976), quoted previously, describe how the needs

18

of a constantly expanding market sees the bourgeoisie scrambling competitively for position all over the globe, thereby creating the phenomenon of modern global imperialism. The first Russian communist leader, Vladimir Ilyich Lenin (1870–1924), developed a more elaborate critique of imperialism as the 'highest and final stage of capitalism' and highlighted its parasitic exploitation of peripheral countries characterized by an increasing gap between rich and poor nations and also leading to wars over control of territory and resources (Lenin, 1986).

The most prominent figures working in this area in the post-Second World War period have been André Gunder Frank and Immanuel Wallerstein. Frank's dependency theory and Wallerstein's world-system analysis uses a deep historical perspective, decentring Europe as the principal agent of historical change in the process. This approach distinguishes it from most versions of globalization which see Europe and the West more generally as at the centre of virtually all world-transforming dynamics, and challenges as well the appropriateness of the Western path to modernity. As with postcolonial theorists, however, Frank sought to 'decentre' Europe, and criticized leading European philosophers, including Karl Marx, for their inherent Eurocentrism. His dependency theory is part of a larger critique of modernization and development theories applied initially to Latin America and then to the Third World in general. It explains underdevelopment in poor, peripheral countries as the exploitative legacy of Western imperialism, colonialism, and capitalism rather than local cultural factors to do with 'traditionalism'. It was, he said, capitalism that had produced 'underdevelopment' and not the allegedly feudal structures of third world countries (Frank, 1998: xvii). Even after independence the underlying structures of exploitation remain while many postcolonial indigenous elites have simply colluded with the 'core' states (generally those of the industrialized North) in perpetuating relations of exploitation. A major focus of dependency theory is therefore on core–periphery relations and how these are embedded in the world system (Frank, 1967; Frank and Gills, 1996).

Wallerstein's world-system approach critiques the totality of exploitative economic and political relations from a sociological as well as historical perspective. He embraces the basic assumptions of dependency theory, but his concept of *world* system is quite deliberate in not using *international*, for it depicts a capitalist world economy which transcends the nation-state model of separate political and economic units in much the same way as 'global' does. Further, his world system 'is a *social* system, one that has boundaries, structures, member groups, rules of legitimation, and coherence' (Wallerstein, 1976: 229 [emphasis added]). In addition, Wallerstein provides a thought-provoking critique of how the very construction of social science forces thinking processes, especially in terms of 'development', along very restricted pathways (Wallerstein, 2001). In taking his unit of analysis as nothing less than the entire world-system, and certainly transcending the nation-state, Wallerstein departed substantially from established social science approaches (see, generally, Wallerstein, Lemert, and Rojas, 2012).

18

KEY POINTS

- The critique of capitalism by Marx and Engels provided a basis for later critiques of traditional theories in the field of global politics. Marx and Engels were also the first to observe how capitalism is implicated in the development of a global system.

- Dependency theory and world systems analysis draw on Marxist thought in critiquing theories of modernization and development, especially in relation to the Third World and the exploitative structure of the global economic and political system.

CRITICAL THEORY

All the theories discussed in this chapter are 'critical' in the sense that they challenge the assumptions of mainstream theories. But within this broader range of critical approaches, critical theory (CT) denotes a particular concern with the ethical notion of emancipation or freedom from oppressive social and material conditions and the promotion of a more just world order. Many contemporary proponents of CT have moved away from the Marxist focus on economics and class struggle and have also found inspiration in the work of Immanuel Kant, long regarded as a contributor to liberal political thought with a strong cosmopolitan vision.

The Italian intellectual Antonio Gramsci (1891–1937) was both an activist and an intellectual who believed strongly in *praxis* which links 'thinking' with 'doing' (**see Box 18.2**). One of his most significant contributions was in highlighting the phenomenon of the *naturalization* of power in the

SHORT BIOGRAPHY BOX 18.2
Antonio Gramsci (1891–1937)

Gramsci was born in 1891 on the Italian island of Sardinia, growing up impoverished circumstances. He won a scholarship to the University of Turin where he studied literature and linguistics and also acquired a knowledge of history and philosophy. He became a founding member of the Italian Communist Party, served as its secretary, and was elected a member of parliament in 1924. Despite having parliamentary immunity from prosecution, Gramsci was imprisoned in 1926 under the fascist regime of Benito Mussolini which had outlawed the Communist Party. Gramsci's impressive intellect had prompted his prosecutor to argue for a substantial prison sentence in order 'to stop this brain from functioning for twenty years'. He died, still in prison, in 1937. Despite very poor health and adverse conditions (not to mention the attempt to prevent his brain from performing), Gramsci produced a fragmented but nonetheless impressive corpus of writings published posthumously under the title *Prison Notebooks*. He is widely regarded as a founding theorist of the links between power, economics and culture, including the political power of cultural institutions such as the mass media. (See, generally, Davidson, 2018.)

Photo 18.2 Antonio Gramsci theorised on the phenomenon of the 'naturalization of power'.
World History Archive/Alamy Stock Photo

creation of hegemony by elites. He argued that ruling classes maintained power and control, even in the absence of constant coercive force, because they make prevailing inequalities seem *natural, inevitable, and even right*. Far from being 'natural', however, inequalities are the product of specific social, political and economic circumstances. They are made to seem natural by those who have the *cultural* power to control 'hearts and minds'. These insights resonate with the Marxist conception of ideology as false consciousness, but the Gramscian approach focuses more on the consensual nature of support for hegemony. If people consider a particular social order to be natural, they are far less inclined to oppose it and even effectively consent to it. Although Gramsci wrote mainly about domestic politics, he recognized that the dynamics of hegemony extended to the global sphere 'between complexes of national and continental civilisations' (Gramsci quoted in Schwartzmantel, 2009: 8).

Later figures, such as Canadian theorist Robert W. Cox, have found Gramsci's insights highly pertinent in explaining the *hegemony of theories and ideas* in the global sphere. This differs from conceptions of hegemony which focus only on material (mainly economic and military) capabilities. Cox is well known for declaring that 'theory is always *for* some one, and *for* some purpose' (1981: 128). Put another way, theories are never neutral in the selection and interpretation of facts—they are reflections of the subjective values and interests of those that devise them and, therefore, tend strongly to support those values and interests. It follows that *facts and values do not exist independently of each other*, so the idea that any theory can be 'value-free', or that knowledge can be totally objective, is insupportable.

Cox argues further that realism is an *ideology of the status quo*. It supports the existing global order and therefore the interests of those who prosper under it. Furthermore, by presenting it as *natural*, the existing order is perceived as inevitable and unchanging in its essentials. Any difficulties that arise within the order are seen as problems to be solved within the parameters *of* that order. The order itself does not come under challenge. Cox and other critical theorists insist, however, that no order is 'natural' or immune from change. All political orders, from that of the smallest community to the world at large, are humanly constructed and can in principle be reconstructed in a more just and equitable manner. CT aims to provide the intellectual framework for emancipation from unfair and unjust social, political, and economic arrangements that benefit the few at the expense of the many. To the extent that liberalism participates in the perpetuation of injustices, especially through capitalism, it is subject to a similar critique. Cox has been a key critic of globalization, arguing that the phenomenon is not simply the inevitable outcome of major, ongoing technical advances but is underpinned by a hegemonic ideology promoting deregulation of both capital and labour, to the considerable disadvantage of the latter (see Griffiths et al., 2009: 169).

The Frankfurt School of the 1920s and 1930s, which included figures such as Theodor Adorno, Herbert Marcuse, and Max Horkheimer, shared with Gramsci a concern for cultural and social factors, therefore placing less emphasis on economics. A more recent figure, Jürgen Habermas, has continued the Frankfurt School's tradition of critical enquiry through new forms of social theory. Habermas's theory of communicative action holds that, under the right conditions, a consensus about 'truth' may be reached. This relies on an **epistemology** which sees knowledge about the social world emerging through a process of continuous dialogue. Because the social sciences cannot proceed as the natural sciences do, they must instead see all action from the perspective of the actors involved (see Smith, 1996: 27–8). Habermas rejects the notion of objective ethical truths that exist independently of any social world. They are made *within* a social world, but one which is wide enough to embrace everyone. This provides the basis for universally valid ethics and so Habermas's **normative** theory is clearly cosmopolitan.

18

Contemporary writers such as Andrew Linklater have extended Habermas's emancipatory concerns to the global sphere, especially with respect to how state boundaries tend to denote the limits of ethical concerns. The most creative critical theories go beyond mere critique of existing theories and practices and put forward alternative visions of how the world *could* be (and *should* be). Linklater's ideas about transformative potentials for the way in which political communities are conceived and structured, for example, set out such a vision. Although modernity has a dark side, he argues that it still carries within it the seeds of the original aims of the Enlightenment which are, in the final analysis, about the emancipation of people from a range of constraints, prejudices, and exploitative practices. And while modernity gave us the Westphalian state system, the 'unfinished project of modernity' envisages a post-Westphalian world in which states as political communities no longer operate in the service of inclusion and exclusion. This transformation, he suggests, seems most likely to occur in the very region which gave rise to that system in the first place and which has since produced the EU, itself a project with considerable normative potential (see Linklater, 1998). Habermas, too, sees very similar possibilities in the European project (**see Box 18.3**). In light of more recent developments with Brexit and the rise of right-wing nationalist populism throughout the continent, however, it seems that the project still has a very long way to go (see Martill and Staiger (eds), 2018).

KEY QUOTE BOX 18.3
Linklater and Habermas on the Transformation of Political Community

Alternative means of organising human beings seem most likely to appear in Western Europe where a lasting balance between the claims of the nation and the species may yet come to be struck. Whether Europe will be the first international region which is permanently transformed by peace rather than by war is unclear. What is clear is that it is improbable that changes in the structure of European international society will be quickly emulated across the world as a whole. Promoting the ideal of a universal communication community in which insiders and outsiders recognise one another as moral equals is essential where the nature of political community has become problematical in the lives of its own members.
(Edited excerpt from Linklater, 1998: 218–19)

It is undisputed that there can be no Europe-wide democratic will-formation capable of enacting and legitimating positively coordinated and effective redistributive policies without an expanded basis of solidarity. Sceptics doubt whether this can happen, arguing that there is no such thing as a European 'people' who could constitute a European state. On the other hand, peoples emerge only with the constitutions of their states. Democracy itself is a legally mediated form of political integration. It is a form that depends, to be sure, on a political culture shared by all citizens. But if we consider the process by which European states of the nineteenth century gradually *created* national consciousness and civic solidarity—the earliest modern form of collective identity—with the help of national historiography, mass communications, and military duty, there is no cause for defeatism. If this artificial form of 'solidarity among strangers' owes its existence to a historically influential abstraction, why should this learning process not continue on, beyond national borders? (Edited excerpt from Habermas, 2003: 97–8)

18

KEY POINTS

- CT provides an intellectual and normative framework promoting a project of emancipation from social, political, and economic arrangements that benefit the few at the expense of the many through hegemonic control.

- CT emphasizes that all political, economic, and cultural orders are humanly *constructed* rather than dictated by nature. Once this is recognized, relations of domination and subordination can be challenged at their foundations rather than simply taken for granted as the way things are and have to be.

CONSTRUCTIVISM

It has been claimed that constructivism has no direct antecedents in traditional international theories although it is conceded that English School approaches, insofar as these have a social orientation, provide useful insights for the contemporary constructivist project (Ruggie, 1998: 11). It is also said that constructivism is not a specific theory of international relations or global politics, but rather a *social* theory with much broader application (McCourt, 2016: 475). There is also a significant tradition of European social theory, developed in earlier periods by classical sociologists such as Emile Durkheim, Max Weber, and Karl Mannheim, from which contemporary constructivists have drawn. Berger and Luckman's influential work, *The Social Construction of Reality* (1966) also broke significant ground in showing how social orders (which embody beliefs, norms, values, interests, rules, institutions, and so on) is an ongoing human production, and never fixed. And if we consider the sphere of global politics through the lens of social constructivist theory, we can see the extent to which it really is a 'world of our making' (Onuf, 1989).

At the broadest level, social constructivism in global politics challenges the way in which both neorealism and neo-liberalism take the essential components (states) and the character of the global or international system (anarchic) for granted, as if states and the system in which they operate were 'just there' rather than emerging as products of human agency and in historically contingent circumstances. Some constructivists are especially critical of the tendency in traditional theories to focus largely on *material* forces (e.g. guns and bombs), arguing that *ideational* forces are equally if not more important. Ideational forces are formed through social interaction and consist of norms, values, rules, and symbols. These influence how agents come to acquire identities and interests and act in the world on the basis of those identities and interests (see, generally, James, Bertucci, and Hayes (eds), 2018).

It is also within the realm of ideas that *meaning* is created, including the meaning of material objects. Alexander Wendt points out, for example, that a gun in the hands of an enemy is a very different thing from the same object in the hands of a friend or ally, adding that 'enmity is a social, not material, relation' (Wendt, 1996: 50). The impact or effect of material objects and forces therefore derives ultimately from social factors and the ways in which actors or agents come to assume identities as enemies or friends (or neither). Wendt takes states as the principal actors in the global system, and so issues of state identity, or more especially how states *construct* identities and interests, feature prominently in his approach (**see Box 18.4**).

18

KEY CONCEPT BOX 18.4
State Identity

The question of identity, and especially state identity, has been a prominent theme in constructivist scholarship. State identity is similar to national identity, but there are differences. National identity may be understood as emerging from affective, intersubjective dynamics operating within a broad group which conceives of itself as 'nation' (that is, 'a people'), on the basis of one or more of the following factors—a shared history, language, religion, culture, ethnicity, and so on. 'The nation' may also lay claim to a particular territory and a right to statehood. As we have seen in Chapter 17, however, few states contain singular nations and a 'national culture' is usually either an amalgam or is based on the characteristics and values of a dominant group. State identity, while perhaps drawing on certain national characteristics, is more of a political/institutional identity oriented to the global or international sphere and its position and interests in that sphere vis-à-vis other states.

State identity is implicated in foreign policy choices, alliances, membership of international organizations and so on, and generally shapes behaviour and interaction in the global sphere. These of course may change over time, sometimes very slowly and sometimes more rapidly, according to circumstances. Japan's identity as an international actor, for example, has changed from that of an aggressive, militaristic state in the earlier part of the twentieth century to a peaceful, democratic member of international society after 1945. Russia's identity in contemporary global politics has been re-constructed in the wake of the break-up of the Soviet Union and the rise to power of Vladimir Putin. The longer-term outcome for the identity of the US as a leading global actor following the Trump presidency remains to be seen.

In addition to state identities, other entities may also acquire identities in the international sphere. The EU, for example, has acquired an identity as global actor over time, projecting certain norms, values and interests according to its self-image as a peaceful, democratic and human rights protective entity that also operates as a large-scale open trading bloc.

A constructivist analysis would look to how all such identities are constructed and re-constructed over time through social processes in both the national and global spheres. One obvious point to be addressed, however, is the extent to which states, like individuals, actually have multiple identities or fluid forms of identification that come into play at different times and under different circumstances, and which can be invoked by state elites according to their interests and opportunities (see Lebow, 2016: 22). This latter point has been developed through 'practice theory'. This suggests that global political actors are driven not so much by 'abstract notions of national interest, identities, or preferences' but rather by 'context-dependent practical imperatives' (McCourt, 2016, 475).

Wendt's version of constructivism does not deny the importance of material force. Rather, it establishes the important connection between material *and* ideational forces, thus providing a better understanding of how 'social facts' are produced. It follows that fundamental institutions, such as states and their sovereign properties, are social rather than material facts, constructed at an intersubjective level by agents (us!). Anarchy or **sovereignty**—or any other concept invented by humans—has no existence or meaning outside of those who think and believe in them. Thus

18

anarchy is simply 'what states make of it' (Wendt, 1992: 391–425). And the same must apply to sovereignty. The things we take for granted as the 'reality' of the world around us possess the same character—the market, the government, the EU, the UN, the US, in fact virtually any entity created and sustained by human agency. One cannot see, feel, hear, smell, taste, or choke on any of these 'things' precisely because they are not material. But they are nonetheless very real in these consequences.

All this casts a different light on the relationship between *agents* and *structures* (people and institutions). This was discussed in Chapter 8 in terms of structuration, with many constructivists emphasizing that agents and structures are *mutually constituted*. Put another way, humans are born into an existing world—one which has both material and ideational aspects—and are shaped by that world as they grow and mature and develop their own ideational perspectives. Existing structures, which always already embody a set of norms and values, shape each emerging generation of agents. But agents also act on existing structures and can change them. After all, these structures were put in place by previous generations rather than set in concrete by nature, so they can in principle be remade or replaced provided there is a sufficient level of *norm change* among relevant actors (see Katzenstein, 1996; Wiener, 2018).

The role of power in the construction of norms, values, and institutions is clearly key to understanding their capacity to endure. Here is where the idea of *social* power is all-important. Again, although it may well be related to material power, social power is much more subtle, reflecting 'the ability to set standards, and create norms and values that are deemed legitimate and desirable, without resorting to coercion or payment' (Van Ham, 2010: 8). The definition of social power provided here resonates with Gramsci's analysis of the role of cultural power in establishing hegemony as well as with the idea of 'soft power', which we consider in relation to diplomacy and foreign policy in Chapter 20.

Constructivism, like other bodies of theory or analytic frameworks, comes in different forms. Some versions like Wendt's is state-centric and tends towards *rationalism* and therefore does not move far from the dominant modes of American social science scholarship. One theorist has also proposed a form of 'realist constructivism', demonstrating that although there are some tensions between these strands of thought, certain key elements can be synthesized (Barkin, 2010). For a theory to be 'rationalist' means that it subscribes to an underlying rationality which directs human behaviour towards particular ends and, further, assumes that knowledge of such matters can be obtained via empirical investigations. This is contrasted with modes of *reflectivist* scholarship, sometimes called post-positivist or interpretive, which reject the positivist/empirical basis of rationalist approaches, thereby challenging the status of the knowledge they claim to produce (Smith 2000: 374–402). Some versions of constructivism argue that it occupies a middle ground between rationalist approaches and reflectivist approaches (mainly postmodernist, poststructuralist, and critical), and creates new areas for both theoretical and empirical investigation (Adler, 1997: 319–63).

There are ongoing developments in the broad field of social theory and constructivism which are incorporating insights from additional areas of social theory including 'actor network theory' which focus, among other things, on the dynamics arising from *relations* between and among actors, rather than the intrinsic properties of actors themselves (whether these be individuals, groups, or institutions). A major work synthesizing aspects of Western social theory with Confucian/Chinese precepts of relationships and relationality is Yaqing Qin's *A Relational Theory of*

18

> **KEY QUOTE** BOX 18.5
> Yaqing Qin Culture and Social Theory

A social theory tends to originate in a particular geo-cultural setting, which shapes the practices of the cultural community and thus defines the efforts to develop theory, too. Social theory is therefore from the very beginning imprinted with the characteristic features of the cultural community of its origin, for it is this community that shapes the background knowledge of its members and thus provides the menu for the theorist to choose throughout the process of her theoretical construction. (Qin, 2018: 3)

World Politics (2018), a work which critiques assumptions of rationality and posits 'culture' as providing the background condition for generating social knowledge, interpretation and practice (**see Box 18.5**). However defined, constructivism has become an increasingly popular approach to the study of global politics for those seeking more complex, socially oriented accounts of the contemporary world.

KEY POINTS

- Constructivist approaches emphasize that the political world is not 'just there' but comes into existence through human agency and in historically contingent circumstances, as illustrated by the variety of political orders evident throughout time and space.

- Constructivism alerts us to the difference between material and ideational forces in the social and political world, as well as to the relationship between them, and how they are implicated in the exercise of power.

- As with other bodies of theory or approaches, constructivism comes in different forms and so there is no one 'correct' way in which its insights can be applied to the study of global politics.

FEMINISM AND GENDER THEORY

Feminism draws from, interacts with, contributes to, and often critiques other schools of theory in analysing the problem of patriarchy and its power dynamics. 'Liberal feminists', for example, will apply certain insights of liberal theory—including the essential equality of all individuals—to critique the way in which conventional liberal theory has at best ignored, or at worst supported, patriarchal structures of authority. Feminism is a principal strand of the broader field of gender theory which is concerned with both femininities and masculinities. However, because the study of gender issues in global politics has been carried out largely by feminist scholars it has been very much concerned with how women have been depicted or, more often than not, written out of the script of global politics.

Photo 18.3 Feminism comes in various forms including Liberal Feminism, Critical Feminism, Feminist Constructivism and Feminist Poststructuralism. *Shutterstock RF: CREATISTA / Shutterstock.com*

Historically, although feminist scholars and activists had been contributing to political thought and to practical developments in women's rights from at least the nineteenth century onwards, it was not until the late 1980s that the apparent absence of women in global politics and economics began to be seriously scrutinized. Attention focused initially on how traditional discourses of IR, because they were founded on masculinist assumptions, excluded women as participants. That the absence of women was made to appear 'normal' or 'natural'—even to many women themselves—was identified as a major problem, exemplifying just why the insights of critical social theory are so important. Many feminists have therefore adopted critical and post-positivist approaches, for as much as any group that finds itself marginalized by a dominant mainstream, feminists have interrogated the extent to which 'knowledge' itself can be constructed to suit male interests.

See Chapter 8 for a discussion of structuration.

As suggested previously, feminism comes in various forms and even within feminist IR, there are different strands (see Chapter 7). The following list is a useful typology which categorizes some of the different theoretical approaches to feminism taken by scholars of global politics (Tickner and Sjoberg, 2010: 198–203).

- **Liberal feminism** highlights the subordination of women in world politics but does not challenge the premises of traditional theories. It is similar to empirical feminism in that it investigates particular problems—say, of refugee women, gendered income inequalities, trafficking of women, rape in war, and so on—usually within a positivist framework. Liberal feminism seeks equality of women in a man's world rather than questioning the foundations of that world.

18

- **Critical feminism** builds explicitly on critical theory, subjecting relations of domination and subordination, the play of power in global politics, and the relationship between material and ideational factors to scrutiny through a gender-sensitive lens. As a theory seeking action and not just interpretation, it promotes a project of emancipation which takes explicit account of women's subordination.

- **Feminist constructivism** criss-crosses the terrain of constructivist theories of global politics. Some concede much methodological ground to positivism, in line with the predominant mode of American constructivism. Others lean towards a post-positivist questioning of the foundations of knowledge. Common themes in feminist constructivism are attention to ideational forces and the essentially social nature of the international sphere.

- **Feminist poststructuralism**, as with poststructuralism (or postmodernism) generally, highlights the construction of meaning through language and, in particular, the relationship between knowledge and power and the extent to which these are reflected in certain binary oppositions. Feminist poststructuralism critiques the way in which binary oppositions such as strong/weak, rational/emotional, and public/private, not to mention masculinity/femininity, have served to empower men at the expense of women.

- **Postcolonial feminism** often goes hand in hand with feminist poststructuralism in exposing certain relations of domination and subordination but focuses critique on how these relations were established through imperialism and colonialism and persist through to the present period. Postcolonial feminists often critique the way in which Western feminists construct knowledge about non-Western women and also tend to treat 'women' as a universal and homogeneous category regardless of differences in culture, social class, race, and geographical location.

Notable for its absence from this typology is a 'realist IR feminism', perhaps because realism, at least as it has developed as a theory of international politics, is so irredeemably masculinist that it cannot accommodate feminist premises. One author, however, identifies a form of 'rationalist feminism' which is strongly empiricist and endorses the assumption that the state is the central actor in international politics and is essentially concerned with its own survival (see Hansen, 2014: 15–16). It should be emphasized, however, that feminist scholarship generally subscribes to the 'realities' of women's lives and their historical exclusion from positions of power but regards none of these realties as fixed or natural. Rather, realities that appear to be simply given must be interrogated, interpreted and contested (see Frazer, 2018: 320–43).

The attention to gender issues forced by feminists has also helped to variegate the concept of masculinity itself (Blanchard, 2003: 1290). Others have pointed out that the 'rugged male warrior' type, often constructed as an ideal, is a stereotype which many 'real' men do not actually fit (Connell cited in Tickner, 1992: 6). We therefore need to recognize the power relations between different kinds of masculinity 'constructed through practices that exclude and include, that intimidate, exploit' and that indicate 'a gender politics within masculinity' (Connell, 2005: 37). Another scholar has investigated the male soldier's gendered construction of his own identity as masculine in relation to his ability to function as a combatant. Such constructions might explain not only the almost complete exclusion of women from warrior ranks (until recently, and then only in some armies) but also the way in which masculinity frequently depends on an 'other' constructed as feminine, and therefore opposite (Goldstein, 2001: 251–2; see also Chisolm and Tidy, 2018).

A particular aspect of war which is often highly gendered is the treatment of 'enemy' civilians. Nowhere was this illustrated more clearly than in the case of the war in Bosnia from 1992 to 1995 which saw rape used as a specific tactic of war. Men and boys were subject to another kind of treatment which brought into currency the term 'ethnic cleansing' (**Box 18.6**).

CASE STUDY BOX 18.6
Gender and Genocide in the Bosnian War (1992–5)

With the end of the Cold War, the formerly communist Federal Republic of Yugoslavia began to disintegrate, generating bitter conflict. The province of Bosnia-Herzegovina, characterized by a multi-ethnic population of Catholic Croats, Orthodox Serbs, and Bosniak Muslims who had lived in relative harmony for years, became the scene of the most gruesome episodes after a referendum for independence in 1992. Some Bosnian Serbs (a minority within the province) dissented and were supported by nationalists in Serbia itself, including the arch-nationalist Serb leader, Slobodan Milošević, who backed Bosnian Serb militia.

The war that ensued saw several notorious episodes of 'ethnic cleansing' now regarded as acts of genocide. The most serious occurred in Srebrenica in July 1995 when an estimated 8,000 Bosniak Muslim men and boys were slaughtered by units of the Army of Republika Srpska (VRS). The subsequent trial of one Serb leader, Radislav Krstić, produced a statement in the Appeals Chamber Judgment following his case before the International Criminal Tribunal for the former Yugoslavia or (ICTY), which summed up the character of the incident:

> By seeking to eliminate a part of the Bosnian Muslims, the Bosnian Serb forces committed genocide. They targeted for extinction the forty thousand Bosnian Muslims living in Srebrenica, a group which was emblematic of the Bosnian Muslims in general. They stripped all the male Muslim prisoners, military and civilian, elderly and young, of their personal belongings and identification, and deliberately and methodically killed them solely on the basis of their identity. The Bosnian Serb forces were aware, when they embarked on this genocidal venture, that the harm they caused would continue to plague the Bosnian Muslims. The Appeals Chamber states unequivocally that the law condemns, in appropriate terms, the deep and lasting injury inflicted, and calls the massacre at Srebrenica by its proper name: genocide... .
> (ICTY, 2004)

Female civilians among the Bosniak Muslims and some other groups were subjected to a different kind of treatment. From an early stage, accounts emerged of women being raped as part of a systematic tactical pattern which included the phenomenon of rape camps where women were subjected to multiple rape, often with the intention of impregnating them with 'Serb' babies. This came to be seen as part of the wider pattern of genocide. In 1995, a charge of rape was brought in the ICTY, the first time that a sexual assault case had ever been prosecuted as a war crime by itself, and not as part of a larger case. The estimates of the number of women raped during the war run as high as 50,000.

The slaughter of men and boys on the one hand, and the systematic rape of women on the other, during this war, illustrate gendered aspects of warfare resulting in the most extreme forms of group violence. In recent years, rape in war (which can also be perpetrated against men as an attack on their masculinity, although it is less common) has achieved much greater prominence as an issue in the narration of war histories generally.

18

> **KEY POINTS**
>
> - Feminism and gender theory provide a very different lens on global politics to those of traditional theories, pushing the boundaries ever wider to incorporate more critical perspectives relevant to every aspect of the field.
> - While sometimes regarded as simply concerned with women's issues, gender theory in global politics is very much concerned with various forms of masculinity and femininity and the way in which they are deployed in both war and peace.

POSTMODERNISM/POSTSTRUCTURALISM

Postmodernism (see Chapter 7) names perhaps the most complex of theoretical fields in the human sciences and is manifest in a confusing array of ideas that challenge, in one way or another, the assumptions of modernity. In the study of global politics, some prefer to describe their approach as 'poststructuralist', which emphasizes the linguistic aspects of meaning and interpretation that produce knowledges (note the plural). For convenience I use the term postmodernism in this chapter.

While sharing some important basic assumptions with critical theory and constructivism, postmodern approaches to global politics are more radical epistemologically, rejecting the idea that we can ever have certain grounds for knowledge. Postmodernism, therefore, rejects more thoroughly the essentially *modernist* assumption that we can describe the world in rational, objective terms. The best we can hope for are fleeting 'moments of clarity' which might allow us to grasp transient truths, but never final, absolute truths resting on permanent and unassailable foundations.

Postmodernism's greatest strength lies in its insights into the relationship between power and knowledge and its capacity for the critique of existing institutions, practices and ideas. Its weakness lies in its inability to go much beyond critique and to map out a programme for positive social and political change, even though it promotes an ethical vision of society. Some would say that, taken to its logical conclusion, postmodernism simply ends in absolute relativism, nihilism, and, ultimately, incoherence. For, if 'there is no truth', the very claim that this is so cannot itself be true. As a further consequence of its relativism—the notion that no 'standard' can be regarded as superior to any other because there is no objective way of adjudicating between them—postmodern approaches also stand accused of creating a pernicious moral vacuum in which good and evil may be regarded simply as competing narratives.

Nonetheless, postmodern strategies provide valuable insights into the *contingent* status of knowledge and the uses to which it may be put in all spheres of politics. Armed with the insight that knowledge is very often a function of power, and that such power can be used to construct metanarratives (understood as embodying comprehensive accounts of history, experience, and knowledge) of enormous importance, we can see how this might operate in concrete contexts. The 'war on terror' which followed the attacks of 11 September 2001 (otherwise known as '9/11'),

18

although not as 'grand' a narrative as an entire theory of history, is a nonetheless a pertinent example of the power/knowledge nexus which exists not just in the hands of a political elite but which pervades a society at large (**see Box 18.7**).

A principal figure in the rise of postmodern thought was Michel Foucault (1926–84), who pioneered a 'genealogical' form of analysis. This interrogates truth claims posing as objective

CASE STUDY BOX 18.7
Positioning Iraq in the Metanarrative of the 'War On Terror'

Photo 18.4 George W. Bush served as the American President from 2001–2009. In 2003 Bush launched the invasion of Iraq, searching for Weapons of Mass Destruction.
National Archives photo

The 'war on terror' was initiated by the attacks of 11 September 2001 ('9/11') on landmark targets in New York and Washington, DC. Two war zones were subsequently occupied by the USA and allies—Afghanistan (in October 2001) and Iraq (in March 2003)—as part of the 'war on terror'. It is widely accepted that Afghanistan was the base for the leader of the group responsible for planning and carrying out the 9/11 attacks. But how did Iraq come to be part of the 'war on terror'?

The following are well established:

1. Al-Qaeda operatives, most of whom were Saudi nationals (*none were Iraqi*), were responsible for the 9/11 attacks in the USA in 2001. Their leader, Osama bin Laden (also a Saudi national) was based in Afghanistan which was governed by the Taliban.

18

The Taliban is a Sunni Muslim fundamentalist political movement which had come to power in Afghanistan during a period of civil war. Although Al-Qaeda and the Taliban are quite separate organizations, they share a common religious ideology.

2. Saddam Hussein, then President of Iraq, had no connection with Afghanistan, Al-Qaeda, or the Taliban. While hostile to the USA (although an ally in an earlier period), he was a secularist and actually repressed Islamic fundamentalism in Iraq.

3. No weapons of mass destruction were ever found in Iraq, which obviously means that there was never any genuine evidence that they existed there prior to the US-led invasion.

4. The presence of terrorists in Iraq *following* the US-led invasion (as evidenced by a relentless campaign of suicide bombing by various factions) is due almost solely to the 'war on terror' itself, as is the rise of the so-called 'Islamic State' which formed in the chaos created by the Iraq War.

Despite the lack of any evidence linking Iraq to the 9/11 attacks, a widespread belief developed, at least among the US public, that Iraq, along with Afghanistan, was the source of the 9/11 attacks. A *Washington Post* poll taken almost two years after the attacks, and around six months after the invasion of Iraq, found that about 70 per cent of Americans believed there was a link between 9/11 and Iraq. How did that link get there? One answer is provided in the same newspaper report which quotes Bush on establishing the link without explicitly telling falsehoods.

If the world fails to confront the threat posed by the Iraqi regime, refusing to use force, even as a last resort, free nations would assume immense and unacceptable risks. The attacks of September the 11th, 2001, showed what the enemies of America did with four airplanes. We will not wait to see what terrorists or terrorist states could do with weapons of mass destruction. (*Washington Post*, Mar. 2003)

The battle of Iraq is one victory in a war on terror that began on September the 11, 2001 . . . The liberation of Iraq is a crucial advance in the campaign against terror. We've removed an ally of al Qaeda, and cut off a source of terrorist funding . . . No terrorist network will gain weapons of mass destruction from the Iraqi regime, because the regime is no more . . . We have not forgotten the victims of September the 11th . . . (May 2003, after declaring major combat in Iraq at an end).
(Milbank and Deane, 2003: A1)

This suggests that the power of the presidential office in the US, supported by a largely uncritical media, succeeded in purveying a particular *metanarrative* about terrorism which was used to justify the war in Iraq despite the lack of evidence (either at the time or subsequently). This further suggests that a large proportion of the US population was especially susceptible to the message. One analysis says that the 9/11 attacks 'not only violated the sovereign immunity of the world's superpower . . . they inevitably unleashed powerfully nationalist feelings and acts of mourning and anger' (Redfield, 4), feelings which served to filter messages in particular ways and to support a military response.

In contrast, support for the war in the UK was much weaker even though former Prime Minister Tony Blair used very similar rhetoric and remains convinced in his own mind that he 'did the right thing'. Indeed, Blair's rhetoric at the time, and since, has been highly moralistic—something that realists see in exactly this kind of 'liberal interventionism'. But lack of broad public support in the UK may be attributed to greater scepticism about the link with 9/11, a more critical press, a more critical attitude towards political leaders generally nurtured by a stronger system of government and opposition, and a less nationalistic political world view among the public at large. We might therefore conclude that the particular power/knowledge nexus generated in the US by the 9/11 attacks, and which supported Bush's rhetorical strategies and narrative, was not as strong in the UK. It should also be noted that in the only other country to send troops in support of the invasion—Australia—public support was also relatively weak, helped by the fact that it was strongly opposed by the Australian Labor Party as well as the Greens (the government of the time was led by conservative Prime Minister John Howard).

Exactly why the USA invaded Iraq, and why some important allies like the UK and Australia went along with it despite no evidence of links with terrorists or of weapons of mass destruction, has been a matter of much speculation with various motives and interests being explored (see, for example, Cramer and Thrall, eds, 2012). But as an important case study, it invites analysis from many different theoretical perspectives.

Questions

1. If we examine the 'regime of truth' as it pertains to Iraq war, what conclusions can we draw about the discourses that supported it?
2. How does the controversy over the 'war on terror' illustrate the relationship between theory and practice?

knowledge about the world while concealing the machinations of power. Foucault argued that each society possesses its own 'regime of truth, its general politics of truth: that is the types of discourse which it accepts and makes function as true . . .'. Foucault further proposed that the human sciences have themselves played a leading role in this concealment, lending a mantle of authority to all kinds of knowledge claims which, although claiming objective status, can be exposed as serving power (Foucault, 1980: 13).

The postmodern problematization of 'truth', 'knowledge' and related issues has also been raised in contemporary discussions of many of US President Trump's claims, the phenomenon of 'fake news', 'alternative facts', Trump attorney Rudi Giuliani's assertion that 'truth isn't truth', and the promulgation of ever more astounding conspiracy theories. Some claim that Trump—and the phenomena that surround him—are the product of postmodern social and political thought. Others suggest that this is not so, but that he can be *explained* through the lens of a postmodern analysis (Hanlon, 2018). **Box 18.8** raises some of the critical issues surrounding the debate in which Trump stands not just as an unusual individual in politics, but as a political phenomenon. The idea of the contingent status of knowledge resonates with Gramscian thought but differs from the latter (and other CT approaches) in its refusal to illuminate an alternative path for social life, for according to its own logic, this would simply end in another 'regime of truth' serving particular

18

KEY DEBATE BOX 18.8
Truth, Reality, and the Trump Phenomenon

Photo 18.5 Fake News: Alternative Facts? A government photographer allegedly edited official pictures of Donald Trump's inauguration to make the crowd appear bigger following a personal intervention from the president. The photos show the inauguration ceremonies of Donald Trump, right, and Barack Obama, left. *U.S. National Park Service*

Many have proposed that the nature of reality and the status of truth have become open questions since Donald Trump decided to enter politics, and even more so after he was elected president. Almost any criticisms of Trump and his policies are decried by him and his loyal supporters as 'fake news' while factual information (such as the relatively smaller size of the crowd at his inauguration compared to that at Obama's, pictured in Photo 18.5) is countered with 'alternative facts'. Trump is also a supporter of a host of conspiracy theories. On climate change, for example, he maintained that 'climate science was a hoax created by the Chinese to make US manufacturing uncompetitive', and that the polar ice caps were not melting but were instead 'at a record level' (Gabbatis, 2018). These claims are a direct repudiation of virtually all available scientific evidence on the subject, but the scientific consensus is explained away by accusing scientists of taking an opportunity 'to wield influence, secure funding or act out a green/Marxist agenda' (ibid.). But it does leave one wondering where the alternative facts to support such claims actually come from.

→

But not all 'conspiracy theories' lack substance. It seems that there is plenty of evidence to implicate the Russian state in a conspiracy to interfere in the US elections of 2016. Moreover, it continued to interfere with the Mueller enquiry set up to investigate exactly who was involved. One news site reported that;

> The Russian operatives unloaded on Mueller through fake accounts on Facebook, Twitter and beyond, falsely claiming that the former FBI director was corrupt and that the allegations of Russian interference in the 2016 election were crackpot conspiracies. One post on Instagram—which emerged as an especially potent weapon in the Russian social media arsena —claimed that Mueller had worked in the past with 'radical Islamic groups'. (Denning, 2018).

Trump has responded with ever more interesting conspiracy theories, some derived from right-wing web sites which implicate the FBI in a conspiracy against Trump, and which have been described as very far 'removed from reality' (Chait, 2018).

In explaining the Trump phenomenon generally, it has been suggested that 'one of the sharpest analytical tools available is the theory of postmodernism' (Heer, 2017), whose proponents

> describe a world where the visual has triumphed over the literary, where fragmented sound bites have replaced linear thinking, where nostalgia ('Make America Great Again') has replaced historical consciousness or felt experiences of the past, where simulacra is indistinguishable from reality, where an aesthetic of pastiche and kitsch (Trump Tower) replaces modernism's striving for purity and elitism, and where a shared plebeian culture of vulgarity papers over intensifying class disparities. In virtually every detail, Trump seems like the perfect manifestation of postmodernism. (Chait, 2018).

Questions
1. Could any theory of politics have *predicted* the 'Trump phenomenon'?
2. How useful is postmodern theory (or any other theory) in explaining 'Trump phenomenon'?

interests. So while proponents of CT have a distinct normative project in making the world a better place, it is difficult for radical postmodernists to entertain such ambitions. Postmodernism does, however, raise awareness of the extent to which knowledge serves power and how the human sciences are implicated in the production of power/knowledge. We must keep in mind, though, that power as such is not necessarily a 'bad' thing; it can also be used for the 'good', for example, in providing for a very significant range of public services as well as regulating social institutions and practices.

In summary, postmodern or poststructuralist analyses of international politics have interrogated various forms of the power/knowledge nexus as well as the grand narratives and discourses which purport to explain the nature and dynamics of the international sphere. Sovereignty,

18

statecraft, anarchy, warfare, borders, identities and interests, and the interpretation of history are all subject to their critical gaze. Postmodernism has therefore gained a foothold in the study of global politics, highlighting the extent to which 'reality' exists not as a concrete, unalterable state of affairs 'out there', but resides ultimately in our mental structures.

KEY POINTS

- Postmodern/poststructural approaches to global politics share some common ground with CT and constructivism in IR but have a much more radical epistemology derived from the rejection of modernist assumptions about knowledge.

- A common criticism is that postmodernism's radical relativism deprives moral arguments in global politics, or any other sphere of social action, of any foundation and permits no adjudication between different standards.

- Despite these criticisms, postmodernism/poststructuralism are valuable in developing critical perspectives on 'regimes of truth' and other narratives and discourses in global politics that serve the machinations of power.

POSTCOLONIAL THEORY

'Postcolonialism' is an interdisciplinary enterprise aimed at critiquing the direct and indirect effects of colonization and its aftermath on subject people. It is not identical to 'subaltern studies' discussed in Chapter 13, although the latter may be regarded as one specific manifestation of postcolonial theory. An important figure in the development of postcolonial thought was Edward Said (1935–2003), whose critical work on 'Orientalism' argued that Europeans—especially the English and French—had long treated the Orient as Europe's major 'cultural contestant'. Thus he argued that Europeans defined *themselves* against, or in contrast with, the people of the Orient. But Orientalism is more than just a style of thought; it is an *activity* dedicated to the production and dissemination of knowledge *about* the Orient and thereby a means of exercising authority over it. In developing his ideas, Said drew on Gramscian notions of hegemony as well as Foucauldian insights into the power/knowledge nexus, which together inform his conception of Orientalism as a hegemonic discourse. Although Said's Orient consisted largely of the Middle East, his ideas have been generalized so that 'Orientalism' is used to designate almost any construction of non-European 'Others' by Europeans or members of 'the West' more generally.

Within the study of global politics, postcolonialism is the medium through which traditional theories, along with other critical approaches, are exposed as largely Eurocentric, the implication being that they not only provide a very partial view of the wider reality of the world, but also are a vital aid in controlling it. 'As a social practice, IR constitutes a space in which certain understandings of the world dominate others, specific interests are privileged over others, and practices of power and domination acquire a normalized form' (Tickner, 2003: 300).

Another postcolonial critique says that traditional approaches possess a 'wilful arrogance' in their basic assumptions about the state of nature, anarchy, and power politics. The authors attack the hybrid beast, 'realism-liberalism', in particular, for its production of 'abstract, ahistorical conceptions of the state, the market, and the individual' which are in fact bound by particular cultural expressions that are essentially 'Western, white, male' (Agathangelou and Ling, 2004: 24–5). But the critique of Western theory extends to many Western feminists who stand accused of portraying the problems of women all over the world through the eyes of a Western female self. Most versions of Marxism, critical theory, postmodernism, and constructivism are similarly tainted with a thoroughgoing Eurocentrism. Postmodernism is therefore generally regarded as anti-Eurocentric, even though it is also quite clearly relies, along with the other critical approaches, on 'Western intellectual traditions, concepts, and methods' (ibid.: 28).

A recent work addressing issues in postcolonial theory, especially those concerning global ethics, adopts a rather unconventional approach which 'rejects the usual hostility to universalism as an imperialist, Eurocentric hoax.' Rather, the author proposes that universalism is inescapable in ethical judgement, and that it is especially so for radical critique in postcolonial societies (Sekyi-Otu, 2018: 1). This suggests that postcolonial scholarship would do well to move away from the tendency to over-invest in the very categories of global politics that they find problematic. Generally speaking, postcolonial critiques have relied on a binary opposition or dichotomy between the West and the non-West. Furthermore, the non-West is often romanticized while the West tends to be demonized. There is certainly plenty in the entity called 'the West' that deserves the most trenchant critiques, from the historical record of European imperialism to the aggression of the USA (supported by the UK and others) in global politics, especially following the attacks of 9/11. But if we buy into the West/non-West dichotomy too uncritically, we risk oversimplifying many global problems and their possible solutions (Lawson, 2006; see also Katzenstein, 2018).

An issue that is directly related to many of the concerns of postcolonial scholarship is the need to 'decolonize the curriculum' and to broaden the range of ideas to which students are exposed. In global politics, as in many other fields of the humanities and social sciences, students are most likely to be exposed only to the ideas developed within a Western tradition dominated by white males. Machiavelli, Hobbes, Marx, Gramsci, Foucault—to name just a few of the most prominent—are studied time and again, indeed as they are in the present volume. Rarely, if ever, do other figures who are non-Western, non-white (or non-male for that matter) make an appearance. Accordingly, 'IR Theory' has been described as a 'Eurocentric monologue' that is badly in need of 'decolonising'. Looking at the methods employed, one critic notes that these are not neutral but 'are constructed in situations that are marked by power relations, ideological agendas, class motivations, patriarchal considerations, imperial designs and other ethical challenges,' and that contestations occur 'only within the Western monologue' (Zondi, 2018: 18, 29). Almost any critical theorist (Western or otherwise) would agree. But given that 'IR theory' has developed historically almost exclusively within the Western academy, it is scarcely surprising.

There is obviously much to be said for opening up discourses about how politics, and especially *global* politics, is studied and it is clear that a diversity of sources, methods, ideas, and approaches is a strength, not a weakness, in any discipline. As we have seen in previous chapters, IR scholarship has not been oblivious to the fact that non-European sources do not feature strongly in IR theory. Is the explanation for this because scholars have simply ignored what is available from other traditions of thought? Is part of the problem that access to sources other than those in English is difficult for most scholars? Or is it because they have not been able to identify something that actually constitutes a body of theory that is distinctively 'IR' from a non-Western source?

18

Over a decade ago, some of these issues were examined in a multi-authored volume entitled *Why is There No Non-Western International Relations Theory?* (Acharya and Buzan eds, 2007). The title suggests that the problem lies in the fact that theorising about 'international relations', as such, has been largely absent in traditions of thought elsewhere. And although classical realism has been able to incorporate a handful of non-Western thinkers, it still remains a 'Western theory'. One possible explanation for this state of affairs is the fact that the international system itself remains a Westphalian system of sovereign states, based squarely on a European model, and globalized through the processes of decolonization. But international systems come and go, and the system that is so familiar to us today will no doubt transform again over time. It may even revert to a system of empires which has, after all, been the most common form of international system in history with the phenomenon appearing on virtually every continent. Given that the rising centres of power are in the Asia-Pacific region, and if there is indeed a close nexus between power and knowledge, it will almost inevitably mean a shift in the sources of theorising. Indeed, there is a very noticeable growth in scholarly output from China in particular, with works drawing increasingly on Chinese traditions of thought such as Confucianism, although the project is still in the early stages (see Qin, 2016). One strand of this project has been conceived as a version of 'moral realism' which takes its cue, not surprisingly, from the rise of China as a global power and the question of political leadership, as set out in **Box 18.9**.

> **KEY QUOTE** BOX 18.9
> Chinese Moral Realism

The theoretical puzzle that moral realism must crack is that of why a rising state is able to displace a dominating hegemon even though it is inferior to the latter in terms of economic base, technical invention, education system, military strength, and political system. Moral realism attributes political leadership to the rise or decline of great powers and categorizes political leadership, according to morality, as inactive, conservative, proactive, or aggressive types at national level, and as tyranny, hegemony, and humane authority at international level. Moral realism is a binary theory which suggests that a state's strength determine strategic interests while types of political leadership determine strategies for achieving those interests. According to moral realist theory it will be possible for China to change the international system in the 21 century if it practices the moral principles of fairness, justice, and civility both at home and abroad.
(Yan, 2016: 1)

18

KEY POINTS

- Postcolonialism seeks to show that traditional theories, along with other critical approaches, are largely Eurocentric and therefore provide only a partial view of the wider reality of the world.

- Postcolonial critiques, however, have often relied on a binary opposition between the West and the non-West which risks oversimplifying many global problems.

GREEN THEORY

Like any other field of theoretical thought in the social sciences, 'green theory' is multifaceted, with many different and often conflicting political approaches to issues concerning the natural environment. It is obviously related directly to the rise of the environmental movement over the last half century or so, prompted in turn by the adverse environmental effects of industrialization. This has turned the environment into an important *political subject* around which various discourses have proliferated. It is said to be distinctive among most contemporary 'single issue' subjects in politics because it comes complete with its own ideology and social movement, neither of which existed before the 1960s (Carter, 2018: 4). The profile of green politics at a practical level, and green theory at an intellectual level, has strengthened in recent years with growing concerns about anthropogenic climate change in particular, as discussed in Chapter 7. These concerns have given rise to the reconceptualization of the current geological era as the 'Anthropocene', understood as an era in which the human impact on the earth's systems has become the dominant force (ibid.).

While there are many different shades of green theory, analysts have identified two main strands—'environmentalism' and 'ecologism'. It is worth reiterating that the latter entails a much more radical approach which goes well beyond what is seen as a mere problem-solving environmental managerialism. Its proponents argue that environmental problems cannot be addressed without radical changes to patterns of production and consumption, let alone basic values and attitudes involving our relationship with the non-human natural world (Dobson, 2012: 2). Rather than the piecemeal management of particular problems, ecologism takes a holistic view, viewing

Photo 18.6 The Extinction Rebellion movement that began in 2019 protested against climate breakdown, biodiversity loss, and the risk of social and ecological collapse.

Shutterstock RF: dpa picture alliance archive/Alamy Stock Photo

18

any particular environmental problem, from acid rain, atmospheric ozone depletion, and the disposal of toxic waste to species extinction, soil erosion, desertification, and climate change as part of a more general pattern of human activity which requires an all-encompassing approach to deal with these ill effects. It therefore attends not just to the parts of a system but takes a 'whole earth' approach, emphasizing the linkages between social, political, cultural, economic, geographic, biological, and any other relevant factors which together form an extensive and highly complex pattern of global interdependence (Lawson, 2015: 228–9).

Most versions of ecologism also entail a theory of morality based on the inherent value of 'nature' rather than of humans and are therefore *ecocentric* rather than *anthropocentric*. Mainstream environmentalism is certainly more likely to look to issues of morality in relation to *human* security as they arise from environmental challenges. Even so, the environment is now also seen as a possible source of traditional security threats. One commentator notes a growing potential for violence and warfare over access to resources, such as water and fuel, that are directly related to environmental problems and which therefore form part of an extended contemporary security agenda (Darby, 2002: xix). We discuss more general ideas about traditional security, human security, and environmental security in the next chapter.

What issues does this raise for IR theory and practice? One response has been a focus on the capacity of states as arguably the most powerful actors in the global system and the only entities capable of bringing about effective action on environmental problems both individually and collectively. Some suggest that increasing state action indicates the 'greening of sovereignty' in the contemporary period as states use their sovereign power to limit the adverse environmental impact of industrialization by regulating a whole range of activities (including corporate activities) involved in resource exploitation, industrial production, infrastructure development, and waste management (see Litfin, 1998: xi). At the global political level, the UN—as an organization of sovereign states—has long been active on the environmental front, recognizing environmental issues as a major human security concern as well as promoting an agenda for the preservation of the earth's natural heritage, not just for the present period but for future generations as well. Indeed, consideration of the interests and well-being of future people (i.e. people who do not even exist yet) adds another key normative dimension to the general field of green political theory in terms of inter-generational justice.

The question of ideological orientations to environmental concerns, as well as to environmental science (and indeed to science more generally) raises some interesting issues for theory. Recent work on the phenomenon of 'anti-science', as it relates to environmental issues, shows that it can come from both right- and left-wing ideological perspectives. The science of climate change, for example, has often come under attacked from those on the political right, while the science associated with genetically modified organisms (GMOs) has usually come from a green-left perspective (see Lawson, 2017: 182–92). On each of these issues, however, there is a strong scientific consensus; on climate change the overwhelming scientific consensus attributes empirically verified increases in long-term climate warming to anthropogenic (mainly industrial) activity which has seen huge quantities of 'greenhouse gases' released into the atmosphere. On the safety of GMOs, there is also a strong scientific consensus that these organisms, provided that they are properly tested and regulated, pose no more risks to the environment than organisms produced by more conventional technologies (Lawson, 2017: 90). Insulin for treating diabetes, incidentally, is produced by genetically modified bacteria, and has been for the best part of half a century.

18

Of course, a scientific consensus on any particular matter does not represent an unassailable Truth, nor is it immune from challenge on the basis of new evidence. Scientists after all deal with probabilities rather than absolute certainties. And among their ranks there are sometimes purveyors of 'bad science' who portray the findings of mainstream climate science as 'fake news'. But a scientific consensus remains the most reliable guide for non-scientists, that is, for the great majority of the public at large, on a range of issues from climate change to GMOs, to the safety of vaccines and the links between tobacco and numerous life-threatening diseases (cancer, diabetes, thrombosis, etc.).

The state of the global environment and the danger to all forms of life posed by various forms of pollution is seen as demanding serious, far-reaching action *now*, and not just at some future point when the problems become overwhelming. A manifesto for Planet Politics (**Box 18.10**) highlights the fact that IR as a set of practices, both intellectual and organizational, must be radically reconfigured if humans and other forms of life are to survive and prosper in an increasingly unviable global environment.

KEY QUOTE BOX 18.10
A Manifesto for Planet Politics

This manifesto is . . . an urgent call for a profound restructuring of international politics and order that can assure the planet's survival, written from a time when its devastation can be seen with an awful clarity. We call for IR and every other relevant discipline to support, enable and clarify this new politics of just ecological entanglement and mutual survival. A complex politics of simple musts: End extinctions! Preserve biodiversity! End deforestation! Repair the oceans! Prevent climate disaster! Decarbonise humanity! Return to social justice! . . .

We fear that the discipline will find our case too difficult and unsettling to hear; that it will repeat its failed rituals and its refusal to value such concerns or support them with credibility, attention, and resources. This would be the ecological sublime, too large and terrible to see. We must fight the comfort we find in disavowal of the climate crisis. We also hope to be heard and for our politics to change. We can see the melting glaciers and surging tides, the dying corals, and acidifying oceans, and predict the disasters they will bring: devastated ecosystems, drowned cities, failed crops, strange new wars, vast streams of human homeless. Or we can continue our diplomacy and our chatter, until our voices are drowned by the risen sea. Animals of the world, unite! (Burke, Fishel, Mitchell, Dalby, and Devine, 2016: 522)

18

KEY POINTS

- The growing importance of green politics at a practical level has seen an equally important growth of 'green theory' at an intellectual level as concerns about the global environment have strengthened.
- An important issue for both green theory and practice is the phenomenon of 'anti-science' in which credible scientific findings, for example on climate change, are challenged as 'fake news'.

CONCLUSION

Whenever we think about the world around us, we do so through a certain set of assumptions concerning the reality of that world. Different theorists obviously see the world in different ways and will interpret facts accordingly. This highlights the point that facts do not simply speak for themselves. Certainly, the different theoretical approaches reviewed in this chapter, and in the previous one, often make them speak in very different ways as well as for different purposes. It follows that the study of global politics cannot be taken simply as a task requiring the unproblematic accumulation and arrangements of the facts that we know (or think we know) about the world. A constructivist would be quick to point out that different theorists see the world in different ways because each has arranged and interpreted the facts about the world in a certain way according to their identities and interests. Similarly, we should not necessarily regard theory as an 'abstraction' from reality but as the means by which it is actually created as well as interpreted. We might then ask whether each theory or way of seeing the world is as good as the next, or whether some are better than others. But rushing to endorse any one theory as the 'right' one is scarcely advisable for students in an early stage of their programme. The important thing is to give each of them serious attention and to allow one's existing beliefs to be challenged.

Some of the issues raised in this chapter also point to a wider debate about the relationship between social and political critique (and its methods), science, and the very idea of 'truth' and 'reality' itself. Good practice in social science of any kind requires high standards of evidence and argument. This does not require mimicking the methods of the natural sciences or relying solely on empirical and quantitative modes of research. But neither should hostility to these methods allow one's judgement to slip into a simple denial of certain 'realities' about the social and political world, whether these are 'socially constructed' or not. Different theories and approaches about how global politics may be best studied or analysed may well be at odds with each other, but it can also be said that methodological as well as theoretical pluralism is a strength rather than a weakness of the discipline. The same considerations apply in 'decolonising the curriculum'—a move which can only benefit scholars of global politics in gaining deeper insights into our highly diverse world.

This leads us to note that, if theory 'creates' the world, then the theories reviewed here can be seen as creating it from a largely 'Western' perspective, for virtually all of them are 'Western' in origin and orientation. It can scarcely be denied that theories in global politics do describe (as well as criticize) an international system and set of practices created in Europe and effectively globalized via processes of colonization and decolonization. Indeed, the theories are themselves products of that very same system. However, if we examine 'Western civilization' in detail, we find that it is the outcome of so many historical and cultural influences, many of which travelled from East Asia and the Pacific, India, the Middle East, and Africa, as well as the Americas, that it is difficult to call it an entirely European project. As the study of global politics and the way in which it is theorized continues to develop and change, and as centres of power themselves shift and change around the world, it will inevitably be enriched by insights from an ever-wider academic community and set of perspectives. Finally, the brief account of green theory and the very 'real-world' issues on which it focuses, remind us that we are indeed 'all in this together'.

18

KEY QUESTIONS

1. How has Marxism impacted on theoretical development in the study of global politics?

2. What are the main elements of Gramsci's notion of hegemony?

3. How does the idea of 'emancipation' contribute to the critical theorization of global politics?

4. What is meant by 'normative theory'?

5. What do constructivists mean when they speak of the world as 'one of our making'?

6. How do 'agents' and 'structures', and 'material' and 'ideational' factors, interact in constructivist theory?

7. What does a 'gender lens' expose in the construction of masculinity and femininity in global politics?

8. What is the relationship between power and knowledge in postmodern approaches to global politics?

9. Can we ever overcome ethnocentrism in the study of global politics?

10. Do postcolonial theories escape the West/non-West dichotomy, or reinforce it?

11. How might one go about 'decolonising the curriculum' in IR theory?

12. What is the difference between environmentalism and ecologism?

13. What are some of the implications of the science of climate change for conceptualizing 'reality'?

14. How can IR be radically reconfigured to meet the challenges of a rapidly deteriorating global environment?

FURTHER READING

Acharya, A. and Buzan, B. (eds) (2010), *Non-Western International Relations Theory: Perspectives on and Beyond Asia* (Abingdon: Routledge).
This book introduces non-Western IR traditions to a Western IR audience, challenging the dominance of Western theory. Contributors emphasize that Western-focused IR theory misrepresents and misunderstands much of world history and seeks to rectify this by introducing the reader to non-Western traditions, literature, and histories which are relevant to how IR is conceptualized.

Dasgupta, S. and Kivisto, P. (eds) (2014), *Postmodernism in a Global Perspective* (New Delhi: Sage).
An interesting set of interdisciplinary essays from leading authors on various themes which revolve around a notion of 'postmodern globalization theory' and include perspectives from feminism, social theory, risk analysis, religion, management studies, and literary criticism. Something for everyone!

Dauvergne, P. (ed.) (2012), *Handbook of Global Environmental Politics* (Cheltenham: Edward Elgar, 2nd edn).
Contains forty short essays by various experts on both theoretical and practical aspects of global environmental politics and includes themes such as democracy, ethics, knowledge/power, sustainability, conflict, governance, regimes, global political economy, and so on.

18

de Jong, S., Icaza, R., and Rutazibwa, O. U. (eds), (2018), *Decolonization and Feminisms in Global Teaching and Learning* (Abingdon: Routledge).

There are seventeen chapters in this very interesting edited collection which range over a number of the issues covered in this chapter, especially in the sections on feminism and postcolonialism.

Edkins, J. (2019), *Routledge Handbook of Critical International Relations* (Abingdon: Routledge).

Provides a wide-ranging collection of chapters by expert scholars which bring together critical theoretical perspectives with real-world problems.

 For additional material and resources, please visit the Online Resources at:
www.oup.com/he/garner4e

18

SECURITY AND INSECURITY

19

READER'S GUIDE

The security of the sovereign state, in a system of states, and existing under conditions of anarchy, has been the traditional focus of studies in global or international politics. Security has therefore been concerned largely with the threats that states pose with respect to each other. This chapter looks first at traditional concepts of security and insecurity, revisiting the Hobbesian state of nature and tracing security thinking through to the end of the Cold War. This is followed by a discussion of ideas about collective security as embodied in the United Nations (UN) and the nature of security cooperation in Europe through the North Atlantic Treaty Organization (NATO). We then consider some pressing security challenges in the post-Cold War period and the broadening of the security agenda to encompass more recent concerns such as environmental security, energy security, cyber security, and the diffuse concept of 'human security'. The last part provides an overview of the 'war on terror', raising further questions concerning how best to deal with non-conventional threats.

SECURITY, INSECURITY, AND POWER POLITICS

Traditional realist approaches to international relations (IR) have taken their cue from a number of classic texts to construct an image of the state of nature characterized by a permanent condition of anarchy. Thomas Hobbes's famous account represents the state of nature as constituting a highly dangerous environment, lacking any effective civil structure. There is no authoritative ruler, no sense of justice or morality, and no security at all for the isolated individuals who exist within it in constant fear. The most powerful individuals prevail over the weaker, although even the powerful must watch their backs constantly. Thus the anarchic state of nature offers the most *insecure* existence imaginable. According to this viewpoint, the solution is to be found in the formation of bounded political communities—states—headed by a sovereign power. This arrangement works to banish anarchy within states, thus providing the conditions for a secure existence. But it does not banish anarchy in the sphere outside of or between states—that is, the international sphere where no sovereign power exists.

For realist scholars of IR, especially neorealists, the study of life *within* the state is regarded as the proper focus for political science, whereas their sole concern is with relations between states in the sphere of international anarchy, as discussed in Chapter 17. Given the nature of anarchy, the international sphere is necessarily the principal locus of insecurity for sovereign states and, therefore, ultimately for the people enclosed within them. Thus the proper concern of IR, for realists, is how to maintain the survival of the sovereign state itself, for it is only when this is taken care of that people can effectively work to achieve 'the good life' within the state **(see Box 19.1)**. We should also note, again, that for realists it is 'the international', rather than 'the global' that best describes their sphere of concern.

None of this means that the international sphere is one of perpetual chaos or warfare. Realist approaches do not regard anarchy as precluding a degree of order and stability. But, given its underlying dynamics, peace and security in the international sphere at any given time are tenuous. Perpetual anarchy thus ensures a state of continuous, underlying *in*security because even in times of apparent peace, it is always ready to unleash its destructive forces when the fragile order weakens or breaks down. As we have seen, this kind of thinking crystallized in realist theory following the breakdown of international order in the lead-up to the Second World War, culminating in the turn to power politics in the post-war period.

The power politics approach to security as worked out by Morgenthau and his successors takes as given the notion of 'peace through strength', where 'strength' is invariably related to military capacity and underpins a robust approach to 'national security'. One scholar notes how

19

> **KEY QUOTE** BOX 19.1
> John Mearsheimer on Security and State Survival

States seek to maintain their territorial integrity and the autonomy of their domestic political order. They can pursue other goals like prosperity and protecting human rights, but those aims must always take a back seat to survival, because if a state does not survive, it cannot pursue those other goals. (Mearsheimer, 2010: 80)

prominent this theme is when foreign policy issues are raised during national election campaigns in the USA. But, although useful politically as a catch phrase, it is rarely explained just how more military power will produce peace (Shimko, 2013: 60). We have seen previously that the power politics approach also involves considerations of both balance of power mechanisms and the security dilemma which ensures a perpetual, competitive struggle for security where, in the final analysis, states can depend only on their own resources. *Self-reliance* is therefore the watchword for security and the ultimate key to survival in the international sphere.

During the Cold War period, the use of the term 'security' by both sides came to denote much more than simple protection against invasion. On the Soviet side, perceptions of security and imperial expansion in Eastern and Central Europe went hand in hand, while on the other side 'any state controlling large geographical areas containing significant quantities of natural resources in a way unacceptable to the US [presented] a threat to the "national security" of the United States' (Young and Kent, 2013: p. xxix).

The evidence since the end of the Cold War, especially with respect to US intervention in Iraq, a country with vast oil resources, suggests that little has changed. A parallel has been drawn with respect to the Libyan conflict of 2011, with one commentator suggesting that if Libya's most significant resource was carrots, there would have been no US-led intervention (Pilger, 2011). On the other hand, it is clear that a major humanitarian crisis was looming as Colonel Gaddafi's forces did not hesitate to target civilians, thus precipitating the UN-authorized intervention to establish a no-fly zone. A statement issued by Canadian Prime Minister Stephen Harper in March 2011 set out a classic idealist position on the humanitarian imperative, complete with a moralizing theme (**see Box 19.2**). Interestingly, Harper was widely regarded as a 'hawk', a term reserved for those who need little persuasion to use military force rather than diplomacy and/or sanctions to achieve objectives. This is comparable to the moralistic position adopted by British Prime Minister Tony Blair in justifying the Iraq war in humanitarian terms. Indeed, Mearsheimer suggests that 'liberal interventionism' is far more hawkish than realism (see, generally, Mearsheimer, 2018).

Another prominent aspect of neorealism relates to the distribution of power in the international system and its effects on the security environment. Reflecting on the history of the state system in Europe from 1648 through to the Second World War, observers of international politics have generally agreed that the system during that period possessed a 'multipolar' character (Mearsheimer, 2010: 85–7). In other words, significant power was distributed among three or more states within the system. The Cold War period, however, was described as 'bipolar' since power was divided largely between the USA and its allies on the one hand, and the USSR and its allies on the other. The structure of bipolarity, together with the deterrent effect of nuclear weapons possessed

19

One either believes in freedom, or one just says one believes in freedom. The Libyan people have shown by their sacrifice that they believe in it. Assisting them is a moral obligation upon those of us who profess this great ideal. (https://www.ctvnews.ca/pm-heads-to-paris-for-emergency-summit-on-libya-1.620539)

Photo 19.1 Harper: One either believes in freedom, or one just says one believes in freedom. *Alamy: dpa picture alliance archive/Alamy Stock Photo*

by both sides, is often said to have produced the 'long peace' of the Cold War period in which major warfare was threatened but did not actually occur. There is no agreement, however, as to whether a multipolar or bipolar system promotes greater security. With respect to the present, it is too soon to tell whether the post-Cold War period of unipolarity, in which the USA appears to have achieved global hegemony, will prove to be more conducive to peace and security in the longer term.

In the meantime, liberal approaches to security have challenged the premises of realism in terms of traditional issues of state security, with considerable success. This is despite the apparent failures of the inter-war system—that is, the League of Nations. Indeed, the strong influence of liberal institutionalism is evident in the extent to which the immediate post-war period saw the re-establishment of overarching international organizations designed to ameliorate the negative effects of anarchy through collective security mechanisms. Foremost among these is the UN, which is the most important institution set up by international treaty (**see Box 19.3**).

> **! KEY CONCEPT** BOX 19.3
> Security Treaties and Alliances

A treaty may take the form of an alliance which is usually defined primarily in security terms as 'a formal agreement between two or more actors—usually states—to collaborate together on perceived mutual security issues' (Evans and Newnham, 1998: 15). The anticipated security benefits of such collaboration depend on the circumstances of each case, but generally include one or more of the following:

- the establishment or strengthening of a system of deterrence;
- a defence pact to operate in the event of a war; and
- some or all of the actors to be precluded from joining other alliances (ibid.).

As instruments for securing international order, treaties and alliances have a very long history. Thucydides refers to treaties between contending forces, while the histories of many other political communities around the world reveal their extensive use. Not all treaties take the form of security alliances, but historically this is the most common form. A treaty may be between formerly hostile parties which see a mutual advantage in establishing more peaceful relations, although this does not guarantee future non-aggression. The non-aggression pact negotiated between Hitler and Stalin on the eve of the Second World War, for example, did not prevent Hitler from launching an invasion of Soviet territory just two years later. A treaty may also be forced on one or more of the parties at the conclusion of hostilities, to the benefit of the victorious side and/or as a punitive mechanism. The Treaty of Versailles is often regarded as a major factor in Hitler's rise to power and support within Germany for his aggressive militarism.

> **KEY POINTS**
>
> - Realists argue that anarchy ensures a state of continuous underlying *insecurity* even during times of apparent peace. Stability under conditions of anarchy is possible through balance of power mechanisms.
> - Liberals are inclined to support humanitarian intervention which realists believe may do more harm than good, and which rarely serves the interests of the intervening state.

THE UNITED NATIONS, COLLECTIVE SECURITY, AND THE SECURITY COUNCIL

As the Second World War drew to a close, a Charter for a new international organization to replace the League of Nations was approved at a meeting in San Francisco by representatives of fifty-one countries in June 1945, with the United Nations Organization coming into official existence on 24 October 1945. Its membership grew steadily as decolonization created newly independent states throughout the following decades, with a further increase occurring after the collapse of the Cold War and the creation of many more sovereign states in the aftermath. Membership of the UN now stands at 192.

The Charter establishes basic principles of order in support of international peace and security to which every new member must sign up. It is thus an international treaty setting out the rights and obligations of its member states as declared in the Preamble to the UN Charter. This states the organization's purpose as being 'to establish conditions under which justice and respect for the obligations arising from treaties and other sources of international law can be maintained'

19

Photo 19.2 The United Nations Organization was founded in 1945. *UN Photo: UN Photo / Eskinder Debebe*

and, further, 'to promote social progress and better standards of life in larger freedom' (United Nations, 1945). There follow nineteen chapters spelling out the more detailed structure of the UN and the various powers and responsibilities of its principle organs.

The Security Council, set up under Chapter V, was originally composed of five permanent members (the UK, the USA, the USSR, France, and China) and six non-permanent members. There are now ten non-permanent members who serve a two-year term. The five permanent members—or 'P5'—each retain veto power over any Security Council decision. This extraordinary power reflects a belief that the new UN would not function without according a special place to the most prominent states, thereby rectifying a perceived weakness of the old League. More generally, the Security Council is primarily responsible for maintaining international peace and security and its functions and powers are set out accordingly. Thus the Security Council embodies the UN's aspirations to provide for 'collective security'—a term encapsulating the notion that true security cannot be obtained through the practice of 'every state for itself' (**see Box 19.4**).

The composition and functioning of the UN Security Council has been subject to many criticisms over the years. One is that the five permanent members (the P5), which hold such a privileged position, reflects circumstances prevailing over sixty-five years ago in a world where decolonization had scarcely begun. The UN's membership has almost quadrupled since then, and many now see the permanent membership as skewed unfairly in favour of the developed world. Certainly, the geographic distribution of the P5 is relatively narrow, with no representation from Africa, the Middle East, South Asia, or South America.

Reform of the permanent membership, however, seems unlikely in the near future. If reform entailed an expanded permanent membership, the veto power would be extended further, making

KEY CONCEPT BOX 19.4
Collective Security

The anarchic character of the international political sphere, and some of the assumptions under-pinning realist approaches, may suggest that in the final analysis security is largely a matter of every state for itself. The best hope for peace and stability from this perspective is in achieving a balance of power. Liberals (and some constructivists), however, believe a superior approach may be found through a collective security arrangement. This means states joining together through a treaty which binds them to supporting each other in case of attack. It therefore functions effec-tively as a defence treaty. The UN is the prime such treaty organization. Others include NATO as well as the Collective Security Treaty Organisation (CSTO) of which Armenia, Kazakhstan, Kyrgyzstan, Russia, Tajikistan, Uzbekistan, Azerbaijan, Belarus, and Georgia are members. The basic principle of such treaties is that an attack on one member state is regarded as an attack on all of them, and all must act collectively to defend against an aggressor.

decisions on vexed issues even more difficult. And, if one new member was admitted to make up the five, who would that be? Brazil, Japan, India, Nigeria, and Egypt are possible claimants, but none would be uncontroversial. On the other hand, if one of the permanent members was to give up their seat at the table, who should, or would, vacate their seat to make way for a new member? It's hard to imagine any of them agreeing to withdraw. If there were no permanent members at all, the dynamics of the Security Council would almost certainly change considerably and there is no guarantee that it would be for the better. Thus reform of the Security Council is highly unlikely in the foreseeable future.

Although lack of reform is often thought to undermine its legitimacy, this does not necessarily diminish whatever efficacy the Security Council possesses (see Hurd, 2008: 199–217). The Libyan intervention in 2011 illustrates sufficient political will among its members to pass a resolution au-thorizing military intervention to establish a no-fly zone to protect civilians. Using Chapter VII of the UN Charter on 'Action with Respect to Threats to the Peace, Breaches of the Peace, and Acts of Aggression', the Security Council resolved to authorize a coalition of member states to take 'all necessary measures ... to protect civilians and civilian populated areas ... while excluding a foreign occupation force of any form'. The resolution went on to set out the terms of a no-fly zone (United Nations Security Council, 2011). Of the P5 members, Russia and China abstained. Soon after the commencement of operations, NATO officially assumed sole responsibility for interna-tional air operations. But NATO forces exceeded their UN mandate and clearly acted to enforce regime change—that is, the total defeat of the Gaddafi regime. This policy succeeded in October 2011, when Gaddafi was killed by insurgents. But, like Iraq, the security situation in Libya has scarcely improved. Rather, it remains wracked with political factionalism and civil war has been ongoing. Libya now also provides yet another theatre for Islamist extremism.

The Security Council has been criticized more recently for failures with respect to both the civil war in Syria and the crisis in Ukraine. The Syrian conflict erupted in 2011 when protests against the authoritarian regime of President Bashar Al-Assad were met with violent repression. Both Russia and China used their veto to block Security Council resolutions on the Assad regime. This was influenced partly by developments in Libya with the Russian Permanent Envoy to the

UN stating that the international community should be alarmed by claims that the NATO interpretation of Security Council resolutions on Libya can serve as a model for the 'responsibility to protect', given what had happened there (cited in Kirsch and Helal, 2014: 431). A monitoring group, based in the UK, estimated the death toll since the start of the war in Syria, which was further complicated by the presence of Islamic State, to be as high as 511,000 as of March 2018. In addition, the United Nations High Commissioner for Refugees (UNHCR) estimated that there were 6.6 million displaced internally with a further 5.6 million around the world (Human Rights Watch, 2019).

The Ukraine crisis emerged from tensions and struggles within the Ukraine over its relationship with the EU (and, by implication, NATO) on the one hand, and Russia on the other. Pro-Russian forces in Crimea, with Russian support, subsequently succeeded in orchestrating the annexation of Crimea by Russia in March 2014. This triggered another movement by pro-Russian separatists across other parts of eastern and southern Ukraine, resulting in widespread violence. Despite denials, there has arguably been clear evidence of direct Russian involvement in the conflict. The role of NATO vis-à-vis Russia and the Ukraine crisis is considered in **Box 19.5**.

Critics of the UN Security Council's failure to effectively mitigate these conflicts, let alone resolve them, highlight serious tensions within the Security Council itself where any of the five veto-wielding permanent member—Russia, China, the USA, the UK, and France—can prevent action being taken on a security issue if it is perceived as impacting on their own national interest. In her outgoing address in 2014, former UN High Commissioner for Human Rights, Navi Pillay, said that 'Short-term geopolitical considerations and national interest, narrowly defined, have repeatedly taken precedence over intolerable human suffering and grave breaches of and long-term threats to international peace and security' (UN, 2014). But the speech also highlighted certain UN successes in promoting positive change—for example, in the ending of apartheid in her home country of South Africa, although that is now a quarter of a century ago.

In the light of the reasoning behind both the UN as a whole and the Security Council in particular, one might ask how different theoretical approaches to IR are reflected. In the first instance, the practical imperatives driving its formation were, once again, based on the experience of warfare and the desire to minimize international conflict. The rhetoric accompanying the various declarations was infused with optimistic visions of a better world in which security was the norm rather than the exception. Further, with membership open to all on equal terms, and a normative commitment to decolonization, the UN reflected a certain egalitarianism while provisions for the social and economic advancement of all nations ensured a proactive role in areas outside mainstream security concerns.

This tendency was strengthened with the Universal Declaration of Human Rights (1948), and an expanded humanitarian role in later years as well as provisions for NGO participation. In short, the UN system may be founded on the sovereign state system, but its basic principles and vision for world order extend beyond this to embrace a range of liberal ideals and a broader interpretation of security. Thus its wide-ranging charter has seen it respond to significant non-military international security concerns such as the environment, health, water, food, natural disasters, cybercrime, and so on.

On the other hand, the structure of the UN's central organ—the Security Council—and the dominance of the P5 reflect a realist concern for the accommodation of power politics even within an 'idealist institution'. In addition, the broader liberal vision for collective international security expressed through the UN remains tied to a traditional state-based vision of world order focused primarily on military issues. So too do other forms of collective security, such as that embodied in NATO, which we examine next.

> **KEY POINTS**
>
> - The UN system is founded on the sovereign state system but its vision for world order extends beyond this to embrace certain liberal ideals and a broader interpretation of security.
> - The Security Council embodies aspirations to 'collective security'—an eminently liberal notion. The provision for five permanent members, however, caters to certain realist notions concerning the role of great powers and moderates its collective security function.

THE ROLE OF NATO

The NATO alliance, instituted in 1948 in the early Cold War period, has played a major role in shaping global order for more than seven decades. The Cold War commenced almost immediately after victory was declared by the 'grand alliance' of forces opposed to the Axis powers in 1945. The common enemy which had held them together was gone, and jockeying for position generated mutual suspicion between the USSR and its erstwhile wartime Western allies. Economic

Photo 19.3 Although seen essentially as a military alliance, the initial reasons for NATO's creation had as much to do with the perceived need to strengthen political will against communism.
NATO https://www.nato.int/cps/en/natohq/photos_156716.htm

19

conditions in Western Europe following the war were dire and rebuilding programmes, sluggish at best. US Secretary of State George Marshall announced a large-scale strategy for delivering economic aid to Europe in June 1947. European recovery was seen as vital to US interests for reasons including the restoration of lucrative markets as well as strengthening Europe generally vis-à-vis the Soviet Union whose communist ideology was seen as a major threat. In 1947, US President Harry S. Truman enunciated a doctrine asserting a leading role for the US in opposing the spread of communism. Together with the 'Marshall Plan', the broad doctrine became known as 'containment' (of communism), a term coined by US diplomat and adviser George Kennan. The 'Truman Doctrine' had long-term international effects, legitimizing the right of the US to intervene in civil wars abroad where communist interests were involved.

It was in this general atmosphere that NATO was established. Although seen essentially as a military alliance, the initial reasons for NATO's creation had as much to do with the perceived need to strengthen political will against communism as with the coordination of strategic military forces to protect Western Europe (Young and Kent, 2013: 85). NATO's initial membership consisted of ten West European states—the UK, France, Denmark, Iceland, Italy, Norway, Portugal, Belgium, the Netherlands, and Luxembourg—plus the USA and Canada. The Soviet response was to establish a rival organization incorporating its communist allies in Eastern and Central Europe, although it was seven years before the Warsaw Pact was formally instituted in 1955 as a 'Treaty of Friendship, Cooperation and Mutual Assistance'.

NATO membership expanded during the Cold War to include Greece, Turkey, West Germany, and Spain, although it suffered a setback when France withdrew from NATO's integrated military structure in 1966 following serious disagreement with the USA in important foreign policy areas. Although France remained a signatory to the 'paper treaty', it remained outside the military structure until 1993. Even then it declined to participate in operations. It was not until 2009 that France was fully reintegrated into NATO's military structure (see Fortmann et al., 2010).

NATO renewed its *raison d'être* in the post-Cold War period as Europe's and the North Atlantic's prime security organization. Its membership expanded again to incorporate a number of former Soviet-dominated countries—the Czech Republic, Hungary, and Poland joined in 1999; Bulgaria, Estonia, Latvia, Lithuania, Romania, Slovakia, and Slovenia in 2004; and Albania and Croatia in 2009 and Montenegro in 2017 to bring its current membership to twenty-nine. As it welcomed the first three of its former communist members in 1999, a new 'strategic concept' was announced at a summit meeting in Washington and a sixty-five-point document released, spelling out NATO's vision of its past, present, and future roles as a pre-eminent international treaty-based security organization. A decade later, NATO's strategic concept was revised again, at least partly in response to the '9/11' attacks on the US (see NATO, 2014). In addition to its military roles, which has seen involvement in Afghanistan, Iraq, Libya, and Syria in recent years, NATO's broad concerns include programmes on 'Science for Peace and Security' (SPS), which assess issues such as climate change and food security (see https://www.nato.int/cps/en/natolive/78209.htm February 2019). For its members, NATO is clearly seen as having a long-term future with a broad security agenda, not just within its own region but globally. For the time being, however, the Ukraine crisis presents an unprecedented challenge in the post-Cold War world (**see Box 19.5**).

Another challenge for NATO has come from a different direction altogether—the USA under the Trump administration. Trump has questioned the value of the alliance, accusing other NATO members of not paying their fair share, and even suggesting it is obsolete. An interview with Ivo

19

BOX 19.5
The Ukraine Crisis and Nato–Russia Relations

The Ukraine crisis appears to be a potential turning point in Euro-Atlantic security . . . most notably the intensifying sense of strategic dissonance between Russia and the West. . . .

Moscow understands European security in very different conceptual terms from the West. Western capitals see the emergence of a Europe 'whole, free and at peace', Moscow sees a continent still fragmented, still dominated by bloc mentality (given US influence in European security), and burdened by ongoing conflict.

Where Western capitals see the 'open door' policy and the enlargement of organisations such as NATO and the EU contributing to wider European stability, Moscow sees the expansion of these organisations destabilising European security. Where Western leaders have sought to emphasise partnership with Russia, including attempting to develop strategic partnership and the creation of numerous seats at the diplomatic table, Moscow sees itself increasingly isolated, the mechanisms for interaction failing to provide Moscow with a voice.

Source: NATO Review, http://www.nato.int/docu/review/2014/russia-ukraine-nato-crisis/Ukraine-crisis-NATO-Russia-relations/EN/index.htm

Daalder, a former US ambassador to NATO from 2009 to 2013, and subsequently president of the Chicago Council on Global Affairs, addresses NATO's contemporary role today, and its importance to the USA. The interviewer is journalist Sean Illing for the news site *Vox* **(Box 19.6)**.

BOX 19.6
President Trump and Nato

Illing

Why does NATO matter in the world of 2018, a world in which the Soviet Union no longer exists?

Daalder

Russia, although it's not the Soviet Union, continues to pursue a policy of trying to undermine the unity of not only the transatlantic alliance but also Europe more generally—and is engaged in active measures to undermine that unity. NATO is the best and strongest counter to Russia's attempts to break NATO apart by interfering in the domestic political systems of its member countries or, as it did in Ukraine, physically invading them.

The second reason is that a Europe in which the US is not engaged is a Europe that is likely to be unstable. That's as true today as it was in 1949. The investment that the US has made to ensure that Europe is peaceful remains a much cheaper investment than if we allowed it to descend into war, in which case we'd inevitably get dragged into the conflict.

Illing

So is that the argument you'd make to a typical US taxpayer who wants to know why he or she should care about what Russia does in the Balkans, or about what is happening in Western Europe?

19

Daalder

Well, the European Union is our No. 1 trading partner and the No. 1 military partner of the US. Our European allies are with us in the Middle East where we're dealing with ISIS and other threats. They're with us in Afghanistan and Iraq. They're the largest investor in our country and therefore they help create jobs. Europe is also the largest market for our goods. As a result of all this, we have a fundamental interest in peace and prosperity in Europe.

Illing

Does Trump have a point when he criticizes other NATO nations for not paying their fair share? Does NATO have a free-rider problem?

Daalder

Yes, he has a point. NATO does have a free-rider problem that is becoming less of a problem but is still there. For a whole host of historical reasons, Europeans invest less in defense than the US, in part because we have a global security role and the US is seen as a country that is committed to the defense of Europe. That doesn't mean Europe doesn't spend money on defense. It does, and in fact the Europeans are currently spending more than any other combination of countries around the world.

Illing

What would happen if NATO was dissolved over night? How different would the world look in the short and medium term?

Daalder

Individual nations in Europe, along with the US, would turn inward and try to figure out a way to provide for their own security without cooperating with other countries. And in a world in which everyone is looking out for themselves and no longer cooperating, suspicions, and fears will go up, which will lead to more defensive measures and perhaps even conflict. So it would create a much more unstable situation overall.

Illing

Could the US sustain its relationships with European powers if it led the effort to scrap NATO?

Daalder

NATO, without the US, is not a viable alliance. The reality is that the US, both politically and militarily, forms the fundamental core of the alliance. If you take the US military out of NATO, you're left with a shell of an infrastructure and a shell of a command structure. And if you take the US politically out of NATO, it's highly unlikely that you'd be able to sustain the alliance given the massive role the US plays in it. So it's hard to see how scrapping NATO wouldn't severely damage our partnerships with European nations.

Illing

Is there a strategic alternative to NATO that could serve the same ends but at less cost for the US and the world?

Daalder

The price that the US pays to NATO is relatively small. In fact, if NATO didn't exist, we'd have to spend more on defense because NATO European countries are paying for US bases, paying to host US troops, and we'd have to pay for much of this ourselves without NATO. We'd have

→

to move thousands of troops back to the US and spend billions of dollars building new bases and new facilities to house them in the US. So it would be vastly more expensive for the US to maintain the military capability it has today without NATO.

More importantly, much of our military spending is not allocated to defend Europe. It's to maintain a global presence, to maintain the freedom of the seas, to have a presence in the Middle East and Asia and other parts of the world. This benefits global security but isn't directly linked to European defense. So this idea that the US military spending is all about NATO or Europe is just wrong.

At the end of the day, NATO provides a support structure that is beneficial to the US and would be more costly to replace.

Source: Sean Illing, Vox.com and Vox Media, Inc.

KEY POINTS

- NATO is essentially a Cold War institution formed in the early post-war period as one mechanism in the effort to contain the spread of communism in Europe.
- Since the end of the Cold War, NATO has developed new strategic concepts to rationalize its ongoing existence as the key security institution in the North Atlantic area.

ALTERNATIVE APPROACHES TO SECURITY

Since at least the 1960s, the peace movement had promoted the idea that genuine security was to be obtained not simply by defeating enemies in war but by working with them to resolve conflicts. Its proponents have argued a case for rethinking security along the lines of 'positive peace', a concept which rejects peace as consisting merely in the absence of violent conflict and which focuses attention on the causes of conflict and their amelioration through cooperative social mechanisms (see Galtung, 1969: 167–91). The peace movement itself was (and remains) multifaceted, taking on different causes and promoting different issues according to time, place, and circumstance. During the Cold War period, various peace activists campaigned against 'hot' warfare in Vietnam, Korea, and other parts of the Third World; against the advancement of nuclear technology for either military or non-military purposes; against poverty, underdevelopment, and neocolonialism in the Third World generally; and for the promotion of grass-roots democracy and social justice in industrialized nations. There were cross-cutting links as well to other social movements, including the women's movement and the environmental movement, both of which advanced their own particular conceptions of security and an alternative agenda for policy-makers well before the end of the Cold War.

Gender theory has provided some interesting and challenging critiques of conventional approaches to security. Although there are very different approaches, a common theme is that global politics in general, and security in particular, are not gender neutral and that a particular masculinist perspective has prevailed. Beyond that, various feminisms have produced different and often conflicting critiques of the gender dimensions of security. One issue that has received

19

long overdue attention in recent years is that of rape in war, an issue highlighted during the war in Bosnia-Herzegovina (see Chapter 18). Before this, there was enormous reluctance to recognize the extent to which rape is used as a widespread tactic in war. The publicity surrounding the situation in the former Yugoslavia also brought long overdue attention to the widespread rape of German women at the end of the Second World War, mainly at the hands of the victorious Red Army, and of the forced prostitution of 'comfort women' used by Japanese forces during the Pacific war: instances of sexual assault in both cases running into the millions.

➔ For a discussion of feminism and gender theory in IR, see Chapter 18.

➔ See Chapter 18, especially **Box 18.5**, for a discussion of gender and rape in warfare.

These are clearly not the only historic cases—soldiers from many other countries and virtually all cultural backgrounds have engaged in rape either en masse or individually, almost always with impunity. It has only very recently been treated seriously in international law. Indeed, the first time that sexual assault was treated separately as a war crime was in 1996 when eight Bosnian Serb military and police officers were indicted in The Hague in connection with the rape of Muslim women in the Bosnian war. A recent study of rape and forced marriage in the context of political violence, and the role of the International Criminal Court (ICC), traces how these actions have been defined and interpreted, and how progressive approaches have been resisted by states with strong patriarchal structures and where conservative religious beliefs underpin legal and social institutions (Baumeister, 2018). The criminalization of sexual violence in war has scarcely prevented the continuation of the practice, but it provides an indication that the practice of rape in war, as something that affects women in particular (although not exclusively), is now treated as an important security issue.

Feminist security studies, more generally, continue to contribute key insights into the extent to which violence frequently has a gendered aspect. But they also highlight the extent to which solutions may be gendered as well. For example, a 2015 UN report noted that women are almost universally portrayed, alongside children, as defenceless, vulnerable victims (see Davies and True, 2019: 7). This feeds into both policy and practice which therefore tend to focus on protecting women and girls *from* men, *by* men, thus perpetuating the inequalities of the gendered dimension, rather than the actual empowerment of women and girls. A strategy based on social and political *empowerment* aimed creating greater equality would see more positive outcomes in terms of prevention.

Another security concern in the post-Cold War period concerned with equality, or lack of it, has been the increasing gap between 'haves' and 'have-nots'—with the former consisting largely of the prosperous, industrialized countries of the northern hemisphere and the latter of underdeveloped countries, most of which lie in the Global South. This has produced a 'North–South' economic/developmental divide with significant security dimensions. Again, concerns about this pre-date the end of the Cold War, as the report of a UN-sponsored commission headed by former West German Chancellor and Nobel Peace Laureate Willy Brandt shows. Published in 1980, this influential report, entitled *North–South: A Programme for Survival*, examined in depth the range of problems arising from significant socio-economic disparities between countries.

A feature of the report was its emphasis on the fact that both North and South had a strong mutual interest in putting an end to dependence, oppression, hunger, and general human distress. It proposed vastly increased aid flows, arguing that the transformation of the global economy would be in the long-term interests of all counties. Although some developed countries saw value in acting on its recommendations, others were tepid at best. US President Ronald Reagan evinced little interest in development issues except where aid was seen as a counter to Soviet influence. But overall aid flows did increase. Just as importantly, the commission opened up new public discourses on the relationship between global development and security by highlighting that narrow military concerns were insufficient in an era of increasing global interdependence. Certainly, by 1989 it was clear that the Cold War had virtually collapsed and that the time for new security thinking in an increasingly globalized world had arrived. Even so, millions remain in dire poverty in the Global South and this is a major factor in contemporary global migration patterns, which better-off states very often see as threatening their border security. This has become a major political issues in Europe (including the UK), in the USA and Australia in particular, where right-wing populism has gathered strength, largely through depicting migrants and asylum seekers as a security threat.

In addition to the plight of millions in the Global South and the multifaceted security threats they faced, attention also turned to the natural environment. Again, concerns were raised well before the end of the Cold War and the UN had held its first major environmental summit in Stockholm in 1972, an event which marked a turning point in global environmental politics. But the post-Cold War world seemed more conducive to expressing environmental concerns explicitly in terms of *security*. The UN again took a lead, organizing an 'earth summit' in Rio de Janeiro in 1992. Although wide-ranging, three major concerns were given particular attention: the state of the world's forests, biodiversity, and climate change. All are interrelated, but it is the latter which has now become the most prominent issue.

The Rio Earth Summit produced the UN Convention on Climate Change (UNFCCC), which set up a framework for intergovernmental efforts to tackle global warming, followed by the Kyoto Protocol (1997) which strengthened the Convention by committing its signatories to binding targets for the reduction of greenhouse gas emissions (see https://unfccc.int/process/the-kyoto-protocol). The US, under the Bush administration, and Australia under the Howard government, however, subsequently pulled out, each claiming that the emissions reduction targets would damage their respective economies and both also claiming that developing countries, which included major emitters such as China and India, should not be given special treatment. Further conferences were held in Copenhagen in 2009, and Cancún in 2010, with the latter establishing a Green Climate Fund intended to raise and disburse US$100 billion a year by 2020 to help poor nations deal with climate impacts and assist low-carbon development. A further 'Conference of the Parties' (COP 21), which refers to the countries that ratified the UNFCCC, was held in Paris in December 2015, which agreed 'to strengthen the global response to the threat of climate change by keeping a global temperature rise this century well below 2 degrees Celsius above pre-industrial levels and to pursue efforts to limit the temperature increase even further to 1.5 degrees Celsius' (https://unfccc.int/process-and-meetings/the-paris-agreement/what-is-the-paris-agreement). In June 2017, President Trump announced that the USA would cease all participation in the agreement to mitigate climate change.

➔ See Chapter 18 for a discussion of environmentalism and ecologism in IR.

The consequences of global warming for security are potentially enormous. Rising sea levels—just one consequence—threaten not just the very existence of small island states, such as Tuvalu and Kiribati in the Pacific, the Maldives and Seychelles in the Indian Ocean, and low-lying countries like Holland and Bangladesh, but also the extensive coastal regions of countries like the USA, Australia, China—and many more. Climate change will also impact adversely on food and water security, not to mention the considerable problems that will inevitably attend mass migration from low-lying areas, with implications for border security as new waves of 'environmental refugees' seek a safe place to live.

19

Other non-traditional security issues to receive more attention in the post-Cold War period include energy security, food and water security (not just in relation to climate change), biosecurity, and border security (the latter with respect to refugees, illicit goods, diseases, etc.). Then there is the increasing problem of cyber security with implications for a huge range of issues from the security of personal data to the military, diplomatic channels, energy installations, financial networks, communications, and so on. As far as Western countries are concerned, some of the major threats to cyber security come not just from organized criminal groups but from state actors, especially Russia, China, and North Korea.

The extent of alleged Russian activity includes a wide range of cyberattacks and interventions aimed at undermining political and social stability in Western countries. Specific examples are interference in the 2016 US presidential elections which prompted the extraordinary Special Counsel investigation by former FBI Director Robert Mueller between 2017 and 2019 on links between Russia and the Trump campaign—an investigation which has itself been hacked. President Trump consistently denied Russian involvement, denouncing the investigation as a 'witch-hunt'. Another notable example were the cyberattacks on the chemical weapons watchdog, the Organisation for the Prohibition of Chemical Weapons, which was looking into the possible involvement of Russian agents in the poisoning of a former Russian double agent, Sergei Skripal, and his daughter in the UK in 2018 (discussed further in Chapter 20). Sports anti-doping authorities have also been targeted in the wake of alleged Russian state-sponsored doping of athletes in various sports.

China has also been accused of cyberattacks and cyber spying, with high-tech companies and other big businesses as well as governments being targeted. Hackers have been accused of stealing technology from industries including aviation, satellites, factory automation, finance and consumer electronics, which of course has been strongly denied by Chinese authorities. A report says that Chinese espionage threats have 'increasingly raised alarm bells among the so-called "five-eyes" countries that share intelligence—the US, the UK, Canada, New Zealand, and Australia—in addition to non-western allies such as Japan' (*Financial Times*, 21 December 2018, https://www.ft.com/content/f5f0b42c-046c-11e9-99df-6183d3002ee1). Tensions have increased since the financial chief of Chinese tech giant Huawei was arrested in Canada on a US warrant relating to charges of fraud in connection with US sanctions on Iran, of providing misleading information to banks, and of stealing trade secrets from a US-based wi-fi operator (*Time*, 28 January 2019, http://time.com/5514960/charges-against-meng-wanzhou-huawei/). China responded by arresting two Canadians in China, with Canada of course protesting in turn. China's ambassador to Canada has been quoted as saying that Canada's actions are 'due to Western egotism and white supremacy' (*Guardian*, 10 January 2019, https://www.theguardian.com/world/2019/jan/09/china-ambassador-canada-white-supremacy-huawei). Both the Russian and Chinese cases obviously raise issues not just for security but also for diplomacy and foreign policy which are further discussed in Chapter 20.

The various forms of security and insecurity concerns mentioned previously draw attention to *securitization theory*. This challenges narrow state-centric and militarist security paradigms and offers new conceptual tools, drawn substantially from constructivist theory, with which to analyse the broad range of issues which have come under the rubric of security in the post-Cold War period. To 'securitize' an issue—say, the flow of refugees from conflict zones or areas of severe economic deprivation into North America, Europe, and Australasia—is to designate these people as constituting an 'existential threat', which requires a special response. Securitization thus goes beyond mere politicization of the issue, taking the issue to a level where it can be depicted as a

> ### ! KEY CONCEPT BOX 19.7
> ### Securitization Theory
>
> Securitisation theory shows us that national security policy is not a natural given, but carefully designated by politicians and decision-makers. According to securitisation theory, political issues are constituted as extreme security issues to be dealt with urgently when they have been labelled as 'dangerous', 'menacing', 'threatening', 'alarming' and so on by a 'securitising actor' who has the social and institutional power to move the issue 'beyond politics'. So, security issues are not simply 'out there' but rather must be articulated as problems by securitising actors. Calling immigration a 'threat to national security', for instance, shifts immigration from a low priority political concern to a high priority issue that requires action, such as securing borders. Securitisation theory challenges traditional approaches to security in IR and asserts that issues are not essentially threatening in themselves; rather, it is by referring to them as 'security' issues that they become security problems. (Eroukhmanoff, 2018)

matter of national security requiring emergency measures. The successful securitization of any given issue, however, depends ultimately on the force of the relevant 'speech act' performed to persuade the audience; in other words, where *saying so* succeeds in rendering any given phenomenon a threat. Similar processes apply to the *de*securitization of an issue (see, generally, Buzan et al., 1998). **Box 19.7** summarizes how securitization theory works.

 Objections to securitization theory have come from both realist and more critical perspectives. The former defend a narrower conception of security in terms of military threats to the state. The latter do not disagree that a broader conception of security is required, but regard securitization theory, as described previously, as missing some crucial points and overemphasizing others. For example, Booth (2007: 167) argues that the salience of a particular security problem does not rely simply on the successful persuasion of a relevant audience who may simply be unreceptive. Using the example of the Rwandan genocide in 1994, he notes that the UN Security Council, when confronted with overwhelming evidence of the massacre, chose not to interpret the event as requiring anything beyond ordinary political action. This did not, however, mean that it was an ordinary 'political' issue for the victims. For them, it was the ultimate security issue of life and death. Booth argues that the relevant audience sometimes needs to be awakened or even created—not simply interpreted. Further, if security is always a speech act, then 'insecurity is frequently a zipped lip' (Booth, 2007: 168).

> ### KEY POINTS
>
> - Social movements such as the peace movement, the women's movement, and the environmental movement have all contributed to alternative conceptualizations of security.
> - The 'North–South' developmental divide as well as crises generating millions of refugees in recent times have significant global security dimensions especially with respect to the border security of better-off states.
>
>

- Environmental security and cyber security are among the major non-conventional security concerns of the twenty-first century.
- Securitization theory challenges conventional security paradigms, offering new conceptual tools with which to analyse a much broader range of contemporary security issues.

POST-COLD WAR CONFLICTS

Despite significant changes in the outlook for global security at the end of the Cold War, and the notion that traditional inter-state security concerns could be put aside to focus on a different range of new security issues, there was one serious inter-state war of the early post-Cold War period—namely, the Gulf War of 1991. But while this episode did bring a focus back on to traditional security concerns, it also prompted visions of a new world order. This stemmed from the fact that the conflict had seen decisive action on the part of the UN Security Council when Iraq's Saddam Hussein broke the golden rule of IR by invading another sovereign state—its neighbour Kuwait. The UN Security Council's Resolution 678 authorized member states cooperating with the official Kuwaiti government to 'use all means necessary' to oust Iraqi forces and restore international peace and security in the area. The unprecedented solidarity of the UN, and the success of multilateral action against Iraq's military aggression, led President George Bush (the elder) to proclaim a new world order in which enduring peace was a real possibility. This was also seen as a triumph for the UN since, in the absence of Cold War constraints, it was now regarded as capable of achieving its original objectives as a vehicle for genuinely effective cooperative security.

But while the prospects for peaceful coexistence between states were being talked up, conflict and violence within states—otherwise known as 'internal conflict'—continued unabated and is seen as a significant ongoing concern. In the early 1990s, there were ongoing conflicts within a number of states from Africa to the Pacific, as well as Northern Ireland and Spain. In addition, the break-up of the former Soviet empire had provoked a flurry of nationalist activity. Not all of this took a violent form, with the formation of the Czech Republic and Slovakia out of the former Czechoslovakia representing a model of peaceful political divorce. The Baltic States too eventually negotiated a peaceful path to independence. The departure of Central Asian republics from the old Soviet Union was accompanied by relatively little violence, although there has been considerable conflict in the Caucasus. New leaders in Moscow were also determined that the Russian Federation should remain intact. Chechnyan separatism, itself expressed in violent terms, has been put down ruthlessly. The Balkans also presented a particularly difficult case. While the secession of Slovenia from Yugoslavia in 1991 was managed with relatively little violence, the subsequent break-up of the Yugoslav state witnessed serious conflict between Croats, Serbs, and Muslims and saw the term 'ethnic cleansing' become part of our vocabulary.

Crises in Africa produced further challenges for a global community struggling to maintain optimism about the prospects for peace and security. As the Cold War receded into history, concerns about fragile and failing states and the associated human costs grew. The experience of Somalia, discussed in Chapter 8, is also widely regarded as having had a significant effect on US

19

attitudes towards the deployment of ground forces overseas. Clarke and Gosende (2003: 145) write that the 'desperate failure of Somalia intruded deeply into the sensibilities of the US Government and public' and that the experience had a profound effect on attitudes to other crises, especially in Rwanda where the US (along with France) forced a reduction of UN forces immediately prior to the 1994 genocide. This event, in which some 800,000 Tutsis and moderate Hutus were massacred by extremist Hutu militia, is regarded as another monumental failure by the UN to act decisively and effectively to prevent an internal conflict from turning into a large-scale tragedy. Similarly, the UN was seen as having failed in the Darfur region of Sudan where the estimates of deaths from genocidal violence starting in 2003 are up to around 400,000. The most recent genocidal activity has been in Myanmar where government forces are blamed for the slaughter and ethnic cleansing of Rohingya people who are Muslim, and ethnically distinct from the majority Buddhist population (see, generally, UN News; https://news.un.org/en/tags/genocide).

Accusations of UN failures are very different from the sentiments expressed at the successful conclusion of Operation Desert Storm in the early post-Cold War period. But they also show that there have been enormous, perhaps inflated, expectations concerning what the UN can achieve under contemporary conditions. The world today is very different from that which emerged at the end of the Second World War and in which the challenges of failing states, civil wars, and large-scale humanitarian disasters were not seen as the major concerns for the UN. However, important conceptual shifts have taken place which appear to have provided the impetus for more robust UN action, as we see next.

KEY POINTS

- The post-Cold War period has seen growing concerns about fragile, failing, and collapsed states which have serious implications for both the security of people within these states as well as for the wider global sphere.

- Although the UN was hailed for its apparent successes in the first Gulf War of the early 1990s, it has since attracted much criticism for its inability to deal adequately with crises elsewhere.

FROM STATE SECURITY TO HUMAN SECURITY AND THE 'RESPONSIBILITY TO PROTECT'

UN intervention in the post-Cold War world has been supported conceptually by new security thinking first articulated explicitly in the *Human Development Report: 1994* (UNDP, 1994). Opening with the claim that: 'The world can never be at peace unless people have security in their daily lives' (ibid.: 1), and a survey of the contrast between the unprecedented prosperity achieved by some and the deepening misery of so many others, the report went on to set out a case for redefining security in 'human' terms, implying a substantial shift away from security defined in terms of state/national security. The 'human' aspect here includes health security, employment security, environmental security, and security from crime as emerging global issues. Security itself was defined in the broadest possible terms as 'safety from the constant threats of hunger, disease, crime

19

and repression' and 'protection from sudden and hurtful disruptions in the pattern of our daily lives—whether in our homes, in our jobs, in our communities or in our environment' (ibid.: 3).

As with previous UN reports, there were both supporters and critics. Among the latter, a common objection was that if virtually everything came under the rubric of 'security' then the term was meaningless. Furthermore, the broadening of the security agenda in this way meant that the important focus on *international* security may be lost. In theoretical terms, it is not hard to see that while realists would be concerned to maintain the international/domestic distinction as a matter of both practical and conceptual importance, those subscribing to alternative ideas about security would welcome the conceptual shift. This has resulted in efforts by policy-makers and others to tackle security at different levels. So, while not neglecting traditional state security needs, more attention has been directed to the multiple levels at which security considerations operate. New security thinking has also prompted a questioning of state legitimacy when it comes to humanitarian crises as **Box 19.8** shows.

KEY DEBATE BOX 19.8
The Responsibility to Protect

An important report issued by the International Commission on Intervention and State Sovereignty (ICISS) in 2001, entitled *The Responsibility to Protect*, was adopted by the UN World Summit in 2005. A central claim is that, while it is the responsibility of sovereign states to protect their own citizens from avoidable catastrophe, if they are unwilling or unable to do so then that responsibility must be borne by the international community (ICISS, 2001). Thus the 'responsibility to protect'—commonly known as 'R2P'—is in the first instance the responsibility of states but may shift to the external realm—the international community—when any state fails in its essential responsibility. The 2005 UN World Summit outcome emphasized the obligations of both individual states and the international community collectively in terms of their responsibility to protect populations from genocide, war crimes, ethnic cleansing, and crimes against humanity:

138. Each individual State has the responsibility to protect its populations from genocide, war crimes, ethnic cleansing and crimes against humanity. This responsibility entails the prevention of such crimes, including their incitement, through appropriate and necessary means. We accept that responsibility and will act in accordance with it. The international community should, as appropriate, encourage and help States to exercise this responsibility and support the United Nations in establishing an early warning capability.

139. The international community, through the United Nations, also has the responsibility to use appropriate diplomatic, humanitarian and other peaceful means, in accordance with Chapters VI and VIII of the Charter, to help protect populations from genocide, war crimes, ethnic cleansing and crimes against humanity. In this context, we are prepared to take collective action, in a timely and decisive manner, through the Security Council, in accordance with the Charter, including Chapter VII, on a case-by-case basis and in cooperation with relevant regional organizations as appropriate, should peaceful means be inadequate and national authorities manifestly fail to protect their

19

→

populations from genocide, war crimes, ethnic cleansing and crimes against humanity. We stress the need for the General Assembly to continue consideration of the responsibility to protect populations from genocide, war crimes, ethnic cleansing and crimes against humanity and its implications, bearing in mind the principles of the Charter and international law. We also intend to commit ourselves, as necessary and appropriate, to helping States build capacity to protect their populations from genocide, war crimes, ethnic cleansing and crimes against humanity and to assisting those which are under stress before crises and conflicts break out.   (United Nations, General Assembly, 2005)

Some have argued that the report did not go far enough in setting out a new framework for UN action in response to crises. A stronger framework would require, for example, limiting the veto power of P5 members when extraordinary circumstances arose, and requiring the UN to do more than merely 'stand ready' to intervene, but actually oblige it to act (Bellamy, 2006). Others, however, see R2P as a crucial *normative* advance in the UN's development, making a significant break with the previous emphasis on the inviolability of state sovereignty (Thakur, 2011*a*). With respect to the Libyan crisis, Ramesh Thakur (2011*b*) writes that the Security Council's authorization of 'all necessary measures' to protect civilians (short of invasion and occupation) marked a historic shift. Instead of the UN merely watching 'haplessly from the sidelines', R2P acted as 'a powerful new galvanizing norm'. But as we have seen, such actions have not produced unambiguous goods in the global system. The Libyan intervention as a specific UN response in line with the 'responsibility to protect' doctrine scarcely produced the desired consequences. It destroyed the existing regime and did little to help set up a viable alternative regime, leaving the door open to a whole array of malign forces including jihadist violence, sectarianism and tribalism. (See Thakur, 2018: ch. 7.)

Questions

1. To what extent does the R2P doctrine set up a tension between the responsibilities of individual states and the international community?
2. How does the debate about R2P reflect the respective positions in the English School debate over pluralism and solidarism discussed in Chapter 17?

19

KEY POINTS

- Traditional security paradigms have been challenged by the shift in emphasis from state security to human security and acknowledgement of the multiple levels at which insecurity occurs.
- The 'responsibility to protect' has highlighted the role that the international community (mainly through the UN) is expected to play when states cannot, or will not, protect their own citizens from harm, although there is no guarantee that well-intentioned intervention will do more good than harm.

SECURITY AND INSECURITY AFTER '9/11'

Developments in new security thinking have taken place against the background of a 'global war on terror', or (GWOT), a term adopted by the Bush administration but officially dropped when President Obama came to power. The attacks on the World Trade Center in New York and the Pentagon in Washington by Al-Qaeda operatives on 11 September 2001 (widely referred to as '9/11') precipitated the US-led invasion of two sovereign states: Afghanistan and Iraq. The GWOT is not easily analysed in terms of traditional security paradigms, even though the US response, in so far as it has involved military force and inter-state warfare, has used traditional methods. The rise of Al-Qaeda and other organizations associated with 'militant Islam', together with the responses by the USA and its allies, illustrates a number of twists and variations on the theme of security (**see Box 19.9**).

As we have seen in Chapter 18, Al-Qaeda, known to be based in Afghanistan with the blessing of the Taliban government, was the prime suspect in the 9/11 attacks. The US demanded that its leader, Osama bin Laden, be handed over by the Taliban government. When it refused to do so, the US and allies attacked just four weeks after. NATO had invoked Article 5 of NATO's

Photo 19.4 One World Trade Center is the main building of the rebuilt World Trade Center complex in Lower Manhattan. *Flickr https://www.flickr.com/photos/zawrotny/8306069668: Dave Z/ Flickr (CC BY 2.0)*

19

CASE STUDY BOX 19.9
The Rise of Islamic Militancy

Islamic radicalism and militancy, which is deeply intertwined with politics in the Middle East region, has been on the rise since at least the 1970s, although the essential background to these developments can be traced back much further. The current geopolitical landscape has been shaped by the outcomes of the First and Second World Wars, colonialism, the authoritarianism of successor regimes in the postcolonial period, and the competing claims of Palestinian and Jewish groups to territory—claims which have acquired an increasing religiosity over the years, in turn fuelling the emergence of extremist, politically driven fundamentalism.

It was under the conditions of the Cold War, however, that Osama bin Laden's Al-Qaeda organization emerged in Afghanistan, a country with a long history of political instability and with strategic significance for the Soviet Union. It became a battleground for competing factions within the country from the early 1970s. While the Soviets supported a Marxist government, the USA, along with Pakistan, Saudi Arabia, China, the UK, and other disparate regimes, generally supported an insurrection led by the Mujahidin, whose name means 'strugglers', also related to the word *jihad* or 'holy struggle'. Initially energized by and partially united in opposition to the Soviet presence in Afghanistan, any coherence the Mujahidin possessed largely dissipated after the Soviet withdrawal in 1989.

Violent conflict between contending factions, as well as with the embattled central government continued until the strongest faction, the Taliban, gained control in 1996, imposing an uncompromising version of Islamic rule. Afghanistan thereafter became a haven for Al-Qaeda, originally formed in Afghanistan during the struggle against the Soviets, but for a time with its main base in Sudan. In 1996, bin Laden shifted to Afghanistan from where he planned attacks on two US embassies in East Africa in 1988 and a US Navy vessel in Yemen in 2000. But the most spectacular attacks, and those with the most far-reaching consequences, were without doubt those of 9/11. These attacks sparked the 'global war on terror'.

Related organizations operating in the contemporary period include Boko Haram, which emerged in Nigeria in 2002. Although undoubtedly inspired and supported by Al Qaeda, the origins of Boko Haram may also be found in a sense of alienation and deprivation among Islamic communities in Nigeria's north. The organization achieved particular notoriety for its abduction of more than 200 schoolgirls in April 2014, many of whom may have been sold into slavery. Another Al Qaeda-related organization in Africa is Somali-based Al Shabaab which made headlines when it killed almost seventy people in an attack on a shopping mall in Nairobi in September 2013, and again in April 2015, with its attack on Garissa University College, in which 147 people were killed. It has been weakened by African Union forces deployed to fight it, but continues with attacks in both Somalia and Kenya. Both Boko Haram and Al Shabaab are dedicated to the establishment of Islamic states and enmity against 'the West' and non-Muslims as well as any rival and/ or moderate Muslim groups. Another group called Abu Sayyaf operates in the Philippines where it has been especially active since 2017, at one stage capturing a city in Mindanao in the south.

Even more infamous in recent times, especially in light of its gruesome execution of hostages, is the organization known variously as ISIL (Islamic State in Iraq and the Levant), ISIS (Islamic

19

→

State in Iraq and Syria), or simply Islamic State (IS), which originally formed as an offshoot of Al-Qaeda in Iraq. It has attracted both Islamist enemies of the Syrian regime as well as Iraqi Sunnis, repressed under a Shia-dominated regime since the overthrow of Saddam Hussein. However, its targets also include Kurds and Christian minorities. It is well known for attracting foreign militants from around the world, including Australians, Canadians, North Americans, Britons, and other Europeans willing to fight, as well as Chechens, Jordanians, and Saudis, among others. Its activities in Iraq have drawn the US and some allies back to military engagement in the country. Abu Sayyaf in the Philippines is, incidentally, an affiliated movement.

IS has sought to establish a 'caliphate' which is, literally, a state governed by the principles of Islam and headed by a Caliph (a ruler understood to be a successor to the prophet Mohamed) although its use of this term, as with almost anything else claimed by IS and the other groups mentioned previously, is opposed by moderate Muslims. Indeed, the great majority of Muslims condemn all the acts of violence and intolerance perpetrated in the name of their religion. This has not prevented the demonization of Islam and its followers in non-Muslim majority countries (including but not limited to the West) by groups and individuals. These include not just minority right-wing groups and individuals who act out their own brands of extremism but also more mainstream political leaders such as US President Trump.

founding charter which declares that an armed attack against one member is an attack on all, in accordance with the principal of collective security. 'Operation Enduring Freedom', as the initial intervention was called, eventually gave way to NATO's International Security Assistance Force (ISAF). Efforts in political reconstruction then saw elections held, a new government put in place, and a programme of infrastructure development commenced. Afghanistan, however, still barely functions as a state and insecurity at multiple levels is the order of the day while corruption is endemic. It took almost a decade to track bin Laden down. He was eventually found in hiding in Pakistan by US special forces in 2011, and executed on the spot.

The war in Iraq, launched in March 2003 by the Bush administration as part of the GWOT, was supported strongly by the UK's then Prime Minister Tony Blair. This intervention, however, lacked the support of either the UN Security Council or NATO. In the Security Council, French opposition to the war was backed by Russia and China. Support for intervention, however, was forthcoming from a 'coalition of the willing', which at one stage included almost fifty countries around the world, although only Poland, Denmark, and Australia sent token military contingents. Canada, a country very closely allied to both the USA and the UK, declined to participate without explicit UN authorization, lack of which rendered the legality of intervention highly questionable.

By almost any measure, the aftermath of the invasion went badly. The years that followed saw Iraq teetering on the brink of civil war between Shia and Sunni factions. And while Al-Qaeda had virtually no presence in Iraq before March 2003, the chaos opened the country up to its operatives, and indeed it became another recruiting ground for both criminal and terrorist organizations. Eight years later, one highly critical report noted that the USA suffered casualties of 4,400 soldiers dead and more than 32,000 seriously wounded; figures that nonetheless pale alongside an estimated 1 million Iraqi civilian deaths as a result of the invasion. The cost to the US economy has been around US$3 trillion (more than sixty times the initial estimate) while the cost

19

to Iraq in terms of infrastructure, environmental damage, and human capital is incalculable. In a 'liberated' Iraq, millions of Iraqis remain displaced, in both Iraq itself as well as around the region, and ordinary citizens remain politically oppressed in the post-war order (see Benjamin and Davis, 2011). The emergence of IS has also contributed to the worst refugee crisis in any region since the Second World War, although the Syrian government is no doubt the root cause of the problem there. As of August 2015, the EU estimated that the total number of Syrians needing humanitarian assistance both within Syria and in neighbouring countries was 12.2 million (see http://ec.europa.eu/echo/files/aid/countries/factsheets/syria_en.pdf).

Another major lesson from the GWOT to date is that the use of conventional military tactics against a non-conventional enemy may not only be ineffectual in defeating that enemy, but create many new problems: while bin Laden was finally killed in May 2011, Al-Qaeda and the Taliban have not only *not* been destroyed but have now been joined by other militant groups including IS; a seemingly never-ending supply of suicide bombers continues to pose a threat to civilian populations in countries around the world; and the prospects for peace and security for the people of both Afghanistan and Iraq remain bleak. Many commentators have argued that terrorism is best dealt with by civil law enforcement agencies and the strengthening of national and international intelligence networks dedicated to the task. A simple news internet search will usually give approximate numbers of attacks foiled each year in countries around the world by civil (police) agencies.

Military force is always a very blunt weapon and its consequences are often both unpredictable and uncontrollable. This led one of the most famous commentators on war, the Prussian military strategist Carl von Clausewitz (1780–1831), to observe that the planning and execution of war necessarily takes place in a kind of twilight where the effects of fog distort and obscure what is going on (see Clausewitz, 1993). The phrase 'the fog of war' is based on this observation. The Chinese Taoist thinker and strategist Sun Tzu, introduced in Chapter 17, advised more than 2,000 years ago that the best victory of all is gained without fighting and outlined various strategies for achieving this end (see Sun Tzu, 2017). These observations point to the fact that much more subtle instruments of politics may be needed to achieve desirable security outcomes in the longer term, especially against highly unconventional threats.

KEY POINTS

- The 9/11 attacks prompted what may be seen as a conventional military response, but against a highly unconventional enemy.
- Although regime change was achieved in both Afghanistan and Iraq through military force, the long-term security outcomes for both countries, as well as the region more generally, remain highly problematic.

19

CONCLUSION

Security and insecurity in the realm of international politics is clearly multifaceted both conceptually and in practical terms. Various institutions, practices, and policies have been developed over the years to cope with different security challenges. These range from those which pose a threat to international peace and security in conventional terms—that is, in terms of armed aggression by one or more states against others in the international system, to other kinds of challenges including internal conflict, genocidal violence and the huge displacement of people they generate; environmental security, food, water, and energy security; cyber security; and threats from non-state actors such as terrorist organizations. In light of all these non-conventional threats, which are the most serious in the contemporary period, we may well question the appropriateness of military responses to date and ask what alternative policy approaches, attuned to the specific dynamics of the various threats, are possible. At the same time, it is important to look critically at conventional notions of state security and to assess these vis-à-vis more expansive notions of human security.

KEY QUESTIONS

1. How does traditional IR theory treat the concept of security and how does it relate to images of the 'state of nature'?

2. Should the nation-state remain central to how security is conceptualized in the present period with respect to both traditional and newer security issues?

3. How have social movements such as the peace movement and the environmental movement challenged traditional militarist approaches to security?

4. In what ways does a gender perspective illuminate non-traditional security issues in IR?

5. What are the main challenges posed for Western democracies by cyberattacks and interventions emanating from authoritarian states.

6. How does securitization theory enhance our critical understanding of the security agenda?

7. How has NATO's role changed in the post-Cold War period and what are the principal threats facing NATO members?

8. Does the concept of 'human security' offer a superior framework for addressing issues in the contemporary period?

9. Is the role of the UN in maintaining international peace and security likely to change significantly following the development of R2P?

10. Are terrorists best dealt with militarily or through law enforcement agencies (i.e. police and the courts) at both national and international levels?

FURTHER READING

Balzacq, T. (ed.) (2011), *Securitization Theory: How Security Problems Emerge and Dissolve* (Abingdon: Routledge).
This provides a new framework for analyzing, not just 'security', but the processes by which security issues emerge, evolve, and dissolve.

Bellamy, A. J. (2014), *The Responsibility to Protect: A Defence* (Oxford: Oxford University Press).
A book-length study of the doctrine and the complex of issues driving the R2P agenda by a leading expert on the subject.

Dodds, F. and Pippard, T. (eds) (2005), *Human and Environmental Security: An Agenda for Change* (London: Earthscan).
An edited collection by leading (mainly non-academic) commentators produced in advance of the UN's 2005 World Summit illustrating the complex links between human and environmental security.

Gentry, C. E., Shepherd, L. J., and Sjoberg, L. (eds) (2018), *Routledge Handbook of Gender and Security* (Abingdon: Routledge).

The core themes of this volume are that gender is conceptually necessary to thinking about central questions of security; analytically important for thinking about cause and effect in security; and politically important for considering possibilities of making the world better in the future.

Gheciu A. and Wohlforth, W. C. (eds) (2018), *The Oxford Handbook of International Security* (Oxford: Oxford University Press).

This volume presents itself as the definitive volume on the state of international security and the academic field of security studies, providing a ***tour de force*** of the most innovative areas of research as well as major developments in established lines of inquiry.

Peterson, C. P., P., Knoblauch, W. M., and Loadenthal, M. (eds) (2019), *The Routledge History of World Peace Since 1750* (Abingdon: Routledge).

A very substantial collection of thirty-four individual chapters by expert contributors in the field of peace studies from across both the humanities and social sciences.

For additional material and resources, please visit the Online Resources at:
www.oup.com/he/garner4e

19

20

DIPLOMACY AND FOREIGN POLICY

READER'S GUIDE

Diplomacy and the conduct of foreign policy are fundamental to relations between political communities. But they are hardly new and have in fact been practised for thousands of years. In the contemporary period, diplomatic and foreign policy practices involve usually fully professionalized state bureaucracies. But alongside formal state diplomatic services are other important actors as well, from NGOs to special envoys or third-party mediators tasked with special missions. There are also special forms of diplomacy such as 'summit diplomacy' and 'public diplomacy', both of which have assumed increasing importance in contemporary practice. Foreign policy behaviour itself is a closely related but distinctive field of study focusing on the strategies that states adopt in their relations with each other and which reflect, in turn, the pressures that governments face in either the domestic or external sphere. In this chapter we also consider the foreign and security policy of the EU which now has a role and an identity as an international actor in its own right and illustrates the fact that, while the state remains the most important entity in the international system, regional bodies must also be counted as actors in diplomacy and foreign affairs. Finally, a brief account of Wikileaks illustrates another, very different, kind of actor in the field.

DIPLOMACY AND STATECRAFT IN GLOBAL HISTORY

If international relations in a conventional sense refers to the pattern of interactions between states in the international system of states, then diplomacy is the principal formal mechanism through which this takes place. Diplomacy is further characterized as embodying primarily peaceful means of conducting such interactions, although some diplomatic behaviour can be very aggressive and threatening. Statecraft is an allied notion denoting the skilful conduct of state affairs or, as some may put it, 'steering the ship of state', usually in the context of external relations. The practice of diplomacy has a very long history, almost certainly reaching beyond the earliest written records. One commentary suggests that the beginnings of diplomacy must have occurred when the first human societies decided it was better to hear the message than to devour the messenger (Hamilton and Langhorne, 2011: 7). To this observation we should add that it also had the advantage of being able to send the messenger back with a response, thereby establishing a basis for ongoing communications. A specific recorded reference to the utility of envoys or messengers may be found in Kautilya's ancient text, the *Arthasástra*, mentioned in Chapter 17, and which states clearly the first principle of diplomacy: *don't shoot the messenger* (**see Box 20.1**).

Diplomacy is known to have existed in ancient China and indeed the pattern of inter-state relations there has been compared directly with those of early modern Europe. For a time, Chinese city-states (called *guo*) enjoyed a certain autonomy which saw alliances and diplomatic practices emerge in a multi-state system well before they did so in Europe, although this effectively ended with the establishment of an overarching empire in 221 BC (Hui, 2005: 4–5). Other studies have investigated historical patterns of diplomacy and trade between China and India, illuminating the role of Buddhism in the process (Tansen, 2003), while evidence has also been found for the practice of alliance diplomacy in the regions covered by the ancient Inca, Aztec, and Mayan empires in the Americas (see Cioffi-Revilla and Landman, 1999: 559–98). There is also ample evidence for diplomatic relations between political communities in pre-modern Africa. A study of West African diplomatic traditions identifies the use of messengers, envoys, and ambassadors along with symbols of diplomatic office, ceremonials and practices of immunity and safe-conduct (Smith, 1989: 12–13).

Formal diplomatic practices between state entities in early modern Europe emerged in Italy where resident embassies had developed by the 1450s. The Florentine political philosopher Niccolò Machiavelli was among the most experienced diplomats of his time as well as one of the best-known commentators on statecraft. The prime responsibility of an ambassador as a servant of the state was well understood by this time, as indicated by an oft-cited observation dating from the late fifteenth century (**see Box 20.2**).

KEY QUOTE BOX 20.1
Kautilya on an Ancient Principle of Diplomacy

Messengers are the mouth-pieces of kings . . . hence messengers who, in the face of weapons raised against them, have to express their mission as exactly as they are entrusted with do not . . . deserve death. (Shamasastry, n.d.: 41)

20

> **KEY QUOTE** BOX 20.2
> Ermolao Barbaro on the First Duty of an Ambassador

The first duty of an ambassador is exactly the same as any other servant of a government, and that is, to do, say, advise, and think whatever may best serve the preservation and aggrandisement of his own state.
(Ermolao Barbaro (1454–93), Venetian noble, scholar, and ambassador at Naples and Rome: cited in Langhorne, 2000: 35)

The practice of maintaining embassies spread to other parts of Europe where, in due course, they became part and parcel of the sovereign state system (Mattingley, 1955: 10). In seventeenth-century France, the administrative machinery for managing foreign policy took on a more advanced form under the guidance of Cardinal de Richelieu (1585–1642), who implemented a system in which information flowed continuously both in and out of Paris, complemented by a method of record-keeping together with a unified and controlled system of management (Langhorne, 2000: 37).

Another significant development was the consolidation of the notion of *raison d'état* (**reason of state**). This expressed the idea that the state amounted to more than its ruler and the expression of his—or occasionally her—wishes (Craig and George, 1990: 5). The term became associated with realist ideas about **machtpolitik** (**power politics**) which also implied the irrelevance of morality in the conduct of relations between states. In realist terms, *raison d'état* requires a statecraft attuned to the inevitability of conflict rather than one seeking justice and perpetual peace. It follows that, however much we might agree that these are highly desirable political goods, the *reality* is that peace and justice in the international sphere remain subordinate to the main business of diplomacy, statecraft, and foreign policy, which is the preservation of the state and the advancement of its interests through whatever means it is prudent to employ. *Raison d'état* has subsequently been absorbed into the notion of '**national interest**' which is the more acceptable face of power politics in the contemporary period. Liberals and others concerned with the promotion of a more ethical approach to global politics, however, would not find 'national interest' cast in amoral terms acceptable. There is now much discussion of '**normative** power', a quality attributed to the EU which proponents of the concept say has been developed precisely in order to escape 'great power mentality' (Manners, 2006: 183; see also Violakis, 2018).

In the wake of the Napoleonic wars, Europe achieved a relatively stable **balance of power** system, initially through the Congress of Vienna (1814–15) at which the great powers were represented mainly by ambassadors and their diplomatic aides. They agreed to establish the **Concert of Europe**, an attempt to institute a formal structure for conducting relations between states as mentioned in Chapter 16. Diplomacy had previously consisted mainly in the representation of the interests of one sovereign state vis-à-vis another (bilateralism), and there was no mechanism for the cooperative management of state relations more generally. Thus in the Concert system we find the first glimmerings of the multilateralism that came to underpin the League of Nations and the UN.

The Concert system declined over the next half-century due at least partly to the rise of **nationalism** which became the principal vehicle of Europe's devastation in the next century.

The years 1914–18 and 1939–45 can scarcely go down in the annals of history as bearing testimony to the capacity of European diplomacy and statecraft to ensure greater peace and stability, or as providing an exemplar of civilized behaviour. Nonetheless, the basic institutions of diplomacy and statecraft in Europe remained integral to the sovereign state system and were carried along with the subsequent global spread of that system. The 1961 Vienna Convention on Diplomatic Relations, which entered into force in April 1964, finally codified in international law well-established rules of diplomacy that all states observe today (for the full document, see http://legal.un.org/ilc/texts/instruments/english/conventions/9_1_1961.pdf).

KEY POINTS

- Diplomacy and statecraft have been a feature of relations between political communities from the earliest times, appearing in various forms in different parts of the world.

- Traditional views of diplomacy and statecraft in international relations incorporate elements of realist thought such as *raison d'état* and *machtpolitik*.

- Contemporary diplomatic methods developed largely within the modern European state system and were codified in international law through the 1961 Vienna Convention on Diplomatic Relations.

DIPLOMACY IN CONTEMPORARY GLOBAL POLITICS

Contemporary diplomatic processes cover virtually all aspects of a state's external or foreign relations from trade and aid to negotiations about territorial borders, international treaties of all kinds, the implementation of international law, the imposition of sanctions, the mediation of hostilities, boundary disputes, framework agreements on matters concerning environmental protection and climate change, and so on. Diplomacy is not identical to foreign policy but is rather a means (although not the only means) by which foreign policy is carried out. Furthermore, diplomacy now extends beyond the pursuit of any given state's own foreign policy objectives, encompassing activities from third-party peace negotiations to Earth summits which have seen extensive multilateral diplomatic activity involving a variety of actors, including numerous NGOs. We have also seen the emergence of 'track two diplomacy', otherwise known as 'backchannel diplomacy', which refers to informal or unofficial diplomatic efforts, sometimes undertaken by private citizens, business people, peace activists, religious figures, or NGOs as well as state actors. It is most commonly deployed in peace negotiations; for example, in preparing the ground for more formal talks by persuading parties in conflict to even agree to negotiate (see Jones, 2015).

The routine business of external affairs is carried out by professional diplomatic services usually located within foreign ministries. In Britain, external affairs are conducted by the Foreign and Commonwealth Office (FCO) while in the US they are a function of the Department of State. Other countries may have a Department of Foreign Affairs and Trade (Australia), or Foreign Affairs and International Trade (Canada), or a Ministry of Foreign Affairs with a separate ministry for trade and related matters (e.g. Japan). Whatever they are called, such departments run diplomatic missions, usually in the form of permanent embassies around the world. Within the Commonwealth,

20

these are called High Commissions—a legacy of Britain's imperial system. Many small, relatively poor states, however, face particular problems in maintaining diplomatic missions abroad due to the high cost of premises and personnel, making it difficult for them to participate on equal terms. As in other spheres, the greater the resources, the greater the clout.

Embassies and consulates (the latter are generally subsidiary to a main embassy) carry out a range of functions from overseeing trade relations, liaising on military matters where there is an alliance with the host country, promoting cultural relations, issuing visas to prospective business people, immigrants, students, or tourists, assisting their own nationals when problems arise, and other consular services. But embassies have, as often as not, also served as bases for intelligence gathering or, to put it more plainly, spying. Where an embassy lists a number of their personnel as 'cultural attachés', one or more are possibly spies. Such personnel may attempt to gather classified information about the host country, or they may in fact operate a surveillance regime focussing on their own nationals within the host country, as illustrated in **Box 20.3**.

The territory or building occupied by an embassy in a foreign country is sometimes regarded, mistakenly, as being effectively 'home soil' of the country concerned, with the same sovereign rights. Article 22 of the Vienna Convention on Diplomatic Relations deals with the inviolability of diplomatic missions, but this does not amount to awarding it the status of sovereign territory. The Article prohibits agents of the receiving state from entering diplomatic premises, except with the consent of the head of the mission. It further provides that the premises of the mission, their furnishings, and any other property within it, as well as the means of transport of the mission, shall be immune from search, requisition, attachment, or execution The receiving state is also responsible for taking all appropriate measures to protect the premises of the mission.

Although it is not common practice for anyone claiming asylum to be able to do so at an embassy, and many embassies explicitly prohibit it, it has occurred. The best-known case is that of Julian Assange, founder of Wikileaks—an organization that publishes confidential documents acquired from governments and other agencies and companies around the world, including diplomatic cables. In a bid to evade arrest warrants over allegations of sexual assault in Sweden, Assange claimed asylum in the Ecuadorian Embassy in London in 2012, where he remained until 2019 when he was evicted. He was fearful of being extradited to the US to face charges over the publication of secret US documents. Assange and Wikileaks have also been implicated with Russia in the 2016 US presidential elections, but that's another story.

Another recent incident on the premises of a diplomatic mission concerns the Saudi Arabian consulate in Istanbul, Turkey, where a dissident Saudi journalist, Jamal Khashoggi was murdered, in October 2018. His body has never been found but Turkish authorities had obtained evidence of Khassogi's violent death in the consulate in the form of audio recordings. After first denying he had been killed there, Saudi authorities, when confronted with the evidence, blamed it on a rogue intelligence agent. Other observers, including the US Central Intelligence Agency (CIA), believe it was on the orders of Saudi Crown Prince Mohammed bin Salman (otherwise known as MBS), who is the heir apparent to the Saudi crown and has a reputation for ruthless crackdowns on any critics.

In a quite separate account of the activities of the Saudi Arabian embassy in London, a long-time observer of diplomatic practices highlights the efforts of officials to spy on Saudi students studying in the UK (**Box 20.3**). The Saudis, however, are not the only ones to use their diplomatic missions abroad to monitor their students. China also keeps a close eye on student activity in the

BOX 20.3
The London Embassy with Thirteen Cultural Attachés

The London embassy of Saudi Arabia has the third largest number of staff of any in the capital, exceeded only by China and the USA. Of these, thirteen are cultural attachés—more than any other.

What do all of these Saudi cultural attachés do? Helpfully, the section of which they are members, the 'Diplomatic Office of the Cultural Bureau' (a.k.a Saudi Arabian Cultural Bureau or SACB), makes it clear that its core functions are exclusively concerned with university-level educational relationships. In so far as this involves Saudi students studying at British universities, of which there are over 8,000 (as of 2018), it is also apparent that the SACB holds them in an iron grip. It is one thing to require reports at the end of every semester on their progress, and to 'urge' them to participate in cultural activities that 'do not conflict with Islamic faith and Saudi traditions'. But the Bureau's stated function also includes the *'supervision and monitoring of the activities of Saudi students and their clubs* [emphasis added].' No wonder Saudi Arabia's cultural attachés represent around a quarter of all diplomatic officers of this class in the British capital.

A report on the Saudi Embassy in Washington also indicates that it has been intimidating Saudi students studying in the United States who voice criticisms of their government; for example, by severing grants, refusing to renew passports, and urging them to return home to an unknown fate.
(Edited extract from G. R. Berridge, 2018)

UK, USA, and Australia, largely through embassy staff, and also uses 'loyal' Chinese students on university campuses to report on dissident activity (see Corr, 2017).

A relatively recent development in diplomatic practice is 'summit diplomacy', a phrase coined by Winston Churchill in the early Cold War period to describe top-level negotiations between key leaders at the time. But it is only in the recent past that heads of government have met more regularly to discuss or negotiate directly (Melissen, 2003: 4). Summit diplomacy itself ranges from ad hoc bilateral summits, such as the summits between President Trump and North Korea's Kim Jong-un on the latter's nuclear weapons programme, to global multilateral summits which include not only heads of government and leading UN figures but in many cases parallel meetings for NGOs as well. Among the largest have been the Earth Summits organized by the UN. Regional or inter-regional summits are now also part and parcel of the regular international scene, with organizations such the Asia-Pacific Economic Cooperation (APEC) forum, the Organization of American States (OAS), and the Asia-Europe Meeting process (ASEM) becoming solidly institutionalized. The Commonwealth, with fifty-four members, has reinvented itself as something of a diplomatic summit club in the postcolonial period, with the Commonwealth Heads of Government Meeting (CHOGM) being held every two years to discuss matters of mutual interest and concern, and formulate policies and initiatives at the highest level. Sometimes, these are seen as little more than opportunities for international socializing at the highest level. The acronym APEC, for example, has been recast as 'A Perfect Excuse for a Chat'. But one should never underestimate the value of high-level diplomatic socialization on a face-to-face basis and its role in building international society.

Although diplomacy is governed by a universal set of rules, variations in diplomatic styles are often said to reflect local cultural or other differences. The Association of Southeast Asian

20

Nations (ASEAN), for example, has promoted the 'ASEAN Way' as a distinctive style of diplomacy. Its emphasis on consensus decision-making and an almost absolute commitment to non-interference in the internal affairs of member states, is said to differ from a 'Western' style of diplomacy. Certainly, the member states of the EU have given considerably less weight to state sovereignty in the interests of political and economic integration. And they have been known to criticize one another openly. To see this as reflecting a great gulf of 'cultural difference' between the two regions, however, belies the fact that the doctrine of state sovereignty is itself a European invention, adopted elsewhere for its political efficacy rather than because it was a good 'cultural fit' in any particular region. As for 'the West', this is not a coherent cultural entity in any case. The diplomatic style of the EU, for instance, has contrasted very strongly with the hawkish approach evinced by the USA under the administration of George W. Bush, although Obama subsequently adopted a less aggressive stance. Diplomacy under the Trump administration has followed no set path although aggressive language and gestures in some circumstances have contrasted with 'softly-softly' approaches in others. What has puzzled some observers is that Trump has been much more at odds with traditional allies (including those in NATO), and relatively soft on countries such as Russia whose interests conflict with those of the US.

Analysis of Trump's diplomatic style also raises the issue of high-level 'personal diplomacy' which has developed over the years since the Second World War, enabled by the rapid development of transport and communications technologies. **Box 20.4** provides both a brief overview of the personal diplomacy styles of US presidents, including a critical commentary on Trump's approach.

BOX 20.4
Personal Diplomacy

History provides us with many examples of the value of leader-to-leader diplomacy. Roosevelt's connection with British Prime Minister Winston Churchill played a central role in the Allied victory during WWII. The bond between Jimmy Carter and Egyptian President Anwar Sadat was crucial to Egyptian-Israeli peace. And Ronald Reagan and Mikhail Gorbachev's relationship was key to the end of the Cold War. Presidents themselves have recognized the importance of leader-to-leader diplomacy. George W. Bush has said 'I placed a high priority on personal diplomacy. Getting to know a fellow world leader's personality, character, and concerns made it easier to find common ground and deal with contentious issues.'

But there are risks as well. Leaders do not always get along. Miscalculation and tension may be as likely as understanding and cooperation. In 1961, US-Soviet relations went from bad to worse after John F. Kennedy and Soviet Premier Nikita Khrushchev met. Khrushchev came away thinking Kennedy was weak and inexperienced. The following year, Khrushchev placed nuclear missiles in Cuba capable of reaching almost every corner of the continental United States. George W. Bush thought he could trust Russian leader Vladimir Putin because 'he looked the man in the eye'. But by the end of his presidency, it was clear that Bush had seriously misjudged the Russian leader.

In his two years in office, Trump has shown himself both following in his predecessors' personal diplomacy footsteps but also breaking from established norms. Since becoming president, he

20

has continued to promote his personal relationships with world leaders. This is normal presidential behaviour. Where Trump differs from his predecessors is in the relationships he promotes and his approach to personal diplomacy. Most striking is his praise of dictators. None have so publicly embraced brutal authoritarians such as Kim Jong-un, Vladimir Putin, and Saudi Crown Prince Mohammed bin Salman. This has a cost. Personal diplomacy is a form of theatre. It sends signals to domestic and international audiences. The leaders a president decides to meet with, praise or attack is a statement of American values and policy. By effusively embracing dictators, Trump's personal diplomacy is at odds with traditional American foreign policy, and critics argue that it emboldens dictators. (Edited extract from Chavez, 2019)

KEY POINTS

- Contemporary diplomatic practice involves different actors including professional diplomatic services, special envoys, heads of government, the UN, NGOs, and regional bodies such as the EU and ASEAN. It may also involve a range of non-state actors in 'track-two diplomacy'.
- Different countries and/or regions are said to possess certain diplomatic styles or orientations, although whether this is due to intrinsic cultural differences is a matter of debate. There are no 'intrinsic cultural differences' between US President Trump and his predecessors but his style is very different.
- Summit diplomacy and personal diplomacy has evolved since the end of World War Two to become a regular feature of the global political landscape.

COLD WAR DIPLOMACY

The study of Cold War diplomatic history is an extensive field dealing with a host of incidents, issues, and crises. These range from the expulsion of diplomats for alleged spying to major crises such as the blockade of West Berlin by the Soviets in 1948/9, and the Cuban missile crisis of 1962, the latter triggered when the Soviets attempted to deploy nuclear warheads in Cuba. The most serious crises were defused by diplomatic means, thus averting major overt conflict. It is commonly believed that the Cuban missile crisis was the closest the world has ever come to 'hot' nuclear warfare, and that the crisis was resolved largely because US President Kennedy and Soviet Premier Khrushchev both recognized that the consequences would be disastrous. Strategic thinking subsequently produced a theory of deterrence known as 'mutually assured destruction' (MAD) which assumed that the possession of incredibly destructive weapons served as the key to preventive strategy. This remains an essential aspect of US foreign and security policy.

Subsequent work on 'nuclear diplomacy' in the Cold War period has sought to answer the question: did the possession of nuclear weapons by both sides actually prevent a Third World War (Gaddis et al., 1999)? There is no clear-cut answer to this question, but what is certain is that, without systems of diplomacy operating, however clumsy they may have seemed at time, the Cold War may well have become the 'hottest' ever. Where diplomacy often did fail, however, was

20

in relation to the Third World which bore the brunt of overt conflict conducted via conventional weaponry during the Cold War period.

Cold War diplomacy also introduced the term *'détente'*—a French word for 'relaxation of tensions'—into the vocabulary of global politics. This applied to a period between 1969 and 1979 when tensions eased due to certain economic and geopolitical circumstances including the fiasco of the Vietnam War (from the US point of view), the souring of Soviet–Chinese relations accompanied by shifting attitudes towards China in the West, the huge cost of the arms race, and the desire to attend more to domestic matters. These factors led to important summit meetings which resulted in the all-important Nuclear Non-Proliferation Treaty (NPT) which opened for signature in 1968. It was subsequently extended indefinitely and currently has 190 signatures, including five nuclear-weapon states—the USA, France, the UK, Russia, and China. Note that the latter are also the five permanent members of the UN Security Council. However, India, Pakistan, and North Korea—all known to possess nuclear weapons—and Israel which maintains secrecy and does not publicly admit to its nuclear weapons—are not signatories.

The safeguards system set up by the NPT is administered by the International Atomic Energy Agency (IAEA). Over recent years, it has expressed considerable concern over Iran's nuclear ambitions. Iran is a signatory to the NPT but is widely believed to have been developing a nuclear weapons programme under the cover of nuclear energy facilities.

The NPT was complemented by other treaties and agreements including the Strategic Arms Limitation Treaty (SALT) dealing with a range of matters concerning missile deployment. The USA under Reagan, however, withdrew from SALT and adopted a more confrontational approach which saw the end of *détente*. Nonetheless, the practices and procedures put in place during the Cold War continue as vital elements of contemporary diplomacy surrounding nuclear energy and weaponry, chemical and biological weapons, and the full range of conventional weapons from weapons of mass destruction to small arms and light weapons, land mines, and so on.

Other aspects of Cold War politics and diplomacy are familiar to us through popular culture, often in the form of fiction and cinema. Although the James Bond genre has been thoroughly reinvented for the post-Cold War world, its Cold War origins are unmistakable in its central theme of spying, an activity that developed close associations with Cold War diplomacy. Real-life dramas featured throughout the Cold War as intelligence gathering by both sides deployed almost any means available. And no better on-the-ground facilities existed than embassies and their diplomatic staff. A common feature of Cold War diplomacy was therefore the expulsion of embassy staff for alleged spying offences. This occurred not only in Europe and the USA, but in Canada, and Australia too where alleged spying activities were met with strong diplomatic responses while anti-communist paranoia became a feature of electoral politics.

Post-Cold War episodes include the expulsion in July 2007 of four Russian diplomats from the UK following the alleged murder by radioactive isotope poisoning of former Russian agent, Alexander Litvinenko, who had become a UK citizen. Moscow's immediate response was a declaration of outrage and denial, followed by the summoning of the British ambassador in Moscow to the Russian foreign office, and then the 'tit-for-tat' expulsion of four British diplomats. A similar pattern was repeated following the March 2018 poisoning of the Skripals in Salisbury in the UK, mentioned in Chapter 19. The evidence points to the use of a deadly nerve agent called Novichok, known to have been developed in Russia, and the presence of Russian state agents in Salisbury at the time of the poisoning. In subsequent developments the UK expelled twenty-three Russian diplomats, following which Russia expelled the same number, and closed down British Council operations in Russia as well. Various of the UK's Western allies, convinced that the blame lay squarely with the Russian state, also responded with diplomatic sanctions. The symbolism and predictability of diplomatic gamesmanship, however, may be read as part and parcel of a system of structured interactions in which countries can express deep dissatisfaction with each other while confining it to a manageable arena.

KEY POINTS

- The Cold War was marked by various crises in which diplomacy played a key role in preventing what may have been a Third World War.

- Cold War diplomacy saw the development of a system of treaties and conventions which continue to play an important role in the ongoing attempt to limit the production and distribution of a wide range of weapons.

- Cold War continuities have been evident in certain diplomatic dramas involving Russia. These also illustrate, among other things, the extent to which diplomacy is at least partly a stage-managed performance albeit with very serious underpinnings.

PUBLIC DIPLOMACY

Public diplomacy refers primarily to the ways in which governments attempt to influence public opinion abroad by utilizing the cultural power of ideas. In practice, it has a history reaching back to at least the nineteenth century, but as a term 'public diplomacy' has achieved prominence only fairly recently in the wake of the Global War on Terror (GWOT) when the violence deployed by the Bush administration to achieve foreign policy goals was contrasted with what might be achieved through other means. It is therefore implicated in the notion of 'soft power' formulated by the American liberal academic Joseph Nye who defines this in terms of the ability to achieve one's end without the use of force or even coercion, effectively by winning 'hearts and minds' (**see Box 20.5**). Interestingly, this has some resonances with Antonio Gramsci's notion of cultural power and the way in which it supports hegemony.

➡ See Chapter 19 for more on Gramscian theory.

In the UK, the FCO has defined public diplomacy as 'a process of achieving the UK's international strategic priorities through engaging and forming partnerships with like-minded organizations and individuals in the public arena'. It emphasizes that public diplomacy goes well beyond traditional government-to-government channels by engaging with NGOs, think tanks, opinion formers, young people, businesses, and individual citizens in a two-way dialogue 'in order to get a better understanding of the changing perceptions of the UK and its policies' (United Kingdom, Foreign and Commonwealth Office, 2011). The two most prominent vehicles of public diplomacy are the British Council, which has primary responsibility for promoting British education and culture internationally through offices around the world (see www.britishcouncil.org/new), and the BBC World Service which provides news and analysis in twenty-seven languages (see www.bbc.co.uk/news/world_radio_and_tv). Both receive funding from the FCO, although both claim to enjoy substantial autonomy.

20

> **KEY CONCEPT** BOX 20.5
> 'Soft Power'

[Soft power] is the ability to get what you want through attraction rather than coercion or payments. It arises from the attractiveness of a country's culture, political ideals, and policies. When our policies are seen as legitimate in the eyes of others, our soft power is enhanced . . . . When you can get others to admire your ideals and to want what you want, you do not have to spend as much on sticks and carrots to move them in your direction. Seduction is always more effective than coercion, and many values like democracy, human rights, and individual opportunity are deeply seductive . . . But attraction can turn to repulsion if we act in an arrogant manner and destroy the real message of deeper values. (Nye, 2004: p. x)

The US State Department has a dedicated Under Secretary for Public Diplomacy and Public Affairs whose mission is 'to support the achievement of US foreign policy goals and objectives, advance national interests, and enhance national security by informing and influencing foreign publics and by expanding and strengthening the relationship between the people and government of the United States and citizens of the rest of the world' (www.state.gov/r). Broadcasting is also a major arm of public diplomacy with Voice of America (VOA), funded by Congress and administered by the US Agency for Global Media (USAGM), which oversees all non-military international broadcasting, reaching an estimated weekly global audience of 275 million with news, information, and cultural programming, utilizing the Internet, mobile and social media, radio, and television (see www.insidevoa.com).

As with other forms of diplomacy, many smaller countries simply do not have the resources to promote themselves abroad. Until recently, relatively wealthy middle powers such as Australia and Canada also lacked specific public diplomacy programmes, although Radio Australia and Radio Canada International, each of which broadcasts in around half a dozen languages, have been operating for decades along with bilateral councils. More attention, however, is now being paid to explicit public diplomacy measures, and in 2007, the Australian senate commissioned a special inquiry into 'Australia's Public Diplomacy: Building Our Image' which produced a long list of recommendations for enhancing Australia's profile in the Asia-Pacific region and beyond (see Parliament of Australia, Senate, 2007). Recent changes in perceptions of Australia's geostrategic region, incidentally, have seen it embrace the term 'Indo-Pacific', with 'Indo' giving more specific emphasize to the Indian Ocean and India itself as a rising power.

As emerging powers, both India and China have also begun to engage in public diplomacy measures, although China has been far more proactive in raising its international profile over the last thirty years or so. This has been all the more important for a country with a poor human rights record and international image problems, especially following the Tiananmen Square massacre in 1989 when tanks confronted unarmed pro-democracy protestors. This incident left lasting impressions on a significant global audience through extensive media coverage. It is commonly believed that this was a major factor in China's failure to win a bid for the Olympic Games in 2000. The rehabilitation of China's image, however, saw a successful bid to host the 2008 games despite ongoing human rights (and other) problems which resulted in a series of protests by individuals and groups around the world when the games were actually held.

20

→ See Chapter 14 for further discussion of Tiananmen Square.

To boost its image internationally, China in 2004 embarked on a project of developing 'Confucius Institutes' around the world. Modelled partly on the British Council, France's Alliance Française, and Germany's Goethe Institut, these have been located mainly in established universities and, along with numerous, 'Confucius classrooms' in schools, aim to promote learning of Chinese language and culture. Since 2004, hundreds of these Institutes have appeared in every region. As of 2019 there were 182 Institutes in European universities (including 29 in the UK alone), 160 in the USA, 126 in Asia, 59 in Africa, and 29 in Oceania. Confucius classrooms in Europe and the USA number around 650 (see http://english.hanban.org/node_10971.htm). A longer-standing institution, China Radio International, has been broadcasting since the 1940s. Its English broadcasting platform can (potentially) reach an audience of nearly 3 billion (see http://english.cri.cn/7146/2013/10/30/2203s795082.htm).

In recent years, concerns have been expressed about Confucius Institutes being used to promote the specific interests of the Chinese Communist Party (CCP) and to wield influence over such issues as Taiwan, Tibet, and China's record on human rights more generally. Accusations of espionage have also been made, although there is no real evidence to date of any serious 'spying' actually being carried out. Reporting on an FBI probe into the activities of the centres on American campuses, one media outlet opined that 'they have become centers for spreading pro-China propaganda and influence activities, including organizing Chinese communist student groups that challenge human rights activists and others' (https://www.washingtontimes.com/news/2018/feb/14/inside-the-ring-fbi-investigating-confucius-instit/).

Similar concerns have been expressed in Australia and the UK where the Institutes have also been branded by critics as 'Trojan horses' and a means by which the CCP can wield influence, not to mention maintaining a watchful eye over its own students studying on those campuses and compromising freedom of expression, a value that is held very strongly in most Western universities and which is seen as threatened by authoritarian influences. Conversely, authoritarian governments often regard Western ideas of freedom of expression (along with the values of liberal democracy and human rights more generally) as a threat to their own values.

Photo 20.1 Xi Jinping, General Secretary of the CCP and President of the People's Republic of China. *Shutterstock RF via DAM: © Getty Images*

20

The issue of advancing public diplomacy through cultural means, as exemplified by the provision of language instruction and accompanying cultural education, is often carried on under the specific label of 'cultural diplomacy', a practice which is related to concepts of soft power and public diplomacy, at least when it is carried out by formal agents of the state or government. A broader understanding, such as the one quoted in **Box 20.6**, takes it beyond the agency of the state and defines it in more diffuse terms.

Some have argued that, although public diplomacy is rarely a decisive factor in the success or otherwise of particular foreign policy initiatives, it functions as an important accessory service, especially in the contemporary period in which media and telecommunications have changed so radically. It is further suggested that the new public diplomacy is shifting the focus from indirectly influencing other governments, which is essentially still a state-to-state interaction, to shaping the attitudes of other societies in a more direct state-to-society interaction (Henriksen, 2006: 1). The need is especially acute for the USA in the present period where, in the Middle East in particular, it has a serious image problem. With the battle for 'hearts and minds' so prominent in international affairs, it is clearly important for states seeking to play a prominent role on the world stage, or to attract attention and support for their various causes, to invest resources in public diplomacy for the 'soft power' it can generate.

It is also interesting to note here the extent to which President Obama started to use new social media as a tool of public diplomacy. Concerted efforts were made to ensure that a major 'address to the Muslim World', delivered at Cairo University in June 2009, reached as large an audience as possible by translating it into Arabic, Persian, Urdu, and around a dozen other languages and disseminating it through Twitter, Facebook, Myspace, YouTube, and other social networking sites as well as regular media outlets (Zeleny, 2009). More generally, new media, itself the product of a new communications age inaugurated by the World Wide Web, has brought diplomacy well and

BOX 20.6
What is Cultural Diplomacy?

Cultural Diplomacy may best be described as a course of actions, which are based on and utilize the exchange of ideas, values, traditions and other aspects of culture or identity, whether to strengthen relationships, enhance socio-cultural cooperation, promote national interests and beyond. Cultural diplomacy can be practiced by either the public sector, private sector or civil society. (http://www.culturaldiplomacy.org/index.php?en_culturaldiplomacy)

This rather bland description should be read together with a more clearly instrumental assessment of the value of cultural diplomacy set out in a 2005 US State Department Report entitled *Cultural Diplomacy: The Linchpin of Public Diplomacy* which states that:

[It] is in our cultural activities that a nation's idea of itself is best represented. And cultural diplomacy can enhance our national security in subtle, wide-ranging, and sustainable ways. Indeed, history may record that America's cultural riches played no less a role than military action in shaping our international leadership, including the war on terror. For the values embedded in our artistic and intellectual traditions form a bulwark against the forces of darkness. (Quoted in Ang, Isar, and Mar, 2016: 4)

truly into the cyber era. And although public diplomacy is usually defined as an activity in which governments and other actors try to get their voices heard and extend their influence, it goes the other way as well. One commentator suggests that the first duty of a public diplomat is actually to listen, something given unprecedented scope through new media (Cull, 2011). We consider some other implications of the new communications age in relation to Wikileaks shortly.

While on the subject of social media and public diplomacy, we must also consider briefly the phenomenon of Trump's 'Twitter diplomacy' which has provoked much commentary in recent times. One media article first described the concerns provoked by Trump's attachment to thinking out loud through Twitter, and the way in which he went completely against all the protocols of the formal diplomatic establishments, 'which regard such heedless commentary as, first, ill-advised in the extreme and, second, plain crass.' On the other hand, the article suggested that we may be witnessing the end of spin and, if so, good riddance.

> **Spin, and the degradation of language it entailed, is a large part of the reason people distrust politicians. They do not like politicians using words in ways ordinary people would not use them. Perhaps it takes the recklessness of Trump to yank language, politics and people back on to the same page, opening the way for a plain-speaking in public life that is less risky and rude than his is, but equally direct.** (Dejevsky, 2017)

In more general terms, we may ask where one draws the line between public diplomacy (usually perceived as a positive thing) and propaganda (usually perceived in negative terms). Propaganda in a neutral sense simply denotes the dissemination or promotion of particular ideas and values. In a slightly more instrumental sense, it implies an attempt to influence beliefs and behaviour rather than an objective presentation of 'the facts'. But, over time, it has acquired more sinister overtones and often conjures up images of deceit, distortion of facts, or even 'brainwashing'. Contemporary variations on the theme of propaganda include 'spin doctoring', otherwise known as 'news management', which has come in for much criticism over the last decade or so, as alluded to by the commentary on Trump's Twitter diplomacy above which is in some respects almost the opposite of spin. While the latter can scarcely be described as carefully crafted, spin attempts to do exactly that through a conscious strategy of minimizing negative images of either politicians or political events while maximizing positive images (see Jowett and O'Donnell, 2006: 2–3). And, although spin is most often played to a domestic audience, it clearly has an important place in the international sphere of diplomacy and statecraft as well. All this suggests that public diplomacy and propaganda are simply different sides of the same coin.

KEY POINTS

- Public diplomacy involves attempts by governments to influence public opinion, mainly in other countries, by promoting positive images of one's country.
- Public diplomacy may be understood as an instrument of 'soft power' in contrast with the methods of power politics.
- Many acts of public diplomacy involve elements of propaganda and 'spin'.

20

FOREIGN POLICY

Foreign policy is generally framed in terms of the strategies that states, or rather those in control of a state at any given time, adopt in their dealings with other actors in the international system or with respect to relevant issues, such as the environment, aid, trade regimes, and so on. Whatever particular issue is at stake, the study of foreign policy invariably links the domestic and international spheres of politics. As Evans and Newnham (1998: 179) put it, foreign policy is often called a 'boundary activity' because it effectively straddles both spheres and mediates between the two.

An important factor affecting a state's foreign policy behaviour is its regional or geopolitical location. For example, although much attention has recently focused on US behaviour in relation to the Middle East, the history of US foreign policy shows how important the Americas have been for forging enduring patterns of foreign policy behaviour. It was in the context of the establishment of independent states in South America, and the attempts by European powers to maintain colonial systems there, that the USA enunciated the 'Monroe doctrine', named for its initiator, President James Monroe. After safely concluding the purchase of Florida from Spain, Monroe announced to Congress in 1823 that the USA would maintain an independent line on its interests in the Americas without reference to European interests. But this did not amount to a declaration of unqualified respect for the sovereignty of the new states emerging in the Americas.

The Monroe doctrine readily evolved into an attitude that political developments in the Americas were not just something that European powers should stay well out of, but something that the USA was entitled to intervene in unilaterally. Subsequent interference by the USA in the internal affairs of Central and South American states—including the undermining or outright overthrow of leftist governments, whether democratically elected or not—may be seen as the logical outcome of the doctrine. In 2005 a well-known right-wing Republican and religious conservative, Pat Robertson, actually declared publicly that the time had come to 'take out' (a euphemism for assassination) the elected socialist President of Venezuela, Hugo Chavez (see BBC, 2005). Robertson subsequently apologized, but the remark nonetheless reflects an important current of thinking among a sector of the US population.

US relations with its northern neighbour, Canada, stand in sharp contrast to those south of its border, despite strong elements of democratic socialism within Canadian politics—reflected in its universal health scheme and much stronger support for public goods generally. One commentator suggests that many Canadians have a self-image as being less individualistic and more 'tolerant' and 'compassionate' than their US neighbours, while to the American left Canada serves as a model of social democracy (Brooks, 2009: 45). More generally, Canada's foreign policy approach is often said to reflect its location in the global system as a 'middle power'—a status it shares with countries like Australia. Canadian and Australian approaches to diplomacy and foreign policy as middle powers, however, may be not simply a function of their size and location in the global system, but also of a particular self-image as 'good international citizens', strongly supporting multilateralism and international institutions like the UN, promoting the notion of a rules-based international order, and contributing substantially to activities such as peace-keeping.

The foreign policy of the UK has followed a different trajectory in its historical development, shaped both by the dynamics of the European region as well as by its colonizing enterprises. It has long been among the 'great powers' in global politics although there has been much talk about its declining status. Former Prime Minister David Cameron, however, insisted his country maintains the 'commercial, military and cultural clout to remain a significant global power' (quoted in Parker and Giles, 2010), while his immediate successor, Theresa May, promoted the idea of 'Global Britain' in the wake of the Brexit vote, which means simply that the UK will need to work harder on its bilateral relations in the absence of the multilateral support network provided by the EU.

The UK has also been deeply enmeshed in 'special relationships' which have been decisive for its foreign policy. Although there are several 'special' relationships, such as the relationship with the former colonial empire through the Commonwealth as well as with fellow EU members, *the* special relationship in recent years has been the Anglo-American relationship. This has ebbed and flowed according to whatever issues in world politics are salient and according to the personalities involved. The term 'special relationship' actually dates from the time when Roosevelt and Churchill forged a close personal alliance during the Second World War. Another strong personal alliance developed between Margaret Thatcher and Ronald Reagan during the latter stages of the Cold War, assisted no doubt by their conservative dispositions and manifest in their shared loathing of communism.

The special relationship was put under intense scrutiny in the post-9/11 period when former Prime Minister Tony Blair offered unwavering support for George W. Bush in the GWOT and, especially, the invasion of Iraq, which was cast by both parties as an integral part of that war even though there was no evidence linking Saddam with Al-Qaeda or the events of 9/11, as set out in Chapter 18. Blair came under much criticism at home for what seemed to be his uncritical endorsement of White House policy and support for a war that turned out to lack any real justification. In an interesting study, published in 2006, comparing the impact of the Falklands War and the Iraq War, it was suggested that, although the idea of the special relationship may have weakened, there is no reason why there should be any significant move away from the relationship. After all, it suggested, 'the problem with Iraq lay not in the special relationship itself' but rather with 'flawed analysis which led to flawed policy' (Freedman, 2006: 74).

More recently, President Trump declared that the relationship had reached the 'highest level of special'. UK Prime Minister of the time, Theresa May, added that 'no two countries do more together to keep their people safe and prosperous.' But Trump was a little less than 'diplomatic' in saying, at the very same joint press conference with May, that how wonderful Boris Johnson would also be as prime minister. 'I said he'll be a great prime minister. He's been very nice to me; he's been saying very good things about me as president. I think he thinks I'm doing a great job, I am doing a great job, that I can tell you, just in case you haven't noticed' (quoted in Walker, 2018).

➜ See Chapter 19 for a discussion of the US-led invasion of Iraq in 2003.

If we look to other parts of the world, and especially the Global South, we may see very similar formal structures operating in terms of both diplomacy and foreign policy, but the challenges, concerns, and approaches may vary according to a range of historical, cultural, economic and other factors. One will often find a particular emphasis on 'South-South' cooperation which may take place bilaterally as well as through regional and other multilateral forums and cover a range of issues from trade to cultural exchanges. There are also efforts to enhance the profile of specific foreign policy approaches as situated in a more authentic cultural context. In South Africa, for example, an official White Paper makes reference to the country's liberation history and goes on to state that its evolving international engagement is based on two central tenets, namely, pan-Africanism and South-South solidarity. It therefore understands its national interest as being 'intrinsically linked to Africa's stability, unity, and prosperity'. There is a further specific reference to anti-colonialism in its foreign policy stance which accords with its liberation history and complements the emphasis on South-South relations (South Africa, 2011: 3).

20

South African foreign policy is also said to be guided by the values of Ubuntu—a word derived from a Bantu language that is understood as akin to a notion of shared humanity embracing positive values such as caring and kindness. It was popularized partly through the writings of Archbishop Desmond Tutu who, along with Nelson Mandela (1918–2013), was among the most prominent figures opposing apartheid rule in South Africa which ended in 1993–4. More recently, Ubuntu has been used to frame both South African domestic and foreign policy approaches, at least at a rhetorical level, and is prominent in the White Paper mentioned previously. In discussing the concept more critically, Qobo and Nyathi (2017) note first that foreign policies are, to a large extent, a projection of domestic values and policies. Thus the Ubuntu concept finds its way into the wider sphere of global politics where its values of pursuing 'common humanity, collaboration, cooperation, and building partnership over conflict' chime with commonly accepted notions of 'good' politics. As in many other cases, however, rhetoric is not matched by performance either at home or abroad, and Ubuntu has been used to conceal patronage and crony-capitalism, especially under former President Jacob Zuma. Even so, the authors contend that Ubuntu remains necessary as a basis for a dialogue on exploring avenues for transformative change. 'This may mean renewal of both domestic and global institutions to better reflect the values associated with Ubuntu, and to facilitate a dialogue about the future of global governance' (Qobo and Nyathi, 2017).

KEY POINTS

- Foreign policy refers to the strategies that governments adopt in their dealings with other actors in the international system.
- The foreign policy behaviour of states (and other actors) is influenced by size, capacity, geopolitical, and/or historical circumstances.
- Formerly colonized countries tend to place much emphasis on the value of South-South cooperation.

THE EU'S COMMON FOREIGN AND SECURITY POLICY

The EU as a foreign policy actor represents a significant departure from the traditional sovereign state model, although it is in Europe that the model was generated in the first place. The EU has been working to develop a Common Foreign and Security Policy (CFSP) in which is also embedded a European Security and Defence Policy (ESDP). A major factor contributing to the development of the CFSP/ESDP, and indeed to the consolidation of the European movement itself, was the end of the Cold War and the perceived need for coordination in regional affairs in the wake of the collapse of Soviet hegemony in Eastern Europe. Beyond the exigencies of these particular circumstances, it has also been suggested that the challenge for the European project was more fundamental: 'From its origins, the ideal or "vocation" of Europe has been to ensure peace between former warring European nation-states and to provide the conditions for geopolitical stability built on the foundations of a commitment to liberal democracy' (Dannreuther, 2004b: 1–2).

The CSFP was embedded in the 1993 Treaty on European Union (otherwise known as the Maastricht Treaty), subsequently refined in the 1999 Amsterdam Treaty and refined again in the Nice Treaty which came into effect in 2003, while the ESDP was given an operational capability in a 2001 meeting of the European Council. The CFSP's basic working profile is set out in **Box 20.7**.

These objectives clearly reflect a desire to export European political norms—especially in respect of human rights, democracy, and 'good governance'—to other parts of the world. As we have seen earlier, it is now said that the EU consciously projects itself as a qualitatively different kind of power in the international sphere—a 'normative power'—staking a claim 'to being a legitimate and thus a more effective international actor' (Farrell, 2005: 453). Further, while 'American unilateralism renews the legitimacy of power politics on the world stage, the normative approach in the European management of international relations sustains the relevance of the very notion of global governance' (Farrell, 2005). This illustrates once again the idea of soft power versus militarism and power politics more generally in achieving foreign policy objectives, **see Box 20.7.**

BOX 20.7
European Union Common Foreign and Security Policy (CFSP)

Photo 20.2 **The European Union has worked to establish political norms.** *Getty Images RF via DAM: Kaliva/Shutterstock.com*

Objectives

Article 11 of the Treaty on European Union defines the following five objectives of the CFSP:

- to safeguard the common values, fundamental interests, independence and integrity of the Union in conformity with the principles of the United Nations Charter;
- to strengthen the security of the Union in all ways;

20

- to preserve peace and strengthen international security, in accordance with the principles of the United Nations Charter, as well as the principles of the Helsinki Final Act and the objectives of the Paris Charter, including those on external borders;
- to promote international cooperation;
- to develop and consolidate democracy and the rule of law, and respect for human rights and fundamental freedoms.

Article 2(b) of Title I TEU (Common provisions) defines the *general objectives of the Union*, which also apply to the framework of the CFSP.

In addition, member states are bound by a clause of *loyalty towards the EU*. Article 11(2) stipulates that they shall:

- support the CFSP actively and unreservedly;
- refrain from any action which is contrary to the interests of the Union or is likely to impair its effectiveness in international relations;
- work together to enhance and develop their mutual political solidarity. (European Union (1993), Treaty on European Union)

(for the consolidated text of the Treaty on European Union, see https://eur-lex.europa.eu/eli/treaty/teu_2012/oj).

KEY POINTS

- The emergence of the EU as a foreign policy actor in its own right represents a significant departure from the traditional state model which Europe itself generated.
- EU foreign policy is founded on a set of ideals which attempt to project 'normative power' and which is comparable in turn to 'soft power'.
- The contrast between EU and US approaches to foreign policy undermines the notion of 'the West' constituting a coherent cultural/political entity in the international sphere, **see Box 20.8**.

KEY DEBATE BOX 20.8
Diplomacy and Foreign Policy after Wikileaks

No account of diplomacy and foreign policy in the contemporary period would be complete without at least a brief account of the Wikileaks saga. Launched in 2006, Wikileaks is self-described as a non-profit media organization providing 'an innovative, secure and anonymous way for independent sources around the world to leak information to our journalists'. It further states: 'The broader principles on which our work is based are the defence of freedom of speech and media publishing, the improvement of our common historical record and the support of the rights of all people to create new history. We derive these principles from the

Photo 20.3 **WikiLeaks founder Julian Assange** *Shutterstock RF: haak78/Shutterstock.com*

Universal Declaration of Human Rights' (https://wikileaks.org/About.html). By the end of 2010, Wikileaks had achieved extraordinary notoriety in global politics generally, and the diplomatic world in particular, due mainly to its release of classified material relating to the wars in Iraq and Afghanistan as well as the acquisition of more than 250,000 US diplomatic cables which it began releasing through a number of highly respected newspapers including the *Guardian*, the *New York Times*, *Le Monde*, *Der Spiegel*, and *El Pais*. In an editorial note accompanying the publication of some material from the confidential cables, the *New York Times* justified it on the basis that 'the documents serve an important public interest, illuminating the goals, success-es, compromises and frustrations of American diplomacy in a way that other accounts cannot match' (*New York Times*, 2010).

  Much of the documents' contents simply confirm what many already knew; for example, that the US administration believe—with good reason—that Russia is run like a 'mafia state'. Some documents, like the analysis provided by a former US Ambassador to Zimbabwe, are models of professional diplomatic reports providing frank, well-informed assessments of the situation in that country. More generally, Wikileaks has revealed the extent to which lies, deceit, and hypocrisy attend the pursuit of 'national interest'. And here the spotlight focuses squarely on the USA. While it has engaged in a concerted campaign against Wikileaks for disseminating classified material, with some US figures even calling for the assassination of Julian Assange, the leaked material has revealed the extent to which the USA is itself prepared to obtain intelligence

20

illicitly (Lawson, 2011). A *Guardian* article also summarized aspects of a 'secret intelligence campaign targeted at the leadership of the UN' including the Secretary General and the representatives of the other permanent Security Council members. One classified directive issued under Hillary Clinton's name in July 2009 sought forensic technical communications details relating to key UN officials, including passwords and personal encryption keys used in private and commercial networks for official communications as well as biometric information such as fingerprints and DNA. The article goes on to note that a 1946 UN convention on privileges and immunities states, among other things, that the premises of the UN 'shall be inviolable' (Booth and Border, 2010). The 1961 Vienna Convention on Diplomatic Relations also provides for the inviolability of a mission's premises, official documents, correspondence, and personnel (see United Nations, 1961).

Most of the documents released via Wikileaks had been redacted, which means that they have been edited prior to publication and, where appropriate, the names of people whose exposure might otherwise put them at risk have been concealed. This did not prevent accusations that Assange has 'blood on his hands' for exposing US operatives or agents to targeting by terrorists. Prominent Republican politician Sarah Palin went so far as to suggest that he should be hunted down just like the leaders of Al-Qaeda and the Taliban (quoted in Beckford, 2010). There is no evidence, however, that anyone was targeted as a result of the leaks. Interestingly, under the George W. Bush administration, and indeed at the instigation of two of his most senior staff, the name of a serving CIA undercover operative, Valerie Plame, was deliberately leaked to the media, possibly endangering her life. Her husband, former US diplomat Joe Wilson, had written an article exposing as false certain claims made by the Bush administration as a justification for the Iraq War. In all this, we may well ponder the distinction between 'national interest' and specific political interests (Lawson, 2011).

Assange himself has already paid a price for the leaks, taking refuge in the Ecuadorian embassy in London from June 2012 to April 2019, following charges brought against him in Sweden for sexual assault. Assange and supporters say these charges were trumped up and politically motivated and opened up the possibility for him to be extradited to the USA on espionage charges. In July 2013, the US Army soldier Chelsea Manning (formerly known as Bradley Manning) was convicted of espionage and sentenced to thirty-five years in prison for supplying Wikileaks with the massive cache of classified documents on the wars in Afghanistan and Iraq, although she was released after only seven years in an act of presidential clemency.

In the meantime, Wikileaks also became implicated in the enquiry into alleged Russian interference in the US Presidential campaign. A statement by Assange in November 2016 defended the release of over 30,000 confidential emails and attachments from the Hilary Clinton campaign, and at the same time said similar material from the Trump campaign would also have been released, if they had possessed it. Assange's message appeared to be especially hostile to Clinton and the Democrats because they had been critical of him and Wikileaks and had alleged collusion with Russia, which Assange denied (https://wikileaks.org/Assange-Statement-on-the-US-Election.html). In January 2019, however, the *New York Times* claimed to have evidence of contact between at least seventeen Trump campaign officials and advisors, Wikileaks, and Russian nationals (Yourish and Buchanan, 2019), while another respected publication, *The Atlantic*, commented on collusion as 'highly likely' with Assange appearing to play an intermediate role (Graham, 2018).

Questions

1. How important is secrecy in the world of diplomacy?
2. Does Wikileaks seriously undermine official diplomatic practice through its public release of otherwise confidential material, or is the threat exaggerated?

CONCLUSION

Diplomacy implies peaceful or at least non-violent interactions between political actors and 'diplomatic solutions' are frequently contrasted with military ones. By the mid-twentieth century the traditional role of diplomacy was certainly understood as a means of maintaining an international order in the interests of peace and stability (Butterfield, 1966: 190). The sections on summit diplomacy and public diplomacy, in particular, further reinforce the image of diplomacy as a peaceful instrument of policy. But diplomacy is not always a process of negotiation between equals. States are not equal in their capacities or capabilities and stronger states are often in a superior bargaining position. Indeed, diplomacy can well be aggressive and coercive, as reflected in the phrase 'gunboat diplomacy' in which the threat of force accompanies negotiations. Clausewitz famously proposed that war is simply 'the continuation of policy by other means' and a necessary instrument of foreign policy. But he also believed that if war had no specific, desirable political purpose, it was both stupid and wrong (Howard, 1966: 197). Diplomacy can certainly be accompanied by the proverbial sabre-rattling and shade into war. But diplomacy at its best is the very antithesis of war. It is a means by which conflicts and disagreements in the international sphere can be resolved peacefully via processes of negotiating, bargaining, and accommodation which spare all parties the prospect of death and destruction through direct violence. In the final analysis, foreign policies attuned to this end are much more likely to serve the 'national interest' than the resort to the far cruder instruments of force.

KEY QUESTIONS

1. What distinguishes diplomacy and statecraft from other forms of political activity?
2. If states are no longer considered the only relevant actors in the international sphere, do they remain the most effective when it comes to diplomatic activity?
3. To what extent has diplomatic practice achieved uniformity throughout the international state system?
4. Are there genuinely different styles of diplomacy according to cultural factors or is the influence of culture in this sense sometimes exaggerated?
5. What role did deterrence play in 'nuclear diplomacy' during the Cold War?
6. Under what circumstances is summit diplomacy most effective?

20

7. What factors are likely to make personal diplomacy succeed or fail?

8. Is public diplomacy simply propaganda on an international scale?

9. To what extent does President Trump's 'Twitter diplomacy' represent a new phenomenon in US diplomacy and foreign policy.

10. What is the Monroe doctrine and how does it illustrate the historic importance of geopolitics in US foreign policy?

11. What is distinctive about South-South foreign relations?

12. Do you believe that the EU can be truly effective as a foreign policy actor in its own right?

13. What long-term impact is Wikileaks likely to have on diplomatic behaviour?

FURTHER READING

Berridge, G. R. (2015), *Diplomacy: Theory and Practice* (Basingstoke: Palgrave Macmillan, 5th edn).
This text combines theoretical and historical perspectives on various styles and modes of diplomacy including discussion of key themes such as the art of negotiation, bilateral and multilateral diplomacy, summit diplomacy, and mediation. The author maintains a website on which he updates his work which extends to many different aspects of diplomacy and diplomatic history. See: https://grberridge.diplomacy.edu/

Bjola, C. and Kornprobst, M. (2018), *Understanding International Diplomacy: Theory, Practice and Ethics* (Abingdon: Routledge, 2nd edn).
This up-to-date text sets out the major trends in the field of diplomacy together with a theoretical approach which understands diplomacy not as a collection of practices or a set of historical traditions, but rather as a form of institutionalized communication. Includes discussion of the Syrian and Ukraine crises as well as problems in the South China sea.

Constantinou, C. M., Kerr, P., and Sharp, P. (eds) (2016), *The Sage Handbook of Diplomacy* (Thousand Oaks, CA: Sage).
Another substantial edited collection with contributions on a variety of diplomatic activity from secret diplomacy, coercive diplomacy, and revolutionary diplomacy to celebrity diplomacy, sports diplomacy, and digital diplomacy.

Hill, C. (2016), *Foreign Policy in the Twenty-First Century* (London: Palgrave, 2nd edn).
Starting with definitions and general background, this book goes on to explore foreign policy issues, concept, and approaches to the subject matter from a variety of perspectives.

Kerr, P. and Wiseman, G. (eds) (2017), *Diplomacy in a Globalising World* (Oxford: Oxford University Press).
The expert contributors to this edited volume of two chapters provide theoretical perspectives and historical background from a variety of Western and non-Western traditions as well as looking at contemporary issues and cases.

Shayam, S. (2018), *How India Sees the World: Kautilya to the 21st Century* (New Delhi: Juggernaut Books).
Authored by a former Indian diplomatic, this is a wide-ranging and very thoughtful book which provides both historical perspectives and contemporary insights on Indian statecraft with special reference to its neighbours in South Asia as well as China.

 For additional material and resources, please visit the Online Resources at:
www.oup.com/he/garner4e

21

INTERNATIONAL ORGANIZATIONS IN GLOBAL POLITICS

READER'S GUIDE

This chapter looks first at the nature of international organizations and the way in which they are generally understood as participants in global politics. It then reviews the rise of international organizations from a historical perspective, with particular reference to developments from the nineteenth century onwards. The chapter goes on to discuss the major intergovernmental institutions that emerged in the twentieth century and which have played such an important role in shaping global order. We look briefly at the League of Nations but most attention is given to its successor, the United Nations (UN), and its various appendages. Then there is the world of non-governmental organizations (NGOs), populated with a bewildering variety of bodies. Some possess significant status in the global sphere, others have little relevance, and still others pose

→

→

dangers. Finally, we consider social movements and their relationship to the contemporary world of international organizations along with the idea of global civil society. In reviewing these institutions, actors, and ideas we should keep in mind that liberal international theory, especially in the form of 'liberal institutionalism', as well as proponents of international society, regard robust international organizations as essential building blocks of global order.

WHAT IS AN INTERNATIONAL ORGANIZATION?

International organizations (IOs), from the UN down to voluntary organizations with constituent members in just a few countries, operate in a sphere which transcends states and the state system in one way or another. This does not mean that they are necessarily more powerful or more important than states but, like states, international organizations exist as tangible institutional products of social and political forces. Beyond that, they comprise clusters of ideas and coalitions of interest at a transnational level and generate purposeful activities in pursuit of certain desired outcomes. As we shall see, some have links with wider social movements. The environmental movement, for example, has generated a numerous IOs at local, national and global levels.

IOs may be public or private organizations, depending on whether they are set up by state actors or by non-state actors. Most are permanent, or at least aspire to an ongoing existence, even if many fall by the wayside. They invariably possess constitutional structures, although the extent to which they possess a legal personality is often unclear. Their power varies enormously, depending on the size and the resources at their disposal. And they come in such diverse forms that it is difficult to pin them down to one clear description. The term international organization also overlaps with international regime. The latter concept originated as a way of understanding international cooperation. As Keohane (1993: 23) explains, highly organized and systematic cooperation characterizes much of global politics, yet there are few rules that are hierarchically enforced. Rather, they are followed voluntarily and cooperatively, becoming embedded in relations of reciprocity. An international regime, though not itself an organization as such, usually incorporates one or more international organizations whose interests centre around a particular issue or theme. A prime example is the global or international human rights regime which revolves around a cluster of important norms and principles that give it its focus. It encompasses many organizations, including—but not limited to—the UN, and operates through processes and rules set up to promote and protect human rights at both national and international levels (see Rittberger and Zangl, 2006: 6–7).

Some definitions encompass multinational corporations, and these do fit a broad conception of what constitutes an international organization. However, multinationals are often treated separately from government and non-profit actors. The *Yearbook of International Organizations* list over 70,000 intergovernmental and non-governmental organizations. Around 40 per cent of these are dormant but, with around 1,200 new organizations being added each year, the field is

21

obviously still growing. The *Yearbook* does not include for-profit organizations such as multinationals (https://uia.org/yearbook).

Another category of IO, also excluded from most standard definitions, encompasses transnational criminal organizations or TCOs. They are included here because they are becoming increasingly important actors. They have been implicated very clearly in the 'new wars' described by Kaldor (2012) as combining traditional aspects of war with organized crime and involving actors at many levels. Whereas organized crime has been very largely a concern for domestic policing agencies in earlier periods, the development of TCOs has required increased policing cooperation in the international sphere to deal with their various activities which include drugs, money laundering, people smuggling, and weapons smuggling. One author notes that the emergence of TCOs results at least partly from the same underlying changes in the global sphere that have proved conducive to the success of transnational corporations. Thus, increased interdependence between states and the permeability of boundaries, developments in international travel and communications, and the globalization of international financial networks 'have facilitated the emergence of what is, in effect, a single global market for both licit and illicit commodities' (Williams, 1997: 316).

The UN Convention Against Transnational Organized Crime, otherwise known as the Palermo Convention, which has additional protocols on people trafficking and smuggling as well as on firearms, entered into force in 2003. It is seen as 'a major step forward in the fight against transnational organized crime and signifies the recognition by Member States of the seriousness of the problems posed by it, as well as the need to foster and enhance close international cooperation in order to tackle those problems' (https://www.unodc.org/unodc/en/organized-crime/intro/UNTOC.html). In addition to their sheer criminality, TCOs are also increasingly seen as threats to both national and international security. In the period after the 9/11 attacks, it was suggested that, even though they are primarily economic actors, they may facilitate the business of terror networks through the provision of money-laundering facilities, false documents, and the procurement of weapons or other material for terrorist purposes. There may also be a growing convergence between some terrorist organizations and organized crime networks (see Sanderson, 2004: 49–61; Dishman, 2005: 237–52). Major participants in the world of TCOs include Italian, Russian and American mafia groups, Chinese Triads, motorcycle gangs like the Hell's Angels, drug cartels, and hybrid entities like the Taliban that merge crime, terrorism, and insurgency (see Sullivan, 2014: 161).

For the remainder of the chapter we focus mainly on those IOs which are more conventionally recognized as such; namely, those set up by states through multilateral agreements, sometimes called intergovernmental organizations or IGOs, and those set up by non-state or non-government actors whose primary business is not strictly commercial (or illicit)—these are the ubiquitous non-governmental organizations or NGOs. An important theme here is the interaction between different organizations in the international sphere that make a model of international politics based almost exclusively on individual sovereign states acting on their own initiative and in their own interest seem very inadequate. At the same time, those who lean heavily in the other direction by exaggerating the importance of IOs can too easily dismiss the crucial role that states play, not simply in organizing their own affairs, but in creating the very world of IOs that may seem to make states less important in many areas. The quote in **Box 21.1** suggests an approach which balances these views.

21

> ❝ **KEY QUOTE** BOX 21.1
> International Organizations

There are two predominant views of international organizations among the general public. The first is a cynical view that emphasizes the dramatic rhetoric and seeming inability to deal with vital problems that are said to characterize international organizations generally and the United Nations in particular. According to this view, mirrored in some realist formulations, international organizations should be treated as insignificant actors on the international stage. The other view is an idealistic one. Those who hold this view envisage global solutions to the problems facing the world today, without recognition of the constraints imposed by state sovereignty. Most of the naïve calls for world government are products of this view. An understanding of international organizations and global governance probably requires that neither view be accepted in its entirety, nor be wholly rejected. International organizations are neither irrelevant nor omnipotent in global politics. They play important roles in international relations, but their influence varies according to the issue area and situation confronted. (Diehl, 2005a: 3)

KEY POINTS

- IOs come in such a variety of forms that they are difficult to define, both with respect to their relationship with states and the state system as well as in terms of their constituent elements.

- Although multinational corporations and terrorist and other criminal organizations operating in the international sphere do constitute IOs of a kind, they are usually treated separately.

- Scholars of global politics interested in the contribution that IOs make to the international system as a whole tend to focus on IGOs and NGOs.

THE EMERGENCE OF INTERNATIONAL ORGANIZATIONS

'History, prior to the nineteenth century, affords relatively few examples of international organizations' (Gerbet, 1981: 28). Although this is a widely accepted view, the myriad IOs of the present era do have important precursors. Previous chapters have shown that certain structures, systems, activities, and ideas which are generally taken as characteristic of contemporary relations between political communities did not simply emerge out of nothing in Western Europe in the modern period and then spread to the rest of the world. So, just as recognizable diplomatic practices have been manifest in different times in different places, so too have recognizable IOs. The earliest known examples appear to have been defensive leagues set up among small, neighbouring states. This was the case in at least one part of China between the seventh and the fifth centuries BC where assemblies met to organize their defences, while in ancient Greece rudimentary IOs were established to arbitrate on issues of mutual concern to a number of city-states (see, generally, Harle, 1998).

Examples of IOs in late medieval Europe include the Hanseatic League which operated between the fourteenth and sixteenth centuries and in which some fifty towns joined forces for the mutual protection of their trading interests, with representatives meeting in a general assembly to decide policy by majority voting. The Swiss confederation, dating from the late 1200s, and the United Provinces of the Netherlands, which emerged in the sixteenth century, although limited territorially, effectively started out as IOs (Gerbet, 1981: 28–9; Klabbers, 2003: 16). The Catholic Church, which held sway throughout much of Europe in earlier periods, may also be counted among the earliest IOs, and one with considerable political as well as cultural power. It was also probably one of the first organizations to establish a near universal presence in the modern period to match its name—'catholic' meaning universal in the sense of 'all-embracing'.

The scale of IOs in earlier times was necessarily constrained by limitations on mobility and communications, as was the phenomenon of globalization itself. As communications and transport technologies developed, so too did the capacity to form ongoing associations which eventually gave rise to formal organizations on a much broader, more inclusive scale, and which were intended to have a more or less permanent existence. The rise of the modern state system, together with technological advances in transport and communications, therefore, saw not only the enhancement of diplomatic networks and practices among states, but also an accompanying growth of organizations designed to facilitate the business of international relations as such. State actors may well have looked first to their own interests, but on a very wide range of matters those interests were likely to be enhanced by cooperation with other states, especially on issues concerning trade. And in turn, international cooperation was best achieved through certain kinds of organizations set up for particular purposes and through which rules and procedures agreed on by member states could be operationalized.

Also discussed in the previous chapter was the Concert of Europe or 'Concert system' which emerged among the great powers in post-Napoleonic Europe. This was not what we would call an IO since it lacked a constitution, a permanent secretariat, and a headquarters and did not meet on a regular basis (see Gerbet, 1981: 32). It may, nonetheless, be seen as a precursor to other major European developments in later years. The Concert system, as we have seen, started with the 1815 Congress of Vienna which provided a benchmark for inter-state cooperation on setting international boundaries and managing waterways (vital for trade) on the continent as well as establishing certain diplomatic protocols. Subsequent conferences generated as part of the Concert system established a pattern of interaction which nurtured important ideas about collective responsibility and a mutual commitment to 'concert together' against threats to the system. Most importantly, it established the idea that state's representatives should meet not merely to sign peace treaties at the end of a war, but also during peaceful periods to prevent war (Archer, 1983: 7). Thus IOs became a vital component of diplomatic processes.

➡ See Chapters 16 and 20 for more on the Concert of Europe.

Although the Concert system virtually ceased to exist after the mid-nineteenth century, the second half of that century did see further ad hoc conferences held on important matters of mutual interest. For example, the 1878 Congress of Berlin met to settle issues in the Balkans following the Russo-Turkish war of 1877–8 and included delegates from the major European powers and observers from several smaller European states with interests in the region as well as representatives of the Ottoman Empire. With the inclusion of the latter, the international element of such conferences was expanded beyond Europe into West Asia. Other treaties and conventions which reached beyond Europe were applied in relation to colonial territories and the USA, often with respect to the navigation of waterways to facilitate trade. The Hague Conferences of 1899 and 1907 established the principle of compulsory arbitration of disputes, giving the development of international law a significant boost.

21

It is noteworthy that the Congress of Vienna was the first significant international forum that took a stand on a broad humanitarian issue by condemning the slave trade as contrary to universal morality (Butler and MacCoby, 2003: 353). This was quite an unusual step for such a conference. But it is no coincidence that it occurred around the time that private organizations, many with a specific philanthropic mission, started to make their presence felt on the international scene as well. The anti-slavery movement in Britain, already active domestically and a prime force behind the Congress resolution, gave rise to an early NGO when its supporters coalesced into the 'Society for the Mitigation and Gradual Abolition of Slavery Throughout the British Dominions' in 1823. Anti-Slavery International, which operates today, was originally founded in 1839 and in 1840 a World Anti-Slavery Convention was held in London (see www.antislavery.org).

Anti-Slavery International is also associated with the International Labour Organization (ILO), itself established by the Treaty of Versailles in 1919 with the status of an autonomous institution but in association with the League of Nations. It survived the demise of the League and is now a UN agency. The early anti-slavery efforts were underpinned by concerted activism on the part of British women who had formed their own local anti-slavery societies and went on to forge international links, especially across the Atlantic. So, in these activities, we also see an emergent women's movement which spread nationally and internationally to take up various causes, including their own liberation. The ILO has also been a Nobel Peace Prize winner, receiving the award on its fiftieth anniversary in 1969 (see, generally, Hughes and Haworth, 2011).

Transport and communications technologies, so essential to both globalization and the emergence of functioning IOs, were themselves among the most important subjects of international agreements and formal associations. For example, the year 1865 saw the foundation of the International Telegraph Union (now the International Telecommunications Union), followed in 1874 by the Universal Postal Union, and in 1890 by the International Union of Railway Freight Transportation (Klabbers, 2003: 18). The two former organizations are now UN specialized agencies, again illustrating continuities in the system of IOs despite the massive disruption of two world wars in the twentieth century. But improvements in transport technologies brought with it other problems, including the more rapid spread of disease, and so concerns about international public health were reflected in the 1853 International Sanitary Convention and subsequent conventions and international offices.

Equally, the rapid development of industry and trade saw the introduction of an International Bureau of Weights and Measures in 1875 while, on the intellectual property front, the Union for the Protection of the Rights of Authors over their Literary and Artistic Property was established in 1884. Private associations at an international level began to outstrip intergovernmental ones in this period, accelerating the trend in internationalism. Such associations were set up in connection with every kind of activity including the humanitarian, religious, ideological, scientific, and technological (Gerbet, 1981: 36).

At the first World Congress of International Organizations held in Brussels in 1910, convened under the auspices of the Union of International Associations, 132 international bodies and thirteen governments were represented. A second world congress in Ghent and Brussels in 1913 saw 169 international associations and twenty-two governments represented. The last world congress of this type (the seventh) was held in 1927 after which the League of Nations assumed responsibility (www.uia.org/history). The overall trend to internationalism in the century before the outbreak of the First World War might have indicated that a new era of peaceful international relations was about to dawn. But other forces, including those of nationalism, were also at work. The death and destruction of 1914–18 was, for a number of key actors, the clarion call for a permanent

IGO supporting a strong framework for international law and designed, above all, to prevent further international conflict, a need reinforced rather than undermined by the Second World War.

KEY POINTS

- Although forms of IO existed before the nineteenth century, in Europe and elsewhere, the Congress of Vienna in 1815 acted as a catalyst for their rapid growth in the nineteenth century, which also helped underpin a nascent body of international law.

- Private organizations also achieved a significant international presence in the nineteenth and early twentieth centuries, those with philanthropic aims contributing to the development of humanitarian principles and the idea of international morality.

- Developments in transport and communications technologies provided a boost to the growth of IOs and themselves became the subject of international agreements and associations along with a host of other agreements.

INTERGOVERNMENTAL ORGANIZATIONS

The supremo of all IGOs is the UN—officially styled the United Nations Organization—with near universal membership of the world's states. Its founding commitment is to 'maintaining international peace and security, developing friendly relations among nations and promoting social progress, better living standards and human rights' (http://www.un.org/en/about-un/). The early development of the UN and the role of the Security Council has already been set out, so we focus here on other aspects of the UN's history, structure, and mission. But first, it is useful to recall the key ideas behind the development of its predecessor organization, the League of Nations. These ideas were to come under attack from realists in later years for their vision of a peaceful global order founded on strong institutions of global governance and an explicit emphasis on the place of morality in the international sphere rather than naked self-interest. The preface to US President Woodrow Wilson's famous Fourteen Points address to the US Congress in January 1918 stands as one of the clearest statements of the idealist vision of global order in that period. The preface was followed by a 'program of the world's peace', the fourteenth point of which proposed the formation of a general association of nations, an idea given substance by the formation of the League of Nations in the immediate aftermath of the war.

➡ See Chapter 17 for a discussion of liberal theory and the League of Nations.

We have seen that the League of Nations has sometimes been described as a failed experiment because it did not prevent the Second World War. It could also be argued, however, that the Second World War illustrated just how important it is to have a strong, functioning IGO to provide for collective security as well as many other matters requiring international support and coordination. In any event, a number of key institutions and practices set up under the League's auspices survived and are enshrined in the present UN system (see Jackson and O'Malley, 2018). Certainly, the latter owes much to the previous experiment in global governance which, in turn, drew on the earlier experiences of the Concert system, thus demonstrating continuity over almost two centuries.

The UN emerged from the wartime cooperation between the major allied powers of the time, with many other states then joining in to create a more truly international body operating under a formal charter setting out the rights and obligations of members. The preamble to the Charter states the general principles and ideals on which the organization is based (**Box 21.2**). The main organs of the UN are set out in the UN's official organizational chart (see www.un.org/aboutun/chartlg.html).

21

BOX 21.2
Preamble to the Charter of the United Nations

Photo 21.1 **The United Nations Flag.** *UN Photo: UN Photo/John Isaac*

We the Peoples of the United Nations Determined

- to save succeeding generations from the scourge of war, which twice in our lifetime has brought untold sorrow to mankind, and
- to reaffirm faith in fundamental human rights, in the dignity and worth of the human person, in the equal rights of men and women and of nations large and small, and
- to establish conditions under which justice and respect for the obligations arising from treaties and other sources of international law can be maintained, and
- to promote social progress and better standards of life in larger freedom,

And for these Ends

- to practice tolerance and live together in peace with one another as good neighbours, and
- to unite our strength to maintain international peace and security, and
- to ensure, by the acceptance of principles and the institution of methods, that armed force shall not be used, save in the common interest, and
- to employ international machinery for the promotion of the economic and social advancement of all peoples.

(www.un.org/en/sections/un-charter/preamble/index.html)

21

The business of the first organ, the Trusteeship Council, set up for the purpose of dealing with eleven non-self-governing trust territories, which had formerly been League of Nations mandate territories, was terminated in 1994 when the last trust territory, administered by the USA, chose self-government and became an independent state. The second, and most powerful, of the UN's organs is, of course, the Security Council, discussed earlier. The third, and some may say the weakest, as well as being the largest, is the General Assembly. A common criticism is that it produces little but endless resolutions which are largely ineffective because there is no mechanism for enforcing them. This illustrates the fact that the UN General Assembly cannot be compared directly to a legislature because, although its resolutions may carry normative force, and guide policy, they cannot have the same legal status as legislation produced by a parliament within a national sphere. However, it would be a mistake to dismiss the significance of the General Assembly as a debating forum. It is the one place where representatives from all states can meet on a more or less equal footing, express views, and debate the full range of issues in international politics. It is, moreover, a key forum for both formal and informal diplomacy and strategic alliances on issues that come up for a vote. This does not necessarily produce desirable outcomes, let alone outcomes that satisfy everyone, but that is in the nature of any political body.

The Economic and Social Council (ECOSOC) has a mandate to initiate studies and reports and to formulate policy recommendations extending over an enormous range of economic and social issues covering living standards; full employment; international economic, social, and health problems; facilitating international cultural and educational cooperation; and encouraging universal respect for human rights and fundamental freedoms. Some of the best-known UN agencies, such as the World Health Organization (WHO), the Food and Agricultural Organization (FAO), the United Nations Educational, Scientific and Cultural Organization (UNESCO), and the World Bank group all fall under its rubric. It has a major role in organizing the many international conferences initiated by the UN and oversees the functional commissions, regional commissions, and other special bodies set out in the organizational chart. Given its scope and size, ECOSOC is by far the largest of the UN's principal organs and expends more than 70 per cent of the human and financial resources of the entire UN system (see www.un.org/ecosoc/en/about-us).

One of ECOSOC's most difficult and controversial functional commissions has been that dealing with human rights, and a brief account of developments in this area illustrates just how problematic it is to achieve coherence in regimes of global governance. The establishment of a Human Rights Commission (HRC) was mandated by the UN's Charter and reflected the abhorrence at the atrocities of the Second World War. Past wars had produced some appalling cases of cruelty and ill-treatment, but the nature of the genocidal policies of Nazi Germany was unprecedented. Beginning with the Universal Declaration of Human Rights (UDHR), which was adopted by the General Assembly in 1948 (**Box 21.3**), the Commission produced a raft of human rights documents and treaties over a period of almost sixty years. The behaviour of many governments around the world over that period, however, demonstrates clearly that the existence of the Charter, or the fact that all members of the UN must endorse the UDHR, is no guarantee that basic human rights will be respected or protected.

➡ For further discussion of human rights, see Chapter 9.

Since the Charter was first drawn up, there has been a strong tendency to divide the broad concept of human rights into two distinct cluster concerns: civil and political rights on the one hand, and economic, social, and cultural rights on the other. The division between the two groups, and whether one group is more important than the other, has been the subject of much debate in

21

BOX 21.3
The Universal Declaration of Human Rights (UDHR)

The UDHR was adopted by the General Assembly of the United Nations on 10 December 1948, reflecting a moment in international history when all member states could agree, at least in principle, to a substantial list of human rights ranging from the basic right to life to a host of economic and social goods. All new members joining the UN must sign up to the UDHR.

The Preamble highlights ideals which 'recognize the inherent dignity and of the equal and inalienable rights of all members of the human family is the foundation of freedom, justice and peace in the world'; it notes the extent to which 'disregard and contempt for human rights have resulted in barbarous acts which have outraged the conscience of mankind'; and heralds 'the advent of a world in which human beings shall enjoy freedom of speech and belief and freedom from fear and want has been proclaimed as the highest aspiration of the common people'.

The Declaration itself contains thirty articles, the first ten of which are set out here:

Article 1: All human beings are born free and equal in dignity and rights. They are endowed with reason and conscience and should act towards one another in a spirit of brotherhood.

Article 2: Everyone is entitled to all the rights and freedoms set forth in this Declaration, without distinction of any kind, such as race, colour, sex, language, religion, political or other opinion, national or social origin, property, birth or other status. Furthermore, no distinction shall be made on the basis of the political, jurisdictional or international status of the country or territory to which a person belongs, whether it be independent, trust, non-self-governing or under any other limitation of sovereignty.

Article 3: Everyone has the right to life, liberty and security of person.

Article 4: No one shall be held in slavery or servitude; slavery and the slave trade shall be prohibited in all their forms.

Article 5: No one shall be subjected to torture or to cruel, inhuman or degrading treatment or punishment.

Article 6: Everyone has the right to recognition everywhere as a person before the law.

Article 7: All are equal before the law and are entitled without any discrimination to equal protection of the law. All are entitled to equal protection against any discrimination in violation of this Declaration and against any incitement to such discrimination.

Article 8: Everyone has the right to an effective remedy by the competent national tribunals for acts violating the fundamental rights granted him by the constitution or by law.

Article 9: No one shall be subjected to arbitrary arrest, detention or exile.

Article 10: Everyone is entitled in full equality to a fair and public hearing by an independent and impartial tribunal, in the determination of his rights and obligations and of any criminal charge against him.

(http://www.un.org/en/universal-declaration-human-rights/index.html)

21

international politics, as illustrated in **Box 21.4**, along with recurrent issues of sovereignty and non-intervention.

The fifth main organ of the UN is the International Court of Justice (ICJ) located in The Hague. As with other parts of the UN system, its origins can be traced to much earlier periods and linked to the gradual development in the modern era of methods of mediation and arbitration of disputes

KEY DEBATE BOX 21.4
The Politics of Human Rights in the UN

Civil and political rights are sometimes seen as possessing a typically 'Western' liberal character unsuited to the cultural context of non-Western countries. The most vocal proponents of this view have come from a number of Middle Eastern and African countries and parts of South East and East Asia, especially China. In addition, economic, social, and cultural rights are often regarded as more urgent for poorer, underdeveloped countries than the right to vote (although human rights activists in such countries generally do not support these kinds of 'culturalist' or 'developmentalist' arguments).

An early division of opinion on the two different clusters of rights gave rise to the development of separate covenants for each and so in 1976 the International Covenant on Civil and Political Rights (ICCPR) and the International Covenant on Economic, Social and Cultural Rights (ICESCR), entered into force. Apart from representing two broad approaches to rights, the covenants also represent a significant attempt to advance the codification of human rights as such and to introduce an international legal framework to support their advancement. Member states are not obliged to sign up to the covenants, but those that do so agree to accept their provisions as legal obligations as well as moral obligations.

The history of human rights issues in the UN has also been plagued by competing conceptions of what the UN can and cannot, or should and should not do, to advance the protection of human rights around the world. On the one hand, the UN is committed to respect for state sovereignty and therefore to the notion that each state is entitled to conduct its own affairs free from external interference. On the other hand, it is committed to the universality of human rights, which implies that it is not only entitled, but also actually enjoined, to act to promote and protect human rights wherever and whenever such action is needed. But any action—even mere criticism of state practices—can be construed as a violation of state sovereignty. The HRC itself was frequently caught between these imperatives and contradictions. Apart from issues of state sovereignty versus universal human rights principles, some countries represented on the Commission at any one time were themselves countries where human rights abuses—often perpetrated by the government—were being carried out. However, countries with poor human rights records—mainly outside 'the West'—complained of being unfairly singled out for criticism. This also led to accusations of attempted interference in the internal affairs of sovereign states. By 2006, the HRC was seen as an ineffectual and largely discredited body. It was replaced by a new Human Rights Council which has revised terms for membership and functions. But it has so far failed to make any real difference due at least partly to the way in which the UN's human rights machinery is still manipulated and undermined by rights abusive regimes which are of course UN members themselves (see Freedman, 2015).

Questions
1. Can human rights really be divided into different categories?
2. Under what circumstances, if any, should state sovereignty be violated to protect human rights?

21

between states. Its immediate predecessor, the Permanent Court of International Justice (PCIJ), was part of the League of Nations system and operated from 1922, until it was dissolved in 1946 to make way for the new UN court. The fifteen judges of the ICJ are elected for nine-year terms by both the United Nations General Assembly and the Security Council. The ICJ functions as something of a world court with the jurisdiction to decide legal disputes submitted to it by states and to give advisory opinions on legal questions at the request of UN organs or authorized agencies. Between May 1947 and January 2019, 176 cases had been entered into its General List (https://www.icj-cij.org/en/cases). Examples of cases pending in 2019 included Islamic Republic of Iran *v.* United States of America over certain Iranian assets; Ukraine *v.* the Russian Federation over both funding of terrorism and racial discrimination; and Palestine *v.* the United States of America over the relocation of the latter's embassy to Jerusalem (https://www.icj-cij.org/en/pending-cases).

One notable case was brought with respect to the application of the Convention on the Prevention and Punishment of the Crime of Genocide (*Bosnia and Herzegovina v. Serbia and Montenegro*) on which judgment was delivered in February 2007. The 171-page judgment dealt with a number of issues, and the case of Srebrenica in particular. This village was the scene of the single biggest massacre in Europe since the end of the Second World War when Serb forces killed approximately 8,000 Bosnian Muslim males. While the court found Serbia and Montenegro not guilty of *deliberately perpetrating a genocide*, it was found guilty of *failing to prevent* a genocide and therefore in breach of its obligations in international law (see https://www.icj-cij.org/en/case/91). This case was separate from the trial of former Serb President Slobodan Milošević which was conducted by a special tribunal, the International Criminal Tribunal for the Former Yugoslavia (ICTY), which was established by a UN Security Council resolution. Milošević's trial ended prematurely with his death in 2006 (although the trial had already run for four years by then) but was nonetheless seen as a landmark case because it was the first time a former head of state had been put on trial before an international criminal tribunal.

➜ For background to the conflict in former Yugoslavia, see Chapter 9.

The sixth and final organ comprises the UN Secretariat and the office of the Secretary-General. The organizational map of the General Assembly alone, which currently brings together 193 member states at least annually, as well as running important offices and conferences and providing services in six official languages (English, French, Arabic, Chinese, Russian, and Spanish), makes clear how extensive the demand for the services of a secretariat are (see, generally, Gordenker, 2010). The Secretary-General also seems to be expected to be everywhere at once and possess an encyclopaedic knowledge not only of the UN system itself, but also of all the world's troubles, both current and potential. In practice, the Secretary-General will often appoint a representative for much routine committee work. One particularly important role for the Secretary-General is to bring matters likely to affect international peace and security to the attention of the Security Council and to report regularly on operations that the UN is involved in. Although the Secretary-General has no authority beyond issuing formal warnings of trouble and delivering information, including anything gleaned from informal discussions, the importance of this function should not be underestimated.

21

The UN has also populated the sphere of IOs with a plethora of agencies and special programmes; the WHO, the FAO, UNICEF, and UNESCO have already been mentioned and the UN's organizational chart lists many more. Some, like UNICEF, are well known but others such as the United Nations Population Fund (UNFPA) are unlikely to register immediately in the minds of the general public. Others have emerged in more recent years to deal with problems unheard of in earlier periods. These include the joint United Nations Programme on HIV/AIDS (UNAIDS). Then there are regional commissions dealing with all the major regions of the world: Africa, Europe, Latin America and the Caribbean, Asia and the Pacific, and Western Asia (more commonly called the Middle East).

The UN and its agencies do not have the IGO field entirely to themselves. There are also a growing number of regional organizations. The EU and ASEAN have been mentioned in previous chapters but there are many others as well, from the African Union (AU) and the Pacific Islands Forum (PIF) to numerous trading blocs such as MERCOSUR in Latin America and the North American Free Trade Agreement (NAFTA). These reflect another significant development in the world of IOs, and that is the trend to regionalization, which we examine in the final chapter. For the moment, we may note that this trend, which has been gathering pace over the last few decades, is likely to have a significant impact in the future, but one which complements rather than undermines the role of the UN. More generally, this points to a future in which IGOs are likely to play an increasingly important role in global order rather than a diminishing one.

KEY POINTS

- The League of Nations is often seen as a failure, but it was nonetheless an important fore-runner to the UN and a number of its institutions have been maintained as part of the latter system.

- The UN is the largest single IGO with five functioning main organs and a plethora of pro-grammes, agencies, commissions, funds, courts, and tribunals involved in different aspects of global governance.

- Although the UN is the principle organ of global governance it does not possess the characteristics of a 'world government' in so far as its constituent members maintain sovereign authority within their own borders and do not form a 'world state'.

NON-GOVERNMENTAL ORGANIZATIONS (NGOS)

The non-state variety of IO sometimes goes by the acronym INGO—which simply stands for *international* non-governmental organization—but for present purposes we shall make do with the more common term NGO. Like IOs in general, NGOs cannot be defined in a completely straightforward way. Generally speaking, however, they share the following characteristics: they are formal rather than ad hoc entities; they aspire to be self-governing according to their own constitutional set-up; they are private in the sense that they operate independently from governments; and they do not make or distribute profits. This describes both national and international bodies, so for those which operate outside of the national sphere, we need to add that they obviously have formal transnational links (see Gordenker and Weiss, 1996: 20).

There are other types of organization which fall somewhere between the government and non-government spheres and, although they often claim to be NGOs, they do not really conform

21

to the description given previously. Gordenker and Weiss identify three significant deviations. The first are 'government-organized non-government organizations' or GONGOs—entities created by governments usually as front organizations for their own purposes (see Chapter 14). These were typically produced by communist countries during the Cold War, but the USA and other Western countries sponsored some as well. Chinese GONGOs in the contemporary period are said to represent an aspect of state corporatism, and little agency of their own (Marchetti, 2018: 22). In this scenario, the functions of civil society remain under state control and surveillance, which severely limits the extent to which they can be seen as part of civil society at all. Today, there is a wide variety of GONGOs, many of which serve dubious causes. The excerpt from an article published in *Foreign Affairs* on the subject of GONGOS, and the dangers that some of them pose, is highly instructive as to their role in the sphere of IOs (**see Box 21.5**).

Another special type of organization is the quasi-autonomous NGO or QUANGO, which is typically funded largely by governments but operates autonomously. Unlike GONGOs, the relationship to government is a transparent one and no subterfuge is intended. The third type is the donor-organized NGO or DONGO. In this case, agencies such as the United Nations Development Program (UNDP) might organize and fund NGOs to coordinate or carry out projects (Gordenker and Weiss, 1996: 20–1). A significant number of other NGOs enjoy consultative status with the UN or, more specifically, one of its councils or agencies. The UN's Economic and Social Council, for example, accords consultative status of some kind to more than 3,000 NGOs ranging from the Adventist Development Relief Agency to the World Press Freedom Committee. These are allied in turn to specific UN agencies such as UNESCO, the FAO, and the WHO.

The practice of according UN consultative status to NGOs dates back to 1946 when ECOSOC granted such status to just over forty NGOs. Growth was steady over the next forty-five years and by 1992 there were more than 700 NGOs with consultative status. As indicated previously, that

> ### ❝ KEY QUOTE BOX 21.5
> #### How Government-Sponsored Groups Masquerade as Civil Society

Behind this contradictory and almost laughable tongue twister [gongo] lies an important and growing global trend that deserves more scrutiny: governments funding and controlling non-governmental organizations (NGOs), often stealthily. Some gongos are benign, others irrelevant. But many . . . are dangerous. Some act as the thuggish arm of repressive governments. Others use the practices of democracy to subtly undermine democracy at home. Abroad, the gongos of repressive regimes lobby the United Nations and other international institutions, often posing as representatives of citizen groups with lofty aims when, in fact, they are nothing but agents of the governments that fund them. Some governments embed their gongos deep in the societies of other countries and use them to advance their interests abroad . . . The globalization and effectiveness of nongovernmental organizations will suffer if we don't find reliable ways of distinguishing organizations that truly represent democratic civil society from those that are tools of uncivil, undemocratic governments.   (Naím, 2007)

21

number has since increased to more than 3,000. There are various rules and criteria governing eligibility. Among the most basic are:

1. the organization must have been in existence (officially registered with the appropriate government authorities as an NGO/non-profit) for at least two years;
2. it must have an established headquarters;
3. it must possess a democratically adopted constitution, authority to speak for its members, a representative structure, appropriate mechanisms of accountability, and democratic and transparent decision-making processes;
4. its basic resources must be derived mainly from contributions of the national affiliates or other components or from individual members; and
5. it must not have been established by governments or intergovernmental agreements (see http://csonet.org/index.php?menu=30).

Many NGOs have a specific philanthropic or humanitarian purpose. Sometimes these are underpinned by religious beliefs but are just as likely to be secular. Many are aligned with broader movements such as the environmental movement, the labour movement, the ecumenical movement, the peace movement, the indigenous rights movement, and the women's movement. More will be said about the role of these broader movements later in this chapter.

Examples of some of the better known NGOs reflecting the ideals of one or other of these movements, or sometimes two or more of them, are the Worldwide Fund for Nature, Greenpeace, the World Council of Churches, the World Peace Council, the International Women's Health Coalition, Médecins Sans Frontières, the Red Cross/Red Crescent, and Amnesty International, to name just a few. A brief account of the Red Cross/Red Crescent Movement provides a case study of how one of the earliest NGOs operating in the international sphere has grown to be the largest humanitarian organization in the world. In addition, it was the prime mover behind the original Geneva Convention which has become the most important international convention relating to the conduct of warfare (**see Box 21.6**).

 CASE STUDY BOX 21.6
The Origins and Development of the International Red Cross/Red Crescent Movement

In 1859, Henry Dunant, a travelling Swiss businessman, witnessed one of the bloodiest battles of the nineteenth century in northern Italy when Napoleon III joined with local forces to drive Austrians from the country. Dunant subsequently published a small book which depicted, among other things, the battlefield after fighting had ceased, describing not just the dead but also the plight of the wounded and their desperate need for care. He went on to devise a plan for national relief societies to aid the wounded of war.

In February 1863, the Société Genevoise d'utilité Publique (Geneva Society for Public Welfare) appointed a committee of five, including Dunant, to consider how the plan could be put into action. This committee, which effectively founded the Red Cross, called for an international conference to pursue Dunant's basic objectives. Dunant put his own time and

21

Photo 21.2 The Red Cross organization is an NGO established in 1881. *dinosmichail/Shutterstock.com*

money into the project, travelling throughout much of Europe to persuade governments to send representatives. The conference was held in October 1863 with thirty-nine delegates from sixteen nations.

Just under a year later, twelve nations signed the International Convention for the Amelioration of the Condition of the Wounded and Sick in Armed Forces in the Field, otherwise known as the Geneva Convention of 1864. The convention provided for guaranteed neutrality for medical personnel and officially adopted the red cross on a field of white as the identifying emblem (the Red Crescent was adopted in most Muslim countries).

Three other conventions were later added to cover naval warfare, prisoners of war, and civilians. Revisions of these conventions have been made periodically, the most extensive being in 1949 relating to the treatment of prisoners of war. The International Committee of the Red Cross remains based in Geneva and the International Federation of Red Cross and Red Crescent Societies has a presence in every country, although in Iran it operates as the Red Lion and Sun. The Red Cross has been associated with four Nobel Peace Prizes, with the very first Nobel Peace Prize being awarded to Henry Dunant himself in 1901 (see https://www.nobelprize.org/prizes/peace/1963/red-cross/history/).

As an example of how national branches work today in situations of violent conflict, 9,000 volunteers with the Syrian Red Crescent (known formally as the Syrian Arab Red Crescent and founded in 1942), have been working with the UN to deliver aid to thousands of internally displaced people in Syria (http://sarc.sy/category/sarc-news/).

KEY POINTS

- IGOs, especially the UN and its agencies, often have a close working relationship with NGOs and have established structures supporting the work of many NGOs.

- Not all NGOS are 'good' in the sense that they make a positive contribution. Some are merely fronts for nefarious activities by dictatorial governments and may work actively to undermine the efforts of other organizations with respect, for example, to human rights issues.

- Many NGOs are also allied with broader movements, thus contributing to a complex web of relationships between different kinds of actors, both state and non-state, in the international sphere.

SOCIAL MOVEMENTS AND GLOBAL CIVIL SOCIETY

The foregoing discussion indicates that many NGOs are involved in philanthropic or humanitarian causes, some of which are embedded in broader social movements. The term 'social movement' is generally understood to denote some kind of collective action, driven by a particular set of social concerns and emerging from society at large rather than through the governmental institutions of the state. Indeed, a feature of many social movements is an oppositional posture vis-à-vis certain aspects of state or governmental activity. In this respect they are often seen as a manifestation of grass-roots democracy expressing or articulating non-mainstream issues and agendas. As we have seen, social movements often transcend the domestic sphere, an early example being the anti-slavery movement. When a movement achieves a transnational profile and popular following, it obviously achieves the status of an international or global social movement. These often reflect shifting coalitions of interests around issue-oriented activities. But, what social movements and the NGOs associated with them usually represent in one way or another is a 'cause', very often in relation to what is perceived as an injustice and/or a danger: Third World poverty, environmental degradation, nuclear weapons, the oppression of indigenous communities, and so on.

To take the latter example, the fact that the concept of indigenous rights has been firmly entrenched in the UN system—and given expression in a raft of measures adopted by some (mainly liberal Western) states with minority indigenous populations—has grown out of a general social movement that in turn gave rise to specific organized entities (NGOs) that have lobbied hard for recognition at local, national, and global levels. The origins of the movement are diffuse, but two general catalysts were the civil rights movement in the US from the 1950s and the anti-apartheid movement in South Africa, both of which attracted wider international sympathy and support, including that of the Anti-Slavery Movement. That sympathy and support was soon extended to minority groups in many states around the world. One major NGO is the International Work Group for Indigenous Affairs (IWEIA). It was founded in 1968 in response to an alarm raised by anthropologists about the ongoing genocide of indigenous peoples in the Amazon. It has gone on to establish a network of researchers and activists to document the situation of indigenous peoples and advocate for their rights (see https://www.iwgia.org/en/about). There is also a World Council of Indigenous People founded in Canada in 1975 and dedicated to 'developing unity among Indigenous peoples throughout

21

the world, strengthening their organizations, and battling the racism, injustice, and dangers they continue to face' (https://canadianhistory.ca/natives/timeline/1970s/1975-the-world-council-of-indigenous-peoples). There is now a UN Permanent Forum on Indigenous Issues (UNPFII), established in 2000, which acts as a high- level advisory body to the Economic and Social Council, and a UN Declaration on the Rights of Indigenous Peoples adopted by the General Assembly in 2007 (https://www.humanrights.gov.au/our-work/un-declaration-rights-indigenous-peoples-1). This very brief account illustrates the linkages between a diffuse movement, based on a rising social consciousness concerning a particular set of problematic issues, and leading in turn to the emergence of organized action in the form of NGOs and, eventually, to a global indigenous rights regime supported by the UN.

These broad social movements and the world of NGOs, taken together, are said to constitute a kind of *global* civil society which has an important role in the general sphere of global governance. The idea of global civil society can also be understood initially in terms of its domestic counterpart discussed in Chapter 14 along with the role of NGOs and interest group politics. Civil society names a sphere of human association not mediated by the state, or at least not directly. Thus it signifies the activities of individuals as participants in groups or collectivities that have a private purpose—private in the sense that they are not part of the realm of formal state or governmental activity. They include professional associations, charities, interest groups, businesses, and so on. Their freedom of organization and articulation of interests is widely regarded as another important manifestation of democracy, and so the repression of civil society organizations and activities is seen as characteristic of authoritarian systems, as discussed in Chapter 15. Many civil society groups are obviously NGOs, but some do not fall easily into the definition of the latter. Also, not all NGOs are connected to social movements. It follows that, although we can often connect NGOs to social movements and in turn class these as part of civil society, we cannot simply conflate the lot into one seamless whole.

➡ See Chapter 14 for a discussion of civil society.

Just as domestic civil society names a sphere that is autonomous of direct government control, so global civil society may be understood as standing apart from the formal, intergovernmental structures of global governance. And as with social movements, global civil society may be regarded not merely as distinct from that sphere, but sometimes positioned in opposition to the realm of formal state-based or state-generated activities. It is, therefore, another avenue through which democratic expression can take place. Certainly, those who look for democratic transformations in the international sphere and promote a form of 'cosmopolitan democracy'—a project involving the extension of democratic accountability to the global sphere, as discussed in Chapter 4—are broadly supportive of the positive role that global civil society has to play in such a process. How ideas of global civil society may be approached from different theoretical perspectives is set out briefly in **Box 21.7**.

Another point to consider is how the plurality of civil society groups around the world, and the notion of global civil society, have most often been analysed through the lens of Western scholarship, and whether this has limited understanding of how civil society groups operate in different contexts and what values they promote. In developing societies, understanding how local groups organize themselves, for example, around gender issues or aid programmes, may require a very different set of conceptualizations about civil society and how it operates, and these may also vary from one local context to the next (see, generally, Kamruzzaman, 2019). One must also take into account some of the power dynamics operating. When it comes to 'doing good', for example, women from the Global North who engage in NGO activities to aid and assist women in the Global South, may not only fail to grasp the different context within which the latter must operate, but generally do so from positions of power and privilege which may perpetuate continuities between the colonial 'civilizing mission' and development (de Jong, 2017: 1–2).

> **BOX** 21.7
> Theorizing Global Civil Society

Different theoretical perspectives can be used to interpret global civil society. Liberals may understand it as providing space for actors which then provide a bottom-up contribution to the effectiveness and legitimacy of the international system as a whole. In essence, it is democracy in action as power is being held to account by the populace. Realists, however, may interpret global civil society as a tool used by the most powerful states to advance their ultimate interests abroad, often promoting and popularising ideas that are key to the national interest. Marxists may see global civil society as political vanguards that can spread a different world view that challenges the dominant order. Finally, some even argue that the concept of civil society as a sphere distinct from the family, state and market remains a Western concept that does not apply easily to societies where the boundaries between these spheres are more blurred (excerpt from Marchetti, 2016).

➡ See Chapter 18 for a discussion of liberalism and realism.

➡ See Chapter 19 for a discussion of Marxism.

At another level, we must also consider whether social movements and the broad sphere of global civil society, and the NGOs which are the principle vehicles of activity in these arenas, present a serious challenge to the traditional structures generated by state sovereignty and the state system. As we have seen, many NGOs have a close association with the UN and its programmes and agencies. So although we may distinguish NGOs from the UN as such, they have come to form an important part of the UN system as a whole. Social movements and global civil society are, therefore, at least partly enmeshed in the web of relations created by IOs including the more formal intergovernmental institutions of global governance.

KEY POINTS

- Global social movements reflect particular sets of concerns coalescing around issues such as the environment, indigenous rights, arms control, and so on, and which engender collective action on a global scale.

- Global civil society, as a sphere of action and interaction standing apart from formal intergovernmental structures and sometimes in opposition to it, constitutes the space within which both international NGOs and social movements more generally operate.

- Both social movements and global civil society are often regarded as enhancing the space and substance of democratic activity at a supranational level.

CONCLUSION

Realist views of how the international or global sphere is organized see states and the state system as the standard units around which almost everyone and everything else revolves, and with international activity of any real consequence being generated by state actors and with state interests firmly in mind. It follows from this view that the role of virtually all other institutions and actors is subordinate, including any form of IO. Indeed, some realists may dismiss the whole

21

project of global governance, composed of the efforts of both state and non-state actors, as of little relevance in the 'real world' of **power politics**. But realist views comprise only one, admittedly influential, view of how the international system works. Liberal views, especially those described as 'liberal institutionalist', occupy a quite different general position. For liberals, it is largely through IOs that the dangerous aspects of international **anarchy** can be ameliorated, and all states have an interest in this. Both the League of Nations and the UN represent a practical manifestation of liberal international theory. As for the fluid realm of NGOs, social movements, and global civil society, these may be seen as an important complement to the more formal sphere of IO and global governance, often acting in concert with it but sometimes opposing and resisting their policies and practices. However we may regard them, IOs have become such an integral part of the international system, and indeed of global or **international society**, that it is difficult to imagine a world without them.

KEY QUESTIONS

1. What are the key characteristics of IOs?
2. How does an international regime differ from an IO?
3. How and why did IOs emerge in the modern period?
4. To what extent has there been a continuity of IOs over the last two centuries?
5. Was the League of Nations a complete failure?
6. On what general principles is the UN founded?
7. Is it possible for the UN to reconcile respect for state sovereignty and respect for universal human rights?
8. Could the UN do more as an IO, or is it expected to do too much as it is?
9. What role do NGOs and social movements play in the global system?
10. How can global civil society enhance opportunities for democratic expression?
11. How might concepts of civil society and social movements differ according to cultural context?
12. How can we deploy IR theory to interpret the role of IOs in global order?

FURTHER READING

Breitmeier, H. (2016), *The Legitimacy of International Regimes* (Abingdon: Routledge).
Explains and critically assesses the role of international regimes and non-state actors in contemporary global order with a particular focus on global environmental regimes and issues of legitimacy and efficacy.

Cogan, J. K., Hurd, I., and Johnstone, I. (2016), *The Oxford Handbook of International Organizations* (Oxford: Oxford University Press).
Covers a very wide range of issues concerning the evolution of IOs including the forces driving their formation, to their accountability under international law, to the multitude of forms they take and the activities they pursue.

21

Karns, M. P. and Mingst, K. A. (2009), *International Organizations: The Politics and Processes of Global Governance* (Boulder, CO: Lynne Rienner).

Covers a wide range of IGOs and NGOs as well as norms and rules, issues of legitimacy and accountability, problems of human rights, development, and the environment relating to IOs. Included are case studies focusing on contemporary concerns such as conflict in the Congo and attempts to combat human trafficking.

Murdie, A. (2014), *Help or Harm: The Human Security Effects of International NGOs* (Stanford, CA: Stanford University Press).

An interesting exploration, with numerous case-study illustrations, of the extent to which international NGOs such as Oxfam or Human Rights Watch make a difference to the cause of promoting human security around the world.

Youngs, R. (2019), *Civic Activism Unleashed: New Hope or False Dawn for Democracy?* (Oxford: Oxford University Press).

Examines the changing nature and increased intensity of civic activism around the world over the last decade with special attention to new types of civic or social movements that emerge without formal leadership and organization.

 For additional material and resources, please visit the Online Resources at: www.oup.com/he/garner4e

21

GLOBAL POLITICAL ECONOMY

READER'S GUIDE

In providing an overview of the field of Global Political Economy (GPE)—also known as International Political Economy (IPE)—this chapter builds on a number of themes introduced in previous sections, including connections with theories of global politics. Once again, theories are discussed from a historical perspective to enable a better appreciation of how ideas, practices, and institutions develop and interact over time. And once again, it will be seen that these theories arose substantially within a European context, although the extent to which these may be applied uncritically to issues of political economy in all parts of the globe must be questioned. Significant issues for GPE include trade, labour, the interaction of states and markets, the nexus between wealth and power, and the problems of development and underdevelopment in the global economy, taking particular account of the North/South divide. The final section discusses the twin phenomena of globalization and regionalization and the way in which these are shaping the global economy and challenging the traditional role of the state. An underlying theme of the chapter is the link between economic and political power.

THE STUDY OF GLOBAL POLITICAL ECONOMY

The study of politics has long been entwined with economic issues, as reflected in the specialist field of political economy, a term which suggests the merging of two significant aspects of social life and which can be traced as far back at least as the moral philosopher Adam Smith (1723–90), who produced an early account of modern industrial society. Since then, the very meaning of political economy has been contested. A recent commentary notes that, for Smith, political economy denoted 'the science of managing a nation's resources so as to generate wealth', while for Karl Marx (1818–83) it was concerned with 'how the ownership of the means of production influenced historic processes'. In the twentieth century it was sometimes taken simply as the interrelationship between economics and politics on the one hand, or a particular methodological approach on the other (Weingast and Whitman, 2006: 3). For present purposes, political economy is taken to be a field of study which lies at the intersection of politics and economics and which is concerned primarily, although not exclusively, with the relationship between states and markets. GPE attempts to make sense of the state/market nexus and the dynamic complex of actors, issues and processes that are involved on a global scale (see Smith, El-Anis, and Farrands, 2017: 3).

The addition of the word 'global' or 'international' to 'political economy' scarcely occurred before the 1970s, and when it did, it was partly in conjunction with the rise of both neoliberalism and neorealism in the theorization of global politics. This is not to suggest that those working in political economy had neglected the international or global dimensions of the field, but rather to say that scholars of traditional international relations on the one hand, and economists on the other, had evinced little interest in each other's work. A significant impetus in the development of GPE was provided by a seminal article published in 1970 by Susan Strange who pointed out that the reciprocal ignorance exhibited by the two disciplines impoverished efforts in both fields to understand the world. IR scholars, she said, had been far too preoccupied with the political and strategic relations between governments, to the exclusion of almost everything else (Strange, 1970: 304). The field has grown enormously since then, reflecting not only increased academic awareness of its importance but also the substantial changes in the global sphere in that period.

As with politics more generally then, GPE cannot confine itself simply to the structural study of institutions or organizations but must also take account of the norms, values, and interests that they reflect. Any arrangement of the global system of production, distribution, and exchange reflects a mix of values and must therefore be understood neither as divinely ordained nor as the fortuitous outcome of mere chance, but rather 'the result of human decisions taken in the context of manmade institutions and . . . self-set rules and customs' (Strange quoted in Balaam and Veseth, 2005: 5).

As suggested previously, many studies in the field take the state and the market to be the two main entities involved. Indeed, it is the 'parallel existence and mutual interaction' of these that create 'political economy' (Gilpin, 1987: 8). The state embodies political forces while the market, famously cast as 'the invisible hand' by Adam Smith, is defined as 'a coordinating mechanism where sellers and buyers exchange goods and services at prices and output levels determined by supply and demand' (Cohn, 2005: 7). The relationship between states and markets is often depicted as one of permanent tension, since the efforts of state actors are primarily concerned with preserving sovereignty and political unity while markets are assumed to thrive on openness and the absence of barriers to trade. But their relationship is also seen as complementary in that state

22

→ See
Chapters 2 and 8
for a discussion
of the state.

action is required to protect property rights, provide infrastructure, and regulate transactions. In turn, where an economy is thriving, which it seems more likely to do where trade barriers are minimal, there is often a proportional strengthening of national political and military power (ibid.).

Students of GPE are obviously concerned mainly with the dynamics produced in the international sphere, and the interactions between states, transnational corporations, international organizations, financial institutions, and so on. But it needs emphasizing once again that the distinction between the domestic and the international is difficult to maintain, especially in the highly interdependent world of the twenty-first century.

KEY POINTS

- GPE sits at the intersection of international politics and economics as well as incorporating other interdisciplinary insights and has developed as a major focus of study within the broader field of global politics over the last five decades.
- Studies in GPE focus mainly on states and markets with the relationship between these consisting in a tangle of complex interactions and processes involving key dynamics of power and wealth.

THE AGE OF MERCANTILISM

The term mercantilism (which derives from the Latin for 'merchant') came to denote a certain cluster of ideas concerning the balance of trade in seventeenth century Europe. As early as 1664, Thomas Mun had argued that national policy should be based on a simple rule: 'to sell more to strangers yearly than we consume of theirs in value' (Mun, 1895: 7). A basic premise of classical mercantilism is that national wealth and military power form a virtuous circle: wealth enhances military power vis-à-vis other states (and in early modern Europe this often meant superior naval power); substantial wealth is acquired through trade; trade is protected by naval power; the wealth generated by trade further enhances naval capacity; and so on. Mercantilism is therefore consistent with the power politics approach to international politics (Smith, El-Anis and Farrands, 2017: 15).

→ See
Chapter 16 for a
discussion of
liberalism and
realism.

The relentless pursuit of trade is justified by its positive contribution to national strength, and so mercantilism is a form of economic nationalism supporting, among other things, trade protectionism. Mercantilism therefore acquired the characteristics of a nationalist discourse which, in a post-feudal age of state-building in Europe, resonated with other ideas about national greatness. It also went hand in hand with justifications of colonialism. In addition, the grounds for legitimate warfare were enlarged to encompass commercial and market considerations. Overall, the legacy of early mercantilist policies was 'to concentrate physical wealth in a few European nation-states, and to create a network of global economic interdependence the remains of which can still be seen today' (Watson, 2004: 3). The key quote in **Box 22.1** provides a brief commentary on the historical trajectory of mercantilism as it relates to European imperialism and colonialism.

Mercantilism was at odds with emergent liberal ideas in both economics and politics more generally. Conservative economic historians depicted mercantilism as *rightly* subordinating economic

22

> **KEY QUOTE** BOX 22.1
> Van den Berg
>
> In 1500s Europe, mercantilism solidified the control of national monarchs over the local power bases that remained from earlier feudal societies. When these alliances between central governments and commercial interests were extended overseas, *mercantilism became colonialism*, which was essentially the joint government-private conquest of foreign territory and resources.
> (Van den Berg, 2015: 270; emphasis added)

to political considerations of national interest, in line with their belief in 'the subordination of the individual to the state and to the exaltation of vigorous nationalism characteristic of mercantilism' (Viner, 1949: 4). An early nineteenth-century defender of mercantilism argued along lines similar to classical realism. Rejecting the 'cosmopolitical' world view of economic liberals which assumes peaceful relations in a politically stable environment, Friedrich List (1789–1846) argued that political economy must start from the premise that relations between states are inherently conflictual, that nationalist rivalries produce the major dynamics with which political economy must grapple, and that 'true political science' must see a world characterized by free trade as 'a very unnatural one' (List, 1991: 54).

Mercantilist thinking declined following the rise of liberal thought but enjoyed a resurgence from the late nineteenth century on into the early twentieth century when nationalism was rife. Liberal ideas supporting free trade suffered a proportionate decline. But the extreme nationalism and trade protectionism of the inter-war years, and their association with the Great Depression as well as the Second World War, gave liberal economic principles in the post-war period a boost, even though mainstream thinking about global politics took a decidedly realist turn at the same time (Cohn, 2005: 71). But since realist theorists evinced little interest in economics, specific mercantilist ideas did not figure prominently in the early post-war period of theorizing of global politics, although they did gather some support in the 1970s and into the 1908s as the architecture of the liberal economic world order came under strain with a global recession, as discussed next. Mercantilism appears to have enjoyed another renaissance under President Trump. Indeed the slogan 'make America great again', and the policy of trade protection that accompanies it, is based squarely on mercantilist premises. This has prompted some critical observers to suggest that his trade policy is stuck in the 80s—the 1680s (Rampell, 2018). We consider aspects of Trump's mercantilism later in this chapter.

KEY POINTS

- Mercantilism is a theory of global political economy based on certain balance of trade principles. Historically, it evinces nationalist, imperialist, and realist elements.
- Mercantilism opposes the ideology of the free market, favouring a strong state which not only provides security but also is actively involved in the economy by promoting protectionist measures.

22

THE RISE OF LIBERAL POLITICAL ECONOMY

By the late eighteenth century, liberal political economy had displaced mercantilism in prominence due largely to Adam Smith's influence. His free trade ideas were based on the division of labour, economic interdependence, and the notion that states in an unregulated global economy would find a productive niche based on absolute advantage. This meant that each state would find the greatest benefit in producing specialized goods most efficiently and trading these with other states, who would do the same. These ideas were further refined by David Ricardo (1772–1823) who expanded Smith's insights by introducing the concept of *comparative* advantage, stating that: 'The same rule which regulates the relative value of commodities in one country, does not regulate the relative value of the commodities exchanged between two or more countries' (Ricardo, 1821: 99). This suggests that, even if one state has no absolute advantage in the production of any particular good, it can at least specialize in the production and export of those it can produce with a relative advantage (Cohn, 2005: 92).

Another important concept underpinning early liberal political economy was laissez-faire (literally, 'let be'), meaning that the state should allow free rein to *individual initiative, competition, the pursuit of self-interest, and the invisible hand of market forces*—all classic elements of liberal political economy. While the pursuit of self-interest may seem attuned only to selfish individual ends, Smith and other liberals believed that the sum of such individual actions adds to overall wealth and prosperity for the community. Liberalism thus described is a theory of the individual *in* society rather than a theory of individual, self-regarding action without reference to a wider social sphere. But because liberal theorists were opposed to mercantilist state practices, and to the abuse of state power more generally, liberal thought acquired a certain anti-statist hue. Even so, most versions of liberalism recognize the state as essential for the organization of political life as well as for legislation to protect rights, especially property rights. In the course of explaining the principle of comparative advantage under a regime of free trade, David Ricardo very succinctly summed up classical liberal political economy ideas, and their implications for the wider world. (**See Box 22.2**.)

John Maynard Keynes (1883–1946) was undoubtedly the most prominent liberal thinker of the twentieth century. But he was certainly no anti-statist and regarded the state as essential to producing the necessary social, political, and economic conditions for human well-being. He also believed that the sum of rational individual actions did not always add up to a rational outcome

> **KEY QUOTE** BOX 22.2
> David Ricardo (1772–1823)

Under a system of perfectly free commerce, each country naturally devotes its capital and labour to such employments as are most beneficial to each. The pursuit of individual advantage is admirably connected with the universal good of the whole. By stimulating industry, by regarding ingenuity, and by using most efficaciously the peculiar powers bestowed by nature, it distributes labour most effectively and most economically: while, by increasing the general mass of production, it diffuses general benefit, and binds together, by one common tie of interest and intercourse, the universal society of nations throughout the civilized world.
(Ricardo, 1821: 99)

22

at the collective level, and so it was important for the state to regulate economic affairs and make adjustments. Certainly, to treat 'the market' as the infallible source of all wisdom was a mistake. Keynes's legacy was embodied to a considerable extent in the post-war global economic order supported in the USA by economists such as John Kenneth Galbraith (1908–2006) who was important in presenting a liberal case for state involvement in economy and society and maintaining a critical stance on simplistic market fundamentalism: 'The notion that [the market] is intrinsically and universally benign is an error of libertarians and unduly orthodox conservatives' (Galbraith, 1984: 39–42).

From the early 1980s, and especially following the end of the Cold War and the apparent triumph of capitalism, a reinvigorated form of market fundamentalism commonly referred to as 'neoliberalism' gained ascendancy, and it has continued to dominate despite the global financial crisis (GFC) of 2008, which we consider in more detail later. As with most 'isms', the term is contested. It has also been associated with an array of quite different political figures, from Margaret Thatcher and Tony Blair in the UK, to Ronald Reagan and George W. Bush in the US, and to Boris Yeltsin and Jiang Zemin, in Russia and China respectively, among others (Steger and Roy, 2010: p. x). At minimum, neoliberal doctrine calls for the privatization of state resources and assets and deregulation of financial and other institutions in the belief that this will produce the conditions under which the market can operate most efficiently and on a self-regulating basis. Indeed, neoliberalism sees free markets as the essential organizing principle for economics, politics, *and* society. The dominance of market logic in virtually all spheres of life has given rise to the notion of 'market society' in which non-market forces and ideas are distinctly subordinate (see Birch, 2017: 2; Zsolnai, 2018: 1). Neoliberalism thus appears to be very different from the socially oriented liberalism not only of Keynes and Galbraith, which supported robust state institutions and a well-regulated form of capitalism, but also from the classical liberalism of Adam Smith and David Ricardo (see Harvey, 2007: 20). A critical perspective would discern the way in which market logic has become naturalized—as if its dominance over all spheres of life is somehow 'natural', and therefore right.

KEY POINTS

- Liberalism displaced mercantilism as the leading theory of political economy with the rise of free trade ideas revolving around the division of labour, interdependence, and comparative advantage. Mercantilist ideas, however, reappear from time to time to challenge liberal orthodoxies.

- Liberal political economy promotes individual initiative, competition, the pursuit of self-interest, and the 'invisible hand' of market forces. Liberals generally believe that the sum of individual actions adds to overall wealth and prosperity although 'social' liberals like Keynes and Galbraith were more sceptical.

- Neoliberalism has become a dominant ideology over the last four decades or so and has tended to subordinate all other economic, political, and social forces to a market logic which stands as the 'natural' order of things.

22

MARXISM AND CRITICAL GPE

The third of the classical theories of political economy is of course Marxism, which, in theorizing such key matters as class struggle, imperialism, exploitation, and technological change, 'contributes an essential critical approach to the operation of contemporary political economy' (Watson, 2004: 9–10). Class analysis and the distribution of wealth are implicit in dependency theory and world system analysis discussed in Chapter 18. Marx's notion of ideology as 'false consciousness' is especially important in analysing how the interests of any ruling class are presented as natural, inevitable, and desirable even for subject classes. This masks the deeper 'truth' about domination and subordination.

Marx's economic theory is concerned to critique the crises produced in capitalism and pays particular attention to the social and political circumstances in which economic development takes place and through which economic institutions emerge. He is especially concerned to expose how capitalism came to dominate production not just on a national scale, but globally. His thought is extended to explain human development in general, including the phenomenon of 'class struggle', a term which highlights the essential conflict of interests between workers and the ruling class. Furthermore, Marx views the *material realities* of the human condition as mediating the whole approach people take to their existence. This in turn forms the basis for what is called Marx's 'materialist conception of history' as set out in **Box 22.3.**

Elsewhere, Marx wrote of a fallacy propagated by defenders of capitalism and liberal political economy which holds that the mode of production is 'encased in eternal *natural* laws independent of history, at which opportunity bourgeois relations are then quietly smuggled in as the inviolable *natural* laws on which society in the abstract is founded' (Marx, [1861] 1973: 87; emphasis added). This, once again, highlights the 'naturalization' of ideas, and hence of power, by ruling classes and resonates with the idea that the political structure of society always reflects 'the prevailing class interests and is never independent of them' (Morrison, 2006: 132). As we saw earlier, these ideas were taken up and elaborated by Antonio Gramsci.

A neo-Gramscian perspective focusing on transnational hegemony and the dynamics of domination and subordination, coercion, and consent has been developed by Robert W. Cox (1981). He suggests that we should not simply accept the global economic or political order as it is, but rather question how it came into being and how it might be transformed altogether—into a more just and

> **KEY QUOTE** BOX 22.3
> Marx's Historical Materialism

In the social production of their existence, men inevitably enter into definite relations which are independent of their will, namely relations of production appropriate to a given stage in the development of the material forces of production. The totality of these relations of production constitutes the economic structure of society, the real foundation, on which arises a legal and political superstructure and to which correspond definite forms of consciousness. The mode of production of material life conditions the general process of social, political and intellectual life. *It is not the consciousness of men that determines their existence, but their social existence that determines their consciousness.* (Marx, 1859; emphasis added)

22

equitable one. The 'new political economy' promoted by Cox and others in the critical tradition also rejects the methodological positivism of conventional realist and liberal approaches which they see as constraining the capacity to think outside the parameters of conventional theory. Thus critical GPE approaches are to be distinguished from conventional approaches because they do not take socio-economic or political structures as neutral or objective but subject to change via human agency. Critical GPE's normative project is to make these changes *for the better* and so to contribute to human emancipation in a broad sense.

Critical approaches to GPE in the contemporary period focus particular attention on the commodification of labour in international markets as part of the broader process of globalization. They are also attuned to gender and race as well as traditional class analysis. But there is still a long way to go before these issues are brought into the mainstream of discussion. As Griffin (2007: 720) argues, in relation to gender, while a gendered analysis is central to a proper understanding of the processes and practice of the global political economy, and while much high-quality work has been done in recent years, it is still seen as a 'women's issue' and therefore as marginal to more important, traditional concerns.

→ See Chapter 18 for a discussion of class analysis and the world system.

International labour migration is itself a massive industry with numerous facets, including significant race, class, and gender dimensions. It rests on wage inequalities between source and destination countries caused by highly uneven development, with labour migration controlled by an economic logic subordinating other social and political concerns (Goss and Lindquist, 1995: 317). The other side of the coin is the search by transnational corporations for ever-cheaper sources of labour. Countries providing low-cost labour are ideal bases for manufacturing industries. While supporters of the capitalist system see this as bringing benefits to the poor on the grounds that any job is better than no job, its critics see it as perpetuating and profiting massively from relations of exploitation. **Box 22.4** highlights significant gender elements in international labour markets.

→ See Chapters 3, 6, and 18 for a discussion of Marxism.

Another point to note is that almost every empirical study to date has found that labour mobility, whether within countries or between countries, increases the prosperity of both the individuals who migrate as well as the countries concerned in both social and economic terms. Yet despite all the evidence supporting the benefits that migrants bring, political opposition to immigrants is widespread. A 2018 World Bank Report highlighting this situation says that:

> Respondents to political opinion polls rate the arrival of immigrants in their countries as among their worst fears. Citizens worried about what migrants and refugees would do to jobs and wages, welfare programs, crime, schools, and their national identity. Frustrated by the public's disregard of their empirical findings, many economists attribute political opposition to cultural and social factors, including xenophobia.
> (www.worldbank.org/en/research/publication/moving-for-prosperity)

CASE STUDY BOX 22.4
Globalization, Labour Markets, and Gender

The global economy depends ultimately on the exploitation of labour, and in particular on the availability of cheap labour in less developed countries. Many of the labour markets are heavily gendered. For example, while Bangladeshi and Indonesian males are employed as migrant workers in construction projects in the Middle East, Singapore, and Malaysia, females from the

22

Philippines and Indonesia are employed as domestic workers. Regulations protecting such migrants are often very weak, leaving many at the mercy of both the companies who arrange the
work contracts—itself an industry—as well as the companies or individuals who employ them.
Even less protected are illegal immigrant workers who are often 'trafficked' into destination
countries. 'Illegals' or 'undocumented' workers are found throughout the world wherever there
is a demand for cheap labour, from the UK and other European countries to the United Arab
Emirates and Kuwait, Singapore, Malaysia, and Japan. Undocumented immigrant labour has
been a very significant part of the US economy for some time, and now makes up around 50
per cent of all farm workers, 15 per cent of construction workers and 9 per cent of service and
domestic workers (e.g. maids, cleaners, and nannies), and many more will be needed as carers for
the aging 'baby boomer' population over the next decade or so (Mayes, 2018).

The 'feminization' of cheap labour is especially prominent in developing countries in South
East and East Asia, parts of Latin America, the Caribbean, and North Africa where increasing
numbers of women work in labour-intensive, low-wage occupations either as domestic workers or in such industries as textiles/garments. One report states that 'Although producing for
some of the most profitable companies in the world [women] are working for poverty wages,
under dreadful conditions . . . Many garment workers are working between 60 and 140 hours of
overtime per week and it is common to be cheated of the overtime pay. Health and safety are
often neglected, workers are denied breaks, and abuses are common—to mention a few of the
problems in the industry.
(https://www.fashionrevolution.org/exploitation-or-emancipation-women-
workers-in-the-garment-industry/).

There is also increased trafficking of women and children made possible under conditions of
globalization. Young women from relatively poorer countries are often deceived into thinking
that they will be offered a good job abroad. For many, it seems to offer a way out of poverty. After arriving in the destination country, however, they soon discover that they have been
brought in to work as prostitutes. And since they are thousands of miles away from home and
have nowhere else to go, it becomes a situation of forced prostitution. It has been an increasing
phenomenon in Europe where young women from poorer areas in Eastern Europe and Russia
have been recruited for the sex industry. Trafficking of women and children, for the sex industry
in particular, is a truly global phenomenon.
(see www.humantraffickingfoundation.org/)

The UN has developed a protocol to prevent, suppress, and punish trafficking to supplement
the UN Convention against Transnational Organized Crime and which defines trafficking in the
following terms:

> 'Trafficking in persons' shall mean the recruitment, transportation, transfer, harbouring
> or receipt of persons, by means of the threat or use of force or other forms of coercion,
> of abduction, of fraud, of deception, of the abuse of power or of a position of vulnera-
> bility or of the giving or receiving of payments or benefits to achieve the consent of a

person having control over another person, for the purpose of exploitation. Exploitation shall include, at a minimum, the exploitation of the prostitution of others or other forms of sexual exploitation, forced labour or services, slavery or practices similar to slavery, servitude or the removal of organs.

(www.ohchr.org/en/professionalinterest/pages/protocoltraffickinginpersons.aspx)

A forced labour protocol also entered into force in 2014. Both the trafficking and forced labour protocols are of course designed to protect adults and children, regardless of gender, from exploitation and outright slavery. In highlighting the extent of the problems involved, however, a 2017 report from the International Labour Organization (ILO) provided the following data which indicates the disproportionate exploitation of women and girls.

- At any given time in 2016, an estimated 40.3 million people are in modern slavery, including 24.9 million in forced labour and 15.4 million in forced marriage.
- It means there are 5.4 victims of modern slavery for every 1,000 people in the world.
- One in four victims of modern slavery are children.
- Out of the 24.9 million people trapped in forced labour, 16 million people are exploited in the private sector such as domestic work, construction or agriculture; 4.8 million persons in forced sexual exploitation, and 4 million persons in forced labour imposed by state authorities.
- Women and girls are disproportionately affected by forced labour, accounting for 99 per cent of victims in the commercial sex industry, and 58 per cent in other sectors.

('Global Estimates of Modern Slavery: Forced Labour and Forced Marriage', Geneva, September 2017, www.ilo.org/global/topics/forced-labour/lang—en/index.htm)

KEY POINTS

- The Marxist tradition of critique is embedded in the social and political relations underscoring the economic sphere. It emphasizes the extent to which the political structure of society reflects the interests of ruling classes and is never independent of them.
- Class analysis remains relevant in a global sphere where low-cost labour migrates or, alternatively, manufacturing industries locate themselves in countries providing cheap and more easily exploited labour.
- Critical GPE is attuned to issues of domination and subordination and is sensitive to issues of class, race, and gender, thereby incorporating a wider range of institutions and practices into analysis.

THE POST-WAR INTERNATIONAL ECONOMIC ORDER

As the Second World War drew to an end, plans for a new international economic order to free up access to markets and raw materials were developed alongside those for new international political institutions. Delegates meeting at Bretton Woods, New Hampshire, in 1944 were also concerned to institute a system which stabilized exchange rates and avoided recreating the conditions which had triggered worldwide depression in the inter-war years. However, contending national interests challenged pure liberal principles and the system which emerged, which Ruggie has characterized as 'embedded liberalism', reflected many compromises: 'unlike the economic nationalism of the thirties it would be multilateral in character; unlike the liberalism of the gold standard and free trade, its multilateralism would be predicated on domestic interventionism' (Ruggie, 1998: 62–84).

Institutionally, the result was the establishment of three major bodies collectively dubbed the 'Bretton Woods institutions'. These were the International Monetary Fund (IMF), the International Bank for Reconstruction and Development (IBRD—later called the World Bank), and the General Agreement on Tariffs and Trade (GATT), which was signed in 1947 as an interim measure until the architecture for a more permanent institution could be worked out. It took until 1995 to establish the World Trade Organization (WTO) (see Wilkinson, 2000). The WTO is now the only global international organization dealing with rules of trade between nations. Its agreements have been 'negotiated and signed by the bulk of the world's trading nations

Photo 22.1 The World Trade Organization is an intergovernmental organization that is concerned with the regulation of international trade between nations. *Shutterstock RF: Hector Christiaen / Shutterstock.com*

and ratified by their parliaments' with the goal of helping 'producers of goods and services, exporters, and importers conduct their business' (www.wto.org/english/thewto_e/whatis_e/whatis_e.htm).

One of the success stories in the early post-war years was the work of the IRBD in Europe and in which the USA played a major role. Fearing communist influence in a badly damaged Europe where millions of people were struggling, US strategy was, as we have seen earlier, to contain that influence partly by rebuilding the economies of Western Europe via the Marshall Plan. Billions in US aid was distributed in ways compatible with securing Europe as a major trading and security partner. In the meantime, the IMF was charged with maintaining a stable exchange rate mechanism and balance of payments regime although it did little in its first few years due to the focus on European reconstruction as well as the rebuilding of Japan and aid packages to Greece and Turkey, also funded largely by the USA. In the late 1950s and 1960s, the IMF's involvement in supplying credits increased, especially as decolonization progressed, and it became a major player in Third World economies. The USA continues to dominate both the IMF and the World Bank, a reflection of its early role in global financial institutions as the major supplier of funds, despite its having become one of the world's largest debtor nations in the present period (see Schuman, 2011).

Although the Bretton Woods institutions remain an important part of international economic architecture, a breakdown nonetheless occurred in the exchange rate mechanism. By the early 1970s, the USA was faced with rising imports and a significant trade imbalance. Huge dollar out-flows providing liquidity for the global economy, although contributing to the USA's considerable prosperity, could not be sustained. Increased interdependence and the recovery of the European and Japanese economies, along with vastly increased financial flows, made it almost impossible to control currency values, producing adverse dynamics (see, generally, Spero and Hart, 1997: 16–21). In 1971, the USA abandoned the dollar gold standard and raised tariffs on imports. Other industrialized countries reacted by strengthening protectionism themselves. This flew in the face of GATT principles supporting free trade, thus hampering reforms. Further trouble was in store with rising inflation, commodity shortages, unaccustomed floating currencies, and then the 'oil shocks' of the mid-1970s when oil-producers quadrupled the price of oil in a year with multiple consequences for the global economy, including recession. In 1975, a meeting of seven leading industrial countries—the USA, the UK, Canada, France, Germany, Italy, and Japan (subsequently called the G7)—met to consider reform of the international monetary system, and amendments to the Articles of Agreement of the IMF were put in place in early 1976. Although this appeared to signal a return to multilateral management, the reforms did little except codify the prevailing 'nonsystem' (Spero and Hart, 1997: 23).

By the early 1980s, in the wake of both global economic developments and the fiasco of the Vietnam War, the status of the USA as the world's leading economic and military powerhouse seemed in decline (Keohane, 1984). The global recession hit most countries hard and the USA was no exception. Liberal economics was identified by conservative commentators as the culprit. One US-based commentator, William R. Hawkins, deployed the term 'neomercantilism' in proposing a form of economic conservatism based more squarely on national interest and dismissing the 'utopianism' of liberal economists' visions of world order based on free trade principles (Hawkins, 1984: 25–39). Five years later, however, the collapse of communism and the apparent triumph of liberal democracy, capitalism, and free market ideology saw neomercantilism and realist GPE

22

overshadowed by strengthening discourses of neoliberal globalization. The new world order proclaimed by liberal triumphalists such as Francis Fukuyama (1989), discussed in earlier chapters, swept all before it in a wave of optimism about the global future. As we shall see shortly, the onset of the GFC in 2008 severely tested neoliberal economic principles. Even before this occurred, policies inspired by neoliberal principles in relation to the 'Global South' were found to have exacerbated rather than eased much of the poverty there, issues we consider next.

KEY POINTS

- The Bretton Woods system emerged after the Second World War as a compromise between liberalism and nationalism. Although the 'system' is said to have collapsed by the early 1970s, the IMF, the World Bank, and the WTO still underpin contemporary global economic governance.

- Following world recession in the 1970s, neomercantilism enjoyed a revival, but the end of the Cold War saw a triumphant liberalism reassert global economic openness as the basis for a prosperous new world order although that is now being challenged by various proponents of economic nationalism, notably US President Trump.

THE NORTH-SOUTH GAP

The North-South developmental gap is a frequent topic of debate in GPE circles and has been for some time. It is sometimes equated with the West/non-West divide, but this can be misleading. One measure of wealth/poverty is demonstrated in a regional pattern of asset holdings which shows that, in the contemporary period, almost 90 per cent of global wealth is heavily concentrated in North America and Europe, but an increasing share is held by high income Asia-Pacific countries which include Japan, South Korea, Taiwan and Singapore as well as Australia and New Zealand (https://www.wider.unu.edu/publication/global-distribution-household-wealth). China, India, and the Philippines are not regarded as wealthy countries—and in fact have a significant problem with poverty—but their share of growth in billionaires is now outpacing all other regions (https://www.knightfrank.com/news/india-leads-global-growth-of-ultra-high-net-worth-individuals-knight-frank-wealth-report-2019-013011.aspx). Sub-Saharan Africa, in contrast, remains the poorest region in the world, and is likely to remain on the bottom of the ladder for some time to come.

In analysing the North–South gap, it is instructive to look back over the last half century to identify some relevant trends and developments. In the 1960s, developing countries had formed the Group of Seventy-Seven (G77), in the wake of the UN Conference on Trade and Development (UNCTAD), to lobby as a bloc in global forums, especially the UN and the GATT. It had limited success. Neither the oil-producing nations who formed their own Organization of Petroleum Exporting Countries (OPEC), nor the countries of the industrialized North, were prepared to contemplate significant concessions to ease the burden of poorer countries. This led to calls for a New International Economic Order (NIEO) under which meaningful reforms could be achieved in aid, foreign investment regimes, the terms of trade, financial arrangements including loans, and a fairer overall monetary system. But little actually happened. By the mid-1970s, there was a rise in protectionism in key industrialized states influenced by neo-mercantilist ideas, accompanied by soaring energy costs, inflation, and increasing indebtedness.

In the meantime, the World Bank and IMF began to promote structural adjustment programmes for poor, underperforming countries. Inspired by neoliberal economic orthodoxies, these included the privatization of state-owned industries and resources, deregulation, strict limitations on public spending, and other austerity measures. Loans were made conditional on governments implementing such measures. The result in many cases was to limit access to health, education, and public utilities even further without significantly improving overall economic performance or alleviating poverty.

The policy measures imposed by the World Bank and IMF—both based in Washington, DC—became known as the 'Washington Consensus', a term originally indicating adherence to a set of broad policy measures which, in addition to privatization and deregulation, included public sector reform, tax reform, fiscal discipline, trade liberalization, property rights, and interest rate and exchange rate reforms. The way in which these were interpreted and implemented is often seen as reflecting the thoroughgoing market fundamentalism supported by neoliberal ideology which, in the wake of capitalism's triumph in the Cold War, seemed unchallengeable (see Williamson, 2009). The 'consensus' appeared to have crumbled by the early 2000s in the wake of evidence that showed poorer economic performance under the policy measures imposed (World Bank, 2005: 34–6), and what remained of it was extinguished by the GFC of 2008.

The spectacular economic growth achieved by China and India in recent years has maintained broad faith in market principles by many policy-makers. However, the gap between rich and poor in these countries has been widening rather than narrowing as the wealth created through economic growth has by no means trickled down to alleviate the poverty of millions. This suggests that, while capitalism as an economic system certainly generates wealth, it does not distribute it effectively or equitably, thus indicating a crucial role for both governments and international organizations like the UN.

With respect to global inequalities, the UN adopted a set of 'Millennium Development Goals' (MDGs) in 2000, with 2015 set as the year by which the number of people living in extreme poverty would be halved—a goal requiring significant funding commitments from richer countries. A 2005 World Summit reaffirmed the MDGs and committed additional funding although progress in many areas remained disappointing. Another five years on, a UN report indicated that very little had changed, especially in sub-Saharan Africa. Although there had been some growth before the GFC, this event hit the poor particularly hard, slowing progress significantly.

By the time of the twentieth anniversary of the UN's World Summit for Social Development in 2015, however, reports were much more upbeat. While acknowledging that progress had been uneven in some areas, with sub-Saharan Africa remaining a major problem area, it was noted that there had been a significant overall decline in world poverty, with the number of people living in extreme poverty reduced by half. The UN has refreshed the MDG project with a post-2015 development agenda called the '2030 Agenda for Sustainable Development' which promises to continue efforts in key areas of concern such as poverty and hunger alleviation, combating disease, improving opportunities for youth, and environmental protection (www.un.org/millenniumgoals).

A 2018 World Bank report says that 'tremendous progress' has been made in reducing extreme poverty over the last few years. Those living in extreme poverty globally fell to a new low of

22

10 per cent in 2015 (the latest year for which figures are available), reflecting continued but slow-ing progress. But rates remain stubbornly high in low-income countries and those affected by conflict and political upheaval. Indeed, the total number of poor in Sub-Saharan Africa has been on the increase. 'In 2015, more extreme poor lived in that region than in the rest of the world combined. By 2030, under all but the most optimistic scenarios, poverty will remain in double dig-its in Sub-Saharan Africa' (www.worldbank.org/en/publication/poverty-and-shared-prosperity). A deeper understanding of the distribution of poverty around the world may be gained by looking at how the 'North–South gap' is theorized (**see Box 22.5**).

KEY DEBATE BOX 22.5
Theorizing the North–South Gap

How does one theorize the North–South gap? In terms of dependency theory, discussed in Chapter 18, the post-war order with its mixture of liberal and mercantile/realist institutions and principles was a recipe for exploitation. World-system analysis also proposes that underdevel-opment and a global division of labour is actually a necessary condition for the maintenance of global capitalism. Other analyses may also emphasize the history of imperialism and find causal factors in the legacy of Western colonialism. However, the record is rather mixed, with some former colonial states now among the world's richest. Singapore, for example, is now ranked in the top ten countries for wealth. Former colonies such as India are home to a large proportion of the world's poor, but also have a fair share of the world's ultra-rich as well as a very large middle class. Indeed, India is now about the sixth wealthiest country in the world, although most of that wealth is privately held. Contemporary neoliberal theory suggest that the 'trickle-down effect' will eventually alleviate the poverty of those at the bottom, but in the meantime the gap between rich and poor in countries like India continues to grow.

In considering issues of income inequality, it is also instructive to look at those countries which have the most equal income. All of the top ten in this category are in the European region, but most are former members of the Soviet Union where a social welfare model developed under the Soviet Union remains in place. The top ten also include Finland and Norway which, although not former communist states, nonetheless have a strong social democratic tradition. This sug-gests that redistributive mechanisms, which are very poorly developed in countries like India, have a very important role to play and that social democratic approaches to the distribution of goods are effective.

Liberal theory has looked to other explanations for the poor performance of many countries of the Global South, particularly in sub-Saharan Africa where an earlier World Bank report found that the best economic performance had occurred in the two countries that had been able to maintain parliamentary democracy—Botswana and Mauritius—and that elsewhere on the con-tinent a crisis of governance underlay a litany of political, social, and economic woes (cited in Williams and Young, 1994: 86). This report is said to have marked a watershed in World Bank thinking about the importance of good governance, where governance is understood generally understood as encompassing all the institutions through which authority is exercised in a coun-try, and includes how governments manage resources and implement policies as well as how

22

those in authority are elected, held accountable, and replaced. Important also are the norms and values that underpin institutions and practices, and which have implications for public goods. Overall, liberal theory suggests that democracy (and strong governance institutions) and development go hand-in-hand while dictatorship is often a recipe for continuing poor growth and maldistribution of resources. On the other hand, Singapore has an authoritarian political system while China, which has recorded spectacular economic growth over the past three decades, remains under communist rule.

More generally, the North–South gap in the distribution of the world's wealth is no doubt due to a complex of causes and the problems it generates cannot be resolved simply by the application of good governance principles and practices, important though these are. Aid is often uncoordinated and misdirected and sometimes merely alleviates symptoms while failing to address causes. Health issues, such as HIV/AIDS, deplete human capital. Countries where women's rights are poorly protected undermine their health and limit their educational opportunities, thereby contributing to continuing cycles of poverty for both men and women. Poverty and instability also go hand in hand, generating humanitarian crises as well as wider security issues which impinge on neighbouring countries as well. No one theory seems capable of addressing all these issues and providing an overall analysis. Perhaps what is required is a multilevel approach combining theoretical insights from economic, political, sociological, and cultural perspectives.

KEY POINTS

- The North–South gap generates serious international political, economic, and social problems and although some markets thrive on the disparities, few actually defend it as fair or just.

- Some programmes inspired by neoliberal economic thinking and formulated by the World Bank and IMF, such as structural adjustment programmes, have been criticized for compounding the problems.

- Critical perspectives on the distribution of wealth and poverty in the world also look to disparities *within* the Global South.

GLOBALIZATION AND REGIONALIZATION IN THE POST-COLD WAR WORLD

If globalization is defined in terms of 'the acceleration and intensification of mechanisms, processes, and activities . . . promoting global interdependence and perhaps, ultimately, global political and economic integration' (Roach, Griffiths, and O'Callaghan, 2014: 140), then it is impossible to separate globalization from the study of GPE. Indeed, some analyses focus almost exclusively on the economic dimensions of the phenomenon, positing liberalizing global market forces as the central dynamic: 'The world economy has internationalized its basic dynamics, it is dominated by uncontrollable market forces, and it has as its principle economic actors and major agents of change truly transnational corporations that owe allegiance to no nation-state and locate wherever on the globe market advantage dictates' (Hirst and Thompson, 1999: 1).

Previous chapters have emphasized the extent to which globalization, in that it involves deepening trends in interconnectedness which transcend state boundaries and controls, challenges the traditional view of international order based on independent sovereign states. We have also seen, in Chapter 8, how this relates to the problems of weakening states in the developed world. Even relatively strong developed states are seen as losing their autonomy and a fair measure of regulatory capacity. But what this means for the capacity of states to deliver a reasonable measure of prosperity and protection in terms of 'human security' to their citizens is a particularly vexed question in the Global South where, as we have seen, structural adjustment programmes have already had a negative impact on state capacity. Further, the 'market' is not geared to anything but producing profits and a strictly economistic approach to explaining and understanding the dynamics of globalized markets cannot address issues of justice, either within or between states.

A major focus in recent years has been on the tax avoidance strategies of multinational corporations which many states have been unable to tackle effectively. A 2017 report estimated global revenue losses to be in the order of US$500 billion annually and noted that the most significant losses occurred in low- and lower middle-income countries, as well as across sub-Saharan Africa, Latin America, the Caribbean, and South Asia (Cobham and Jansky, 2017: 1). Within the EU, corporations such as Google, Microsoft, Apple, Amazon, Starbucks, Gap, and IKEA have been identified as costing tax revenue alone up to US76 billion a year (Chew, 2016).

There have also been significant revelations about the extent of offshore tax havens used by the super-rich, including celebrities, business people, sports stars, politicians, and public officials from around the world as well as fraudsters, money launderers and dealers in illicit goods. The 'Panama Papers', which refer to some 11.5 million files leaked in April 2016 from the database of the world's fourth largest offshore financial services provider, Mossack Fonseca, based in Panama, have revealed details of tax havens and offshore companies set up to hide the assets of political, business, and other figures from Russia, China, the US, and the UK and dozens of other countries. As the US Justice Department launched an enquiry in April 2016 into widespread international tax avoidance schemes, then President Obama said that 'the leak from Panama illustrated the scale of tax avoidance involving Fortune 500 companies and running into trillions of dollars worldwide' (Neate, 2016). Offshore schemes are not necessarily illegal, but they do offer ways and means of hiding assets from public scrutiny as well as simply avoiding paying tax and thereby holding back vast sums that could otherwise be used for public goods—schools and colleges, hospitals and health services, roads and bridges, environmental projects, and so on.

Another aspect of global economic development that has attracted significant attention over the last two decades is the enormous growth in some Asia-Pacific economies and the prospects for a 'Pacific Century'. Despite the setbacks of a regional financial crisis in the late 1990s, and some fallout from the GFC, the Asia-Pacific boom has continued, with the growth of China and India attracting particular attention. But what has been especially interesting about developments in the region is the extent to which many states, or rather their governments, have been proactive in creating the conditions for growth in the global economy. It has therefore hardly been a case of states versus markets but rather states *promoting* markets as part of a broader developmental strategy.

State governments have also been active agents in the promotion of regionalization. This is a complex integrative process incorporating cultural and social dimensions as well as political and economic ones although, as with globalization, the primary dynamic of regionalization is usually seen to be economic. However, many regionalizing processes have an important security dimension as well. For example, the Association of Southeast Asian Nations (ASEAN), one of the longest-standing regional organizations outside Europe, was founded primarily for the purpose of securing regional peace in the Cold War period and has only lately been concerned with economic issues. The African Union (AU), whose predecessor organization—the Organization of African Unity (OUA)—had a strong political emphasis with support for decolonization and opposition to apartheid in South Africa at the top of its agenda for many year, now looks to supporting integration and development across the continent although there is still a strong political and security focus as well. One of Latin America's longest standing regional organizations, Mercosur, is focused specifically on promoting free trade among its members as well as greater ease of movement among people. The Gulf Cooperation Council (GCC) is an alliance of six countries in the Arabian Peninsula (Bahrain, Kuwait, Oman, Qatar, Saudi Arabia, and the United Arab Emirates) promoting economic, security, cultural and social cooperation to their mutual advantage. They have a particular interest in oil, given that they hold about half of all the world's oil reserves between them, although they also have a strong interest in diversifying their resource base.

Although some have seen regionalization as leading to the consolidation of rival trading blocs which threaten global multilateralism, others see it as perfectly compatible with global integration (Haggard, 1997: 20). Indeed, in some parts of the world, it is regarded as a means of participating more effectively in a globalized economy by creating opportunities for economic growth via free trade and other arrangements within a regional framework. Regionalization on this account is part of the broader globalization process itself rather than a negative reaction against it.

Outside the EU—and in addition to ASEAN, the AU, and Mercosur—regionalization has been proceeding apace in the Middle East, in the areas covered by the former USSR, South Asia, the Pacific, and the Caribbean. There are also organizations covering huge swathes of the globe. The Asia-Pacific Economic Cooperation (APEC) forum, for example, has grown from an initial twelve participants in 1989, to a current membership of twenty-one comprising Australia, Brunei, Canada, Chile, China, Hong Kong, Indonesia, Japan, Malaysia, Mexico, New Zealand, Papua New Guinea, Peru, Philippines, Russia, Singapore, South Korea, Taiwan, Thailand, the USA, and Vietnam. Its 'region' reaches half-way round the world with its member countries being home to close to 3 billion people and their economies representing approximately around 60 per cent of world GDP and nearly 50 per cent of world trade. In describing its purposes in broad outline, the organization declares that:

> APEC ensures that goods, services, investment and people move easily across borders. Members facilitate this trade through faster customs procedures at borders; more favorable business climates behind the border; and aligning regulations and standards across the region. For example, APEC's initiatives to synchronize regulatory systems is a key step to integrating the Asia-Pacific economy. A product can be more easily exported with just one set of common standards across all economies.

(See www.apec.org/About-Us/About-APEC)

22

While regionalization is clearly occurring in most parts of the world, the extent to which it has become institutionalized varies considerably. It is usually held to be most advanced, but by no means complete, in Europe. The EU itself has been a long time in the making—almost five decades passed from the time of the founding of the European Movement in 1943 to the Maastricht Treaty of 1992. Brexit is no doubt a substantial set-back for the European project, and perhaps for Britain itself. At the time of writing, however, the future of both Britain and the EU in a post-Brexit world is unclear and it will take several years before the consequences can be properly assessed. In the short-term, the value of British pound dropped significantly, falling to a thirty-one-year low against the US dollar by January 2017. In January 2019, it was reported that financial services companies had already moved about £800bn in staff, operations, and customer funds to Europe since the referendum (www.ft.com/content/c9d2a2ca-1262-11e9-a581-4ff78404524e). Other indicators showed that UK economic growth had slowed in the last quarter of 2018, and had been irregular over the previous three years, although the 'trade spat' between the USA and China were a factor as well (www.bbc.com/news/business-46835078).

There are also ongoing financial problems in Europe. A sovereign debt crisis, triggered partly by the GFC, revealed additional problems within the Eurozone, especially in Greece, Portugal, and Ireland. 'Sovereign debt' refers simply to money owed by governments, and a crisis occurs when governments cannot meet loan repayments or interest. Bailouts by other financial institutions such as the IMF are usually conditional on governments adopting austerity measures in public sector spending. In Greece, this led to significant social and political unrest as public spending cuts deepened and unemployment rose, triggering further concerns about 'financial contagion' affecting not only the Eurozone but US financial institutions as well. Apart from illustrating the high level of interdependence produced by both globalization and regionalization, the Greek case in particular, including the crisis of 2015 which nearly precipitated the 'Grexit' (the Greek exit from the Eurozone), illustrates the extent to which both governments and financial institutions require constraints. The most recent problem economy in Europe is Italy's where a combination of factors including market volatility (triggered partly by Brexit) and a very poorly managed financial system have seen a significant proportion of Italy's debt treated as 'junk' which has serious implications for interest rates on their loans. This has left Italian banks in major trouble, although the EU will not support a bailout funded by taxpayers money (https://www.investopedia.com/terms/e/european-sovereign-debt-crisis.asp). In the wake of this crisis, a growing number of Italians have been attracted to populist/nationalist political parties, although it is doubtful whether these hold any sort of solution to problems generated largely within Italy itself.

Experiments in regional integration in other parts of the world are generally far less institutionalized and there is little evidence elsewhere of a willingness to compromise or 'pool' sovereignty to enhance integration, a factor which has been key to the EU's success. While states in other regions may cooperate closely on a range of matters, integration is fairly superficial. National sovereignty is jealously guarded by many states, some of which were still colonies only a generation ago and which cling tenaciously to an almost absolute principle of non-interference in their 'sovereign affairs', especially when it comes to matters of human rights.

Another important development is inter-regionalism—itself a phenomenon that reinforces regionalization. A notable example is the Asia-Europe Meeting (ASEM) process established in the mid-1990s. Formed primarily to enhance economic relations, it has political and cultural pillars as well. 'Europe' initially consisted of the EU for the purposes of the meeting process, while the Asian membership included all the ASEAN countries plus China, Japan, and South Korea. India, Mongolia, Pakistan, as well as the ASEAN Secretariat joined in 2008, and in 2010 Australia, New Zealand, and Russia joined in a separate category. In 2012, Norway and Switzerland joined on the European side while Bangladesh joined as an Asian member. Summit meetings are held biennially and, in between, more than fifty ministerial and officials' meetings occur annually, maintaining dialogue over finance, trade, culture, education, disaster preparedness, transport, immigration, climate change, piracy at sea, information technology, food security, development, employment, energy security, global governance, and other relevant topics (see www.aseminfoboard.org/about/overview).

In summary, although regional schemes have existed for decades, a definite pattern of strengthening regionalization in the post-Cold War period is clear. It is driven primarily by economic factors but virtually all of the regional associations aspire to closer social and political ties as well. The other observable pattern is the continuing development of an overarching tripolar economic system based on the 'macro-regions' of Europe, North America, and Asia—the principle powerhouses of the global economy. The formation of ASEM is generally viewed as strengthening the third leg of that system, balancing the already strong North American–European and North American–Asian legs. Seen from this perspective, globalization and regionalization are, indeed, complementary dynamics in the global economy.

We have also seen, however, that while globalization and regionalization may well be complementary in nurturing processes of economic liberalization, they may also be complementary in undermining the economic role and functions of the nation-state. Trade liberalization and financial deregulation are all about easing state-imposed restraints, if not dispensing with them altogether, even though state actors are in many cases responsible for macroeconomic policy allowing such developments.

Outside of the academy, dissent and critique emanates from broad social movements manifest in 'anti-globalization' protests—now regular occurrences at various global or regional forums. Most participants are peaceful protesters gathering under the banners of various NGOs with concerns ranging from labour rights to environmental issues, consumer protection, peace advocacy, and so on. Others are self-described anarchists whose tactics range from civil disobedience to violence, mainly against commercial property and security personnel.

An early manifestation of 'global protest' was the 'Battle for Seattle' in November 1999 when around half a million demonstrators converged on a WTO ministerial meeting. The 2007 APEC meeting in Sydney saw thousands of security personnel deployed to lock down the entire city centre for several days to forestall the vigorous protests which had become a feature of the various gatherings of regional or global organizations since Seattle. Estimated costs for the G8 and G20 meetings held in Canada in 2010, bringing together leaders of the world's richest nations, were reported to be a staggering US$1.1 billion, with security by far the most expensive item. In comparison, the G20 held in Brisbane in 2014 cost a relatively modest AUD$500 million, of which AUD$100 million was spent on security. In Hamburg, in 2017, in addition to the cost of hosting the summit and providing security, the destruction of property during riots at the G20 meeting, where up to 100,000 protesters gathered, ran to about 12 million euros (www.g20.utoronto.ca/factsheets/factsheet_costs-g20.html).

While anarchists—who are by definition anti-statist—get most of the media attention, many of the protesters are concerned with issues that have actually been the traditional preserve of the state and who see the processes of globalization and regionalization as undermining the rights and interests of ordinary people in a variety of ways. As mentioned previously, these include labour rights and consumer protection as well as environmental issues. This has prompted much debate on the role of the state, and indeed the future of sovereignty in a globalizing world. The role of the state has also come under scrutiny again in the wake of the GFC, which we consider briefly in the final section.

22

KEY POINTS

- Globalization and regionalization are complex integrative processes driven predominantly by a liberal economic logic while incorporating social and political dimensions.

- Some critical GPE approaches welcome the openings provided by globalization for new social movements while remaining critical of adverse economic consequences for marginalized groups.

- Both globalization and regionalization have been seen as undermining the traditional role of the state, an unwelcome development from the perspective of neomercantilist/realist approaches as well as from traditional leftist perspectives concerned with the negative impact on state provision for social protection and welfare.

FINANCIAL CRISES IN THE GLOBAL SYSTEM

From the Great Depression of the inter-war period, to the GFC of 2008 and subsequent crises in the Eurozone, the global economic system has been subject to significant fluctuations in its fortunes. The GFC followed a period of rapid growth in the USA and the development of increasingly complex financial products. The latter products involved the securitization of high-risk loans, mainly in the form of mortgages which had encouraged people with insufficient means to buy into a fast-rising housing market. From around 2006, interest rates started to climb, and many could not meet repayments, precipitating an increase in bank foreclosures. With an avalanche of defaults, the 'housing bubble' burst. Financial institutions were left holding significantly devalued assets and from early 2007, a number faced collapse. One of the largest investment banks, Lehman Brothers, declared bankruptcy in September 2008. Institutional failure created a liquidity crisis and loans for thousands of businesses as well as mortgages became increasingly difficult to obtain. When banks stop lending, precipitating a 'credit crunch', the economy contracts, unemployment rises, and recession sets in.

The spate of financial institutional failure also saw massive government bailouts. By early 2009, financial institutions as well as the car industry in the USA had been propped up by a government commitment of a staggering 12.2 trillion dollars (*New York Times*, 2009). The idea that markets are efficient self-regulators and perform best when left alone by governments now seemed ludicrous. The 'efficient market hypothesis' was declared dead at a meeting of the World Economic Forum in Davos in January 2009. Former US Federal Reserve Chairman Alan Greenspan had previously admitted that he had made a big mistake by 'assuming that banks' self-interest would prevent them doing anything that would threaten their own survival' (Wighton, 2009).

Heavy exposure to the high-risk strategies of US loan schemes saw a number of European economies hit very hard. The UK banking industry was badly mauled and government bailouts followed. In Iceland, three major banks failed and had to be nationalized, bringing the Icelandic economy itself to the brink of collapse. Icelandic banks had also attracted significant investments from other European institutions, including pension funds, lured by what seemed to be attractive interest rates in fairly safe investments. By 2010, a sovereign debt crisis in the Eurozone emerged with Greece, Portugal, Spain, Italy, and Ireland the hardest hit.

Of course, a 'global' crisis generally means just that, and we have noted already the adverse impact on poverty reduction measures in the global South. The only developed economies to escape recession were Poland, Israel, South Korea, and Australia. The Australian case is discussed in **Box 22.6**.

Australia's story contrasts with Greece, one of the countries hardest hit by Europe's sovereign debt crisis, where government debt, as of 2019, stands about 178 per cent of GDP. Harsh austerity measures imposed by the terms of a European Central Bank's bailout deal precipitated significant political fallout in 2015 following the election of a new left-wing government which sought to ease the burden of poverty and unemployment resulting from the austerity measures but which ultimately failed to force its agenda through in the face of the enormous pressures imposed by the financial institutions. There have been numerous commentaries and critiques of the GFC and its impact on the global economy, probing both proximate and deeper causes as well as looking at lessons learnt. Well-known financier and businessman, turned liberal philanthropist, Hungarian-American George Soros has provided a sharp commentary on economic theory in the wake of the crisis which also has implications for how we view the 'science' of politics, **see Box 22.7**.

CASE STUDY BOX 22.6
Australia and the GFC

In 2008, when the GFC struck economies around the world, Australia's proved resilient. At the time, Australia had a population of 21.25 million, a GDP of almost US$50,000 per capita and zero debt. It had enjoyed a substantial period of economic growth attributable to a decade-long commodities boom, favourable terms of trade, and an immigration programme bringing skilled workers in particular into the country. Unemployment was at a thirty-year low although inflation was relatively high at 4.2 per cent. Australian commodities are often emphasized in the success story of the economy, but the service sector in fact makes up around 65 per cent of the economy. The budget surplus for 2008/09 was projected to be just over AUD$27 million.

As the GFC wrought havoc in other advanced economies, a combination of factors kept the Australian economy on a stable footing. These included continued strong commodity exports to China; continued population growth through immigration; prudential regulation of financial institutions meaning relatively low levels of 'toxic debt' which meant banks maintained a high credit rating; a well-timed announcement by the Labour government that it would guarantee bank deposits and keep credit flowing; a cut in interest rates by the Reserve Bank; and a fiscal stimulus package which included direct payments to households and a boost to the housing sector as well as public spending on infrastructure—the latter a typically Keynesian strategy (Tanner, 2009). There was no talk of austerity but rather the opposite. The Labour government made a decision to borrow 52 billion to fund a major stimulus package.

Australia's deficit increased significantly, due partly to the funding for stimulus measures, but also to falls in the demand for commodities. As of the March 2019 quarter, the current account deficit stood at only 2.9 billion. Australia also holds a world record in continuous economic growth (i.e. with no technical recession) for thirty years. Despite these figures, Australia has experienced very slow wages growth, the gap between rich and poor has widened, household debt is very high, and an ageing population poses problems for the future—all issues affecting most other advanced economies to varying degrees in the present period.

22

> ## KEY QUOTE BOX 22.7
> ### George Soros on 'The Anatomy of a Crisis'

Economic theory has modelled itself on theoretical physics. It has sought to establish timelessly valid laws that govern economic behaviour and can be used reversibly both to explain and to predict events. But instead of finding laws capable of being falsified through testing, economics has increasingly turned itself into an axiomatic discipline consisting of assumptions and mathematical deductions . . .

Rational expectations theory and the efficient market hypothesis are products of this approach. Unfortunately they proved to be unsound. To be useful, the axioms must resemble reality . . . rational expectations theory was pretty conclusively falsified by the crash of 2008 which caught most participants and most regulators unawares. The crash of 2008 also falsified the Efficient Market Hypothesis because it was generated by internal developments within the financial markets, not by external shocks, as the hypothesis postulates.

The failure of these theories brings the entire edifice of economic theory into question. Can economic phenomena be predicted by universally valid laws? I contend that they can't be, because the phenomena studied have a fundamentally different structure from natural phenomena. The difference lies in the role of thinking. Economic phenomena have thinking participants, natural phenomena don't. The thinking of the participants introduces an element of uncertainty that is absent in natural phenomena. The uncertainty arises because the participants' thinking does not accurately represent reality . . .

We really have to rethink our view of the financial markets quite profoundly; recognizing that instead of perfect knowledge and perfect information our understanding is inherently imperfect and that applies to market participants and regulators and social scientists alike. (Soros, 2010)

Photo 22.2 George Soros is a Hungarian-American investor and philanthropist. *https://www. georgesoros.com/press-resources/: georgesoros.com*

> **KEY POINTS**
>
> - The GFC is the latest in a series of 'boom and bust' episodes in the global capitalist economy, the first of which was the Great Depression of the late 1920s and early 1930s which also started in the USA. Both illustrate the phenomena of financial 'contagion' made possible by the interconnectedness of a globalized economy, although the case of Australia illustrates that domestic economic policy still matters.
> - The GFC has tested neoliberal approaches to the relationship between states and markets in advanced industrialized economies and found them wanting, just as they have been in relation to economic development in the global South.

GLOBALIZATION AND THE TRUMP PHENOMENON

The 'Trump phenomenon' has been discussed in various places throughout this book. Like Brexit it is, in large measure, an expression of nationalism embodied in the slogan 'America first'. But it has profound implications for political economy and amounts to a form of neo-mercantilism. The Trump administration's trade policies reflect a belief that protectionism—that is, shielding domestic industries and businesses from cheaper foreign imports or competition—will provide overall benefits to the US economy and 'make America great again'. Most economic theories do not support this belief but rather highlight the opposite effect which emerges when less efficient domestic industries are sheltered from competition and consumer goods become more expensive. The classic liberal theories of both Adam Smith and David Ricardo, discussed earlier in this chapter, were among the first to highlight the efficiencies of market liberalization in contrast with the fallacies of economic nationalism. The Trump administration has not only abandoned the Trans-Pacific Partnership (TPP)—a trade agreement between the US and 11 other countries around the Asia-Pacific which was on the point of being ratified—but has also introduced tariffs on billions of dollars' worth of goods from China, Mexico, the EU, and Canada. In turn, each of these countries are now imposing tariffs on exports from the US, and China has also devalued its currency to keep its exports competitive. In turn, the Trump administration has branded China a 'currency manipulator' (https://www.investopedia.com/trading/chinese-devaluation-yuan/).

The idea that no-one wins a trade war, least of all the country that starts one, is partly borne out by the fact the US trade deficit increased in 2018, although others may say that it would take more time to see the positive benefits accrue. But since US exports are overwhelmingly in the service sector rather than in goods, protectionism through tariffs still makes little sense. In addition, trade is not a zero-sum game in which there are only winners or losers. A well-regulated trade regime can produce gains for all, although that result is not automatic. Job losses caused by uncompetitive industries closing down clearly impact whole communities if alternative employment is not readily available. In this respect, government has a role to play in assisting such communities.

The only real support for protectionism comes not from the Republican Party but from Trump's 'base'. How that particular sector of the population can be characterized generally has been the subject of much speculation, but at the very least it is essentially nationalistic and 'anti-foreign'— and therefore remains supportive of Trump's protectionism as well as his anti-immigrant stance. Even so, it appeared to diminish somewhat with the prolonged government shut-down over

December–January 2018–19 when Trump failed to get US$5.7 billion worth of funding for his Mexican border wall approved by Congress, and China has also devalued its currency to keep its exports competitive. In turn, the Trump administration has branded China a 'currency manipulator' (https://www.investopedia.com/trading/chinese-devaluation-yuan/). On a related matter, we have seen earlier in this chapter the extent to which the US economy relies on undocumented immigrant workers in the agricultural sector in particular, and so a programme that is genuinely effective in targeting these workers could spell disaster in that sector of the economy as well.

The overall legacy of the Trump phenomenon for the US economy—and the global economy with which it is so intimately connected—is still far from clear. That it has been a disruptive force in global trade and competition is certainly evident enough, but the longer-term consequences will take some years to play out. At another level, one commentator has pointed out that Trump's beliefs and actions highlight the extent to which politics and economics are so strongly entwined. 'For globalization is not a spontaneous economic process: it is built on a political foundation.' This foundation has been built up over years of political interaction between governments on a global scale which has produced a raft of institutions, regulations, and practices enabling businesses to interact productively across national boundaries and within a rules-based framework (Oatley, 2019: i). The USA has been one of the principal architects of that order, as well as one of its main beneficiaries. Yet it is the very foundation of this order that Trump has sought to overturn.

The Trump phenomenon, as such, is unique to the contemporary USA, and Trump himself certainly seems to be one of a kind. But some elements of his agenda have been evident elsewhere, especially in Europe and the UK where nationalism and its logical accompaniments—anti-immigrant, anti-EU, and anti-globalization sentiments—have been on the rise. As with Trump's neo-mercantilist policies, any assessment of the long-term effects will obviously have to wait. One thing is certain, though, and that is that the unfettered pace of liberalization—which is one of the essential underpinnings of globalization—cannot be taken for granted and the benefits that it is meant to deliver will need to be spread more equitably to avoid backlash from those who perceive themselves as the ultimate losers. Trump undertook to deliver more benefits to those missing out to date, but critics suggest that his tax cuts for the USA's wealthiest classes are scarcely a good start for redistributing benefits:

KEY POINTS

- The Trump phenomenon is in some ways unique to the USA, but its nationalist and anti-globalization underpinnings are evident elsewhere, especially in the UK and parts of Europe.

- The liberalizing aspects of globalization with respect to both trade and the movement of labour appear to have brought greater prosperity to many, yet these have produced much of the resentment now expressed in support for the Trump agenda.

CONCLUSION

It is evident that the proper study of politics at either the national or global level entails due attention to the relationship between states and markets and between political and economic power. We have also seen that theories of GPE developed over the last few centuries parallel those in the more general field of politics. Mercantilism and realism, together with doctrines of nationalism and sovereignty, form a theoretical cluster which, although not entirely coherent, together produce a distinctive world view in which nation-states are the ultimate repository of political, social, and economic life and ought to be defended as such. Many traditional social democrats as well as the more conservative proponents of communitarianism would agree.

Liberal perspectives, while acknowledging the importance of states, generally embrace a world view which shifts the focus from discrete social, political and economic communities to the myriad overlapping ties between these communities. Aided by the revolution in transport, communications, and other forms of technology, these ties have produced a thoroughly interdependent world which can only benefit from a continued softening of sovereign state boundaries to provide a truly global market for goods and services. The twin phenomena of globalization and regionalization both reflect and support a liberal view of world order.

Critical GPE challenges the assumptions of both realists and liberals, urging attention to the vested interests that lie behind them and the injustices they mask. While levels of socio-economic well-being vary considerably within countries, critical GPE sees the North–South gap in the global economy as a standing indictment of both mercantilist and liberal (especially neoliberal) approaches. The GFC has served to reinforce critiques of the latter. The challenge is to move from incremental problem-solving approaches to a stance on theory and practice which probes the deeper historical development of opportunities and constraints as well as future trajectories. Some critical approaches do not oppose all aspects of globalization and find much to be welcomed in the challenge to sovereignty. Underpinned by a normative cosmopolitanism, while also recognizing the claims of localism; critical GPE sees the emergence of global and regional social movements as vehicles for positive change as well as providing an ongoing practical critique of both liberal and realist approaches.

KEY QUESTIONS

1. In what sense does classical mercantilism see national wealth and military power forming a virtuous circle?

2. How does liberal theory justify the pursuit of economic self-interest?

3. How relevant is class analysis to contemporary GPE?

4. How do gender-sensitive studies contribute to GPE?

5. What are the main features of critical GPE and how does it add to traditional Marxist perspectives?

6. What does the North–South gap tell us about justice and injustice in the global economy?

7. What is meant by the terms 'structural adjustment' and 'good governance' and how do they reflect liberal political and economic principles?

8. What are some of the main concerns expressed through the 'global protest' movement?

9. Are globalization and/or regionalization genuine threats to the future of the nation-state as the foundation of world order?

10. What does the GFC tell us about the relationship between states and markets?

11. What are the basic features of the 'Trump phenomenon' and to what extent are these evident outside the USA?

22

FURTHER READING

Amoore, L. (ed.) (2005), *The Global Resistance Reader* (London: Routledge).
Claims to be the first comprehensive account of the exponential rise of transnational social movements in opposition to the financial, economic, and political hegemony of major international organizations such as the WTO, World Bank, and IMF with discussion of conceptual issues, substantive themes, and case studies.

Cafruny, A., Talani, L. S., and Martin, G. P. (eds) (2016), *The Palgrave Handbook of Critical International Political Economy* (London: Palgrave Macmillan).
This collection challenges mainstream assumptions in GPE and demonstrates the value of critical theory.

Eagleton-Pierce, M. (2016), *Neoliberalism: The Key Concepts* (Abingdon: Routledge).
Provides a critical guide to a whole vocabulary of political economy that has developed around the idea of 'neoliberalism' over the last four decades or so.

Engel, U., Zinecker, H., Mattheis, F., Dietze, A., and Plötze, T. (eds) (2017), *The New Politics of Regionalism: Perspectives from Africa, Latin America and Asia-Pacific* (Abingdon: Routledge).
The contributors approach regionalism as one pattern of transformation and territorialization in a changing global order engaged in by different actors under varying circumstances and challenging state-centric perspectives on a number of different levels.

Ravenhill, J. (ed.) (2017), *Global Political Economy* (Oxford: Oxford University Press, 5th edn).
A detailed introduction to the subject matter of GPE with expert contributors covering theoretical approaches, global trade, finance and production, the implications of globalization for the state, and issues concerning the environment, the global South, and regionalism.

van der Pijl, K. (2015), *Handbook of the International Political Economy of Production* (Cheltenham: Edward Elgar).
Provides an interesting and comprehensive overview of the changing world of global production including the geography of why and where jobs are moving in manufacturing and services. Specific topics include the human and natural basis on which production rests, the consequences of exploitation and marginalization on body and mind, sex work, biotechnology, and issues of ecological rebalancing.

 For additional material and resources, please visit the Online Resources at:
www.oup.com/he/garner4e

23

CONCLUSION: TOWARDS A GLOBALIZING, POST-WESTERN-DOMINATED WORLD

BY PETER FERDINAND

READER'S GUIDE

This chapter brings together the threads of the various arguments that have run throughout the book. It argues first that the study of political philosophy, political institutions, and international relations are closely interlinked. Second, it argues that the study of politics cannot be divorced from the study of other social sciences—economics, philosophy, law, sociology, psychology, and also history. In fact, globalization has made those connections more important. Third, it suggests that the study of politics should be seen as a genuinely international and comparative enterprise, which does not automatically assume the pre-eminence of the sovereign state, nor a privileged position for Europe or the USA. The global financial crisis has accelerated trends of rising powers in other parts of the world and undermined the capacity of Western states to serve as exemplars. Having said that, we must acknowledge that more works have been written on political systems there than in other parts of the world, and scholars located in the West have tended to dominate academic publishing.

THE STUDY OF POLITICS IN CONTEXT

This book has been divided into three equal parts—political philosophy, political institutions, and international relations. Yet the ideas and institutions that they present are closely interlinked. Certainly, global politics is part of the same intellectual universe as the study of political theories, institutions, and comparative politics. The study of normative political philosophy, for example, cannot be kept apart from the empirical study of political institutions and the latter clearly operate at both domestic and international levels. Political systems are dependent for their stability upon their legitimacy, the reasons why members of that society believe them to be appropriate and acceptable—therefore they have recourse to ideas in order to legitimize them. Where sufficient members of a society believe the political system to be illegitimate, political rulers will need to employ a significant degree of coercion to remain in power.

Of course, most states explicitly set out to educate and/or socialize their people into supporting them, which is yet another argument in favour of seeing the connection between the normative and empirical dimensions of politics. Nevertheless, what people think democracy is and how they assess it, for example, is inseparable from the way in which they make it operate. The discussion of the concepts of 'power' and 'justice', which were presented largely in the context of domestic political systems, is equally valid for the international arena. There is obviously a connection between national political systems and the global one. The international system as it has developed on Westphalian principles assumes equality and equal sovereignty between nation-states. The Montevideo criteria for determining recognition of one state by another, as discussed in Chapter 16, include the capacity of national governments to control all of their territory. For many states, especially in the developing world, stability depends at least as much on a benign international environment as on domestic circumstances.

➜ See Chapter 16 for a discussion of the Montevideo Convention.

This book is also based on another fundamental assumption, namely that the study of politics is eclectic, overlapping with other disciplines in terms of subject matter, theories, and methods. These overlaps occur mainly in the social sciences, but they include history and philosophy as well. In the latter case, political philosophy has traditionally been preoccupied with identifying the polity that will enable human beings to live the good life, and in this quest moral and political philosophy become largely inseparable. Similarly, one of the recurring themes of this volume has been the impact of history on the spread of both European-type states and the Westphalian state system around the world.

In the social sciences, economics is a discipline with a high degree of formal abstraction, yet there is an increasing recognition that institutions play a key role in determining many economic outcomes—exemplified by the New Institutionalist school. The global financial crisis has reinforced the view that economic modelling, however sophisticated, cannot provide a complete picture of how economies actually operate. The study of political economy—domestic and international—is based on methods from politics and economics. In addition, economic abstractions form the basis of rational choice theories of politics, such as the economic theory of democracy examined in Chapter 4. Here, it is assumed that political parties and voters have the utility-maximizing characteristics of actors—businesses and consumers—in the economic sphere. Parties will therefore be preoccupied with winning political power and voters will be concerned with exercising electoral choice in a way that will further their interests.

➜ See Chapter 4 for a discussion of the economic theory of democracy.

The overlap between sociology and politics is equally apparent. For example, social stratification clearly plays a big part in the emergence of politicians and in voting patterns. The study of power,

23

examined in Chapter 3, employs concepts and models of society developed by political sociologists. Chapter 10 emphasized the overlap between law and politics in determining the rules that decide who gets what, when, and how in society. Psychology too overlaps with the study of politics. For example, Chapter 11 illustrated ways in which it can contribute to our understanding of voting behaviour, and many themes in political philosophy are dependent on assumptions made about human nature. In addition, policy studies often involve methods of analysis and data derived from a great variety of disciplines, not just social science ones. Studies of environmental policy-making, for instance, can involve approaches drawn from natural sciences too—indeed, policy analysis often benefits from scientific or technological understanding. It is evident, then, that a sophisticated understanding of political processes, whether national or international, will often require insights derived from other disciplines. This should not be taken to imply, however, that politics is simply a hybrid discipline made up of concepts and modes of analysis borrowed from other disciplines. It clearly has its own specific preoccupations—most notably, political obligation, political ideologies, political institutions, and political behaviour at both the domestic and international levels, focusing on recurring regularities in political thinking and action. Some, echoing Aristotle, even see it as the master human science.

THE IMPACT OF GLOBALIZATION

The distinctions between domestic and international politics and between the domestic politics of individual nation-states, as this book has shown, have been further eroded by trends in globalization. Here are some examples:

1. Economic crises in individual states are more difficult to prevent from spreading to others. The most recent example is the 'subprime' mortgage crisis in the USA which caused four British as well as a few German banks to require state intervention, and hundreds of billions of dollars of losses in banks worldwide. The Eurozone has seen similar evidence of 'contagion' in 2011 spreading fears of collapse in Greece, and Ireland, to Portugal, Spain, and Italy. The renewed Greek financial crisis in 2015 has posed a new existential threat to the euro, which has combined with simultaneous fears of a serious slowdown in the Chinese economy to unsettle markets. All of this has a serious effect on the economic policies of governments around the world.

2. There have been increasing flows of people across national borders in search of work or refuge. In Britain, for instance, the 2011 Census showed that 11.9 per cent of the population had been born abroad, as compared with 6.7 per cent in the 1991 census. Migrant workers and their families play a significant role not only in the political life of their new countries, but also often as diasporas of the countries from which they came. This is especially well documented for politics in the USA and is an increasingly frequent phenomenon within the EU, but it can be found elsewhere around the world too. As China develops into a global economic and political power, its diaspora in South East Asia and Africa becomes increasingly relevant to its foreign policy.

3. Concern for the environment has also become pre-eminently a global issue, as states increasingly accept the need jointly to move towards policies of sustainable development, which will constrain the domestic policy choices of individual states.

4. There has been an increase in regional organizations where states agree to pool elements of their sovereignty in exchange for the promise of coordinated policies and action. For

23

centuries, states have done this in the form of military alliances. In more recent decades, however, this has spread to organizations with economic and non-military political objectives. The best example of this is the EU, which has the closest ties between its members of all regional organizations, but there has been a proliferation of them elsewhere, for example, ASEAN, Mercosur, NAFTA, and so on.

→ See Chapter 20 for a discussion of regionalism.

5. As discussed in Chapter 15, since the 1970s, there have been two waves of democratization spreading around the world. The collapse of one authoritarian regime sometimes encourages opponents in other ones, as happened in Eastern Europe, then the former Soviet Union between 1989 and 1991, and the 'Arab Spring' of 2011—hence the 'wave'-like phenomenon. And then political actors within states look elsewhere for ideas on political organization; for example, constitutional provisions, electoral arrangements, ways of running electoral campaigns, the reorganization of civil services, and so on. Equally, democratic states also sometimes seek to promote the spread of democracy through various forms of external assistance, ranging from training in the techniques of political professionalism to outright intervention, while authoritarian states may also cooperate to try to stay in power.

6. Ideas for the reform of policies in specific areas spread through international epistemic communities of professionals who share common orientations towards the most effective ways of delivering the policy objectives, irrespective of the particular state in which they live. Ideas of reforms to welfare policies, for example, spread from the USA to Western Europe. Ideas on educational policies have spread around the EU as individual states have been confronted with the evidence from league tables of achievements of their pupils in mastering basic skills. Equally important has been the role of the Intergovernmental Panel on Climate Change—a group of climate scientists from around the world who have played a significant role in getting the issue of global warming on to the political agenda.

7. The proliferation and globalization of media institutions and sources of information, accelerated by the rise of the Internet and other forms of electronic communication as outlined in Chapter 14, have facilitated the emergence of the beginnings of a global civil society; that is, transnational organizations of political activists. Whether it is organizations such as Greenpeace, Médecins sans Frontières, Amnesty International, Oxfam, Caritas, the Red Crescent, the World Wide Fund for Nature, or events such as Live Aid concerts, they all raise concerns above the level of the nation-state.

→ See Chapter 14 for a discussion on the impact of the media.

Globalization presents enormous challenges to the academic study of politics. Above all, it has made the study of international politics that much more important. Political philosophers, too, will have to reorient their focus from the nation-state, the character of which, since the sixteenth century, they have helped to shape. Globalization has, at the very least, increased the pressures on the state, complicating the activities of national governments. According to the economist Rodrik (2011), it is impossible for states simultaneously to pursue all three goals of democracy, national self-determination, and economic globalization—they have to choose two, and in recent years the tendency in Western states has been to pursue economic globalization and democracy, thereby eroding their capacity to control the national economy.

Another trend challenges governments from the opposite direction, from below, in the form of decentralization. Subunits of nation-states demand greater autonomy or independence. The declaration of independence by Kosovo from Serbia is a recent example. It was preceded by the disintegration of the former Soviet Union and the former Yugoslavia which gave rise to many new sovereign states, or which in some cases restored sovereignty to previously independent countries. Elsewhere in the world we have seen successful bids for independence in East Timor and South Sudan, while there are continuing demands for independence for the Basque country, Northern Cyprus, and the Kurds, and secessionist movements in Tibet, the Philippines, and Thailand, to name just a few. At the same time the state is being eroded at another level through the spread of neo-liberal market ideas which advocate a clearer separation of the state from market operations, exemplified by the increasing trend towards establishing the independence of central banks from government intervention, which makes state control of the national economic less direct. Rapley (2006) also emphasized the role of criminal gangs in carving out and controlling 'statelets' of neighbourhoods that coexist in delicate, 'often symbiotic' relationships with nation-states. Examples include the favelas in Brazil, the ganglands of Kingston, Jamaica, and several cities in northern Mexico, not to mention the drug lords of Afghanistan and Myanmar. Often, these gangs are linked with broader networks of transnational crime, challenging the traditional state from both outside and inside.

➡ See Chapter 10 for an analysis of the collapse of the former Yugoslavia.

All of this has contributed to the 'hollowing out' of the state evoked in Chapters 2 and 13, with forces both above and below national governments sucking the vitality out of the state, the institution that has dominated both the practice and the study of politics around the world. Certainly, according to Savoie (2010), it has eviscerated traditional expectations of democratic accountability. It is now much more difficult to know whom to blame for policy failures in Western democracies, let alone punish them in elections. Some commentators, such as Scholte (2005), have even gone so far as to identify 'globalization' with the deterritorialization of social, economic, and technical processes, which flow around the globe without significant obstacle. Others counter this by pointing to a different form of state activity at the international level, namely transnationalism. Slaughter (1997), for instance, has pointed to the rise of new networks of nodes of cooperation between branches of national governments. She points to the increasing webs of relations that link the courts and ministries of justice of individual states. This leads them to cooperate in new approaches to solving problems and sometimes to convergence. Certainly, judges in one jurisdiction are often more aware now of the thinking of judges in others on similar issues—and this applies not just to the EU, which has the greatest integration of a supranational court with national ones. According to Slaughter (1997: 184), '[t]he state is not disappearing; it is disaggregating into its separate, functional distinct parts'. Yet the protracted Eurozone crisis since 2011 is a stark reminder that network arrangements may find decisive, quick decision-making problematic. International markets move rapidly, and they expect national political decision-makers to keep up. Failure to do so invites speculation against currencies. So while the state may be in decline, its often-foretold demise is still a long way off.

➡ See Chapters 2 and 13 for discussion of the 'hollowing out' of the state.

NEW MEDIEVALISM

The end of the Cold War certainly transformed global politics and our understanding of it. One approach to the changing international order—the most optimistic—was the 'End of History' thesis of Fukuyama (1992). This proclaimed the victory of the West not merely in material terms, but also in ideological terms. The liberal democratic and capitalist model of politics and economics had prevailed over communist authoritarianism, and the future convergence of the rest of the world to the Western model seemed assured, even if it was likely to take some time. Although Eastern Europe has, indeed, mostly evolved in that direction, while most of South East Asia and East Asia have at least embraced the capitalist part of the model, convergence around the core values and practices of liberal democracy and capitalism has not yet occurred in other important parts of the world, especially in the Middle East. Furthermore, the failure of Anglo-American intervention to ignite that kind of support in Iraq has provoked a great deal of justified scepticism about the ability of these core Western countries to export their preferred model of politics and economics.

➡ See Chapter 2 for a description of 'new medievalism'.

An alternative scenario has been promoted in the form of a 'new medievalism', mentioned in Chapter 2, which denotes a coming era characterized by multiple and overlapping international authority and loyalties. This scenario has at least two variants. One variant stresses the lack of established order, even anarchy, resulting from the weakening of the nation-state as an institution, as outlined in Chapters 2 and 8. At its most extreme, the 'new medievalism' emphasizes the erosion of traditional sources of stability and the lack of any adequate alternative to replace it. Above all, this is attributed to the 'hollowing out' of state capacity. As emphasized in Chapters 8 and 16, the nation-state has generally been much weaker in the developing world for decades, but the phenomenon is now growing in the developed world as well. From this perspective, order in the global international system, for long predicated on the pre-eminence of nation-states, is now under threat and as yet no alternative structure of order has emerged to replace it. In other words, the world is moving towards greater anarchy, as was supposedly the case in the Middle Ages. The alternative variant accepts the erosion of traditional poles of authority but instead argues that the Middle Ages were not as anarchic or 'dark' as is sometimes presented. There were sources of order and authority which restrained tendencies to anarchy. Advocates of this point of view generally rely on European parallels and emphasize the importance of universal authorities such as the Catholic Church and the Holy Roman Empire. There was no international system as we conceive of it in today's terms, but it was not chaotic. Conflict between various centres of power would erupt, spread, and then die down—it was not endemic. According to the more positive view of the Middle Ages, it was a time of international pluralism, with conflict restrained or moderated by overarching, mainly religious, ideologies. Admittedly, this is another version of the world seen through European lenses, for it takes no account of what was happening in other parts of the world at the same time. It thus universalizes the European experience without taking account of the many imperial systems, stretching from Africa through to China, and the Americas, as surveyed in Chapter 15.

➡ See Chapter 8 discussion of the problems of weakening states.

➡ See Chapter 8 for a discussion of weak states in the developing world.

➡ See Chapter 15 for a discussion of states and empires in world history.

Those who take this more positive view of the Middle Ages suggest that there are alternative poles of authority that prevent chaos today. Friedrichs (2001), for example, argues that the post-international world is held together by the organizational claims of the surviving nation-state system and the transnational market economy, bolstered by international organizations such as the United Nations (UN), the International Monetary Fund (IMF), and the World Trade Organisation (WTO). He suggests that this is analogous to the medieval system which was held together by the competing universalistic claims of Empire and Church.

Yet many signs suggest that global governance, i.e. the 'steering' of the global system, is encountering more and more challenges, and institutions are failing to cope (Alexandroff and Cooper, 2010). The trend is towards the weaker kind of medievalism. The attempt at a fundamental reform of the UN in 2005 failed acrimoniously, with the consequence that at best there will only be incremental change (Weiss, 2009). The WTO has failed to conclude the Doha Round of

23

further trade liberalization. The IMF struggled to find the resources to cope with the global financial crisis. Global environmental negotiations also broke down in acrimony at the Copenhagen conference in December 2009. And the attempt to involve more states from the developing world in global decision-making by boosting the role of the Group of Twenty (G20) group of countries at the expense of the Group of Eight (G8) brought only temporary results.

Whether one believes that the world is becoming more anarchic or that it retains the capacity for self-stabilization, the permeability of national boundaries and of the power of national governments by outside forces seems indisputable. This makes the connection between the study of domestic and international politics, and the need for political philosophers to theorize these developments, even stronger.

DECENTRING THE WEST? THE RISE OF THE SOUTH?

Whether or not the new system is stable or more anarchic, one political trend does seem to be emerging across the globe. This is the rise of new centres of power. This is so, even though the USA continues unchallenged as the sole superpower, with an economy that will remain the most powerful in the world for the next two decades, with conventional and nuclear military resources that dwarf all others, and with a significant claim to soft power too, despite the travails of Iraq. Until recently, the EU was emerging as a more powerful and cohesive economic and political power on the world stage. It sometimes seeks to offer a different approach to international politics—one based more on diplomacy and on establishing standards for law-based international behaviour. Despite its failings, it has achieved the most basic objective of banishing inter-state war from the European continent, at least since 1945 and with good prospects of that continuing into the future. Given the experience of the three major Franco-German wars between 1870 and 1945, this is a great achievement. Furthermore, the gradual integration that has taken place has led to much greater prosperity. All this has made the EU a standard against which regional integration projects in other parts of the world are measured, although we must be careful not to assume it is a model that other regional projects can, and must, follow, especially given the Eurozone crisis of 2011.

➜ See Chapter 20 for a discussion of the different diplomatic styles of the USA and EU.

From this perspective the 'West' appears as powerful now as at any time since the end of the Second World War. A Western model of modernity could seem as influential and attractive as ever. And yet other actors in the world are gaining in confidence, as is illustrated in **Box 23.1**, which summarizes the contrasting views of a former Singaporean diplomat turned academic, Kishore Mahbubani, of the head of the STRATFOR consulting firm in the USA, George Friedman, and of a senior long-time State Department official and academic, Joseph Nye.

Even the US National Intelligence Council (2008) recognized the heavy probability of increasing multilateralism and multipolarity over the next fifteen years, where it had downplayed it only four years earlier. The updated version of its report in 2012 confirmed the continuing diffusion of global power in the world to 2030.

The global financial crisis that broke in the USA, in the second half of 2007, has accelerated the trend. What it has revealed is that the increasing role of the state in Western societies, as highlighted by the secular rise in state finance as a share of national GDP throughout the twentieth century (**see Table 8.1**), has become fiscally unsustainable. In recent years, the USA and other Western states have relied on borrowing from global financial markets to provide the scale of

23

KEY DEBATE BOX 23.1
Is the West in Decline? Is Asia becoming Dominant?

Mahbubani on the rise of the East over the West:

Sometimes the hardest things to see are the largest things.

At the height of Western power, when Western influence extended into virtually every corner of the world, the West essentially wrapped the globe with several layers of Western influence. The enormity of Western power made the world believe that there was only one way forward . . .

The unraveling of Western influence is a complex process. It has many different strands. The West has to understand that this is the major historical trend of our time, that it defines our era . . .

The process of de-Westernization is much deeper than the story of anti-Americanism . . . Many in the West want to believe that this bout of anti-Americanism is just a passing phase caused by the harsh and insensitive policies of one administration . . .

This is a mirage. The mindsets of the largest populations within Asia—the Chinese, the Muslims, and the Indians—have been changed irrevocably. Where once they may have happily borrowed Western lenses and Western cultural perspectives to look at the world, now with growing cultural self-confidence, their perceptions are growing further and further apart . . .

History teaches us that leadership in any era is provided by emerging powers. For example, when America replaced the UK as the world's leading power, it moved naturally to providing global leadership. By the same logic, China should eventually take over the mantle of global leadership from America. In its own way it is providing global inspiration, if not leadership. (Mahbubani, 2008: 127–31, 237–8)

Friedman on the new 'American century':

We are now in an America-centric age. To understand this age, we must understand the United States, not only because it is so powerful but because its culture will permeate the world and define it. Just as French culture and British culture were definitive during their times of power, so American culture, as young and barbaric as it is, will define the way the world thinks and lives. So studying the twenty-first century means studying the United States.

If there were only one argument that I could make about the twenty-first century, it would be that the European century has ended and that the North American age has begun, and that North America will be dominated by the United States for the next hundred years. The events of the twenty-first century will pivot around the United States. That doesn't guarantee that the United States is necessarily a just or moral regime. It certainly does not mean that the United States has yet developed a mature civilization. It does mean that in many ways the history of the United States will be the history of the twenty-first century. (Friedman, 2010: 14)

Nye on the durability of American power:

Any effort to assess American power in the coming decades should recall how many earlier efforts have been wide of the mark. It is chastening to remember how wildly exaggerated were American estimates of Soviet power in the 1970s and of Japanese power in the 1980s . . .

As an overall assessment, describing the twenty-first century as one of American decline is likely to be inaccurate and misleading . . . America has many problems, but it is not in absolute decline, and even in relative terms, it is likely to remain more powerful than any single state in the coming several decades. The real problem for the United States is not that it will be overtaken by China or another contender, but that it will be faced with a rise in the power resources of many others—both states and non-state actors. This diffusion of power will make the United States relatively less able to control others. Entropy [i.e. increasing disorder] may become a greater challenge than China. Moreover, the world will face an increasing number of new transnational issues which will require power *with* others as much as power *over* others. (Nye, 2015: 116–17; emphasis in original)

financing for activities for which their taxpayers were unwilling to pay directly. The problem was further exacerbated by the mushrooming US deficit on foreign trade (Reinhart and Rogoff, 2009). Ironically, many states had been reducing their fiscal share of GDP before the crisis broke (Tanzi, 2011: 95), but they were caught out by events in 2007–8. This dependency on external borrowing turned toxic when large financial institutions such as banks ran into their own liquidity and credibility crisis and needed state bailouts. The consequence, according to Gagnon and Hinterschweiger (2011) is that Western states will need to do much more over the next twenty-five years to reduce this level of public debt to avoid another, even bigger, crisis. As a consequence, Western states will find their freedom of manoeuvre much more restricted for years to come.

Basic demographic trends reinforce this trend of a fundamental shift in global power, as can be seen from **Table 23.1**.

This cites the current UN median projection of world population growth over the period to 2030. What it shows is that in the period 2010–30 the world population is expected to grow by 1.3 billion, but within that overall figure the European population will shrink both absolutely and relatively by roughly 35 million, so that it will be roughly equal with the population of South America and the Caribbean. While the population of North America is expected to rise by 59 million, the population of Africa will rise both absolutely and relatively by 414 million, i.e. a fifth more than the entire North American population of 348 million in 2010, while the population of Asia is expected to rise by 739 million, with the Indian population beginning to overtake China's.

Four states or groups of states exemplify the change. First, there is the rise of powerful states in Asia and of the region as a whole. This is graphically symbolized by the change in foreign exchange reserves there. Where, in 1980, Pacific Asia held 12.37 per cent of global reserves, by the end of 2009 this figure had risen to 56.57 per cent. Japan has been an economic giant for

23

Table 23.1 Regional distribution of world population, selected years (%)

	1990	2010	2030
Africa	11.8	14.4	17.2
Asia (including Middle East)	60.2	60.7	60.1
Europe (including Russia to the Urals)	13.7	10.5	8.4
Latin America and the Caribbean	8.4	8.7	8.7
North America	5.4	5.1	5.0
Oceania	0.5	0.5	0.5
World (in millions)	5,264	6,830	8,130

Source: http://www.un.org/esa/population/publications/longrange2/World-Pop2300final.pdf

some decades, but now China, and more recently India, have come into focus as both economic and military contenders for great power status. China is sometimes presented in the USA as the country most likely to challenge American ascendancy in the coming decades. Whether or not this turns out to be the case, there is no doubting the significance of the change compared with the twentieth century and, indeed, the second half of the nineteenth, when China was so preoccupied with internal disorder and its consequences that it was unable to play a leading role in world affairs. Now the 'rise' of China has become a standard topic of discussion and debate, including inside China itself. Books are written with eye-catching titles such as *When China Rules the World* (Jacques, 2009). India's economic take-off since the early 1990s adds further pressure to the challenge to the West. According to the most recent US National Intelligence Council report (2012: 15), 'by 2030, Asia will have surpassed North America and Europe combined in terms of global power, based upon GDP, population size, military spending, and technological investment'.

The second big change is the increasing self-confidence of the Islamic world. Throughout the nineteenth and twentieth centuries, the Islamic world declined significantly vis-à-vis the West. The dissolution of its most powerful grouping—the Ottoman Empire—led to both military occupation by Western countries and, equally importantly, a sense of inferiority in the face of Western modernity, as exemplified by the Ataturk secularist revolution of the 1920s mentioned in Chapter 8. Even the use of the oil 'card' by Saudi Arabia and others in the 1970s did not essentially change this. Now, things are different. Younger generations of Muslims, it seems, feel more self-assured, less deferential towards the West. The same is true of various Islamic governments. Having said that, we must remain very careful not to draw a simplistic dividing line between the 'Islamic world' and 'the West'. The Islamic world is not united. Turkey is a member of NATO—a largely 'Western' alliance, as well as a candidate for EU membership. Many Islamic countries are allies of the USA in the war on terror. There are many overlapping interests and even alliances between the Islamic world and the West, but there are also many between the Islamic world and the East.

➡ See Chapter 8 for a description of Turkey's radical reforms.

The third big change is the resurgence of Russia. In one sense this does not represent such a big break with recent history. After all, the Soviet Union was the rival superpower from the end of the Second World War until the Union's collapse in 1991. Russia's reappearance as a global player should not, then, be so surprising. What is significant about Russia's resurgence is the regime's greater disdain for supposed Western superiority, even as it continues sometimes to proclaim itself as of the West; and this is in spite of the fact that the West lavished considerable resources, both financial and advisory, on Russia to try to smooth its transition from a communist regime to, hopefully, democracy and a market economy. The intervention by Russia and Russians in Crimea and Eastern Ukraine in 2014 has further widened the rift with the West and stimulated greater official enthusiasm for a 'Eurasian' rather than Western identity.

Fourth, there is the increasing international prominence of the BRICS states (Brazil, Russia, India, China, and South Africa). Originally highlighted as a disparate group with the potential for dramatic returns on foreign investment, it has gradually evolved into a forum that now holds annual summits for foreign policy cooperation and to provide international leadership, especially for developing states in their dealings with the developed world. Their most recent innovation was the establishment of a BRICS Development Bank that might compete with the World Bank.

All these new actors demand greater respect. This is symptomatic of a wider change of attitude in other parts of the world towards the 'West'. It is no longer the object of the same deference as during most of the nineteenth and twentieth centuries. While its levels of economic development and technological prowess remain undisputed, it is no longer seen to embody the only path to 'modernity', a path that nations in other parts of the world are obliged to follow if they are going to achieve the same levels of development. Indeed, there is an increasing body of people who argue that the Western style and level of development is out of keeping with the new priority of an ethic of environmentally friendly, sustainable development. They advocate a search for alternative solutions. China is often presented as the state most likely to challenge the West, and it is true that books now appear there that look forward to a dominant China that embodies different (and superior) civilizational values (Zhang, 2012, 2014). Indian writers too put forward their country as a source of alternative, more genuinely plural, global values and receive endorsement from current Prime Minister Modi (Malhotra, 2013). Equally, the developing world's refusal, despite enormous pressure from the USA, to agree to binding commitments on reducing carbon emissions, at least until they are given the resources to cope with the consequences, reveals a much more confident persona. This behaviour is predicated on the developing world's insistence that developed countries have been largely responsible for climate change and therefore should take action to deal with it.

This inclination resonates with the emergence of two other schools of political analysis. The first is the 'subaltern studies' school described in Chapter 14. This rejects the idea of automatically assigning superiority and paying greater attention to the 'winners' of development. These 'winners' include both elites within individual states and also, internationally, the developed world. Instead, from this perspective, analysts should pay more attention to the 'subalterns', i.e. the underdogs. The latter point is encapsulated in the title of an article by the American academic and black activist Cornel West (1991), 'Decentring Europe', as well as a book by the Indian anthropologist Dipak Chakrabarty (2000), *Provincializing Europe*; that is, treating Europe 'merely' as the equal of other regions of the world.

➡ See Chapter 14 for a discussion of subaltern studies.

To some extent this approach echoes postmodernism, as briefly outlined in Chapter 7 and further discussed in Chapter 17. The orientation underlying it is the rejection of deference to 'god-like' scientific authorities. Rather, it encourages and advocates pluralism. It has been criticized, with some justice, for taking this too far, for excessive relativism. Postmodernists are more noted for seeking to undermine the claims to objectivity of particular academic authorities than for establishing the validity of alternative claims. Yet, the basic principle underlying this book is compatible with their outlook. We do not believe that Western political systems should automatically enjoy greater esteem than those in other parts of the world. Politics in other parts of the world is equally deserving of study.

➡ See Chapter 7 for a discussion of postmodernism.

It is certainly true that, as was repeatedly emphasized in the second section of the book, Western ideas (explored in Part 1) and institutions have spread around the world and in many ways set the standard for what could be regarded as 'modern' political systems. It is a historical fact that democracy, for example, spread from Europe and the USA to other parts of the world in the twentieth century. 'Political science' is often seen as primarily a Western academic discipline; and although critics continue to argue that 'Western' political institutions such as political parties are inappropriate for non-Western societies with different traditions, it is striking that viable alternative forms of political activism and political organization have proved remarkably limited. In the 1960s and 1970s, for instance, leaders of Third World states such as Sukarno in Indonesia and Nyerere in Tanzania advocated forms of political organization and decision-making that were more in keeping with the traditions of village societies; yet these alternative forms have not prospered. To some extent this was the result of other dimensions of modernization. Increasing urbanization, for example, undermined the appeal of traditional rural forms of decision-making.

➡ See Chapter 18 for a further discussion of postmodernism.

➡ See Chapter 12 for a discussion of the problems facing parties.

It is worth reiterating, however, that there is no obvious logical reason why forms of political organization found in the West should acquire automatic pre-eminence. Nor is it obvious that political institutions in the West are all in rude health. One of the arguments underlying Chapter 12 was that political parties in the West suffer from great problems, not least the lack of esteem in which they are held by their potential supporters. Concepts underlying such forms are not always easily translated from Western, especially Anglophone, contexts to other parts of the world. Chapter 14, for example, showed how the concept of 'civil society' was based on assumptions derived from Western experience which were not easily translated into Islamic or Asiatic societies. Chapter 15 referred to the increasing disconnect between politicians and voters across most of the Western world. Yet, we all tend to assess political institutions in other countries through lenses that were fashioned in our own societies. The state, political parties, interest groups, and federalism—these are just some of the key terms of political discourse which look and behave differently from one political system to another. Just because we think we know what they mean in systems with which we are familiar, does not mean that they are identical elsewhere.

➡ See Chapter 14 for a discussion of civil society.

POLITICS IN A GLOBALIZING WORLD: THE END OF POWER AS WE HAVE KNOWN IT?

All of this suggests that domestic politics and international relations are mutating. According to Naim (2013), power in general has become more difficult to exercise, whether it be by governments, political leaders, or business leaders. Government at home has become more fraught. Authorities face more challenges than ever before. The regional shifts in global power outlined above are one key facet of this challenge. Another is the constraint on national governments posed by the need to attract foreign capital. Already at the end of the 1990s, the American commentator Thomas Friedman identified the challenge of the 'golden straitjacket', i.e. the need for governments to appeal to international markets and investors. His idea is encapsulated in **Box 23.2**.

KEY QUOTE BOX 23.2
Friedman on the Neo-Liberal 'Golden Straitjacket'

To fit into the Golden Straitjacket a country must either adopt, or be seen as moving toward, the following golden rules: making the private sector the priority engine of its economic growth, maintaining a low rate of inflation and price stability, shrinking the size of the state bureaucracy, maintaining as close to a balanced budget as possible, if not a surplus, eliminating and lowering tariffs on imported goods, removing restrictions on foreign investment, getting rid of quotas and domestic monopolies, increasing exports, privatizing state-owned industries and utilities, deregulating capital markets, making its currency convertible, opening its industries, stock, and bond markets to direct foreign ownership and investment, deregulating its economy to promote as much domestic competition as possible, eliminating government corruption, subsidies and kickbacks as much as possible, opening its banking and telecommunications systems to private ownership and competition, and allowing its citizens to choose from an array of competing pension options and foreign-run pension and mutual funds. When you stitch all of these pieces together you have the Golden Straitjacket.   (Friedman, 1999: 86–7)

Friedman remarked that the consequence of governments adopting such a Golden Straitjacket is that the economy grows but politics shrinks. In other words, the range of policy alternatives is narrowed to technocratic ones, even in democracies. Citizens in democracies find their preferences ever more subordinated to financial markets. The global financial crisis has intensified that trend, as heavily indebted governments impose austerity so as to satisfy lenders, whether domestic or foreign, even if it means savage cuts in living standards. Most countries have experienced this challenge, but it is exemplified in the Eurozone, with Greece the most obvious example. If Gagnon and Hinterschweiger (2011) are right, dealing with this problem will continue to define the parameters of political debate in many countries for at least another decade.

All of this means that it will become even more important to understand such challenges, incorporate them into the analysis of how politics operates around the world, and devise ways of coping with them. Moreover, political philosophers as well as international relations scholars will have to engage more than they have done with the ideas underlying non-Western political practice. Two key themes emphasized in this book have been, first, the declining importance of the sovereign state, and second, the growing significance of non-Western parts of the world. Both present enormous challenges for the political analyst. The impact of globalization reinforces the importance of the study of international politics and the need for political philosophers to reorient their traditional focus on the state. Likewise, the growing significance of the non-Western world will have to be taken into account by students of comparative politics and international relations. Political philosophers too will have to engage more than they have done with the ideas underlying non-Western political practice. This does not mean that the state has, or is likely to, become a peripheral concern of the political analyst. Nor does it mean that politics in Europe or the USA will become unimportant. Describing and analysing politics in the West and their impact on world affairs will remain absorbing. The evolution of these political systems and the ideas underlying them will still attract wide interest and offer alternative possible reforms for each other when

23

the systems or individual institutions run into difficulties. What happens on both sides of the Atlantic will also have a major impact on world affairs for decades to come. Trump's vow to 'make America great again' is an attempt to reverse the trend of increasing globalization. Nevertheless, the previous dominance of the state and Western theory and practice has been eroded. It is uncertain where these developments will lead, and because of this the study of politics at the beginning of the twenty-first century will continue to be exciting and invigorating.

KEY QUESTIONS

1. Is the global rise of Asia credible, likely, or coordinated?
2. Does it matter if Asia becomes more dominant? To whom, and why?
3. How should the USA respond? How should people outside the USA respond? Is Trump's strategy credible?
4. Has the global financial crisis intensified globalization or revived the power of national states?
5. Is it good or bad if political power is becoming more difficult to exercise? Does it make the world a safer or more dangerous place?
6. Does the 'Golden Straitjacket' bring greater benefits or problems for democracies? Should they try to escape from it? What is the evidence from Greece and the Eurozone more generally? What about the UK?
7. Has China avoided the 'Golden Straitjacket' and prospered? If so, how?
8. Is the shift of global power from the West to the East inevitable?
9. Where will the Islamic world figure if power does shift from the West to the East?

FURTHER READING

Ehteshami, A. (2007), *Globalization and Global Politics in the Middle East: Old Games, New Rules* (London and New York: Routledge).
A thoughtful survey of the impact of globalization on the Middle East.

EUISS (2014), *A Changing Global Environment* (Paris: Chaillot Paper 133 C), (http://www.iss.europa.eu/uploads/media/Chaillot_Paper_133_-_A_changing_global_environment.pdf).
A European analysis of trends in global affairs, especially as they affect the EU.

Friedman, T. (1999), *The Lexus and the Olive Tree* (London and New York: HarperCollins).
A widely quoted analysis of the impact of globalization around the world and some of the resistance that it engendered.

Mahbubani, K. (2008), *The New Asian Hemisphere: The Irresistible Shift of Global Power to the East* (New York: Public Affairs).
A passionate advocacy of the Asian century.

Malhotra, R. (2013), *Being Different: An Indian Challenge to Western Universalism* (Noida, Uttar Pradesh: HarperCollins).
The author presents traditional Indian ways of thinking as a more appropriate basis for genuinely plural, global values.

23

Naim, M. (2013), *The End of Power: From Boardrooms to Battlefields and Churches to States, Why Being in Charge Isn't What it Used to Be* (New York: Basic Books).
A thought-provoking commentary on the way that power, and especially political power, is becoming increasingly hobbled.

Naughton, B. (2010), 'China's distinctive system: Can it be a model for others?' *Journal of Contemporary China*, 19(65): 437–60.
An attempt to identify what is special about China's economic system and development by one of the foremost analysts of the Chinese economy.

Nye, J. S. (2015), *Is the American Century Over?* (Cambridge and Malden, MA: Polity).
A well-balanced analysis of the opportunities and challenges facing the world's still most powerful nation.

Poirson, T. and Oprisko, R. (eds) (2015), *Caliphates and Islamic Global Politics* (Bristol: E-International Relations).
Updates Ehteshami with more recent developments in the Middle East, including the rise of ISIS/ISIL.

Shambaugh, D. (2014), *China Goes Global: The Partial Power* (New York: Oxford University Press).
A wide-ranging, persuasive analysis by one of America's foremost China-watchers.

US National Intelligence Council (2012), *Global Trends 2030: Alternative Worlds* (Washington, DC) (http://www.dni.gov/files/documents/GlobalTrends_2030.pdf).
The most recent set of scenarios for global trends as seen from Washington, DC.

Zhang, W. (2012), *The China Wave: Rise of a Civilizational State* (Hackensack, NJ: World Century).
This portrays the rise of China as a civilizational challenge to the West.

 For additional material and resources, please visit the Online Resources at:
www.oup.com/he/garner4e

23

GLOSSARY

Agency In social science literature denotes the fact of something happening or existing because of an actor's action. The contrast is with a state of affairs that is chiefly determined by impersonal factors (historical, economic, etc.) over which human actors have little control. Hence the frequent use of the combined term structure-agency to pose the question whether background factors or human action were the primary causes.

Alternative member model A hybrid voting system that combines strengths of both majoritarianism and proportional representation: votes are cast both for individual candidates within a constituency and for a general list of candidates from separate parties.

Amoral familism The exaltation of family interests above all other moral considerations, originally coined by the sociologist Banfield to describe social relations in Sicily.

Anarchy In its simplest sense anarchy denotes an absence of political rule or sovereign authority. In traditional International Relations theory, states are said to exist in an anarchic international sphere because there is no sovereign authority standing above individual states.

Anthropocentric An ethic which prioritizes the interests of humans over all other forms of life.

Arrow's impossibility theorem A mathematical theorem formulated by the economist Kenneth Arrow which shows the impossibility of determining the 'optimal' ranking of preferences by members of a society when no alternative choice receives an absolute majority.

Authoritarian Refers to rule which is unaccountable and restrictive of personal liberty.

Authority A situation whereby an individual or group is regarded as having the right to exercise power and is thereby acting legitimately.

Balance of payments Refers to a country's international economic transactions over a certain period showing the sum of all ingoing and outgoing sums between individuals, businesses, and government agencies in that country in relation to those in the rest of the world.

Balance of power A system of relations between states where the goal is to maintain an equilibrium of power, thus preventing the dominance of any one state.

Behaviouralism An approach that stresses the importation of the scientific method in the study of social phenomena. Objective measurement of the social world is the goal, values to be completely jettisoned from social enquiry.

Bicameralism The principle of having two separate chambers of a national parliament.

Bipolarity In international politics generally describes a distribution of power in which two states possess a preponderance of economic, military, and political power and influence either internationally or in a particular region. Bipolarity during the Cold War referred to the power and influence of the USA *vis-à-vis* that of the USSR.

Bourgeoisie Term appearing frequently in Marxist analysis and referring to a merchant and/or propertied class possessing essential economic power and control.

Cartel parties A type of party that has evolved from the **mass party** with more limited membership and dominated by professional politicians.

Citizenship The granting of social and political rights to enable individuals to participate in state decision-making.

Civic culture A variety of **political culture**, where citizens predominantly feel capable of taking an active part in politics.

Civic nationalism Refers to loyalty to the institutions and values of a particular political community; sometimes presented as a more moderate form of nationalism.

Civil society Consists of institutions, such as interest groups, which stand in an intermediary position between the individual and the state. See also **international civil society**.

Class analysis Associated with traditional Marxism which places socio-economic class (e.g. proletariat, peasantry, bourgeoisie, aristocracy) at the centre of virtually all political analysis.

Classical liberalism Emphasizes that the state's role should be limited to ensure internal and external security and to ensure that private property rights are enforced.

Cohabitation Occurs when a country's president comes from one party and the prime minister from a different one.

Cold War A description of the states system existing between the end of the Second World War in 1945 and the collapse of Soviet communism by the early 1990s. On the one side was the United States, the dominant power in the West; on the other was the Soviet Union, the dominant power in the East.

Colonialism A mode of domination involving the subjugation of one population group and their territory to another, usually through settling the territory with sufficient people from the colonizing group to impose direct or indirect rule over the native population and to maintain control over resources and external relations. It is a common manifestation of **imperialism** but is not identical with it.

Communitarianism A strand of thought which argues that individuals gain their rights and duties within particular communities. It is often contrasted with **cosmopolitanism**.

Complex interdependence See also **interdependence**. While interdependence in IR refers to the notion developed mainly in liberal theory that states in fact are interconnected through a web of relations, primarily in the economic field, which makes warfare less likely (and less desirable as a foreign policy strategy), *complex* interdependence simply introduces more variables as relevant to the equation, therefore deepening the complexity of interdependence and strengthening the case for seeing the world as far more pluralistic than, say, neorealist theories allow.

Concert of Europe Term used to designate a largely informal agreement among the major powers of nineteenth-century Europe to act together—or 'concert' together—on matters of mutual concern. It emerged following the Congress of Vienna (1814–15) and was manifest principally in irregular diplomatic meetings and conferences aimed at the peaceful resolution of differences.

Consociational democracy A means whereby the elites of different parts of a heterogeneous community can share power and integrate society.

Constituency An electoral district.

Constitution The complex of relations between a state's governing institutions and the people, including the understandings that are involved. Most of these relations are usually codified in a single document.

Constitutionalism The principle that assigns a special significance to constitutions and rule of law in national life.

Constructivism Sometimes called *social* constructivism, it refers to the notion that the 'reality' of the world around us is constructed intersubjectively through social interaction which gives meaning to material objects and practices; thus 'reality' is not simply an objective truth detached from a social base.

Coordinated market economies Where firms depend more heavily on non-market relationships to coordinate their activities than in liberal Anglo-American economies; more typically found in continental Europe.

Corporatism Traditionally, corporatism referred to the top–down model where the state, as in the fascist model, incorporates economic interests in order to control them and civil society in general. Modern societal or neocorporatism, on the other hand, reflects a genuine attempt by governments to incorporate economic interests, trade union and business interests, into the decision-making process.

Cosmopolitan democracy A system of popular control of supranational institutions and processes.

Cosmopolitanism A position which holds that humans ought to be regarded as a single moral community to which universal principles apply irrespective of national boundaries.

Cultural pluralism The descriptive fact of the existence of different norms of behaviour determined by culture. Can be regarded as normatively desirable or undesirable deductive method.

Deductive method The process of reasoning whereby a logically certain conclusion can be derived from one or more premises or statements.

Deliberative democracy A model of democracy emphasizing the role of discussion and

debate as a means of reaching rational, legitimate, and altruistic decisions.

Democracy Refers to a political system in which there is self-government.

Democratic elitism An attempt, most associated with Joseph Schumpeter, to reconcile elitism with democracy. According to this model, voters have the opportunity to choose between competing teams of leaders.

Democratic peace A thesis which holds that countries that are governed democratically do not go to war against each other.

Democratization The introduction of a democratic system or democratic principles.

Deontological An ethical theory which holds that certain end states (as in the case of a natural right) are to be upheld because they are right in themselves, irrespective of the consequences which accrue from them in particular circumstances.

Deterrence Both a theory and a strategy in IR based on the notion that the possession of powerful weapons will deter aggression by other countries. During the Cold War, *nuclear* deterrence was a widely supported strategy.

Developmental state A state, such as Japan, which prioritizes economic resources for rapid development, and which uses carrots and sticks to induce private economic institutions to comply.

Dichotomy A division into two mutually exclusive or contradictory entities or groups such as 'the West' and the 'non-West'.

Direct democracy Refers to a system whereby the people rule directly and not through representatives.

Duverger's Law The conclusion by the French political scientist Maurice Duverger that first-past-the-post electoral systems lead to two-party systems.

Ecocentric An ethic which removes humans from the centre of the moral universe and accords intrinsic value to non-human parts of nature.

Ecological modernization A version of sustainable development which seeks to show how liberal capitalist societies can be reformed in an environmentally sustainable way.

Ecologism An ideology that stresses the interdependence of all forms of life, and which is often used to denote the moral dethroning of humans.

Economic nationalism Based on, concerned with, or verifiable by observation or experience rather than theory or pure logic.

Elitism In a normative sense refers to the rule of the most able. From an empirical perspective it refers to the existence of a ruling group beyond popular control in all societies of any complexity.

Elitist theory of democracy See **democratic elitism**.

Emancipation A common theme in Critical Theory which denotes a normative aspiration to liberate people from unfair economic, social and political conditions.

Embedded autonomy The insulation of state economic policy-makers in **developmental states** from short-term political pressures.

Empire Shares a common etymology with **imperialism** and denotes a system in which one country or centre of power dominates and controls other, weaker countries either directly or indirectly using either force, the threat of force, or some other means of coercion.

Empirical Based on, concerned with, or verifiable by observation or experience rather than theory or pure logic.

Empirical analysis Refers to the measurement of factual information, of what is rather than what ought to be.

Enlightenment A seventeenth- and eighteenth-century intellectual and cultural movement that emphasized the application of reason to knowledge in a search for human progress.

Epistemic communities Groups of specialists in various countries who share a common approach to a policy area that transcends national differences.

Epistemology Refers to the task of establishing what can be known about what exists.

Ethnic cleansing A term which emerged during the breakup of the former Yugoslavia and which referred to attempts to physically rid (i.e. 'cleanse') a particular area of people from a certain ethnic group by either driving them out or murdering them.

Ethnic nationalism Refers to loyalty to a shared inheritance based on culture, language, or religion.

Ethnocentrism The tendency to see and interpret the world primarily from the perspective of one's own cultural, ethnic, or national group. It often entails elements of hierarchy in that one tends to regard one's own culture as superior, or at least preferable, to others.

Ethnosymbolism The manipulation of mainly cultural symbols to strengthen national identity.

Executive The branch of government responsible for the execution of policy. It is conceptually separate from the other two branches of government—legislative and judicial—and it comprises ministers (whether elected or not) and all government officials.

Federalism The principle that within a state, different territorial units have the authority to make certain policies without interference from the centre.

Fordism Refers to a form of large-scale mass-production that is homogeneous both in terms of the products made and also in terms of the repetitive jobs that came with it.

General will A concept, associated with Rousseau, which holds that the state ought to promote an altruistic morality rather than the selfish interests of individuals.

Global governance This term extends the concept of **governance** as defined below, and refers loosely to the 'architecture' constituted by various authoritative political, social, and economic structures and actors that interconnect and interact in the absence of actual 'government' in the global sphere.

Global justice The application of principles of justice at a global rather than a national level.

Global south This term corresponds more or less to what was commonly referred to as the 'Third World'. It designates poorer, underdeveloped countries most of which lie geographically south of the equator. Correspondingly, it requires a 'North' which is sometimes used as an alternate designation for 'the West'.

Globalization A term used to describe the process of increasing economic, political, social, and cultural interdependence which has, for good or ill, reduced the autonomy of sovereign states.

Good governance A set of principles formulated by international financial institutions to make the government of developing states fair, effective, and free from corruption.

Governance A term often preferred now to government since it reflects the broader nature of modern government which includes not just the traditional institutions of government but also the other inputs into decisions that steer society such as subnational and supranational institutions, the workings of the market, and the role of interest groups.

Harm principle A position, associated with John Stuart Mill, that actions are to be allowed unless the effect of them is to harm others.

Hegemony Generally embodies the concept of political, social, and economic domination. In IR it may refer to the general dominance of a particular country over others. It was developed as an important concept in Critical Theory by Antonio Gramsci and is used to theorize relations of domination and subordination in both domestic and international spheres.

Human nature Refers to innate and immutable human characteristics. Hobbes, for instance, regards the competitive and self-serving nature of humans as necessitating an all-powerful state. Other strands of thought either regard human nature in a more positive light or, as with Marx, suggest that human character depends upon the social and economic structure of society.

Humanitarian intervention This term implies direct intervention by one country, or a group of countries, in the internal affairs of another country, on the grounds that such intervention is justified by humanitarian concerns relating, for example, to genocide. See also **intervention**.

Idealism This term has invited numerous interpretations in philosophy, politics, and international relations. For the purposes of IR, it is usually taken to refer to a particular school of liberal thought which emerged in the wake of the First World War and which envisaged opportunities for significant positive change in world affairs and which aimed in particular at eliminating warfare. It remains an appropriate designation for any school of thought in IR which promotes visions of a better world order in which peace and justice are the order of the day.

Identity politics Sometimes referred to as the politics of difference, identity politics is a cultural movement based on a demand for recognition and respect by particular groups of people centered on their race, ethnicity, gender, sexual orientation or nationality. For identity groups on the progressive left identity politics is about redressing negative perceptions by re-asserting the value and dignity of the particular oppressed group.

Illiberal democracy Describes states where competitive elections are held but in which there is relatively little protection of rights and liberties, and state control over the means of communication ensures that governing parties are rarely defeated at the polls.

Imperialism Literally, 'to command', and denoting the exercise of power by one group over another. It is sometimes used synonymously with **colonialism** but is broader in its application because it does not necessarily involve actual physical occupation of the territory in question or direct rule over the subjugated people.

Inductive method Inductive reasoning is a method of reasoning in which the premises are viewed as supplying some evidence for the truth of the conclusion.

Insider groups Interest groups enjoying a privileged relationship with government.

Institutions Regular patterns of behaviour that provide stability and regularity in social life; sometimes these patterns are given organizational form with specific rules of behaviour and of membership.

Interdependence The notion developed mainly in liberal theory that states in fact are interconnected through a web of relations, primarily in the economic field, which makes warfare less likely (and less desirable as a foreign policy strategy).

Interest groups Political actors who seek collectively to press specific interests upon governments (sometimes also called pressure groups).

Intergenerational justice Principles of justice relating to non-contemporaries; i.e. between those living now and those still to be born.

International civil society Refers broadly to the realm of non-state actors, including interest groups and voluntary associations, in the international sphere.

International regime An idea developed by Stephen Krasner which encapsulates the way in which groups of actors in certain issue areas converge around a set of principles, norms, rules, and procedures. An example is the international human rights regime.

International society A concept associated with the English School of International Relations indicating that the condition of anarchy in the international sphere does not preclude the development of a society of states characterized by peaceful working relations.

Internationalism Refers to both a belief in the benefits of international political and economic cooperation and a movement that advocates practical action in support of these objectives.

Intervention In international relations, usually refers to direct intervention by one or more states in the internal affairs of another, by either military or non-military means. *Humanitarian* intervention refers to any intervention which is claimed to have a primarily humanitarian purpose, such as intervening to prevent genocide.

Intragenerational justice Principles of justice relating to contemporaries, that is those who are living at the same time.

Iron triangles Groups of politicians, officials, and outside experts who regularly formulate government policy in particular issue areas to the exclusion of wider social groups.

Issue networks Looser groups of officials and outsiders who regularly share ideas in particular policy areas.

Legal positivism A form of legal theory that asserts that law is simply what the state says it is.

Legislatures Institutions of government which have the power of making, amending and repealing laws in a society. The term is often used interchangeably with 'parliament', but whereas the latter term focuses upon the role of the chamber(s) as an arena for debates over laws and policies, the term 'legislature' focuses more upon its law-making role.

Liberal democracy Describes states—such as the USA, the United Kingdom, and India—which are characterized by free and fair elections involving universal suffrage, together with a liberal political framework consisting of a relatively high degree of personal liberty and the protection of individual rights.

Liberal institutionalism Closely associated with liberal internationalism, this concept focuses more attention on the ability of international institutions to ameliorate the negative effects of anarchy in the international system.

Machtpolitik See **power politics**.

Marxism The political and economic theories of Karl Marx and Friedrich Engels, later developed by their followers to form the basis of communism.

Marxist See **Marxism**.

Mass parties Political parties typically in the first half of the twentieth century that attracted millions of grass-roots members.

Mercantilism The economic theory that trade generates wealth and is stimulated by the accumulation of profitable balances, which a government should encourage by means of protectionism.

Meritocratic theory of justice Advocates distributing resources to those who display some merit, such as innate ability, and therefore deserve to be rewarded.

Metanarrative This concept, sometimes called a 'grand narrative', refers to a total philosophy or historical explanation of the social and political world presented as an ultimate truth.

Methodology Refers primarily to the particular way(s) in which knowledge is produced. Methodologies vary considerably depending on the type of research being carried out to produce knowledge in different fields—historical, anthropological, linguistic, biological, medical, etc. Different methodologies invariably incorporate their own assumptions and rationales about the nature of knowledge, although these are not always stated explicitly.

Modernism A movement towards modifying traditional beliefs in accordance with modern ideas.

Modernist See **modernism**.

Modernity Modernity is a temporal and cultural phenomenon linked not only to the rise of industrialization in Europe and North America but also to profound changes in social and political thought which are closely associated with the intellectual movement known as the Enlightenment.

Monism The view that there are no fundamental divisions in phenomena.

Nation A named community, often referred to as 'a people', usually occupying a homeland and sharing one or more cultural elements, such as a common history, language, religion, customs, etc. Nations may or may not have a state of their own.

National interest A concept closely associated with *raison d'état* and power politics. It suggests that the interests of the state (or at least of one's own state) is paramount over any other consideration in the international sphere. Although regarded as a foundational concept in realist approaches it is as easily used to justify idealist approaches as well indicating that what is actually in the national interest may be highly contested.

Nationalism In politics and international relations, nationalism refers to doctrine or ideology which holds that 'the nation' is more or less entitled to political autonomy, usually in a state of its own.

Natural law Law conceived as both universal and eternal, applying to all people in all places and at all times, because it derives either from 'nature' or God as distinct from local laws arising within specific communities.

Natural rights Rights which humans are said to possess irrespective of the particular legal and political system under which they live.

Negative liberty Holds that liberty can be increased by removing external obstacles, provided by physical incarceration or law, to it.

Neoliberalism A modified form of liberalism tending to favour free-market capitalism.

Nepotism The practice among those with power or influence of favouring relatives or friends, especially by giving them jobs.

Neo-medievalism A system of governance resembling Europe in the Middle Ages where authority belongs to an overlapping array of local, national, and supranational institutions.

New liberalism A version of liberalism that advocates a more positive role for the state than classical liberalism. Argues that the state, in correcting the inequities of the market, can increase liberty by creating greater opportunities for individuals to achieve their goals.

New Public Management An approach to the reform of government bureaucracies in the 1990s that sought to introduce methods of business administration.

Night-watchman state A model in which the state concentrates on ensuring external and internal security, playing little role in civil society and the economy where the economic market is allowed to operate relatively unhindered.

Non-governmental organizations (NGOs) A term applying to almost any organization that operates independently from government, whether at the local, national, or international level.

Normative Relating to rules, or making people obey rules, especially rules of behaviour.

Normative analysis Refers to analysis which asks ought rather than is type questions, therefore forming the basis of political philosophy. It does not seek to ask, therefore, whether democracy, or freedom, or a pluralist state exists, but whether these outcomes are desirable ones.

Ontology Relates to what exists. It asks what is there to know? Is there, for instance, a political world out there capable of being observed or is the reality, to at least some degree, created by the meanings or ideas we impose upon it?

Original position A device used by John Rawls to denote a position where individuals meet to decide the rules of justice governing the society in which they are to live.

Outsider groups Interest groups that enjoy no special relationship with the government and thus seek to press their case from the outside.

Parliamentarianism The principle that governments are formed by prime ministers, rather than heads of state, who are primarily responsible to parliament.

Paternalism The practice, often associated with conservatism, of restricting the liberty of individuals in order to benefit them.

Patriarchy Refers to male domination and corresponding female oppression.

Perestroika The policy of attempted restructuring of the Soviet political system under President Gorbachev in the late 1980s.

Pluralist See **pluralism**.

Pluralism Originated as a normative argument against monism or sameness. In political theory it is most associated with a theory of the state which holds that political power is diffuse, all organized groups having some influence on state outputs. In IR it is associated with one of two main approaches adopted by the 'English School' as well as with neoliberal theory which highlights the multiplicity, or plurality, of forces at work in the international system.

Plurality A simple majority in voting (sometimes also known as first-past-the-post), as distinct from an absolute majority (i.e. 50 per cent plus one).

Policy communities Groups of officials and experts in particular policy areas who regularly consult each other.

Political culture The aggregate attitudes of members of a society towards the institutions of rule and how they should operate.

Political obligation A central preoccupation of political theorists asking why, if at all, individuals ought to obey the state. There have been a variety of different answers to this question ranging from the divine right of kings to rule to the modern claim that democracy is the basis for authority.

Political party A group of political activists who aspire to form or be part of the government on the basis of a programme of policies.

Political system The totality of institutions within a state and all the connections between them.

Polyarchy A term coined by Robert Dahl. It refers to a society where government outcomes are a product of the competition between groups. The rule of minorities, not majorities, is postulated as the normal condition of pluralist democracies.

Populism A political approach that strives to appeal to ordinary people who feel that their concerns are disregarded by established elite groups.

Positive discrimination Refers to the practice of discriminating in favour of those disadvantaged groups who, it is argued, would remain disadvantaged unless affirmative action was taken in their favour.

Positive liberty A theory which holds that liberty can be increased either by state action or by removing internal obstacles such as immorality or irrationality.

Postivist See **positivism**.

Positivism An approach which believes it is possible to generate empirical statements without any evaluative connotations. At an extreme level, the so-called logical positivists argue that only empirical statements, together with those that are true by definition, are meaningful, thereby ruling out the value of normative statements.

Postmodernism A multi-faceted theoretical approach which challenges the certainties and dualisms of modernism. It therefore promotes pluralism and difference.

Power The ability to make others do something that they would not have chosen to do.

Power politics (machtpolitik) A view of politics associated with realism and which generally takes morality and justice to be irrelevant to the conduct of international relations, a view predicated in turn on the notion that 'might is right'.

Presidentialism The principle that the president of a republic is the head of the government.

Principal-agent relations Identifies the differentiation of roles between the giver of instructions, usually in government administration, and the implementer.

Procedural justice The distribution of goods according to a set of rules, irrespective of the outcome.

A family of voting systems that make their highest priority a close approximation between the votes given to all the parties putting up candidates and the number of seats into which this is translated in parliament.

Protectionism An economic strategy, usually associated with a national policy of trade restriction in the form of tariffs and quotas, which attempts to protect domestic industries, businesses, and jobs from competition from abroad.

Public space The arena (real or virtual) in which any member of society is free to express views on any issue of interest to the public. Sometimes associated with the German philosopher Habermas, who stressed its key importance for democracy and the difficulty of maintaining it under capitalism.

Realism Denotes a complex array of theories and ideas in the human sciences, especially philosophy, sociology, politics, and international relations. In the latter, it names a general approach to theory which takes power politics, national interest, and similar concepts as foundational to action in the international sphere, and opposes idealism in liberal and critical theories.

Reason of state (raison d'état) See **national interest**.

Rechtsstaat Literally, a law-based state, as distinct from a state where the ruler or executive is free to adopt policies and change them as they see fit.

Regionalization A process in which a number of states in a given geographical area come together for mutually beneficial purposes, often forming a regional association. Some, like the EU, are highly institutionalized and have myriad economic, social, and political interconnections, while others may have minimal rules and less ambitious purposes.

Religious fundamentalism Referrs to the belief of an individual or a group of individuals in the absolute authority of a sacred religious text or teachings of a particular religious leader, prophet, and/or God.

Representative democracy Refers to a system whereby the people choose others to represent their interests, rather than making decisions themselves.

Rule of law The principle that everyone in a state, the executive included, is subject to the same impersonal laws.

Secularism In political terms, it refers to the removal of religion from a privileged position in the state.

Security dilemma A concept in international relations, developed principally in realist thought, in which the condition of anarchy is seen to prompt states to engage in self-regarding behaviour in order to survive. The dilemma arises when efforts by one state to enhance its own security (such as acquiring superior weaponry) provokes insecurity in another state, which may then respond by building up its own military capacity.

Self-determination A doctrine that emerged in the early twentieth century in relation to the right of 'peoples' (nations) to determine their own political future, thus embodying elements of both democracy and nationalism.

Semantic analysis In political studies, refers to an analysis of the meaning of key terms and concepts—such as democracy and freedom—which can be separated from a normative analysis of such concepts.

Social capital The aggregate set of attitudes and networks that enable members of a society willingly to cooperate in pursuit of joint projects.

Social contract A device used by a number of political thinkers, most recently John Rawls, to justify a particular form of state. It is conceived as a voluntary agreement that individuals make in a state of nature, which is a society before government is set up.

Social constructivism See **constructivism**.

Social Darwinism The application of Darwin's theory of natural selection to social life. It was used by the social theorist Herbert Spencer to justify a *laissez-faire* approach to social policy to ensure that only the fittest survive.

Social democratic See **social democracy**.

Social democracy An approach which, after the Russian Revolution in 1917, became associated with liberal democracies that engaged in redistributive policies and the creation of a welfare state.

Social justice The principle that goods ought to be distributed according to a principle based on need, merit, or pure equality.

Social movement Refers to largely informal broad-based movements composed of groups and individuals coalescing around key issue areas on a voluntary and often spontaneous basis. Examples include the environmental movement, women's movement, peace movement, and anti-globalization movement.

Solidarism A term applied to a branch of thought in English School International Relations theory which seeks to promote greater protection of human rights internationally, even where this overrides, at least in principle, the rights of states to nonintervention in domestic politics.

Sovereignty Refers to self-government either at the level of the individual or at the level of the state. To say a state is sovereign is to claim that it has a monopoly of force over the people and institutions in a given territorial area.

State A two-level concept: (*a*) the government executive of a country, sometimes also known as a nation-state; (*b*) the whole structure of political authority in a country.

Statecraft The skilful conduct of state affairs, usually in the context of external relations.

State of nature A concept with a long history in political and social thought which posits a hypothetical vision of how people lived before the institution of civil government and society. There are various competing versions of the state of nature, some portraying it as dangerous while others see it in a more positive light.

Structural adjustment Used in application to economic policies imposed on countries—usually poor and underdeveloped—by the World Bank and the International Monetary Fund as a condition for obtaining loans, so as to reduce fiscal deficits. Specific policies have included privatization, cuts in government expenditure on public services, devaluation, tariff cuts, and so on.

Structuration A concept derived from the sociologist Anthony Giddens, which here designates all the factors that both constrain and also provide resources for the functioning of a political system.

Sustainable development A term that seeks to denote the compatibility between environmental protection and economic growth.

Totalitarian Refers to an extreme version of authoritarian rule, in which the state controls all aspects of society and the economy.

Totalitarianism See **totalitarian**.

Unicameralism The principle of having a single chamber of a national parliament.

Unilateralism Refers to the tendency of a state to pursue its preferred foreign policy strategies regardless of whether there is support from international bodies (such as the

UN or NATO) or indeed regardless of any international law.

Utilitarianism A consequentialist ethical theory which argues that the behaviour of individuals and governments should be judged according to the degree to which their actions maximize pleasure or happiness.

Utopia Refers to an ideal state of affairs which does not exist but which can be aimed for. The search for utopias is seen by some as a worthwhile exercise to expand the limits of human imagination, and by others as a recipe for illiberal, authoritarian, and even totalitarian societies.

REFERENCES

Acharya, Amitav, and Barry Buzan (eds) (2007), 'Why Is There No Non-Western IR Theory', special issue of *International Relations of the Asia-Pacific* 7(3): 285–470.

Acharya, Amitav, and Barry Buzan (2019), *The Making of Global International Relations: Origins and Evolution of IR at its Centenary* (Cambridge: Cambridge University Press).

Adam, Robert (2017), 'Government Advisers in Decline but Earning More', https://www.instituteforgovernment.org.uk/blog/governmentadvisers-decline-earning-more

Ai, Janette (2015), *Politics and Traditional Culture: The Political Use of Traditions in Contemporary China* (New Jersey: World Scientific).

Ajani, Gianmaria (2019), 'Russian Liberalism and the Rule of Law: Notes from Underground', in Riccardo Mario Cucciolla (ed.), *Dimensions and Challenges of Russian Liberalism: Historical Drama and New Prospects* (Switzerland: Springer), pp. 15–26.

Alagappa, Harish (2016), 'The Decline and Fall of Indian Liberalism', in Ronald Meinardus (ed.) (2016), *What Does It Mean to be a Liberal in India* (New Delhi: Academic Foundation).

Ali, T. (2002), *The Clash of Fundamentalisms* (London: Verso).

Anderson, Berit and Brett Horvath (2017), 'Scout: The Rise of the Weaponized AI Propaganda Machine', https://yaleglobal.yale.edu/content/scout-rise-weaponized-ai-propaganda-machine

Ang, Ien, Yudhishthir Raj Isar, and Phillip Mar (eds) (2016), *Cultural Diplomacy: Beyond the National Interest?* (Abingdon: Routledge).

Appiah, Kwame Anthony (2015), *Cosmopolitanism: Ethics in a World of Strangers* (London: Penguin).

Arblaster, A. (1984), *The Rise and Decline of Western Liberalism* (Oxford: Basil Blackwell).

Arblaster, A. (2002), *Democracy* (Milton Keynes: Open University Press).

Archibugi, D. (1995), 'From the United Nations to Cosmopolitan Democracy', in D. Archibugi and D. Held (eds), *Cosmopolitan Democracy: An Agenda for a New World Order* (Cambridge: Polity Press).

Arneson, R. (2000), 'The Priority of the Right over the Good Rides Again', in P. Kelly (ed.), *Impartiality, Neutrality and Justice: Re-reading Brian Barry's Justice as Impartiality* (Edinburgh: Edinburgh University Press), pp. 60–86.

Ashworth, Lucian M. (2018), 'The Origins of International Relations', https://www.bisa.ac.uk/index.php/research-articles/539-the-origins-ofinternational-relations

Atlantic, The (2018), 'The Grim Conclusions of the Largest-Ever Study of Fake News', https://www.theatlantic.com/technology/archive/2018/03/largest-study-ever-fake-news-mit-twitter/555104/

Avineri, S., and A. de-Shalt (eds) (1992), *Communitarianism and Individualism* (Oxford: Oxford University Press).

Ayer, A. J. (1971), *Language, Truth and Logic* (Harmondsworth: Penguin, 2nd edn).

Bachrach, P. (1967), *The Theory of Democratic Elitism* (London: London University Press).

Bachrach, P., and M. Baratz (1963), 'Decisions and Non-decisions', *American Political Science Review*, 57: 632–42.

Bachrach, P., and M. Baratz (1970), *Power and Poverty: Theory and Practice* (New York: Oxford University Press).

Bachtiger, Andre, John S. Dryzek, Jane Mansbridge, and Mark Warren (eds) (2018), *The Oxford Handbook of Deliberative Democracy* (Oxford: Oxford University Press).

Bailey, Matthew (2011), 'The Uses and Abuses of British Political Fiction, or How I Learned to Stop Worrying and Love Malcolm Tucker', *Parliamentary Affairs* 64(2): 281–95.

Baiocchi, Gianpaolo (2005), *Militants and Citizens: The Politics of Participatory Democracy in Porto Alegre* (Stanford, CA: Stanford University Press).

Barrett, M. (1988), *Women's Oppression Today* (London: Verso).

Barry, B. (1970), *Sociologists, Economics and Democracy* (Basingstoke: Collier Macmillan).

Barry, B. (1999), 'Sustainability and Intergenerational Justice', in A. Dobson, *Fairness and Futurity: Essays* on Sustainability and Justice (Oxford: Oxford University Press).

Barry, B. (2001), *Culture and Equality: An Egalitarian Critique of Multiculturalism* (Cambridge: Polity Press).

Barry, J. (1999), *Rethinking Green Politics* (London: Sage).

Barry, N. (2000), *An Introduction to Modern Political Thought* (Basingstoke: Macmillan, 4th edn).

Barry, N. (2006), 'Defending Luck Egalitarianism', *Journal of Applied Philosophy* 23(1): 89–107.

Baumeister, Hannah (2018), *Sexualised Crimes, Armed Conflict and the Law: The International Criminal Court and the Definitions of Rape and Forced Marriage* (Abingdon: Routledge).

Bayly, C. A. (2012), *Recovering Liberties: Indian Thought in the Age of Liberalism and Empire* (Cambridge: Cambridge University Press).

Beitz, C. (1979), *Political Theory and International Relations* (Princeton: Princeton University Press).

Bell, D. (1960), *The End of Ideology* (Glencoe, IL: Free Press).

Bell, Daniel (2006), *Beyond Liberal Democracy: Political Thinking for an East Asian Context* (Princeton and Oxford: Princeton University Press).

Bell, Daniel (2008), *China's New Confucianism: Politics and Everyday Life in a Changing Society* (Princeton and Oxford: Princeton University Press).

Bell, Duncan (2014), 'What is Liberalism?', *Political Theory* 42(6): 682–715.

Bell, Duncan (2016), *Reordering the World: Essays on Liberalism and Empire* (Princeton and Oxford: Princeton University Press).

Benn, S. (1971), 'Privacy, Freedom and Respect for Persons', in J. Pennock and J. Chapman (eds), *Nomos XIII Privacy* (New York: Atherton).

Bentham, J. (1948), *An Introduction to the Principles of Morals and Legislation* (New York: Hafner Press).

Berlin, I. (1969), *Four Essays on Liberty* (Oxford: Oxford University Press).

Bernstein, E. (1961), *Evolutionary Socialism* (New York: Schocken Books).

Berridge, G. R. (2015), *Diplomacy: Theory and Practice* (Basingstoke: Palgrave Macmillan, 5th edn).

Berridge, G. R. (2018), 'Which London Embassy Needs 13 Cultural Attaches', 10 December, https://grberridge.diplomacy.edu/ viewed February 2019.

Bevir, R., and R. A. W. Rhodes (2002), 'Interpretive Theory', Marsh and G. Stoker (eds), *Theory and Methods in Political Science* (Basingstoke: Palgrave), pp. 131–52.

Bian, Yanjie (2018), *Guanxi, How China Works* (Cambridge: Polity).

Billington, James H. (2004), *Russia in Search of Itself* (Washington, DC: Woodrow Wilson Center Press).

Biorcio, Roberto (2014), *L'aggressività dei populismi* (Milan: Casa della Cultura).

Biorcio, Roberto (2015), *Il populismo nella politica italiana. Da Bossi a Berlusconi, da Grillo a Renzi* (Milan: Passato Prossimo/Presente Italiano).

Birch, Kean (2017), *A Research Agenda for Neoliberalism* (Cheltenham: Edward Elgar).

Bjola, Corneliu, and Markus Kornprobst (2018), *Understanding International Diplomacy: Theory, Practice and Ethics* (Abingdon: Routledge).

Blom-Hansen, J. (2000), 'Still Corporatism in Scandinavia?', *Scandinavian Political Studies* 23(2): 157–78.

Blowers, A. (1984), *Something in the Air: Corporate Power and the Environment* (London: Harper & Row).

Bogart, Karen (1998), 'Asian Values and their Impact upon Business Practices', in Josiane Cauquelin, Paul Lim and Birgit Mayer-Konig (eds), *Asian Values: Encounter with Diversity* (Richmond: Curzon Press), pp. 139–63.

Bogdanor, Vernon (2019), *Beyond Brexit: Towards a British Constitution* (London: I.B. Tauris).

Bookchin, M. (1971), *Post Scarcity Anarchism* (Berkeley, CA: Ramparts).

Booysen, Susan (2011), *The African National Congress and the Regeneration of Political Power* (Johannesburg: Wits University Press).

Bourchier, David (2015), *Illiberal Democracy in Indonesia: The Ideology of the Family State* (Abingdon and New York: Routledge).

Bramwell, A. (1989), *Ecology in the Twentieth Century* (New Haven, CN: Yale University Press).

Brandt, R. (1992), *Morality, Utilitarianism, and Rights* (Cambridge: Cambridge University Press).

Breitbart, Andrew (2012), *Righteous Indignation: Excuse Me While I Save the World* (Boston, MA: Grand Central).

Britten, S. (1977), *The Economic Consequences of Democracy* (London: Temple Smith).

Browers, Michaelle (2013), 'Islamic Political Ideologies', in Michael Freeden, Lyman Tower Sargent, and Marc Stears (eds), *The Oxford Handbook of Political Ideologies* (Oxford: Oxford University Press), pp. 627–43.

Brown, D. (2000), *Contemporary Nationalism: Civic, Ethnocultural and Multicultural Politics* (London: Routledge).

Brownmiller, S. (1975), *Against Our Will: Men, Women and Rape* (New York: Simon & Schuster).

Bryson, V. (1999), *Feminist Debates* (Basingstoke: Macmillan).

Burke, Anthony, Stefanie Fishel, Audra Mitchell, Simon Dalby, and Daniel J. Levine (2016), 'Planet Politics: A Manifesto from the End of IR', *Millennium* 44(3): 499–523.

Burke, E. [1790] (1968), *Reflections on the Revolution in France* (Harmondsworth: Penguin).

Burnham, J. (1941), *The Managerial Revolution* (New York: Day).

Buruma, Ian, and Avishai Margalit (2004), *Occidentalism: A Short History of Anti-Westernism* (London: Atlantic Books).

Butler, J. (2007), *Gender Trouble: Feminism and the Subversion of Identity* (Abingdon, Routledge).

Caney, S. (2008), 'Human Rights, Climate Change and Discounting', *Environmental Politics* 17(4): 536–55.

Canovan, Margaret (2002), 'Taking Politics to the People as the Ideology of Democracy', in Yves Meny and Yves Surel (eds), *Democracies and the Populist Challenge* (Basingstoke: Palgrave), pp. 25–44.

Carruthers, P. (1992), *The Animals Issue* (Cambridge: Cambridge University Press).

Carter, Neil (2018), *The Politics of the Environment: Ideas, Activism, Policy* (Cambridge: Cambridge University Press, 3rd edn).

Casaleggio, Roberto and Beppe Grillo (2011), *Siamo in guerra per una nuova politica. La rete contro i partiti* (Milan: Chiarelettere).

Cauquelin, Josiane, Paul Lim, and Birgit Mayer-Konig (eds) (1998), *Asian Values: Encounter with Diversity* (Richmond: Curzon Press).

Chait, Jonathan (2018), 'Trump's Latest FBI Conspiracy Theory Is His Craziest Yet', *Intelligencer*, 5 June, http://nymag.com/ intelligencer/2018/06/trumps-latest-fbiconspiracy-theory-is-his-craziest-yet.html, viewed 9/2/2019.

Chapman, Richard Allen (1975), 'Leviathan Writ Small: Thomas Hobbes on the Family', *American Political Science Review* 69(1): 76–90.

'Charter 08' (2008), http://politica-china.org/ wp-content/uploads/1231502360charter_08_Engligh.pdf

Chatterjee, Partha (2010), 'The Poverty of Western Political Theory', in Aakash Singh and Silika Mohapatra (eds) (2010), *Indian Political Thought* (Abingdon: Routledge), pp. 287–99.

Chavez, Tizoc (2019), 'Personal Diplomacy Has Long Been a Presidential Tactic, But Trump Adds a Twist', *The Conversation*, 23 January, https://www.theguardian.com/business/2016/apr/19/panamapapers-us-justice-department-investigation-taxavoidance

Cheek, Timothy (2006), *Living with Reform: China since 1989* (New York: PalgraveMacmillan).

Cheeseman, Nic, and Brian Klaas (2018), *How to Rig an Election* (New Haven, CT: Yale University Press).

Cherki, Alice (2006), *Frantz Fanon: a Portrait* (Ithaca, NY: Cornell University Press).

Chew, Jonathan (2016), '7 Corporate Giants Accused of Evading Billions in Taxes', *Fortune International*, 11 March, http://fortune.com/2016/03/11/applegoogle-taxes-eu/.

Chisolm, Amanda, and Joanna Tidy (eds) (2018), *Masculinities at the Margins: Beyond the Hegemonic in the Study of Militaries, Masculinities and War* (Abingdon: Routledge).

Chun, Shan (2009), 'On Chinese Cosmopolitanism (Tian Xia)', *Culture Mandala: Bulletin of the Centre for East-West Cultural & Economic Studies* 8(2): 20–9

Cobham, Alex, and Petr and Jansky (2017), 'Global Distribution of Revenue Loss from Tax Avoidance', WIDER Working Paper 2017/55, March, UNUWIDER, https://www.wider.unu.edu/sites/default/files/wp2017-55.pdf

Cohen, G. (1979), 'Capitalism, Freedom and the Proletariat', in A. Ryan (ed.), *The Idea of Freedom* (Oxford: Oxford University Press).

Coker, Christopher (2019), *The Rise of the Civilizational State* (Cambridge: Polity).

Colomer, Josep M. (2017), 'Empires versus States', *Politics* (Oxford: Oxford Research Encyclopaedias), http://oxfordre.com/politics/view/10.1093/acrefore/9780190228637.001.0001/acrefore-9780190228637-e-608

Confucius (1938), *The Analects* (trans. and annotated by Arthur Waley) (London: George Allen & Unwin).

Constantinou, Costas M., Pauline Kerr, and Paul Sharp (eds) (2016), *The Sage Handbook of Diplomacy* (Thousand Oaks, CA: Sage).

Cook, David (2005), *Understanding Jihad* (Berkeley, CA: University of California Press).

Cooper, Ian (2013), 'Bicameral or Tricameral: National Parliaments and Representative Democracy in the European Union', *Journal of European Integration* 35(5): 531–46.

Corr, Anders (2017), 'Ban Official Chinese Student Organizations Abroad', *Forbes* 4. Cramer, Jane K., and A. Trevor Thrall (eds) (2012), *Why Did the United States Invade Iraq?* (Abingdon: Routledge).

Crenshaw, Kimberle, (1989), 'Demarginalizing the Intersection of Race and Sex: A Black Feminist Critique of Antidiscrimination Doctrine, Feminist Theory and Antiracist Politics,' University of Chicago Legal Forum, 1989(1): Article 8: 139–67, http://chicagounbound.uchicago.edu/uclf/vol1989/iss1/8 *University of Chicago Legal Forum*

Crenson, M. (1971), *The Un-Politics of Air Pollution* (Baltimore: Johns Hopkins University Press).

Crick, B. (1962), *In Defence of Politics* (London: Weidenfeld & Nicolson).

Crosland, C. A. R. (1980), *The Future of Socialism* (London: Jonathan Cape).

Cucciolla, Riccardo Mario (ed.) (2019), *Dimensions and Challenges of Russian Liberalism: Historical Drama and New Prospects* (Berlin: Springer), June, https://www.forbes.com/sites/anderscorr/2017/06/04/ban-official-chinese-student-organizationsabroad/#6b3615f35bbc viewed 15 Februrary 2008.

Cunningham, F. (2002), *Theories of Democracy* (London: Routledge).

Dahl, R. (1958), 'A Critique of the Ruling Elite Model', *American Political Science Review*, 52(2): 463–99.

Dahl, R. (1963), *Who Governs?* (New Haven, CN: Yale University Press).

Dahl, R. (1971), *Polyarchy* (New Haven, CN: Yale University Press).

Dahl, R. (1991), *Modern Political Analysis* (Englewood Cliffs, NJ: Prentice-Hall, 5th edn).

D'Ancona, Matthew (2017), *Post-Truth: The New War on Truth and How to Fight Back* (London: Ebury Press).

Daniels, N. (1975), *Reading Rawls* (New York: Basic Books).

Davidson, Alastair (2018), *Antonio Gramsci: Towards an Intellectual Biography* (Chicago: Haymarket Books).

Davies, Nick (2009), *Flat Earth News: An Award-Winning Reporter Exposes Falsehood, Distortion and Propaganda in the Global Media* (London: Vintage).

Davies, Sara, and Jacqui True (eds) (2019), 'WPS: A Transformative Agenda', *The Oxford Handbook of Women, Peace and Security* (Oxford: Oxford University Press).

Davutoglu, Ahmet (2014), *Strategijska dubina* (Belgrade: Glasnik).

Dearlove, J., and P. Saunders (2000), *Introduction to British Politics* (Cambridge: Polity Press, 3rd edn).

Dejevsky, Mary (2017), 'In Defence of Donald Trump's Twitter Diplomacy', *Guardian*, 6 February, https://www.theguardian.com/commentisfree/2017/feb/05/in-defence-oftwitter-diplomacy viewed 1 March 2019.

De Jong, Sarah (2017), *Complicit Sisters: Gender and Women's Issues Across North-South Divides* (New York: Oxford University Press).

Delannoi, Gil, and Oliver Dowlen (eds) (2010), *Sortition: Theory and Practice* (Exeter: Imprint Academic).

De La Torre, Miguel (ed.) (2008), *The Hope of Liberation in World Religions* (Waco, TX: Baylor University Press).

Deneen, Patrick J. (2018), *Why Liberalism Failed* (New Haven: Yale University Press).

Denli, Özlem (2018), *Liberal Thought and Islamic Politics in Turkey* (Baden-Baden: Nomos).

Denning, Steve (2018), 'How Russia is Still Running Interference for Trump', *Forbes*, 19 December, https://www.forbes.com/sites/stevedenning/2018/12/19/how-putin-augmentstrumps-disinformation-against-the-russiaprobe/#6e66b58749a0

deSouza, Peter Ronald, and Sridharan, E. (eds) (2006), *India's Political Parties* (New Delhi: Sage).

Dessel, Enrique (1996), 'A Note on Liberation Theology', in Leslie Bethell (ed.), *Ideas and Ideologies in Twentieth Century Latin America* (Cambridge: Cambridge University Press), pp. 275–83.

Devetak, Richard (2018), *Critical International Theory: An Intellectual History* (Oxford: Oxford University Press).

Devlin, P. (1965), *The Enforcement of Morals* (Oxford: Oxford University Press).

Diamond, L. (2015), 'Facing Up to the Democratic Recession', *Journal of Democracy* 26, 1: 141–55.

Dikotter, Frank (2010), *Mao's Great Famine: The History of China's Most Devastating Catastrophe, 1958–62* (London: Bloomsbury).

Dikotter, Frank (2017), *The Cultural Revolution: A People's History, 1962–76* (London: Bloomsbury).

Dobson, A. (1996), 'Democratising Green Theory: Preconditions and Principles', in B. Doherty and M. de Geus (eds), *Democracy and Green Political Thought* (London: Routledge), pp. 132–48.

Dobson, A. (2007), *Green Political Thought* (London: Unwin Hyman, 4th edn).

Dobson, Andrew (2012), *Green Political Thought* (Abingdon: Routledge).

Doherty, B. and M. de Geus (eds) *Democracy and Green Political Thought* (London: Routledge).

Donaldson, S., and W. Kymlicka (2011), *Zoopolis: A Political Theory of Animal Rights*. New York: Oxford University Press.

Donovan, J., and C. Adams, (2007), *The Feminist Care Tradition in Animal Ethics* (New York: Columbia University Press).

Downs, A. (1957), *An Economic Theory of Democracy* (New York: Harper & Row).

Dryzek, J. (2010), *Foundations and Frontiers of Deliberative Governance* (Oxford: Oxford University Press).

Dryzek, J., and P. Dunleavy (2009), *Theories of the Democratic State* (Basingstoke: Palgrave).

Duducu, Jem (2018), *The Sultans: The Rise and Fall of the Ottoman Rulers and their World: A 600 Year History* (Amberley Publishing: Stroud).

Duncan, G., and S. Lukes (1964), 'The New Democracy', in S. Lukes (ed.), *Essays in Social Theory* (London: Macmillan).

Dunleavy, P., and B. O'Leary (1987), *Theories of the State* (Basingstoke: Macmillan).

Dunleavy, P., and H. Ward (1981), 'Exogenous Voter Preferences and Parties with State Power: Some Internal Problems of Economic Theories of Party Competition', *British Journal of Political Science* 11: 351–80.

Dunn, Kevin C. (2001), 'Introduction: Africa and International Relations Theory', in Kevin C. Dunn and Timothy M. Shaw (eds), *Africa's Challenge to International Relations Theory* (Basingstoke: Palgrave).

Dworkin, A. (1981), *Pornography: Men Possessing Women* (London: Women's Press).

Dworkin, R. (1978), *Taking Rights Seriously* (London: Duckworth).

Dworkin, R. (1987), *Taking Rights Seriously* (London: Duckworth).

Dye, T. (2000), *The Irony of Democracy* (London: Harcourt Brace).

Eatwell, Roger, and Matthew Goodwin (2018), *National Populism: The Revolt Against Liberal Democracy* (London: Pelican).

Eckersley, R. (1992), *Environmentalism and Political Theory* (London: UCL Press).

Eckersley, R. (2004), *The Green State* (Cambridge, MA: MIT Press).

Economist, The (2018), 'Britain's Good-chap Model of Government Is Coming Apart', https://www.economist.com/britain/2018/12/18/britainsgood-chap-model-of-government-is-coming-apart

Edkins, Jenny (2019), *Routledge Handbook of Critical International Relations* (Abingdon: Routledge).

Eickelman, Dale F., and James Piscatori (2018), *Muslim Politics* (Princeton, NJ: Princeton University Press).

Ekeli, K. (2009), 'Constitutional Experiments: Representing Future Generations through Submajority Rules', *Journal of Political Philosophy* 17(4): 440–61.

Elischer, Sebastian (2013), *Political Parties in Africa: Ethnicity and Party Formation* (Cambridge: Cambridge University Press).

Eroukhmanoff, Clara (2018), 'Securitization Theory: An Introduction', *E-International Relations*, 14 January, https://www.e-ir.info/2018/01/14/securitisation-theory-an-introduction/

Esposito, John L. (1999), *The Islamic Threat: Myth or Reality?* (New York: Oxford University Press, 3rd edn).

EU (European Union) (2018), 'The EU in Brief', 4 July, https://europa.eu/european-union/about-eu/eu-in-brief_en

European Court of Human Rights (2019), 'Guide on Article 8 of the European Convention on Human Rights', https://www.echr.coe.int/Documents/Guide_Art_8_ENG.pdfref

Faludi, S. (1991), *Backlash: The Undeclared War Against American Women* (New York: Crown).

Fanon, Frantz (2001), *The Wretched of the Earth* (London: Penguin Classics).

Fassbender, Bardo (2011), 'Westphalia: Peace of', *Oxford Public International Law*, https://opil.ouplaw.com/view/10.1093/law:epil/9780199231690/law-9780199231690-e739

Festenstein, M., and M. Kenny (2005), *Political Ideologies* (Oxford: Oxford University Press).

Ferdinand, Peter (2012), *Governance in Pacific Asia: Political Economy and Development from Japan to Burma* (New York: Continuum).

Ferdinand, Peter (2016), 'Westward Ho—The China Dream and "One Belt, One Road": Chinese Foreign Policy under Xi Jinping', *International Affairs* 92(4): 941–57.

Firestone, S. (1972), *The Dialectic of Sex* (London: Paladin).

Fish, Stephen and Matthew Koenig (2011), *The Handbook of National Legislatures: A Global Survey* (Cambridge: Cambridge University Press).

Fishkin, J., Jowell, R., and Luskin, R. (2002), 'Considered Opinions: Deliberative Polling in Britain', *British Journal of Political Science* 32: 455–87.

Flinders, M. (2012), *Defending Politics: Why Democracy Matters in the Twenty-First Century* (Oxford: Oxford University Press).

Floridia, Antonio (2018), 'The Origins of the Deliberative Turn', in Andre Bachtiger, John S. Dryzek, Jane Mansbridge, and Mark Warren (eds) *The Oxford Handbook of Deliberative Democracy* (Oxford: Oxford University Press).

Forbes (2018), 'China Now Boasts More Than 800 Million Internet Users', https://www.forbes.com/sites/niallmccarthy/2018/08/23/china-nowboasts-more-than-800-million-internet-users-and-98-of-them-are-mobile-infographic/

Foucault, M. (1977), *Discipline and Punishment* (Harmondsworth: Penguin).

Fox, W. (1984), 'Deep Ecology: A New Philosophy of Our Times', *The Ecologist* 14(5): 199–200.

Fox, W. (1995), *Toward a Transpersonal Ecology: Developing New Foundations for Environmentalism* (Totnes: Resurgence).

Frank, Andre Gunder (1998), *ReOrient: Global Economy in the Asian Age* (Berkeley: University of California Press).

Frazer, Elizabeth (2018), 'Feminism and Realism', in Matt Sleat (ed.), *Politics Recovered: Realist Thought in Theory and Practice* (New York: Columbia University Press).

Freeden, M. (1996), *Ideologies and Political Theory* (Oxford: Oxford University Press).

Freeden, Michael, and Andrew Vincent (eds) (2012), *Comparative Political Thought: Theorizing Practices* (London: Routledge).

Freeden, M., L. Sargent, and M. Stears (2015), *The Oxford Handbook of Political Ideologies* (Oxford: Oxford University Press).

Freedman, Rosa (2015), *Failing to Protect: The UN and the Politicisation of Human Rights* (Oxford: Oxford University Press).

Freeman, S. (2007), *Rawls* (London: Routledge).

Frey, R. K. (1983), *Rights, Killing and Suffering* (Oxford: Clarendon Press).

Friedan, B. (1963), *The Feminine Mystique* (Harmondsworth: Penguin).

FT (2019), 'Liberalism Has Outlined Its Purpose', https://www.ft.com/video/a49cfa25-610e-438c-b11d-5dac19619e08?playlist-name=editorspicks&playlist-offset=3

Fukuyama, F. (1992), *The End of History and the Last Man* (Harmondsworth: Penguin).

Fukuyama, Francis (2014), *Political Order and Political Decay: From the Industrial Revolution to the Globalization of Democracy* (London: Profile Books).

Fukuyama, F. (2018), *Identity: Contemporary Identity Politics and the Struggle for Recognition* (London: Profile).

Fung, Edmund S. K. (2010), *The Intellectual Foundations of Chinese Modernity* (Cambridge: Cambridge University Press).

Gabbatis, John (2018), 'Americans Who Believe in Conspiracy Theories about 9/11 and Princess Diana's Death More Likely to Doubt Climate Change', *Independent*, 9 May, https://www.

independent.co.uk/environment/climate-changeconspiracy-theory-new-world-order-jfk-princessdiana-a8343291.html viewed 8 February 2019.

Gabrielson, T., Hall, C., Meyer J., and Schlosberg, D. (eds) (2016), *The Oxford Handbook of Environmental Political Theory* (Oxford: Oxford University Press).

Gallie, W. (1955/6), 'Essentially Contested Concepts', *Proceedings of the Aristotelian Society*, 56(1): 167–98.

Gamble, A. (1994), *The Free Economy and the Strong State* (London: Macmillan, 2nd edn).

Gamble, A. (2000), *Politics and Fate* (Cambridge: Polity Press).

Garner, R. (2005), *The Political Theory of Animal Rights* (Manchester: Manchester University Press).

Garner, R. (2013), *A Theory of Justice for Animals: Animal Rights in a Nonideal World* (New York: Oxford University Press).

Garner, R. (2017), 'Animals and Democratic Theory: Beyond an Anthropocentric Account', *Contemporary Political Theory* 164: 459–77.

Garner, R. (2019), *Environmental Political Thought: Interests, Values and Inclusion*, (London: Red Globe Press).

Garnham, N. (2001), 'Public Sphere and the Media', in Neil J. Smelser and Paul B. Bailes (eds), *International Encyclopedia of the Social and Behavioral Sciences* (Amsterdam: Elesevier), pp. 12585–90.

Gerth, H., and C. Wright Mills (1946), *From Max Weber: Essays in Sociology* (London: Routledge & Kegan Paul).

Gilligan, C. (1982), *In a Different Voice* (Cambridge, MA: Harvard University Press).

Giscard d'Estaing, Valery (2004), 'A Better European Bridge to Turkey', *Financial Times*, 24 November.

Gluck, Carol (1985), *Japan's Modern Myths: Ideology in the Late Meiji Period* (Stanford, CA: Stanford University Press).

Goodin, R. (1992), *Green Political Theory* (Cambridge: Polity Press).

Goodin, R. (2007), 'Enfranchising All Affected Interests and Its Alternatives', *Philosophy and Public Affairs* 35(1): 40–68.

Goodwin, B. (2014), *Using Political Ideas* (Chichester: John Wiley & Sons, 6th edn).

Goody, Jack (1996), *The East in the West* (Cambridge: Cambridge University Press).

Gordenker, Leon (2010), The UN Secretary-General and Secretariat (Abingdon: Routledge, 2nd edn).

Gorz, A. (1985), *Paths to Paradise* (London: Pluto).

Graham, David A. (2018), 'Is Wikileaks a Russian Front?', *The Atlantic*, 29 November, https://www.theatlantic.com/politics/archive/2018/11/wikileaks-trump-mueller-roger-stone-jeromecorsi/576940/, viewed 2 March 2019.

Gramsci, A. (1971), *Selections from Prison Notebooks* (London: Lawrence & Wishart).

Gray, T. (1991), *Freedom* (Atlantic Highlands, NJ: Humanities Press International Inc.).

Greer, G. (1970), *The Female Eunuch* (New York: McGraw-Hill).

Greer, Jed, and Kavaljit Singh (2000), 'A Brief History of Transnational Corporations', *Global Policy Forum*, https://www.globalpolicy.org/empire/47068-a-brief-history-of-transnationalcorporations.html

Griffiths, James (2019), *The Great Firewall of China: How to Build and Control an Alternative Version of the Internet* (London: Zed books).

Gupta, Dipankar (2000), *Interrogating Caste: Understanding Hierarchy and Difference in Indian Society* (Gurgaon: Penguin).

Gutierrez, Gustavo (1971), *A Theology of Liberation: History, Politics And Salvation* (London: SCM Press).

Gutmann, A., and D. Thompson (1996), *Democracy and Disagreement* (Cambridge, MA: Harvard University Press).

Habermas, Jurgen (1989), *The Structural Transformation of the Public Sphere: An Enquiry into a Category of Bourgeois Society* (Cambridge: Polity).

Hague, R., and M. Harrop (2007), *Comparative Government and Politics* (Basingstoke: Palgrave, 7th edn).

Hajer, M. (1997), *The Politics of Environmental Discourse* (Oxford: Clarendon Press).

Hale, Charles A. (1996), 'Political Ideas and Ideologies in Latin America, 1870–1930', in Leslie Bethell (ed.), *Ideas and Ideologies in Twentieth-Century Latin America* (Cambridge: Cambridge University Press), pp. 133–205.

Hale, Charles A. (2010), *El pensamiento político en Mexico y Latinoamerica. Articulos y escritos breves,* ed. Gabriel Torres Puga and Josefina Zoraida Vazquez (Mexico, DF: El Colegio de Mexico).

Hale, Henry (2004), 'Yabloko and the Challenge of Building a Liberal Party in Russia', *Europe Asia Studies* 56(7): 993–1030.

Hale, William, and Ergun Ozbudun (2011), *Islamism, Democracy and Liberalism in Turkey: The Case of the AKP* (London: Routledge).

Halisi, C. R. D. (1999), *Black Political Thought in the Making of South African Democracy* (Bloomington, IN: Indiana University Press).

Hallaq, Wael B. (2014), *The Impossible State: Islam, Politics, and Modernity's Moral Predicament* (New York: Columbia University Press).

Hallin, Daniel C., and Paolo Mancini (2004), *Comparing Media Systems: Three Models of Media and Politics* (Cambridge and New York: Cambridge University Press).

Hallin, Daniel C., and Paolo Mancini (eds) (2012), *Comparing Media Systems beyond the Western World* (Cambridge and New York: Cambridge University Press).

Hanlon, Aaron (2018), 'Postmodernisn Didn't Cause Donald Trump. It Explains Him', *Washington Post*, 31 August, https://www.washingtonpost.com/outlook/postmodernism-didnt-causetrump-it-explains-him/2018/08/30/0939f7c4-9b12-11e8-843b-36e177f3081c_story.html?noredirect=on&utm_term=.3da4cb9ad91f viewed 8 January 2019.

Hannan, Daniel (2016), *Why Vote Leave* (London: House of Zeus).

Hansen, Emmanuel (1977), *Frantz Fanon: Social and Political Thought* (Columbus, OH: Ohio State University Press).

Hansen, Lene (2014), 'Ontologies, Epistemologies and Methodologies', in Laura J. Shepherd (ed.), *Gender Matters in Global Politics: A Feminist Introduction to International Relations* (Abingdon: Routledge, 2nd edn).

Hardin, G. (1968), 'The Tragedy of the Commons', *Science* 162: 1243–8.

Hardman, Isabel (2018), *Why We Get the Wrong Politicians* (London: Atlantic Books).

Harrison, Jackie (2006), *News* (Abingdon: Routledge).

Hart, Roderick P., and Rebecca LaVally (2017), 'Not a Fourth Estate but a Second Legislature', in Kate Kenski and Kathleen Hall Jamieson (eds), *The Oxford Handbook of Political Communication* (Oxford and New York: Oxford University Press).

Hart, H. (1967), 'Are There Any Natural Rights', in A. Quinton (ed.), *Political Philosophy* (Oxford: Oxford University Press).

Hay, C. (1997), 'Divided by a Common Language: Political Theory and the Concept of Power', *Politics* 17(1): 45–52.

Hay, C. (1999), 'Marxism and the State', in A. Gamble, D. Marsh, and T. Tant (eds), *Marxism and Social Science* (London: Macmillan).

Hay, C. (2002), *Political Analysis* (Basingstoke: Palgrave).

Hay, C., and Lister, M. (2006), 'Introduction', in C. Hay, M. Lister, and D. Marsh (eds.), *The State: Theories and Issues* (Basingstoke: Palgrave), pp. 1–20.

Hayward, T. (2005), *Constitutional Environmental Rights* (Oxford: Oxford University Press).

Heater, D. (1999), *What is Citizenship?* (Cambridge: Polity Press).

Heer, Jeet (2017), 'America's First Postmodern President', *New Republic*, 8 July, https://newrepublic.com/article/143730/americas-firstpostmodern-president viewed 8 February 2019.

Heffernan, R. (2000), *New Labour and Thatcherism: Political Change in Britain*. (Basingstoke: Palgrave Macmillan).

Hegel, G. W. F. (1942), *Philosophy of Right* (Oxford: Oxford University Press).

Heilbroner, R. (1974), *An Inquiry into the Human Prospect* (New York: Norton).

Held, D. (1989), *Political Theory and the Modern State* (Cambridge: Polity Press).

Held, D. (2006), *Models of Democracy* (Cambridge: Polity Press, 3rd edn).

Held, D., and A. Leftwich (1984), 'A Discipline of Politics?', in A. Leftwich (ed.), *What is Politics? The Activity and its Study* (Oxford: Blackwell).

Henry (2007), 'Simplify and Exaggerate', http://crookedtimber.org/2007/01/19/simplify-andexaggerate/

Hewitt, C. (1974), 'Policy-making in Postwar Britain: A National-level Test of Elitist and Pluralist Hypotheses', *British Journal of Political Science* 4(2): 187–216.

Heywood, A. (2013), *Politics* (Basingstoke: Palgrave Macmillan, 4th edn).

Heywood, A. (2015), *Political Theory: An Introduction* (Basingstoke: Palgrave Macmillan, 4th edn).

Heywood, A. (2017), *Political Ideologies: An Introduction* (London: Palgrave, 6th edn).

Hill, Christopher (2016), *Foreign Policy in the Twenty-First Century* (London: Palgrave, 2nd edn).

Hill, Fiona, and Clifford Gaddy (2012), 'Putin and the Uses of History', *The Public Interest*, 117(January–February): 21–31.

Hirst, P. (1996), *Associative Democracy: New Forms of Economic and Social Governance* (Cambridge: Polity Press).

Hitler, A. (1926/1969), *Mein Kampf* (London: Hutchinson).

Hobbes, T. (1651/1992), *Leviathan* (Cambridge: Cambridge University Press).

Hoffman, J. (1995), *Beyond the State* (Cambridge: Polity Press).

Hoffman, J., and P. Graham (2006), *Introduction to Political Theory* (Harlow: Pearson).

Hughes, Steve, and Nigel Haworth (2011), *International Labour Organization (ILO): Coming in From the Cold* (Abingdon: Routledge).

Human Rights Watch (2019), 'World Report', https://www.hrw.org/world-report/2019/countrychapters/syria viewed 13 February 2019.

Huntington, S. (1996), *The Clash of Civilizations* (New York: Simon & Schuster).

Hurrell, Andrew (2016), 'Beyond Critique: How to Study Global IR?', *International Studies Review* 18(1): 149–51.

Hyams, K. (2015), 'Political Authority and Obligation', in C. MacKinnon (ed.), *Issues in Political Theory* (Oxford: Oxford University Press, 3rd edn) pp. 8–29.

Imamoto, Shizuka (2018), *Rejection of Racial Equality Bill* (Chennai: Notion Press).

iNews (2018), 'All the Times Boris Johnson Flat-out Lied', https://inews.co.uk/news/uk/times-borisjohnson-flat-lied/

Inglehart, R., C. Haerpfer, A. Moreno, C. Welzel, K. Kizilova, J. Diez-Medrano, M. Lagos, P. Norris, E. Ponarin, and B. Puranen et al. (eds) (2014). *World Values Survey: Round Six–Country-Pooled Datafile Version*. Madrid: JD Systems Institute, http://www.worldvaluessurvey.org/WVSDocumentationWV6.jsp

Jackson, Robert (2018), 'Sovereignty in World Politics: A Glance at the Conceptual and Historical Landscape', in Neil Walker (ed.), *Relocating Sovereignty* (Abingdon: Routledge).

Jackson, Simon, and Alanna O'Malley (eds) (2018), *The Institution of International Order: From the League of Nations to the United Nations* (Abingdon: Routledge).

Jackson, T. (2009). *Prosperity without Growth: Economics for a Finite Planet* (London: Earthscan).

Jaggar, A. (1983), *Feminist Politics and Human Nature* (Lanham, MD: Rowman & Littlefield).

James, Patrick, Mariano E. Bertucci, and Jarrod Hayes (eds) (2018), *Constructivism Reconsidered: Past, Present, and Future* (Ann Arbor, MI: University of Michigan Press).

Jeffreys, S. (2013), *Gender Hurts: A Feminist Analysis of the Politics of Transgenderism* (London: Routledge).

Jenner, W. J. F. (1992), *The Tyranny of History: The Roots of China's Rise* (Harmondsworth: Allen Lane).

Jessop, B. (1990), *State Theory* (Cambridge: Polity Press).

Jessop, B. (2015), *The State: Past, Present, Future* (Cambridge: Polity Press).

Jodhka, Surinder S. (2012), *Caste* (New Delhi: Oxford University Press).

Johnson, C. (1995), *Japan: Who Governs? The Rise of the Developmental State* (New York: Norton).

Jones, P. (1994), *Rights* (Basingstoke: Macmillan).

Jones, Peter (2015), *Track Two Diplomacy in Theory and Practice* (Stanford: Stanford University Press).

Judis, John B. (2018), *The Nationalist Revival: Trade, Immigration, and the Revolt Against Globalization* (New York: Columbia Global Reports).

Kaehne, Axel (2007), *Political and Social Thought in Post-Communist Russia* (London: Routledge).

Kaldor, Mary (2012), *New and Old Wars: Organised Violence in a Global Era* (Cambridge: Polity Press).

Kamali, Mohammad Hashim (2002), *Freedom, Equality and Justice in Islam* (Cambridge: Islamic Texts Society).

Kamruzzaman, Palash (ed.) (2019), *Civil Society in the Global South* (Abingdon: Routledge).

Katzenstein, Peter J. (2018), 'Second Coming? Reflections on a Global Theory of International Relations', *Chinese Journal of International Politics* 11(4): 373–90.

Kaufmann, E. (2018), *Whiteshift: Populism, Immigration and the Future of White Majorities* (London: Allen Lane).

Kautilya (1992), *The Arthashastra* (Gurgaon: Penguin Random House).

Kautilya (2016), *The Arthashatra* (London: Penguin).

Kaviraj, Sudipta (2011), 'On the Enchantment of the State: Indian Thought on the Role of the State in the Narrative of Modernity', in Akhil Gupta and K. Sivaramakrishnan (eds), *The State in India After Liberalization: Interdisciplinary Perspectives* (London: Routledge), pp. 31–48.

Kaviraj, Sudipta (2012), *The Trajectories of the Indian State* (Ranikhat: Orient Blackswan).

Kaviraj, Sudipta (2013), 'On the Historicity of the Political: *Rajaniti* and Politics in Modern Indian Thought', in Michael Freeden and Andrew Vincent (eds), *Comparative Political Thought* (London: Routledge), pp. 24–39.

Kaviraj, Sudipta (2001), 'In Search of Civil Society', in Sudipta Kaviraj and Sunil Khilnani (eds), *Civil Society: History and Possibilities* (Cambridge: Cambridge University Press), pp. 287–323.

Keane, John (2009), *The Life and Death of Democracy* (London: Simon Schuster).

Keating, M., and D. McCrone (eds) (2013), *The Crisis of Social Democracy in Europe* (Edinburgh: Edinburgh University Press).

Kejriwal, Arvind (2015), *Swaraj* (London: HarperCollins).

Kelsay. John (2015), 'Jihad', in Gerhard Bowering (ed.), *Islamic Political Thought: An Introduction* (Princeton, NJ: Princeton University Press), pp. 86–104.

Keohane, Robert O. (1986), 'Reciprocity in International Relations', *International Organization* 40(1): 1–27.

Kerr, Pauline, and Geoffrey Wiseman (eds) (2017), *Diplomacy in a Globalising World* (Oxford: Oxford University Press).

Khilnani, Sunil (1999), *The Idea of India* (Harmondsworth: Penguin).

Khomiakov, Vladimir (2018). *Gosudarstvennaia ideologiia—eto prosto* (Moscow: Knizhnii mir).

Kitchen, M. (1976), *Fascism* (Basingstoke: Macmillan).

Koditschek, Theodore (2011), *Liberalism, Imperialism, and the Historical Imagination: Nineteenth-Century Visions of a Greater Britain* (Cambridge: Cambridge University Press).

Kohn, H. (1944), *The Idea of Nationalism* (London: Macmillan).

Kornhauser, W. (1960), *The Politics of Mass Society* (Glencoe, IL: Free Press).

Kukathas, C., and P. Pettit (1990), *Rawls: A Theory of Justice and its Critics* (Oxford: Polity Press).

Kumagai, Fumie (1996), *Unmaking Japan Today: The Impact of Traditional Values on Modern Japanese Society* (Westport, CT: Praeger).

Kymlicka, W. (1995), *Multicultural Citizenship: A Liberal Theory of Minority Rights* (Oxford: Oxford University Press).

Kymlicka, W. (2002), *Contemporary Political Philosophy* (Oxford: Oxford University Press, 2nd edn).

Lacorne, Denis (2019), *The Limits of Tolerance* (New York: Columbia University Press).

Lal, Priya (2015), *African Socialism in Postcolonial Tanzania: Between the Village and the World* (Cambridge: Cambridge University Press).

Larsen, S. (ed.), (2001), *Fascism Outside of Europe* (New York: Columbia University Press).

Laslett, P. (1956), 'Introduction', *Philosophy, Politics and Society*, 1st ser. (Oxford: Blackwell).

Lasswell, H. (1936), *Politics: Who Gets What, When, How?* (New York: McGraw-Hill).

Lawson, Stephanie (2017), 'IR Theory in the Anthropocene: Time for a Reality Check?', in Synne L. Dyvik, Jan Selby, and Rorden Wilkinson (eds), *What's the Point of International Relations?* (Abingdon: Routledge).

Lebow, Richard Ned (2016), *National Identities and International Relations* (Cambridge: Cambridge University Press).

Lebra, Takiye Sugiyama (1976), *Japanese Patterns of Behavior* (Hawaii: University of Hawaii Press).

Leftwich, A. (ed.) (1984), *What is Politics? The Activity and its Study* (Oxford: Blackwell).

Leopold, A. (1949), *A Sand County Almanac* (Oxford: Oxford University Press).

Levitsky, S., and L. Way (2002), 'Assessing the Quality of Democracy', *Journal of Democracy* 13(2) (Apr.): 51–65.

Levitsky, Steven, James Loxton, and Brandon Van Dyck (2016), 'Introduction: Challenges of partybuilding in Latin America', in Steven Levitsky,

James Loxton and Brandon Van Dyck (eds), *Challenges of Party-Building in Latin America* (Cambridge: Cambridge University Press), pp. 1–48.

Lewis, Michael (2018), *The Fifth Risk* (London: Allen Lane).

Li, He (2015), *Political Thought and China's Transformation* (Basingstoke: Palgrave Macmillan).

Liberal International (2019), 'Our Mission: Liberalism', https://liberal-international.org/who-we-are/our-mission/

Liebig, Michael (2013), 'Kautilya's Relevance for India Today', *India Quarterly* 69(2): 99–116.

Liebig, Michael (2014), *Endogene politisch-kulturelle Resourcen. Die Relevanz des Kautilya-Arthashastra für das moderne Indien* (Baden-Baden: Nomos).

Liebig, Michael, and Saurabh Mishra (eds) (2017), *The Arthashastra in a Transcultural Perspective: Comparing Kautilya with Sun-Zi, Nizam al-Mulk, Barani and Machiavelli* (New Delhi: Pentagon Press).

Lijphart, A., and M. Crepaz (1991), 'Corporatism and Consensus in Eighteen Countries: Conceptual and Empirical Linkages', *British Journal of Political Science*, 21: 235–46.

Lilla, M. (2017), *The Once and Future Liberal: After Identity Politics* (New York: Harper Collins).

Lindblom, C. (1977), *Politics and Markets* (New York: Basic Books).

Linklater, A. (2008), 'Globalization and the Transformation of Political Community', in J. Baylis, S. Smith, and P. Owens (eds), *The Globalization of World Politics* (Oxford: Oxford University Press).

Lively, J. (1975), *Democracy* (Oxford: Blackwell).

Lo, Mbaye (2019), *Political Islam, Justice and Governance* (Basingstoke: Palgrave Macmillan).

Locke, J. (1690/1988), *Two Treatises of Government* (Cambridge: Cambridge University Press).

Lowndes, V., D. Marsh, and G. Stoker (eds) (2018), *Theory and Methods in Political Science* (London: Palgrave, 4th edn).

Lowy, Michael (1996), *The War of Gods: Religion and Politics in Latin America* (London: Verso).

Lukes, S. (2005), *Power: A Radical View* (Basingstoke: Palgrave Macmillan, 2nd edn).

MacIntyre, A. (1985), *After Virtue: A Study in Moral Theory* (London: Duckworth, 2nd edn).

MacKinnon, C. (1989), *Towards a Feminist Theory of the State* (London: Harvard University Press).

Macpherson, C. B. (1962), *The Political Theory of Possessive Individualism* (Oxford: Oxford University Press).

Macpherson, C. B. (1966), *The Real World of Democracy* (Oxford: Oxford University Press).

Macpherson, C. B. (1977), *The Life and Times of Liberal Democracy* (Oxford: Oxford University Press).

Mahbubani, Kishore (2008), *The New Asian Hemisphere: The Irresistible Shift of Global Power to the East* (New York: Public Affairs).

Mainwaring, Scott (ed.) (2018), *Party Systems in Latin America: Institutionalization, Decay, and Collapse* (Cambridge: Cambridge University Press).

Makgoba, M. W. (1998), 'Oppositions, Difficulties, and Tensions between Liberalism and African Thought', in R. W. Johnson and David Welsh (eds), *Ironic Victory: Liberalism in Post-liberation South Africa* (Oxford: Oxford University Press), pp. 265–92.

Marchetti, Raffaele (2016) 'Global Civil Society', *E-International Relations*, 28 December, https://www.e-ir.info/2016/12/28/global-civil-society/

Marchetti, Raffaele (2018), 'Dynamic of Interaction between Governments and Civil Society Organizations', in Raffaele Marchetti (ed.), *Government–NGO Relationships in Africa, Asia, Europe and MENA* (Abingdon: Routledge).

Marcuse, H. (1964), *One-Dimensional Man: Studies in the Ideology of Advanced Industrial Society* (Boston, MA: Beacon).

Marietta, Morgan, and David C. Barker (2019), *One Nation, Two Realities: Duelling Facts in American Democracy* (New York: Oxford University Press).

Marquand, D. (1988), *The Unprincipled Society* (London: Jonathan Cape).

Marr, Andrew (2004), *My Trade* (London: Macmillan).

Moore, Martin (2019), *Democracy Hacked: How Technology is Destabilizing Politics* (London: Oneworld).

Marschall, Stefan (2015), *Parlamentarismus* (Baden-Baden: Nomos, 2nd edn).

Marshall, T. H. (1950), *Citizenship and Social Class, and Other Essays* (Cambridge: Cambridge University Press).

Martell, L. (1994), *Ecology and Society* (Cambridge: Polity Press).

Martill, Benjamin and Uta Staiger (eds) (2018), *Brexit and Beyond: Rethinking the Futures of Europe* (London: UCL Press).

Martin, Guy (2012), *African Political Thought* (Basingstoke: Palgrave).

Marx, Karl (1859), *A Contribution to the Critique of Political Economy*, https://www.marxists.org/archive/marx/works/1859/critique-pol-economy/preface.htm

Marx, K., and F. Engels (1848/1976), *The Communist Manifesto* (Harmondsworth: Penguin).

Mauzy, D., and R. Milne (2002), *Singapore Politics: Under the People's Action Party* (London: Routledge).

Mayes, Suzanne (2019), 'Why Care About Undocumented Immigrants? For One Thing They've Become Vital to Key Sectors of the US Economy', *The Conversation*, 15 January, https://theconversation.com/why-care-about-undocumented-immigrantsfor-one-thing-they've-become-vital-to-key-sectorsof-the-us-economy-98790 viewed 6 March 2019.

McElroy, W. (1995), *A Woman's Right to Pornography* (New York: St Martin's Press).

McIntosh, M. (1978), 'The State and the Oppression of Women', in A. Kuhn, and A. Wolpe (eds), *Feminism and Materialism* (London: Routledge & Kegan Paul).

McLellan, D. (1980), *The Thought of Karl Marx* (Basingstoke: Macmillan).

Meadows, D., et al. (1972), *The Limits to Growth* (New York: Universe).

Mearsheimer, John (2018), *The Great Delusion: Liberal Dreams and International Realities* (New Haven: Yale University Press).

Mehta, V. R. (1996), *Indian Political Thought: An Interpretation* (New Delhi: Manohar).

Mellor, M. (1997), *Feminism and Ecology* (Cambridge: Polity).

Menchik, Jeremy (2016), *Islam and Democracy in Indonesia: Tolerance Without Liberalism* (Cambridge: Cambridge University Press).

Miliband R. (1972), *Parliamentary Socialism* (London: Merlin).

Miliband, R. (1978), *The State in Capitalist Society* (New York: Basic Books).

Mill, J. S. (1970), *The Subjection of Women* (Cambridge, MA: MIT Press).

Mill, J. S. (1972), *Utilitarianism, On Liberty, and Considerations on Representative Government* (London: Dent).

Miller, D. (1976), *Social Justice* (Oxford: Clarendon Press).

Miller, D. (1990), *Market, State and Community: Theoretical Foundations to Market Socialism* (Oxford: Clarendon Press).

Millett, K. (1971), *Sexual Politics* (New York: Granada Publishing).

Mills, C. Wright (1956), *The Power Elite* (New York: Oxford University Press).

Minford, P. (2010), 'The Banking Crisis: A Rational Interpretation', *Political Studies*, 8(1): 40–54.

Mishra, Pankaj (2013), *From the Ruins of Empire: The Revolt Against the West and the Remaking of Asia* (Harmondsworth: Penguin).

Mitchell, J. (1971), *Woman's Estate* (Harmondsworth: Penguin).

Mohan, C. Raja (2015), *Modi's World: Expanding India's Sphere of Influence* (Noida: Uttar Pradesh: HarperCollins).

Møller, J., and Skaaning, S.-E. (2013), 'Regime types and democratic sequencing', *Journal of Democracy*, 24(1): 144.

Mookherjee, M. (2015), 'Multiculturalism', in C. McKinnon (ed.), *Issues in Political Theory* (Oxford: Oxford University Press).

Morse, Richard M. (1999), *El espejo de Prospero. Un estudio de la dialectica del Nuovo Mundo* (Mexico, DF: Siglo XXI, 2nd edn).

Mouffe, C. (2005), *On the Political* (London: Routledge).

Mouffe, C. (2018), *For a Left Populism* (London: Verso).

Mourdaukoutas, Panos (2018), 'What is China Doing in Africa?', *Forbes*, 4 August, https://www.forbes.com/sites/panosmourdoukoutas/2018/08/04/china-is-treating-africa-the-same-way-europeancolonists-did/#5a343537298b

Mudde, C. (2007), *Populist Right Parties in Europe* (Cambridge: Cambridge University Press).

Mudde, C. (2018), 'How Populism became the Concept that Defines Our Age', *Guardian*, 22 November.

Mudde, Cas, and Cristobal Rovero Kaltwasser (2017), *Populism: A Very Short Introduction* (Oxford: Oxford University Press).

Mulder, Niels (1996), *Inside Thai Society: Interpretations of Everyday Life* (Amsterdam: The Pepin Press).

Mulder, Niels (2003), *Southeast Asian Images* (Chiang Mai: Silkworm).

Mulhall, S., and A. Swift (1996), *Liberals and Communitarians* (Oxford: Blackwell).

Mutz, D. (2008), 'Is Deliberative Democracy a Falsifiable Theory?', *Annual Review of Political Science* 11: 21–38.

Nagel, T. (1987), 'Moral Conflict and Political Legitimacy', *Philosophy and Public Affairs*, 16(3): 215–40.

Neate, Rupert (2016), 'Panama Papers: US Launches Criminal Inquiry into Tax Avoidance Claims', *Guardian*, 19 April, https://www.theguardian.com/business/2016/apr/19/panama-papers-usjustice-department-investigation-tax-avoidance

Nettl, J. P. (2019), *Rosa Luxemburg* (London: Verso).

Neuberger, B. (2006), 'African Nationalism', in G. Delanty and K. Kumar (eds), *The Sage Handbook of Nations and Nationalism* (London: Sage).

Niemeyer, S. (2004), 'Deliberation in the Wilderness: Displacing Symbolic Politics', *Environmental Politics* 13(2): 347–72.

Niskanen, W. (1971), *Bureaucracy and Representative Government* (Chicago: Aldine).

Norloff, Carla (2015), 'Hegemony', *Oxford Bibliographies*, https://www.oxfordbibliographies.com/view/document/obo-9780199743292/obo-9780199743292–0122.xml

Nozick, R. (1974), *Anarchy, State and Utopia* (Oxford: Blackwell).

Oakeshott, M. (1962), *Rationalism in Politics and Other Essays* (New York: Routledge, Chapman & Hall).

Oatley, Thomas (2019), *International Political Economy* (New York: Routledge, 6th edn).

Oborne, Peter and Tom Roberts (2017), *How Trump Thinks: His Tweets and the Birth of a New Political Language* (London: House of Zeus).

Ohmae, K. (1995), *The End of the Nation State* (London: Harper Collins).

Open secrets (2016), '2016 Presidential Race', https://www.opensecrets.org/pres16/

Ophuls, W. (1973), 'Leviathan or Oblivion', in H. Daly (ed.), *Toward a Steady State Economy* (San Francisco: Freeman), pp. 215–30.

O'Sullivan, N. (1976), *Conservatism* (London: Macmillan).

Pabst, Adrian (2016), 'Brexit and the Destiny of the EU: From Secular Market-State to Civic Commonwealth?', *ABC Religions and Ethics*, 14 June, https://www.abc.net.au/religion/brexitand-the-destiny-of-the-eu-from-secular-marketstate-to-ci/10096876 viewed 7 February 2019.

Pabst, Adrian (2019), *Liberal World Order and Its Critics: Civilisational States and Cultural Commonwealths* (Abingdon: Routledge).

Page, E. (2006), *Climate Change, Justice and Future Generations* (Cheltenham: Edward Elgar).

Parekh, B. (2000), *Rethinking Multiculturalism: Cultural Diversity and Political Theory* (Cambridge, MA: Harvard University Press).

Parekh, Bhikhu (2010), 'The Poverty of Indian Political Theory', in Aakash Singh and Palese, Michela (2018), 'The Irish Abortion Referendum: How a Citizens' Assembly Helped to Break Years of Political Deadlock', https://www.electoral-reform.org.uk/the-irish-abortionreferendum-how-a-citizens-assembly-helped-tobreak-years-of-political-deadlock/

Parkinson, J. (2006), *Deliberating in the Real World* (Oxford: Oxford University Press).

Passmore, K. (2014), *Fascism: A Very Short Introduction* (Oxford: Oxford University Press).

Pateman, C. (1970), *Participation and Democratic Theory* (Cambridge: Cambridge University Press).

Pateman, C. (1988), *The Sexual Contract* (Oxford: Polity Press).

Pateman, C. (1989), *The Disorder of Women* (Oxford: Polity Press).

Patterson, Thomas E. (2017), 'Game versus Substance in Political News', in Kate Kenski and Kathleen Hall Jamieson (eds), *The Oxford Handbook of Political Communication* (Oxford and New York: Oxford University Press), pp. 377–90.

Pederson, Susan (2015), *The Guardians: The League of Nations and the Crisis of Empire* (Oxford: Oxford University Press).

Pepper, D. (1993), *Eco-Socialism: From Deep Ecology to Social Justice* (London: Routledge).

Peters, Rudolph (2016), *Jihad: A History in Documents* (Princeton, NJ: Markus Wiener, 3rd edn).

Phillips, A. (1995), *The Politics of Presence* (Oxford: Clarendon Press).

Plamenatz, J. (1963), *Man and Society*, Vol 2 (London: Longman).

Plant, R. (1991), *Modern Political Thought* (Oxford: Basil Blackwell).

Platonov, O. A. (eds) (2016), *Russkaia Doktrina: Gosudarstvennaia Ideologiia Epokhi Putina* (Moscow: Institut Russkoi Tsivilizatsii, 3rd edn).

Pogge, T. (1989), *Realizing Rawls* (Ithaca, NY: Cornell University Press).

Pogrebinschi, Thamy (2018), 'Deliberative Democracy in Latin America', in Andre Bachtiger, John S. Dryzek, Jane Mansbridge, and Mark Warren (eds), *The Oxford Handbook of Deliberative Democracy* (Oxford: Oxford University Press).

Polsby, N. (1980), *Community Power and Political Theory* (New Haven, CN: Yale University Press, 2nd edn).

Popper, K. (1962), *The Open Society and its Enemies*, ii. *Hegel and Marx* (London: Routledge & Kegan Paul).

Porritt, J. (1984), *Seeing Green* (Oxford: Basil Blackwell).

Poulantzas, N. (1973), *Political Power and Social Classes* (London: New Left Books).

Poulantzas, N. (1976), 'The Capitalist State: A Reply to Miliband and Laclau', *New Left Review*, 95: 63–83.

Prakash, Gyan (2010), 'Subaltern Studies as Postcolonial Criticism', in Aakash Singh and Silika Mohapatra (eds), *Indian Political Thought* (Abingdon: Routledge), pp. 215–26.

Prospect magazine (2019), 'Does Britain Need a Proper Constitution?', https://www.prospectmagazine.co.uk/magazine/does-britain-need-constitutiondebate-sionaidh-douglas-scott-adam-tomkins

Pye, Lucian (1968), 'Political Culture', in D. L. Sills and R. K. Merton (eds), *International Encyclopedia of the Social Sciences* (New York: Macmillan), pp. 218–24.

Pye, Lucian W. (1985), *Asian Power and Politics: The Cultural Dimensions of Authority* (Cambridge, MA: Belknap Press).

Qin, Yaqing (2011), 'Development of International Relations Theory in China: Progress through Debates' *International Relations of the Asia-Pacific* 11(2): 231–57.

Qin, Yaqing (2016), 'Recent Developments Towards a Chinese School of IR Theory', *E-International Relations*, 26 April, https://www.e-ir.26-Garner4e-Ref-v1.indd 573 12/14/19 8:10 PMinfo/2016/04/26/recent-developments-toward-achinese-school-of-ir-theory/

Qobo, Mzukisi and Nceku Nyanthi (2017), 'Ubuntu, Foreign Policy and Radical Uncertainty in South Africa and the World', *Africa Portal*, 20 September, https://www.africaportal.org/features/ubuntu-foreign-policy-and-radicaluncertainty-south-africa-and-world/

Qvortrup, Matt (ed.) (2018), *Referendums Around the World* (Basingstoke: Palgrave Macmillan).

Raskin, Marcus (2004), *Liberalism: the Genius of American Ideals* (Lanham, MD: Rowman & Littlefield).

Rauf, Imam Feisal Abdul (2015), *Defining Islamic Statehood: Measuring and Indexing Contemporary Muslim States* (Basingstoke: Palgrave Macmillan).

Rawls, J. (1971), *A Theory of Justice* (Cambridge, MA: Harvard University Press).

Rawls, J. (1993), *Political Liberalism* (New York: Columbia University Press).

Rawls, J. (1999), *The Law of Peoples* (Cambridge, MA: Harvard University Press).

Reid, A. (2010), *Imperial Alchemy: Nationalism and Political Identity in Southeast Asia* (Cambridge: Cambridge University Press).

Reporters Without Borders (2019), 'Press Freedom Index', https://rsf.org/en/ranking

Reyes Heroles, Jesus (1974), *El liberalismo mexicano. La integración de las ideas* (vol. 3) (Mexico, DF: Fonda de Cultura Economica, 2nd edn).

Robertson, D. (1976), *A Theory of Party Competition* (London: Wiley).

Robertson, David (1993), *The Penguin Dictionary of Politics* (Harmondsworth: Penguin).

Robertson, R. (1992), *Globalization: Social Theory and Global Culture* (London: Sage).

Rohlen, Thomas P. (1989), 'Order in Japanese Society: Attachment, Authority, and Routine', *Journal of Japanese Studies* 15(1): 5–40.

Rosen, Lawrence (2000), *The Justice of Islam: Comparative Perspectives on Islamic Law and Society* (New York: Oxford University Press).

Rosen, Lawrence (2010), 'Islamic Concepts of Justice', in Akbar S. Ahmed and Tamara Sonn (eds), *The Sage Handbook of Islamic Studies* (London: SAGE), pp. 69–82.

Ross-Smith, Nicholas (2018), 'Can Neo-classical Realism become a Genuine Theory of International Relations', *Journal of Politics* 80(2): 742–49.

Rousseau, J. (1913), *The Social Contract and Discourses* (London: Dent).

Roy, Himanshu (2011), 'Gandhi: Swaraj and Satyagraha', in Mahendra Prasad Singh and Himanshu Roy (eds), *Indian Political Thought: Themes and Thinkers* (Delhi: Pearson).

Russell, B. (1938), *Power: A New Social Analysis* (London: Allen & Unwin).

Russkaia narodnaia liniia (2010), 'Modernizatsii Rossii Meshaiut Russkie', http://ruskline.ru/news_rl/2010/9/15/modernizacii_rossii_meshayut_russkie/

Said, Edward (2003), *Orientalism* (Harmondsworth: Penguin).

Savigny, H., and L. Marsden (2011), *Doing Political Science and International Relations: Theories in Action* (Basingstoke: Palgrave).

Saward, M (2001), 'Reconstructing Democracy: Current Thinking and New Directions', *Government and Opposition* 36(4): 559–81.

Schain M., A. Zolberg, and P. Hossay (eds) (2002), *Shadows Over Europe: The Development and Impact of the Extreme Right in Western Europe* (Basingstoke: Palgrave Macmillan).

Schudson, Michael (2008), *Why Democracies Need an Unlovable Press* (Cambridge: Polity).

Schumacher, E. (1973), *Small is Beautiful: Economics as if People Mattered* (London: Blond & Briggs).

Schumpeter, J. (1961), *Capitalism, Socialism and Democracy* (New York: Harper & Row).

Scott, J. (1990), *Domination and the Arts of Resistance* (New Haven, CN: Yale University Press).

Scruton, R. (2001), *The Meaning of Conservatism* (Basingstoke: Palgrave Macmillan, 3rd edn).

Sekyi-Otu, Ato (2018), *Left Universalism: Africacentric Essays* (New York: Routledge).

Seth, Sanja7 (2013), 'Postcolonial Theory and the Critique of International Relations', in Sanjay Seth (ed.), *Postcolonial Theory and International Relations: A Critical Introduction* (Abingdon: Routledge).

Sheikh, Naveed S. (2015), 'Reclaiming Jihad as a Strategy of Conflict Transformation', *Peace Review: A Journal of Social Justice* 27: 288–95.

Shepard, William E. (1996), *Sayyid Qutb and Islamic Activism: A Translation and Critical Analysis of Social Justice in Islam* (Leiden: E.J. Brill).

Shimko, Keith L. (2013), *International Relations: Perspective, Controversies and Readings* (Boston: Wadsworth Cengage Learning, 4th edn).

Shiraishi, Saya (1997), *Young Heroes: The Indonesian Family in Politics* (Ithaca, NY: Southeast Asia Program, Cornell University).

Shorten, A. (2016), *Contemporary Political Theory* (London: Palgrave).

Silika Mohapatra (eds), *Indian Political Thought* (Abingdon: Routledge), pp. 19–30.

Singer, P. (2002), *One World: The Ethics of Globalization* (Melbourne: Text Publishing).

Singh, Aakash, and Silika Mohapatra (eds) (2010), *Indian Political Thought* (Abingdon: Routledge).

Singh, Mahendra Prasad, and Himanshu Roy (eds) (2011), *Indian Political Thought: Themes and Thinkers* (Delhi: Pearson).

Slaughter, A. (2003), *A New World Order* (Princeton: Princeton University Press).

Smith, G. (2003), *Deliberative Democracy and the Environment* (London: Routledge).

Smith, Graham and Corinne Wales (2000), 'Citizens' Juries and Deliberative Democracy', *Political Studies* 48(1): 51–65.

Smith, Robert Sydney (1989), *Warfare & Diplomacy in Pre-Colonial West Africa* (Madison, University of Wisconsin Press, 2nd edn).

Smith, Roy, Imad El-Anis, and Christopher Farrands (2017), *International Political Economy in the 21st Century: Contemporary Issues and Analyses* (Abingdon: Routledge, 2nd edn).

So Cheese (2012), 'How Many Cheeses Are There in France?', www.socheese.fr/la-question/article/combien-la-france-compte-t-elle-de?lang=en

Sono, Themba (1998), 'Why Are There So Few Black Liberals?', in R. W. Johnson and David Welsh (eds), *Ironic Victory: Liberalism in post-liberation South Africa* (Oxford: Oxford University Press), pp. 307–20.

South Africa (2011), 'Building a Better World: The Diplomacy of Ubuntu', White Paper on South Africa's Foreign Policy, final draft 13 May, https://www.sahistory.org.za/archive/building-better-worlddiplomacy-ubuntu

Sridharan, E. (2010), 'The Party System', in Niraja Gopal Jayal and Pratap Bhanu Mehta (eds), *The Oxford Companion to Politics in India* (Oxford: Oxford University Press), pp. 117–35.

Stanish, Charles (2017), *The Evolution of Human Cooperation: Ritual and Social Complexity in Stateless Societies* (Cambridge: Cambridge University Press).

Steiner, J., Bachtiger, A., Sporndli, M., and Steenbergen, M. (eds) (2004), *Deliberative Politics in Action. Analysing Parliamentary Discourse* (Cambridge, Cambridge University Press).

Stoker, G. (2006), *Why Politics Matter* (Basingstoke: Palgrave).

Stoker, G., and D. Marsh (2002), 'Introduction', in D. Marsh and G. Stoker (eds), *Theory and Methods in Political Science* (Basingstoke: Palgrave), pp. 1–16.

Sullivan, John P. (2014), 'Transnational Crime', in Mary Kaldor and Iavor Rangelov (eds), *The Handbook of Global Security* (Malden, MA: John Wiley & Sons).

Sumption, Jonathan (2019), *Trials of the State: Law and the Decline of Politics* (London: Profile).

Sunstein, Cass (2017), *#Republic* (Princeton, NJ: Princeton University Press).

Sun Tzu (2017), *The Art of War* (New York: Quarto Publishing).

Surkov, Vladislav (2007), 'Russkaia Politicheskaia Kul'tura. Vzgliad iz Utopii (Chast' 2)', www.surkov.info/russkaya-politicheskaya-kultura-vzglyad-izistorii-chast-2

Surkov, Vladislav (2018), 'The Loneliness of the Half-Breed', *Russia in Global Affairs*, https://eng.globalaffairs.ru/book/The-Loneliness-of-the-Half-Breed-19575

Susskind, Jamie (2018), *Future Politics: Living Together in a World Transformed by Tech* (Oxford: Oxford University Press).

Sydney Morning Herald (2010), '"I Am the People," Chavez Tells Followers Ahead of Polls', https://www.smh.com.au/world/i-am-the-people-chaveztells-followers-ahead-of-polls-20100124-mryf.html

Sylvest, Casper (2004), 'Interwar Internationalism, the British Labour Party, and the Historiography of International Relations', *International Studies Quarterly* 48(2): 409–32.

Swift, A. (2014), *Political Philosophy: A Beginners Guide for Students and Politicians* (Cambridge: Polity, 3rd edn).

Talmon, J. (1952), *The Origins of Totalitarian Democracy* (London: Secker & Warburg).

Taylor, P. (1986), *Respect for Nature* (Princeton: Princeton University Press).

Temelkuran, Ece (2019), *How to Lose a Country: The 7 Steps from Democracy to Dictatorship* (London: 4th Estate).

Teschke, Benno (2003), *The Myth of 1648: Class, Geopolitics, and the Making of Modern International Relations* (London: Verso).

Thakur, Ramesh (2018), *Reviewing the Responsibility to Protect: Origins, Implementation and Controversies* (Abingdon: Routledge).

Thomas, G. (1993), *An Introduction to Ethics* (London: Duckworth).

Tierney, Stephen (2007), *Multiculturalism and the Canadian Constitution* (Vancouver: University of British Columbia).

Tilly, C. (1975), 'Reflections on the History of European State-making', in C. Tilly (ed.), *The Formation of National States in Western Europe* (Princeton: Princeton University Press).

Tocqueville, Alexis de (2000), *Democracy in America* (Chicago: Chicago University Press).

Tombs, David (2002), *Latin American Liberation Theology* (Boston, MA: Brill).

Trevor Roper, H. (1947), *The Last Days of Hitler* (London: Macmillan).

Tronto, J. (1993), *Moral Boundaries: The Political Argument for an Ethic of Care* (New York: Routledge).

Tuğal, Cihan (2016), *The Fall of the Turkish Model: How the Arab Uprisings Brought Down Islamic Liberalism* (London: Verso).

UK (United Kingdom) (2018), 'UK Foreign Policy in a Shifting World', House of Lords, Select Committee on International Relations, 5th Report of Session 2017–19, 18 December, https://publications.parliament.uk/pa/ld201719/ldselect/ldintrel/250/250.pdf

UNAA (United Nations Association of Australia) (2017), *The United Nations and the Rules-Based International Order* (Canberra: UNAA).

UNESCAP (United Nations Economic and Social Commission for Asia and the Pacific) (2009), 'What Is Good Governance?', 10 July, https://www.unescap.org/resources/what-good-governance

Vaishnav, Milan (2017), *When Crime Pays: Money and Muscle in Indian Politics* (London: Yale University Press).

Vajpayi, Ananya (2012), *Righteous Republic: The Political Foundations of Modern India* (Cambridge, MA: Harvard University Press).

Vertovec, Steven (2009), *Transnationalism* (Abingdon: Routledge).

Viktorov, V. V. (2009), *Rossiiskaia Tsivilizatsiia. Tendentsii Razvitiia Ot Istokov K Sovremennosti* (Moscow: Vuzovskii uchebnik).

Vincent, A. (1995), *Modern Political Ideologies* (Oxford: Blackwell, 2nd edn).

Violakis, Petros (2018), *Europeanisation and the Transformation of EU Security Policy: Post-Cold War Developments in the Common Security and Defence Policy* (Abingdon: Routledge).

Waldron, J. (1989), 'Legislation and Moral Neutrality', in R. Goodin and A. Reeve (eds), *Liberal Neutrality* (London: Routledge), pp. 61–83.

Walker, Peter (2018), '"The Highest Level of Special": Trump Praises US Relationship with UK', *Guardian*, 14 July, https://www.theguardian.com/us-news/2018/jul/13/the-highest-level-of-special-trump-praises-usrelationship-with-uk viewed 1 March 2019.

Wallerstein, Immanuel, Charles C. Lemert, and Carlos Aguirre Rojas (2012), *Uncertain Worlds: World-Systems Analysis in Changing Times* (Abingdon: Routledge).

Walzer, M. (1985), *Spheres of Justice* (New York: Basic Books).

Walzer, M. (1990), 'The Communitarian Critique of Liberalism', *Political Theory*, 18(1): 6–23.

Walzer, M. (1994), *Thick and Thin: Moral Arguments at Home and Abroad* (Notre Dame, IN: University of Notre Dame Press).

Wang, Yingmei, and Wang, Jinjing (2013), *Zhongguo Meng* (Beijing: Guojia Xingzheng Xueyuan).

Wang, Zheng (2012), *Never Forget National Humiliation: Historical Memory in Chinese Politics and Foreign Relations* (New York: Columbia University Press).

Weale, A. (2007), *Democracy* (Basingstoke: Palgrave, 2nd edn).

Westergaard, J., and H. Resler (1975), *Class in a Capitalist Society* (London: Heinemann).

Wiarda, Howard J. (2001), *The Soul of Latin America: The Cultural and Political Tradition* (New Haven, CT: Yale University Press).

Wiarda, Howard J. (2014), *Political Culture, Political Science, and Identity Politics* (Farnham: Ashgate).

Wiener, Antje (2018), *Contestation and Constitution of Norms in Global International Relations* (Cambridge: Cambridge University Press).

Wike, Richard and Janell Fetterolf (2018), 'Liberal Democracy's Crisis of Confidence', *Journal of Democracy* 29(4): 136–50.

Wilkinson, R. and Pickett, K. (2009), *The Spirit Level: Why More Equal Societies Almost Always Do Better* (London: Penguin).

Wilson, Lord Richard (2013), 'Public Sphere and Political Experience', in Christian J. Emden and David Midgley (eds), *Beyond Habermas: Democracy, Knowledge, and the Public Sphere* (Oxford: Berghahn), pp. 1–16.

Wissenburg, M. (1993), 'The Idea of Nature and the Nature of Distributive Justice', in A. Dobson and P. Lucardie (eds), *The Politics of Nature: Explorations in Green Political Thought* (London: Routledge), pp. 3–20.

Wolf, Margery (1968), *The House of Lim: A Study of a Chinese Farm Family* (New York: Apple-Century-Crofts).

Wolff, J. (1996), *An Introduction to Political Philosophy* (Oxford: Oxford University Press).

Wolff, R. P. (1970), *In Defence of Anarchism* (New York: Harper & Row).

Wolff, R. (1977), *Understanding Rawls* (Princeton: Princeton University Press).

Wolmar, Christian (2002), *Down the Tube: the Battle for London's Underground* (London: Aurum).

Woods, K. (2014), *Human Rights* (Basingstoke: Palgrave Macmillan).

Woolstonecraft, M. (1792/1978), *Vindication of the Rights of Women* (Harmondsworth: Penguin).

World Commission on Environment and Development (1987), *Our Common Future* (Oxford: Oxford University Press).

World Values Survey, (2019), 'Findings and Insights—Live Cultural Map', www.worldvaluessurvey.org/WVSContents.jsp

Worth, Owen (2012), '"Accumulating the Critical Spirit", Rosa Luxemburg and Critical IPE', *International Politics* 49(2), 136–53.

Wright, A. (1979), *G.D.H. Cole and Socialist Democracy* (Oxford: Clarendon Press).

Wright, A. (1996), *Socialisms* (London: Routledge).

Xi, Jinping (2014), *The Governance of China* (Beijing: Foreign Languages Press).

Yan, Xuetong (2016), 'Political Leadership and Power Redistribution', *Chinese Journal of International Relation* 9(1): 1–26.

Yang, H., and D. Zhao (2015), 'Performance Legitimacy, State Autonomy and China's Economic Miracle', *Journal of Contemporary China* 24(91): 64–82.

Yeşiltaş, Murat (2014), 'Turkey's Quest for a "New International Order": The Discourse of Civilization and the Politics of Restoration', *Perceptions* Winter, XIX(4): 43–76.

YouGov (2019), 'Are MPs Elected to Exercise Their Own Judgement or Do Their Constituents' Bidding?', https://yougov.co.uk/topics/politics/articlesreports/2019/08/13/are-mps-elected-exercisetheir-own-judgement-or-do

Young, I. (2000), *Inclusion and Democracy* (Oxford: Oxford University Press).

Yourish, Karen, and Larry Buchanan (2019), 'Trump and His Associates Had More Than 100 Contacts with Russians before the Inauguration', *New York Times*, 19 January, https://www.nytimes.com/interactive/2019/01/26/us/politics/trump-contacts-russians-wikileaks.html viewed 2 March 2019.

Yu, Dan (2009), *Confucius from the Heart: Ancient Wisdom for Today's World* (London: Macmillan).

Zakaria, F. (2003), *The Future of Freedom: Illiberal Democracy at Home and Abroad* (London: Norton).

Zakaria, Fareed (1994), 'Culture is Destiny: A Conversation with Lee Kuan Yew', *Foreign Affairs* 74(2) March–April: 109–26.

Zhang, Weiwei (2012), *The China Wave: Rise of a Civilizational State* (Hackensack, NJ: World Century).

Zondi, Siphamandla (2018), 'Decolonising International Relations and Its Theory: A Critical Conceptual Meditation', *Politikon* 45(1): 16–31.

Zsolnai, Laszlo (2018), *Ethics, Meaning, and Market Society* (New York: Routledge).

Zygar', Mikhail (2016), *Vsia Kremliovskaia Rat* (Moscow: Intellektual'naia Literatura).

INDEX